THE JNDI API
Tutorial and Reference

The JNDI API Tutorial and Reference Companion CD-ROM

The JNDI API Tutorial and Reference Companion CD-ROM is loaded with development kits and documentation, including the content and code of the book. Be sure to read and consent to the license agreements associated with each product.

TABLE 32: Development Kits on *The JNDI API Tutorial and Reference* Companion CD-ROM.

Development Kits	Version
Java 2 SDK, Standard Edition	1.2.2
Java Naming and Directory Interface (JNDI)	1.2.1
Also includes browser demo and these service providers:	
LDAP	1.2.2
COS Naming	1.2.1
RMI Registry	1.2.1
NIS	1.2.1
File System	1.2 Beta 2
Java Authentication and Authorization Service (JAAS)	1.0
Java Secure Socket Extension (JSSE)	1.0.1
RMI over IIOP	1.0.1

TABLE 33: Documentation on *The JNDI API Tutorial and Reference* Companion CD-ROM.

Documentation
The JNDI Tutorial
JNDI API Architecture
JNDI SPI Architecture
The Java Tutorial
JDBC Database Access Tutorial
RMI over IIOP Programmer's Guide
Java Secure Socket Extension (JSSE) User's Guide

TABLE 34: Specifications on *The JNDI API Tutorial and Reference* Companion CD-ROM.

Specifications	Version
JNDI Specification (javadoc)	1.2.1
Java 2 Platform API Documentation (javadoc)	1.2.2
Java Authentication and Authorization Service (JAAS) (javadoc)	1.0
Java Secure Socket Extension (JSSE) (javadoc)	1.0.1
RMI over IIOP Specification (javadoc)	1.0.1
Selected Internet Drafts and RFCs	

TABLE 35: Miscellaneous on *The JNDI API Tutorial and Reference* Companion CD-ROM.

And More...
Java Code Conventions
Java Programming Language Glossary
The Java Platform White Paper
Java Security Code Guidelines

The `index.html` file on the CD-ROM is the central HTML page that links you to all of its contents. To view this page, use the Open Page command or its equivalent in your Internet browser. On some platforms, you can simply double click on the HTML page to launch it in your browser.

Check out the latest Sun Microsystems' Java Programming Language product releases at

`http://java.sun.com/products/`

See this book's Web page at `http://java.sun.com/products/jndi/tutorial` for pointers to the latest versions of this content.

More Tutorials: You can join the Java Developer Connection (`http://java.sun.com/jdc/`) to gain access to many other Java-related tutorials. Join today, it's free!

The JNDI API Tutorial and Reference Companion CD-ROM

The JNDI API Tutorial and Reference Companion CD-ROM is loaded with development kits and documentation, including the content and code of the book. Be sure to read and consent to the license agreements associated with each product.

TABLE 32: Development Kits on *The JNDI API Tutorial and Reference* Companion CD-ROM.

Development Kits	Version
Java 2 SDK, Standard Edition	1.2.2
Java Naming and Directory Interface (JNDI)	1.2.1
Also includes browser demo and these service providers:	
LDAP	1.2.2
COS Naming	1.2.1
RMI Registry	1.2.1
NIS	1.2.1
File System	1.2 Beta 2
Java Authentication and Authorization Service (JAAS)	1.0
Java Secure Socket Extension (JSSE)	1.0.1
RMI over IIOP	1.0.1

TABLE 33: Documentation on *The JNDI API Tutorial and Reference* Companion CD-ROM.

Documentation
The JNDI Tutorial
JNDI API Architecture
JNDI SPI Architecture
The Java Tutorial
JDBC Database Access Tutorial
RMI over IIOP Programmer's Guide
Java Secure Socket Extension (JSSE) User's Guide

TABLE 34: Specifications on *The JNDI API Tutorial and Reference* Companion CD-ROM.

Specifications	Version
JNDI Specification (javadoc)	1.2.1
Java 2 Platform API Documentation (javadoc)	1.2.2
Java Authentication and Authorization Service (JAAS) (javadoc)	1.0
Java Secure Socket Extension (JSSE) (javadoc)	1.0.1
RMI over IIOP Specification (javadoc)	1.0.1
Selected Internet Drafts and RFCs	

TABLE 35: Miscellaneous on *The JNDI API Tutorial and Reference* Companion CD-ROM.

And More...
Java Code Conventions
Java Programming Language Glossary
The Java Platform White Paper
Java Security Code Guidelines

The `index.html` file on the CD-ROM is the central HTML page that links you to all of its contents. To view this page, use the Open Page command or its equivalent in your Internet browser. On some platforms, you can simply double click on the HTML page to launch it in your browser.

Check out the latest Sun Microsystems' Java Programming Language product releases at

`http://java.sun.com/products/`

See this book's Web page at `http://java.sun.com/products/jndi/tutorial` for pointers to the latest versions of this content.

More Tutorials: You can join the Java Developer Connection (`http://java.sun.com/jdc/`) to gain access to many other Java-related tutorials. Join today, it's free!

THE JNDI API
Tutorial and Reference

Building Directory-Enabled Java™ Applications

Rosanna Lee
and
Scott Seligman

ADDISON-WESLEY

Boston • San Francisco • New York • Toronto • Montreal
London • Munich • Paris • Madrid
Capetown • Sydney • Tokyo • Singapore • Mexico City

Library of Congress Cataloging-in-Publication Data
Lee, Rosanna.
     JNDI API tutorial and reference / Rosanna Lee, Scott Seligman.
         p. cm. -- (The Java series)
     ISBN 0-201-70502-8 (alk. paper)
         1. JNDI 2. Application program interfaces (Computer software) 3. Java (Computer program language) 4. Directory services (Computer network technology) I. Seligman, Scott. II. Title. III. Series.

     QA76.76.A63 L44 2000
     005.2'762--dc21   00-036361

The publisher offers discounts on this book when ordered in quantity for special sales. For more information, please contact:
     Pearson Education Corporate Sales Division; One Lake Street; Upper Saddle River, NJ 07458
     (800) 382-3419; corpsales@pearsontechgroup.com
Visit Addison-Wesley on the Web at www.awl.com/cseng/

Text printed on recycled and acid-free paper.

ISBN 0-201-70502-8
1 2 3 4 5 6 7 8 9 – MA – 04 03 02 01 00
First Printing, June 2000

To the JNDI Team

—*R.L.*

To Shoshi and Shana

—*S.S.*

Contents

Contents

List of Figures

List of Tables

Preface

How to Use This Book

This book teaches you how to write directory-enabled Java™ applications by using the Java Naming and Directory Interface™ (JNDI). It is divided into two parts: a tutorial and a reference.

It is intended as a tutorial and reference only for the JNDI and not for the rest of the Java platform. For a tutorial-style presentation of the class libraries in the rest of the Java platform, see *The Java™ Tutorial* and *The JFC Swing Tutorial*, by Mary Campione and Kathy Walrath, and *The Java™ Tutorial Continued*, by Mary Campione, Kathy Walrath, Alison Huml, and the Tutorial team. For a reference-style presentation of the class libraries in other parts of the Java platform, see *The Java™ Class Libraries* books by Patrick Chan, Rosanna Lee, and Douglas Kramer. This book also does not explain any part of the Java programming language. Several books are available for learning the language. These include *The Java™ Programming Language*, by Ken Arnold and James Gosling, and *The Java™ Language Specification*, by James Gosling, Bill Joy, and Guy Steele.

Following is an overview of this book.

Tutorial

The first part of this book is a tutorial. It is modeled after *The Java Tutorial*, by Mary Campione and Kathy Walrath.

Trails and Lessons

The tutorial consists of six trails—programming lessons grouped together by topic. To learn about a certain topic, go to the **Table of Contents**, decide which trail meets your needs, and go through the lessons in that trail. For example, if you are interested in writing a service provider, select the **Building a Service Provider** trail.

You can read the tutorial sequentially or select trails in any order. However, some of the beginner trails are prerequisites for the more advanced trails.

The first page of a trail contains a high-level overview of the trail. It lists, describes, and provides references to all of the lessons on the trail. It also provides a detailed table of contents of the lessons in the trail.

Each lesson begins with an introduction to the material in the lesson. Most lessons contain many examples. Trying the examples as you go along will help you to understand the concepts discussed in each lesson.

Links

The online version of this tutorial is filled with hyperlinks to sections inside and outside of the tutorial. In this hardcopy version of the tutorial, these hyperlinks have been handled as follows.

- A link to a section, lesson, or trail within the tutorial is replaced by a cross reference, annotated by a page number.
- A link to a method, class, interface, or package in the JNDI has been removed. Use instead the reference part of this book to look up the item.
- A link to an Internet RFC or Internet-draft has been removed. These documents may be accessed both from the CD that accompanies this book and the Web site at http://www.ietf.org.
- A link to an external document or software has been replaced by the item's URL. These files may also be found on the accompanying CD.
- A link to a sample program or configuration file has been removed. Simply find the file on the accompanying CD (see later in this Preface for instructions).

Examples

All of the code examples in the tutorial have been compiled and run by using the following software.

- The FCS version of the Java™ 2 SDK, Standard Edition, v1.2 on either Solaris or Windows NT or both
- The 1.2.1 version of the JNDI class libraries
- The 1.2.2 version of the LDAP service provider
- The 1.2 Beta 2 version of the file system service provider

Most of the complete examples are available both online from the JNDI Web site (http://java.sun.com/products/jndi/tutorial) and on the accompanying CD. This tutorial is located in the Tutorials/jndi directory on the CD. Each trail resides in its own directory, under which are located subdirectories for each lesson within the trail. The examples and related files used in a lesson are found in the src subdirectory of the lesson's directory. For example, the examples in the **Naming Operations** lesson in **The Basics** trail are found in the Tutorials/jndi/basics/naming/src directory. Tools and utilities for configuring the examples are found in the directories `Tutorials/jndi/config/fs` and `Tutorials/jndi/config/LDAP`.

We strongly encourage you to try the examples that accompany this tutorial as you go along. To do that, you will need the JNDI classes and a v1.1.2 or higher version of the Java platform software, such as the JDK software (`http://java.sun.com/products/jdk`). The JDK provides a compiler that you can use to compile Java programs. It also provides an interpreter for running Java applications. To run Java applets, you can use the JDK Applet Viewer or any Java-compatible Web browser, such as the HotJava™ browser.

Online Version

The complete online tutorial is available both on the accompanying CD and from the JNDI Web site. The title page of each lesson contains a URL for the corresponding lesson online.

Reference

The second part of this book is a reference. Its format is similar to a dictionary's in that it is designed to optimize the time that it takes for you to look up information about a class or class member.

Package Overviews

The package overviews briefly describe each package and its classes. Each overview includes a general description about the package, as well as diagrams that show the inheritance hierarchy of its classes.

Alphabetical Reference of Classes

This part covers the alphabetical listing of the classes from the following five packages:

```
javax.naming
javax.naming.directory
javax.naming.event
javax.naming.ldap
javax.naming.spi
```

The classes are ordered alphabetically without regard to package. Each is described in its own chapter that contains a picture of the class hierarchy, a class description, a member summary, and descriptions for each member. Most examples for the class or items within the class are found in the tutorial part of this book.

Class Hierarchy Diagram

Each chapter starts with a class diagram like that shown in Figure i. This diagram shows all of the ancestors of the class, its siblings, its immediate descendents, and any interfaces that it

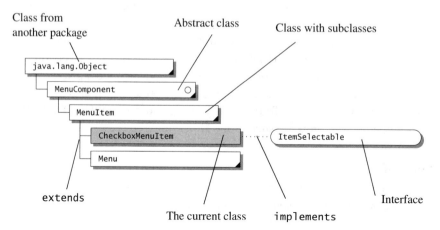

FIGURE i: Class Hierarchy Diagram.

implements. In these diagrams, if a package name precedes a class or interface name, then the class or interface is not in the same package as the current class.

In the diagrams, the different kinds of Java entities are distinguished visually as follows:

- The interface: A rounded rectangle
- The class: A rectangle
- The abstract class: A rectangle with an empty dot
- The final class: A rectangle with a black dot
- Classes with subclasses: A rectangle with a small black triangle in the lower-right corner

The class or interface being described in the current chapter is shaded grey. A solid line represents extends and a dotted line represents implements.

Class Description

In the class description, we describe all of the properties of the class. For example, the discussion of the properties of the Context interface includes information on how names and environment properties are treated. Describing in one place all of a class's available properties and how they behave makes learning all of the class's capabilities much easier than if that data is scattered throughout the member descriptions.

Any terminology used in the member descriptions is introduced and described in the class descriptions. For more information at any time, you should go to the class description.

Member Summary

The member summary is intended to help you quickly grasp the key points of the class. It groups the members into categories that are specific to that class. For example, in the Name interface the *Update Methods* category lists all methods concerning updates. It is intended as a quick summary of the class's members, so it does not contain any syntax information other than the name of the member.

As an example, following is the member summary for `Attributes`. Notice that all overloads of a method or constructor share the same entry.

MEMBER SUMMARY	
Update Methods	
`put()`	Adds a new attribute to this attribute set.
`remove()`	Removes an attribute from this attribute set.
Copy Method	
`clone()`	Makes a copy of this attribute set.
Query and Access Methods	
`get()`	Retrieves the attribute with the given attribute identifier from this attribute set.
`getAll()`	Retrieves an enumeration of the attributes in this attribute set.
`getIDs()`	Retrieves an enumeration of the identifiers of the attributes in this attribute set.
`isCaseIgnored()`	Determines whether the attribute set ignores the case of attribute identifiers when retrieving or adding attributes.
`size()`	Retrieves the number of attributes in this attribute set.

Member Descriptions

The member descriptions appear in alphabetical order within a class chapter regardless of what kind of method or field they are. This is done to make locating a member proceed as fast as possible.

Overloaded methods are grouped in one member description because they share very similar functionality. The different overloaded forms are typically provided as a convenience for the programmer when specifying parameters. For instance, some overloads eliminate parameters by providing common defaults. To describe overloads with missing parameters, we use a phrase of the form "if the parameter p is not specified, then it defaults to the value 3.14." Other overloads take different representations of a value. For example, one overload could take a particular parameter as an integer, whereas another could take the same parameter as a string that contains an integer.

Each member description contains some or all of the following fields.

PURPOSE   A brief description of the purpose of this member

SYNTAX   The syntactic declaration of this member

DESCRIPTION   A full description of this member

PARAMETERS	The parameters accepted by this member, if any, listed in alphabetical order
RETURNS	The value and its range returned by this member, if any
EXCEPTIONS	The exceptions and errors thrown by this member, if any, listed in alphabetical order
SEE ALSO	Other related classes or members, if any, listed in alphabetical order
OVERRIDES	The method that this member overrides, if any
EXAMPLE	A code example that illustrates how this member is used (usually a reference to an example in the tutorial part of this book)

Typographical Conventions Used in This Book

`Lucida Sans Typewriter` is used for examples, syntax declarations, class names, method names, values, and field names. *Italic* is used when defining a new term and for emphasis.

Additional Information about This Book

Errata and additional information about this book and other books in the Java Series are available at the following URL:

```
http://java.sun.com/docs/books/
```

Please send feedback about this book to the following:

```
jndi-book@java.sun.com
```

Acknowledgments

We want to thank the many people who helped to make this book possible.

The JNDI team, who developed the technology. Over the years, team members have included R. Vasudevan, Rosanna Lee, Scott Seligman, Vincent Ryan, Jonathan Bruce, and Jon Ruiz.

The Novell JNDI team, led by Michael Mackay, Kent Boogert, Michael Simpson, Steve Holbrook, Jim Sermersheim, Bruce Bergeson, and Steven Merrill. Without Novell's technical, as well as nontechnical, support, the JNDI wouldn't exist.

The Ivy team, who developed the technology on which a lot of the JNDI is based. Over the years, team members have included R. Vasudevan, Rosanna Lee, Kamal Anand, Greg White-head, Anil Gangolli, Sanjay Dani, Joseph Pallas, Caveh Jalali, Scott Seligman, Vincent Ryan, and Aravindan Ranganathan.

The Sun management, including David "Kip" Kipping, Lou Delzompo, Sandeep Khanna, Bob Bressler, Sharada Achanta, John Fowler, Maxine Erlund, and Bonnie Kellett. They provided the environment and support for us to innovate and develop the JNDI and Ivy technologies.

Partners, customers, and readers who provided valuable feedback on the JNDI technology and online tutorial.

Mary Campione, Kathy Walrath, and Alison Huml, authors of the Java tutorial books, who provided the inspiration, model, and tools for writing the online tutorial.

Odile Sullivan-Tarazi, Dale Green, and Jim Inscore, who assisted in the production of the online tutorial.

Mike Hendrickson, executive editor for this book at Addison-Wesley, who helped coordinate the many tasks and people needed to complete it.

Laura Michaels, who improved the readability of this book under tremendous time pressure.

Patrick Chan, who provided the package and class diagrams in this book.

Sarah Weaver, Rosemary Simpson, Lisa Friendly, Tim Lindholm, Heather Peterson, and Julie DiNicola, all of whom played a part in the production of this book and were wonderful to work with.

Rosanna Lee
Palo Alto, California
Scott Seligman
Cupertino, California
April 2000

## PART I

Tutorial

Getting Started

The lessons in the **Getting Started** trail offer a quick introduction to the Java Naming and Directory Interface™ (JNDI), providing the background information for understanding the rest of the material in this tutorial. They touch on the fundamental concepts in naming and directory systems, give a brief JNDI overview, and show how to write a simple Java™ application that uses the JNDI. If you are already familiar with naming and directory concepts, then you can skip this trail and proceed to **The Basics** trail (page 37).

- The **Naming and Directory Concepts** lesson (page 7) talks about fundamental concepts in naming and directory systems. It describes the role of such services in computer systems and what it means for an application to be *directory-enabled*.

- The **JNDI Overview** lesson (page 17) describes the JNDI architecture and gives a quick rundown of its three major components: the naming model, the directory model, and the service provider model.

- The **Examples** lesson (page 25) provides two examples that use the JNDI. The first shows how to look up an object, and the second shows how to read an attribute from a directory service.

- The **Common Problems** lesson (page 31) contains descriptions and solutions to common problems that you might encounter when you first start using the JNDI.

Naming and Directory Concepts

This lesson explains naming and directory concepts in detail and discusses how Java programs can use naming and directory services. It also defines common terms related to such services. These terms are summarized at the end of the lesson in a glossary.

Naming Concepts

A fundamental facility in any computer is the *naming service*—the means by which names are associated with objects and objects are found based on their names. When using almost any computer program or system, you are always naming one object or another. For example, when you use an electronic mail (e-mail) system, you must provide the name of the recipient to whom you want to send mail. To access a file in the computer, you must supply its name. A naming service allows you to look up an object given its name.

A naming service's primary function is to map people-friendly names to objects, such as addresses, identifiers, or objects typically used by computer programs. For example, the Internet Domain Name System (DNS) maps machine names (such as www.sun.com) to IP addresses (such as 192.9.48.5). A file system maps a filename (for example, c:\bin\autoexec.bat) to a file handle that a program can use to access the contents of the file. These two examples also illustrate the wide range of scale at which naming services exist—from naming an object on the Internet to naming a file on the local file system.

Names

To look up an object in a naming system, you supply it the name of the object. The naming system determines the *syntax* that the name must follow. This syntax is sometimes called the naming system's *naming convention*.

For example, the UNIX™ file system's naming convention is that a file is named from its path relative to the root of the file system, with each component in the path separated from left to right using the forward slash character ("/"). The UNIX pathname, /usr/hello, for example, names a file hello in the file directory usr, which is located in the root of the file system.

The DNS naming convention calls for components in the DNS name to be ordered from right to left and delimited by the dot character ("."). Thus the DNS name sales.Wiz.COM names a DNS entry with the name sales, relative to the DNS entry Wiz.COM. The DNS entry Wiz.COM, in turn, names an entry with the name Wiz in the COM entry.

The Lightweight Directory Access Protocol (LDAP) naming convention orders components from right to left, delimited by the comma character (","). Thus the LDAP name cn=Rosanna Lee,o=Sun,c=US names an LDAP entry cn=Rosanna Lee, relative to the entry o=Sun, which in turn, is relative to c=us. The LDAP has the further rule that each component of the name must be a name/value pair with the name and value separated by an equals character ("=").

Bindings

The association of a name with an object is called a *binding*. For example, a filename is *bound* to a file.

The DNS contains bindings that map machine names to IP addresses. An LDAP name is bound to an LDAP entry.

References and Addresses

Depending on the naming service, some objects cannot be stored directly; that is, a copy of the object cannot be placed inside the naming service. Instead, they must be stored by reference; that is, a *pointer* or *reference* to the object is placed inside the naming service. A reference is information about how to access an object. Typically, it is a much more compact representation that can be used to communicate with the object, while the object itself might contain a lot more state information. Using the reference, you can contact the object and obtain more information about the object.

For example, an airplane object might contain a list of the airplane's passengers and crew, its flight plan, its fuel and instrument status, and its flight number and departure time. By contrast, an airplane object reference might contain only its flight number and departure time. The reference is a much more compact representation of information about the airplane object and can be used to obtain additional information. A file object, for example, is accessed using a *file reference*, also called a *file handle*. A printer object, for example, might contain the state of the printer, such as its current queue and the amount of paper in the paper tray. A printer object reference, on the other hand, might contain only information on how to reach the printer, such as its print server name and printing protocol.

Although in general a reference can contain any arbitrary information, it is useful to refer to its contents as *addresses* (or communication endpoints): specific information about how to access the object.

For simplicity, this tutorial uses "object" to refer to both objects and object references when a distinction between the two is not required.

Contexts

A *context* is a set of name-to-object bindings. Every context has an associated naming convention. A context provides a lookup (*resolution*) operation that returns the object and may provide operations such as those for binding names, unbinding names, and listing bound names. A name in one context object can be bound to another context object (called a *subcontext*) that has the same naming convention.

For example, a file directory, such as /usr, in the UNIX file system is a context. A file directory named relative to another file directory is a subcontext (some UNIX users refer to this as a subdirectory). That is, in a file directory /usr/bin, the directory bin is a subcontext of usr. In another example, a DNS domain, such as COM, is a context. A DNS domain named relative to another DNS domain is a subcontext. For example, in the DNS domain Sun.COM, the DNS domain Sun is a subcontext of COM.

Finally, an LDAP entry, such as c=us, is a context. An LDAP entry named relative to another LDAP entry is a subcontext. For example, in the LDAP entry o=sun,c=us, the entry o=sun is a subcontext of c=us.

Naming Systems and Namespaces

A *naming system* is a connected set of contexts of the same type (they have the same naming convention) and provides a common set of operations. For example, a system that implements the DNS protocol is a naming system. A system that communicates using the LDAP is a naming system.

A naming system provides a naming service to its customers for performing naming-related operations. A naming service is accessed through its own interface. For example, the DNS offers a naming service that maps machine names to IP addresses. The LDAP offers a naming service that maps LDAP names to LDAP entries. A file system offers a naming service that maps filenames to files and directories.

A *namespace* is the set of names in a naming system. For example, the UNIX file system has a namespace consisting of all of the names of files and directories in that file system. The DNS namespace contains names of DNS domains and entries. The LDAP namespace contains names of LDAP entries.

Directory Concepts

Many naming services are extended with a *directory service*. A directory service associates names with objects and also allows such objects to have *attributes*. Thus you not only can look up an object by its name but also get the object's attributes or search for the object based on its attributes.

An example is the telephone company's directory service. It maps a subscriber's name to his address and telephone number. A computer's directory service is very much like a telephone company's directory service in that both can be used to store information such as telephone numbers and addresses. The computer's directory service is much more powerful, however, because it is available online and can be used to store a variety of information that can be utilized by users, programs, and even the computer itself and other computers.

A *directory object* represents an object in a computing environment. A directory object can be used, for example, to represent a printer, a person, a computer, or a network. A directory object contains *attributes* that describe the object that it represents.

Attributes

A directory object can have *attributes*. For example, a printer might be represented by a directory object that has as attributes its speed, resolution, and color. A user might be represented by a directory object that has as attributes the user's e-mail address, various telephone numbers, postal mail address, and computer account information.

An attribute has an *attribute identifier* and a set of *attribute values*. An attribute identifier is a token that identifies an attribute independent of its values. For example, two different computer accounts might have a `"mail"` attribute; `"mail"` is the attribute identifier. An attribute value is the contents of the attribute. The e-mail address, for example, might have an attribute identifier of `"mail"` and the attribute value of `"john.smith@somewhere.com"`.

Directories and Directory Services

A *directory* is a connected set of directory objects. A *directory service* is a service that provides operations for creating, adding, removing, and modifying the attributes associated with objects in a directory. The service is accessed through its own interface.

Many examples of directory services are possible. The Novell Directory Service (NDS) is a directory service from Novell that provides information about many networking services, such as the file and print services. Network Information Service (NIS) is a directory service available on the Solaris operating system for storing system-related information, such as that relating to machines, networks, printers, and users. The Netscape Directory is a general-purpose directory service based on the Internet standard LDAP.

Searches and Search Filters

You can look up a directory object by supplying its name to the directory service. Alternatively, many directories, such as those based on the LDAP, support the notion of a *search*. When you search, you supply not a name but a query consisting of a logical expression in which you specify the attributes that the object or objects must have. The query is called a *search filter*. This style of searching is sometimes called *reverse lookup* or *content-based searching*. The directory service searches for and returns the objects that satisfy the search filter.

For example, you can query the directory service to find all users that have the attribute "age" greater than 40 years. Similarly, you can query it to find all machines whose IP address starts with "192.113.50."

Combining Naming and Directory Services

Directories often arrange their objects in a hierarchy. For example, the LDAP arranges all directory objects in a tree, called a *directory information tree (DIT)*. Within the DIT, an organization object, for example, might contain group objects that might in turn contain person objects. When directory objects are arranged in this way, they play the role of naming contexts in addition to that of containers of attributes.

Directory-Enabled Java Applications

Directory service is a vital component of network computing. By using a directory service, you can simplify applications and their administration by centralizing the storage of shared information. As the use of the Java programming language to write practical applications in a network environment increases, the ability to access directory services will become essential.

Traditional Use of the Directory

A *directory-enabled application* is an application that uses a naming or directory service. Directory-enabled Java applications and applets, like any other program running on the network, can use the directory in the traditional way, that is, to store and retrieve attributes of directory objects. A Java mail client program, for example, can use the directory as an address book for retrieving the addresses of mail recipients. A Java mail transfer agent program can use it to retrieve mail routing information. And a Java calendar program can use it to retrieve user preference settings.

Applications can share the common infrastructure provided by the directory. This sharing makes applications that are deployed across the system, and even the network, more coherent and manageable. For example, printer configuration and mail routing information can be stored in the directory so that it can be replicated and distributed for use by all printer-related and mail-related applications and services.

The Directory as an Object Store

In addition to using the directory in the traditional way, Java applications can also use it as a repository for Java objects, that is, to store and retrieve Java objects. For example, a Java print client program should be able to look up a printer object from the directory and send a data stream to the printer object for printing.

Glossary

Table 1 lists terms introduced in this lesson. It also contains some terms that will be introduced later in this tutorial; they are listed here for completeness.

TABLE 1:   Glossary.

Term	Definition
address	A specification of a communication endpoint.
alias	An object that contains the name of another object. The use of aliases allows one object to be named using different names.
application resource file	An optional properties file named `jndi.properties` found in the classpath of the application/applet using the JNDI. All of the properties contained in all application resource files in the classpath are collected and added to the environment of the initial context.
atomic name	An indivisible component of a name, as defined by the naming convention of the context in which the name is bound.
attribute	Information associated with a directory object. An attribute consists of an attribute identifier and a set of attribute values.
binding	The association of a name with an object.
composite name	A name that spans multiple naming systems.
composite name resolution	The process of resolving a name that spans multiple naming systems.
composite namespace	The arrangement of namespaces from autonomous naming systems to form one logical namespace.
compound name	A name in the namespace of a single naming system. It is a sequence of zero or more atomic names composed according to the naming convention of that naming system.
context	An object whose state is a set of bindings that have distinct atomic names.

TABLE 1:   Glossary.

Term	Definition
context factory	A specialization of an object factory. It accepts information about how to create a context, such as a reference, and returns an instance of the context.
control	A modifier that accompanies an LDAP v3 request or an LDAP v3 response. A control that accompanies a request is called a *request control*. A control that accompanies a response is called a *response control*.
control factory	A class that narrows a control into one of a more specific type.
directory	A connected set of directory objects.
directory entry	Same as *directory object*.
directory object	An object that is in the directory. Sometimes called a *directory entry*.
directory service	A service that provides operations for creating, adding, removing, and modifying the attributes associated with objects in a directory.
event listener	An object that receives notification of events.
event source	An object that fires (generates) events.
environment properties	Properties used to specify various preferences and properties that define the environment in which naming and directory services are accessed.
federated namespace	Same as composite namespace.
federated naming service	A service that provides operations on a federated naming system.
federated naming system	An aggregation of autonomous naming systems that cooperate to support the name resolution of composite names through a standard interface. Each member of the federation has autonomy in its choice of operations and naming conventions.
initial context	The starting point for the resolution of names for naming and directory operations.
junction	A binding in one naming system whose reference identifies a context in another naming system.
link reference	A reference that contains a composite name. It is a symbolic link that can span multiple naming systems.
name	A people-friendly identifier for identifying an object or a reference to an object.
name resolution	The process of resolving a name to the object to which it is bound.
namespace	A set of all names in a naming system.
naming convention	The set of syntactic rules that govern how a name is generated. These rules determine whether a name is valid or invalid in the context in which the name is used.

Continued

TABLE 1:   **Glossary.**

Term	Definition
naming service	A service that provides the operations on a naming system.
naming system	A connected set of contexts of the same type (they have the same naming convention).
next naming system	The subordinate naming system in a federation of naming systems.
object factory	A producer of objects that accepts some information about how to create an object, such as a reference, and then returns an instance of that object.
operational attribute	An attribute maintained and used for administrative purposes. It is not visible to clients unless explicitly requested.

provider resource file	An optional properties file named `[prefix/]jndiprovider.properties`, where *prefix* is the package name of the service provider's class and each period character is converted to a forward slash ("/") character. This file is used by the JNDI when determining the values of the following JNDI-defined properties:
	`java.naming.factory.object`
	`java.naming.factory.state`
	`java.naming.factory.control`
	`java.naming.factory.url.pkgs`

referral	An object that contains the name(s) and location(s) of other object(s). It is a generalization of an alias.
reference	Information for accessing an object. It contains one or more addresses for communicating or referring to an object.
request control	A control that accompanies an LDAP v3 request sent by the client. The JNDI has two types of request controls: those that are associated with connection establishment, called *connection request controls*, and those that are associated with a context, called *context request controls*.
response control	A control that accompanies an LDAP v3 response sent by the server.
schema	A set of rules that specifies the types of objects that a directory may contain and the mandatory and optional attributes that directory objects of different types are to have. It may also specify the structure of the namespace and the relationship between different types of objects.
search filter	A logical expression that specifies the attributes that the directory objects being requested should have. It is used by the directory to locate those objects.
service provider	An implementation of a context or initial context that can be plugged in dynamically to the JNDI architecture to be used by the JNDI client.

TABLE 1:   Glossary.

Term	Definition
state factory	A factory that accepts an object and returns data representing the object to be stored in (and acceptable to) the underlying naming/directory service.
subcontext	A context that is bound in another context of the same type (it has the same naming convention).
unsolicited notification	A notification sent by an LDAP v3 server not in response to any client request.

JNDI Overview

The Java Naming and Directory Interface™ is an application programming interface (API) that provides naming and directory functionality to applications written using the Java™ programming language. It is defined to be independent of any specific directory service implementation. Thus a variety of directories—new, emerging, and already deployed—can be accessed in a common way.

Architecture

The JNDI architecture consists of an API and a service provider interface (SPI). Java applications use the JNDI API to access a variety of naming and directory services. The SPI enables a variety of naming and directory services to be plugged in transparently, thereby allowing the Java application using the JNDI API to access their services. See Figure 1.

Packaging

The JNDI is included in the Java 2 SDK, v1.3. It is also available as a Java Standard Extension for use with the JDK™ v1.1 and Java 2 SDK, v1.2. It extends the v1.1 and v1.2 platforms to provide naming and directory functionality.

To use the JNDI, you must have the JNDI classes and one or more service providers. The Java 2 SDK, v1.3 includes three service providers for the following naming/directory services:

- Lightweight Directory Access Protocol (LDAP)
- Common Object Request Broker Architecture (CORBA) Common Object Services (COS) name service
- Java Remote Method Invocation (RMI) Registry

Other service providers can be downloaded from the JNDI Web site (`http://java.sun.com/ products/jndi`) or obtained from other vendors. When using the JNDI as a Standard Extension on the JDK v1.1 and Java 2 SDK, v1.2, you must first download the JNDI classes and one

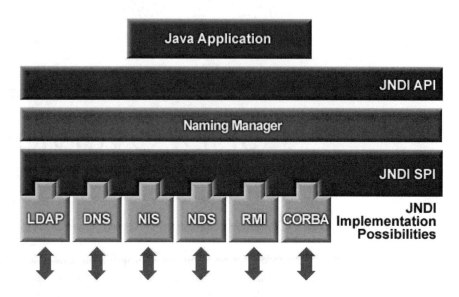

FIGURE 1:   JNDI Architecture.

or more service providers. See the **Preparations** lesson (page 41) for details on how to install the JNDI classes and service providers.

The JNDI is divided into five packages:

- `javax.naming`
- `javax.naming.directory`
- `javax.naming.event`
- `javax.naming.ldap`
- `javax.naming.spi`

Naming Package

The `javax.naming` package contains classes and interfaces for accessing naming services.

Context

The naming package defines a `Context` interface, which is the core interface for looking up, binding/unbinding, and renaming objects and creating and destroying subcontexts.

The most commonly used operation is `lookup()`. You supply `lookup()` the name of the object that you want to look up, and it returns the object bound to that name. For example, the following code fragment looks up a printer and sends a document to the printer object to be printed.

```
Printer printer = (Printer)ctx.lookup("treekiller");
printer.print(report);
```

Names

Every naming method in the Context interface has two overloads: one that accepts a Name argument and one that accepts a java.lang.String name. Name is an interface that represents a *generic name*—an ordered sequence of zero or more components. For the methods in the Context interface, a Name argument that is an instance of CompositeName represents a composite name, so you can name an object using a name that spans multiple namespaces. A Name argument of any other type represents a compound name. (Names are covered in the **Beyond the Basics** trail (page 79).) The overloads that accept Name are useful for applications that need to manipulate names, that is, composing them, comparing components, and so on.

A java.lang.String name argument represents a composite name. The overloads that accept java.lang.String names are likely to be more useful for simple applications, such as those that simply read in a name and look up the corresponding object.

Bindings

listBindings() returns an enumeration of name-to-object bindings. Each binding is represented by an instance of the Binding class. A binding is a tuple containing the name of the bound object, the name of the object's class, and the object itself.

list() is similar to listBindings(), except that it returns an enumeration of Name-ClassPair. NameClassPair contains an object's name and the name of the object's class. list() is useful for applications such as browsers that want to discover information about the objects bound within a context but that don't need all of the actual objects. Although list-Bindings() provides all of the same information, it is potentially a much more expensive operation.

References

Objects are stored in naming and directory services in different ways. A service that supports storing Java objects might support storing an object in its serialized form. However, some naming and directory services do not support the storing of Java objects. Furthermore, for some objects in the directory, Java programs are but one group of applications that access them. In this case, a serialized Java object might not be the most appropriate representation. A reference might be a very compact representation of an object, whereas its serialized form might contain a lot more state (see the **Naming Concepts** lesson (page 8)).

The JNDI defines the Reference class to represent a reference. A reference contains information on how to construct a copy of the object. The JNDI will attempt to turn references looked up from the directory into the Java objects that they represent so that JNDI clients have the illusion that what is stored in the directory are Java objects.

The Initial Context

In the JNDI, all naming and directory operations are performed relative to a context. There are no absolute roots. Therefore the JNDI defines an *initial context*, InitialContext, which provides a starting point for naming and directory operations. Once you have an initial context, you can use it to look up other contexts and objects.

Exceptions

The JNDI defines a class hierarchy for exceptions that can be thrown in the course of performing naming and directory operations. The root of this class hierarchy is NamingException. Programs interested in dealing with a particular exception can catch the corresponding subclass of the exception. Otherwise, they should catch NamingException.

Directory Package

The javax.naming.directory package extends the javax.naming package to provide functionality for accessing directory services in addition to naming services. This package allows applications to retrieve attributes associated with objects stored in the directory and to search for objects using specified attributes.

The Directory Context

The DirContext interface represents a *directory context*. It defines methods for examining and updating attributes associated with a directory object.

You use getAttributes() to retrieve the attributes associated with a directory object (for which you supply the name). Attributes are modified using modifyAttributes(). You can add, replace, or remove attributes and/or attribute values using this operation.

DirContext also behaves as a naming context by extending the Context interface. This means that any directory object can also provide a naming context. For example, a directory object for a person might contain attributes about that person as well as provide a context for naming objects, such as the person's printers and file system relative to that person directory object.

Searches

DirContext contains methods for performing content-based searching of the directory. In the simplest and most common form of usage, the application specifies a set of attributes—possibly with specific values—to match and submits this attribute set to the search() method. Other overloaded forms of search() support more sophisticated search filters.

Event Package

The `javax.naming.event` package contains classes and interfaces for supporting event notification in naming and directory services. Event notification is described in detail in the **Beyond the Basics** trail (page 111).

Events

A `NamingEvent` represents an event that is generated by a naming/directory service. The event contains a *type* that identifies the type of event. For example, event types are categorized into those that affect the namespace, such as "object added," and those that do not, such as "object changed." A `NamingEvent` also contains other information about the change, such as information about the object before and after the change.

Listeners

A `NamingListener` is an object that listens for `NamingEvents`. Each category of event type has a corresponding type of `NamingListener`. For example, a `NamespaceChangeListener` represents a listener interested in namespace change events and an `ObjectChangeListener` represents a listener interested in object change events.

To receive event notifications, a listener must be registered with either an `EventContext` or an `EventDirContext`. Once registered, the listener will receive event notifications when the corresponding changes occur in the naming/directory service.

LDAP Package

The `javax.naming.ldap` package contains classes and interfaces for using features that are specific to the LDAP v3 that are not already covered by the more generic `javax.naming.directory` package. In fact, most JNDI applications that use the LDAP will find the `javax.naming.directory` package sufficient and will not need to use the `javax.naming.ldap` package. This package is primarily for those applications that need to use "extended" operations, controls, or unsolicited notifications.

"Extended" Operations

In addition to specifying well-defined operations such as search and modify, the LDAP v3 (RFC 2251) specifies a way to transmit yet-to-be defined operations between the LDAP client and the server. These operations are called *"extended" operations*. An "extended" operation may be defined by a standards organization such as the Internet Engineering Task Force (IETF) or by a vendor.

Controls

The LDAP v3 (RFC 2251) allows any request or response to be augmented by yet-to-be defined modifiers, called *controls*. A control sent with a request is a *request control*, and a control sent with a response is a *response control*. A control may be defined by a standards organization such as the IETF or by a vendor. Request controls and response controls are not necessarily paired; that is, there need not be a response control for each request control sent, and vice versa.

Unsolicited Notifications

In addition to the normal request/response style of interaction between the client and server, the LDAP v3 also specifies *unsolicited notifications*—messages that are sent from the server to the client asynchronously and not in response to any client request.

The LDAP Context

The `LdapContext` interface represents a context for performing "extended" operations, sending request controls, and receiving response controls. Examples of how to use these features are described in the **Controls and Extensions** lesson (page 289).

Service Provider Package

The `javax.naming.spi` package provides the means by which developers of different naming/directory service providers can develop and hook up their implementations so that the corresponding services are accessible from applications that use the JNDI.

Plug-In Architecture

The `javax.naming.spi` package allows different implementations to be plugged in dynamically. These implementations include those for the initial context and for contexts that can be reached from the initial context.

Java Object Support

The `javax.naming.spi` package supports implementors of `Context.lookup()` and related methods to return Java objects that are natural and intuitive for the Java programmer. For example, if you look up a printer name from the directory, then you likely would expect to get back a printer object on which to operate. This support is provided in the form of object factories.

This package also provides support for doing the reverse. That is, implementors of Context.bind() and related methods can accept Java objects and store the objects in a format acceptable to the underlying naming/directory service. This support is provided in the form of state factories.

Multiple Naming Systems (Federation)

JNDI operations allow applications to supply names that span multiple naming systems. In the process of completing an operation, one service provider might need to interact with another service provider, for example to pass on the operation to be continued in the next naming system. The javax.naming.spi package provides support for different providers to cooperate to complete JNDI operations.

Examples

This lesson contains two examples.[1] The first example shows you how to look up an object from a naming service, in this case the file system. The second example shows you how to read an attribute from a directory service, in this case an LDAP directory.

If you have problems compiling or running these examples, then see the **Common Problems** lesson (page 31). That lesson describes problems that you might encounter when trying to compile and run the examples or when using the JNDI in general and offers solutions that you can try.

Naming Example

This example shows you how to write a program that looks up an object whose name is passed in as a command-line argument. It uses a service provider for the file system. Therefore the name that you supply to the program must be a filename. You do not need to understand details about the service provider at this point.

Importing the JNDI Classes

Using your favorite text editor, create a file named `Lookup.java`. You can import either the entire package or only individual classes and interfaces. The following code imports each class that is used from the `javax.naming` package.

```
import javax.naming.Context;
import javax.naming.InitialContext;
import javax.naming.NamingException;
```

---

[1] See the **Preface** for instructions on how to find the examples on the accompanying CD.

Creating an Initial Context

In the `main()` method of the program, create an initial context. Indicate that you're using the file system service provider by setting the *environment properties* parameter (represented by a `Hashtable` class) to the `InitialContext` constructor, as follows.

```
Hashtable env = new Hashtable();
env.put(Context.INITIAL_CONTEXT_FACTORY,
    "com.sun.jndi.fscontext.RefFSContextFactory");
Context ctx = new InitialContext(env);
```

How to set up the parameters for this constructor is explained in more detail in **The Basics** trail (page 49).

Looking Up an Object

Next, use `Context.lookup()` to look up an object. The following code looks up the object bound to the name supplied in the command line:

```
Object obj = ctx.lookup(name);
```

Catching NamingException

The creation of the initial context and the `lookup()` method can throw a `NamingException`. For this reason, you need to enclose these calls inside a `try/catch` clause. Here's the code fragment repeated with the `try/catch` clause.

```
try {
    // Create the initial context
    Context ctx = new InitialContext(env);

    // Look up an object
    Object obj = ctx.lookup(name);

    // Print it
    System.out.println(name + " is bound to: " + obj);

} catch (NamingException e) {
    System.err.println("Problem looking up " + name + ": " + e);
}
```

Compiling the Program

Next, you compile the source file using the Java™ compiler. To compile the program, you must have access to the JNDI classes. If you are using the Java 2 SDK, v1.3, then the JNDI classes are already included. Otherwise, you can include the classes either by setting the CLASSPATH variable to include the `jndi.jar` that you downloaded from the JNDI Web site (or copied from the accompanying CD) or by installing `jndi.jar` as an installed extension. See the **Preparations** lesson (page 41) for details on how to install the JNDI classes and service providers.

If the compilation succeeds, then the compiler will create a file named `Lookup.class` in the same directory (folder) as the Java source file (`Lookup.java`). If the compilation fails, then make sure that you typed in and named the program exactly as shown here, using the capitalization shown. If you are still having problems, then see the **Common Problems** lesson (page 31) for help.

Running the Program

To run the program, you need access to the JNDI classes, the file system service provider, and your example class (`Lookup.class`). See the compilation step for instructions on including access to the JNDI classes. To include the file system service provider classes (`fscontext.jar`), either include `fscontext.jar` in your CLASSPATH variable or install it as an extension. Note that the archive `fscontext.jar` is *not* included with the Java 2 SDK, v1.3. See the **Preparations** lesson (page 41) for details on how to install the JNDI classes and service providers. Finally, include the directory that contains your `Lookup.class` file in your the CLASSPATH variable.

To run the program, supply the name of a file in your file system, as follows:

```
# java Lookup /tmp
```

Or as follows:

```
# java Lookup \autoexec.bat
```

If you supply a file directory, then you will see something like the following.

```
# java Lookup /tmp
/tmp is bound to: com.sun.jndi.fscontext.RefFSContext@1dae083f
```

If the name that you supplied is a file, then you will see something like this:

```
/tmp/f is bound to: //tmp/f
```

If you have any trouble running this example, then see the **Common Problems** lesson (page 32).

Directory Example

This example shows you how to write a program that retrieves attributes from a directory object. It uses an LDAP service provider to access an LDAP service.

Importing the JNDI Directory Classes

Using your favorite text editor, create a file named Getattr.java. You can import either the entire package or only individual classes and interfaces. The following code imports each class that is used from the javax.naming and javax.naming.directory packages.

```
import javax.naming.Context;
import javax.naming.directory.InitialDirContext;
import javax.naming.directory.DirContext;
import javax.naming.directory.Attributes;
import javax.naming.NamingException;
```

Creating an Initial Directory Context

In the main() method of the program, create an initial directory context. This is similar to creating an initial context in the previous naming example, except that you use the constructor for InitialDirContext.

```
Hashtable env = new Hashtable();
env.put(Context.INITIAL_CONTEXT_FACTORY,
    "com.sun.jndi.ldap.LdapCtxFactory");
env.put(Context.PROVIDER_URL, "ldap://localhost:389/o=JNDITutorial");

DirContext ctx = new InitialDirContext(env);
```

Similar to the naming example, indicate that you're using the LDAP service provider by setting the Hashtable parameter to the InitialDirContext constructor appropriately. Details on how to set up the parameters for this constructor are given in **The Basics** trail (page 49). For now, the only thing to understand is that the program by default identifies an LDAP server on the local machine. If your LDAP server is located on another machine or is using another port, then you need to edit the LDAP URL ("ldap://localhost:389/o=JNDITutorial") accordingly. Instructions for setting up a sample LDAP server for this tutorial are given in the **Preparations** lesson (page 43).

Getting a Directory Object's Attributes

Next, use getAttributes() to get an object's attributes. The following code retrieves all of the attributes associated with the object bound to the name "cn=Ted Geisel, ou=People":

```
Attributes attrs = ctx.getAttributes("cn=Ted Geisel, ou=People");
```

Extracting the Desired Attribute

From a set of attributes, Attributes, you can ask for a particular attribute by using Attributes.get() and then from that attribute get its value. The following line first gets the surname attribute "sn" and then invokes Attribute.get() on it to get its value:

```
attrs.get("sn").get();
```

Catching NamingException

The method calls shown so far can throw a NamingException. For this reason, you need to wrap these calls inside a try/catch clause. Here's the code fragment repeated with the try/catch clause.

```
try {

    // Create the initial directory context
    DirContext ctx = new InitialDirContext(env);

    // Ask for all attributes of the object
    Attributes attrs = ctx.getAttributes("cn=Ted Geisel, ou=People");

    // Find the surname attribute ("sn") and print it
    System.out.println("sn: " + attrs.get("sn").get());

} catch (NamingException e) {
    System.err.println("Problem getting attribute:" + e);
}
```

Compiling the Program

Next, compile the source file using the Java compiler. As with the naming example, to do this you need access to the JNDI classes.

If the compilation succeeds, then the compiler creates a file named Getattr.class in the same directory (folder) as the Java source file (Getattr.java). If the compilation fails, then make sure that you typed in and named the program exactly as shown here, using the capitalization shown. If you are still having problems, then see the **Common Problems** lesson (page 31) for help.

Running the Program

As with the naming example, you need access to both the JNDI classes and your example class (Getattr.class). You also need access to the LDAP service provider classes (ldap.jar and providerutil.jar). If you are using the Java 2 SDK, v1.3, then these classes are already included.

Here's an example of a command line for running Getattr and the output it generates.

```
# java Getattr
sn: Geisel
```

Recall that the program was configured using the following property.

```
env.put(Context.PROVIDER_URL, "ldap://localhost:389/o=JNDITutorial");
```

With this configuration, this command queries the LDAP server on machine localhost that is listening on port 389, serving the "o=JNDITutorial" namespace. (See the **Preparations** lesson (page 49) for details on this configuration step.) It asks for the attributes of the entry "cn=Ted Geisel, ou=People". Once it has the attributes, it extracts the surname attribute ("sn"). If you have any trouble running this example, then see the **Common Problems** lesson (page 32).

Common Problems (and Their Solutions)

This lesson describes common problems that you might encounter when using the JNDI and gives their solutions. The problems are classified as follows:

- Compilation
- Runtime
- Web browser

Compilation Problems

Here are the most common problems that you might encounter when compiling a program that uses the JNDI classes.

Class or Package Not Found

Problem: You get "Package javax.naming not found" or a similar error complaining about missing classes.

Cause: You did not include the JNDI classes (jndi.jar) in your CLASSPATH when you compiled your program, or you did not install the JNDI classes properly as an extension, or you mistyped the class or package name.

Solution: The Java™ 2 SDK, v1.3 includes the JNDI classes. If you are using this version and get a class or package not found error, then double-check the spelling of the package and class.

If you are not using the Java 2 SDK, v1.3, then you need to download the JNDI classes and include them in your development environment. The way that you include the JNDI classes depends on your development environment.

If you are using the Java 2 SDK, v1.2, then make sure that jndi.jar is in the *JAVA_HOME/* jre/lib/ext directory, where *JAVA_HOME* is the directory that contains the SDK. If you are using the javac compiler from the JDK™ v1.1, then add jndi.jar either to your CLASSPATH environment variable or to the -classpath option in your javac command line. See the **Preparations** lesson (page 45) for more details.

Incompatible Java Platform Versions

Problem: You get compilation failures complaining about missing java.* packages or classes.
Cause: You are using an old version of the Java platform.
Solution: You need to use the Java v1.1.2 or higher. See http://java.sun.com/products/jdk/.

Runtime Problems

Here are the most common problems that you might encounter when you try to run a successfully compiled program that uses the JNDI classes.

Class Not Found

Problem: You get a NoClassDefFoundError when running your program.
Cause: You did not include the JNDI classes (jndi.jar) in your classpath, or you did not install the JNDI classes properly.
Solution: The Java 2 SDK, v1.3 includes the JNDI classes, so if you are using this version you should not get this error.

If you are not using the Java 2 SDK, v1.3, then the way that you include the JNDI classes in your *execution* environment depends on that environment. If you are using the Java 2 SDK, v1.2, then make sure that jndi.jar is in the *JAVA_HOME/*jre/lib/ext directory, where *JAVA_HOME* is the directory that contains the Java Runtime Environment (JRE). Note that on some platforms, separate jre/lib/ext directories exist for the JRE and the SDK. Make sure that the JNDI JARs have been installed in both jre/lib/ext directories. If you are using the java interpreter from the JDK v1.1, then add the JARs either to your CLASSPATH environment variable or to the -classpath option in your java command line.

For an applet, you need to make the JNDI and provider classes available to that applet (for example, by adding them to the archive option).

No Initial Context

Problem: You get a NoInitialContextException.

Cause: You did not specify which implementation to use for the initial context. Specifically, the `Context.INITIAL_CONTEXT_FACTORY` environment property was not set to the class name of the factory that will create the initial context. Or, you did not make available to the program the classes of the service provider named by `Context.INITIAL_CONTEXT_FACTORY`.

Solution: Set the `Context.INITIAL_CONTEXT_FACTORY` environment property to the class name of the initial context implementation that you are using. See **The Basics** trail (page 49) for details.

If the property was set, then make sure that the class name was not mistyped and that the class named is available to your program (either in its classpath or installed in the `jre/lib/ext` directory of the JRE). The Java 2 SDK, v1.3 includes service providers for LDAP, COS naming, and the RMI registry. All other service providers must be installed and added to the execution environment.

Connection Refused

Problem: You get a `CommunicationException`, indicating "connection refused."

Cause: The server and port identified by the `Context.PROVIDER_URL` environment property is not being served by the server. Perhaps someone disabled or turned off the machine on which the server is running. Or, maybe you mistyped the server's name or port number.

Solution: Check that there is indeed a server running on that port, and restart the server if necessary. The way that you perform this check depends on the LDAP server that you are using. Usually, an administrative console or tool is available that you can use to administer the server. You may use that tool to verify the server's status.

Connection Fails

Problem: The LDAP server responds to other utilities (such as its administration console) but does not seem to respond to your program's requests.

Cause: The server does not respond to LDAP v3 connection requests. Some servers (especially public servers) do not respond correctly to the LDAP v3, ignoring the requests instead of rejecting them. Also, some LDAP v3 servers have problems handling a control that Sun's LDAP service provider automatically sends and often return a server-specific failure code.

Solution. Try setting the environment property `"java.naming.ldap.version"` to `"2"`. The LDAP service provider by default attempts to connect to an LDAP server using the LDAP v3; if that fails, then it uses the LDAP v2. If the server silently ignores the v3 request, then the provider will assume that the request worked. To work around such servers, you must explicitly set the protocol version to ensure proper behavior by the server.

If the server is a v3 server, then try setting the following environment property before creating the initial context:

```
env.put(Context.REFERRAL, "throw");
```

This will turn off the control that the LDAP provider sends automatically. (See the **Referrals** lesson (page 259) for details.)

Program Hangs

Problem: The program hangs.

Causes: Some servers (especially public ones) won't respond (not even with a negative answer) if you attempt to perform a search that would generate too many results or that would require the server to examine too many entries in order to generate the answer. Such servers are trying to limit the amount of resources that they expend on a per-request basis.

Or, you tried to use Secure Socket Layer (SSL) against a server/port that does not support it, and vice versa (that is, you tried to use a plain socket to talk to an SSL port).

Solution: If your program is hanging because the server is trying to restrict the use of its resources, then retry your request using a query that will return a single result or only a few results. This will help you to determine whether the server is alive. If it is, then you can broaden your initial query and resubmit it.

If your program is hanging because of SSL problems, then you need to find out whether the port is an SSL port and then set the `Context.SECURITY_PROTOCOL` environment property appropriately. If the port is an SSL port, then this property should be set to `"ssl"`. If it is not an SSL port, then this property should not be set.

Name Not Found

Problem: You get a `NameNotFoundException`.

Causes: When you initialized the initial context for the LDAP, you supplied a root-distinguished name. For example, if you set the `Context.PROVIDER_URL` environment property for the initial context to `"ldap://ldapserver:389/o=JNDITutorial"` and subsequently supplied a name such as `"cn=Joe,c=us"`, then the full name that you passed to the LDAP service was `"cn=Joe,c=us,o=JNDITutorial"`. If this was really the name that you intended, then you should check your server to make sure that it contains such an entry.

Also, the Netscape Directory Server returns this error if you supply an incorrect distinguished name for authentication purposes. For example, the LDAP provider will throw a `NameNotFoundException` if you set the `Context.SECURITY_PRINCIPAL` environment property to `"cn=Admin,o=Tutorial"`, and `"cn=Admin,o=Tutorial"` is not an entry on the LDAP server. The correct error for the Netscape Directory Server to return actually should be something related to authentication, rather than "name not found."

Solution: Verify that the name that you supplied is that of an entry existing on the server. You can do this by listing the entry's parent context or using some other tool such as the directory server's administration console.

Web Browser Problems

Here are some problems that you might encounter when trying to deploy an applet that uses the JNDI classes.

Cannot Authenticate by Using CRAM-MD5

Problem: You get an `AppletSecurityException` when an applet running inside Netscape Communicator attempts to authenticate using CRAM-MD5 to the LDAP server.
Cause: Netscape Communicator disables access to the `java.security` packages. The LDAP provider used the message digest functionality provided by `java.security.MessageDigest` for implementing CRAM-MD5.
Solution: Use the Java Plug-in.

Cannot Connect to Arbitrary Hosts

Problem: You get an `AppletSecurityException` when your applet attempts to communicate with a directory server that is running on a machine different from the one from which the applet was loaded.
Cause: Your applet was not signed, so it can connect only to the machine from which it was loaded. Or, if the applet was signed, the browser has not granted the applet permission to connect to the directory server machine.
Solution: If you want to allow the applet to connect to directory servers running on arbitrary machines, then you need to sign *both* your applet *and* all of the JNDI JARs that your applet will be using. For information on signing JARs, see `http://java.sun.com/products/jdk/1.1/docs/guide/security/index.html`.

Cannot Access System Properties for Configuration

Problem: You get an `AppletSecurityException` when your applet attempts to set up the environment properties using system properties.
Cause: Web browsers limit access to system properties and throw a `SecurityException` if you attempt to read them.
Solution: If you need to obtain input for your applet, then try using applet `params` instead.

The Basics

The lessons in this trail explain how to write applications that access naming and directory services. They give you the basics of how to interact with the directory using the JNDI, from preparing the environment, to looking up objects from the namespace, to searching the directory.

- The **Preparations** lesson (page 41) covers how to set up your environment to compile and run JNDI programs.
- The **Naming Opereations** lesson (page 53) explains how to perform naming operations, such as looking up objects and removing them from the naming service.
- The **Directory Operations** lesson (page 59) discusses how to perform directory operations, including searching and modifying entries in the directory.

Preparations

Before you begin, you need to do two things. First, make sure that you have the required software. The first section lists that software.

Second, you need to perform some programmatic setup. The last part of this lesson details how to do this, including how to create an initial context and how to handle the exceptions that JNDI methods can throw.

In addition, a section is included that explains what to expect from the examples in this tutorial. The examples are intended as guides for you to follow when building your own applications. You can run them to observe the behavior described. When you write your own applications and run them against servers that you or others have set up, the behavior that you observe might be dramatically different.

Required Software

Following is a list of the software/systems that you need:

- Java™ platform software
- JNDI software
- Service provider software
- Naming and directory server software

Java Platform Software

To run applications or applets that use the JNDI, you need v1.1.2 or higher of the Java platform software (such as the Java 2 Software Development Kit (SDK) or Java Development Kit (JDK™ software).

To run the applets, you can use any Java-compatible Web browser, such as HotJava™, Netscape Communicator or Navigator v4, or Internet Explorer v5. To ensure that your applets take full advantage of the latest features of the Java platform software, you can use the Java Plug-in with your Web browser.

JNDI Software

The JNDI class libraries are already included with the Java 2 SDK, v1.3. If you are using another version of the SDK, then you can use the JNDI software available both on the accompanying CD and from the JNDI Web site (`http://java.sun.com/products/jndi`). In addition, all sample code from this tutorial, as well as the tutorial itself, are available both on the accompanying CD and from that site.

Service Provider Software

The JNDI API is a generic API for accessing any naming or directory service. Actual access to a naming or directory service is enabled by plugging in a service provider under the JNDI. An overview of the JNDI architecture and the role of service providers is given in the **JNDI Overview** lesson (page 17).

A *service provider* is software that maps the JNDI API to actual calls to the naming or directory server. Typically, the roles of the service provider and naming/directory server differ. In the terminology of client/server software, the JNDI and the service provider are the *client* (called the *JNDI client*) and the naming/directory server is the *server*.

Clients and servers may interact in many ways. In one common way, they use a network protocol so that the client and server can exist autonomously in a networked environment. The server typically supports many different clients, not only JNDI clients, provided that the clients conform to the specified protocol. The JNDI does not dictate any particular style of interaction between JNDI clients and servers. For example, at one extreme the client and server could be the same entity.

You need to obtain the classes for the service providers that you will be using. For example, if you plan to use the JNDI to access an LDAP directory server, then you need software for an LDAP service provider.

The Java 2 SDK, v1.3 comes with service providers for LDAP, COS naming, and the RMI registry. If you are using an earlier version of the SDK, then you need to get the service providers. The accompanying CD contains several service providers, including one for the LDAP. In addition, the JNDI Web site lists service providers that you can download.

This tutorial uses two service providers:

- The file system service provider for the naming examples
- The LDAP service provider for the directory and event notification examples

The file system service provider can be obtained from the accompanying CD or the JNDI Web site.

When using the file system service provider, you don't need to set up a server because you can use your local file system as the server. When using the LDAP service provider, you need either to set up your own server or to have access to an existing server, as explained next.

Naming and Directory Server Software

Once you have obtained the service provider software, you then need to set up or have access to a corresponding naming/directory server. Setting up a naming/directory server is typically the job of a network system administrator. Different vendors have different installation procedures for their naming/directory servers. Some require special machine privileges before the server can be installed. You should consult the naming/directory server software's installation instructions.

For the naming examples in this tutorial, you'll use the file system.

For the directory examples in this tutorial, you need access to an LDAP server. You can download a free, publicly available LDAP server from OpenLDAP (http://www.openldap.org). See the next part of this lesson for information on populating the LDAP server with content for running this tutorial's examples.

Publicly accessible servers are also available at the following URLs:

```
ldap://ldap.Bigfoot.com
ldap://ldap.four11.com
ldap://ldap.InfoSpace.com
```

Contents of the Directory

Once you've set up the directory,[1] or have directed your program to communicate with an existing directory, what sort of information can you expect to find there? You can get two kinds of information from the directory: bindings and attributes.

The directory can be viewed as consisting of *name-to-object bindings*. That is, each object in the directory has a corresponding name. You can retrieve an object in the directory by looking up its name. If you are using a naming service such as the file system (as you will be doing in some of this tutorial's examples), then the objects are files and they are bound to filenames.

Also stored in the directory are attributes. An object in the directory, in addition to having a name, also has an optional set of attributes. You can ask the directory for an object's attributes, as well as ask it to search for an object that has certain attributes.

This trail gives examples of accessing both kinds of information. The specifics of exactly what you can access from a naming or directory service depend on how the particular service has been laid out and what information has been added into it.

---

[1]See the **Preface** for instructions on how to find the configuration tools and files used in this tutorial on the accompanying CD.

Directory Schema

A *schema* specifies the types of objects that a directory may contain. This tutorial populates the directory with entries, some of which require special schema definitions. To accommodate these entries, you must first either turn off schema-checking in the server or add the schema files that accompany this tutorial to the server. Both of these tasks are typically performed by the directory server's administrator.

This tutorial has two schema files that you must install:

- Schema for Java objects (see **Appendix**)
- Schema for CORBA objects (see **Appendix**)

The format of these files is a formal description that possibly cannot be directly copied and pasted into server configuration files. Specifically, the attribute syntaxes are described in terms of RFC 2252.

Different directory servers have different ways of configuring their schema. This tutorial includes some tools for installing the Java and CORBA schemas on directory servers that permit their schemas to be modified via the LDAP. It also includes tools for updating an existing directory that has older versions of these schemas. Following is a list of tasks the tools can perform.

1. Create Java schema (`CreateJavaSchema.java`).
2. Create CORBA schema (`CreateCorbaSchema.java`).
3. Update directory entries that use an outdated Java schema (`UpdateJavaSchema.java`).
4. Update directory entries that use an outdated CORBA schema (`UpdateCorba-Schema.java`).

Follow the instructions in the accompanying README file to run these programs. The README file and the tools are available both on the accompanying CD and from the JNDI Web Site.

Note 1: If you are using Netscape Directory Server v4.1, then you must update the schema. If you are updating the schema by manually updating its configuration files, then first locate the `java-object-schema.conf` file in the server installation at the directory named

    NETSCAPE-DIRECTORY-HOME/slapd-*SERVER-ID*/config/

The contents of `java-object-schema.conf` are out-of-date. You must replace them with the schema in **Appendix**. See Note 2 for further instructions.

If you are updating the schema using the Java programs that accompany this tutorial, then first locate the `ns-schema.conf` file in the server installation at the directory named

    NETSCAPE-DIRECTORY-HOME/slapd-*SERVER-ID*/config/

Comment out the line that contains `java-object-schema.conf` because that schema is out-of-date. Restart the server and use the `CreateJavaSchema` program to install the updated schema. You need to manually remove the reference to the old schema from the list of built-in schemas in `ns-schema.conf`. This is because the server does not permit such built-in schemas to be modified via the LDAP.

Note 2: The Network Directory Server v4.1 (and earlier releases) has a different way of identifying attribute syntaxes than RFC 2252. For that server, you should use the following substitutions:

"case ignore string" for the attributes with the Directory String syntax
(1.3.6.1.4.1.1466.115.121.1.15)
"binary" for the attributes with the Octet String syntax (1.3.6.1.4.1.1466.115.121.1.40)

Providing Directory Content for This Tutorial

To set up the file system namespace, run the Setup program. This program creates a file sub-tree that provides a common frame of reference for discussing what to expect in terms of listing and looking up objects from the file system. To run this program, give it the name of the directory in which to create the tutorial test namespace. For example, typing the following

```
# java Setup /tmp/tutorial
```

creates a directory /tmp/tutorial and populates it with directories and files.

In the directory examples in this trail, the results shown reflect how the LDAP directory has been set up using the configuration file (tutorial.ldif) that accompanies this tutorial. If you are using an existing server, or a server with a different setup, then you might see different results. Before you can load the configuration file (tutorial.ldif) into the directory server, you must follow the instructions for updating the server's schema.

Installation Note: Access Control. Different directory servers handle access control differently. Some examples in this trail perform updates to the directory. Therefore you need to take server-specific actions to make the directory updatable in order for those examples to work. For the Netscape Directory Server, add the aci entry suggested in the netscape.aci.ldif file to the dn: o=JNDITutorial entry to make the entire directory updatable.

Packages and Classpath

To use the JNDI in your program, you need to set up its compilation and execution environments.

Importing the JNDI Classes

Following are the JNDI packages:

- javax.naming
- javax.naming.directory
- javax.naming.event
- javax.naming.ldap
- javax.naming.spi

The examples in this trail use classes and interfaces from the first two packages. You need to import these two packages into your program or import individual classes and interfaces that you use. The following two lines import all of the classes and interfaces from the two packages `javax.naming` and `javax.naming.directory`.

```
import javax.naming.*;
import javax.naming.directory.*;
```

Compilation Environment

To compile a program that uses the JNDI, you need access to the JNDI classes. Java 2 SDK, v1.3 already includes the JNDI classes, so if you are using it you need not take any further actions.

If you are using an older version of the Java SDK, then you need to obtain the JNDI classes, which are available both on the accompanying CD and from the JNDI Web site.

If you are using Java 2 SDK, v1.2, then you can install the JNDI classes as an installed extension. Copy the `jndi.jar` archive file to the *JAVA_HOME*/`jre/lib/ext` directory, where *JAVA_HOME* is the directory that contains the SDK.

If you are not using the JNDI as an installed extension, or are using JDK v1.1, then copy the `jndi.jar` archive file to its permanent location and add its location to your classpath. You can do this by setting the CLASSPATH variable to include the absolute filename of the `jndi.jar` archive file.

Execution Environment

To run a program that uses the JNDI, you need access to the JNDI classes and classes for any service providers that the program uses. The JRE (Java 2 Runtime Environment) v1.3 already includes the JNDI classes and service providers for LDAP, COS naming, and the RMI registry. If you are using some other service providers, then you need to download and install their archive files in the *JAVA_HOME*/`jre/lib/ext` directory, where *JAVA_HOME* is the directory that contains the JRE.

If you are using an older version of the JRE, then you need to obtain the JNDI classes, which are available both on the accompanying CD and from the JNDI Web site. This Web site also lists some service providers. You may download these providers or use providers from the accompanying CD or other vendors.

If you are using the JRE v1.2, then you can install the JNDI classes as an installed extension. Copy the `jndi.jar` archive file to the *JAVA_HOME*/`jre/lib/ext` directory, where *JAVA_HOME* is the directory that contains the JRE.

If you are not using the JNDI as an installed extension or are using the JRE v1.1, then copy the JNDI and service provider archive files to their permanent location and add that location to your classpath. You can do that by setting the CLASSPATH variable to include the absolute filenames of the archive files. For the examples in this trail, you'll need the file system and

LDAP service providers. To provide for this, include the filenames `fscontext.jar`, `ldap.jar`, and `providerutil.jar` in your CLASSPATH variable.

Naming Exceptions

Many methods in the JNDI packages throw a `NamingException` when they need to indicate that the operation requested cannot be performed. Commonly, you will see a `try/catch` wrapper around the methods that can throw a `NamingException`, as follows.

```
try {
    Context ctx = new InitialContext();
    Object obj = ctx.lookup("somename");
} catch (NamingException e) {
    // Handle the error
    System.err.println(e);
}
```

Exception Class Hierarchy

The JNDI has a rich exception hierarchy stemming from the `NamingException` class. The class names of the exceptions are self-explanatory and are listed later in this discussion. To handle a particular subclass of `NamingException`, you catch the subclass separately. For example, the following code specifically treats the `AuthenticationException` and its subclasses.

```
try {
    Context ctx = new InitialContext();
    Object obj = ctx.lookup("somename");
} catch (AuthenticationException e) {
    // Attempt to reacquire the authentication information
    ...
} catch (NamingException e) {
    // Handle the error
    System.err.println(e);
}
```

Enumerations

Operations such as `Context.list()` and `DirContext.search()` return a `Naming-Enumeration`. In these cases, if an error occurs and no results are returned, then `NamingException` or one of its appropriate subclasses will be thrown at the time that the method is invoked. If an error occurs but there are some results to be returned, then a `NamingEnumeration` is returned so that you can get those results. When all of the results are exhausted, invoking `NamingEnumeration.hasMore()` will cause a `NamingException` (or one of its subclasses) to be thrown to indicate the error. At that point, the enumeration becomes invalid and no more methods should be invoked on it.

For example, if you perform a search() and specify a count limit (*n*) of how many answers to return, then the search() will return an enumeration consisting of at most *n* results. If the number of results exceeds *n*, then when NamingEnumeration.hasMore() is invoked for the *n + 1* time, a SizeLimitExceededException will be thrown. See the count limit discussion in this trail (page 69) for sample code.

Examples in This Tutorial

In the inline sample code that is embedded within the text of this tutorial, the try/catch clauses are usually omitted for the sake of readability. Typically, because only code fragments are shown here, only the lines that are directly useful in illustrating a concept are included. You will see appropriate placements of the try/catch clauses for NamingException if you look in the source files that accompany this tutorial.

Exceptions in the javax.naming Package

Following are the exceptions contained in the javax.naming package:

```
NamingException
    CannotProceedException
    CommunicationException
    ConfigurationException
    ContextNotEmptyException
    InsufficientResourcesException
    InterruptedNamingException
    InvalidNameException
    LimitExceededException
        SizeLimitExceededException
        TimeLimitExceededException
    LinkException
        LinkLoopException
        MalformedLinkException
    NameAlreadyBoundException
    NameNotFoundException
    NamingSecurityException
        AuthenticationException
        AuthenticationNotSupportedException
        NoPermissionException
```

```
NoInitialContextException
NotContextException
OperationNotSupportedException
PartialResultException
ReferralException
ServiceUnavailableException
```

Exceptions in the javax.naming.directory Package

Following are the exceptions contained in the javax.naming.directory package:

```
NamingException
    AttributeInUseException
    AttributeModificationException
    InvalidAttributeIdentifierException
    InvalidAttributesException
    InvalidAttributeValueException
    InvalidSearchControlsException
    InvalidSearchFilterException
    NoSuchAttributeException
    SchemaViolationException
```

Exceptions in the javax.naming.ldap Package

Following are the exceptions contained in the javax.naming.ldap package:

```
NamingException
    ReferralException
        LdapReferralException
```

The Initial Context

Before performing any operation on a naming or directory service, you need to acquire an *initial context*—the starting point into the namespace. This is because all methods on naming and directory services are performed relative to some context. To get an initial context, you must follow these steps.

1. Select the service provider of the corresponding service that you want to access.
2. Specify any configuration that the initial context needs.
3. Call the InitialContext constructor.

Select the Service Provider for the Initial Context

You can specify the service provider to use for the initial context by creating a set of *environment properties* (a Hashtable) and adding the name of the service provider class to it. Environment properties are described in detail in the **Beyond the Basics** trail (page 95).

For example, if you are using the LDAP service provider from Sun Microsystems, then your code would look like the following.

```
Hashtable env = new Hashtable();
env.put(Context.INITIAL_CONTEXT_FACTORY,
    "com.sun.jndi.ldap.LdapCtxFactory");
```

To specify the file system service provider from Sun Microsystems, you would write code that looks like the following.

```
Hashtable env = new Hashtable();
env.put(Context.INITIAL_CONTEXT_FACTORY,
    "com.sun.jndi.fscontext.RefFSContextFactory");
```

You can also use *system properties* to specify the service provider to use. See the **Beyond the Basics** trail (page 95) for details.

Supply the Information Needed by the Initial Context

Clients of different directories might need various information for contacting the directory. For example, you might need to specify on which machine the server is running and what information is needed to identify the user to the directory. Such information is passed to the service provider via *environment properties*. The JNDI specifies some generic environment properties that service providers can use. Your service provider documentation will give details on the information required for these properties.

For example, suppose that the program is using the LDAP service provider. This provider requires that the program specify the location of the LDAP server, as well as user identity information. To provide this information, you would write code that looks as follows.

```
env.put(Context.PROVIDER_URL, "ldap://ldap.wiz.com:389");
env.put(Context.SECURITY_PRINCIPAL, "joeuser");
env.put(Context.SECURITY_CREDENTIALS, "joepassword");
```

This tutorial uses the file system and LDAP service providers from Sun Microsystems. For the examples that use the file system, supply as the provider URL the URL corresponding to the path that you gave to the Setup program. For example, if you used the directory /tmp/tutorial in the Setup program, your code would look as follows.

```
env.put(Context.PROVIDER_URL, "file:/tmp/tutorial/");
```

The examples that use the LDAP assume that a server has been set up on the local machine at port 389 with the root-distinguished name of "o=JNDITutorial" and that no authentication is required for updating the directory. They include the following code for setting up the environment.

```
env.put(Context.PROVIDER_URL, "ldap://localhost:389/o=JNDITutorial");
```

If you are using a directory that is set up differently, then you will need to set up these environment properties accordingly. For example, if the directory is running on another machine, then you will need to replace "localhost" with the name of that machine.

Creating the Initial Context

You are now ready to create the initial context. To do that, you pass to the InitialContext constructor the environment properties that you created previously:

```
Context ctx = new InitialContext(env);
```

Now that you have a reference to a Context object, you can begin to access the naming service.

To perform directory operations, you need to use an InitialDirContext. To do that, use one of its constructors:

```
DirContext ctx = new InitialDirContext(env);
```

This statement returns a reference to a DirContext object for performing directory operations.

Names

Notice that the Context and DirContext interfaces include overloaded forms of each method: one that accepts a java.lang.String name and one that accepts a Name. Each pair of these overloaded methods is equivalent in that if the Name and java.lang.String parameters are simply different representations of the same name, then the overloaded versions of the same methods behave in the same way.

For the purposes of this trail, you can just think of and use the name parameter as a name in the target namespace (such as that of your LDAP server). For a more thorough discussion of names, see the **Beyond the Basics** trail (page 79).

Naming Operations

You can use the JNDI to perform naming operations, including read operations and operations for updating the namespace. The following operations are described in this lesson:

- Looking up an object
- Listing the contents of a context
- Adding, overwriting, and removing a binding
- Renaming an object
- Creating and destroying subcontexts

Configuration

The examples in this lesson[1] use the file system service provider. They assume that you have set up a sample file namespace using the configuration program (Setup) that accompanies this trail. See the **Preparations** lesson (page 41) for instructions on running this program. If you use another service provider or choose to use another part of the file namespace, then the behavior will differ from what is shown here.

The initial context used in these examples is initialized using the following environment properties.

```
    //Set up the environment for creating the initial context
Hashtable env = new Hashtable();
env.put(Context.INITIAL_CONTEXT_FACTORY,
    "com.sun.jndi.fscontext.RefFSContextFactory");
env.put(Context.PROVIDER_URL, "file:/tmp/tutorial");
Context ctx = new InitialContext(env);
```

---

[1]See the **Preface** for instructions on how to find the examples on the accompanying CD.

Looking Up an Object

To look up an object from the naming service, use `Context.lookup()` and pass it the name of the object that you want to retrieve. Suppose that there is an object in the naming service with the name `"report.txt"`. To retrieve the object, you would write

```
Object obj = ctx.lookup("report.txt");
```

The type of object that is returned by `lookup()` depends both on the underlying naming system and on the data associated with the object itself. A naming system can contain many different types of objects, and a lookup of an object in different parts of the system might yield objects of different types. In this example, `"report.txt"` happens to be bound to a file (`java.io.File`). You can cast the result of `lookup()` to its target class.

For example, the following code looks up the object `"report.txt"` and casts it to `File`.

```
import java.io.File;
...
File f = (File)ctx.lookup("report.txt");
```

The complete example is in the file `Lookup.java`.

Listing a Context

Instead of getting a single object at a time, as with `Context.lookup()`, you can list an entire context by using a single operation. There are two methods for listing a context: one that returns the bindings and one that returns only the name-to-object class name pairs.

The Context.list() Method

`Context.list()` returns an enumeration of `NameClassPair`. Each `NameClassPair` consists of the object's name and its class name. The following code fragment lists the contents of the `"awt"` directory (that is, the files and directories found in the `"awt"` directory).

```
NamingEnumeration list = ctx.list("awt");

while (list.hasMore()) {
    NameClassPair nc = (NameClassPair)list.next();
    System.out.println(nc);
}
```

Running this example yields the following output.

```
# java List

accessibility: javax.naming.Context
color: javax.naming.Context
datatransfer: javax.naming.Context
dnd: javax.naming.Context
event: javax.naming.Context
```

```
font: javax.naming.Context
geom: javax.naming.Context
im: javax.naming.Context
image: javax.naming.Context
peer: javax.naming.Context
print: javax.naming.Context
swing: javax.naming.Context
```

The Context.listBindings() Method

Context.listBindings() returns an enumeration of Binding. Binding is a subclass of Name-ClassPair. A binding contains not only the object's name and class name but also the object. The following code enumerates the awt context, printing out each binding's name and object.

```
NamingEnumeration bindings = ctx.listBindings("awt");

while (bindings.hasMore()) {
    Binding bd = (Binding)bindings.next();
    System.out.println(bd.getName() + ": " + bd.getObject());
}
```

Running this example yields the following output.

```
# java ListBindings

accessibility: com.sun.jndi.fscontext.RefFSContext@1dacd52e
color: com.sun.jndi.fscontext.RefFSContext@1dacd551
datatransfer: com.sun.jndi.fscontext.RefFSContext@1dacd584
dnd: com.sun.jndi.fscontext.RefFSContext@1dacd5b6
event: com.sun.jndi.fscontext.RefFSContext@1dacd5e8
font: com.sun.jndi.fscontext.RefFSContext@1dacd61b
geom: com.sun.jndi.fscontext.RefFSContext@1dacd64d
im: com.sun.jndi.fscontext.RefFSContext@1dacd62a
image: com.sun.jndi.fscontext.RefFSContext@1dacd65c
peer: com.sun.jndi.fscontext.RefFSContext@1dacd68f
print: com.sun.jndi.fscontext.RefFSContext@1dacd6c1
swing: com.sun.jndi.fscontext.RefFSContext@1dacd6f3
```

Terminating a NamingEnumeration

A NamingEnumeration can be terminated in one of three ways: naturally, explicitly, or unexpectedly.

- When NamingEnumeration.hasMore() returns false, the enumeration is complete and effectively terminated.
- You can terminate an enumeration explicitly before it has completed by invoking Naming-Enumeration.close(). Doing this provides a hint to the underlying implementation to free up any resources associated with the enumeration.
- If either hasMore() or next() throws a NamingException, then the enumeration is effectively terminated.

Regardless of how an enumeration has been terminated, once terminated it can no longer be used. Invoking a method on a terminated enumeration yields an undefined result.

Why Two Different List Methods?

`list()` is intended for browser-style applications that just want to display the names of objects in a context. For example, a browser might list the names in a context and wait for the user to select one or a few of the names displayed to perform further operations. Such applications typically do not need access to all of the objects in a context.

`listBindings()` is intended for applications that need to perform operations on the objects in a context en masse. For example, a backup application might need to perform "file stats" operations on all of the objects in a file directory. Or a printer administration program might want to restart all of the printers in a building. To perform such operations, these applications need to obtain all of the objects bound in a context. Thus it is more expedient to have the objects returned as part of the enumeration.

The application can use either `list()` or the potentially more expensive `listBindings()`, depending on the type of information it needs.

Adding, Replacing, and Removing a Binding

The `Context` interface contains methods for adding, replacing, and removing a binding in a context.

Adding a Binding

`Context.bind()` is used to add a binding to a context. It accepts as arguments the name of the object and the object to be bound.

```
// Create the object to be bound
Fruit fruit = new Fruit("orange");
// Perform the bind
ctx.bind("favorite", fruit);
```

This example creates an object of class `Fruit` and binds it to the name `"favorite"` in the context `ctx`. If you subsequently looked up the name `"favorite"` in `ctx`, then you would get the `fruit` object. Note that to compile the `Fruit` class, you need the `FruitFactory` class.

If you were to run this example twice, then the second attempt would fail with a `Name-AlreadyBoundException`. This is because the name `"favorite"` is already bound. For the second attempt to succeed, you would have to use `rebind()`.

Adding or Replacing a Binding

rebind() is used to add or replace a binding. It accepts the same arguments as bind(), but its semantics are such that if the name is already bound, then it will be unbound and the newly given object will be bound.

```
// Create the object to be bound
Fruit fruit = new Fruit("lemon");

// Perform the bind
ctx.rebind("favorite", fruit);
```

This example, when run, will replace the binding created by the bind() example.

Removing a Binding

To remove a binding, you use unbind().

```
// Remove the binding
ctx.unbind("favorite");
```

This example, when run, removes the binding that was created by the bind() or rebind() example.

Renaming an Object

You can rename an object in a context by using Context.rename().

```
// Rename to old_report.txt
ctx.rename("report.txt", "old_report.txt");
```

This example renames the object that was bound to "report.txt" to "old_report.txt". After verifying that the object got renamed, the program renames it to its original name ("report.txt"), as follows.

```
// Rename back to report.txt
ctx.rename("old_report.txt", "report.txt");
```

Creating and Destroying a Context

The Context interface contains methods for creating and destroying a *subcontext*, a context that is bound in another context of the same type. In a file system, this corresponds to creating and removing a subdirectory.

Creating a Context

To create a context, you supply to `createSubcontext()` the name of the context that you want to create.

```
// Create the context
Context result = ctx.createSubcontext("new");
```

This example creates a new context, called "new", that is a child of `ctx`. If you list the context `ctx`, then you will see that there is now an entry for "new".

Destroying a Context

To destroy a context, you supply to `destroySubcontext()` the name of the context to destroy.

```
// Destroy the context
ctx.destroySubcontext("new");
```

This example destroys the context "new" in the context `ctx`.

Directory Operations

You can use the JNDI to perform directory operations, including the following:

- Reading an object's attributes
- Modifying an object's attributes
- Searching the directory
- Performing hybrid naming and directory operations

This lesson describes each of these operations. Before using any of them, you should read the section on the use of attribute names (page 60) that apply to all of these operations.

Configuration

The examples in this lesson[1] use the LDAP service provider. They assume that you have set up a sample namespace using the content described in the **Preparations** lesson (page 43). If you use another service provider or choose to use another part of the LDAP namespace, then the behavior will differ from what is shown here.

The initial context used in these examples is initialized using the following environment properties.

```
// Set up the environment for creating the initial context
Hashtable env = new Hashtable();
env.put(Context.INITIAL_CONTEXT_FACTORY,
    "com.sun.jndi.ldap.LdapCtxFactory");
env.put(Context.PROVIDER_URL, "ldap://localhost:389/o=JNDITutorial");
DirContext ctx = new InitialDirContext(env);
```

---

[1]See the **Preface** for instructions on how to find the examples on the accompanying CD.

Attribute Names

An attribute consists of an *attribute identifier* and a set of *attribute values*. The *attribute identifier*, also called *attribute name*, is a string that identifies an attribute. An *attribute value* is the content of the attribute and its type is not restricted to that of string. You use an attribute name when you want to specify a particular attribute for either retrieval, searches, or modification. Names are also returned by operations that return attributes (such as when you perform reads or searches in the directory).

When using attribute names, you need to be aware of certain directory server features so that you won't be surprised by the result. These features are described in the next subsections.

Attribute Type

In directories such as the LDAP, the attribute's name identifies the attribute's type and is often called the *attribute type name*. For example, the attribute name "cn" is also called the attribute type name. An attribute's type definition specifies the syntax that the attribute's value is to have, whether it can have multiple values, and equality and ordering rules to use when performing comparison and ordering operations on the attribute's values.

Attribute Subclassing

Some directory implementations support *attribute subclassing*, in which the server allows attribute types to be defined in terms of other attribute types. For example, a "name" attribute might be the superclass of all name-related attributes; "commonName" might be a subclass of "name". For directory implementations that support this, a request for the "name" attribute might return the "commonName" attribute.

When accessing directories that support attribute subclassing, you must be aware that the server might return attributes that have names different from those that you requested. To minimize the chance of this, use the most derived subclass.

Attribute Name Synonyms

Some directory implementations support synonyms for attribute names. For example, "cn" might be a synonym for "commonName". Thus a request for the "cn" attribute might return the "commonName" attribute.

When accessing directories that support synonyms for attribute names, you must be aware that the server might return attributes that have names different from those you requested. To help prevent this from happening, use the canonical attribute name instead of one of its synonyms. The *canonical attribute name* is the name used in the attribute's definition; a synonym is the name that refers to the canonical attribute name in its definition.

Language Preferences

An extension to the LDAP v3 (RFC 2596) allows you to specify a language code along with an attribute name. This resembles attribute subclassing in that one attribute name can represent several different attributes. An example is a "description" attribute that has two language variations:

```
description: software
description;lang-en: software products
description;lang-de: Softwareprodukte
```

A request for the "description" attribute would return all three attributes.

When accessing directories that support this feature, you must be aware that the server might return attributes that have names different from those that you requested.

Reading Attributes

To read the attributes of an object from the directory, use DirContext.getAttributes() and pass it the name of the object for which you want the attributes. Suppose that an object in the naming service has the name "cn=Ted Geisel, ou=People". To retrieve this object's attributes, you'll need code that looks like this:

```
Attributes answer = ctx.getAttributes("cn=Ted Geisel, ou=People");
```

You can then print the contents of this answer as follows.

```
for (NamingEnumeration ae = answer.getAll(); ae.hasMore();) {
    Attribute attr = (Attribute)ae.next();
    System.out.println("attribute: " + attr.getID());
    /* Print each value */
    for (NamingEnumeration e = attr.getAll(); e.hasMore();
        System.out.println("value: " + e.next()))
        ;
}
```

This produces the following output.

```
# java GetattrsAll

attribute: sn
value: Geisel
attribute: objectclass
value: top
value: person
value: organizationalPerson
value: inetOrgPerson
attribute: jpegphoto
value: [B@1dacd78b
attribute: mail
value: Ted.Geisel@JNDITutorial.com
attribute: facsimiletelephonenumber
```

```
value: +1 408 555 2329
attribute: telephonenumber
value: +1 408 555 5252
attribute: cn
value: Ted Geisel
```

Returning Selected Attributes

To read a selective subset of attributes, you supply an array of strings that are attribute identifiers of the attributes that you want to retrieve.

```
// Specify the ids of the attributes to return
String[] attrIDs = {"sn", "telephonenumber", "golfhandicap", "mail"};

// Get the attributes requested
Attributes answer = ctx.getAttributes("cn=Ted Geisel, ou=People",
    attrIDs);
```

This example asks for the "sn", "telephonenumber", "golfhandicap", and "mail" attributes of the object "cn=Ted Geisel, ou=People". This object has all but the "golfhandicap" attribute, so three attributes are returned in the answer. Following is the output of the example.

```
# java Getattrs
```

```
attribute: sn
value: Geisel
attribute: mail
value: Ted.Geisel@JNDITutorial.com
attribute: telephonenumber
value: +1 408 555 5252
```

Modifying Attributes

The DirContext interface contains methods for modifying the attributes and attribute values of objects in the directory.

Using a List of Modifications

One way to modify the attributes of an object is to supply a list of modification requests (ModificationItem). Each ModificationItem consists of a numeric constant indicating the type of modification to make and an Attribute describing the modification to make. Following are the three types of modifications:

- ADD_ATTRIBUTE
- REPLACE_ATTRIBUTE
- REMOVE_ATTRIBUTE

Modifications are applied in the order in which they appear in the list. Either all of the modifications are executed, or none are.

The following code creates a list of modifications. It replaces the "mail" attribute's value with a value of "geisel@wizards.com", adds an additional value to the "telephonenumber" attribute, and removes the "jpegphoto" attribute.

```
// Specify the changes to make
ModificationItem[] mods = new ModificationItem[3];

// Replace the mail attribute with a new value
mods[0] = new ModificationItem(DirContext.REPLACE_ATTRIBUTE,
    new BasicAttribute("mail", "geisel@wizards.com"));

// Add an additional value to "telephonenumber"
mods[1] = new ModificationItem(DirContext.ADD_ATTRIBUTE,
    new BasicAttribute("telephonenumber", "+1 555 555 5555"));

// Remove the "jpegphoto"
mods[2] = new ModificationItem(DirContext.REMOVE_ATTRIBUTE,
    new BasicAttribute("jpegphoto"));
```

After creating this list of modifications, you can supply it to modifyAttributes() as follows.

```
// Perform the requested modifications on the named object
ctx.modifyAttributes(name, mods);
```

Using Attributes

Alternatively, you can perform modifications by specifying the type of modification and the attributes to which to apply the modification.

For example, the following line replaces the attributes (identified in orig) associated with name with those in orig:

```
ctx.modifyAttributes(name, DirContext.REPLACE_ATTRIBUTE, orig);
```

Any other attributes of name remain unchanged.

Both of these uses of modifyAttributes() are demonstrated in the sample program (Modattrs.java). This program modifies the attributes by using a modification list and then uses the second form of modifyAttributes() to restore the original attributes.

Searching the Directory

One of the most useful features that a directory offers is its *yellow pages*, or *search*, service. You can compose a query consisting of attributes of entries that you are seeking and submit that query to the directory. The directory then returns a list of entries that satisfy the query. For example, you could ask the directory for all entries of a bowling average greater than 200 or all entries that represent a person with a surname beginning with "Sch."

The DirContext interface provides several methods for searching the directory, with progressive degrees of complexity and power. The various aspects of searching the directory are covered in the following sections:

- Basic Search
- Search Filters
- Search Controls

Basic Search

The simplest form of search requires that you specify the set of attributes that an entry must have and the name of the target context in which to perform the search.

The following code creates an attribute set `matchAttrs`, which has two attributes "tele-phonenumber" and "mail". It specifies that the qualifying entries must have a surname ("sn") attribute with a value of "Geisel" and a "mail" attribute with any value. It then invokes Dir-Context.search() to search the context "ou=People" for entries that have the attributes specified by `matchAttrs`.

```
// Specify the attributes to match
// Ask for objects that have a surname ("sn") attribute
// with the value "Geisel" and the "mail" attribute
Attributes matchAttrs = new BasicAttributes(true); // ignore case
matchAttrs.put(new BasicAttribute("sn", "Geisel"));
matchAttrs.put(new BasicAttribute("mail"));

// Search for objects that have those matching attributes
NamingEnumeration answer = ctx.search("ou=People", matchAttrs);
```

You can then print the results as follows.

```
while (enum.hasMore()) {
    SearchResult sr = (SearchResult)enum.next();
    System.out.println(">>>" + sr.getName());
    printAttrs(sr.getAttributes());
}
```

`printAttrs()` is similar to the code in the `getAttributes()` example that prints an attribute set.

Running this example produces the following result.

```
# java SearchRetAll

>>>cn=Ted Geisel
attribute: sn
value: Geisel
attribute: objectclass
value: top
value: person
value: organizationalPerson
value: inetOrgPerson
attribute: jpegphoto
value: [B@1dacd78b
attribute: mail
value: Ted.Geisel@JNDITutorial.com
attribute: facsimiletelephonenumber
value: +1 408 555 2329
attribute: cn
```

```
value: Ted Geisel
attribute: telephonenumber
value: +1 408 555 5252
```

Returning Selected Attributes

The previous example returned all attributes associated with the entries that satisfy the speci-fied query. You can select the attributes to return by passing search() an array of attribute identifiers that you want to include in the result. After creating the matchAttrs as shown pre-viously, you also need to create the array of attribute identifiers, as shown next.

```
// Specify the ids of the attributes to return
String[] attrIDs = {"sn", "telephonenumber", "golfhandicap", "mail"};

// Search for objects that have those matching attributes
NamingEnumeration answer = ctx.search("ou=People", matchAttrs,
    attrIDs);
```

This example returns the attributes "sn", "telephonenumber", "golfhandicap", and "mail" of entries that have an attribute "mail" and a "sn" attribute with the value "Geisel". This example produces the following result. (The entry does not have a "golfhandicap" attribute, so it is not returned.)

```
# java Search

>>>cn=Ted Geisel
attribute: sn
value: Geisel
attribute: mail
value: Ted.Geisel@JNDITutorial.com
attribute: telephonenumber
value: +1 408 555 5252
```

Search Filters

In addition to specifying a search using a set of attributes, you can specify a search in the form of a search filter. A *search filter* is a search query expressed in the form of a logical expression. The syntax of search filters accepted by DirContext.search() is described in RFC 2254.

The following search filter specifies that the qualifying entries must have an "sn" attribute with a value of "Geisel" and a "mail" attribute with any value:

```
(&(sn=Geisel)(mail=*))
```

The following code creates a filter and default search controls, SearchControls, and uses them to perform a search. The search is equivalent to the one presented in the basic search example.

```
// Create the default search controls
SearchControls ctls = new SearchControls();

// Specify the search filter to match
// Ask for objects that have the attribute "sn" == "Geisel" and
```

```
// the "mail" attribute
String filter = "(&(sn=Geisel)(mail=*))";

// Search for objects using the filter
NamingEnumeration answer = ctx.search("ou=People", filter, ctls);
```

Running this example produces the following result.

```
# java SearchWithFilterRetAll
```

```
>>>cn=Ted Geisel
attribute: sn
value: Geisel
attribute: objectclass
value: top
value: person
value: organizationalPerson
value: inetOrgPerson
attribute: jpegphoto
value: [B@1dacd75e
attribute: mail
value: Ted.Geisel@JNDITutorial.com
attribute: facsimiletelephonenumber
value: +1 408 555 2329
attribute: cn
value: Ted Geisel
attribute: telephonenumber
value: +1 408 555 5252
```

Quick Overview of Search Filter Syntax

The search filter syntax is basically a logical expression in prefix notation (that is, the logical operator appears before its arguments). Table 2 lists the symbols used for creating filters.

TABLE 2: **Search Filter Symbols.**

Symbol	Description
&	conjunction (i.e., *and*—all in the list must be true)
|	disjunction (i.e., *or*—one or more alternatives must be true)
!	negation (i.e., *not*—the item being negated must not be true)
=	equality (according to the matching rule of the attribute)
~=	approximate equality (according to the matching rule of the attribute)
>=	greater than (according to the matching rule of the attribute)
<=	less than (according to the matching rule of the attribute)
=*	presence (i.e., the entry must have the attribute but its value is irrelevant)
*	wildcard (indicates zero or more characters can occur in that position); used when specifying attribute values to match
\	escape (for escaping "*", "(", or ")" when they occur inside of an attribute value)

Each item in the filter is composed using an attribute identifier and either an attribute value or symbols denoting the attribute value. For example, the item "sn=Geisel" means that the "sn" attribute must have the attribute value "Geisel" and the item "mail=*" indicates that the "mail" attribute must be present.

Each item must be enclosed within a set of parentheses, as in "(sn=Geisel)". These items are composed using logical operators such as "&" (conjunction) to create logical expressions, as in "(& (sn=Geisel) (mail=*))".

Each logical expression can be further composed of other items that themselves are logical expressions, as in "(| (& (sn=Geisel) (mail=*)) (sn=L*))". The last example requests either entries that have both a "sn" attribute of "Geisel" and the "mail" attribute or entries whose "sn" attribute begins with the letter "L."

For a complete description of the syntax, see RFC 2254.

Returning Selected Attributes

The previous example returned all attributes associated with the entries that satisfy the specified filter. You can select the attributes to return by setting the search controls argument. You create an array of attribute identifiers that you want to include in the result and pass it to SearchControls.setReturningAttributes(). (Search controls are discussed further in the next section.) Here's an example.

```
// Specify the ids of the attributes to return
String[] attrIDs = {"sn", "telephonenumber", "golfhandicap", "mail"};
SearchControls ctls = new SearchControls();
ctls.setReturningAttributes(attrIDs);
```

This example is equivalent to the **Returning Selected Attributes** example in the **Basic Search** section (page 64). Running it produces the following results. (The entry does not have a "golfhandicap" attribute, so it is not returned.)

```
# java SearchWithFilter

>>>cn=Ted Geisel
attribute: sn
value: Geisel
attribute: mail
value: Ted.Geisel@JNDITutorial.com
attribute: telephonenumber
value: +1 408 555 5252
```

Search Controls

The **Search Filters** section (page 65) showed how you can use the SearchControls argument to select the attributes that are returned with entries in a search operation. You can use this argument also to control other aspects of the search. Following are the available controls:

- The attributes to return
- The scope in which the search is to occur

- The maximum number of entries to return
- The maximum number of milliseconds to wait
- Whether to return the Java object associated with the entry
- Whether JNDI links are dereferenced during the search

Returning Java objects is described in the **Java Objects and the Directory** trail (page 183). JNDI links are described in the **Beyond the Basics** trail (page 142).

Search Scope

The default SearchControls specifies that the search is to be performed in the named context (SearchControls.ONELEVEL_SCOPE). This default is used in the examples in the **Search Filters** section (page 65).

In addition to this default, you can specify that the search be performed in the *entire subtree* or only in the named object.

Search the Subtree. A search of the entire subtree searches the named object and all of its descendants. To make the search behave in this way, pass SearchControls.SUBTREE_SCOPE to SearchControls.setSearchScope() as follows.

```
// Specify the ids of the attributes to return
String[] attrIDs = {"sn", "telephonenumber", "golfhandicap", "mail"};
SearchControls ctls = new SearchControls();
ctls.setReturningAttributes(attrIDs);
ctls.setSearchScope(SearchControls.SUBTREE_SCOPE);

// Specify the search filter to match
// Ask for objects that have the attribute "sn" == "Geisel" and
// the "mail" attribute
String filter = "(&(sn=Geisel)(mail=*))";

// Search the subtree for objects by using the filter
NamingEnumeration answer = ctx.search("", filter, ctls);
```

This example searches the context ctx's subtree for entries that satisfy the specified filter. It finds the entry "cn=Ted Geisel, ou=People" in this subtree that satisfies the filter.

```
# java SearchSubtree

>>>cn=Ted Geisel, ou=People
attribute: sn
value: Geisel
attribute: mail
value: Ted.Geisel@JNDITutorial.com
attribute: telephonenumber
value: +1 408 555 5252
```

Search the Named Object. You can also search the named object. This is useful, for example, to test whether the named object satisfies a search filter. To search the named object, pass SearchControls.OBJECT_SCOPE to setSearchScope().

```
// Specify the ids of the attributes to return
String[] attrIDs = {"sn", "telephonenumber", "golfhandicap", "mail"};
SearchControls ctls = new SearchControls();
ctls.setReturningAttributes(attrIDs);
ctls.setSearchScope(SearchControls.OBJECT_SCOPE);

// Specify the search filter to match
// Ask for objects that have the attribute sn == Geisel and
// the "mail" attribute
String filter = "(&(sn=Geisel)(mail=*))";

// Search the subtree for objects by using the filter
NamingEnumeration answer =
    ctx.search("cn=Ted Geisel, ou=People", filter, ctls);
```

This example tests whether the object "cn=Ted Geisel, ou=People" satisfies the given filter.

```
# java SearchObject

>>>
attribute: sn
value: Geisel
attribute: mail
value: Ted.Geisel@JNDITutorial.com
attribute: telephonenumber
value: +1 408 555 5252
```

The example found one answer and printed it. Notice that the name of the result is the empty string. This is because the name of the object is always named relative to the context of the search (in this case, "cn=Ted Geisel, ou=People").

Count Limit

Sometimes, a query might produce too many answers and you want to limit the number of answers returned. You can do this by using the count limit search control. By default, a search does not have a count limit—it will return all answers that it finds. To set the count limit of a search, pass the number of maximum desired answers to SearchControls.setCountLimit().

The following example sets the count limit to 1.

```
// Set the search controls to limit the count to 1
SearchControls ctls = new SearchControls();
ctls.setCountLimit(1);
```

If the program attempts to get more than the count limit number of results, then a SizeLimit-ExceededException will be thrown. So if a program has set a count limit, then it should either differentiate this exception from other NamingExceptions or keep track of the count limit and not request more than that number of results.

Specifying a count limit for a search is one way of controlling the resources (such as memory and network bandwidth) that your application consumes. Other ways to control the resources consumed are to narrow your search filter (be more specific about what you seek), start your search in the appropriate context, and use the appropriate scope.

Time Limit

A time limit on a search places an upper bound on the amount of time that the search operation will block waiting for the answers. This is useful when you don't want to wait too long for an answer. If the time limit specified is exceeded before the search operation can be completed, then a `TimeLimitExceededException` will be thrown.

To set the time limit of a search, pass the number of milliseconds to `Search-Controls.setTimeLimit()`. The following example sets the time limit to 1 second.

```
// Set the search controls to limit the time to 1 second (1000 ms)
SearchControls ctls = new SearchControls();
ctls.setTimeLimit(1000);
```

To get this particular example to exceed its time limit, you need to reconfigure it to use either a slow server or a server that has lots of entries. Alternatively, you can use other tactics to make the search take longer than 1 second.

A time limit of zero means that no time limit has been set and that calls to the directory will wait indefinitely for an answer.

Hybrid Naming and Directory Operations

The **Naming Operations** lesson (page 56) discussed how you can use `bind()`, `rebind()`, and `createSubcontext()` in the `Context` interface to create bindings and subcontexts. The `Dir-Context` interface contains overloaded versions of these methods that accept attributes. You can use these `DirContext` methods to associate attributes with the object at the time that the binding or subcontext is added to the namespace. For example, you might create a `Person` object and bind it to the namespace and at the same time associate attributes about that object.

Before you go on: The examples in this lesson require that you make additions to the schema. You must either turn off schema-checking in the LDAP server or add the schema that accompanies this tutorial to the server (see **Appendix**). Both of these tasks are typically performed by the directory server's administrator. See the **Preparations** lesson (page 43) for details.

Creating a Context That Has Attributes

To create a context that has attributes, you supply to `DirContext.createSubcontext()` the name of the context that you want to create and its attributes.

```
// Create attributes to be associated with the new context
Attributes attrs = new BasicAttributes(true); // case-ignore
Attribute objclass = new BasicAttribute("objectclass");
objclass.add("top");
objclass.add("extensibleObject");
```

```
attrs.put(objclass);

// Create the context
Context result = ctx.createSubcontext("cn=Fruits", attrs);
```

This example creates a new context called "cn=Fruits" that has an attribute "objectclass" with two values, "top" and "extensibleObject", in the context ctx. If you list the context ctx, then you will see that it now contains an entry for "cn=Fruits".

```
# java Create

ou=Groups: javax.naming.directory.DirContext
ou=People: javax.naming.directory.DirContext
cn=Fruits: javax.naming.directory.DirContext
```

Adding a Binding That Has Attributes

DirContext.bind() is used to add a binding that has attributes to a context. It accepts as arguments the name of the object, the object to be bound, and a set of attributes.

```
// Create the object to be bound
Fruit fruit = new Fruit("orange");

// Create attributes to be associated with the object
Attributes attrs = new BasicAttributes(true); // Case-ignore
Attribute objclass = new BasicAttribute("objectclass");
objclass.add("top");
objclass.add("extensibleObject");
attrs.put(objclass);
attrs.put("color", "orange");
attrs.put("flavor", "sweet");

// Perform the bind
ctx.bind("cn=favorite, cn=Fruits", fruit, attrs);
```

This example creates an object of class Fruit and binds it to the name "cn=favorite" into the context named "cn=Fruits", relative to ctx. This binding has three attributes: "objectclass", "color", and "flavor". If you subsequently looked up the name "cn=favorite, cn=Fruits" in ctx, then you would get the fruit object. If you then got the attributes of "cn=favorite, cn=Fruits", you would get those attributes with which the object was created. Following is this example's output.

```
# java Bind

orange
attribute: flavor
value: sweet
attribute: color
value: orange
attribute: objectclass
value: top
value: extensibleObject
value: javaObject
value: javaNamingReference
```

```
attribute: javaclassname
value: Fruit
attribute: javafactory
value: FruitFactory
attribute: javareferenceaddress
value: #0#fruit#orange
attribute: cn
value: favorite
```

The extra attributes and attribute values shown are used to store information about the object (fruit). These extra attributes are discussed in more detail in the **Java Objects and the Directory** trail (page 195).

If you were to run this example twice, then the second attempt would fail with a Name-AlreadyBoundException. This is because the name "cn=favorite" is already bound in the "cn=Fruits" context. For the second attempt to succeed, you would have to use rebind().

Replacing a Binding That Has Attributes

DirContext.rebind() is used to add or replace a binding and its attributes. It accepts the same arguments as bind(). However, rebind()'s semantics require that if the name is already bound, then it will be unbound and the newly given object and attributes will be bound.

```
// Create the object to be bound
Fruit fruit = new Fruit("lemon");

// Create attributes to be associated with the object
Attributes attrs = new BasicAttributes(true); // case-ignore
Attribute objclass = new BasicAttribute("objectclass");
objclass.add("top");
objclass.add("extensibleObject");
attrs.put(objclass);
attrs.put("color", "yellow");
attrs.put("flavor", "sour");

// Perform bind
ctx.rebind("cn=favorite, cn=Fruits", fruit, attrs);
```

When you run this example, it replaces the binding that the bind() example created.

```
# java Rebind

lemon
attribute: flavor
value: sour
attribute: color
value: yellow
attribute: objectclass
value: top
value: extensibleObject
value: javaObject
value: javaNamingReference
attribute: javaclassname
value: Fruit
attribute: javafactory
```

```
value: FruitFactory
attribute: javareferenceaddress
value: #0#fruit#lemon
attribute: cn
value: favorite
```

Beyond the Basics

The lessons in the **Beyond the Basics** trail provide in-depth information on advanced JNDI topics. Before embarking on this trail, you should have a good grasp of the JNDI fundamentals. If you do not, then proceed first to **The Basics** trail (page 37).

- The **What's in a Name** lesson (page 79) discusses the use of string names and structured names in the JNDI. It gives details about the different types of names and describes utilities for parsing and constructing names.
- The **Environment Properties** lesson (page 95) describes how to configure the JNDI using environment properties, system properties, applet parameters, application resource files, and provider resource files.
- The **Event Notification** lesson (page 111) describes how to use event notification in the JNDI.
- The **URLs** lesson (page 123) describes the different uses of URLs in the JNDI.
- The **Federation** lesson (page 131) describes what federation is and how it is supported by the JNDI.
- The **Miscellaneous** lesson (page 139) discusses various topics, including class loading, link references, and naming policies.

8

What's in a Name?

Having gone through some of the trails in this tutorial, such as **The Basics** trail (page 37), the **Java Objects and the Directory** trail (page 151), or the **Tips for LDAP Users** trail (page 201), you probably have used some of the examples to access or update data in a naming or directory service. You were able to use these examples, or write programs of your own that use the JNDI, even though you had very little detail about the name argument that is used pervasively throughout the JNDI. This is because the concept of a name is so ubiquitous that we all share some common preconceived notions of what it is and how to use it. The JNDI methods support such common notions and, for the most part, treat names in an intuitive manner. Consequently, not much discussion of how to specify a name is necessary.

This lesson covers the different types of names and their uses in the JNDI. It is intended for applications that need to do more than just pass name parameters to methods. The lesson first discusses the use of string names and structured names and why the JNDI contains both. It then describes the two different types of structured names: composite and compound. The last part shows how to handle names that include special characters and how to parse and compose names.

See the **URLs** lesson (page 123) for a discussion of how URLs are treated as names in the JNDI.

String Names versus Structured Names

Each naming method in the `Context` and `DirContext` interfaces has two overloaded forms: one that accepts a string name (`java.lang.String`) and one that accepts a structured name (`Name`). For example, `lookup()` has two forms:

- `lookup(java.lang.String)`
- `lookup(javax.naming.Name)`

String Names

The overloads that accept a `java.lang.String` name are convenience forms that allow the methods to be invoked without the caller's having to construct a `CompositeName` instance. The `String` name argument passed to these overloads represents a *composite name* and follows the syntactic rules specified in the `CompositeName` class.

For example, the following two invocations of `lookup()` are equivalent.

```
Object obj1 = ctx.lookup("cn=Ted Geisel, ou=People, o=JNDITutorial");
```

```
CompositeName cname = new CompositeName(
    "cn=Ted Geisel, ou=People, o=JNDITutorial");
Object obj2 = ctx.lookup(cname);
```

Structured Names

The overloads that accept a `Name` accept an instance of `CompositeName`, `CompoundName`, or any other class that implements the `Name` interface.

If the object is an instance of `CompositeName`, then it is treated as a composite name. A *composite name* is a name that can span multiple naming systems, not just the naming system on which the method is invoked. See the **Composite Names** section (page 81) of this lesson for examples of how to use composite names. In the degenerate case, the name spans only the naming system on which the method is invoked. In the **Tips for LDAP Users** trail (page 201), for instance, all of the examples use string names from the LDAP namespace. Note that even in this degenerate case, the name is still a composite name; that is, it is a composite name having a single component.

If the object is not an instance of `CompositeName`, then it is treated as a *compound name*— a name that spans only one namespace. See the **Compound Names** section (page 86) of this lesson for examples of how to use compound names.

When to Use Which

Typically, your program would use a string name if it was supplied a string name by the user. It would use a `Name` instance if it was composing the name by using input from the user. For example, in a namespace browser application, as the user traverses different parts of the namespace, the application might need to compose names that direct the browser toward those parts of the namespace. It could do so by creating string representations of the names for those parts of the namespace and by being cognizant of and using the appropriate naming syntax(es). Or, it could use `Name` instances created with the help of utilities provided by the JNDI.

See the **Handling Special Characters** section (page 90) of this lesson about how best to accommodate special characters in a name that conflicts with the JNDI composite name syntax.

Composite Names

Recall that a composite name is a name that spans multiple naming systems. Here's an example of a composite name:

```
cn=homedir,cn=Jon Ruiz,ou=People/tutorial/report.txt
```

This is the string representation of a composite name that contains two parts: an LDAP name, `"cn=homedir, cn=Jon Ruiz, ou=People"`, and a filename, `"tutorial/report.txt"`. When you pass this string to a `Context` method, such as `lookup()`, in the namespace set up as recommended by this tutorial (see the **Preparations** lesson (page 43)), the method will resolve through the LDAP directory to the file system and return the target object (a file). The mechanics of how this is accomplished by the underlying service provider implementations are described in the **Federation** lesson (page 131).

Here's an example.

```
File f = (File)ctx.lookup(
    "cn=homedir,cn=Jon Ruiz,ou=People/tutorial/report.txt");
```

String Representation

A composite name is made up of *components*. You can think of a component as a segment of the composite name that belongs to a single naming system. Each component is separated by a forward slash character ("/").

For example, the name

```
cn=homedir, cn=Jon Ruiz, ou=People/tutorial/report.txt
```

has three components:

1. `cn=homedir, cn=Jon Ruiz, ou=People`
2. `tutorial`
3. `report.txt`

The first component belongs to the LDAP namespace, and the second two belong to the file system namespace. As you can see from this example, multiple components from the *same* namespace are allowed (`"tutorial"` and `"report.txt"` are both from the file system namespace), but one component cannot span more than one namespace. (See the discussion on this in the **Federation** lesson (page 131).)

In addition to the forward slash character ("/"), the composite name syntax allows three other special characters: the backslash character ("\"), the single quotation character ("'"), and the double quotation character ("""). The slash, backslash, and quotation characters are called *meta characters*, which means they have special meanings when they occur in a composite name. The backslash character is the *escape character*. When the escape character precedes a meta character, the meta character is treated literally and not interpreted according to its special meaning. For example, in the string a\/b, the forward slash character is escaped by the backslash character and therefore is not treated as a composite name component separator. See the **Handling Special Characters** section (page 90) of this lesson for a more detailed discussion of meta characters.

The quotation characters are provided so that you can use the meta characters within a composite name component without having to escape them. When a component is quoted, its first and last characters must be (the same) quotation characters. A single quotation character must be matched by a single quotation character, and a double quotation character must be matched by a double quotation character. Here are three examples of the same component written by using escapes and quotation characters.

```
a\/b\/c\/d
"a/b/c/d"
'a/b/b/d'
```

Two different quotation characters are permitted so as to allow quoting when a quotation character already exists in the component. For example, a component containing a double quotation character can be represented as either \"ab or '"ab'.

A composite name can be *empty*, that is, it contains zero components. An empty composite name is represented by the empty string.

A composite name component can be *empty*, that is, it contains an empty string. A leading component separator (the composite name string begins with a separator) denotes a leading empty component. A trailing component separator (the composite name string ends with a separator) denotes a trailing empty component. Adjacent component separators denote an empty component. Here are examples of each.

```
/abc
abc/
abc//xyz
```

See the discussion in the **Handling Special Characters** section (page 90) of this lesson about how best to accommodate special characters in a name that conflicts with the JNDI composite name syntax.

The CompositeName Class

The CompositeName class is the structural form of a composite name. The constructor accepts a string representation of a composite name and parses it into components according to the composite name syntax.

Here's an example that uses the constructor to parse a composite name and then prints its components.

```
String name = // Composite name to parse
CompositeName cn = new CompositeName(name);
System.out.println(cn + " has " + cn.size() + " components: ");
```

```
for (int i = 0; i < cn.size(); i++) {
    System.out.println(cn.get(i));
}
```

Running this example with an input of a/b/c produces the following results.

```
a/b/c has 3 components:
a
b
c
```

The CompositeName class contains methods to access components, to modify a Composite-
Name, to compare two CompositeNames for equality, and to get the string representation of a
CompositeName.

Accessing Components of a Composite Name

Here are the methods that you can use to access components of a composite name:

- get(int posn)
- getAll()
- getPrefix(int posn)
- getSuffix(int posn)
- clone()

To retrieve the component at a particular position within a CompositeName, you use get().
The previous constructor example shows an example of its use.

getAll() returns all of the components of a CompositeName as an enumeration. You iterate through the enumeration to get each component. The constructor example can be rewritten
using an enumeration, as shown next.

```
try {
    CompositeName cn = new CompositeName(name);
    System.out.println(cn + " has " + cn.size() + " components: ");
    for (Enumeration all = cn.getAll(); all.hasMoreElements();) {
        System.out.println(all.nextElement());
    }
} catch (InvalidNameException e) {
    System.out.println("Cannot parse name: " + name);
}
```

You can also get a CompositeName's suffix or prefix as a CompositeName instance. Here's
an example that gets the suffix and prefix of a composite name.

```
CompositeName cn = new CompositeName("one/two/three");
Name suffix = cn.getSuffix(1);   // 1 <= index < cn.size()
Name prefix = cn.getPrefix(1);   // 0 <= index < 1
```

When you run this program, it generates the following output.

```
two/three
one
```

To make a copy of a CompositeName, you use clone().

Modifying a Composite Name

Following are the methods that you can use to modify a composite name:

- add(String comp)
- add(int posn, String comp)
- addAll(Name comps)
- addAll(Name suffix)
- addAll(int posn, Name suffix)
- remove(int posn)

After creating a CompositeName instance, you can add and remove components from it. Here's an example that appends a CompositeName to an existing CompositeName, adds components to the front and the end, and removes the second component.

```
CompositeName cn = new CompositeName("1/2/3");
CompositeName cn2 = new CompositeName("4/5/6");
System.out.println(cn.addAll(cn2));          // 1/2/3/4/5/6
System.out.println(cn.add(0, "abc"));        // abc/1/2/3/4/5/6
System.out.println(cn.add("xyz"));           // abc/1/2/3/4/5/6/xyz
System.out.println(cn.remove(1));            // 1
System.out.println(cn);                      // abc/2/3/4/5/6/xyz
```

Comparing a Composite Name

Following are the methods that you can use to compare two composite names:

- compareTo(Object name)
- equals(Object name)
- endsWith(Name name)
- startsWith(Name name)
- isEmpty()

You can use compareTo() to sort a list of CompositeName instances. Here's an example that uses compareTo() to implement the Bubble Sort algorithm.

```
private static void sort(CompositeName[] names) {
    int bound = names.length-1;
    CompositeName tmp;
    while (true) {
        int t = -1;
        for (int j=0; j < bound; j++) {
            int c = names[j].compareTo(names[j+1]);
            if (c > 0) {
                tmp = names[j];
                names[j] = names[j+1];
                names[j+1] = tmp;
                t = j;
            }
        }
        if (t == -1) break;
        bound = t;
    }
}
```

equals() lets you determine whether two CompositeNames are syntactically equal. Two CompositeNames are equal if they both have the same (case-exact matched) components in the same order.

With startsWith() and endsWith(), you can learn whether a CompositeName starts or ends with another CompositeName; that is, whether a CompositeName is a suffix or prefix of another CompositeName.

The convenience method isEmpty() enables you to determine whether a CompositeName has zero components. You can also use the expression size() == 0 to perform the same check.

Here are examples of using some of these comparison methods.

```
CompositeName one = new CompositeName("cn=fs/o=JNDITutorial/tmp/a/b/c");
CompositeName two = new CompositeName("tmp/a/b/c");
CompositeName three = new CompositeName("cn=fs/o=JNDITutorial");
CompositeName four = new CompositeName();

System.out.println(one.equals(two));        // false
System.out.println(one.startsWith(three));  // true
System.out.println(one.endsWith(two));      // true
System.out.println(one.startsWith(four));   // true
System.out.println(one.endsWith(four));     // true
System.out.println(one.endsWith(three));    // false
System.out.println(one.isEmpty());          // false
System.out.println(four.isEmpty());         // true
System.out.println(four.size() == 0);       // true
```

Getting the String Representation

Following is the method that you can use to get the string representation of a composite name:

```
toString()
```

When you use the CompositeName constructor, you supply the string representation of a composite name and get back a CompositeName instance. To do the reverse, that is, to get the string representation of a CompositeName instance, you use toString(). The result of toString() can be fed back to the constructor to produce a CompositeName instance that is equal to the original CompositeName instance. Here's an example.

```
CompositeName cn = new CompositeName(name);
String str = cn.toString();
System.out.println(str);
CompositeName cn2 = new CompositeName(str);
System.out.println(cn.equals(cn2));// true
```

CompositeName as an Argument to Context Methods

A CompositeName instance passed to methods in the Context and DirContext interfaces is treated as a composite name. Here is an example that looks up an object by first creating a CompositeName instance that represents its name.

```
// Create the initial context
Context ctx = new InitialContext(env);
```

```
// Parse the string name into CompositeName
Name cname = new CompositeName(
    "cn=homedir,cn=Jon Ruiz,ou=people/tutorial/report.txt");

// Perform the lookup using CompositeName
File f = (File) ctx.lookup(cname);
```

Compound Names

A *compound name* is a name in a single naming system. Here's an example of a compound name:

```
cn=homedir, cn=Jon Ruiz, ou=People
```

This is the string representation of an LDAP name that contains three components:

1. ou=People
2. cn=Jon Ruiz
3. cn=homedir

Relationship of a Compound Name to a Composite Name

When you pass a string name to a `Context` method, such as `lookup()`, the method expects a composite name. The composite name might have just one component. You may pass an LDAP string name, for instance to `lookup()`. The only restriction to keep in mind concerns whether the string name contains characters that conflict with the composite name syntax. In that case, those characters need to be properly escaped or quoted. For example, the compound name cn=a/b needs to be specified as cn=a\/b to prevent it from being interpreted as a composite name that has two components.

When you pass a `Name` argument to a `Context` method, such as `lookup()`, the method can accept either a composite name or a compound name, as explained in a previous section. To have the argument interpreted as a composite name, use an instance of `CompositeName`.

String Representations

As shown in the previous example, a compound name consists of components. The components are separated according to the naming system's syntax. For example, in the LDAP, components are ordered from right to left and separated by a comma character ("."). Thus the string representation of the following components

```
ou=People
cn=Jon Ruiz
cn=homedir
```

is

```
cn=homedir, cn=Jon Ruiz, ou=People
```

The CompoundName Class

The CompoundName class is a convenience class for representing the structural form of a compound name. Its constructor accepts a string representation of the compound name and a set of properties that describe the naming syntax of the name. The set of properties and the CompoundName class are intended to be flexible enough to describe the syntaxes of most naming systems. However, implementors may choose to provide their own implementations of compound names that are either subclasses of CompoundName or any class that implements the Name interface.

Typically, you use the CompoundName constructor only if you are writing a service provider. As an application developer, you usually encounter compound names (either CompoundName or direct implementations of Name) when you want to parse a name from a particular naming system.

Here's an example that gets the name parser for a context in a naming system and uses the parser to parse a name from that naming system.

```
NameParser parser = ctx.getNameParser("");
Name compoundName = parser.parse(compoundStringName);
```

Manipulating a Compound Name

Notice that NameParser.parse() returns an object that implements the Name interface. This interface is implemented by both the CompositeName and CompoundName classes. This means that you can access and update the components of a compound name in a way similar to how you would a composite name.

Following is example code that replaces the second component of a compound name and adds components to the head and tail of the name.

```
// Get the parser for this namespace
NameParser parser = ctx.getNameParser("");

// Parse the name
Name cn = parser.parse("cn=John,ou=People,ou=Marketing");

// Remove the second component from the head
System.out.println(cn.remove(1));          // ou=People

// Add to the head (first)
System.out.println(cn.add(0, "ou=East"));
          // cn=John,ou=Marketing,ou=East

// Add to the tail (last)
System.out.println(cn.add("cn=HomeDir"));
          // cn=HomeDir,cn=John,ou=Marketing,ou=East
```

Running this program produces the following output.

```
ou=People
cn=John, ou=Marketing, ou=East
cn=HomeDir, cn=John, ou=Marketing, ou=East
```

Note that the notions of *head* and *tail* are independent of the name's syntax. For example, the LDAP syntax specifies that components are ordered right to left. This means that the rightmost component is the head and the leftmost component the tail. For such a name, a component added to the head ("cn=East") is added to the right and a component added to the tail ("cn=HomeDir") is added to the left.

Following is the output produced by a modified version of the previous example. This example uses UNIX filename syntax instead of the LDAP syntax.

```
People
East/Marketing/John
East/Marketing/John/HomeDir
```

Compound Name as an Argument to Context Methods

A Name instance that is *not* a CompositeName passed to methods in the Context and DirContext interfaces is treated as a compound name. Following is an example that looks up an LDAP entry by using a compound name. It first gets a context handle into an LDAP namespace. Then it obtains a parser for that namespace by calling Context.getNameParser(), which is then used to parse an LDAP string name into a compound name. The compound name is subsequently used in the lookup() call.

```
// Create the initial context
Context ctx = new InitialContext(env);

// Get the parser for the namespace
NameParser parser = ctx.getNameParser("");

// Parse the string name into the compound name
Name compound = parser.parse("cn=Jon Ruiz,ou=people");

// Perform the lookup using the compound name
Object obj = ctx.lookup(compound);
```

Fully Qualified Compound Names

Sometimes you want to obtain the fully qualified name of an object. For example, in the DNS, you might want to know a machine's fully qualified Internet name so that it can be used in Kerberos authentication or as an address for Internet mail delivery. In the LDAP, a fully qualified distinguished name might be inserted into an X.509 certificate or be given out as an e-mail address or as part of a URL.

The use of this fully qualified name is typically outside the scope of the JNDI. That is, once the name is obtained, it is passed to and used in other subsystems rather than fed back into one of the JNDI APIs. Furthermore, the definition of *fully qualified* is determined by the service provider and/or underlying naming/directory system.

The JNDI provides `Context.getNameInNamespace()` for obtaining an object's fully qualified name, relative to its own namespace. That is, the result is a name in the namespace served by the underlying naming system.

Here's an example that looks up an entry (`"cn=Jon Ruiz, ou=people"`) and then invokes `getNameInNamespace()` to get its fully qualified LDAP name.

```
// Create the initial context
Context ctx = new InitialContext(env);

// Perform the lookup
Context jon = (Context)ctx.lookup("cn=Jon Ruiz,ou=people");

String fullname = jon.getNameInNamespace();
```

When you run this program, it produces the following output.

```
cn=Jon Ruiz, ou=people, o=JNDItutorial
```

Name Parsers

To *parse* a name means to use its string representation (`java.lang.String`) to obtain its structural representation (`Name`). The JNDI provides a name parser for composite names and a generic interface for compound name parsers. Service providers provide the actual implementations of name parsers for compound names exported by their namespaces.

Parsing Composite Names

To parse a composite name, you pass its string representation to the `CompositeName` constructor. For example, the following code parses a string name into a structured name, `CompositeName`.

```
// Parse the string name into CompositeName
Name cname = new CompositeName(
    "cn=homedir,cn=Jon Ruiz,ou=people/tutorial/report.txt");
```

See the **Composite Names** section (page 81) for examples of how to access and change the components of a `CompositeName`.

Parsing Compound Names

To parse a compound name, you use the `NameParser` interface. This interface contains a single method:

```
Name parse(String name) throws InvalidNameException;
```

First, however, you must obtain a `NameParser` from the service provider that supports the namespace. Here is an example that obtains name parsers for the LDAP namespace and file namespace.

```
// Create the initial context
Context ctx = new InitialContext();

// Get the parser for LDAP
NameParser ldapParser =
    ctx.getNameParser("ldap://localhost:389/o=jnditutorial");

// Get the parser for filenames
NameParser fsParser = ctx.getNameParser("file:/");
```

See the **Compound Names** section (page 86) for more examples of how to get a `NameParser` instance.

Once you have an instance of a `NameParser`, you can use its `parse()` method to parse compound names. As a continuation of the example, you can use `ldapParser` to parse an LDAP string name into its structural form, as follows.

```
// Parse the name using the LDAP parser
Name compoundName = ldapParser.parse(
    "cn=John Smith, ou=People, o=JNDITutorial");
```

Similarly, you can use `fsParser` to parse a filename, as follows.

```
// Parse the name using the LDAP parser
Name compoundName = fsParser.parse(
    "tmp/tutorial/beyond/names/parse.html");
```

Note that each parser determines the syntax of names that it will accept. If you supply a valid filename that is not a legal LDAP name to an LDAP parser, then you will get an `InvalidName-Exception`.

See the **Compound Names** section (page 86) for examples of how to access and change the components of a compound name.

Although `parse()` returns a `Name`, `NameParser` is intended to be used only for compound names and not for composite names. The object returned by `parse()` might or might not be an instance of `CompoundName`. The only requirement is that it implements the `Name` interface. The exact type of the object returned depends on the service provider implementation.

Handling Special Characters

A naming convention, such as that for the LDAP or the file system, typically has meta characters. For example, in the LDAP, if one of the following characters appears in the name, then it must be preceded by the escape character, the backslash character ("\"):

- A space or "#" character occurring at the beginning of the string
- A space character occurring at the end of the string
- One of the characters ",", "+", """, "\", "<", ">", or ";"

When you are specifying a name to one of the `Context` methods, you not only must pay attention to the special characters and naming convention of the underlying naming system. You also need to be concerned about the JNDI composite name syntax, which also defines special characters. The combination of the two syntaxes might lead to many levels of escaping.

For example, suppose that you have a "cn" attribute whose value contains a backslash character:

```
backslash\a
```

The LDAP requires that the backslash character be escaped in a name. Therefore when you use this attribute as an LDAP name, you must precede the backslash character in its value with another backslash character, as follows:

```
cn=backslash\\a
```

The backslash character is also a special character in the JNDI, so if you supply this string name as a composite name, then you must escape the backslashes, again by preceding each with a backslash character:

```
cn=backslash\\\\a
```

If you specify this as a literal in the Java programming language, then you need to follow the Java programming language requirements and escape a backslash within a string literal with yet another backslash:

```
String cname = "cn=backslash\\\\\\\\a";
```

String Names as Composite Names

You need to keep in mind that the string names that you pass to the `Context` methods are composite names. To avoid any surprises if a name contains special characters that might conflict with the JNDI composite name syntax, you should use the `Context` methods that accept a `Name`. Two ways are available for doing this. The first way is to use a `CompositeName`. You create a `CompositeName` object and then append the naming system-specific name (such as an LDAP name) to it. Here is an example.

```
String dn = ...; // An LDAP-distinguished name
Name composite = new CompositeName().add(dn);
Object obj = ctx.lookup(composite);
```

Applying this technique to the previous LDAP sample name, you would no longer need to add escapes for the JNDI syntax manually because that would be handled automatically by the `CompositeName` class.

```
Name composite = new CompositeName().add("cn=backslash\\\\a");
Object obj = ctx.lookup(composite);
```

The second way is to use a compound name. You create a compound name by parsing the naming system-specific name (such as an LDAP name). Here is an example.

```
String dn = ...; // An LDAP-distinguished name
NameParser ldapParser = ctx.getNameParser("");
Name compound = ldapParser.parse(dn);
Object obj = ctx.lookup(compound);
```

Applying this technique to the previous LDAP sample name, you would no longer need to add escapes for the JNDI syntax because you are not using JNDI composite names.

```
Name compound = ldapParser.parse("cn=backslash\\\\a");
Object obj = ctx.lookup(compound);
```

Dynamic Name Composition

For name composition, you typically use the methods in the Name interface. The **Composite Names** section (page 81) explained how to add components to a composite name and the **Compound Names** section (page 86) discussed how to add components to a compound name.

These methods are useful when you know that you are dealing with either composite names or compound names. But what if you have a composite name and you need to add a component? Would you use the composite name syntax or the compound name syntax? If compound, which compound name syntax? Developers who write applications such as namespace browsers often face this question. It can be difficult to answer without a lot of insight and knowledge about the context in which the name is bound and how it was resolved.

For example, suppose that the name "cn=homedir, cn=Jon Ruiz, ou=People" is bound to an object in a different naming system—specifically, a file system context. To add a filename component to this name, you use the composite name syntax. This is because you are traversing from an LDAP namespace to the file namespace.

```
cn=homedir, cn=Jon Ruiz, ou=People/tutorial
```

When you add yet another filename component to the result, you should use the filename syntax. For example, in Windows, adding the component "report.txt" results in the name

```
cn=homedir, cn=Jon Ruiz, ou=People/tutorial\report.txt
```

To add an LDAP component to the name "cn=Jon Ruiz, ou=People", you would use the LDAP name syntax:

```
cn=homedir, cn=Jon Ruiz, ou=People
```

In all three examples, you use a different naming syntax. The rules of when to use which syntax become difficult to figure out, as well as to program.

To assist in this task, the JNDI provides Context.composeName() for composing names dynamically depending on federated namespace boundaries. You give this method two arguments: the name that you want to append and the name of this context (relative to one of its ancestor contexts). You need to supply the latter because, in general, a context does not know its name, especially its name relative to other contexts through which you might have resolved to get there.

The implementation of this method is supplied by the service provider. This puts the onus of figuring out namespace boundaries and which naming syntax to use on the service provider instead of the application developer.

Following is an example that performs the compositions described here.

```
// Create the initial context
Context ctx = new InitialContext(env);

// Compose a name within the LDAP namespace
Context ldapCtx = (Context)ctx.lookup("cn=Jon Ruiz,ou=people");
String ldapName = ldapCtx.composeName("cn=homedir",
    "cn=Jon Ruiz,ou=people");
System.out.println(ldapName);

// Compose a name when it crosses into the next naming system
Context homedirCtx = (Context)ctx.lookup(ldapName);
String compositeName = homedirCtx.composeName("tutorial", ldapName);
System.out.println(compositeName);

// Compose a name within the File namespace
Context fileCtx = (Context)ctx.lookup(compositeName);
String fileName = fileCtx.composeName("report.txt", compositeName);
System.out.println(fileName);
```

The names of the variables used in this example are only for illustrative purposes. The application does not need to know whether it is interacting with an LDAP context, a file system context, or a context that connects the two.

Note: The v1.2 Beta version of the file system service provider does not implement `composeName()` properly. If you run this example on a Windows platform, then the last filename composition uses a forward slash character ("/") instead of a backslash character.

This method also has an overloaded form that accepts `Name` instead of `java.lang.String` arguments. If you use the `Name` form, then make sure that both arguments are of the same type. For example, don't mix a `CompositeName` with a `CompoundName`.

Environment Properties

The **Preparations** lesson (page 49) discussed how to set up a `Hashtable` object, populate it with some properties, and then use it as a parameter to the `InitialContext` constructor. Here is an example.

```
Hashtable env = new Hashtable();
env.put(Context.INITIAL_CONTEXT_FACTORY,
    "com.sun.jndi.ldap.LdapCtxFactory");
env.put(Context.PROVIDER_URL, "ldap://localhost:389/o=JNDITutorial");
Context ctx = new InitialContext(env);
```

Almost every example in this book uses a similar pattern. The data in the `Hashtable` is called *environment properties*, or simply *environment*. The use of the `Hashtable` as shown is but one way to specify environment properties.

This lesson describes in detail what environment properties are, where they come from, and how they are used by the JNDI. It also describes how to update environment properties and how to customize a service provider using properties.

Overview

The JNDI is a generic interface. To access any naming/directory service, you must specify the service provider to use. This is but one piece of configuration information. Depending on the naming/directory service and the service provider, you might need to specify other configuration information, for example telling the service provider to which server to use. You specify configuration information in the JNDI by using environment properties. Although this section describes many environment properties, in general you need to specify only a few properties.

Following are the different types of environment properties, categorized by their scope and applicability:

- Standard
- Service-specific

- Feature-specific
- Provider-specific

Standard JNDI Environment Properties

The JNDI defines environment properties that are standard across all service providers. Not all standard environment properties are applicable to all service providers. But when a service provider does use one of these properties, it must interpret the property according to the definition specified by the JNDI.

These properties have the prefix `"java.naming."` The `Context` and `LdapContext` interfaces declare constants for these properties. Table 3 shows the list of the standard JNDI environment properties.

TABLE 3: Standard JNDI Environment Properties.

Property Name	Description
`java.naming.applet`	An instance of `java.applet.Applet`. The applet parameters of this applet instance are used to obtain certain environment properties. See the next section for details. *Constant*: `Context.APPLET` *Default*: None.
`java.naming.authoritative`	A string (`"true"` or `"false"`) that specifies the authoritative source of the service requested. If you set this property to `"true"`, then you are asking the service provider to use the most authoritative source for the service (such as a master server). Otherwise, the source need not be (but can be) authoritative. *Constant*: `Context.AUTHORITATIVE` *Default*: `"false"`.
`java.naming.batchsize`	The string representation of an integer that specifies the preferred batch size to use when returning data via the service's protocol. See the **Searches** lesson (page 256) for details and an example. *Constant*: `Context.BATCHSIZE` *Default*: Provider's default. *Example*: `"10"`
`java.naming.dns.url`	A URL string that specifies the DNS host and domain names to use for the "jndi" URL context implementation. *Constant*: `Context.DNS_URL` *Default*: None. *Example*: `"dns://dnsserver/wiz.com"`

TABLE 3: **Standard JNDI Environment Properties.**

Property Name	Description
`java.naming.factory.control`	Colon-separated list of class names of control factories. Each class must implement the `ControlFactory` interface. This property is used by `ControlFactory.get-ControlInstance()`, which in turn is used by service providers. See the **Controls and Extensions** lesson (page 298) for details. *Constant*: `LdapContext.CONTROL_FACTORIES` *Default*: The empty list. *Example*: `"com.wiz.jndi.ldap.ControlFactory:\` `vendorX.ldap.VendorXControlFactory"`
`java.naming.factory.initial`	Class name of the initial context factory. Class must implement the `InitialContextFactory` interface. This class is instantiated by the `InitialContext` constructor. You must set this property, unless you pass only URL names to the `InitialContext` methods. *Constant*: `Context.INITIAL_CONTEXT_FACTORY` *Default*: None. *Example*: `"com.sun.jndi.ldap.LdapCtxFactory"`
`java.naming.factory.object`	Colon-separated list of class names of object factories. Each class must implement the `ObjectFactory` or `DirObjectFactory` interface. This property is used by `NamingManager.getObjectInstance()` and `DirectoryManager.getObjectInstance()`, which in turn are used by service providers. See the **Java Objects and the Directory** trail (page 185) for details. *Constant*: `Context.OBJECT_FACTORIES` *Default*: The empty list. *Example*: `"com.wiz.jndi.ldap.AttrsTo-Remote:com.wiz.jndi.ldap.AttrsToCorba"`
`java.naming.factory.state`	Colon-separated list of class names of state factories. Each class must implement the `StateFactory` or `DirState-Factory` interface. This property is used by `Naming-Manager.getStateToBind()` and `DirectoryManager.getStateToBind()`, which in turn are used by service providers. See the **Java Objects and the Directory** trail (page 171) for details. *Constant*: `Context.STATE_FACTORIES` *Default*: The empty list. *Example*: `"com.wiz.jndi.ldap.RemoteTo-Attrs:com.wiz.jndi.ldap.CorbaToAttrs"`

Continued

TABLE 3:   **Standard JNDI Environment Properties.**

Property Name	**Description**
`java.naming.factory.url.pkgs`	Colon-separated list of package prefixes of URL context factories. The prefix consists of the URL scheme id and a suffix to construct the class name, as follows: *prefix.scheme.scheme*URLContextFactory For example, suppose that the prefix is `"vendorZ.jndi"` and the URL scheme is `"ldap"`. Then the complete class name is `vendorZ.jndi.ldap.ldapURLContext-Factory`. Each class whose name is constructed in this manner must implement the `ObjectFactory` or `DirObjectFactory` interface and follow the rules for processing URL names. The package prefix `"com.sun.jndi.url"` is always appended to the end of the list specified by this property. This property is used when a URL name is passed to the `InitialContext` methods. See the **URLs** lesson (page 123) for more information. *Constant*: `Context.URL_PKG_PREFIXES` *Default*: The empty list. *Example*: `"com.wiz.jndi.url:vendorZ.jndi"`
`java.naming.language`	A string specifying the preferred language to use with this service. The values of this property are defined by RFC 1766. *Constant*: `Context.LANGUAGE` *Default*: Provider's default. *Example*: `"en-US"`
`java.naming.provider.url`	A URL string for configuring the service provider specified by the `"java.naming.factory.initial"` property. *Constant*: `Context.PROVIDER_URL` *Default*: Provider's default. *Example*: `"ldap://localhost:389/o=JNDITutorial"`
`java.naming.referral`	A string specifying how the service provider should handle referrals; one of `"throw"`, `"ignore"`, or `"follow"`. See the **Referrals** lesson (page 259) for details and examples. *Constant*: `Context.REFERRAL` *Default*: Provider's default. *Example*: `"throw"`

TABLE 3: **Standard JNDI Environment Properties.**

Property Name	Description
`java.naming.security.authentication`	A string specifying the type of authentication to use; one of "none", "simple", or "strong" or a provider-specific string. See the **Security** lesson (page 221) for details and examples. *Constant*: `Context.SECURITY_AUTHENTICATION` *Default*: Provider's default. *Example*: "simple"
`java.naming.security.credentials`	An object specifying the credentials of the entity performing the authentication. Its type is determined by the service provider. See the **Security** lesson (page 221) for details and examples. *Constant*: `Context.SECURITY_CREDENTIALS` *Default*: Provider's default. *Example*: A `char[]` containing "secret."
`java.naming.security.principal`	A string that specifies the identity of the entity performing the authentication. See the **Security** lesson (page 221) for details and examples. *Constant*: `Context.SECURITY_PRINCIPAL` *Default*: Provider's default. *Example*: "cn=Directory Manager, o=JNDITutorial"
`java.naming.security.protocol`	A string specifying the security protocol to use. See the **Security** lesson (page 221) for details and an example. *Constant*: `Context.SECURITY_PROTOCOL` *Default*: Provider's default. *Example*: "ssl"

Service-Specific Environment Properties

Service-specific environment properties are common across all service providers that implement a particular service or protocol. For example, several different service providers might implement the LDAP. These providers would use LDAP-specific environment properties.

Service-specific properties have the prefix "java.naming.*service*." For example, the LDAP-specific properties have the prefix "java.naming.ldap." and the CORBA-specific properties have the prefix "java.naming.corba." Note that these are JNDI-related environment properties used by the JNDI service providers. A service or subsystem such as CORBA or the RMI might define other properties unrelated to the JNDI. See the **Miscellaneous** lesson (page 237) for examples of LDAP-specific environment properties.

Feature-Specific Environment Properties

Feature-specific environment properties are common across all service providers that implement a particular feature. For example, the LDAP service provider and a *VendorX* service provider might both use the SASL for authentication. These providers would then use SASL-specific environment properties when configuring that feature.

Feature-specific properties have the prefix `"java.naming.`*feature*`."` For example, the SASL-specific properties have the prefix `"java.naming.security.sasl."` Note that these are JNDI-related environment properties used by the JNDI service providers. A feature or subsystem such as the SASL might define other properties unrelated to the JNDI. See the **Security** lesson (page 230) for some examples of SASL-specific properties.

Provider-Specific Environment Properties

Provider-specific environment properties are properties used by only one service provider. For example, Sun's LDAP service provider has a property for turning on tracing. (See the example in the **Frequently Asked Questions** lesson (page 306).) A provider-specific property should have a prefix that reflects its uniqueness, commonly the package name of the service provider. For example, the Sun LDAP provider's trace property is named `"com.sun.jndi.ldap.trace.ber"`.

Specifying Environment Properties

You can specify environment properties to the JNDI by using the environment parameter to the `InitialContext` constructor and application resource files. Several JNDI standard environment properties could be specified also by using system properties and applet parameters, as described later in this section.

Application Resource Files

To simplify the task of setting up the environment required by a JNDI application, you may distribute *application resource files* along with application components and service providers. An application resource file has the name `jndi.properties`. It contains a list of key/value pairs presented in the properties file format (see `java.util.Properties`). The key is the name of the property (for example, `"java.naming.factory.object"`) and the value is a string in the format defined for that property.

Here is an example of an application resource file.

```
java.naming.factory.object=\
    com.sun.jndi.ldap.AttrsToCorba:com.wiz.from.Person
java.naming.factory.state=\
    com.sun.jndi.ldap.CorbaToAttrs:com.wiz.from.Person
java.naming.factory.control=com.sun.jndi.ldap.ResponseControlFactory
```

```
java.naming.factory.initial=com.sun.jndi.ldap.LdapCtxFactory
java.naming.provider.url=ldap://localhost:389/o=jnditutorial
com.sun.jndi.ldap.netscape.schemaBugs=true
```

Notice that no restrictions apply regarding the type of environment property that you can have in this file.

The JNDI automatically reads the application resource files from all components in the applications' classpaths and *JAVA_HOME*/lib/jndi.properties, where *JAVA_HOME* is the file directory that contains your JRE (Java Runtime Environment). The JNDI then makes the properties from these files available to the service providers and other components that need to use them. Therefore these files should be considered *world-readable* and should not contain sensitive information, such as clear-text passwords.

Note: Except for *JAVA_HOME*/lib/jndi.properties, application resource files are supported only when you use the Java 2 platform. If you use the JDK[TM] software v1.1, then you can see only *JAVA_HOME*/lib/jndi.properties.

For example, following is a program that lists a context without specifying any environment properties in the InitialContext constructor.

```
InitialContext ctx = new InitialContext();
NamingEnumeration enum = ctx.list("");
```

If you run this program with the jndi.properties file shown previously, then it will list the contents of the o=jnditutorial entry on the specified LDAP server.

The use of application resource files to specify any JNDI environment properties allows the JNDI to be configured with minimal programmatic setup. By using the *JAVA_HOME*/lib/jndi.properties file, you can also configure the JNDI for all applications and applets that use the same Java interpreter.

If you use application resource files, then you must remember to grant your applet or application permission to read all of the application resource files.

System Properties

A *system property* is a key/value pair that the Java runtime defines to describe the user, system environment, and Java system. The runtime defines and uses a set of default system properties. Other properties can be made available to a Java program via the -D command line option to the Java interpreter. For example, running the interpreter as follows

```
# java -Dmyenviron=abc Main
```

adds the property myenviron with the value abc to the list of system properties visible to the program Main. The java.lang.System class contains static methods for reading and updating system properties. The ability to read or update any system property is controlled by the security policy of the Java runtime system.

The JNDI reads the following standard JNDI properties from the system properties:

```
java.naming.factory.initial
```

```
java.naming.factory.object
```

```
java.naming.factory.state
```

```
java.naming.factory.control
```

```
java.naming.factory.url.pkgs
```

```
java.naming.provider.url
```

```
java.naming.dns.url
```

When set as system properties, these environment properties affect the contexts of all applications or applets (if the applet is allowed permission to read these properties).

Using the same program in the previous application resource file example, specify the initial context factory to use by giving the initial context to use on the command line. Here are two examples.

```
# java -Djava.naming.factory.initial=com.sun.jndi.ldap.LdapCtxFactory\
    -Djava.naming.provider.url=ldap://localhost:389/o=jnditutorial\
    List
```

```
# java -Djava.naming.factory.initial=\
        com.sun.jndi.fscontext.RefFSContextFactory\
    -Djava.naming.provider.url=file:/tmp \
    List
```

The first example uses LDAP, and the second uses the file system.

The use of system properties to specify standard JNDI environment properties allows the JNDI to be configured with minimal programmatic setup. However, they are probably convenient to use only from scripts. This is because items with long property names must be specified on the command line. Also, applets generally do not have permission to read arbitrary system properties and must be explicitly granted permission to do so.

Applet Parameters

You can pass parameters to an applet by using simple key/value pairs. They are specified in the HTML file that references the applet. How you specify them depends on the applet context. For example, if the applet is referenced from an `applet` tag, then you specify the parameters by using the `param` tag. Here is an example.

```
<param
    name=java.naming.factory.initial
    value=com.sun.jndi.ldap.LdapCtxFactory>

<param
    name=java.naming.provider.url
    value=ldap://localhost:389/o=jnditutorial>
```

If the applet is referenced from the Java Plug-in, then you specify its parameters by using key/value pairs. Here is an example.

```
java.naming.provider.url="ldap://localhost:389/o=jnditutorial"
java.naming.factory.initial="com.sun.jndi.ldap.LdapCtxFactory"
```

For the JNDI to access an applet's parameters, you must set the `Context.APPLET("java.naming.applet")` environment property. The JNDI reads the following standard JNDI properties from the applet parameters:

`java.naming.factory.initial`

`java.naming.factory.object`

`java.naming.factory.state`

`java.naming.factory.control`

`java.naming.factory.url.pkgs`

`java.naming.provider.url`

`java.naming.dns.url`

Here is an example that adds a single property (`"java.naming.applet"`) to the environment.

```
// Put this applet instance into the environment
Hashtable env = new Hashtable();
env.put(Context.APPLET, this);

// Pass the environment to the initial context constructor
Context ctx = new InitialContext(env);

// List the objects
NamingEnumeration enum = ctx.list(target);
while (enum.hasMore()) {
    out.println(enum.next());
}
ctx.close();
```

The JNDI then obtains the necessary environment properties from the applet parameters (shown previously).

This use of applet parameters to specify standard JNDI environment properties allows the JNDI to be configured in the same way that an applet typically performs configuration for other subsystems or components. System properties and application resource files are not good mechanisms for applets to depend on. This is because applets typically cannot read system properties or arbitrary files (including `jndi.properties`).

A Context's Environment

You can use application resource files, the environment parameter, system properties, and applet parameters to specify environment properties. What if you use more than one of these mechanisms at the same time?

Initialization

When you use any of the constructors from the following classes, you can supply a `Hashtable` parameter that contains environment properties: `InitialContext`, `InitialDirContext`, and `InitialLdapContext`. The initial context's environment is initialized from the following two sources, in the order specified.

1. The constructor's environment parameter. If the property is one of

   `java.naming.factory.initial`

   `java.naming.factory.object`

   `java.naming.factory.state`

   `java.naming.factory.control`

   `java.naming.factory.url.pkgs`

   `java.naming.provider.url`

   `java.naming.dns.url`

   and it does not occur in the environment parameter, then it is obtained from the applet parameters, and if not present there, from the system properties.

2. All application resource files (`jndi.properties`).

So the environment, effectively, is the union of the environment parameter and all application resource files, with the additional rule that some standard properties could be obtained from applet parameters or system properties.

If one of the following properties is found in both of these two sources or in more than one application resource file, then all of the property's values are concatenated into a single colon-separated list. For other properties, only the first value found is used.

   `java.naming.factory.object`

   `java.naming.factory.state`

   `java.naming.factory.control`

   `java.naming.factory.url.pkgs`

When the constructor is called, the JNDI constructs an environment according to these rules and passes the result to the underlying service provider. When you invoke methods that obtain context objects derived from the initial context, such as `Context.lookup()`, the environment of the parent context is inherited.

Note that possibly not all of the environment properties will apply to a context. The context, however, is always required to record them and pass them on to any derived contexts.

Getting a Context's Environment

To obtain a context's environment, you use `getEnvironment()`. Here is an example.

```
// Initial environment with various properties
Hashtable env = new Hashtable();
env.put(Context.INITIAL_CONTEXT_FACTORY,
    "com.sun.jndi.fscontext.FSContextFactory");
env.put(Context.PROVIDER_URL, "file:/");
env.put(Context.OBJECT_FACTORIES, "foo.bar.ObjFactory");
env.put("foo", "bar");

// Call the constructor
Context ctx = new InitialContext(env);

// See what environment properties you have
System.out.println(ctx.getEnvironment());
```

When you run this example with the following application resource file in your classpath:

```
java.naming.factory.object=\
    com.sun.jndi.ldap.AttrsToCorba:com.wiz.from.Person
java.naming.factory.state=\
    com.sun.jndi.ldap.CorbaToAttrs:com.wiz.from.Person
java.naming.factory.control=com.sun.jndi.ldap.ResponseControlFactory
java.naming.factory.initial=com.sun.jndi.ldap.LdapCtxFactory
java.naming.provider.url=ldap://localhost:389/o=jnditutorial
com.sun.jndi.ldap.netscape.schemaBugs=true
```

you get the following results.

```
com.sun.jndi.ldap.netscape.schemaBugs=true
java.naming.factory.object=foo.bar.ObjFactory:\
    com.sun.jndi.ldap.AttrsToCorba:com.wiz.from.Person
java.naming.factory.initial=com.sun.jndi.fscontext.FSContextFactory
foo=bar
java.naming.provider.url=file:/
java.naming.factory.state=\
    com.sun.jndi.ldap.CorbaToAttrs:com.wiz.from.Person
java.naming.factory.control=com.sun.jndi.ldap.ResponseControlFactory
```

Notice the following from this output.

- The properties found in only one source—"foo" from the environment parameter, and "`com.sun.jndi.ldap.netscape.schemaBugs`" from the application resource file—are in the resulting environment.
- The list-of-factories properties (e.g., "`java.naming.factory.object`") that occur in both sources are merged, with the one from the environment parameter occurring first in the list.
- All other properties (e.g., "`java.naming.factory.initial`") that occur in both sources take their values from the environment parameter.

Users often mistakenly update the result of getEnvironment() and then expect that the context's environment has been updated accordingly. Depending on the underlying provider implementation, updating the results of getEnvironment() might have no effect. In fact, you should think of the result of getEnvironment() as an immutable, read-only object and not attempt to update it. See the next section for instructions on how to update a context's environment.

Updating a Context's Environment

You can change a context's environment by using addToEnvironment() and removeFrom-Environment().

Following is an example that creates an initial context and then gets a context derived from that initial context (via lookup()). It then updates the environments of the initial context and the derived context.

```
// Initial environment with various properties
Hashtable env = new Hashtable();
env.put(Context.INITIAL_CONTEXT_FACTORY,
    "com.sun.jndi.fscontext.FSContextFactory");
env.put(Context.PROVIDER_URL, "file:/");
env.put(Context.OBJECT_FACTORIES, "foo.bar.ObjFactory");
env.put("foo", "bar");

// Call the constructor
Context ctx = new InitialContext(env);

// Get the child context
Context child = (Context)ctx.lookup("tmp");

// See what properties the initial context has
System.out.println(ctx.getEnvironment());

// Replace foo in the parent
ctx.addToEnvironment("foo", "baz");

// Add a new property to the parent
ctx.addToEnvironment("com.wiz.jndi.wizProp", "wizards");

// Remove an attribute from the parent
ctx.removeFromEnvironment(Context.OBJECT_FACTORIES);

// Remote the property from the child
child.removeFromEnvironment(Context.PROVIDER_URL);

// See what environment properties you have after updates
System.out.println(">>>>> Parent context: ");
System.out.println(ctx.getEnvironment());

// See what environment properties the child has after updates
System.out.println(">>>>> Child context: ");
System.out.println(child.getEnvironment());
```

Following is the output from running the example. Notice that these updates affect only the Context instance on which they are performed.

```
{
com.sun.jndi.ldap.netscape.schemaBugs=true,
java.naming.factory.object=\foo.bar.ObjFactory:\
    com.sun.jndi.ldap.AttrsToCorba:com.wiz.from.Person,
java.naming.factory.initial=com.sun.jndi.fscontext.FSContextFactory,
foo=bar,
java.naming.provider.url=file:/,
java.naming.factory.state=com.sun.jndi.ldap.CorbaToAttrs:\
    com.wiz.from.Person,
java.naming.factory.control=com.sun.jndi.ldap.ResponseControlFactory
}

>>>>> Parent context:
{
com.sun.jndi.ldap.netscape.schemaBugs=true,
com.wiz.jndi.wizProp=wizards,
java.naming.factory.initial=com.sun.jndi.fscontext.FSContextFactory,
foo=baz,
java.naming.provider.url=file:/,
java.naming.factory.state=com.sun.jndi.ldap.CorbaToAttrs:\
    com.wiz.from.Person,
java.naming.factory.control=com.sun.jndi.ldap.ResponseControlFactory
}

>>>>> Child context:
{
com.sun.jndi.ldap.netscape.schemaBugs=true,
java.naming.factory.object=foo.bar.ObjFactory:\
    com.sun.jndi.ldap.AttrsToCorba:com.wiz.from.Person,
java.naming.factory.initial=com.sun.jndi.fscontext.FSContextFactory,
foo=bar,
java.naming.factory.state=com.sun.jndi.ldap.CorbaToAttrs:\
    com.wiz.from.Person,
java.naming.factory.control=com.sun.jndi.ldap.ResponseControlFactory
}
```

Scope of Changes

As the previous example showed, changing the environment properties of one context does not affect any of its derived contexts. However, contexts that are derived in the future from this context will inherit the updated environment.

Defaults

Some environment properties have defaults. For example, an implementation might by default ignore referrals unless the "java.naming.referral" environment property has been set to "throw" or "follow". When such a property is removed by using removeFromEnvironment(), the default value effectively becomes the property's value, even though the actual default value might not necessarily show up when you examine the context's properties by using getEnvironment().

Verifying the Update

After updating a context's environment, you can verify the update immediately by using getEnvironment(). However, often an environment property represents a behavioral aspect of the context, for example the credentials to use when logging on to the server. In such cases, there is no guarantee that just because the property has been updated, the context has verified the correctness and applicability of the property. This is because doing that might require server interaction. The next time that the context needs to use the property, the verification will occur. A failure might be indicated then.

For example, suppose that you used addToEnvironment() three times to update the client's identity, credentials, and authentication type. Suppose also that you supplied the wrong credentials. Then the next time that you invoke a method that requires authentication on the context, the underlying service provider will attempt to authenticate by using the updated properties. However, the authentication will fail because of the wrong credentials and you will get an AuthenticationException.

Customizing a Service Provider

Environment properties allow an application and its user to customize the usage of the JNDI. You can customize a particular service provider by using a provider resource file. Like an application resource file, a provider resource file contains key/value pairs presented in the properties file format (see java.util.Properties).

A provider resource file has the name

```
[prefix/]jndiprovider.properties
```

where *prefix* is the package name of the provider's context implementation, with each period character converted to a forward slash character. For example, suppose that the context implementation's class name is com.sun.jndi.ldap.LdapCtx; its provider resource filename would be "com/sun/jndi/ldap/jndiprovider.properties". Whereas a single application can use multiple application resource files, there is at most one provider resource file per service provider. In fact, the provider resource file is typically bundled with the service provider and is loaded using the same class loader that loads the service provider.

Usage

The provider resource file serves two purposes. First, it allows the service provider to be built without being hardwired to components, such as object and state factories, and at the same times allows some defaults to be specified.

Second, it can be used as a deployment mechanism. For example, suppose that you get an LDAP service provider from a vendor. You can customize that provider by adding, for example, some object and state factories suitable for your enterprise, such as factories for accounting and employee objects. When that LDAP provider is subsequently used by your applications within your enterprise, those factories will be used automatically without the application's or user's having to specify the relevant properties via application resource files, system properties, applet parameters, or initial context environment parameters.

The degree to which you can manipulate a service provider's provider resource file depends on how the provider has been packaged. For example, if the provider is packaged as a JAR, then you can supply an updated provider resource file for the provider by first extracting the contents of the JAR and then repackaging it with the updated provider resource file. Note that this procedure is not recommended for the service providers that are packaged in the Java 2 SDK/JRE, Standard Edition, v1.3. For those service providers, you should not try to update their provider resource files. Instead, use application resource files as described previously in this lesson.

Affected Properties

Although a provider resource file can contain any property, the JNDI looks only for the following from a provider resource file:

```
java.naming.factory.object
java.naming.factory.state
java.naming.factory.control
java.naming.factory.url.pkgs
```

Unlike the contents of an application resource file, the contents of a provider resource file are not added to the environment. Instead, those contents augment the value of the environment supplied to the following methods.

- `NamingManager.getObjectInstance(Object, Name, Context, Hashtable)`
- `DirectoryManager.getObjectInstance(Object, Name, Context, Hashtable, Attributes)`
- `NamingManager.getStateToBind(Object, Name, Context, Hashtable)`
- `DirectoryManager.getStateToBind(Object, Name, Context, Hashtable, Attributes)`
- `ControlFactory.getControlInstance(Control, Context, Hashtable)`

When a service provider calls one of these methods, it supplies an instance of the `Context` from which the method is being called and the context's environment. The JNDI uses the context's class loader to find the provider resource file and appends the value of the property (relevant for the method) to the same property found in the environment. It then uses the resulting property as the ordered list of factories to search.

For example, suppose that the LDAP service provider, implemented by using the class `com.sun.jndi.ldap.LdapCtx`, calls `DirectoryManager.getObjectInstance()`. The JNDI will find the value of the `"java.naming.factory.object"` property from the `com/sun/jndi/ldap/jndiprovider.properties` file and append that to the value of the `"java.naming.fac-`

tory.object" property found in the environment parameter (Hashtable). The JNDI will then use this list of factories to find an object factory that returns a non-null answer.

A service provider is free to access the provider resource file for other properties, but that behavior is provider-specific.

Event Notification

As the naming/directory service plays an increasingly important role in the computing environment, the need to provide administration and monitoring tools to help manage changes in the service also increases. For such tools and other applications, the traditional request/response style of interaction needs to be augmented with an asynchronous notification model that allows applications to register interest in changes in the service.

The `javax.naming.event` package contains classes and interfaces for supporting event notification. It uses an event model similar to that used by the Java™ Abstract Windowing Toolkit (AWT) and JavaBeans,™ both of which are part of the Java 2 platform. The model is essentially that events are fired by event sources. An event listener registers with an event source to receive notifications about events of a particular type.

In the JNDI, event sources are objects that implement either the `EventContext` or `EventDirContext` interface. Event listeners are objects that implement the `NamingListener` interface or one of its subinterfaces.

This lesson describes the different types of event listeners available in the JNDI and how to register them to receive event notifications. It also describes how to register for unsolicited notifications that might be generated by LDAP servers.

Client and Server Configuration

The examples in this lesson use the LDAP service provider. They assume that you have set up a sample namespace using the content described in the **Preparations** lesson (page 43). If you use another service provider or choose to use another part of the LDAP namespace, then the behavior will differ from what is shown here.

The initial context used in these examples is initialized using the following environment properties.

```
// Set up the environment for creating the initial context
Hashtable env = new Hashtable();
env.put(Context.INITIAL_CONTEXT_FACTORY,
```

```
            "com.sun.jndi.ldap.LdapCtxFactory");
    env.put(Context.PROVIDER_URL, "ldap://localhost:389/o=JNDITutorial");
```

Also, the LDAP server must support the Persistent Search control (Internet-draft draft-ietf-ldapext-psearch-02.txt). The Netscape Directory Server v4.1 supports this control.

Event Listeners

A listener in the JNDI is represented by the NamingListener interface. This is the root interface for objects that handle events generated by the JNDI. Typically, an object implements a subinterface of NamingListener rather than directly implementing NamingListener.

The javax.naming.event package contains two subinterfaces of NamingListener: ObjectChangeListener and NamespaceChangeListener. The javax.naming.ldap package contains one subinterface: UnsolicitedNotificationListener. This subinterface is discussed in the **LDAP Unsolicited Notifications** section (page 120).

Handling Errors

The NamingListener interface not only serves as the root interface, but also specifies how a registered listener is to be notified of errors. It defines a single method: namingException-Thrown(). This method is invoked by the service provider when an error occurs while the provider is collecting data for generating events that the listener is seeking. For example, the server might have gone offline or cannot collect any more data in that part of the directory. When that occurs, the service provider deregisters the listener and invokes namingException-Thrown() on the listener to notify it of the problem. This allows the listener to take action, such as notifying the application's user that the lack of events is due to a problem rather than the nonoccurrence of events.

See the **Listener Registration** section (page 115) for details on how to handle errors when registering listeners.

Handling Namespace Changes

NamespaceChangeListener handles events that affect the namespace, including the addition, removal, and renaming of an object. An object that implements this interface must provide definitions for the three methods declared in the interface, as well as for namingException-Thrown() (from the NamingListener interface).

Here is an example of a NamespaceChangeListener.

```
public class SampleNCListener implements NamespaceChangeListener {
    private String id;

    public SampleNCListener(String id) {
        this.id = id;
    }
```

```
    public void objectAdded(NamingEvent evt) {
        System.out.println(id + ">>> added: " + evt.getNewBinding());
    }
    public void objectRemoved(NamingEvent evt) {
        System.out.println(id + ">>> removed: " + evt.getOldBinding());
    }

    public void objectRenamed(NamingEvent evt) {
        System.out.println(id + ">>> renamed: " + evt.getNewBinding() +
            " from " + evt.getOldBinding());
    }

    public void namingExceptionThrown(NamingExceptionEvent evt) {
        System.out.println(id +
            ">>> SampleNCListener got an exception");
        evt.getException().printStackTrace();
    }
}
```

When an object has been added, getOldBinding() will always return null because it wasn't in the namespace prior to its being added. When an object has been removed, getNewBinding() will always be null because it won't be in the namespace after it has been removed. More details about the old and new bindings are in the **Naming Events** section (page 118).

Handling Object Changes

ObjectChangeListener handles events that affect an object's contents, for example if an object's binding has been replaced with another or one of an object's attributes has been removed or replaced.

An object that implements the ObjectChangeListener interface must provide definitions for objectChanged() as well as for namingExceptionThrown() (from the NamingListener interface).

Here is an example of an ObjectChangeListener.

```
public class SampleOCListener implements ObjectChangeListener {
    private String id;

    public SampleOCListener(String id) {
        this.id = id;
    }
    public void objectChanged(NamingEvent evt) {
        System.out.println(id + ">>> object changed: " +
            evt.getNewBinding() + " from " + evt.getOldBinding());
    }

    public void namingExceptionThrown(NamingExceptionEvent evt) {
        System.out.println(id +
            ">>> SampleOCListener got an exception");
        evt.getException().printStackTrace();
    }
}
```

Even though this example displays both the old and new bindings for an object that has changed, some or all of that information might not be available if it is not supplied by the service provider or naming/directory server. More details about the old and new bindings are given in the **Naming Events** section (page 118).

Note that removing an object is a namespace change and not an object content change. An application interested in both should use a listener that implements both NamespaceChange-Listener and ObjectChangeListener, as described next.

Handling More Than One Type of Change

If you are interested in both namespace changes and object content changes, then you should define one listener that implements both interfaces. In that way, the service provider might be able to optimize the resources used for the registration by collecting data about both types of change with one request to the server. It can also reduce the number of listeners that the provider must manage as well as your application's code size.

Here is an example of a listener that implements both NamespaceChangeListener and ObjectChangeListener.

```java
public class SampleListener
implements NamespaceChangeListener, ObjectChangeListener {
    private String id;

    public SampleListener(String id) {
        this.id = id;
    }

    public void objectAdded(NamingEvent evt) {
        System.out.println(id + ">>> added: " + evt.getNewBinding());
    }
    public void objectRemoved(NamingEvent evt) {
        System.out.println(id + ">>> removed: " + evt.getOldBinding());
    }

    public void objectRenamed(NamingEvent evt) {
    System.out.println(id + ">>> renamed: " + evt.getNewBinding() +
        " from " + evt.getOldBinding());
    }

    public void objectChanged(NamingEvent evt) {
        System.out.println(id + ">>> object changed: " +
            evt.getNewBinding() + " from " + evt.getOldBinding());
    }

    public void namingExceptionThrown(NamingExceptionEvent evt) {
        System.out.println(id +
            ">>> SampleNCListener got an exception");
        evt.getException().printStackTrace();
    }
}
```

Listener Registration

To receive event notifications, a listener registers with an event source. In the JNDI, the event sources implement either the EventContext or EventDirContext interface. To get an event source, you must look it up using the naming/directory service. That is, you perform a lookup() on an object and then cast the result to an EventContext or EventDirContext. Whether a context supports either of these interfaces is optional. A context that supports neither does not support event notification.

Here is an example that looks up a name from the initial context and casts it to an Event-DirContext.

```
// Get the EventDirContext for registering the listener
EventDirContext ctx = (EventDirContext)
    (new InitialDirContext(env).lookup("ou=People"));
```

To get an event source for the initial context itself, use the empty string as the name argument to lookup(). Here is an example.

```
EventDirContext ctx = (EventDirContext)
    (new InitialDirContext(env).lookup(""));
```

EventContext is intended for applications that can name the object of interest. You register a listener to receive notifications by using EventContext.addNamingListener().

Here is an example that registers a NamespaceChangeListener with a context.

```
// Get the event context for registering the listener
EventContext ctx = (EventContext)
    (new InitialContext(env).lookup("ou=People"));

// Create the listener
NamingListener listener = new SampleNCListener("nc1");

// Register the listener for namespace change events
ctx.addNamingListener("ou=Objects,cn=Rosanna Lee",
    EventContext.ONELEVEL_SCOPE, listener);
```

Target and Scope

The object named by the name parameter to addNamingListener() is called the *target*. The second parameter specifies the *scope*. The scope identifies whether the listener is to receive notifications on one of the following:

- Only the target (OBJECT_SCOPE)
- The immediate children of the target (which must be a context) (ONELEVEL_SCOPE)
- The target and all of its descendants (SUBTREE_SCOPE)

Here is an example that adds listeners by using the same target but three different scopes.

```
// Get the event context for registering the listeners
EventContext ctx = (EventContext)
```

```
        (new InitialContext(env).lookup("ou=People"));

    String target = ...;

    // Create the listeners
    NamingListener oneListener = new SampleListener("ONELEVEL");
    NamingListener objListener = new SampleListener("OBJECT");
    NamingListener subListener = new SampleListener("SUBTREE");

    // Register the listeners by using different scopes
    ctx.addNamingListener(target, EventContext.ONELEVEL_SCOPE,
        oneListener);
    ctx.addNamingListener(target, EventContext.OBJECT_SCOPE,
        objListener);
    ctx.addNamingListener(target, EventContext.SUBTREE_SCOPE,
        subListener);
```

After registering the listeners, this program creates a thread that makes namespace changes to the LDAP server. It makes changes to the target, the children of the target, and the grandchildren of the target. The listener registered for object scope will receive the two notifications for changes applied to the target. The listener registered for one-level scope won't receives notifications for these two changes but will receive notifications for the changes applied to the children. The listener registered for subtree scope will get notifications for all of the changes.

Registration Errors

addNamingListener() can throw a NamingException when it encounters an error while registering the listener. However, there is no guarantee that the data supplied will be verified immediately at registration time. For example, some verification might require possibly open-ended server interaction. When an error occurs in this case, the service provider will invoke the listener's namingExceptionThrown() method to notify it of the problem. Therefore the application must be prepared to handle the error regardless of whether it occurs at registration time or asynchronously in the listener's code.

Nonexistent Targets

Some service providers/services might allow registration for nonexistent targets. That is, in the previous example, the entry named by target might not need to exist at the time that addNamingListener() is called. To check whether this feature is supported, you use targetMustExist(). Here is an example.

```
    // Get the event context for registering the listener
    EventContext ctx =
        (EventContext)new InitialContext(env).lookup("");

    // Create the listener
    NamingListener listener = new MyListener();
    String target = ...;
```

```
// Check whether the object exists so that you don't wait
// forever for a nonexistent object
if (!ctx.targetMustExist()) {
    // Check that the object exists before continuing
    // If lookup fails, an exception will be thrown
    // and you would skip registration
    ctx.lookup(target);
}

// Register the listener
ctx.addNamingListener(target, EventContext.ONELEVEL_SCOPE,
    listener);
```

This example does not want to register an ObjectChangeListener for a nonexistent object, so it first checks whether the context requires the object to exist. If the context does not, then the program performs a lookup(). The example also uses a listener that implements NamespaceChangeListener so that it can detect when the object has disappeared, at which point the listener notifies the user and deregisters itself.

```
public void objectRemoved(NamingEvent evt) {
    System.out.println(">>> removed: " +
        evt.getOldBinding().getName());
    deregisterSelf(evt.getEventContext());
}
private void deregisterSelf(EventContext ctx) {
    System.out.println("Deregistering listener...");
    synchronized (ctx) {
        try {
            ctx.removeNamingListener(this);
        } catch (NamingException e) {
            System.out.println("Listener removal problem: " + e);
        }
    }
}
```

Using Search Filters

If you want to be more selective about the objects for which you register interest, then you can use a search filter. The EventDirContext interface contains addNamingListener() overloads that accept a search filter, in the same way that some of the search methods in the DirContext interface do.

Here is an example that registers interest only in objects that have the object class "java-object".

```
// Get the event DirContext for registering the listener
EventDirContext ctx = (EventDirContext)
    (new InitialDirContext(env).lookup("ou=People"));

// Create the listener
NamingListener listener = new SampleNCListener("nc1");

// Set up the search constraints
SearchControls constraints = new SearchControls();
```

```
constraints.setSearchScope(SearchControls.SUBTREE_SCOPE);

// Register the listener for namespace change events for
// entries identified using a search filter
// In this example, register interest in namespace changes to
// objects that have the object class "javaobject"
ctx.addNamingListener("cn=Rosanna Lee", "(objectclass=javaobject)",
    constraints, listener);
```

The filter applies to existing objects and to those that come into existence after the registration.

Deregistration

A registered listener becomes unregistered in any of three ways.

1. When `Context.close()` is invoked on the event source, any registered listeners are automatically deregistered.
2. When a listener receives an error notification via `namingExceptionThrown()`, it is automatically deregistered.
3. When a listener is explicitly removed via a call to `EventContext.removeNamingListener()`, it is deregistered.

An example of explicit deregistration is shown in the **Nonexistent Targets** section (page 116).

Naming Events

After a `NamespaceChangeListener` or `ObjectChangeListener` has been registered with an event source, it will get event notifications in the form of `NamingEvents`. An instance of this class contains information about the event, such as its type and event source, and information about the object that caused the event to be fired. Typically, an event source creates an instance of `NamingEvent` and passes it to naming listeners. The naming listeners then can use the `NamingEvent` instance's access methods to obtain information about the event.

Event Type

A `NamingEvent` contains a *type* that identifies the type of event. An event type could be, for example, *object-added* or *object-changed*. Event types are categorized into those that affect the namespace (such as an object-added type) and those that do not (such as an object-changed type). Here are the event types defined in the `NamingEvent` class.

- `NamingEvent.OBJECT_CHANGED`: An object's content has changed. For example, one of its attribute has been removed or perhaps its binding has been replaced.
- `NamingEvent.OBJECT_ADDED`: A new object has been added to the namespace.
- `NamingEvent.OBJECT_REMOVED`: An existing object has been removed from the namespace.

• NamingEvent.OBJECT_RENAMED: An existing object has been given another name. Note that not all naming services support the generation of *rename* events. For example, an object being renamed might be manifested as an object removal followed by an object addition.

The event type is obtained using getType().

Event Source

An *event source* is the entity that fired the event and the object with which the listener has registered. It is an instance of EventContext or EventDirContext. See the **Listener Registration** section (page 115) for more information about these two interfaces.

The event source is obtained by using getEventContext() or java.util.Event-Object.getSource(). These methods differ only in that getEventContext() returns the result as an EventContext whereas getSource() returns the result as a java.lang.Object, so you don't need to cast the result.

You can use the event source to obtain more information about the object or objects reachable from it. If you do use this method, you must synchronize access to it. This is because implementations of Context are not guaranteed to be thread-safe (and EventContext is a sub-interface of Context).

Here is some listener code that uses the event source.

```
Attributes attrs;

// Get the event source
EventContext ctx = evt.getEventContext();

// Get the name of the object that changed
// Should really check for null binding first
String which = evt.getNewBinding().getName();

// Lock the event source
synchronized(ctx) {
    attrs = ctx.getAttributes(which, new String[]{"objectclass"});
}
// Do something useful with attrs
```

Other Information

A NamingEvent contains, in addition to the event's type and source, the old and new bindings of the object that caused the event, as well as any additional information. You use getNewBinding() to obtain a Binding instance that describes the state of the object *after* the event occurred. The Binding contains the name of the object, the object itself, and its attributes. Any and all of this data might be missing if the server or service provider cannot provide it.

You use getOldBinding() to get similar information about the object *before* the event occurred.

Note that the name in the old and new bindings is relative to the event source. For example, suppose that your program uses the following code to register a listener.

```
EventContext ctx = (EventContext)
    (new InitialContext(env).lookup("ou=People"));

// Create the listener
NamingListener listener = new SampleNCListener("nc1");

// Register the listener for namespace change events
ctx.addNamingListener("ou=Objects,cn=John Smith",
    EventContext.ONELEVEL_SCOPE, listener);
```

When the object "cn=String" is added beneath "ou=Objects", the name in the binding of the NamingEvent will have the name "cn=String, ou=Objects, cn=John Smith".

In addition, you can use getChangeInfo() to obtain any additional change information that the server or service provider has supplied. For example, the server might send an identifier that identifies the change.

LDAP Unsolicited Notifications

The LDAP v3 (RFC 2251) defines an *unsolicited notification*—a message that is sent by an LDAP server to the client without any provocation from the client. An unsolicited notification is represented in the JNDI by the UnsolicitedNotification interface.

Because unsolicited notifications are sent asynchronously by the server, you can use the same event model used for receiving notifications about namespace changes and object content changes. You register interest in receiving unsolicited notifications by registering an UnsolicitedNotificationListener with an EventContext or EventDirContext.

Here is an example of an UnsolicitedNotificationListener.

```
public class UnsolListener
    implements UnsolicitedNotificationListener {
    public void notificationReceived(
        UnsolicitedNotificationEvent evt) {
        System.out.println("received: " + evt);
    }
    public void namingExceptionThrown(NamingExceptionEvent evt) {
        System.out.println(">>> UnsolListener got an exception");
            evt.getException().printStackTrace();
    }
}
```

Following is an example that registers an implementation of UnsolicitedNotification-Listener with an event source. Note that only the listener argument to EventContext.add-NamingListener() is relevant. The name and scope parameters are not relevant to unsolicited notifications.

```
// Get the event context for registering the listener
EventContext ctx = (EventContext)
(new InitialContext(env).lookup("ou=People"));

// Create the listener
NamingListener listener = new UnsolListener();

// Register the listener with the context (all targets equivalent)
ctx.addNamingListener("", EventContext.ONELEVEL_SCOPE, listener);
```

When running this program, you need to point it at an LDAP server that can generate unsolicited notifications and prod the server to emit the notification.

A listener that implements `UnsolicitedNotificationListener` can also implement other `NamingListener` interfaces, such as `NamespaceChangeListener` and `ObjectChange-Listener`.

URLs

A *Uniform Resource Locator* (URL) is a string that specifies the location of a resource on the Web. The specification of a URL's syntax and semantics are described in RFC 1738. In summary, the syntax is

> *scheme* **:** *scheme-specific-parts*

where *scheme* identifies the URL's type. For example, the following is a URL for the `ldap` scheme:

```
ldap://localhost:389/cn=Ted Geisel, ou=People, o=JNDITutorial
```

URL strings are used in several places in the JNDI. Their usage can be categorized into two groups: names and addresses. They are used as names as follows:

- As names to the initial context (page 123)
- As names returned by naming enumerations (page 127)

They are used as addresses as follows:

- As references for federation (page 128)
- As data for configuration (page 129)

This lesson describes these uses of URL strings in the JNDI. See the **Referrals** lesson (page 259) for descriptions and examples of how URL strings are used as LDAP referrals.

URLs as Names to the Initial Context

In the JNDI, every name is resolved relative to a context. To begin, you typically create an initial context by using one of the constructors from the `InitialContext`, `InitialDirContext`, or `InitialLdapContext` class. The **Environment Properties** lesson (page 95) contains examples of how to use these constructors.

Once you have an instance of a `Context`, you can look up other contexts and perform naming operations relative to those contexts. The names supplied to all of those contexts are *relative names*. That is, they are interpreted relative to the context to which they are supplied.

The closest thing to an *absolute name* in the JNDI is a URL string. In the JNDI, you can supply a URL string to the methods in the `InitialContext` and `InitialDirContext` classes. (The `InitialLdapContext` class does not declare any method that accepts a name argument, although the class does inherit all of the methods from the `InitialContext` and `InitialDirContext` classes.)

Client's View

When you supply a URL string, that is, a string of the form

> *scheme* : *scheme-specific-parts*

to an `InitialContext` or `InitialDirContext` method, such as `lookup()`, the name is treated as a URL string rather than a name relative to the initial context. Here is an example that looks up an object using an LDAP URL string.

```
Object obj = new InitialContext().lookup(
    "ldap://localhost:389/cn=homedir,cn=Jon Ruiz,"
    "ou=People,o=jnditutorial");
```

The `InitialContext` class (and subclasses) diverts the method invocation so that it is processed by the corresponding *URL context implementation* rather than any underlying initial context implementation. That is, if you had set the `Context.INITIAL_CONTEXT_FACTORY` environment property, then it would not have been used in the `lookup()` call. Instead, the JNDI would find and use the URL context implementation for the `ldap` URL scheme. Notice from the previous example that no `Context.INITIAL_CONTEXT_FACTORY` property was specified to the `InitialContext` constructor.

The JNDI's ability to accept arbitrary URL strings from the `InitialContext` class (and subclasses) allows you to access any namespace for which you have an implementation. Thus you are not restricted by the namespace offered by the implementation named by the `Context.INITIAL_CONTEXT_FACTORY` property. For example, suppose that you name a file system service provider by using the `Context.INITIAL_CONTEXT_FACTORY` environment property. Using the same `InitialContext` instance, you can access an LDAP namespace by specifying an LDAP URL string and you can access a CORBA namespace by specifying a CORBA URL string.

How URL Strings Are Processed

When the `InitialContext` class receives a URL string as a name argument to one of its methods, it looks for a URL context implementation. It does this by using the `Context.URL_PKG_PREFIXES` environment property. This property contains a colon-separated list of package prefixes. Each item in the list is a fully qualified package prefix of a URL context factory. The factory name is constructed using the following rule:

package_prefix . scheme . scheme`URLContextFactory`

The package prefix `"com.sun.jndi.url"` is always appended to the end of this list.

Typically, a service provider that supplies a context implementation will also supply a URL context implementation so that it can handle URL strings passed to the `InitialContext`. However, this is not a requirement and some service providers might not supply any URL context implementations. Suppose that the `Context.URL_PKG_PREFIXES` property contains

`com.widget:com.wiz.jndi`

Also suppose that the following URL string is supplied to the `lookup()` method of the `InitialContext` class:

`ldap://localhost:389/cn=homedir, cn=Jon Ruiz, ou=People, o=JNDITutorial`

The JNDI then will look for the following classes:

`com.widget.ldap.ldapURLContextFactory`

`com.wiz.jndi.ldap.ldapURLContextFactory`

`com.sun.jndi.url.ldap.ldapURLContextFactory`

It next tries to instantiate each class in turn and invokes `ObjectFactory.getObject-Instance(Object, Name, Context, Hashtable)` until one of them produces a non-null answer. The answer, which is a context, is then used to carry out the originally intended method, using the URL string as the name argument.

Next, suppose that the JNDI successfully instantiated the `com.wiz.jndi.ldap.ldapURL-ContextFactory` class and obtains a context from it. The JNDI then invokes `lookup()` on the context and supplies it `"ldap://localhost:389/cn=homedir, cn=Jon Ruiz, ou=People, o=JNDITutorial"` as the string name argument.

If the JNDI cannot find a URL context factory that returns a non-null answer, then the input URL string is passed to the underlying initial context implementation (i.e., that implementation specified in the `Context.INITIAL_CONTEXT_FACTORY` environment property).

See the **Building a Service Provider** trail (page 357) for descriptions on how to write a URL context implementation.

Relationship to the Underlying Initial Context

You need to understand that no relationship exists between the implementation named by the `Context.INITIAL_CONTEXT_FACTORY` environment property and any URL context implementation other than all can be accessed via the same `InitialContext` instance. For example, suppose that you have the following environment property settings:

`java.naming.factory.initial=com.wiz.jndi.ldap.LdapContextFactory`

`java.naming.factory.url.pkgs=`

If you supply the name "ldap://localhost:389/o=JNDITutorial" to Initial-Context.lookup(), then the list of URL context factory classes that the JNDI will try is

```
com.sun.jndi.url.ldap.ldapURLContextFactory
```

If the service provider came with a URL context factory, then the provider should supply an application resource file (jndi.properties) that contains the factory's package prefix. See the **Environment Properties** lesson (page 95) for a description of application resource files. If the provider has a URL context factory but has not specified a package prefix for it in an application resource file, then you should specify it in your program or application resource file so that the JNDI can find the factory.

Relationship to Composite Names

To specify a URL string as part of a composite name to the methods in the InitialContext class, make it the first component of a composite name. By doing this, you, in effect, use the URL string to name a context in which to continue operation on the rest of the name's components.

Here is an example that creates a CompositeName that consists of an LDAP URL string as the first component and filenames as the remaining components.

```
String url = "ldap://localhost:389/cn=homedir,cn=Jon Ruiz,ou=people,"
    "o=JNDITutorial";

// Create a CompositeName in which the first component is a URL string
Name name = new CompositeName().add(url);

// Add the other components
name.add("tutorial").add("report.txt");

// Perform the lookup by using CompositeName
System.out.println(ctx.lookup(name));
```

You can't specify composite name components as part of the URL string itself because doing so might conflict with the URL's syntax.

More Than Just Names

Some URLs, such as those for the LDAP (RFC 2255), specify more than name components. The LDAP URL syntax allows you to specify the scope of the search and the search query, as well as the attributes to return. See the **Miscellaneous** lesson (page 246) for more information and an example of how query components in a URL string are used.

URLs as Names Returned by Naming Enumerations

You can enumerate the contents of a context by using `list()`, `listBindings()`, or `search()`. When you invoke one of these, you get back a `NamingEnumeration`. Each item of the enumeration is an instance of `NameClassPair` or one of its subclasses. To get the name of the item, that is, the name of the object relative to the target context (the context that you're listing or searching), you use `NameClassPair.getName()`. The string name returned by this method is a composite name. For example, you should be able to feed this name back into one of the `Context` methods of the target context.

However, sometimes the underlying service or service provider cannot return a name relative to the target context, for example if the item was retrieved by following a referral or an alias. When a relative name cannot be returned, the service provider returns a URL string. You use this URL string by passing it to the `InitialContext` methods, as described in the previous section.

To determine whether the name returned by `getName()` is relative, you use `NameClassPair.isRelative()`.

Following is an example that searches a context for entries whose `"cn"` attribute starts with the letter "S." It then retrieves the `"telephonenumber"` attribute of the item by using `DirContext.getAttributes()`. You could have done this much more easily by using the `SearchControls` argument to request the attributes. Here, the attribute retrieval is separated out so that the use of `isRelative()` can be illustrated.

When the example gets an item containing a URL string as a name (that is, `isRelative()` returns `false`), it uses the `InitialContext` to process the URL string.

```
// Set up the environment for creating the initial context
Hashtable env = new Hashtable(11);
env.put(Context.INITIAL_CONTEXT_FACTORY,
    "com.sun.jndi.ldap.LdapCtxFactory");
env.put(Context.PROVIDER_URL, "ldap://localhost:489/o=JNDItutorial");

// Enable referrals so that you get some nonrelative names
env.put(Context.REFERRAL, "follow");

// Create the initial context
DirContext initCtx = new InitialDirContext(env);

// Get the target context
DirContext targetCtx = (DirContext)initCtx.lookup("ou=All");

SearchControls constraints = new SearchControls();
constraints.setSearchScope(SearchControls.SUBTREE_SCOPE);

// Perform the search on the target context
NamingEnumeration enum = targetCtx.search("", "(cn=S*)", constraints);
Attributes attrs;
NameClassPair item;
```

127

```
String[] attrIds = new String[]{"telephonenumber"};

// For each answer found, get its "telephonenumber" attribute
// If relative, resolve it relative to the target context
// If not relative, resolve it relative to the initial context
while (enum.hasMore()) {
    item = (NameClassPair)enum.next();
    System.out.println(">>>>>" + item.getName() + " ");
    if (item.isRelative()) {
        attrs = targetCtx.getAttributes(item.getName(), attrIds);
    } else {
        attrs = initCtx.getAttributes(item.getName(), attrIds);
    }
    System.out.println(attrs);
}
```

Here is the output from running this program.

```
>>>>>ldap://localhost:389/cn=Scott Seligman, ou=People, o=JNDITutorial
{telephonenumber=telephonenumber: +1 408 555 5252}
>>>>>ldap://localhost:389/cn=Samuel Clemens, ou=People, o=JNDITutorial
{telephonenumber=telephonenumber: +1 408 555 0186}
>>>>>ldap://localhost:389/cn=Spuds Mackenzie, ou=People, o=JNDITutorial
{telephonenumber=telephonenumber: +1 408 555 4420}
>>>>>ldap://localhost:389/cn=S. User,ou=NewHires,o=JNDITutorial
No attributes
```

See also the **Referrals** lesson (page 259) and **Dereferencing Aliases** section (page 241) for more examples and descriptions.

URLs as References for Federation

Federation is the process of "hooking" together naming systems so that the aggregate system can process composite names. One basic means by which you federate systems is to bind the reference of one naming system in a context in another naming system. The **Storing Objects in the Directory** lesson (page 158) contains descriptions of the Reference class and how to store and read references from the directory.

The contents of a reference used for federation is unrestricted, but a useful and common type of reference is one that contains a URL string. You can create a Reference for a URL string by creating a StringRefAddr whose type is "URL" and whose content is the URL string.

Here is an example of a reference to a file system context.

```
// Create the file system reference
Reference fsRef = new Reference("javax.naming.Context",
    new StringRefAddr("URL", "file:/tmp"));
```

You can then bind this reference in another naming system, such as the LDAP:

```
ldapCtx.bind("cn=fs", fsRef);
```

The LDAP and file system are now *federated.*

Next, you supply a name to the LDAP service provider that spans both the LDAP naming system and the file system:

```
Object obj = ldapCtx.lookup("cn=fs/tutorial/report.txt");
```

Although the name "cn=fs" is in the LDAP naming system, it is naming an object in the file system, the object (context) named by the URL string "file:/tmp".

When the LDAP service provider processes the "cn=fs" entry, it asks the JNDI to return the context identified by that entry so that it can continue the operation. The service provider does this by using NamingManager.getContinuationContext() and Directory-Manager.getContinuationDirContext(), which are explained in the **Building a Service Provider** trail (page 371). The JNDI, when given a reference that contains a "URL" String-RefAddr and no factory class name, will turn the URL string in the reference into a context by using the same algorithm used for locating a URL context implementation, as explained in the **URLs as Names to the Initial Context** section (page 123) of this lesson. In the previous example, the JNDI uses the file URL context implementation to process the URL string "file:/tmp". It then uses the resulting context to process the remainder of the name, "tutorial/report.txt".

URLs as Data for Configuration

A URL string is used in configuration in either of two ways. One way is as a referral. A *referral* is basically configuration data on an LDAP server. See the **Referrals** lesson (page 259) for details. The other way is to configure the initial context implementation. This use is described in this section.

The JNDI defines an environment property Context.PROVIDER_URL for configuring the initial context implementation. Here's an example that configures the initial context implemented by a file system service provider, com.sun.jndi.fscontext.FSContextFactory.

```
// Initialize environment with various properties
Hashtable env = new Hashtable();
env.put(Context.INITIAL_CONTEXT_FACTORY,
    "com.sun.jndi.fscontext.FSContextFactory");
env.put(Context.PROVIDER_URL, "file:/");

// Call the constructor
Context ctx = new InitialContext(env);
```

The URL string in this case is a file URL that specifies the file directory root for the implementation.

Here is an example that configures the initial context of Sun's LDAP service provider.

```
// Initialize environment with various properties
Hashtable env = new Hashtable();
env.put(Context.INITIAL_CONTEXT_FACTORY,
    "com.sun.jndi.ldap.LdapCtxFactory");
env.put(Context.PROVIDER_URL, "ldap://localhost:389/o=jnditutorial");
```

```
// Call the constructor
Context ctx = new InitialContext(env);
```

In this example, the URL string supplied is an `ldap` URL. It specifies the LDAP server's machine and port number and the distinguished name of the root naming context ("o=jndi-tutorial").

From these two examples, you can see that the format of the provider URL string is service provider-specific. The provider determines the URL schemes that it supports. Also, most providers specify a default value for the `Context.PROVIDER_URL` property. For example, Sun's file system service provider specifies that if the `Context.PROVIDER_URL` property has not been specified, then the default provider URL names the root of the file system.

Federation

Recall that federation is the process of "hooking" together naming systems so that the aggregate system can process composite names—names that span the naming systems. Many examples of composite names and federation are possible in the computing world, for example URLs (RFC 1738) and the World Wide Web. One way that the JNDI federation model differs from these models is that it provides a single programmatic interface for accessing federations. Not just one API for one federation, but one API for many different types of federations.

Federation is a first-class concept in the JNDI. You can use composite names and federation as naturally as you would noncomposite names and single naming systems. You simply supply a name, and the JNDI and service providers take care of any federation and name resolution issues. The JNDI model of federation is based on the X/Open Federated Naming (XFN) model. The XFN is a C language-based standard for accessing multiple, possibly federated, naming and directory services. Those readers familiar with the XFN will find many similarities between the XFN and the JNDI, not just in terms of federation, but also in many other respects.

How does a composite name get processed by the underlying federation of naming systems? This lesson answers this question from an API user's perspective. It provides descriptions and concepts that help an API user or service provider developer understand how federation works. Details and examples of how to implement support for federation in a service provider are described in the **Building a Service Provider** trail (page 371).

To answer this question, this lesson addresses the following three lower-level questions.

- How does a service provider for a naming system determine which component(s) to process and which to pass on? (page 132)
- How does a service provider process the component(s) intended for it? (page 134)
- How does a service provider "pass on" processing to the service provider for the next naming system? (page 136)

Naming System Boundaries

The **What's in a Name?** lesson (page 79) explains in detail how to use a composite name to express a name that spans multiple naming systems. This section explains how a service provider determines which components of the composite name to process and which to pass on. In effect, the service provider needs to determine the *naming system boundary* that separates its components from those of its (downstream) neighbor.

Strong and Weak Separation

The example in the **What's in a Name?** lesson has the following composite name:

```
cn=homedir, cn=Jon Ruiz, ou=People/tutorial/report.txt
```

This composite name has three components:

1. `cn=homedir, cn=Jon Ruiz, ou=People`
2. `tutorial`
3. `report.txt`

The first component belongs to the LDAP naming system, and the second two belong to the (UNIX) file system. As this example shows, a composite name can have multiple (possibly consecutive) components from the same naming system ("tutorial" and "report.txt" are both from the file system), but one component cannot span more than one naming system. So, the correspondence between the composite name component separator—the forward slash character ("/")—and naming system boundaries might not be one-to-one.

In this lesson, service providers are categorized by whether they treat the composite name component separator as a naming system boundary. Those that do support *strong separation*, and those that don't support *weak separation*.

- A provider that supports strong separation processes a composite name by consuming the leading component of the name and leaving the remaining components for other naming systems.
- A provider that supports weak separation does not necessarily treat the separator as a naming system boundary. When processing a composite name, it consumes as many leading components as appropriate for the underlying naming system.

The primary factor for determining whether a provider supports strong or weak separation is the syntax of the underlying naming system. If that system has a flat namespace or a hierarchical namespace with a compound name component separator that does not conflict with the composite name component separator, then the corresponding service provider will support strong separation. Otherwise, the provider most likely will support weak separation. Of course, it can get around the syntax conflict issue and support strong separation by requiring that any compound name component separator be escaped or quoted. This requirement might be inconvenient for users of that provider, but it might be the only way by which some providers can support federation. (See later in this lesson.)

Service providers that support strong separation include those for the LDAP, the Windows file system, and the RMI registry. The LDAP naming system is hierarchical and has the comma character (",") as its compound name component separator. The Windows file system is hierarchical and has the backslash character ("\") as the separator. Neither of these separators conflicts with the composite name component separator. The RMI registry namespace is a flat namespace. Service providers that support weak separation include those for the COS naming service and the UNIX file system.

Conditions for Supporting Weak Separation

Weak separation is convenient because it makes composite names look cleaner (fewer quotation marks or escapes are required). Also, this allows users to be less cognizant of naming system boundaries. However, not all service providers can support weak separation. Certain restrictions may force a provider to support strong separation. For example, if the namespace syntax is hierarchical and uses the forward slash character ("/") as its separator but names are arranged right to left, then the provider cannot use weak separation. This because the conflicting direction prevents any sensible determination of naming system boundaries.

If the naming system is terminal (components from that naming system can appear only at the end of a composite name), then the service provider can support weak separation. For example, suppose that a spreadsheet application's namespace has a left-to-right syntax and uses the forward slash character as the component separator. Suppose also that it names spreadsheet cells that will always be terminal; that is, things will not be named relative to a spreadsheet cell. In this case, the service provider for the spreadsheet naming system can support weak separation. Given a composite name, it will consume all of its components.

If the naming system is nonterminal but the service provider can determine the naming system boundary syntactically, then it can support weak separation. In this case, the service provider would use a syntactic rule to determine how many components from a composite name to consume. For example, the compound name components from the naming system might have a distinguishing characteristic that allows the provider to select the components.

As a specific example, a DCE X.500 name looks like this:

```
c=us/o=wiz/ou=people
```

A provider for this naming system can support weak separation by looking for components that have a key/value pair separated by an equals character ("="). It will, however, restrict the types of naming systems that can be federated directly beyond its naming system. In the previous example, a naming system that has names that consist of key/value pairs separated by an equals character cannot be federated.

If the naming system is nonterminal but the service provider can determine the naming system boundary dynamically, then it can support weak separation. The underlying naming system must be able to return residual unresolved components of names. To determine which components to consume, the provider will resolve the entire composite name and, based on the result of the resolution, use any residual to determine what is not in its naming system.

The Current Naming System

Regardless of whether a service provider supports strong or weak separation, once it has determined the components of the composite name that it should process, it needs to process them. How it does this depends on whether its participation in the name's resolution is as an intermediate naming system or a terminal naming system.

An *intermediate naming system* is a naming system that is involved only in the resolution of the composite name. It is responsible for passing on the operation to its target context. The *terminal* (or *target*) naming system is the system that contains the context in which the operation is carried out. In other words, the terminal naming system is the system named by the tail component(s) of a composite name. In the following sample composite name:

```
cn=homedir, cn=Jon Ruiz, ou=People/tutorial/report.txt
```

the LDAP directory is an intermediate naming system and is responsible for resolving the name "cn=homedir, cn=Jon Ruiz, ou=People". The UNIX file system is the terminal or target naming system and is responsible for performing the requested context operation on the name "tutorial/report.txt".

Processing for a terminal naming system is not very interesting: The provider merely carries out the requested context operation. For example, if the context method invoked was Context.list(), then the service provider would invoke list(), using its components from the composite name, as if it was not in a federation and then return the results of list() to the caller.

By contrast, processing for an intermediate naming system is much more interesting. The provider's job is to determine the reference to the *next naming system*, or *nns*, when given its components from the composite name. This reference is called the *next naming system pointer*, or *nns pointer*. In the previous example, the LDAP provider must determine the nns pointer for the LDAP name "cn=homedir, cn=Jon Ruiz, ou=People".

Retrieving NNS Pointers

A service provider can support retrieval of the nns pointer in either of two ways. One way is to use an *explicitly* named nns pointer, also called a *junction*. The second way is via an *implicit* nns pointer.

Junctions

A *junction* is the binding of a name to an nns pointer; in the previous example, "cn=homedir, cn=Jon Ruiz, ou=People" is a junction. This name is bound to a reference to a file system context. If you perform a `Context.lookup()` on the name, then you will get back not an LDAP entry but a `Context` instance for a directory (`/tmp`) in the file system.

A context may contain an unlimited number of junctions. Moreover, a junction is usually indistinguishable from other normal (nonjunction) names in the context, although this depends on the naming policy of the underlying naming system.

Implicit NNS Pointers

A service provider also can support retrieval of the nns pointer via an *implicit* nns pointer. An implicit nns pointer is named by using the composite name component separator, the forward slash character ("/"). Suppose that the name "`corp.wiz.com`" names an object in the current naming system. Then the name "`corp.wiz.com/`" will name its nns pointer.

An implicit nns pointer is used when a naming system's native entries cannot or should not be used directly to hold an nns pointer. It can be determined *statically* or *dynamically*.

Static Implicit NNS Pointers.

A static implicit nns pointer is constructed by using data found in the current naming system. For example, suppose that you store nns pointers in the DNS by using TXT records. When the DNS provider processes the name "`corp.wiz.com/`", it will use the data in the TXT record of the "`corp.wiz.com`" entry to construct the nns pointer.

Dynamic Implicit NNS Pointers.

An implicit nns pointer can also be determined dynamically, based on the types and content of the objects bound in the current naming system. This is useful when the result of resolving a composite name's components in the current naming system does not indicate any nns information. The only conclusion that the service provider can draw is that resolution was completed in the current naming system and should proceed to the next naming system.

For example, suppose that the composite name "`lib/xyz.zip/part1/abc`" consists of two parts: "`lib/xyz.zip`" and "`part1/abc`". "`lib/xyz.zip`" names a file in the ZIP format, and "`part1/abc`" names an entry in the ZIP file. The resolution of "`lib/xyz.zip`" results in a file object and does not indicate which nns to use for continuing the operation on "`part1/abc`".

To support a dynamic implicit nns pointer, the JNDI defines a special `Reference` called an *nns reference*. This reference has an address type "`nns`" and an address content that is the resolved object. In the ZIP file example, the resolved object is the ZIP file itself and the file system service provider would construct an nns reference as follows.

```
Reference ref = new Reference("java.io.File",
    new RefAddr("nns") {
        public Object getContent() {
            return theFile;
        }
    });
```

The Next Naming System

Once a service provider has determined the nns pointer by using the techniques described in the previous section, it next must turn the nns pointer into a context, called the *continuation context*, and continue the operation in that context. To do this, the JNDI provides the following utility methods.

- `NamingManager.getContinuationContext(CannotProceedException cpe)`
- `DirectoryManager.getContinuationDirContext(CannotProceedException cpe)`

The argument to these methods is a `CannotProceedException`.

The purpose of these methods is to get a context in the nns in which to continue the operation by using the nns pointer and other information in the `CannotProceedException`.

The Continuation Context

The JNDI obtains the continuation context based on information supplied in the `CannotProceedException`. The service provider must complete the information in the `CannotProceedException`. Table 4 describes the fields of this exception.

The JNDI uses the information in the exception to find an *object factory*, described in the **Object Factories** lesson (page 185), which returns an instance of `Context`. If the JNDI cannot find an appropriate context in which to continue the operation, then it throws the `CannotProceedException` received from the service provider.

TABLE 4:   CannotProceedException Fields for Federation.

Field	Description
resolved name	The name of the resolved object, relative to the starting context for this operation.
resolved object	The nns pointer. This is used as the object argument to the object factory.
remaining name	The part of the composite name that remains to be processed.
"alt" name	The name of the resolved object, relative to the "alt" name context. This is used as the name argument to the object factory.
"alt" name context	The context in which to resolve "alt" name. This is used as the context argument to the object factory.
environment	The environment of the current context. This is used as the environment argument to the object factory.
remaining new name	The remaining name to be used as the "new name" argument for `Context.rename()`.

Resolving through Subinterfaces

Notice from the previous description that the object factory that produces the continuation context must return an instance of Context. The instance does not need to implement other subinterfaces of Context. This is because it does not make sense to require intermediate naming systems to implement all of the subinterfaces of the terminal naming system. For resolution to be successful, the JNDI has the following two requirements.

- The providers for the originating and terminal naming system must implement the subinterface.
- The providers for all other intermediate naming systems must implement either the subinterface or both the Resolver and Context interfaces.

The Resolver interface is intended to allow resolution to proceed through a provider that does not support the interface to one that does. DirectoryManager.getContinuationDirContext() automatically uses the Resolver interface when necessary. See the **Building a Service Provider** trail (page 379) for details.

Completing the Operation

After the provider gets a continuation context, it invokes the originally intended context operation on the continuation context by using as the name argument the remaining components of the composite name. Here is an example that does this for DirContext.search().

```
DirContext cctx = DirectoryManager.getContinuationDirContext(cpe);
answer = cctx.search(cpe.getRemainingName(), matchingAttrs);
```

The processing then continues to the next naming system. There, the following three-step procedure repeats until the terminal naming system is reached.

1. Determine the composite name components to process.
2. Process the result of Step 1.
3. Continue to the next naming system.

At this point, the actual operation is carried out.

Miscellaneous

This lesson discusses the following miscellaneous advanced topics:

- Class loading (page 139)
- Link references (page 142)
- Naming policies (page 144)
- Threads and synchronization (page 146)
- Security (page 148)

Class Loading

The JNDI is an API defined independent of any specific naming or directory service implementation. For an application, applet, servlet, or any program unit to use the JNDI, it must specify the service provider to use and have access to the provider's class files. A single program might use more than one provider. Furthermore, the program and/or providers might use object factories, state factories, and control factories, all of whose class files must also be made available to the JNDI. In addition, the JNDI needs access to application resource files (see the **Application Resource Files** section (page 100)) provided by the program, providers, and other components. In all of these cases, the JNDI needs to load in class and resource files. This section explains how the JNDI uses class loaders and how you can affect its use of them.

Background on Class Loaders

The class loader is the means by which Java™ classes and resources are loaded into the JRE. It controls the policies ranging from where to load class definitions to the data format of the class definitions.

In the JDK™ 1.1 and earlier releases, no relationship exists between various class loaders. A system class loader is responsible for loading in the Java runtime, the application, and classes and resources in the application's classpath. An applet class loader is responsible for loading applets and their related classes and resources, possibly over the network by communicating with a Web server.

In the Java 2 Platform, Standard Edition, v1.2 and later releases, class loaders have a hierarchical relationship. Each class loader has a parent class loader. When a class loader is asked to load a class or resource, it consults its parent class loader before attempting to load the item itself. The parent in turn consults its parent, and so on. So it is only after *all* of the ancestor class loaders cannot find the item that the current class loader gets involved.

A *bootstrap class loader* is responsible for loading in the Java runtime. It is the "root" in the class loader hierarchy. The system class loader is a descendant of the bootstrap class loader. It is responsible for loading in the application, as well as for loading classes and resources in the application's classpath.

The Java 2 platform also introduced the notion of *context class loader*. A thread's context class loader is, by default, set to the context class loader of the thread's parent. The hierarchy of threads is rooted at the *primordial thread* (the one that runs the program). The context class loader of the primordial thread is set to the class loader that loaded the application. So unless you explicitly change the thread's context class loader, its context class loader will be the application's class loader. That is, the context class loader can load the classes that the application can load. This loader is used by the Java runtime such as RMI (Java Remote Method Invocation) to load classes and resources on behalf of the user application. The context class loader, like any Java 2 platform class loader, has a parent class loader and supports the same delegation model for class loading described previously.

Class Loading on the JDK 1.1 Software

When you use the JNDI with the JDK 1.1 software, you must place the JNDI JARs, service provider JARs, and JARs or class files containing factories in the application's classpath. If you're using an applet, then you must place those JARs and class files in the applet's codebase directory and/or archive locations. Consequently, the class loader that loads the JNDI JARs is typically the same as the one that loads in the application and the factories.

Note that you cannot use JNDI application resource files with the JDK 1.1 software. See the **Application Resource Files** section (page 100) for details.

Class Loading on the Java 2 Platform

When you use the JNDI with the Java 2 platform, the class loader that loads the JNDI classes typically differs from the one that loads in the application. For example, in the Java 2 SDK, v1.3, the JNDI classes are loaded by the bootstrap class loader whereas the application classes are loaded by the system class loader. In the Java 2 SDK, v1.2, if you install the JNDI as an installed extension, then the JNDI classes are loaded by the class loader responsible for loading installed extensions, whereas the application classes are loaded by the system class loader. As a result, if the JNDI were to use its class loader to load service providers and factories, then it might not see the same classes as the application. Therefore, to try to see what the application can see, the JNDI uses the calling thread's context class loader when it is loading in classes for the service providers, factories, and application resource files.

In rare circumstances, you want to change a thread's context class loader to affect how the JNDI finds classes. This might occur, for example, when the environment that you're working in does not set the context class loader properly. For example, a bug in the Java 2 SDK, Standard Edition, v1.2.2 causes the AWT (Abstract Window Toolkit) not to set the listener threads' context class loader to be the class loader that loaded the applet. Consequently, callback methods invoked by the listener threads do not have access to service providers and factories that the applet can otherwise load explicitly. Or, you might want to add an additional repository of JARs and class files that contains special providers and factories to your applications/applets. To change a thread's context class loader, you use `Thread.setContextClassLoader()`.

Here is an example.

```
ClassLoader prevCl =
    Thread.currentThread().getContextClassLoader();

// Create the class loader by using the given URL
// Use prevCl as parent to maintain current visibility
ClassLoader urlCl =
    URLClassLoader.newInstance(new URL[]{new URL(url)}, prevCl);
try {
    // Save the class loader so that you can restore it later
    Thread.currentThread().setContextClassLoader(urlCl);

    // Expect that the environment properties are in the
    // application resource file found at "url"
    Context ctx = new InitialContext();

    System.out.println(ctx.lookup("tutorial/report.txt"));

    // Do something useful with "ctx"
    ...
} catch (NamingException e) {
    // Handle the exception
    ...
} finally {
    // Restore
    Thread.currentThread().setContextClassLoader(prevCl);
}
```

This example creates a `URLClassLoader` that loads classes from a specified codebase URL. It then creates an initial context and performs other JNDI operations within the context of that class loader. In this example, the class loader affects how the initial context was initialized (via an application resource file found by the new class loader), as well as the result of `lookup()` (via the object factory named in the application resource file and the class file of the factory found by the new class loader). To run this program, you supply a codebase URL as follows:

```
# java ChangeClassLoader file:/some/directory/somewhere/
```

In that codebase, you can specify a `jndi.properties` file. In this example, the following `jndi.properties` file is in the codebase directory.

```
java.naming.factory.initial=com.sun.jndi.fscontext.FSContextFactory
java.naming.provider.url=file:/tmp
java.naming.factory.object=FooObjectFactory
```

In the same codebase directory is the class definition for `FooObjectFactory`, which when given a `java.io.File` object always returns the string `"foo"`. When you run this program, you see this output:

```
foo
```

If you do not see this output, then check the correctness of the codebase URL argument. Remember, if you are naming a codebase directory, then you should include a trailing forward slash character in the URL.

Class Loading from Prespecified Locations

In some cases, the location of class files is specified explicitly. For example, you can specify an object factory's codebase in its `Reference`. When the JNDI reads such an object from the naming or directory service, it will use a class loader for the codebase named in the `Reference` to obtain the class files for the factory. The parent of that class loader is the thread's context class loader.

Link References

A *link reference* is a symbolic link that can span multiple naming systems. It is represented by the `LinkRef` class. Its content is a URL string or a composite name. If the first component of the composite name is the string `"."` (a string consisting of a period character ("`.`")), then the composite name is to be resolved relative to the context in which the link reference is bound. Otherwise, the URL or composite name is to be resolved relative to the initial context.

Relationship to Context Operations

You bind a link reference, like any other object, in a context by using `Context.bind()` and its related methods. The underlying service provider must support binding `Reference` and `Referenceable` objects. When you subsequently perform a `Context.lookup()` or other context operation involving the link reference, the link reference is automatically dereferenced.

For example, suppose that the following composite name is in the initial context:

```
some/where/over/there
```

You create a link reference to `"some/where"` and bind it to the name `"here"` in the initial context. Subsequently listing the context by using the name `"here/over/there"` is effectively the same as using the name `"some/where/over/there"`.

A link reference is not dereferenced only when you use `Context.lookupLink()`. In this case, a link reference bound to the terminal component of the composite name is returned as is without being dereferenced. In the previous example, if you invoke this statement:

```
Object obj = ctx.lookupLink("here");
```

then the result will be a `LinkRef` that contains the composite name `"some/where"`. If the name that you supply to `lookupLink()` contains a component bound to a link reference as a nonterminal component, then the link reference will still be dereferenced. In the previous example, if you invoke this statement:

```
Object obj = ctx.lookupLink("here/over/there");
```

then the result will be the object bound to `"some/where/over/there"`.

Note: Support for link references is implemented by the underlying service provider. Neither Sun's LDAP service provider nor its file system service provider currently supports link references.

Relationship to Aliases, Referrals, URL References, and Other Symbolic Links

Symbolic links are common in naming and directory systems. For example, the UNIX file system supports symbolic links for files and directories, the LDAP supports aliases and referrals, and the JNDI supports URL references (see the **URLs** lesson (page 128)). The JNDI link reference differs from all of these.

An *LDAP alias* is an LDAP entry that contains the distinguished name of another LDAP entry on the same LDAP server. LDAP servers are responsible for dereferencing aliases. A link reference differs from an alias in that it is not LDAP-specific and can name objects outside of the LDAP namespace or server. Unlike an alias, a link reference is processed on the client side (by the service provider).

An *LDAP referral* is an LDAP entry that contains the URL of another LDAP entry, possibly on another LDAP server. The URL need not be an LDAP URL, but the entry it names must be an LDAP entry. LDAP clients are responsible for dereferencing referrals. A link reference differs from a referral in that it is not LDAP-specific; it need not name another LDAP entry. A link reference can be *relative*; that is, it can name another object relative to the context in which the link reference is bound. A referral always contains an absolute URL.

A UNIX symbolic link contains a relative or absolute name of a file or directory. It differs from a link reference in that it can name only another file or directory.

A link reference differs from a URL reference in that it is explicitly typed and designed to support links, whereas a URL reference is intended primarily to support federation. URL references are processed by URL context factories/implementations. Link references are supported by service providers, which are responsible for dereferencing them and performing link loop or link limit detections.

Naming Policies

As mentioned earlier in this lesson, the JNDI is defined independent of any specific naming and directory service implementation. This allows a variety of naming and directory systems to be accessed in a common way. However, for it to offer true independence, common policies are required that specify *how* the naming and directory should be used. Without these policies, you might be able to use the same API to access the data, but how you find and use that data would still be directory-dependent. The lack of policy is a problem not only for multiple naming and directory systems, but also for single naming/directory systems such as the LDAP. Without general agreement on how the data in the directory is to be organized and used, a single system can easily deteriorate into an unmanageable mess. For example, suppose that two applications need to associate data with a user in an enterprise. If each application chooses its own policy regarding how to name and represent a user in the directory, then the directory will contain two representations of the same user. Furthermore, users of each application will have to learn each representation and how to name it.

Types of Policies

There are two categories of policies:

- Naming policies that specify how objects are named relative to each other and the common names to use.
- Directory policies, called schema, that specify the attributes that objects in the directory should have and the names and syntaxes of those attributes.

The LDAP defines attribute syntaxes (RFC 2252) and user-related schema (RFC 2256). Many other proposals for specifying other domain-specific schema are available, such as for mail and security. In addition, efforts are underway to standardize the schema across different directory systems (see RFC 2307). Further, several proprietary schemas have emerged in the LDAP space from vendors such as Netscape and Microsoft. Some applications that are based on servers from those vendors have dependencies on the proprietary schemas.

In the naming policy area, naming policies have been defined in the X.500. Most LDAP systems follow a common naming convention at the higher levels of the naming tree (for example, how to name countries, organizations, and departments). Less agreement exists on lower levels. However, some servers, such as the Active Directory from Microsoft, have defined their own naming policies.

The DNS has defined naming policies at the higher levels of the naming tree. It is used primarily to name machines and domains on the Internet and Intranet, so naming policies for other entities are less relevant.

In terms of a composite naming policy, the HTTP and FTP URLs have set the de facto standard. Namely, the first component of the URL names the host/domain using the DNS. After the first component, there is a proprietary namespace.

The Java 2 Platform Enterprise Edition Naming Policies

The JNDI does not define any naming policy on its own. However, one important platform that does define a limited set of naming policies for using the JNDI is the Java 2 Platform, Enterprise Edition (J2EE™). It defines a logical namespace that application components (such as Enterprise JavaBeans, servlets, and JavaServer Pages (JSP)) can use to name resources, components, and other data. The namespace is provided to a component by its *container*, the entity that executes the component. Typically, a component has a *deployment descriptor* that contains, among other data, information about the logical names and types of resources and components that the component needs or references. An administrator, using information from the deployment descriptor, maps the logical namespace to bindings in the namespace of the actual environment into which the component is being deployed. The container uses this mapping to present the logical namespace to the component. See the J2EE specification for details.

The enterprise namespace is rooted in a URL context for the java URL scheme. For example, you might use a name such as "java:comp/env/jdbc/Salary" from the initial context to name the Salary database. Details about URL contexts are discussed in the **URLs** lesson (page 123). By using a URL context, the policy avoids any conflicts with names in the initial context configured by the Context.INITIAL_CONTEXT_FACTORY environment property.

At the root context of the namespace is a binding with the name "comp", which is bound to a subtree reserved for component-related bindings. The name "comp" is short for component. There are no other bindings at the root context. However, the root context is reserved for the future expansion of the policy, specifically for naming resources that are tied not to the component itself but to other types of entities such as users or departments. For example, future policies might allow you to name users and organizations/departments by using names such as "java:user/alice" and "java:org/engineering".

In the "comp" context are two bindings: "env" and "UserTransaction". The name "env" is bound to a subtree that is reserved for the component's environment-related bindings, as defined by its deployment descriptor. "env" is short for environment. The J2EE recommends (but does not require) the following structure for the "env" namespace.

- Enterprise JavaBeans™ are placed under the "ejb" subtree. For example, a Payroll EJB might be named "java:comp/env/ejb/Payroll".
- Resource factory references are placed in subtrees differentiated by their resource manager type. Here are some examples:

- "jdbc" for JDBC™ DataSource references
- "jms" for JMS connection factories
- "mail" for JavaMail connection factories
- "url" for URL connection factories

For example, a JDBC Salary database might have the name "java:comp/env/jdbc/Salary".

The "env" context might also contain bindings for other types of configuration data (such as strings and wrappers around primitive data types) that the component needs, as defined in the component's deployment descriptor. No policy is recommended or required for these bindings; they can be placed at the root of the "env" context or be partitioned by subtrees based on their logical relationships or types. For example, you might have bindings for a string and a numeric parameter that are named using "java:comp/env/CompanyName" and "java:comp/env/PrimeRate", respectively.

The name "UserTransaction" is bound to a javax.transaction.UserTransaction object. The component that looks up this object from the namespace (by using the name "java:comp/UserTransaction") can use it to start, commit, or abort transactions.

Threads and Synchronization

The JNDI defines synchronous access to naming and directory systems. Like most other APIs defined for the Java platform, asynchronous access is achieved by using multiple threads.

When you use multiple threads in your program, remember that the JNDI specifies that concurrent access to the *same* Context instance is not guaranteed to be thread-safe. Although some service providers might guarantee thread-safety for the same Context instance, it is best to use synchronization so that the code is portable across different service provider implementations. When you use multiple threads to access *different* Context instances, they need not be synchronized.

Here is an example that creates two threads, each listing a different Context instance.

```
// Create the contexts
Context ctx1 = new InitialContext(env);
Context ctx2 = (Context)ctx1.lookup("ou=People");

// Create the threads
Thread thread1 = new ListThread(ctx1, "ONE");
Thread thread2 = new ListThread(ctx2, "TWO");

// Let them work
thread1.start();
thread2.start();
```

Each thread's run() method looks as follows.

```
public void run() {
    try {
        NamingEnumeration enum = ctx.list("");
        while (enum.hasMore()) {
```

```
            System.out.println(label + ": " + enum.next());
        }
    } catch (NamingException e) {
        System.out.println(label + ": " + e);
    }
}
```

When you run this program, you will see the following output.

```
# java DiffCtx

ONE: ou=Groups: javax.naming.directory.DirContext
ONE: ou=People: javax.naming.directory.DirContext
ONE: ou=Staff: javax.naming.directory.DirContext
ONE: ou=NewHires: javax.naming.directory.DirContext
TWO: cn=Ted Geisel: javax.naming.directory.DirContext
ONE: cn=favDrink: javax.naming.directory.DirContext
TWO: cn=Jon Ruiz: javax.naming.directory.DirContext
TWO: cn=Scott Seligman: javax.naming.directory.DirContext
...
```

Note that despite the fact that both Context instances are derived from the same InitialContext instance, you need not lock their access. However, if you modify the example slightly so that you use two threads to list the *same* Context instance, then you need to lock the Context instance. In the following modified example, the thread's run() method looks like this.

```
public void run() {
    try {
        // Lock for multithreaded access
        synchronized (ctx) {
            NamingEnumeration enum = ctx.list("");
            while (enum.hasMore()) {
                System.out.println(label + ": " + enum.next());
            }
        }
    } catch (NamingException e) {
        System.out.println(label + ": " + e);
    }
}
```

When you run this example, it generates the following output.

```
# java SameCtx

ONE: ou=Groups: javax.naming.directory.DirContext
ONE: ou=People: javax.naming.directory.DirContext
ONE: ou=Staff: javax.naming.directory.DirContext
ONE: ou=NewHires: javax.naming.directory.DirContext
ONE: cn=favDrink: javax.naming.directory.DirContext
TWO: ou=Groups: javax.naming.directory.DirContext
TWO: ou=People: javax.naming.directory.DirContext
TWO: ou=Staff: javax.naming.directory.DirContext
TWO: ou=NewHires: javax.naming.directory.DirContext
TWO: cn=favDrink: javax.naming.directory.DirContext
```

Security

The JNDI does not define a security model. Rather, it uses the security models that are in place in the underlying Java platform and in the underlying naming/directory service. However, in terms of security support, the JNDI does provide security-related environment properties that allow the JNDI client to specify commonly needed security-related information. These properties are listed in the **Environment Properties** lesson (page 95). Following is a brief summary of them.

- `Context.SECURITY_AUTHENTICATION` (`"java.naming.security.authentication"`): Specifies the authentication mechanism to use.
- `Context.SECURITY_PRINCIPAL` (`"java.naming.security.principal"`): Specifies the name of the user/program that is doing the authentication. Depends on the value of the `Context.SECURITY_AUTHENTICATION` property.
- `Context.SECURITY_CREDENTIALS` (`"java.naming.security.credentials"`): Specifies the credentials of the user/program that is doing the authentication. Depends on the value of the `Context.SECURITY_AUTHENTICATION` property.
- `Context.SECURITY_PROTOCOL` (`"java.naming.security.protocol"`): Specifies the security protocol to use.

Service providers are encouraged to use these properties when they apply to accessing the underlying naming/directory service. However, providers may use other means to authenticate their clients, such as the Java Authentication and Authorization Service (`http://java.sun.com/products/jaas`).

Environment Properties

You need to keep in mind that the environment properties contain possibly security-sensitive information (such as passwords). You also need to understand that when you supply environment properties to a service provider (by using the `InitialContext` constructors), they are passed by the provider to factories (see the **Object Factories** (page 185), **State Factories** (page 171), and **Response Control Factories** (page 298) lessons for details). You should ensure that all factories and providers that you use can be trusted with possibly security-sensitive information.

Application resource files, as described in the **Environment Properties** lesson (page 100), allow you to easily specify environment properties. The JNDI will read and use all application resource files in the classpath. Because environment properties can affect the factories that you use (see the next section), you should be careful about the class definitions and application resource files that you include in your classpath.

Factories

The JNDI architecture is designed to be very flexible. You can dynamically choose service providers, as well as customize them by using object factories, state factories, and response control factories. Thus, depending on the configuration of providers and factories, a program's behavior can vary dramatically.

This flexibility, though powerful, has security implications. You should ensure that the factories used are trusted. Malicious factories can return wrong or intentionally misleading data or corrupt your underlying naming/directory service. Because naming/directory services are often used to store security-related information, you should take extra precaution to include only valid and trusted factories.

Instances of Context

An instance of Context or one of its subinterfaces is a possibly authenticated connection to the underlying naming/directory service. It can be returned by various methods in the JNDI API and SPI, including the following:

- Context.lookup()
- Context.listBindings()
- DirContext.createSubcontext()
- DirContext.getSchema()
- Attribute.getAttributeDefinition()
- LdapContext.newInstance()
- DirectoryManager.getContinuationDirContext()
- DirectoryManager.getObjectInstance()
- NamingManager.getInitialContext()
- NamingExceptionEvent.getEventContext() and getSource() (from java.util.Event Object)
- Context.lookupLink()
- Context.createSubcontext()
- various forms of DirContext.search()
- DirContext.getSchemaClassDefinition()
- Attribute.getAttributeSyntaxDefinition()
- NamingManager.getContinuationContext()
- NamingManager.getObjectInstance()
- NamingManager.getURLContext()
- NamingEvent.getEventContext() and getSource() (from java.util.EventObject)
- UnsolicitedNotificationEvent.getSource() (from java.util.EventObject)

Context instances are also passed to object, state, and control factories.

As with environment properties, you should not pass Context instances to untrusted service providers, factories, or any other untrusted code.

Java Objects and the Directory

Traditionally, directories have been used to store data. Users and programmers think of the directory as a hierarchy of directory entries, each containing a set of attributes. You look up an entry from the directory and extract the attribute(s) of interest. For example, you can look up a person's telephone number in the directory. Alternatively, you can search the directory for entries that have a particular set of attributes, for example all persons in the directory with the surname Smith. Examples of this type of use of the directory are covered in **The Basics** trail (page 59).

For applications written in the Java™ programming language, Java objects are typically shared. For such applications, it makes sense to be able to use the directory as a repository for Java objects. The directory provides a centrally administered, and possibly replicated, service for use by Java applications distributed across a network. For example, an application server might use the directory for registering objects that represent the services that it manages so that a client can later search the directory to locate those services as needed.

The JNDI provides an object-oriented view of the directory, thereby allowing Java objects to be added to and retrieved from the directory without requiring the client to manage data representation issues. This trail discusses the use of the directory for storing and retrieving Java objects.

- The **Storing Objects in the Directory** lesson (page 155) describes how serializable objects, referenceable objects, remote objects, and objects with attributes can be stored in the directory.
- The **State Factories** lesson (page 171) describes the role of state factories and their use by applications and service providers.
- The **Reading Objects from the Directory** (page 179) lesson describes the different ways that objects can be read from the directory.
- The **Object Factories** (page 185) lesson describes the role of object factories and their use by applications and service providers.
- The **Representation in the Directory** lesson (page 195) describes the format in which objects are stored in directories, such as LDAP directories.

Storing Objects in the Directory

Applications and services can use the directory in different ways to store and locate objects. For example, an application might store (a copy of) the object itself, a reference to an object, or attributes that describe the object. In general terms, a Java™ object's serialized form contains the object's state and an object's reference is a compact representation of addressing information that can be used to contact the object. Some examples are given in the **Naming Concepts** lesson (page 7). An object's attributes are properties that are used to describe the object; attributes might include addressing and/or state information.

Which of these three ways to use depends on the application/system that is being built and how it needs to interoperate with other applications and systems that will share the objects stored in the directory. Another factor is the support provided by the service provider and the underlying directory service.

Programmatically, all applications use one of the following methods when storing objects in the directory:

- `Context.bind()`
- `DirContext.bind()`
- `Context.rebind()`
- `DirContext.rebind()`

The application passes the object that it wants to store to one of these methods. Then, depending on the types of objects that the service provider supports, the object will be transformed into a representation acceptable to the underlying directory service.

This lesson shows how to create different types of objects and store them in the directory.

- Java serializable objects
- `Referenceable` objects and JNDI `References`
- Objects with attributes (`DirContext`)
- RMI objects (including those that use IIOP)
- CORBA objects

Before you go on: The examples in this lesson use the LDAP directory. The initial context used is initialized using the following environment properties.

```
// Set up the environment for creating the initial context
Hashtable env = new Hashtable();
env.put(Context.INITIAL_CONTEXT_FACTORY,
    "com.sun.jndi.ldap.LdapCtxFactory");
env.put(Context.PROVIDER_URL, "ldap://localhost:389/o=JNDITutorial");
```

Schema: To run these examples successfully, you must either turn off schema-checking in the server or add the Java schema and the CORBA schema that accompany this tutorial to the server (see **Appendix**). Both of these tasks are typically performed by the directory server's administrator. See the **Preparations** lesson (page 43) for more information.

Software Requirements: In addition to the software requirements listed in the **Preparations** lesson (page 41), you also need the following archive files when using the examples related to RMI and CORBA: `ldapbp.jar` and `rmiregistry.jar`. `ldapbp.jar` can be downloaded as part of the LDAP service provider from the JNDI Web site. It is also available on the CD that accompanies this book. `rmiregistry.jar` is available as part of the Java 2 SDK, v1.3, so, if you are using that SDK, then you won't need to add `rmiregistry.jar` separately. Otherwise, you can download it from the JNDI Web site or obtain it from the accompanying CD.

To try the CORBA and RMI/IIOP examples, you need the CORBA classes. If you are using the Java 2 SDK, v1.2 or higher releases, then you already have those classes. Otherwise, you need to install the Java IDL, a version of which comes with the RMI-IIOP Standard Extension (which you can download from `http://java.sun.com/products/rmi-iiop/` or obtain it from the accompanying CD).

If you are not using the Java 2 SDK, v1.3 and you want to try the RMI example that uses IIOP, then you need to install the RMI-IIOP Standard Extension.

Serializable Objects

To *serialize* an object means to convert its state to a byte stream so that the byte stream can be reverted back into a copy of the object. A Java object is *serializable* if its class or any of its superclasses implements either the `java.io.Serializable` interface or its subinterface, `java.io.Externalizable`. *Deserialization* is the process of converting the serialized form of an object back into a copy of the object.

For example, the `java.awt.Button` class implements the `Serializable` interface, so you can serialize a `java.awt.Button` object and store that serialized state in a file. Later, you can read back the serialized state and deserialize it into a `java.awt.Button` object.

The Java platform specifies a default way by which serializable objects are serialized. A (Java) class can override this default serialization and define its own way of serializing objects of that class. The *Object Serialization Specification* describes object serialization in detail (`http://java.sun.com/products/jdk/1.2/docs/guide/serialization/`).

When an object is serialized, information that identifies its class is recorded in the serialized stream. However, the class's definition ("class file") itself is not recorded. It is the responsibility of the system that is deserializing the object to determine how to locate and load the necessary class files. For example, a Java application might include in its classpath a JAR file that contains the class files of the serialized object(s) or load the class definitions by using information stored in the directory, as explained later in this lesson.

Binding a Serializable Object

You can store a serializable object in the directory if the underlying service provider supports that action, as does Sun's LDAP service provider.

The following example invokes `Context.bind()` to bind an AWT button to the name "cn=Button". To associate attributes with the new binding, you use `DirContext.bind()`. To overwrite an existing binding, use `Context.rebind()` and `DirContext.rebind()`.

```
// Create the object to be bound
Button b = new Button("Push me");

// Perform the bind
ctx.bind("cn=Button", b);
```

You can then read the object back using `Context.lookup()`, as follows.

```
// Check that it is bound
Button b2 = (Button)ctx.lookup("cn=Button");
System.out.println(b2);
```

Running this example produces the following output.

```
# java SerObj
java.awt.Button[button0,0,0,0x0,invalid,label=Push me]
```

Specifying a Codebase

Note: The procedures described here are for binding a serializable object in a directory service that follows the schema defined in RFC 2713. These procedures might not be generally applicable to other naming and directory services that support binding a serializable object with a specified codebase.

When a serialized object is bound in the directory as shown in the previous example, applications that read the serialized object from the directory must have access to the class definitions necessary to deserialize the object. Alternatively, you can record a *codebase* with the serialized object in the directory, either when you bind the object or subsequently by adding an attribute by using `DirContext.modifyAttributes()`. You can use any attribute to record this codebase and have your application read that attribute from the directory and use it appropriately. Or you can use the "javaCodebase" attribute specified in RFC 2713. In the latter case, Sun's LDAP service provider will automatically use the attribute to load the class definitions as needed. "javaCodebase" should contain the URL of a codebase directory or a JAR file. (Note that JAR files work only with the Java 2 platform.) If the codebase contains more than one URL, then each URL must be separated by a space character.

The following example resembles the one for binding a java.awt.Button. It differs in that it uses a user-defined Serializable class, Flower, and supplies a "javaCodebase" attribute that contains the location of Flower's class definition. Here's the code that does the binding.

```
String codebase = ...;

// Create the object to be bound
Flower f = new Flower("rose", "pink");

// Perform the bind, and specify the codebase
ctx.bind("cn=Flower", f, new BasicAttributes("javaCodebase",codebase));
```

When you run this example, you must supply the URL of the location at which the class file Flower.class was installed. For example, if Flower.class was installed at the Web server web1, in the directory example/classes, then you would run this example as follows.

```
# java SerObjWithCodebase http://web1/example/classes/

pink rose
```

Afterward, you may remove Flower.class from your classpath and run any program that looks up or lists this object.

Referenceable Objects and References

You can think of the serialized state of an object as a copy of the object in a different representation. Sometimes it is not appropriate to store that representation in the directory. This is because the serialized state might be too large or it might be inadequate for your needs (the application, for example, might need more information than can be supplied by the serialized form). Or you might need the object in a different form.

For reasons such as these, the JNDI defines a *reference* for use when (the serialized form of) an object cannot be stored in the directory directly. You store an object with an associated reference in the directory *indirectly* by storing its reference. It might be useful to think of the distinction between a serialized object and a JNDI reference as that between a copy of a Java object and a Java object reference.

What's in a Reference?

A reference is represented by the class `Reference`. A `Reference` consists of an ordered list of addresses and class information about the object being referenced. Each address is represented by a subclass of `RefAddr` and contains information on how to construct the object.

References are commonly used to represent connections to a network service such as a database, directory, or file system. Each address may then identify for that service a *communication endpoint* that contains information on how to contact the service. Multiple addresses might arise for various reasons, such as the need for replication or multiple access points (that is, the object offers interfaces over more than one communication mechanism).

A reference also contains information to assist in creating an instance of the object to which the reference refers. It contains the Java class name of that object, as well as the class name and location of the object factory to be used to create the object.

Referenceable Objects

An object whose class implements the `Referenceable` interface has an associated reference. The `Referenceable` interface has one method, `getReference()`, which returns the reference of the object.

The following example shows a `Fruit` class that implements the `Referenceable` interface.

```
public class Fruit implements Referenceable {
    String fruit;

    public Fruit(String f) {
        fruit = f;
    }

    public Reference getReference() throws NamingException {
        return new Reference(
            Fruit.class.getName(),
            new StringRefAddr("fruit", fruit),
            FruitFactory.class.getName(),
            null);              // Factory location
    }

    public String toString() {
        return fruit;
    }
}
```

The reference of a `Fruit` instance consists of a single address (of class `StringRefAddr`). This address contains the fruit type with which the instance was created. For example, if the instance was created using `new Fruit("orange")`, then its address type would be `"fruit"` and its address contents `"orange"`. The reference contains two additional pieces of information: the fully qualified name of the `Fruit` class (in this case, simply `"Fruit"`) and the fully qualified name of the *object factory* class that can be used to create instances of `Fruit` (in this case, "FruitFactory"). Object factories are described in the **Object Factories** lesson (page 185).

Binding a Referenceable Object

You might remember the Fruit class from the **Adding a Binding That Has Attributes** example (page 71). The following example is a simplification of that example.

After creating an instance of Fruit, you invoke Context.bind(), DirContext.bind(), Context.rebind(), or DirContext.rebind() to add it to the directory.

```
// Create the object to be bound
Fruit fruit = new Fruit("orange");
...

// Perform the bind
ctx.bind("cn=favorite", fruit);
```

The service provider implementation of bind()/rebind() first extracts the reference from the object being bound (by using Referenceable.getReference()) and then stores that reference in the directory. When that object is subsequently looked up from the directory, its corresponding object factory will convert the reference into an instance of the object (conversion details are described in the **Object Factories** lesson (page 185)).

```
// Read the object back
Fruit f2 = (Fruit) ctx.lookup("cn=favorite");
System.out.println(f2);
```

This produces the following output, "orange", produced by Fruit.toString().

```
# java RefObj

orange
```

From the perspective of the application using JNDI, it is dealing only with bind() and lookup(). The service provider takes care of getting the reference from the object and converting it to/from the actual object itself.

Note that you can store a Referenceable object in the directory only if the underlying service provider supports it. Sun's LDAP service provider supports storing both References and Referenceable objects.

Binding a Reference

Binding a Referenceable object is more elegant than binding a Reference directly. This is because you can simply bind the object instead of first getting its reference. However, you can also bind a Reference directly. See the **Remote Objects** section (page 165) for an example of binding a Reference.

Objects with Attributes

If the object that you're attempting to bind is neither Serializable nor Referenceable, then you can still bind it if it has attributes, provided that binding DirContext objects is a feature supported by the underlying service provider. Sun's LDAP service provider supports this feature.

Interoperability

Binding DirContext objects is especially useful for interoperability with non-Java applications. An object is represented by a set of attributes, which can be read and used by non-Java applications from the directory. The same attributes can also be read and interpreted by a JNDI service provider, which, in conjunction with an object factory, converts them into a Java object.

For example, an object might have, as some of its attribute values, URLs that the JNDI service provider could use to generate an instance of a Java object that the application could use. These same URLs could be used also by non-Java applications.

Binding an Object by Using Its Attributes

The following example shows a Drink class that implements the DirContext interface. Most DirContext methods are not used by this example and so simply throw an OperationNot-SupportedException.

```
public class Drink implements DirContext {
    String type;
    Attributes myAttrs;

    public Drink(String d) {
        type = d;
        myAttrs = new BasicAttributes(true);  // Case ignore
        Attribute oc = new BasicAttribute("objectclass");
        oc.add("extensibleObject");
        oc.add("top");

        myAttrs.put(oc);
        myAttrs.put("drinkType", d);
    }

    public Attributes getAttributes(String name)
        throws NamingException {
        if (! name.equals("")) {
            throw new NameNotFoundException();
        }
        return (Attributes)myAttrs.clone();
    }

    public String toString() {
```

```
                return type;
        }
        ...
    }
```

The `Drink` class contains the "objectclass" and "drinkType" attributes. The "object-class" attribute contains two values: "top" and "extensibleObject". The "drinkType" attribute is set by using the string passed to the `Drink` constructor. For example, if the instance was created by using `new Drink("water")`, then its "drinkType" attribute will have the value "water".

The following example creates an instance of `Drink` and invokes `Context.bind()` to add it to the directory.

```
// Create the object to be bound
Drink dr = new Drink("water");

// Perform the bind
ctx.bind("cn=favDrink", dr);
```

When the object is bound, its attributes are extracted and stored in the directory.

When that object is subsequently looked up from the directory, its corresponding object factory will be used to return an instance of the object. The object factory is identified by the `Context.OBJECT_FACTORIES` environment property when the initial context for reading the object is created. Conversion details are described in the **Object Factories** lesson (page 185).

```
Hashtable env = ...;
// Add property so that the object factory can be found
env.put(Context.OBJECT_FACTORIES, "DrinkFactory");

// Create the initial context
DirContext ctx = new InitialDirContext(env);

// Read back the object
Drink dr2 = (Drink) ctx.lookup("cn=favDrink");
System.out.println(dr2);
```

This produces the following output, "water", produced by `Drink.toString()`.

```
# java DirObj

water
```

From the perspective of the application using the JNDI, it is dealing only with `bind()` and `lookup()`. The service provider takes care of getting the attributes from the object and converting them to/from the actual object itself.

Note that you can store a `DirContext` object in the directory only if the underlying service provider supports that.

Remote Objects

The RMI (Java Remote Method Invocation) system is a mechanism that enables an object on one Java virtual machine to invoke methods on an object in another Java virtual machine. Any object whose methods can be invoked in this way must implement the `java.rmi.Remote` interface. When such an object is invoked, its arguments are *marshalled* and sent from the local virtual machine to the remote one, where the arguments are *unmarshalled* and used. When the method terminates, the results are marshalled from the remote machine and sent to the caller's virtual machine.

To make a remote object accessible to other virtual machines, a program typically registers it with the RMI registry. The program supplies to the registry the string name of the remote object as well as the object itself. When a program wants to access a remote object, it supplies the object's string name to the registry that is on the same machine as the remote object. The registry returns to the caller a reference (called a *stub*) to the remote object. When the program receives the stub for the remote object, it can invoke methods on the object (through the stub).

A program can also obtain references to remote objects as a result of remote calls to other remote objects or from other naming services. For example, the program can look up a reference to a remote object from an LDAP server that supports the schema defined RFC 2713.

The string name accepted by the RMI registry has the syntax

```
rmi://hostname:port/remoteObjectName
```

where *hostname* and *port* identify the machine and port, respectively, on which the RMI registry is running and *remoteObjectName* is the string name of the remote object. *hostname*, *port*, and the prefix, `"rmi:"`, are optional. If *hostname* is not specified, then it defaults to the local host. If *port* is not specified, then it defaults to 1099. If *remoteObjectName* is not specified, then the object being named is the RMI registry itself. See the RMI specification (`http://java.sun.com/products/jdk/rmi/`) for details.

RMI can be supported by using the Java Remote Method Protocol (JRMP) and the Internet Inter-ORB Protocol (IIOP). The JRMP is a specialized protocol designed for RMI; the IIOP is the standard protocol for communication between CORBA objects. RMI over IIOP allows Java remote objects to communicate with CORBA objects that might be written in a non-Java programming language.

Some service providers, such as Sun's LDAP service provider, support the binding of `java.rmi.Remote` objects into directories. When `java.rmi.Remote` objects and/or RMI registries are bound into an enterprise-wide shared namespace such as the LDAP, RMI clients can look up `java.rmi.Remote` objects without knowing on which machine the objects are running.

Binding a Remote Object

Before you go on: To run this example, you need the Java 2 Platform, v1.2 or higher release. You also need `ldapbp.jar`, as stated in the introduction of this lesson (page 155).

The following example defines a `java.rmi.Remote` interface `Hello` that has one method, `sayHello()`.

```
public interface Hello extends Remote {
    public String sayHello() throws RemoteException;
}
```

It also defines an implementation of this interface, `HelloImpl`.

```
public class HelloImpl extends UnicastRemoteObject implements Hello {
    public HelloImpl() throws RemoteException {
    }

    public String sayHello() throws RemoteException {
        return ("Hello, the time is " + new java.util.Date());
    }
}
```

This example also creates an instance of `HelloImpl` and binds it in the directory, assigning it the name `"cn=RemoteHello"`.

```
// Create the remote object to be bound, and give it a name
Hello h = new HelloImpl();

// Bind the object to the directory
ctx.bind("cn=RemoteHello", h);
```

After the object has been bound in the directory, an application can look it up by using the following code.

```
Hello h2 = (Hello)ctx.lookup("cn=RemoteHello");
h2.sayHello();
```

To run this example, you must do the following.

1. Compile `Hello.java`, `HelloImpl.java` and this example:

   `# javac Hello.java HelloImpl RemoteObj.java`

2. Run `rmic` with `HelloImpl` as the argument to produce the stubs for the remote object:

   `# rmic HelloImpl`

3. Copy `Hello.class`, `HelloImpl.class` and the class files generated by `rmic` to a directory on a Web server.

4. Specify the directory in Step 3 as the codebase to the Java interpreter.

   `# java -Djava.rmi.server.codebase=http://web1/example/classes/ RemoteObj`

RemoteObj does not terminate, because it created the remote object HelloImpl that other RMI clients can contact and use. However, this program will terminate eventually, when the remote object becomes garbage collected. To prevent the object's being garbage collected, you must maintain a (live) reference to the remote object. If you had registered the object in the RMI registry instead, then maintaining a reference would not be necessary because the registry would automatically maintain a reference to the object.

When you later look up this object from the directory, the directory will return the bound HelloImpl remote object. The RMI will automatically download the necessary class files from the codebase specified in the "java.rmi.server.codebase" property. See the **Reading Objects from the Directory** lesson (page 179) for an example.

Binding a Remote Object by Using a Reference

Before you go on: This example requires that you have started the RMI registry on your machine. You also need rmiregistry.jar, as stated in the introduction of this lesson (page 155).

The following example uses the same Hello and HelloImpl classes used in the previous example. It creates a Reference containing an RMI URL ("rmi://mymachine/hello") and binds it in the directory.

```
String rmiurl = "rmi://mymachine/hello";

// Create the reference containing the (future) location of the object
Reference ref = new Reference("Hello", new StringRefAddr("URL", rmiurl));

// Bind the object to the directory
ctx.bind("cn=RefHello", ref);
```

It then creates an instance of HelloImpl and binds it in the local RMI registry by using the same RMI URL ("rmi://mymachine/hello").

```
// Create the remote object to be bound
Hello h = new HelloImpl();

// Bind the object to the RMI registry
ctx.rebind(rmiurl, h);
```

After the object has been bound in both the directory and the RMI registry, an application can look up the object by using the following code.

```
Hello h2 = (Hello)ctx.lookup("cn=RefHello");
System.out.println(h2.sayHello());
```

In effect, this method has one more level of indirection than the previous example offered. The information stored in the directory (the Reference) is actually a pointer to information stored in another naming service (the RMI registry), which in turn, contains the reference to the `java.rmi.Remote` object.

To run this example, you must do the following.

1. Perform Steps 1–3 from the previous example.
2. Compile this example:

```
# javac RemoteRef.java
```

3. Specify the codebase directory as the codebase to the Java interpreter.

```
# java -Djava.rmi.server.codebase=http://web1/example/classes/ RemoteRef
```

RemoteRef does not terminate, because it created the remote object `HelloImpl` that other RMI clients can contact and use.

When you later look up this object from the directory, the directory will return the bound `HelloImpl` remote object. The RMI will automatically download the necessary class files from the codebase specified in the `"java.rmi.server.codebase"` property. See the **Reading Objects from the Directory** lesson (page 179) for an example.

Binding a Remote Object That Uses IIOP

Before you go on: This example requires that you have `ldapbp.jar`, as stated in the introduction of this lesson (page 155). If you are not using the Java 2 SDK, v1.3, then you also need to install the RMI-IIOP Standard Extension (`http://java.sun.com/products/rmi-iiop`). If you are not using the Java 2 SDK, v 1.2 or higher release, then you also need to install Java IDL, a version of which comes with the RMI-IIOP Standard Extension.

The procedure for binding a `java.rmi.Remote` object that uses IIOP or JRMP is identical as far as the JNDI is concerned. From the user/application's perspective, they differ only in how the stubs for the `java.rmi.Remote` object are generated. Looking up the object presents a bigger difference: When the object is looked up from the directory (or some other naming service), the result must be narrowed by using `javax.rmi.PortableRemoteObject.narrow()` instead of the Java type cast operator.

The following example uses the `Hello` interface from the JRMP example. It defines an implementation of this interface, `RiHelloImpl`, that is analogous to `HelloImpl`, except that it extends from `javax.rmi.PortableRemoteObject` instead of from `java.rmi.server.Uni-castRemoteObject`.

```
public class RiHelloImpl extends PortableRemoteObject implements Hello {
    public RiHelloImpl() throws RemoteException {
    }

    public String sayHello() throws RemoteException {
        String date = new String((new java.util.Date()).toString());
```

```
        return ("RMI/IIOP hello | " + date);
    }
}
```

The example creates an instance of RiHelloImpl and binds it in the directory, assigning it the name "cn=RmiiiopHello".

```
// Create the remote object to be bound, and give it a name
Hello h = new RiHelloImpl();

// Bind the object to the directory
ctx.bind("cn=RmiiiopHello", h);
```

After the object has been bound in the directory, an application can look it up by using the following code.

```
// Look up the object
org.omg.CORBA.Object cobj =
    (org.omg.CORBA.Object)ctx.lookup("cn=RmiiiopHello");

// Narrow the object to the desired type
Hello robj = (Hello)PortableRemoteObject.narrow(cobj, Hello.class);

// Invoke the method
System.out.println(robj.sayHello());
```

To run this example, you must do the following.

1. Compile Hello.java, RiHelloImpl.java and this example:

   ```
   # javac Hello.java RiHelloImpl RmiiiopObj.java
   ```

2. Run rmic with RiHelloImpl as the argument and the "-iiop" option to produce the IIOP stubs for the remote object:

   ```
   # rmic -iiop RiHelloImpl
   ```

3. Copy Hello.class, RiHelloImpl.class and the class files generated by rmic to a directory on a Web server.

4. Specify this directory as the codebase to the Java interpreter.

   ```
   # java -Djava.rmi.server.codebase=http://web1/example/classes/ RmiiiopObj
   ```

RmiiiopObj does not terminate, because it created the remote object RiHelloImpl that other RMI clients can contact and use.

When you later look up this object from the directory, the directory will return the bound RiHelloImpl remote object. The RMI will automatically download the necessary class files from the codebase specified in the "java.rmi.server.codebase" property. See the **Reading Objects from the Directory** lesson (page 179) for an example.

CORBA Objects

CORBA (Common Object Request Broker Architecture) defines a language-independent framework for objects to invoke methods on each other. Before an object can invoke a method on another object, it must first obtain a reference to the object. The target object can use different ways to make its reference known to other objects. The traditional way is to use a naming service, such as the Common Object Services (COS) Name Service. Another way is to publish its object reference in an LDAP server that supports the schema defined RFC 2714. Using the JNDI, the code to use either of these ways are the same. You can select the underlying naming service or directory to use at runtime by selecting the initial context to use. The example shown in this section uses an LDAP directory.

Binding a CORBA Object Reference

Before you go on: To run this example, you need `ldapbp.jar`, as stated in the introduction of this lesson (page 155). If you are not using the Java 2 SDK, v1.2 or higher release, then you also need to install the Java IDL, a version of which comes with the RMI-IIOP Standard Extension (`http://java.sun.com/products/rmi-iiop`).

The following example first defines an interface, `HelloApp`, by using the Interface Description Language (IDL).

```
module HelloApp {
    interface hello
    {
        string sayHello();
    };
};
```

It then defines an implementation of this interface, `helloServant`.

```
class helloServant extends HelloApp._helloImplBase {
    public String sayHello() {
        return "\nHello world !!\n" + new java.util.Date();
    }
}
```

Next, it creates an instance of `helloServant` and binds it to the directory, assigning it the name `"cn=CorbaHello"`.

```
// Create and initialize the ORB
ORB orb = ORB.init(args, null);

// Create the servant, and register it with the ORB
helloServant helloRef = new helloServant();
orb.connect(helloRef);
```

```
// Let the service provider use the ORB
env.put("java.naming.corba.orb", orb);

// Create the initial context
DirContext ctx = new InitialDirContext(env);

// Bind the object to the directory
ctx.bind("cn=CorbaHello", helloRef);
```

After the object has been bound in the directory, an application can look it up by using the following code.

```
// Look up and narrow the object
HelloApp.hello h2 = HelloApp.helloHelper.narrow(
    (org.omg.CORBA.Object)ctx.lookup("cn=CorbaHello"));

// Invoke the method
System.out.println(h2.sayHello());
```

To run this example, you must do the following.

1. Run the IDL compiler (idltojava) with HelloApp.idl as the argument to produce the stubs for the CORBA object:

   ```
   # idltojava HelloApp
   ```

   This generates a directory HelloApp that contains .java and .class files.

2. Compile this example:

   ```
   # javac CorbaObj.java
   ```

3. Run the example:

   ```
   # java CorbaObj
   ```

   If you want the helloServant created by the example to hang around for other CORBA clients to access, then run the program with the -wait parameter:

   ```
   # java CorbaObj -wait
   ```

When you later look up this object from the directory, the directory will return the bound helloServant CORBA object. See the **Reading Objects from the Directory** lesson (page 179) for an example.

State Factories

The **Storing Objects in the Directory** lesson (page 155) gave examples of binding several types of objects. What if you want to bind yet another type of object that differs from all of the types shown so far? What determines the types of objects that a service provider is willing to bind?

The JNDI provides a general framework for transforming objects supplied to Context.bind() and related methods into a format acceptable to a service provider. This framework uses *state factories*. A state factory transforms an object into another object. The input is the object and optional attributes, supplied to Context.bind(), and the output is another object and optional attributes, to be stored in the underlying naming service or directory. A service provider can be preconfigured with a set of state factories. For example, Sun's LDAP service provider has state factories for storing RMI and CORBA objects. The application can configure additional state factories for a service provider to use.

This lesson first describes how to write a state factory. It then discusses how service providers use state factories and concludes with an example of how to write a custom state factory.

Writing a State Factory

A state factory implements either the StateFactory or DirStateFactory interface. State-Factory has one method: getStateToBind().

```
public Object getStateToBind(
    Object obj,
    Name name,
    Context nameCtx,
    Hashtable environment)
    throws NamingException;
```

DirStateFactory is a subinterface of StateFactory and declares an additional method: getStateToBind().

171

```
public DirStateFactory.Result getStateToBind(
    Object obj,
    Name name,
    Context nameCtx,
    Hashtable environment,
    Attributes inAttrs)
    throws NamingException;
```

This method accepts as an argument the object to be bound (obj). The name and nameCtx arguments are provided to the state factory in case the factory requires additional information from the directory. The env argument is the environment properties of the context that is using the state factory. See the **Beyond the Basics** trail (page 95) for details about environment properties. The DirStateFactory version of the method accepts an additional inAttrs (Attributes) argument, which contains the attributes to be bound with obj.

StateFactory versus DirStateFactory

You should use a StateFactory with a context that implements the Context interface. Use a DirStateFactory with a context that implements the DirContext interface. For example, a COS naming service provider implements only the Context interface. Because no Attributes parameter can be passed to the service provider, and consequently, not to the state factory, the service provider will use only getStateToBind() as defined in the StateFactory interface. By contrast, an LDAP service provider typically implements the DirContext interface and will use getStateToBind() as defined in the DirStateFactory interface.

Accessibility

The state factory class must not only implement the StateFactory/DirStateFactory interface and provide an implementation for getStateToBind(). It also must be public and must have a public constructor that accepts no arguments.

Job Description

Typically, a state factory is quite simple and small. Its main role is to perform some transformation on the input and produce an object (and/or attributes) suitable for storing by the service provider. For example, a state factory for an LDAP service provider might accept an object and some attributes and return a set of attributes that is the union of the input attributes and the attributes that represent the object. A state factory for a COS naming service provider might, for example, accept a java.rmi.Remote object and return its CORBA *tie* object.

In general, a close relationship exists between the representation of the object as it is stored in the underlying naming service or directory and the state factory that does the transformation. For example, if an object is represented as a set of attributes in the directory, then the corresponding state factory must return attributes for representing the object.

If All Else Fails

A state factory is usually very specific regarding the types of transformations that it will handle. For example, one factory might accept only CORBA objects, whereas another might accept only objects that implement a specific interface. In fact, in many cases, as explained in the next section, the JNDI will ask a state factory to attempt the transformation by using input that was intended for another state factory. It is common for a single service provider to use multiple state factories. Therefore, if a state factory finds that it does not support the type of input supplied, then it should return `null`. The factory should throw an exception only when it encounters an error while processing the input that it should otherwise accept. Throwing an exception precludes other state factories from being tried.

Interaction Between State Factories and Service Providers

A service provider acts as the go-between for the application and the directory when the application stores or retrieves Java objects from the directory. When you write a service provider, you need to perform this go-between role by following the rules outlined in this section for storing objects in the directory.

The following detailed description is intended for developers writing service providers. The insight it offers into the go-between role of service providers might also interest API users.

Relevant Methods

When accepting objects to be bound into the underlying naming/directory service, the service provider should use the guidelines described in this section. An object can be bound by using one of the following methods:

- `Context.bind()`
- `DirContext.bind()`
- `Context.rebind()`
- `DirContext.rebind()`

Minimal Set of Acceptable Types

A service provider should try to support binding and rebinding objects that are or do one of the following:

- Instances of `Reference`
- Implement the `Referenceable` interface

- Implement the `java.io.Serializable` interface
- Implement the `DirContext` interface

It should check whether an object is in these four categories in the order listed because this order is most likely to capture the intent of the client. For example, a `Reference` is `Serializable`, so if you perform the `Serializable` check first, then no `Reference` objects will ever be stored in the reference format (they would all be serialized).

Framework Support

A service provider should use state factories configured with the provider and application. This allows the service provider to be customized to support arbitrary types of objects (for which a corresponding state factory is available).

The JNDI framework provides utility methods that service providers can use to access state factories. A service provider that implements only the `Context` interface should use `NamingManager.getStateToBind()`. A service provider that implements the `DirContext` interface should use `DirectoryManager.getStateToBind()`.

These methods traverse the list of state factories specified in the `Context.STATE_FACTORIES` environment property and the provider resource file and try to find a factory that yields a non-`null` answer. (See the **Beyond the Basics** trail (page 95) for details about environment properties and the provider resource file.)

Here's an example of how a `DirContext` implementation might use state factories.

```
// First, use state factories to do a transformation
DirStateFactory.Result res = DirectoryManager.getStateToBind(
    obj, name, ctx, env, inAttrs);
obj = res.getObject();
Attributes outAttrs = res.getAttributes();

// Check for Referenceable
if (obj instanceof Referenceable) {
    obj = ((Referenceable)obj).getReference();
}

// Store different formats
if (obj instanceof Reference) {
    // Store as ref and add outAttrs
} else if (obj instanceof Serializable) {
    // Serialize and add outAttrs
} else if (obj instanceof DirContext) {
    // Grab attributes, and merge with outAttrs
} else {
    ...
}
```

When the provider gets an object (`obj`) and attributes (`inAttrs`) from the client to bind into the directory, it invokes `getStateToBind()` to get a possibly updated pair of object/attributes. If no state factories return a non-`null` answer, then `getStateToBind()` returns the original pair of object and attributes. In either case, the provider stores the results in the underlying directory in a format acceptable to the directory.

Examples

Here are some examples of how state factories are used in the examples from this lesson and the **Storing Objects in the Directory** lesson (page 155).

- **Reference example** (page 160). `Fruit` is a `Referenceable` object. The service provider extracts its reference by using `Referenceable.getReference()` and stores the reference into the directory. No state factory is used.

- **Attributes example** (page 161). `Drink` is a `DirContext` object. The service provider extracts its attributes by using `DirContext.getAttributes()` and stores the attributes into the directory. No state factory is used.

- **Serialization example** (page 157). No state factory is used. The service provider serializes the `java.awt.Button` object and stores its serialized form into the directory.

- **Remote reference example** (page 165). The service provider stores the `Reference` in the directory. No state factory is used.

- **Remote (JRMP) object example** (page 164). A state factory (bundled with the service provider) turns the `java.rmi.Remote` object into a marshalled object, which is then stored by the service provider into the directory.

- **Remote (IIOP) object example** (page 166). A state factory (bundled with the service provider) turns the `java.rmi.Remote` object into a stringified CORBA object reference, which is then stored by the service provider into the directory.

- **CORBA example** (page 168). A state factory (bundled with the service provider) turns the CORBA object into a stringified CORBA object reference, which is then stored by the service provider in the directory.
- **Custom object example** (page 175). The state factory `PersonStateFactory` turns a `Person` object into a set of attributes, which is then stored by the service provider into the directory. `PersonStateFactory` is identified in the application resource file used by the client program (`CustomObj`).

The remainder of this section describes the state factory `PersonStateFactory`.

Custom Object Example

This example illustrates how an arbitrary type (e.g., `Person`) can be stored and read back from the directory by using custom state and object factories.

```
// Create the object to be bound
Person john = new Person("Smith", "John Smith");
```

175

Examples

```
// Perform the bind
ctx.rebind("cn=John Smith", john);

// Read back the object
Person john2 = (Person) ctx.lookup("cn=John Smith");
```

Although this example uses both a state factory and an object factory, the focus is on the state factory. See the **Object Factories** lesson (page 185) for a detailed discussion of object factories.

Sun's LDAP service provider is used for this example. When Context.bind() is invoked on this provider, it uses DirectoryManager.getStateToBind() to retrieve the state of the object to be bound. This example specifies in the jndi.properties file the factories that it uses.

```
java.naming.factory.initial=com.sun.jndi.ldap.LdapCtxFactory
java.naming.factory.state=PersonStateFactory
java.naming.factory.object=PersonObjectFactory
```

(See the **Beyond the Basics** trail (page 95) for details about environment properties.)

The PersonStateFactory accepts an instance of Person and returns a DirState-Factory.Result instance that contains the attributes representing the Person object.

```
public DirStateFactory.Result getStateToBind(
        Object obj, Name name, Context ctx, Hashtable env,
        Attributes inAttrs) throws NamingException {

    // Only interested in Person objects
    if (obj instanceof Person) {
        Attributes outAttrs;
        if (inAttrs == null) {
            outAttrs = new BasicAttributes(true);
        } else {
            outAttrs = (Attributes)inAttrs.clone();
        }

        // Set up the object class
        if (outAttrs.get("objectclass") == null) {
            BasicAttribute oc =
                new BasicAttribute("objectclass", "person");
            oc.add("top");
            outAttrs.put(oc);
        }

        Person per = (Person)obj;
        // Mandatory attributes
        if (per.surname != null) {
            outAttrs.put("sn", per.surname);
        } else {
            throw new SchemaViolationException(
                "Person must have surname");
        }
        if (per.commonName != null) {
            outAttrs.put("cn", per.commonName);
        } else {
            throw new SchemaViolationException(
```

```
                    "Person must have common name");
        }

        // Optional attributes
        if (per.passwd != null) {
            outAttrs.put("userPassword", per.passwd);
        }
        if (per.phone != null) {
            outAttrs.put("telephoneNumber", per.phone);
        }
        if (per.seeAlso != null) {
            outAttrs.put("seeAlso", per.seeAlso);
        }
        if (per.desc != null) {
            outAttrs.put("description", per.desc);
        }

        //System.out.println("state factory: " + outAttrs);
        return new DirStateFactory.Result(null, outAttrs);
    }
    return null;
}
```

Reading Objects from the Directory

The **Storing Objects in the Directory** lesson (page 155) discussed different ways in which Java objects (or rather information about Java objects) are stored in a directory. Each of that lesson's examples demonstrated that once the object is stored, you can simply use Context.lookup() to get a copy of the object back from the directory, regardless of what type of information was actually stored. This is made possible by object factories. A brief discussion of how object factories are used by lookup() is included in the **Lookups** section (page 179) of this lesson.

You can get the object back not only by using lookup(), but also when you list a context and when you search a context or its subtree. In all of these cases, object factories might be involved. This lesson describes also how these operations interact with object factories. Object factories are discussed in detail in the **Object Factories** lesson (page 185).

Lookups

The serialization example (page 157) showed that an object stored (serialized) in a directory can be read back by using lookup().

```
// Check that the object is bound
Button b2 = (Button)ctx.lookup("cn=Button");
System.out.println(b2);
```

Similarly, in the reference example (page 160), attributes example (page 161), remote object examples (page 163), the CORBA object example (page 168), and the custom object example (page 175), you could simply use lookup() to retrieve the stored object.

Object Factories

In the attributes example (page 161), the environment used to create the initial context had an additional property, Context.OBJECT_FACTORIES. This property specifies the class names of one or more object factories to use when turning information stored in the directory into Java objects expected by the application.

When the object is represented as a reference in the directory, the reference contains the class name and, optionally, the location of the object factory. Consequently, the reference example (page 160) did not need to set the Context.OBJECT_FACTORIES property. Similarly, when an object is serialized, it typically needs only to be deserialized and not transformed any further. This was the case with the previous java.awt.Button example (page 157), so again, no object factory was specified.

In the attributes example, what is stored to represent the Drink object is simply a collection of attributes, so you need to specify an object factory, DrinkFactory, to use to convert those attributes to a Drink object.

Although no factories were specified explicitly in the remote (page 163) and CORBA (page 168) object examples, object factories were preconfigured into the LDAP service provider that was used. (See the **Beyond the Basics** trail (page 95) for details about environment properties and how they are used to configure service providers.) The custom object example (page 175) also used an object factory. There, the factory was specified by using an application resource file (see the **Beyond the Basics** trail (page 100) for details).

Object factories are described in more detail in the **Object Factories** lesson (page 185).

Type of Object

The type of object returned by lookup() is determined by the object factory and/or the service provider. In the remote object examples, the object looked up is a java.rmi.Remote object. In the RMI/IIOP object and CORBA object examples, the object looked up is a CORBA object. Following are some examples of how an object is used after it has been looked up from the directory.

The following code looks up a remote object bound by using the directly bound and reference examples.

```
// Read from the directory
Hello h = (Hello)ctx.lookup(name);
// Execute the remote method
System.out.println(h.sayHello());
```

To successfully run this example, the RMI requires that you specify a security manager and a security policy.

```
# java -Djava.security.manager -Djava.security.policy=.policy\
    LookupRemote cn=RemoteHello
```

After performing the `lookup()`, you can cast the result to a `Hello` class and invoke a method on it.

Note: The stub and server files must have been placed in the location specified by the server programs (i.e., that specified by the `"java.rmi.server.codebase"` property), as directed by the binding examples (page 163).

The following code looks up a CORBA object bound by using the CORBA object example.

```
// Look up the object
org.omg.CORBA.Object cobj =
    (org.omg.CORBA.Object)ctx.lookup("cn=CorbaHello");

// Narrow the object to the right type
HelloApp.hello h2 = HelloApp.helloHelper.narrow(cobj);

// Invoke the method on the object
System.out.println(h2.sayHello());
```

After performing the `lookup()`, you must use the appropriate `narrow()` method to narrow the object to the right type and then invoke the appropriate method on the object.

Note: You must copy to the classpath, or otherwise make available in the classpath, the class files generated by `idltojava` (i.e., the `HelloApp` directory and its contents) in the binding example (page 168).

Lists

The **Naming Operations** lesson (page 54) showed you how to list a context using the `Context.list()` and `Context.listBindings()` methods. This section describes how these methods are affected by object factories.

List

When you use `Context.list()`, you get back an enumeration of `NameClassPair`. You can invoke `getClassName()` on each `NameClassPair` to obtain the class name of the object in that binding.

For example, if you list the context that you used to bind the various objects in the **Storing Objects in the Directory** lesson (page 155), then you get the following output.

```
# java List

ou=Groups: javax.naming.directory.DirContext
ou=People: javax.naming.directory.DirContext
cn=Button: java.awt.Button
cn=Flower: Flower
cn=favorite: Fruit
cn=favDrink: javax.naming.directory.DirContext
cn=RefHello: Hello
cn=CorbaHello: javax.naming.directory.DirContext
cn=RmiiiopHello: javax.naming.directory.DirContext
cn=RemoteHello: HelloImpl
```

For each binding, the Java class name was determined based on information stored in the directory, without an instance of the object in the binding necessarily having to be created. No object factory was involved.

List Bindings

When you use Context.listBindings(), you get back an enumeration of Binding. You can invoke getObject() on each Binding to obtain the object in that binding. The result of get-Object() is the same as that obtained by looking up the object by using Context.lookup().

For example, if you list the bindings in the context that you used to bind the various objects in the **Storing Objects in the Directory** lesson (page 155), then you get the following output.

```
# java -Djava.security.manager -Djava.security.policy=.policy\
    ListBindings

ou=Groups: com.sun.jndi.ldap.LdapCtx:com.sun.jndi.ldap.LdapCtx@1dacd730
ou=People: com.sun.jndi.ldap.LdapCtx:com.sun.jndi.ldap.LdapCtx@1dacd8ae
cn=Button: java.awt.Button: java.awt.Button\
    [button0,0,0,0x0,invalid,label=Push me]
cn=Flower: Flower: pink rose
cn=favorite: Fruit: orange
cn=favDrink: Drink: water
cn=RemoteHello: HelloImpl_Stub: HelloImpl_Stub[RemoteStub\
    [ref: [endpoint:[129.111.111.111:44999](remote),objID:\
    [-68dff7b3:d975735a08:-8000, 0]]]]
cn=RefHello: HelloImpl_Stub: HelloImpl_Stub[RemoteStub [ref:\
    [endpoint:[129.111.111.111:45006](remote),objID:\
    [2bf4308e:d975745b44:-8000, 0]]]]
cn=CorbaHello: com.sun.CORBA.idl.CORBAObjectImpl:\
    com.sun.CORBA.idl.CORBAObjectImpl:\
    com.sun.CORBA.idl.GenericCORBAClientSC@84675dd2
cn=RmiiiopHello: com.sun.CORBA.idl.CORBAObjectImpl:\
    com.sun.CORBA.idl.CORBAObjectImpl:\
    com.sun.CORBA.idl.GenericCORBAClientSC@ac6b5dd2
```

Notice that the "cn=favDrink" entry and a few others now have a more precise class name (Drink, HelloImpl_Stub). This is because instantiating the object (by the corresponding object factory) provided more class information. Notice also that the remote object HelloImpl was returned as a stub to the real object.

Note 1: You must run this example by using the Java 2 Platform, v1.2 or higher release because some of the object factories require that platform.

Note 2: The -Djava.security.manager option specifies that the default security manager be used, and the -Djava.security.policy=.policy option specifies that the .policy file be used for the security policy. These two options are needed when you are listing/looking up the java.rmi.Remote objects. In the policy file, you need to grant permission to connect to and accept connections from the Web server and the machine on which the remote objects are running.

Searches

The **Directory Operations** lesson (page 63) showed how to use the various Dir-Context.search() methods. When you perform a search using a SearchControls parameter, you can control what gets returned in each SearchResult. Specifically, if you invoke Search-Controls.setReturningObjFlag() with true and pass that to search(), then each entry in the SearchResult will contain the corresponding Java object.

The following example searches the context used to bind the various objects in the **Storing Objects in the Directory** lesson (page 155) and prints each result's object (class name and object reference).

```
SearchControls ctls = new SearchControls();
ctls.setReturningObjFlag(true);

// Specify the search filter to match any object
String filter = "(objectclass=*)";

// Search for objects by using the filter
NamingEnumeration answer = ctx.search("", filter, ctls);
```

The output of this example is as follows.

```
# java -Djava.security.manager -Djava.security.policy=.policy Search
ou=Groups: com.sun.jndi.ldap.LdapCtx:com.sun.jndi.ldap.LdapCtx@723fdc9a
ou=People: com.sun.jndi.ldap.LdapCtx:com.sun.jndi.ldap.LdapCtx@642fdc9a
cn=Fruits: com.sun.jndi.ldap.LdapCtx:com.sun.jndi.ldap.LdapCtx@63afdc9a
cn=Button: java.awt.Button: \
    java.awt.Button[button0,0,0,0x0,invalid,label=Push me]
cn=Flower: Flower: pink rose
cn=favorite: Fruit: orange
cn=favDrink: Drink: water
cn=CorbaHello: com.sun.CORBA.idl.CORBAObjectImpl:\
```

```
        com.sun.CORBA.idl.CORBAObjectImpl:\
        com.sun.CORBA.idl.GenericCORBAClientSC@8a9e173a
cn=RemoteHello: HelloImpl_Stub:HelloImpl_Stub[RemoteStub\
        [ref: [endpoint:[129.111.111.111:46547](remote),\
        objID:[75de816d:d98468df8c:-8000, 0]]]]
cn=RefHello: HelloImpl_Stub: HelloImpl_Stub[RemoteStub \
        [ref: [endpoint:[129.111.111.111:46550](remote),\
        objID:[272f25a1:d9846946ca:-8000, 0]]]]
cn=Custom: com.sun.jndi.ldap.LdapCtx: com.sun.jndi.ldap.LdapCtx@db7a1739
cn=John Smith: Person: My name is Smith, John Smith.
cn=RmiiiopHello: com.sun.CORBA.idl.CORBAObjectImpl:\
        com.sun.CORBA.idl.CORBAObjectImpl:\
        com.sun.CORBA.idl.GenericCORBAClientSC@ac6b5dd2
```

The same notes that apply to the list bindings example (page 182) also apply to this example.

Object Factories

If you have tried some of the examples in the **Reading Objects from the Directory** lesson (page 179), then you likely have noticed the use of *object factories*. An object factory is a producer of objects. It accepts some information about how to create an object, such as a reference, and then returns an instance of that object. Both the representation and the nature of the information that an object factory expects and accepts as valid are determined by the object factory and are closely tied to how that information is stored in the directory.

This lesson first describes how to write an object factory. It then discusses some other uses of object factories, in addition to those already seen in this trail, as well as the way in which factories relate to service providers. It concludes with three examples of object factories:

- One for a reference
- One for a set of attributes
- One for a custom Java object class

Writing an Object Factory

An object factory implements either the `ObjectFactory` or `DirObjectFactory` interface. `ObjectFactory` has one method: `getObjectInstance()`.

```
public Object getObjectInstance(
    Object info,
    Name name,
    Context nameCtx,
    Hashtable environment)
    throws Exception;
```

`DirObjectFactory` is a subinterface of `ObjectFactory` and declares an additional method: `getObjectInstance()`.

```
public Object getObjectInstance(
    Object info,
    Name name,
```

```
          Context nameCtx,
          Hashtable environment,
          Attributes attrs)
          throws Exception;
```

This method accepts as arguments information about the object (`info`) and the name of the object (`name`) relative to the context (`nameCtx`) in which it is bound. The `env` argument is the environment properties of the context that is using the object factory. See the **Beyond the Basics** trail (page 95) for details about environment properties. The `DirObjectFactory` version of the method accepts an additional `attrs` (`Attributes`) argument, which contains (some or all of) the attributes associated with `obj`.

ObjectFactory versus DirObjectFactory

You should use an `ObjectFactory` with a context that implements only the `Context` interface. Use a `DirObjectFactory` with a context that implements the `DirContext` interface.

For example, a COS naming service provider implements only the `Context` interface. Because `Attributes` is not relevant in that scenario, only `getObjectInstance()` as defined in the `ObjectFactory` interface is relevant for that service provider. By contrast, an LDAP service provider typically implements the `DirContext` interface and will use `getObject-Instance()` as defined in the `DirObjectFactory` interface. The `Attributes` parameter is used by the service provider to pass along any attributes associated with `info` to the factory so that the factory does not have to fetch the attributes itself. For example, when a service provider does a `Context.lookup()`, it can pass to `getObjectInstance()` any attributes that it read from the server about the object's being looked up.

Accessibility

The object factory class must not only implement the `ObjectFactory`/`DirObjectFactory` interface and provide an implementation for `getObjectInstance()`. It also must be public and must have a public constructor that accepts no arguments.

Job Description

Typically, an object factory is quite simple and small. Its main role is to collect the information necessary to create an instance of the intended object's class and then to invoke that class's constructor. However, the complexity of the objects that it creates can vary significantly. For example, the object factory examples given in this lesson are pretty trivial; the objects that they create are also trivial. By contrast, an LDAP object factory creates an LDAP context, which creates and manages connections to an LDAP server. In this case, a relatively simple object factory is creating a very complex object.

In general, the information that an object factory uses to create objects comes from the directory. Consequently, a close relationship exists between the representation of the objects as stored in the directory and the object factory that creates the objects by using that information. For example, if the object is represented as a set of attributes in the directory, then the corresponding object factory must know to extract information from those attributes so as to create the object.

If All Else Fails

An object factory is usually very specific regarding the types of transformations that it will handle. In fact, in many cases, as explained in the **Interaction Between Object Factories and Service Providers** section (page 188), the JNDI will ask an object factory to try to create an instance of an object that was intended for another object factory. A single service provider commonly uses multiple object factories. Therefore if an object factory finds that it cannot create an object based on the arguments supplied, then it should return `null`. Only if the object factory knows for sure that it is supposed to create the object, but it can't, should it throw an exception. Throwing an exception precludes other object factories from being tried.

Other Uses

The object factory is actually a general mechanism used throughout the JNDI. In this lesson, object factories are used to transform information stored in the directory into Java objects that applications can use. And typically, these objects are objects that the application uses directly (such as a `Person` object or a `Drink` or `Fruit` object).

The following discussion introduces you to other uses of object factories. It is intended as background information for API users. Developers of service providers can find full discussions of these topics in the **Beyond the Basics** trail (page 131) and the **Building a Service Provider** trail (page 357).

Federation and Context Factories

You saw how an object can be bound into the directory. What if the object happens to be the root of another naming system? In the LDAP, for example, you can bind an object that is the root of a file system. You can then supply an object factory whose role it is to convert the information stored in the LDAP directory about the file system into the *root* context of the file system. This type of object factory is called a *context factory*. Given information about the context object to create, a context factory will create and return an instance of `Context`.

The file system in this example is called the nns (see the **Federation** lesson (page 134)). Just as the nature of the information stored in a directory about a Java object can vary (from a reference to attributes to a serialized object), so can the nature of the information stored in a directory about the nns. In the file system example, you might store a URL that identifies the file system's server and protocol information as a JNDI reference.

By storing nns information in a directory, you are federating naming systems, thereby allowing them to resolve composite names. See the **Federation** lesson (page 131) for details.

URL Context Factories

A special kind of context factory is a *URL context factory*, which creates contexts for resolving URLs or contexts whose locations are specified by URLs. For example, an LDAP URL context factory can create a context for accepting arbitrary LDAP URLs. The same LDAP URL context factory can create a context identified by an LDAP URL. That context will then be able to resolve names relative to the location specified by the URL.

URL context factories are used for federation and are also used by the *initial context* to resolve and process requests for URLs. In fact, in the remote reference example (page 165), the remote object is stored in the directory as a reference that contains an RMI URL. When the object is looked up from the directory, the JNDI uses an RMI URL context factory to look up and return the object from the RMI registry named in the URL.

Interaction Between Object Factories and Service Providers

A service provider acts as the go-between for the application and the directory when the application stores or retrieves Java objects from the directory. When you write a service provider, you need to perform this go-between role by following the rules outlined in this section for reading objects from the directory.

The following detailed description is intended for developers writing service providers. The insight it offers into the go-between role of service providers might also interest API users.

Relevant Methods

When returning objects to the JNDI client application, the service provider should use the guidelines described in this section. An object can be returned by using one of the following methods:

- `Context.lookup()`
- `Context.lookupLink()`
- `Binding.getObject()`
- `SearchResult.getObject()`

Framework Support

A service provider should use object factories configured with the provider and application. This allows the provider to be customized to support arbitrary types of objects (for which a corresponding object factory is available).

The JNDI framework provides utility methods that service providers can use to access object factories. A provider that implements only the `Context` interface should use `Naming-Manager.getObjectInstance()`. A provider that implements the `DirContext` interface should use `DirectoryManager.getObjectInstance()`. These methods interact with the object factories to produce a Java object that represents the information in the directory. Which object factories are used depends on the object read from the directory. If the object is a reference, then these methods use the object factory class named in the reference. If the reference contains a URL, then these methods use the corresponding URL context factory. Otherwise, they traverse the list of object factories specified in the `Context.OBJECT_FACTORIES` environment property and the provider resource file and try to find a factory that yields a non-`null` answer. (See the **Beyond the Basics** trail (page 95) for details about environment properties and the provider resource file.)

Federation

As explained in the **Other Uses** section (page 187) of this lesson, object factories also play a role in federation. How a service provider uses object factories to support federation is described in the **Building a Service Provider** trail (page 371).

Examples

Here are some examples of how object factories are used to read the objects created in the **Storing Objects in the Directory** lesson (page 155) and the **State Factories** lesson (page 171).

- **Reference example** (page 160). The object factory `FruitFactory` is used because its class name is identified in the reference. The factory creates an instance of `Fruit`.
- **Attributes example** (page 161). The client programs (lookup, list, and search) set the `Context.OBJECT_FACTORIES` environment property to `"DrinkFactory"` so that `NamingManager.getObjectInstance()` will load and instantiate `DrinkFactory` to create an instance of `Drink`.
- **Serialization example** (page 157). No object factory is used. The serialized object (an instance of `java.awt.Button`) is returned unchanged by `NamingManager.getObject-Instance()`.
- **Remote reference example** (page 165). The RMI URL context factory turns the RMI URL stored in a reference in the directory into an RMI stub found in the RMI registry.
- **Remote (JRMP) object example** (page 164). An object factory (bundled with the service

provider) turns the marshalled object of the RMI stub stored in the directory back into an RMI stub.

- **Remote (IIOP) object example** (page 166). An object factory (bundled with the service provider) turns the stringified CORBA object reference stored in the directory into a live CORBA object.
- **CORBA example** (page 168). An object factory (bundled with the service provider) turns the stringified CORBA object reference stored in the directory into a live CORBA object.
- **Custom object example** (page 175). The object factory `PersonObjectFactory` turns an LDAP entry (represented by a set of attributes) into a `Person` object. `PersonObject-Factory` is identified in the application resource file used by the client program (`Custom-Obj`).

The remainder of this section describes the object factories `FruitFactory`, `DrinkFactory`, and `PersonObjectFactory`.

Reference Example

The reference example (page 160) illustrates how an instance of a `Referenceable` class `Fruit` is stored in and subsequently looked up from the directory. When the reference is looked up from the directory, `Context.lookup()` turns the data read from the directory into an instance of `Fruit`.

```
Fruit f2 = (Fruit) ctx.lookup("cn=favorite");
```

This happens because of the following.

1. The service provider being used (Sun's LDAP service provider) invoked `Directory-Manager.getObjectInstance()` and supplied to the method the data (a reference) that the provider read from the directory for the entry `"cn=favorite"`.
2. The reference identified `FruitFactory` as the object factory's class name.
3. `FruitFactory.getObjectInstance()` returned an instance of `Fruit`.

`FruitFactory.getObjectInstance()` is simple. It first verifies that it can do something with the data. That is, it checks that the data is a `Reference` containing an address of type `"fruit"` and that the reference is for objects of class `Fruit`. If this verification fails, then the factory returns `null` so that other factories, if any, can be attempted. If it succeeds, then the content of the address (in this case, `"orange"`) is used to create a new instance of `Fruit`, which is then returned.

The definition of `FruitFactory.getObjectInstance()` is as follows.

```
public Object getObjectInstance(Object obj, Name name, Context ctx,
    Hashtable env) throws Exception {
    if (obj instanceof Reference) {
        Reference ref = (Reference)obj;
        if (ref.getClassName().equals(Fruit.class.getClassName())) {
            RefAddr addr = ref.get("fruit");
            if (addr != null) {
```

```
                    return new Fruit((String)addr.getContent());
                }
            }
        }
        return null;
    }
```

Attributes Example

The attributes example (page 161) illustrates how an instance of a DirContext class Drink is stored and subsequently looked up from the directory. When the Drink object's attributes are looked up from the directory, Context.lookup() turns those attributes into an instance of Drink.

```
    Drink d2 = (Drink) ctx.lookup("cn=favDrink");
```

This happens because of the following.

1. The service provider being used (Sun's LDAP provider) invoked Directory-Manager.getObjectInstance() and supplied to the method the data (a DirContext) that the provider read from the directory for the entry "cn=favDrink".

2. The client program identified the object factory (DrinkFactory) to use when it created the initial context.

```
    // Add property so that object factory can be found
    env.put(Context.OBJECT_FACTORIES, "DrinkFactory");
```

3. DrinkFactory.getObjectInstance() returned an instance of Drink.

DrinkFactory.getObjectInstance() first verifies that the object is intended for its factory. It does this by checking that the object is a DirContext and that it contains a "drink-Type" attribute. If this verification fails, then the method returns null. Otherwise, it gets the value of the "drinkType" attribute (in this case, "water") and uses it to create an instance of Drink.

The definition of DrinkFactory.getObjectInstance() is as follows.

```
public Object getObjectInstance(Object obj, Name name, Context ctx,
    Hashtable env, Attributes inAttrs) throws Exception {
    if (obj instanceof DirContext) {
        try {
            Attribute dt;
            if (inAttrs != null &&
                (dt=inAttrs.get("drinktype")) != null) {
                String drinkType = (String)dt.get();
                return new Drink(drinkType);
            }
        } catch (NamingException e) {
            // Debug
            System.err.println(e);
            e.printStackTrace();
        }
    }
}
```

Examples

```
            // Return null to indicate that other factories should be tried
            return null;
    }
```

Custom Object Example

The custom object example (page 175) illustrates how an instance of a user-defined class Person is stored and subsequently looked up from the directory. When the Person object's attributes are looked up from the directory, the Context.lookup() method turns these attributes into an instance of Person.

```
Person john2 = (Person) ctx.lookup("cn=John Smith");
```

This was possible because of the following.

1. The service provider being used (Sun's LDAP provider) invoked Directory-Manager.getObjectInstance() and supplied to the method the object (an LDAP context object) and attributes that the provider read from the directory for the entry "cn=John Smith".
2. The client program identified the object factory (PersonObjectFactory) to use by using an application resource file that named PersonObjectFactory as one of the object factories to try.
3. PersonObjectFactory.getObjectInstance() returned an instance of Person.

PersonObjectFactory.getObjectInstance() first verifies that the object is intended for its factory. It does this by checking that the "objectclass" attribute has a value of "person". If this verification fails, then the method returns null. Otherwise, it constructs an instance of Person by supplying the constructor values obtained from the entry's other attributes, such as the "surname" and "commonname" attributes.

The definition of PersonObjectFactory.getObjectInstance() is as follows.

```
public Object getObjectInstance(Object obj, Name name,
    Context ctx, Hashtable env, Attributes attrs) throws Exception {
    // Only interested in Attributes with "person" objectclass
    // System.out.println("object factory: " + attrs);
    Attribute oc = (attrs != null ?
        attrs.get("objectclass") : null);
    if (oc != null && oc.contains("person")) {
        Attribute attr;
        String passwd = null;

        // Extract the password
        attr = attrs.get("userPassword");
        if (attr != null) {
            passwd = new String((byte[])attr.get());
        }
        Person per = new Person(
            (String)attrs.get("sn").get(),
            (String)attrs.get("cn").get(),
            passwd,
            (attr=attrs.get("telephoneNumber")) != null ?
```

```
            (String)attr.get() : null,
        (attr=attrs.get("seealso")) != null ?
            (String)attr.get() : null,
        (attr=attrs.get("description")) != null ?
            (String)attr.get() : null);
    return per;
}
return null;
}
```

Representation in the Directory

The representation of Java objects in a naming or directory system varies depending on the system. This lesson describes the representations of Java objects in the LDAP directory and in the file system. It is intended for developers of service providers, although API users might find it interesting as well.

LDAP Directories

The details of how LDAP attributes are used to store data about Java objects are described in RFC 2713. RFC 2714 describes how CORBA object references are stored in an LDAP directory. This section offers a quick summary of those documents. It is intended primarily for developers of LDAP service providers and of object/state factories for LDAP directories. API users will generally not need this information. Service providers and object/state factories implement the details here so that API users can simply use methods such as `Context.bind()` and `Context.lookup()` as described in the **Storing Objects in the Directory** lesson (page 155) and the **Reading Objects from the Directory** (page 179) lesson.

Developers of LDAP service providers and object/state factories, as well as those needing to add the Java/CORBA schema to servers, should consult these documents in addition to reading this section.

Types of Objects

As indicated in the **State Factories** lesson (page 173), service providers are encouraged to support storing the following types of objects:

- Referenceable objects
- Reference objects
- java.io.Serializable objects
- DirContext objects

In addition to these types, Sun's LDAP provider has state factories that support storing java.rmi.Remote and CORBA objects.

The Java objects are represented in the LDAP as subclasses of the "javaObject" abstract object class. This object class defines the attributes listed in Table 5.

TABLE 5:   **Common LDAP Attributes for Storing a Java Object.**

LDAP Attribute Name	Content
javaClassName (mandatory)	The *distinguished* class name of the object
javaClassNames	All other names of classes and interfaces implemented by the object
javaCodebase	The location of the object's class files
javaDoc	The location of the object's class document
description	The textual description of the object

DirContext Objects

A DirContext object is stored straightforwardly in the directory as an LDAP entry that has attributes. In other words, an LDAP service provider extracts the attributes by using Dir-Context.getAttributes("") and stores them in the directory. When such an entry is read from the directory, it is returned as a DirContext (unless an object factory was used).

Referenceable Objects

A Referenceable object is represented in the directory by its reference (Reference-able.getReference()). A Reference is represented in the directory as a "javaNaming-Reference" object class. This object class defines the attributes listed in Table 6.

TABLE 6:   **LDAP Attributes for Storing a Referenceable Object.**

LDAP Attribute Name	Content
javaClassName (mandatory)	Reference.getClassName()
javaFactoryName	Reference.getFactoryClassName()
javaCodebase	Reference.getFactoryClassLocation()
javaReferenceAddress	Reference.get()

"javaReferenceAddress" is a multivalued attribute consisting of one or more values. Each value represents a RefAddr. Details of how a RefAddr is encoded are given in RFC 2713. See the **Tips for LDAP Users** trail (page 245) for an example.

An LDAP entry that has these attributes must include "javaObject "and "javaNaming-Reference" in its list of object classes. When these attributes are read from an LDAP entry, they are used to construct a Reference, which is then used to construct an object represented by the information in the reference.

Serializable Objects

A java.io.Serializable object is represented in the directory as a "javaSerialized-Object" object class. This object class defines the attributes listed in Table 7.

TABLE 7:   **LDAP Attributes for Storing a Serialized Object.**

LDAP Attribute Name	Content
javaClassName (mandatory)	Object.getClass().getName()
javaSerializedData (mandatory)	Serialized form of the object
javaClassNames	Names of all interfaces and classes implemented by the object
javaCodebase	URLs of directories or JAR files containing classes of the serialized object

An LDAP entry that has these attributes must include "javaObject" and "javaSerial-izedObject" in its list of object classes. When these attributes are read from an LDAP entry, they are used to reconstruct a copy of the serialized object. The content of the "javaSerial-izedData" attribute is deserialized into a java.lang.Object. If the "javaCodebase" attribute is available, then the classes needed for the deserialization are loaded from the specified codebase.

Marshalled Objects

To *marshal* an object means to record its state and codebase(s) in such a way that when the marshalled object is *unmarshalled*, a copy of the original object is obtained, possibly by automatically loading the class definitions of the object. You can marshal any object that is serializable or remote (that is, it implements the java.rmi.Remote interface).

Marshalling is like serialization, except that it also records codebases. It differs from serialization in that it treats remote objects specially. If an object is a java.rmi.Remote object, then marshalling records the remote object's stub, instead of the remote object itself. As with serialization, when an object is marshalled the entire tree of objects rooted at the object is marshalled. When it is unmarshalled, the tree is reconstructed. A marshalled object is represented by the `java.rmi.MarshalledObject` class. This class is represented in the directory as a "javaMarshalledObject" object class. This object class defines the attributes listed in Table 8.

TABLE 8:   **LDAP Attributes for Storing Marshalled Object.**

LDAP Attribute Name	Content
`javaClassName` (mandatory)	`Object.getClass().getName()` (of the unmarshalled object)
`javaSerializedData` (mandatory)	Serialized form of the marshalled object
`javaClassNames`	Names of all interfaces and classes implemented by the (unmarshalled) object

An LDAP entry that has these attributes must include "javaObject" and "javaMarshalledObject" in its list of object classes. When these attributes are read from an LDAP entry, they are used to reconstruct a copy of the marshalled object. The content of the "javaSerializedData" attribute is deserialized into a `java.rmi.MarshalledObject`. An object factory responsible for marshalled objects can then unmarshal the object by invoking `java.rmi.MarshalledObject.get()`.

CORBA Objects

The CORBA objects are represented in the LDAP as subclasses of the "corbaObject" abstract object class. This object class defines the attributes listed in Table 9.

TABLE 9:   **Common LDAP Attributes for Storing a CORBA Object.**

LDAP Attribute Name	Content
`corbaRepositoryId`	Ids of the interfaces implemented by the object
`description`	Textual description of the object

A CORBA object is stored in the directory by recording its CORBA object reference. A CORBA object reference is represented in the directory as a "corbaObjectReference" object class. This object class defines the attribute listed in Table 10.

An LDAP entry that has this attribute must include "corbaObject" and "corbaObjectReference" in its list of object classes. When this attribute is read from an LDAP entry, it is

TABLE 10: **LDAP Attributes for Storing a CORBA Object Reference.**

LDAP Attribute Name	Content
corbaObjectReference (mandatory)	Stringified form of the CORBA object reference

used to reconstruct the stringified object reference, which then is used by an object factory to get the corresponding "live" CORBA object.

Remote Objects

A `java.rmi.Remote` object that uses the JRMP protocol is stored in the directory either as a `Reference` that contains an RMI URL or as a marshalled object. A `java.rmi.Remote` object that uses the IIOP protocol is stored in the directory as a CORBA object; that is, the CORBA object reference of the object's CORBA tie is stored.

Schema

The Java schema and the CORBA schema that you need to add to your directory are included with this tutorial (**Appendix**). See RFC 2713 and RFC 2714 for details.

File System

Sun's file system service provider supports storing Java objects in the file system. Specifically, it supports the binding of `Referenceable` objects. Such objects are stored as a set of properties in a file called `.bindings`. The parent directory that contains this `.bindings` file is the parent *context* of these bindings.

For example, if you have a file directory called `food`, then you can add a binding to it as follows:

```
ctx.bind("food/fav", new Fruit("orange"));
```

The binding for `"fav"` will be stored in the file `food/.bindings`. You can subsequently look up the object

```
Fruit f = (Fruit) ctx.lookup("food/fav");
```

See **The Basics** trail (page 53) for more examples.

Tips for LDAP Users

The lessons in the **LDAP** trail provide details on the mapping between the LDAP and the JNDI. They also give hints and tips for accessing the LDAP service through the JNDI.

- The **Comparison of the LDAP and JNDI Models** lesson (page 207) gives an overview of the LDAP and describes the differences and similarities between the JNDI and the LDAP.
- The **Security** lesson (page 221) shows how to use different security authentication mechanisms and SSL (Secure Socket Layer) to access the LDAP service.
- The **Miscellaneous** lesson (page 237) shows how to perform various tasks such as reading nonstring attributes and dealing with LDAP aliases and URLs.
- The **Searches** lesson (page 249) explains search filters in more detail. It also explains how the LDAP "compare" operation relates to the JNDI search methods and how the LDAP "search" operation is related to other JNDI methods.
- The **Referrals** lesson (page 259) explains how LDAP referrals work and how you can use them from within the JNDI.
- The **Schema** lesson (page 271) describes schema information that is available from the LDAP and how it can be accessed from the JNDI.
- The **Controls and Extensions** lesson (page 289) describes how to use LDAP controls and extensions.
- The **Frequently Asked Questions** lesson (page 305) answers many of the questions that you might have when using the JNDI to access the LDAP service.

Before you go on: The **Preparations** lesson (page 45) described how to set up the software required to use the JNDI to run the examples in this tutorial. The **Directory Operations** lesson (page 59) explained how to set the `Context.INITIAL_CONTEXT_FACTORY` and `Context.PROVIDER_URL` environment properties to contact the LDAP server that you are using. This trail contains more LDAP-specific examples and requires that additional data be added to the LDAP server (such as for setting up aliases and referrals). To do this, add the entries found in `ldaptrail.ldif`, available both on the accompanying CD and from the JNDI Web Site, to the LDAP server that you set up according to the **Preparations** lesson. This task is typically performed by the directory server's administrator.

Comparison of the LDAP and JNDI Models

The *Lightweight Directory Access Protocol* (LDAP) is a network protocol for accessing directories. It is based on the *X.500*, a CCITT standard for directory services that is part of the OSI suite of services.

This lesson describes the differences and similarities in the LDAP and JNDI models. It begins by giving an overview of the X.500. Then it describes the LDAP (v2 and v3) and its related standards. The remainder of the lesson discusses how LDAP concepts are represented in the JNDI, including how LDAP operations and error codes map to JNDI methods and exceptions.

X.500 Overview

The X.500 directory service is a global directory service. Its components cooperate to manage information about objects such as countries, organizations, people, machines, and so on in a worldwide scope. It provides the capability to look up information by name (a *white-pages* service) and to browse and search for information (a *yellow-pages* service).

The information is held in a *directory information base* (DIB). Entries in the DIB are arranged in a tree structure called the *directory information tree* (DIT). Each entry is a named object and consists of a set of attributes. Each attribute has a defined attribute type and one or more values. The directory schema defines the mandatory and optional attributes for each class of object (called the *object class*). Each named object may have one or more object classes associated with it.

The X.500 namespace is hierarchical. An entry is unambiguously identified by a *distinguished name* (DN). A distinguished name is the concatenation of selected attributes from each entry, called the *relative distinguished name* (RDN), in the tree along a path leading from the root down to the named entry.

Users of the X.500 directory may (subject to access control) interrogate and modify the entries and attributes in the DIB.

For more information on the X.500, refer to the CCITT X.500 (1988/1993)/ISO Directory.

Naming Convention

Although the concepts of distinguished names and relative distinguished names are core to the X.500 model, the X.500 standard itself does not define any string representation for names. What is communicated between the X.500 components is the *structural form* of names. The reasoning behind this is that the standard is sufficient to allow different implementations to interoperate. String names are never communicated between different implementations. Instead, they are necessary only for interaction with end-users. For that purpose, the standard allows any representation, not necessarily only string representations.

Systems that are based on the X.500, such as the LDAP, the DCE Directory, Novell's NDS, and Microsoft's Active Directory, each define its own string representation. For example, in the LDAP, a DN's RDNs are arranged right to left, separated by the comma character (","). Here's an example of a name that starts with "c=us" at the top and leads to "cn=Rosanna Lee" at the leaf.

```
cn=Rosanna Lee, ou=People, o=Sun, c=us
```

Here's an example of the same name using the string representation of the DCE Directory and Microsoft's Active Directory.

```
/c=us/o=Sun/ou=People/cn=Rosanna Lee
```

The convention for these systems is that RDNs are ordered left to right and separated by the forward slash character ("/").

Protocols

The X.500 standard defines a protocol (among others) for a client application to access the X.500 directory. Called the *Directory Access Protocol* (DAP), it is layered on top of the Open Systems Interconnection (OSI) protocol stack.

Application Programming Interfaces

The X.500 standard itself does not define an API for accessing the directory. Again, the X.500 standard is mainly concerned with interoperability between directory clients and directory servers and between different directory servers.

One standard API that has been defined for the X.500 is the X/Open Specifications API to Directory Services (XDS), a C language-based API that client programs use for accessing X.500 directories.

LDAP v2

The Internet community, recognizing the need for an X.500-like service but faced with different underlying network infrastructure (TCP/IP instead of OSI), designed a new protocol based on the X.500 DAP, called *Lightweight* DAP, or LDAP. RFC 1777 defines what is now called *version 2* of the LDAP (or LDAP v2).

The goal of the LDAP v2 was a protocol that could be easily implemented, with special focus on being able to build small and simple clients. One way that it attempted to achieve simplification was to use a lot of strings and to minimize wherever possible the use of structures. DNs, for example, are represented in the protocol as strings, as are attribute type names and many attribute values.

The protocol consists of the client's sending requests to the server, to which the server responds, though not necessarily in the same order in which the requests were sent. Each request is tagged with an ID so that requests and responses can be matched. The protocol works over either TCP or UDP, although the TCP version is most commonly used.

Because of the focus on clients, the LDAP community also defined standards for the string representation of DNs (RFC 1779), search filters (RFC 1960), and attribute syntaxes (RFC 1778), for a C language-based API (RFC 1823), and for the format of URLs for accessing LDAP services (RFC 1959).

Operations

Table 11 lists the operations defined in the LDAP v2.

TABLE 11:   **LDAP v2 Operations.**

Operation	Description
bind	Used to start a connection with the LDAP server. The LDAP is a connection-oriented protocol. The client specifies the protocol version and the client authentication information.
unbind	Used to terminate the connection with the LDAP server.
add	Used to add a new entry. The client specifies the name of the new entry and a set of attributes for the new entry.
delete	Used to remove an existing entry. The client specifies the name of the entry to remove.

Continued

TABLE 11:   LDAP v2 Operations.

Operation	Description
search	Used to search the directory. The client specifies the starting point (*base object*) of the search, the search scope (either the object only, its children, or the subtree rooted at the object), and a *search filter* (RFC 1960). It can also supply other information to control the search, such as the names of the attributes to return and the size and time limits. The search results consist of LDAP entries (and the attributes requested) that satisfy the filter.
modify	Used to modify an existing entry. The client specifies the name of the entry to be modified and a list of modifications. Each modification consists of an attribute and information regarding whether its values are to be added, deleted, or replaced.
modify RDN	Used to change the RDN of the last component of an existing entry (that is, to assign the entry a new name in the same context). The client specifies the DN for the entry and the new RDN.
compare	Used to test whether an entry has an attribute/value pair. The client specifies the name of the entry and the name and value to check.
abandon	Used to terminate an outstanding request.

LDAP v2 Compared to the X.500 Standard

At a very high level, the LDAP v2 looks a lot like the X.500. Both define a hierarchical DIT consisting of entries having DNs. Each entry consists of a set of attributes. Both directories can be searched by using search filters that contain (at the structural level) more or less the same elements. The operations defined by both protocols (such as "search") are very similar.

Of course, many implementation differences exist between the X.500 and the LDAP. Most notably, their underlying protocol stacks are different. The X.500 protocols sit on top of the session/presentation layer of the OSI stack, whereas the LDAP runs on top of TCP. Furthermore, the X.500 standard is comprehensive, with details specified to maximize interoperability in client/server and server/server interactions. By contrast, the LDAP v2 standard, because of its goals, is much more minimal.

LDAP v3

The LDAP v3 (RFC 2251) is designed to address some of the limitations of the LDAP v2 in the areas of internationalization, authentication, referral, and deployment. It also allows new features to be added to the protocol without also requiring changes to the protocol. This is done by using *extensions* and *controls*.

Internationalization

Internationalization is addressed via an international character set (ISO 10646) to represent protocol elements that are strings (such as DNs). Version 3 also differs from version 2 in that it uses UTF-8 to encode its strings.

Authentication

The LDAP v2 supported three types of authentication: anonymous, simple (clear-text password), and Kerberos v4.

The LDAP v3 uses the Simple Authentication and Security Layer (SASL) authentication framework (RFC 2222) to allow different authentication mechanisms to be used with the LDAP. SASL specifies a challenge-response protocol in which data is exchanged between the client and the server for the purposes of authentication.

Several SASL mechanisms are currently defined: DIGEST-MD5, CRAM-MD5, Anonymous, External, S/Key, GSSAPI, and Kerberos v4. An LDAP v3 client can use any of these SASL mechanisms, provided that the LDAP v3 server supports them. Moreover, new (yet-to-be defined) SASL mechanisms can be used without changes to the LDAP having to be made.

Referrals

A *referral* is information that a server sends back to the client indicating that the requested information can be found at another location (possibly at another server). In the LDAP v2, servers are supposed to handle referrals and not return them to the client. This is because handling referrals can be very complicated and therefore would result in more-complicated clients. As servers were built and deployed, referrals were found to be useful, but not many servers supported server-side referral handling. So a way was found to retrofit the protocol to allow it to return referrals. This was done by placing the referral inside of the error message of a "partial result" error response.

The LDAP v3 has explicit support for referrals and allows servers to return the referrals directly to the client.

Deployment

A common protocol such as the LDAP is useful for ensuring that all of the directory clients and servers "speak the same language." When many different directory client applications and directory servers are deployed in a network, it also is very useful for all of these entities to talk about the same objects. For example, if applications App1 and App2 both need to associate data with a user, then it makes sense for the directory to have a common notion of *user* that both applications can use rather than each going off and defining its own.

A *directory schema* specifies, among other things, the types of objects that a directory may have and the mandatory and optional attributes that each type of object may have. The LDAP v3 defines a schema (RFC 2252 and RFC 2256) based on the X.500 standard for common objects found in the network, such as countries, localities, organizations, users/persons, groups, and devices. It also defines a way for a client application to access the server's schema so that it can find out the types of objects and attributes that a particular server supports.

The LDAP v3 further defines a set of syntaxes for representing attribute values (RFC 2252).

Extensions

In addition to the repertoire of predefined operations, such as "search" and "modify," the LDAP v3 defines an "extended" operation. The "extended" operation takes a request as an argument and returns a response. The request contains an identifier that identifies the request and the arguments of the request. The response contains the results of performing the request. The pair of "extended" operation request/response is called an *extension*. For example, there can be an extension for Start TLS, which is a request for the client to the server to activate the Start TLS protocol.

These extensions can be standard (defined by the LDAP community) or proprietary (defined by a particular directory vendor).

Controls

Another way to add new features is by using a *control*. The LDAP v3 allows the behavior of any operation to be modified through the use of controls. Any number of controls may be sent along with an operation, and any number of controls may be returned with its results. For example, you can send a Sort control along with a "search" operation that tells the server to sort the results of the search according to the "name" attribute.

Like extensions, such controls can be standard or proprietary.

Additional Differences

Table 12 lists additional differences between the LDAP v3 and v2.

LDAP v3 Compared to the X.500 Standard

The LDAP v3 has many more features than the LDAP v2 and therefore departs from one of original goals of the LDAP v2—to have small and simple clients. The LDAP v3 supports a larger subset of the X.500 features than does the LDAP v2.

TABLE 12: **Differences between LDAP v2 and LDAP v3.**

Feature	Description
bind	The "bind" operation is optional and can be sent multiple times during a session. If a client requests an operation to be performed without doing an explicit bind, then the client is treated as "anonymous." The client can also send a "bind" operation in the middle of a session to change the client's credentials (without sending an unbind first).
modify DN	The "modify DN" operation allows you to rename an entry to any other part of the namespace. (That is, you are not restricted to the same context, as in the case of the LDAP v2.) The client specifies the DN of the entry, the new RDN, and the (optional) DN of the new parent for the new RDN. If the optional DN of the new parent is not specified, then the parent of the original entry is used.
search filter	The LDAP v3 defines an updated search filter representation (RFC 2254) that supports the ISO 10646 character set, supports extensible matches, and uses the UTF-8 encoding.
operational attributes	*Operational attributes* are maintained by servers for administrative purposes. They are not visible to client applications unless those applications explicitly ask for them. They are used to hold such information as time stamps and a *subschema subentry* (which is a pointer to schema information about the entry). The LDAP v3 defines these operational attributes and subschema entries and allows clients to access them.
LDAP URL	The LDAP v3 defines an updated LDAP URL format (RFC 2255) to support extensions.

JNDI Mapping

Both the JNDI and LDAP models define a hierarchical namespace in which you name objects. Each object in the namespace may have attributes that can be used to search for the object. At this high level, the two models are similar, so it is not surprising that the JNDI maps well to the LDAP.

This section discusses how the LDAP maps to the JNDI. Some topics, such as referrals and schema, are discussed only briefly here and in more detail in other lessons in this trail.

Models

You can think of an LDAP entry as a JNDI `DirContext`. Each LDAP entry contains a name and a set of attributes, as well as an optional set of child entries. For example, the LDAP entry `"o=JNDITutorial"` may have as its attributes `"objectclass"` and `"o"`, and it may have as its children `"ou=Groups"` and `"ou=People"`.

In the JNDI, the LDAP entry "o=JNDITutorial" is represented as a context with the name "o=JNDITutorial" that has two subcontexts, named: "ou=Groups" and "ou=People". An LDAP entry's attributes are represented by the Attributes interface, whereas individual attributes are represented by the Attribute interface. See the next part of this lesson for details on how the LDAP operations are accessed through the JNDI.

Federation

Whereas the LDAP model covers a single namespace, the JNDI model deals with multiple namespaces linked via *federation*. The LDAP namespace is but one of many namespaces that can be accessed through the JNDI.

Names

As a result of federation, the names that you supply to the JNDI's context methods can span multiple namespaces. These are called *composite names*. When using the JNDI to access an LDAP service, you should be aware that the forward slash character ("/") in a string name has special meaning to the JNDI. If the LDAP entry's name contains this character, then you need to escape it with the backslash character ("\"). For example, an LDAP entry with the name "cn=O/R" must be presented as the string "cn=O\\/R" to the JNDI context methods. See the **What's in a Name?** lesson (page 90) for details.

LDAP names as they are used in the protocol are always fully qualified names that identify entries that start from the root of the LDAP namespace (as defined by the server). Following are some examples of fully qualified LDAP names.

```
cn=John Smith, ou=Marketing, o=Some Corporation, c=gb

cn=Ted Geisel, ou=People, o=JNDITutorial
```

In the JNDI, however, names are always *relative*; that is, you always name an object relative to a context. For example, you can name the entry "cn=Ted Geisel" relative to the context named "ou=People, o=JNDITutorial". Or you can name the entry "cn=Ted Geisel, ou=People" relative to the context named "o=JNDITutorial". Or, you can create an initial context that points at the root of the LDAP server's namespace and name the entry "cn=Ted Geisel, ou=People, o=JNDITutorial".

In the JNDI, you can also use LDAP URLs to name LDAP entries. See the LDAP URL discussion in the **Miscellaneous** lesson (page 246).

Searches

One of the most important aspects of the LDAP is its search model. You can search for entries in an LDAP server by specifying a search filter. The JNDI's DirContext interface supports

LDAP-style searches and search filters. The results of searches are returned in an enumeration of `SearchResult`. Searches are discussed in detail in the **Searches** lesson (page 249).

Referrals

LDAP-style referrals are supported with the `ReferralException`. Referrals are discussed in detail in the **Referrals** lesson (page 259).

Schema

The JNDI contains methods in the `DirContext` and `Attribute` interfaces for retrieving an LDAP entry's or an LDAP attribute's schema. The schema is discussed in detail in the **Schema** lesson (page 271).

Controls and Extensions

LDAP v3-style controls and extensions are supported using the `javax.naming.ldap` package and are described in detail in the **Controls and Extensions** lesson (page 289).

Java Objects

Beyond basic LDAP functionality such as accessing LDAP entries and searching the directory, the JNDI also supports the notion of Java objects' being integrated into the directory. Thus you can think of the LDAP directory as a repository for Java objects, that is, as an integral part of the environment in which you develop and deploy your Java applications. This topic is discussed in detail in the **Java Objects and the Directory** trail (page 151).

LDAP Operations and JNDI Mapping

The LDAP defines a set of operations or requests (see RFC 2251). In the JNDI, these map to operations on the `DirContext` and `LdapContext` interfaces (which are subinterfaces of `Context`). For example, when a caller invokes a `DirContext` method, the LDAP service provider implements the method by sending LDAP requests to the LDAP server.

Table 13 shows how operations in the LDAP correspond to JNDI methods.

TABLE 13:   Comparison of LDAP and JNDI Operations.

LDAP Operation	Corresponding JNDI Methods
bind	The corresponding way of creating an initial connection to the LDAP server in the JNDI is the creation of an `InitialDirContext`. When the application creates an initial context, it supplies client authentication information via environment properties. To change that authentication information for an existing context, use `Context.addToEnvironment()` and `Context.removeFromEnvironment()`.
unbind	`Context.close()` is used to free resources used by a context. It differs from the LDAP "unbind" operation in that within a given service provider implementation, resources can be shared among contexts, so closing one context won't free all of the resources if those resources are being shared with another context. Make sure to close all contexts if your intent is to free all resources.
search	The corresponding method in the JNDI is the overloading of `DirContext.search()` that accepts a *search filter* (RFC 2254). See **The Basics** trail (page 65) for an example. Also, see the **Searches** lesson (page 249) for more examples.
modify	The corresponding method in the JNDI is the overloading of `DirContext.modifyAttributes()` that accepts an array of `DirContext.ModificationItems`. See **The Basics** trail (page 62) for an example.
add	The corresponding methods in the JNDI are `DirContext.bind()` and `DirContext.createSubcontext()`. You can use either to add a new LDAP entry. Using `bind()`, you can specify not only a set of attributes for the new entry but also a Java object to be added along with the attributes. See **The Basics** trail (page 70) for examples of both.
delete	The corresponding methods in the JNDI are `Context.unbind()` and `Context.destroySubcontext()`. You can use either to remove an LDAP entry.
modify DN/RDN	The corresponding method in the JNDI is `Context.rename()`. See the **Miscellaneous** lesson (page 244) for more details.
compare	The corresponding operation in the JNDI is a suitably constrained `DirContext.search()`. See the **Searches** lesson (page 253) for an example.
abandon	When you close a context, all of its outstanding requests are abandoned. Similarly, when you close a `NamingEnumeration`, the corresponding LDAP "search" request is abandoned.
extended operation	The corresponding method in the JNDI is `LdapContext.extendedOperation()`. See the **Controls and Extensions** lesson (page 301) for more details.

LDAP Status Codes and JNDI Exceptions

The LDAP defines a set of status codes that are returned with LDAP responses sent by the LDAP server (see RFC 2251). In the JNDI, error conditions are indicated as checked exceptions that are subclasses of `NamingException`. See **The Basics** trail (page 47) for an overview of the JNDI exception class hierarchy.

The LDAP service provider translates the LDAP status code that it receives from the LDAP server to the appropriate subclass of `NamingException`. Table 14 shows the mapping between LDAP status codes and JNDI exceptions.

TABLE 14: **Mapping LDAP Status Codes to JNDI Exceptions.**

LDAP Status Code	Meaning	Exception or Action
0	Success	Report success.
1	Operations error	`NamingException`
2	Protocol error	`CommunicationException`
3	Time limit exceeded.	`TimeLimitExceededException`
4	Size limit exceeded.	`SizeLimitExceededException`
5	Compared false.	Used by `DirContext.search()`. Does not generate an exception.
6	Compared true.	Used by `DirContext.search()`. Does not generate an exception.
7	Authentication method not supported.	`AuthenticationNotSupportedException`
8	Strong authentication required.	`AuthenticationNotSupportedException`
9	Partial results being returned.	If the environment property `"java.naming.referral"` is set to `"throw"` or the contents of the error do not contain a referral, then throw a `PartialResultException`. Otherwise, use the contents to build a referral.
		Continued

TABLE 14: Mapping LDAP Status Codes to JNDI Exceptions.

LDAP Status Code	Meaning	Exception or Action
10	Referral encountered.	If the environment property `"java.naming.referral"` is set to `"ignore"`, then ignore. If the property is set to `"throw"`, then throw a `ReferralException`. If the property is set to `"follow"`, then the LDAP provider will process the referral. If the `"java.naming.ldap.referral.limit"` property has been exceeded, then throw a `LimitExceededException`.
11	Administrative limit exceeded.	`LimitExceededException`
12	Unavailable critical extension requested.	`OperationNotSupportedException`
13	Confidentiality required.	`AuthenticationNotSupportedException`
14	SASL bind in progress.	Used internally by the LDAP provider during authentication.
16	No such attribute exists.	`NoSuchAttributeException`
17	An undefined attribute type.	`InvalidAttributeIdentifierException`
18	Inappropriate matching	`InvalidSearchFilterException`
19	A constraint violation.	`InvalidAttributeValueException`
20	An attribute or value already in use.	`AttributeInUseException`
21	An invalid attribute syntax.	`InvalidAttributeValueException`
32	No such object exists.	`NameNotFoundException`
33	Alias problem	`NamingException`
34	An invalid DN syntax.	`InvalidNameException`
35	Is a leaf.	Used by the LDAP provider; usually doesn't generate an exception.
36	Alias dereferencing problem	`NamingException`
48	Inappropriate authentication	`AuthenticationNotSupportedException`
49	Invalid credentials	`AuthenticationException`
50	Insufficient access rights	`NoPermissionException`
51	Busy	`ServiceUnavailableException`
52	Unavailable	`ServiceUnavailableException`
53	Unwilling to perform	`OperationNotSupportedException`
54	Loop detected.	`NamingException`

TABLE 14:   **Mapping LDAP Status Codes to JNDI Exceptions.**

LDAP Status Code	Meaning	Exception or Action
64	Naming violation	`InvalidNameException`
65	Object class violation	`SchemaViolationException`
66	Not allowed on a nonleaf.	`ContextNotEmptyException`
67	Not allowed on RDN.	`SchemaViolationException`
68	Entry already exists.	`NameAlreadyBoundException`
69	Object class modifications prohibited.	`SchemaViolationException`
71	Affects multiple DSAs.	`NamingException`
80	Other	`NamingException`

Security

An LDAP service provides a generic directory service. It can be used to store information of all sorts, from information about entities on the network, such as users, printers, and computers, to locations of file systems, to application configuration information. All LDAP servers have some system in place for controlling who can read and update the information in the directory. For example, although some of the information in the directory might be publicly readable by all, most of that information probably cannot be updated by all. Other parts of the directory might be readable/updatable only by those to whom the directory administrator has granted appropriate access.

To access the LDAP service, the LDAP client first must authenticate itself to the service. That is, it must tell the LDAP server who is going to be accessing the data so that the server can decide what the client is allowed to see and do. If the client authenticates successfully to the server, then when the server subsequently receives a request from the client, it will check whether the client is allowed to perform the request. This process is called *access control*.

The LDAP standard has proposed ways in which LDAP clients can authenticate to LDAP servers (RFC 2251 and `draft-ietf-ldapext-authmeth-04.txt`). These are discussed in general in the **LDAP Authentication** section (page 222) and **Authentication Mechanisms** section (page 224). This lesson also contains descriptions of how to use the anonymous, simple, and SASL authentication mechanisms.

Access control is supported in different ways by different LDAP server implementations. It is not discussed in this lesson.

Another security aspect of LDAP service is the way in which requests and responses are communicated between the client and the server. Many LDAP servers support the use of secure channels to communicate with clients, for example to send and receive attributes that contain secrets, such as passwords and keys. LDAP servers use SSL for this purpose. This lesson also shows how to use SSL with the LDAP service provider.

LDAP Authentication

In the LDAP, authentication information is supplied in the "bind" operation. In LDAP v2, a client initiates a connection with the LDAP server by sending the server a "bind" operation that contains the authentication information.

In the LDAP v3, the "bind" operation serves the same purpose, but it is optional. A client that sends an LDAP request without doing a "bind" is treated as an *anonymous client* (see the **Anonymous Authentication** section (page 225) for details). In the LDAP v3, this operation may be sent at any time, possibly more than once, during the connection. A client can send a "bind" request in the middle of a connection to change its identity. If the request is successful, then all outstanding requests that use the old identity on the connection are discarded and the connection is associated with the new identity.

The authentication information supplied in the "bind" operation depends on the *authentication mechanism* that the client chooses. See the next section for a discussion of the authentication mechanism.

Authenticating to the LDAP by Using the JNDI

In the JNDI, authentication information is specified in environment properties. When you create an initial context by using the `InitialDirContext` class (or its superclass or subclass), you supply a set of environment properties, some of which might contain authentication information. You can use the following environment properties to specify the authentication information.

- `Context.SECURITY_AUTHENTICATION` (`"java.naming.security.authentication"`).
  Specifies the authentication mechanism to use. For the Sun LDAP service provider, this can be one of the following strings: `"none"`, `"simple"`, or *sasl_mech*, where *sasl_mech* is a space-separated list of SASL mechanism names. See the next section for a description of these strings.
- `Context.SECURITY_PRINCIPAL` (`"java.naming.security.principal"`).
  Specifies the name of the user/program doing the authentication and depends on the value of the `Context.SECURITY_AUTHENTICATION` property. See the next few sections in this lesson for details and examples.
- `Context.SECURITY_CREDENTIALS` (`"java.naming.security.credentials"`).
  Specifies the credentials of the user/program doing the authentication and depends on the value of the `Context.SECURITY_AUTHENTICATION` property. See the next few sections in this lesson for details and examples.

When the initial context is created, the underlying LDAP service provider extracts the authentication information from these environment properties and uses the LDAP "bind" operation to pass them to the server.

The following example shows how, by using a simple clear-text password, a client authenticates to an LDAP server.

```
// Set up the environment for creating the initial context
Hashtable env = new Hashtable();
env.put(Context.INITIAL_CONTEXT_FACTORY,
    "com.sun.jndi.ldap.LdapCtxFactory");
env.put(Context.PROVIDER_URL, "ldap://localhost:389/o=JNDITutorial");

// Authenticate as S. User and the password "mysecret"
env.put(Context.SECURITY_AUTHENTICATION, "simple");
env.put(Context.SECURITY_PRINCIPAL,
    "cn=S. User, ou=NewHires, o=JNDITutorial");
env.put(Context.SECURITY_CREDENTIALS, "mysecret");

// Create the initial context
DirContext ctx = new InitialDirContext(env);

// ... do something useful with ctx
```

Using Different Authentication Information for a Context

If you want to use different authentication information for an existing context, then you can use `Context.addToEnvironment()` and `Context.removeFromEnvironment()` to update the environment properties that contain the authentication information. Subsequent invocations of methods on the context will use the new authentication information to communicate with the server.

The following example shows how the authentication information of a context is changed to "none" after the context has been created.

```
// Authenticate as S. User and the password "mysecret"
env.put(Context.SECURITY_AUTHENTICATION, "simple");
env.put(Context.SECURITY_PRINCIPAL,
    "cn=S. User, ou=NewHires, o=JNDITutorial");
env.put(Context.SECURITY_CREDENTIALS, "mysecret");

// Create the initial context
DirContext ctx = new InitialDirContext(env);

// ... do something useful with ctx

// Change to using no authentication
ctx.addToEnvironment(Context.SECURITY_AUTHENTICATION, "none");

// ... do something useful with ctx
```

Authentication Failures

Authentication can fail for a number of reasons. For example, if you supply incorrect authentication information, such as an incorrect password or principal name, then an `AuthenticationException` is thrown.

Here's an example that is a variation of the previous example. This time, an incorrect password causes the authentication to fail.

```
// Authenticate as S. User and give an incorrect password
env.put(Context.SECURITY_AUTHENTICATION, "simple");
env.put(Context.SECURITY_PRINCIPAL,
    "cn=S. User, ou=NewHires, o=JNDITutorial");
env.put(Context.SECURITY_CREDENTIALS, "notmysecret");
```

This produces the following output.

```
javax.naming.AuthenticationException: [LDAP: Invalid Credentials]
    at java.lang.Throwable.<init>(Compiled Code)
    at java.lang.Exception.<init>(Compiled Code)
      ...
```

Because different servers support different authentication mechanisms, you might request an authentication mechanism that the server does not support. In this case, an `Authentica-tionNotSupportedException` will be thrown.

Here's an example that is a variation of the previous example. This time, an unsupported authentication mechanism ("custom") causes the authentication to fail.

```
// Authenticate as S. User and the password "mysecret"
env.put(Context.SECURITY_AUTHENTICATION, "custom");
env.put(Context.SECURITY_PRINCIPAL,
    "cn=S. User, ou=NewHires, o=JNDITutorial");
env.put(Context.SECURITY_CREDENTIALS, "mysecret");
```

This produces the following output.

```
javax.naming.AuthenticationNotSupportedException: Unsupported\
    value for java.naming.security.authentication property.
    at java.lang.Throwable.<init>(Compiled Code)
    at java.lang.Exception.<init>(Compiled Code)
    at javax.naming.NamingException.<init>(Compiled Code)
      ...
```

Authentication Mechanisms

Different versions of the LDAP support different types of authentication. The LDAP v2 defines three types of authentication: anonymous, simple (clear-text password), and Kerberos v4.

The LDAP v3 supports anonymous, simple, and SASL authentication. SASL is the Simple Authentication and Security Layer (RFC 2222). It specifies a challenge-response protocol in which data is exchanged between the client and the server for the purposes of authentication and establishment of a security layer on which to carry out subsequent communication. By using SASL, the LDAP can support any type of authentication agreed upon by the LDAP client and server.

This lesson contains descriptions of how to authenticate by using anonymous, simple, and SASL authentication.

Specifying the Authentication Mechanism

The authentication mechanism is specified by using the `Context.SECURITY_AUTHENTICATION` environment property. The property may have one of the values given in Table 15.

TABLE 15:   Values for the "java.naming.security.authentication" Property.

Property Value	Description
sasl_mech	A space-separated list of SASL mechanism names. Use one of the SASL mechanisms listed (e.g., "`CRAM-MD5`" means to use the CRAM-MD5 SASL mechanism described in RFC 2195).
`none`	Use no authentication (anonymous).
`simple`	Use weak authentication (clear-text password).

The Default Mechanism

If the client does not specify any authentication environment properties, then the default authentication mechanism is "`none`". The client will then be treated as an anonymous client.

If the client specifies authentication information without explicitly specifying the `Context.SECURITY_AUTHENTICATION` property, then the default authentication mechanism is "`simple`".

Anonymous Authentication

As just stated, the default authentication mechanism is "`none`" if the client does not specify any authentication environment properties. If the client sets the `Context.SECURITY_AUTHENTICATION` environment property to "`none`", then the authentication mechanism is "`none`" and all other authentication environment properties are ignored. You would want to do this explicitly only to ensure that any other authentication properties that might have been set are ignored. In either case, the client will be treated as an anonymous client. This means that the server does not know or care who the client is and will allow the client to access (read and update) any data that has been configured to be accessible by any unauthenticated client.

Because none of the directory examples in **The Basics** trail (page 59) set any of the authentication environment properties, all of them use anonymous authentication.

Here is an example that explicitly sets the `Context.SECURITY_AUTHENTICATION` property to "`none`" (even though doing this is not strictly necessary because that is the default).

```
// Set up the environment for creating the initial context
Hashtable env = new Hashtable();
env.put(Context.INITIAL_CONTEXT_FACTORY,
```

```
        "com.sun.jndi.ldap.LdapCtxFactory");
env.put(Context.PROVIDER_URL, "ldap://localhost:389/o=JNDITutorial");

// Use anonymous authentication
env.put(Context.SECURITY_AUTHENTICATION, "none");

// Create the initial context
DirContext ctx = new InitialDirContext(env);

// ... do something useful with ctx
```

Simple Authentication

Simple authentication consists of sending the LDAP server the fully qualified DN of the client (user) and the client's clear-text password (see RFC 2251). This mechanism has security problems because the password can be read from the network. To avoid exposing the password in this way, you can use the simple authentication mechanism within an encrypted channel (such as SSL), provided that this is supported by the LDAP server.

Both the LDAP v2 and v3 support simple authentication.

To use the simple authentication mechanism, you must set the three authentication environment properties as follows.

- Context.SECURITY_AUTHENTICATION. Set to "simple".
- Context.SECURITY_PRINCIPAL. Set to the fully qualified DN of the entity that is being authenticated (e.g., "cn=S. User, ou=NewHires, o=JNDITutorial"). It is of type java.lang.String.
- Context.SECURITY_CREDENTIALS. Set to the password of the principal (e.g., "mysecret"). It is of type java.lang.String, char array (char[]), or byte array (byte[]). If the password is a java.lang.String or a char array, then it is encoded by using UTF-8 for the LDAP v3 and ISO-Latin-1 for the LDAP v2 for transmission to the server. If the password is a byte[], then it is transmitted as is to the server.

See the example earlier in this section that illustrates how to use simple authentication.

Note: If you supply an empty string, an empty byte/char array, or null to the Context.SECURITY_CREDENTIALS environment property, then the authentication mechanism will be "none". This is because the LDAP requires the password to be nonempty for simple authentication. The protocol automatically converts the authentication to "none" if a password is not supplied.

SASL Authentication

Software Requirement: When using the SASL examples, you need the `ldapbp.jar` and `jaas.jar` archive files in addition to the software requirements listed in the **Preparations** lesson (page 41). These can be downloaded as part of the LDAP service provider from the JNDI Web site. They are also included on the CD that accompanies this book.

The LDAP v3 protocol uses the SASL to support *pluggable authentication*. This means that the LDAP client and server can be configured to negotiate and use possibly nonstandard and/or customized mechanisms for authentication, depending on the level of protection desired by the client and the server. The LDAP v2 protocol does not support the SASL.

Several SASL mechanisms are currently defined:

- Anonymous (RFC 2245)
- CRAM-MD5 (RFC 2195)
- DIGEST-MD5
- External (RFC 2222)
- GSSAPI mechanisms
- Kerberos v4 (RFC 2222)
- Kerberos v5
- SecurID
- Secure Remote Password
- S/Key (RFC 2222)
- X.509

SASL Mechanisms Supported by LDAP Servers

Of the mechanisms on the previous list, popular LDAP servers (such as those from Netscape and Innosoft) currently support CRAM-MD5 and External. An Internet-draft (`draft-ietf-ldapext-authmeth-04.txt`) proposes the use of DIGEST-MD5 as the mandatory default mechanism for LDAP v3 servers.

Here is a simple program for finding out the list of SASL mechanisms that an LDAP server supports.

```
// Create the initial context
DirContext ctx = new InitialDirContext();

// Read supportedSASLMechanisms from the root DSE
Attributes attrs = ctx.getAttributes("ldap://localhost:389",
    new String[]{"supportedSASLMechanisms"});
```

Here is the output produced by running this program against a server that supports the External SASL mechanism.

```
{supportedsaslmechanisms=supportedSASLMechanisms: EXTERNAL}
```

Specifying the Authentication Mechanism

To use a particular SASL mechanism, you specify its Internet Assigned Numbers Authority (IANA)-registered mechanism name in the `Context.SECURITY_AUTHENTICATION` environment property. You can also specify a list of mechanisms for the LDAP provider to try. This is done by specifying an ordered list of space-separated mechanism names. The LDAP provider will use the first mechanism for which it finds an implementation.

Here's an example that asks the LDAP provider to try to get the implementation for the DIGEST-MD5 mechanism and, if that's not available, use the one for CRAM-MD5:

```
env.put(Context.SECURITY_AUTHENTICATION, "DIGEST-MD5 CRAM-MD5");
```

You might get this list of authentication mechanisms from the user of your application. Or you might get it by asking the LDAP server, via a call similar to that shown previously. The LDAP provider itself does not consult the server for this information. It simply attempts to locate and use the implementation of the specified mechanisms.

Sun's LDAP provider has built-in support for the CRAM-MD5 and External SASL mechanisms; you can add support for additional mechanisms. See the **Using Arbitrary SASL Mechanisms** section (page 232).

Specifying the "Bind" Distinguished Name

SASL authentication consists of the client and the server exchanging SASL messages embedded inside LDAP "bind" requests and responses. The "bind" request contains a name field, which is the DN of the directory object that the client wishes to authenticate as. The field's value may be `null` (that is, not specified), depending on the SASL mechanism (which may embed the DN within the credentials that it exchanges with the server).

The value of the `Context.SECURITY_PRINCIPAL` environment property is used as the "bind" DN.

Specifying Input for the Authentication Mechanism

Some mechanisms, such as External, require no additional input—the mechanism name alone is sufficient for the authentication to proceed. The External example (page 234) shows how to use the External SASL mechanism.

Most other mechanisms require some additional input. Depending on the mechanism, the type of input might vary. Following are some common inputs required by mechanisms.

- **Authentication id**. The identity of the entity performing the authentication.
- **Authorization id**. The identity of the entity for which access control checks should be made if the authentication succeeds.
- **Authentication credentials**. For example, a password or a key.

The authentication and authorization ids might differ if the program (such as a proxy server) is authenticating on behalf of another entity. The authentication id is specified by using the `Context.SECURITY_PRINCIPAL` environment property. It is of type `java.lang.String`.

The password/key of the authentication entity is specified by using the `Context.SECURITY_CREDENTIALS` environment property. It is of type `java.lang.String`, char array (`char[]`) or a byte array (`byte[]`). If the password is a byte array, then it is transformed into a char array by using an UTF-8 encoding.

By default, the value of the `Context.SECURITY_PRINCIPAL` environment property, in addition to being the authentication id, is also used as the authorization id. If you need to specify an authorization id that differs from the authentication id, then use the `"java.naming.security.sasl.authorizationId"` environment property. Its value must be of type `java.lang.String`.

The CRAM-MD5 example (page 229) shows how to use the `Context.SECURITY_PRINCIPAL` and `Context.SECURITY_CREDENTIALS` properties for CRAM-MD5 authentication.

If a mechanism requires input other than those already described, then you need to define a callback object for the mechanism to use. See the **Callback** section (page 230) for an example of how to do this.

CRAM-MD5 Authentication

CRAM-MD5 authentication is one of the SASL mechanisms that was at one point proposed as a required mechanism for LDAP v3 servers. It has since been superseded by DIGEST-MD5. However, some existing servers, such as the Netscape Directory Server, support CRAM-MD5. Because the use of SASL is part of the LDAP v3 (RFC 2251), servers that support only the LDAP v2 do not support CRAM-MD5.

When using the CRAM-MD5 mechanism, the LDAP server sends some data to the LDAP client. The client responds by encrypting the data with its password by using the MD5 algorithm. The LDAP server then uses the client's stored password to determine whether the client used the right password.

To use the CRAM-MD5 authentication mechanism, you must set the authentication environment properties as follows.

- `Context.SECURITY_AUTHENTICATION`. Set to the string `"CRAM-MD5"`.
- `Context.SECURITY_PRINCIPAL`. Set to the principal name. According to `draft-ietf-ldapext-authmeth-01.txt`, the name should be either the string `"dn:"`, followed by the fully qualified DN of the entity being authenticated, or the string `"u:"`, followed by the user id. Which of these two forms is required depends on the LDAP server implementation. Examples of each are `"dn: cn=C. User,ou=NewHires,o=JNDITutorial"`, and `"u: cuser"`. An earlier draft of this proposal did not include the use of the `"dn:"` prefix, so some servers might simply accept the fully qualified DN of the entity being authenticated (e.g., `"cn=C. User, ou=NewHires, o=JNDITutorial"`). Check with the LDAP server that you are using to see what name it expects. In any case, the data type of this property must be `java.lang.String`.

- Context.SECURITY_CREDENTIALS. Set to the password of the principal (e.g., "mysecret"). It is of type java.lang.String, char array (char[]), or byte array (byte[]). If the password is a java.lang.String or char[], then it is encoded by using UTF-8 for transmission to the server. If the password is a byte[], then it is transmitted as is to the server.

The following example shows how a client performs authentication by using CRAM-MD5 to an LDAP server.

```
// Set up the environment for creating the initial context
Hashtable env = new Hashtable();
env.put(Context.INITIAL_CONTEXT_FACTORY,
    "com.sun.jndi.ldap.LdapCtxFactory");
env.put(Context.PROVIDER_URL, "ldap://localhost:389/o=JNDITutorial");

// Authenticate as C. User and the password "mysecret"
env.put(Context.SECURITY_AUTHENTICATION, "CRAM-MD5");
env.put(Context.SECURITY_PRINCIPAL,
    "cn=C. User, ou=NewHires, o=JNDITutorial");
env.put(Context.SECURITY_CREDENTIALS, "mysecret");

// Create the initial context
DirContext ctx = new InitialDirContext(env);

// ... do something useful with ctx
```

Note: The Netscape Directory Server v4.1 supports the CRAM-MD5 authentication mechanism only if you install some additional software on the server. Otherwise, attempting to use CRAM-MD5 with the server results in a CommunicationException's being thrown. See the server's documentation for instructions on how to obtain and install the software.

Callbacks for SASL Mechanisms

A SASL mechanism is always given the authorization id, either that specified by the "java.naming.security.sasl.authorizationId" or Context.SECURITY_PRINCIPAL environment property. All other input is supplied on-demand, that is, on the request of the mechanism.

By default, the LDAP provider supplies the authentication id and credentials by using, respectively, the Context.SECURITY_PRINCIPAL and Context.SECURITY_CREDENTIALS environment properties. If a SASL mechanism requires input other than these, or if you prefer to supply the input through a different means, then you can define a *callback handler object* for the mechanism to use. To do this, you set the "java.naming.security.sasl.callback" environment property to the callback handler object, as explained next.

Callback Handler

The LDAP provider uses the javax.security.auth.callback package from the Java Authentication and Authorization Service (http://java.sun.com/products/jaas). The object contained in the "java.naming.security.sasl.callback" environment property must be of type javax.security.auth.callback.CallbackHandler. When a SASL mechanism requires input, it invokes CallbackHandler.handle() and supplies the list of callbacks that it needs in order to get that input. A mechanism must use the javax.security.auth.callback.NameCallback when asking for the authentication id and use the javax.security.auth.callback.PasswordCallback when asking for the authentication credentials. To obtain other input, the mechanism will use one of the callbacks defined in the javax.security.auth.callback package or any other callback that implements the javax.security.auth.callback.Callback interface. The callback handler must be able to handle the type of callback requested by a mechanism, so the application that creates/uses the callback handler must have some knowledge about what the mechanism requires.

Here is an example of a callback handler that handles NameCallback and PasswordCallback by reading the data from Standard Input.

```
public class SampleCallbackHandler implements CallbackHandler {
    public void handle(Callback[] callbacks)
        throws java.io.IOException, UnsupportedCallbackException {
        for (int i = 0; i < callbacks.length; i++) {
            if (callbacks[i] instanceof NameCallback) {
                NameCallback cb = (NameCallback)callbacks[i];
                cb.setName(getInput(cb.getPrompt()));
            } else if (callbacks[i] instanceof PasswordCallback) {
                PasswordCallback cb = (PasswordCallback)callbacks[i];
                String pw = getInput(cb.getPrompt());
                char[] passwd = new char[pw.length()];
                pw.getChars(0, passwd.length, passwd, 0);
                cb.setPassword(passwd);
            } else {
                throw new
                    UnsupportedCallbackException(callbacks[i]);
            }
        }
    }
    /**
    * A reader from Standard Input. In real world apps, this would
    * typically be a TextComponent or similar widget.
    */
    private String getInput(String prompt) throws IOException {
        System.out.print(prompt);
        BufferedReader in = new BufferedReader(
            new InputStreamReader(System.in));
        return in.readLine();
    }
}
```

CRAM-MD5 by Using a Callback Handler

Here's a modified version of the CRAM-MD5 example that gets its password by using a callback handler instead the `Context.SECURITY_CREDENTIALS` environment property. The CRAM-MD5 mechanism needs the authorization id and the password as input. The authorization id is obtained from the `Context.SECURITY_PRINCIPAL` property. All other input required by the CRAM-MD5 mechanism is supplied by `SampleCallbackHandler`.

```
// Set up the environment for creating the initial context
Hashtable env = new Hashtable(11);
env.put(Context.INITIAL_CONTEXT_FACTORY,
    "com.sun.jndi.ldap.LdapCtxFactory");
env.put(Context.PROVIDER_URL, "ldap://localhost:389/o=JNDITutorial");
env.put(Context.SECURITY_AUTHENTICATION, "CRAM-MD5");

// Specify bind DN as C. User
env.put(Context.SECURITY_PRINCIPAL,
    "cn=C. User, ou=NewHires, o=JNDITutorial");

// If the authorization id differs, set using
// java.naming.security.sasl.authorizationId property
// env.put("java.naming.security.sasl.authorizationId", "u:cuser");

// Specify the callback to use for fetching the
// authentication id/password
env.put("java.naming.security.sasl.callback",
    new SampleCallbackHandler());

// Create the initial context
DirContext ctx = new InitialDirContext(env);

// ... do something useful with ctx
```

Using Arbitrary SASL Mechanisms

Note: The descriptions and examples presented here are based on a preview of a proposed Java SASL API standard. Although these examples work with version 1.2 of the LDAP provider, the APIs are still subject to change, depending on the evolution of the Java SASL API (`draft-ietf-weltman-java-sasl-03.txt`).

The LDAP provider has built-in support for the CRAM-MD5 and External SASL mechanisms. To use other SASL mechanisms, you must make the classes for the mechanisms available to your program (for example by adding them to your classpath) and set the `"javax.security.sasl.client.pkgs"` environment property to the package name of the *factory* class that creates implementations for those mechanisms.

Here is an example that uses a package (`examples`) that contains a custom SASL mechanism.

```
// Specify the package name for SASL to search for the
// mechanism factories
env.put("javax.security.sasl.client.pkgs", "examples");

// Use the bogus SASL mechanism name
env.put(Context.SECURITY_AUTHENTICATION, "SAMPLE");
```

The program first adds the package examples to the list of packages to search for SASL mechanisms (actually, *mechanism factories*). It then requests a SASL mechanism ("SAMPLE") from that package.

When you run the program, the "SAMPLE" SASL mechanism implementation class (SampleMech) prints a debug message to indicate that it has been invoked. When the program communicates with the LDAP server, the server will return an AuthenticationNot-SupportedException because "SAMPLE" is a bogus mechanism. You can use a similar technique to access a SASL mechanism that the LDAP server does support. Do this by using an appropriate value for the SASL mechanism name and the package name of the mechanism implementation. SASL mechanism implementations are typically provided by vendors and must follow the interfaces and guidelines outlined in the Java SASL API.

SSL and Custom Sockets

The simple and CRAM-MD5 authentication mechanisms authenticate the LDAP client to the LDAP server. They do not provide any other security features, such as ensuring that requests sent to the server on that authenticated connection are from the same client or protecting the privacy of the data exchanged between client and server.

To provide higher levels of security for communicating with clients, most LDAP servers allow their services to be accessed through SSL. Such servers support SSL ports in addition to normal (unprotected) ports. To use this service, the client needs to specify the port number of the SSL port in the Context.PROVIDER_URL property and use SSL sockets when communicating with the server.

By default, Sun's LDAP service provider uses plain sockets when communicating with the LDAP server. To request that SSL sockets be used, set the Context.SECURITY_PROTOCOL property to "ssl".

In the following example, the LDAP server is offering SSL at port 636. To run this program, you must enable SSL on port 636 on your LDAP server. This procedure is typically carried out by the directory's administrator.

```
// Set up the environment for creating the initial context
Hashtable env = new Hashtable();
env.put(Context.INITIAL_CONTEXT_FACTORY,
    "com.sun.jndi.ldap.LdapCtxFactory");
env.put(Context.PROVIDER_URL, "ldap://localhost:636/o=JNDITutorial");

// Specify SSL
env.put(Context.SECURITY_PROTOCOL, "ssl");
```

```
// Authenticate as S. User and the password "mysecret"
env.put(Context.SECURITY_AUTHENTICATION, "simple");
env.put(Context.SECURITY_PRINCIPAL,
    "cn=S. User, ou=NewHires, o=JNDITutorial");
env.put(Context.SECURITY_CREDENTIALS, "mysecret");

// Create the initial context
DirContext ctx = new InitialDirContext(env);

// ... do something useful with ctx
```

To run this program, you need to have an SSL package that implements the `javax.net.SocketFactory` interface (for details, see `http://java.sun.com/security/ssl/API_users_guide.html`). The SSL package must be available in your execution environment (such as the HotJava Browser or the Java Web Server) or be added to your classpath. Currently, Sun also provides a standalone SSL implementation, Java Secure Socket Extension (`http://java.sun.com/products/jsse`). See later in this section (page 235) for additional information about Java SSL packages.

Note: If you use SSL to connect to a server on a port that is *not* using SSL, then your program will hang. Similarly, if you use a plain socket to connect to a server's SSL socket, then your application will hang. This is a characteristic of the SSL protocol.

Using SSL with the External SASL Mechanism

SSL provides authentication and other security services at a lower layer than the LDAP. Since authentication has already been done, the LDAP layer can use that authentication information from SSL by using the External SASL mechanism.

The following example is like the previous SSL example, except that instead of using simple authentication, it uses the External SASL authentication. By its using External, you do not need to supply any principal or password information, because they get picked up from the SSL.

```
// Set up the environment for creating the initial context
Hashtable env = new Hashtable(11);
env.put(Context.INITIAL_CONTEXT_FACTORY,
    "com.sun.jndi.ldap.LdapCtxFactory");
env.put(Context.PROVIDER_URL, "ldap://localhost:389/o=JNDITutorial");

// Principal and credentials will be obtained from the connection
env.put(Context.SECURITY_AUTHENTICATION, "EXTERNAL");

// Specify SSL
env.put(Context.SECURITY_PROTOCOL, "ssl");
```

```
// Create the initial context
DirContext ctx = new InitialDirContext(env);

// ... do something useful with ctx
```

Using Custom Sockets

When you set the Context.SECURITY_PROTOCOL property to "ssl", the LDAP provider will use the socket factory javax.net.ssl.SSLSocketFactory to attempt to create an SSL socket to communicate with the server. To use a different SSL package, you need to set the "java.naming.ldap.factory.socket" environment property to the class name of the socket factory that will produce SSL sockets. This class must implement the javax.net.Socket-Factory interface (see http://java.sun.com/security/ssl/API_users_guide.html for details).

SSL sockets are but one type of socket. You can probably think of other types of sockets that might be useful, such as those for bypassing firewalls. You can use the "java.naming.ldap.factory.socket" environment property to specify other types of sockets to use. This is useful for setting the socket factory on a per connection basis. To set the socket factory for all sockets used in a program, use java.net.Socket.setSocketFactory(). Note that if Context.SECURITY_PROTOCOL is set to "ssl", then the "java.naming.ldap.factory.socket" property should specify a socket factory that produces SSL sockets.

Here is an example that creates an initial context by using a custom socket factory.

```
// Set up the environment for creating the initial context
Hashtable env = new Hashtable();
env.put(Context.INITIAL_CONTEXT_FACTORY,
    "com.sun.jndi.ldap.LdapCtxFactory");
env.put(Context.PROVIDER_URL, "ldap://localhost:555/o=JNDITutorial");

// Specify the socket factory
env.put("java.naming.ldap.factory.socket",
    "com.widget.socket.MySocketFactory");

// Create the initial context
DirContext ctx = new InitialDirContext(env);

// ... do something useful with ctx
```

Java SSL Packages

Other Java APIs, such as RMI, use SSL. The RMI documentation includes a list of issues related to RMI-SSL, including the Java SSL packages available within and outside of the United States. For details, see

http://java.sun.com/products/jdk/1.2/docs/guide/rmi/SSLInfo.html

Miscellaneous

The directory examples in **The Basics** trail (page 59) showed how you can access the LDAP directory by using the JNDI packages. This lesson contains tips for affecting the behavior of the LDAP service provider. Following are the topics covered:

- How to specify which protocol version (2 or 3) to use
- How to read nonstring attributes from the directory
- How to suppress the return of attribute values
- How to control the dereferencing of aliases
- How to rename an LDAP entry
- How to control how references are stored
- How to use LDAP URLs

Protocol Versions

The LDAP is available as version 2 and version 3. As discussed in the **Comparison of the LDAP and JNDI Models** lesson (page 207), the two versions differ and many features (such as referrals and pluggable authentication mechanisms) that are part of version 3 are not available in version 2. But for the most part, when you use the JNDI to access the LDAP service, you will see no difference between the two versions.

Sun's LDAP service provider supports both versions. The selection of which version to use depends primarily on which version the LDAP server supports. By default, the LDAP provider first uses version 3 to communicate with the specified LDAP server. If the server does not support that version, then the LDAP provider attempts to communicate by using version 2. The LDAP provider handles the selection automatically, so seldom does the client need to explicitly request that a particular version be used.

Only in a few circumstances would you want to explicitly specify the protocol version. One is if the LDAP server with which you want to communicate fails to indicate that it does not support version 3. Some public servers exhibit this behavior, and an attempt to communicate with them by using version 3 results either in a hung client (because the server does not respond to the version) or a protocol error (because the server responds with an incorrect error code). Or, you might want to specify the version explicitly if you want your program to use only that version and to fail if the contacted server does not support the version. For example, your program might need to make updates to the server's published schema; this makes sense only for version 3.

To specify the protocol version, you use the `"java.naming.ldap.version"` environment property. Here is an example that asks for version 2 of the protocol.

```
// Set up the environment for creating the initial context
Hashtable env = new Hashtable(11);
env.put(Context.INITIAL_CONTEXT_FACTORY,
    "com.sun.jndi.ldap.LdapCtxFactory");
env.put(Context.PROVIDER_URL, "ldap://localhost:389/o=JNDITutorial");

env.put("java.naming.ldap.version", "2");

// Create the initial context
DirContext ctx = new InitialDirContext(env);

// ... do something useful with ctx
```

To ask for version 3, simply replace the 2 with a 3, as follows:

```
env.put("java.naming.ldap.version", "3");
```

Attributes

Because most of the operations on the LDAP directory center around attributes, you need to understand how to use those attributes through the JNDI.

An LDAP entry's attributes are represented by the `Attributes` interface, whereas individual attributes are represented by the `Attribute` interface. To create attributes for use in your program, use the `BasicAttributes` and `BasicAttribute` classes.

Here is an example that creates two attributes, `"oc"` and `"photo"`, and puts them into an `Attributes` object.

```
// Create a multivalued attribute that has four String values
BasicAttribute oc = new BasicAttribute("objectClass", "top");
oc.add("person");
oc.add("organizationalPerson");
oc.add("inetOrgPerson");

// Create an attribute by using a byte array
BasicAttribute photo = new BasicAttribute("jpegPhoto", buf);

// Create the attribute set
BasicAttributes attrs = new BasicAttributes(true);
attrs.put(oc);
attrs.put(photo);
```

Attribute Names

You identify an attribute through the use of its *attribute name*, which is sometimes called the *attribute identifier* or *attribute type name*. The **Directory Operations** lesson (page 60) discusses attribute names, specifically attribute subclassing, attribute name synonyms, and the syntax for specifying language preferences. These features might not be supported by all LDAP server implementations.

LDAP attribute names are case-insensitive. Thus two attribute names, such as "object-class" and "objectClass", both would be interpreted to refer to the same attribute. If you are using the BasicAttributes class to represent LDAP attributes, then you should pass true for the ignoreCase parameter to its constructors. Here are some examples.

```
Attributes attrs1 = new BasicAttributes(true);

Attributes attrs2 = new BasicAttributes("objectClass", "top", true);
```

Options

The LDAP v3 allows *options* to be appended to an attribute name. Each option is preceded by a semicolon character (";"). Options are like attribute subclassing. That is, an attribute named without the option is treated as the superclass of an attribute named with an option. The only option defined by the protocol is *binary* (indicated by using the string ";binary"), which means that the attribute's value should be transmitted in binary format (regardless of its actual syntax). This option is reserved for transmitting ASN.1 encoded data (such as certificates: "caCertificate;binary"). Servers that support attribute subclassing may support identification of the attribute without its binary option, but it is best always to include the binary option in the attribute name.

Operational Attributes

The LDAP v3 supports the notion of *operational attributes*, which are attributes associated with a directory object for administrative purposes. The access control list for an object, for example, is an operational attribute. In DirContext.getAttributes() and Dir-Context.search(), you can supply null as the list of attributes to return and therefore can specify that all attributes associated with the requested objects be returned. The attributes returned, however, do not include operational attributes. To retrieve operational attributes, you must name them explicitly.

Attribute Values

An LDAP attribute can have a single value or multiple, unordered values. Whether an attribute is allowed to have more than one value is dictated by the attribute's definition in the directory's schema. Both single and multivalued attributes are represented in the JNDI as an Attribute. In the previous example, a multivalued attribute and a single-valued attribute are created.

The JNDI is very flexible in how attribute values can be represented because such values are declared as `java.lang.Object`. When you use the JNDI to access or update attributes stored in a particular directory, the types of the attribute values depend on the directory and, to some extent, on the corresponding service provider. For the LDAP directory, Sun's LDAP provider represents attribute values as either `java.lang.String` or `byte[]`. `byte` arrays are used to represent attribute values with nonstring attribute syntaxes. Strings are used to represent the values of all other syntaxes.

For an arbitrary attribute, no programmatic way is available to determine whether its syntax is a nonstring. Manual ways are available, of course, and involve looking up the attribute and its syntax in documents such as RFC 2256. The LDAP service provider has a built-in list of attribute names that it knows contain nonstring values and allows clients to add to that list. Table 16 gives that built-in list.

TABLE 16:   Attributes Returned as byte[].

Attribute Name	Attribute OID
All attribute names containing ";binary".	
photo	0.9.2342.19200300.100.1.7
personalSignature	0.9.2342.19200300.100.1.53
audio	0.9.2342.19200300.100.1.55
jpegPhoto	0.9.2342.19200300.100.1.60
javaSerializedData	1.3.6.1.4.1.42.2.27.4.1.8
thumbnailPhoto	1.3.6.1.4.1.1466.101.120.35
thumbnailLogo	1.3.6.1.4.1.1466.101.120.36
userPassword	2.5.4.35
userCertificate	2.5.4.36
cACertificate	2.5.4.37
authorityRevocationList	2.5.4.38
certificateRevocationList	2.5.4.39
crossCertificatePair	2.5.4.40
x500UniqueIdentifier	2.5.4.45

When you read one of these attributes from the LDAP directory, its value will be of type `byte[]`.

Specifying Additional Nonstring Attributes

If your program uses an attribute whose value should be returned as a `byte` array but the attribute's name is not on the list in Table 16, then you need to add the name to the list of nonstring attributes. You do this by using the "java.naming.ldap.attributes.binary" environment property. Its value is a string of space-separated attribute names.

For example, the following environment property setting informs the LDAP provider that the values of the attributes named "mpegVideo" and "mySpecialKey" are to be returned as byte arrays.

```
env.put("java.naming.ldap.attributes.binary", "mpegVideo mySpecialKey");
```

Suppressing the Return of Attribute Values

The LDAP v3 allows you to specify that only attribute type names (and not attribute values) be returned. To do this by using the JNDI, you set the "java.naming.ldap.typesOnly" environment property. This property affects DirContext.getAttributes() and DirContext.search(). When you specify that objects are to be returned (by passing true to SearchControls.setReturningObjFlag()) and then you invoke search(), this property is ignored because attribute values are required to generate the object.

Here's an example that gets a list of an entry's attribute names.

```
// Indicate that you want only the type names
env.put("java.naming.ldap.typesOnly", "true");

// Create the initial context
DirContext ctx = new InitialDirContext(env);

// Get the attributes
Attributes attrs = ctx.getAttributes("cn=Ted Geisel, ou=People");
```

This example produces the following output.

```
{sn=sn: No values,
 objectclass=objectclass: No values,
 jpegphoto=jpegphoto: No values,
 mail=mail: No values,
 facsimiletelephonenumber=facsimiletelephonenumber: No values,
 telephonenumber=telephonenumber: No values, cn=cn: No values}
```

Dereferencing Aliases

In the X.500, you can set a leaf entry to point to another object in the namespace. Called an *alias* entry, it contains the DN of the object to which it is pointing. When you look up an object by using the alias, the alias is *dereferenced* so that what is returned is the object pointed to by the alias's DN.

You can use aliases to organize the directory's namespace so that as the namespace evolves, old names may be used. Suppose, for example, that in the "o=Wiz, c=us" company, the departments "ou=hardware" and "ou=software" are merged into "ou=engineering". You can move the contents of "ou=hardware" and "ou=software" to "ou=engineering" and change the entries "ou=hardware" and "ou=software" into alias entries that point to "ou=engineering".

In the LDAP, aliases are supported in the same way as in the X.500.

When you use Sun's LDAP service provider, you can control how aliases are dereferenced in one of four ways, by using the "java.naming.ldap.derefAliases" environment property, as shown in Table 17. If this environment property is not set, then the default is "always".

TABLE 17:   Values for the "java.naming.ldap.derefAliases" Property.

Property Value	Description
always	Always dereference aliases.
never	Never dereferences aliases.
finding	Dereferences aliases only *during* name resolution.
searching	Dereferences aliases only *after* name resolution.

In the LDAP, these four modes of alias dereferencing affect only the "search" operations. No dereferencing is done for the update operations "modify," "add," and "delete." Similarly, in the JNDI, no dereferencing is done for the update methods in the Context and DirContext interfaces. The "java.naming.ldap.derefAliases" environment property affects all methods that read from the directory.

Note also that the "dereference links" flag in the SearchControls class is not related to aliases.

Dereferencing Aliases Example

The following example demonstrates how the "java.naming.ldap.derefAliases" environment property affects the "search" operation. It accepts as a command-line argument one of the four settings for "java.naming.ldap.derefAliases" listed in Table 17. If no argument has been specified, then the environment property is not set (which is equivalent to setting it to "always").

For this example, the directory has been set up with two aliases, as follows. (See Figure 2.)

- "ou=Staff" is an alias that points to "ou=People". If you list the context of "ou=Staff", then you will see the contents of the "ou=People" context.
- "cn=Newbie, ou=People" is an alias that points to the "cn=J. Duke, ou=NewHires" entry.

After setting the environment property, the example performs a search on the "ou=Staff" context for all entries whose "cn" attribute begins with "J." Here's the code fragment that sets the environment property and performs the search.

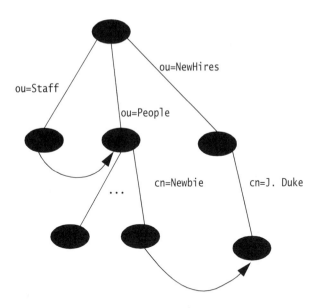

FIGURE 2:   Server Configuration for Dereferencing Aliases Example.

```
if (args.length > 0) {
    // Set the dereference flag as requested
    env.put("java.naming.ldap.derefAliases", args[0]);
}

// Create the initial context
DirContext ctx = new InitialDirContext(env);

// Perform the search
NamingEnumeration answer = ctx.search("ou=Staff", "(cn=J*)", null);
```

Table 18 summarizes the results of running this program with different arguments to the command line.

TABLE 18:   Results from Dereferencing Aliases Example.

Command Line Arguments	Result
(none)	Three entries: "cn=Jon Ruiz", "cn=John Fowler", and "cn=J.Duke"
always	Three entries: "cn=Jon Ruiz", "cn=John Fowler", and "cn=J.Duke"
never	Zero (because the "ou=Staff" alias is never dereferenced)
finding	Two entries: "cn=Jon Ruiz" and "cn=John Fowler" (because the "cn=Newbie" alias is never dereferenced)
searching	Zero (because the "ou=Staff" alias is never dereferenced)

Note: The Netscape Directory Server v4.1 does not support aliases. If you run this example using that server, then the results will be as if the setting is `"never"`.

When you run these examples, the names of the entries (`NameClassPair.getName()`) that you get back are LDAP URLs containing the fully qualified names of the entries. If you invoke `NameClassPair.isRelative()` on them, then the method returns `false`. This is because when the alias is followed, it reaches another part of the namespace that is no longer named relative to the `"ou=Staff"` context.

Renaming Objects

You use `Context.rename()` to rename an object in the directory. In the LDAP v2, this corresponds to the "modify RDN" operation that renames an entry within the same context (that is, renaming a sibling). In the LDAP v3, this corresponds to the "modify DN" operation, which is like "modify RDN," except that the old and new entries need not be in the same context. You can use `Context.rename()` to rename a leaf entry or an interior node. The following code renames an interior node from `"ou=NewHires"` to `"ou=OldHires"`:

```
ctx.rename("ou=NewHires", "ou=OldHires");
```

Note: The Netscape Directory Server v4.1 does not support renaming interior nodes. If you run this example, then you will get a `ContextNotEmptyException`.

Renaming to a Different Part of the DIT

With the LDAP v3, you can rename an entry to a different part of the DIT. To do this by using `Context.rename()`, you must use a context that is the common ancestor for both the new and the old entries. For example, to rename `"cn=C. User, ou=NewHires, o=JNDITutorial"` to `"cn=C. User ou=People, o=JNDITutorial"`, you must use the context named by `"o=JNDITutorial"`. Following is an example that demonstrates this. If you try to run this example against an LDAP v2 server, then you will get an `InvalidNameException` because version 2 does not support this feature.

```
ctx.rename("cn=C. User, ou=NewHires", "cn=C. User, ou=People");
```

Note: The Netscape Directory Server v4.1 does not support renaming with different parent nodes. If you run this example by using that server, then you will get a CommunicationException (indicating a "protocol error").

Keeping the Old Name Attributes

In the LDAP, when you rename an entry, you have the option of keeping the entry's old RDN as an attribute of the updated entry. For example, if you rename the entry "cn=C. User" to "cn=Claude User", then you can specify whether you want the old RDN "cn=C. User" to be kept as an attribute.

To specify whether you want to keep the old name attribute when you use Context.rename(), use the "java.naming.ldap.deleteRDN" environment property. If this property's value is "true" (the default), then the old RDN is removed. If its value is "false", then the old RDN is kept as an attribute of the updated entry.

```
// Set the property to keep RDN
env.put("java.naming.ldap.deleteRDN", "false");

// Create the initial context
DirContext ctx = new InitialDirContext(env);

// Perform the rename
ctx.rename("cn=C. User, ou=NewHires", "cn=Claude User,ou=NewHires");
```

Storing Objects

The **Java Objects and the Directory** trail (page 151) showed you how to store and read Java objects from the directory. Specifically, the **LDAP Directories** section (page 195) discussed how Java objects are represented as attributes in an LDAP directory. If you have not yet gone through that trail, then before going further you might want to at least read through that trail to understand some of the terminology used here.

The **LDAP Directories** section (page 195) and RFC 2713 describe the representation of a Reference as multiple LDAP attributes. By default, the hash character ("#") is used to encode the RefAddr in the Reference. If this character already appears in the contents of the RefAddr, then you need to use another character. You do this by setting the "java.naming.ldap.ref.separator" environment property to a string that contains the separator character.

Here's an example. If you run the reference example (page 160) and then examine the "cn=favorite" entry in the directory, then you will see the following attributes.

```
objectclass: top, javaContainer, javaObject, javaNamingReference
javaclassname: Fruit
```

```
javafactory: FruitFactory
javareferenceaddress: #0#fruit#orange
cn: favorite
```

You can modify this example to use the colon character (":") as the separator, as follows.

```
// Ask to use ":" as the encoding character
env.put("java.naming.ldap.ref.separator", ":");

// Create the initial context
DirContext ctx = new InitialDirContext(env);

// Create the object to be bound
Fruit fruit = new Fruit("orange");

// Perform the bind
ctx.rebind("cn=favorite", fruit);
```

The modified program produces the following attributes.

```
objectclass: top, javaContainer, javaObject, javaNamingReference
javaclassname: Fruit
javafactory: FruitFactory
javareferenceaddress: :0:fruit:orange
cn: favorite
```

LDAP URLs

RFC 2255 describes the syntactic format of LDAP v3 URLs. The format contains all of the elements necessary to specify an LDAP "search" operation, with provisions for supporting future version 3 extensions:

```
ldap://host:port/dn?attributes?scope?filter?extensions
```

Authentication information may be specified in the `extensions` portion of the URL. See the RFC for a complete description of the format.

URLs play a role in several places in the JNDI. This section describes how LDAP URLs can be used with the LDAP service provider.

URL as a Name to the Initial Context

If you pass an LDAP URL to the methods in `InitialContext` or `InitialDirContext`, then the JNDI will look for a context implementation (called a *URL context implementation*) to process the LDAP URL.

Here is an example that performs a search from the initial context, using an LDAP URL as the name argument.

```
// Create the initial context
DirContext ctx = new InitialDirContext();

// Perform the search by using URL
```

```
NamingEnumeration answer = ctx.search(
    "ldap://localhost:389/ou=People,o=JNDITutorial",
    "(sn=Geisel)", null);
```

This example produces the following output.

```
>>>cn=Ted Geisel
{sn=sn: Geisel,
 objectclass=objectclass: top, person, organizationalPerson,\
    inetOrgPerson,
 jpegphoto=jpegphoto: [B@1dacd78a,
 mail=mail: Ted.Geisel@JNDITutorial.com,
 facsimiletelephonenumber=facsimiletelephonenumber:\
    +1 408 555 2329,
 telephonenumber=telephonenumber: +1 408 555 5252,
 cn=cn: Ted Geisel}
```

You might have noticed that you did not need to set up any environment properties to perform this search. This is because the JNDI automatically searches for the URL context implementation. If the URL context implementation is not found, it will use only the implementation specified by the environment properties (if any). For an LDAP URL, it looks for a class with the name `ldapURLContextFactory` from package locations specified by the environment property `Context.URL_PKG_PREFIXES` (`"java.naming.factory.url.pkgs"`). This property contains a list of package prefixes separated by colon characters (":"). If no class with the right name is found in these packages, then the package `com.sun.jndi.url.ldap` is searched.

Query Components in a URL

With the exception of the `DirContext.search()` methods, when an LDAP URL is passed as a name to the initial context, the URL should *not* contain any query ("?") components. If it does, then an `InvalidNameException` is thrown by the LDAP service provider.

For the `search()` methods, if a URL contains query components, then all other arguments (including the filter and `SearchControls`) are ignored. The query components of the URL and its defaults are used instead. For example, if an LDAP URL containing a scope component is supplied, then that scope overrides any scope setting that is passed in an argument. If the URL contains other query components but not the scope, then the LDAP URL's default scope ("base object") is used.

Here is an example that performs a subtree search by using a filter of `"(sn=Geisel)"`.

```
// Perform the search by using URL
NamingEnumeration answer = ctx.search(
"ldap://localhost:389/ou=People,o=JNDITutorial??sub?(sn=Geisel)",
    "" /* ignored*/, null /* ignored */);
```

Note: Version 1.2 of Sun's LDAP provider does not treat query components properly.

URL for Configuring Service Providers

To configure an LDAP service provider, you typically supply an LDAP URL in the `Context.PROVIDER_URL("java.naming.provider.url")` environment property. The LDAP service provider uses this URL to configure its connection to the directory server. Only the *host*, *port*, and *dn* parts of the URL are relevant in this setting. Supplying other parts of the URL results in a `ConfigurationException`.

URL for Specifying Referrals

An LDAP referral contains a list of one or more URLs. To process an LDAP referral, the service provider uses the information in these URLs to create connections to the LDAP servers to which they refer. Multiple LDAP URLs in a single referral are treated as alternatives, each followed until one succeeds. The complete URL (including any query components) is used.

You set up referrals by creating *referral* entries in the directory that contain the "REF" attribute. This attribute contains one or more referral URLs (usually LDAP URLs). See the **Referrals** lesson (page 267) for details on referrals.

URL as a Name in NamingEnumeration

When you perform a `Context.list()`, `Context.listBindings()`, or `DirContext.search()`, you get back a `NamingEnumeration`. Each item in this enumeration is an instance or subclass of `NameClassPair`. When the name of the item (`NameClassPair.getName()`) is not relative to the target context, the name is returned as a URL. You can use `NameClassPair.isRelative()` to check whether the name is relative. One main reason why the name might not be relative is because a referral was followed. In this case, the name of the object is that in the referred namespace and not the one at which the operation was initiated. See the **URLs** lesson (page 123) for more details and an example.

URL as an Argument to getObjectInstance()

When an LDAP namespace is federated under another namespace (such as DNS), the information that is stored in the superior namespace might be an LDAP URL. In such a scenario, a `lookup()`/`list()`/`search()` method invocation in the superior namespace will return a `Reference` that contains the LDAP URL for the LDAP namespace. The service provider for the superior namespace will then pass the `Reference` to `NamingManager.getObjectInstance()` or `DirectoryManager.getObjectInstance()` to create an instance of an LDAP context. See the **Beyond the Basics** trail (page 131) for details on federation.

Searches

The **Directory Operations** lesson (page 63) described how to perform basic searches and how to use search filters and search controls.

This lesson describes LDAP searches in more detail. It discusses how the different search methods and other methods in the `DirContext` interface map to the LDAP "search" and "compare" operations. It also explores search results returned by the search methods and how to control the batch size of search results returned by the server.

Context Search Methods

The `DirContext` interface provides the following search methods:

- `search(Name name, Attributes matchingAttrs)`
- `search(Name name, Attributes matchingAttrs, String[] retAttrs)`
- `search(Name name, String filter, SearchControls ctls)`
- `search(Name name, String filterExpr, Object[] filterArgs,
    SearchControls ctls)`

Each of these methods has a corresponding overloaded form that accepts a `java.lang.String` name instead of `Name` as the first argument.

Using Matching Attributes

The first form, `search(Name name, Attributes matchingAttrs)`, is equivalent to the second form, `search(Name name, Attributes matchingAttrs, String[] retAttrs)`, with `null` supplied as the `retAttrs` argument:

```
search(name, matchingAttrs, null);
```

The **Basic Search** examples (page 64) show how to use both of these methods.

In these methods, the `matchingAttrs` argument is converted into an RFC 2254 string filter that is a conjunctive expression of the attributes from `matchingAttrs`. For example, a `matchingAttrs` containing the following attributes:

```
sn: Geisel
mail: (No value)
```

is translated into the string filter `"(&(sn=Geisel)(mail=*))"`.

Each attribute value is treated as a *literal*—that is, the attribute in the directory entry is expected to contain exactly that value. Therefore, if the attribute value contains a star character ("*") or other special characters defined in RFC 2254, then the LDAP provider will apply the appropriate encoding rules. For example, a `matchingAttrs` containing the following attributes:

```
sn: Geisel
mail: *
```

is translated into the string filter `"(&(sn=Geisel)(mail=\2a))"`. In this case, the directory entry must contain a `"mail"` attribute whose value is the string `"*"`.

If the attribute value is a `byte` array, then it is encoded by using the notation for encoding nonstring attributes, as described in RFC 2254. For example, a `matchingAttrs` containing the following attribute:

```
jpegphoto: 82 12 38 4e 23 e3 (byte array)
```

is translated into the string filter `"(jpegphoto=\82\12\38\4e\23\e3)"`.

Using String Filters

The **Search Filters** section (page 65) offers a quick overview of search filter syntax and contains examples of how to use the third form of the search method, `search(Name name, String filter, SearchControls ctls)`. The string filter follows the syntax specified in RFC 2254, except that Unicode characters are also allowed. Using Unicode characters is preferable to using encoded UTF-8 octets.

For example, in the Java programming language, you can specify the Greek letter *alpha* as the Unicode character \u03b1. To search for an entry whose attribute value contains this character, you can use the string `"\u03b1"` or `"\ce\b1"` (with appropriate escapes for the backslash characters ("\") if you're using that character as a literal string in the Java programming language). The Unicode form is the preferred form. The LDAP service provider will translate Unicode characters into their corresponding UTF-8 representation for transmission to the server.

Using String Filters with Arguments

The fourth form of the search method, search(Name name, String filterExpr, Object[] filterArgs, SearchControls ctls), allows you to construct the string filter by using a filter expression filterExpr and an array of arguments filterArgs.

The filterExpr argument can contain strings of the form "{*n*}", where the *n*th element of filterArgs replaces the occurrence of the "{*n*}" string in filterExpr in the resulting string filter. Each "{*n*}" string may appear as an attribute name, an attribute value, or a component of the attribute value. (Or more precisely, each "{*n*}" string may appear in place of "attr" or "value" in Section 4 of RFC 2254.)

During the substitution, the objects in filterArgs are encoded as follows.

- Each byte in a byte array (byte[]) is encoded as a string, according to RFC 2254. For example, the array {0, 1, 10, 100} is encoded as the string "\00\01\0a\64".
- Strings are treated as literals; "*" and other special characters defined in RFC 2254 that appear in the string are encoded according to the rules in RFC 2254. For example, a string of "*" is encoded as the string "\2a". Therefore, to use special characters in the filter, you must put them in the string expression filterExpr.
- Objects that are neither a String nor a byte[] are converted to their string form via Object.toString() and then the rules for String apply.

Here's an example that demonstrates the use of this method.

```
// Specify the filter arguments
byte[] key = {(byte)0x61, (byte)0x62, (byte)0x63, (byte)0x64,
    (byte)0x65, (byte)0x66, (byte)0x67};
String name = "User";

// Perform the search
NamingEnumeration answer = ctx.search("ou=NewHires",
    "(&(mySpecialKey={0}) (cn=*{1}))",      // Filter expression
    new Object[]{key, name},                // Filter arguments
    null);                                  // Default search controls
```

The filter expression specifies two substitutions: the contents of the byte array key replaces "{0}" and name replaces "{1}". Note the use of the wildcard for the "cn" portion of the filter in the filter expression. Running this example produces the following output.

```
>>>cn=S. User
{myspecialkey=myspecialkey: abcdefg,
 sn=sn: User,
 objectclass=objectclass: top, person, organizationalPerson,
    inetOrgPerson, extensibleObject,
 mail=mail: suser@JNDITutorial.com,
 userpassword=userpassword: [B@1dacd79e,
 cn=cn: S. User
}
```

Other Context Methods

Other methods in the interface, in addition to `search()`, read from the directory:

- `getAttributes()`
- `lookup()`
- `lookupLink()`
- `list()`
- `listBindings()`

Because the LDAP "search" operation is the primary way in which data is to be read from the directory, all of these other methods use the LDAP "search" operation in one way or another. This section describes how each method uses this operation. Examples of how to use each method are available in **The Basics** trail (page 37).

getAttributes()

`getAttributes()` retrieves attributes associated with the named entry. This method comes in two forms (ignoring the overloads that accept `java.lang.String` names instead of `Name` names):

- `getAttributes(Name name)`
- `getAttributes(Name name, String[] retAttrs)`

The first form is equivalent to the second form, with `null` supplied as the `retAttrs` argument:

```
getAttributes(name, null);
```

The `retAttrs` argument contains the list of attributes to retrieve. If `retAttrs` contains an attribute with the special name `"*"`, or if `retAttrs` is `null`, then all attributes of the named entry are retrieved. This method is equivalent to performing an LDAP "search" operation using the string filter `"(objectclass=*)"` and a search scope of `SearchControls.OBJECT_SCOPE` and asking that the requested attributes be returned.

lookup() and lookupLink()

`lookup()` and `lookupLink()` return the object bound to the name. If a `java.io.Serializable`, `Reference`, or `Referenceable` object was previously bound to the name, by using either `bind()` or `rebind()`, then the result of these methods will be an object constructed by using the attributes used for storing Java objects. See the **Representation in the Directory** lesson (page 195) for details. Otherwise, a `DirContext` object representing the named entry is returned.

These methods are implemented by using an LDAP "search" operation with the string filter `"(objectclass=*)"` and a search scope of `SearchControls.OBJECT_SCOPE` and asking for all of the entry's attributes. If the entry contains Java object-related attributes, then those attributes are used to reconstruct the object, as described in the **Representation in the Directory** lesson (page 195). The result is then passed to the object factory mechanism, `NamingManager.getObjectInstance()`, before being returned to the caller. See the **Reading Objects from the Directory** lesson (page 179) for details.

list() and listBindings()

`list()` and `listBindings()` list the named context and return an enumeration of `NameClassPair` or `Binding`, respectively. These methods are implemented by using an LDAP "search" operation with the string filter `"(objectclass=*)"` and a search scope of `SearchControls.ONELEVEL_SCOPE`. `list()` asks for the `"objectClass"` and `"javaClassName"` attributes so that the class name of each entry can be determined (`NameClassPair.getClassName()`). If the `"javaClassName"` attribute does not exist, then the class name is `"javax.naming.directory.DirContext"`. The name of each entry (`NameClassPair.getName()`) either is relative to the named context or is an LDAP URL. The latter is used if a referral or alias has been followed.

`listBindings()` resembles `list()`, except that it asks for all of the entry's attributes. It will attempt to create for each item in the enumeration an object (to be returned by `Binding.getObject()`) similar to the way that `lookup()` creates an object from the data read from the directory.

The LDAP "Compare" Operation

The LDAP "compare" operation allows a client to ask the server whether the named entry has an attribute/value pair. This allows the server to keep certain attribute/value pairs secret (i.e., not exposed for general "search" access) while still allowing the client limited use of them. Some servers might use this feature for passwords, for example, although it is insecure for the client to pass clear-text passwords in the "compare" operation itself.

To accomplish this in the JNDI, use suitably constrained arguments for the following methods:

- `search(Name name, String filter, SearchControls ctls)`
- `search(Name name, String filterExpr, Object[] filterArgs, SearchControls ctls)`

First, the filter must be of the form "(*name=value*)". You cannot use wildcards. Second, the search scope must be `SearchControls.OBJECT_SCOPE`. Finally, you must request that no attributes be returned.

Here's an example.

```
// Value of the attribute
byte[] key = {(byte)0x61, (byte)0x62, (byte)0x63, (byte)0x64,
    (byte)0x65, (byte)0x66, (byte)0x67};
```

```
    // Set up the search controls
    SearchControls ctls = new SearchControls();
    ctls.setReturningAttributes(new String[0]);        // Return no attrs
    ctls.setSearchScope(SearchControls.OBJECT_SCOPE);// Search obj only

    // Perform the search
    NamingEnumeration answer = ctx.search("cn=S. User, ou=NewHires",
        "(mySpecialKey={0})", new Object[]{key}, ctls);
```

If the compare is successful, then the resulting enumeration will contain a single item whose name is the empty name and that contains no attributes.

Search Results

When you use the search methods in the `DirContext` interface, you get back a `NamingEnumeration`. Each item in `NamingEnumeration` is a `SearchResult`, which contains the following information:

- Name
- Object
- Class name
- Attributes

Name

Each `SearchResult` contains the name of the LDAP entry that satisfied the search filter. You obtain the name of the entry by using `getName()`. This method returns the *composite name* of the LDAP entry *relative* to the *target context*. The target context is the context to which the name parameter resolves. In LDAP parlance, the target context is the *base object* for the search. Here's an example.

```
    NamingEnumeration answer = ctx.search("ou=NewHires",
        "(&(mySpecialKey={0}) (cn=*{1}))",     // Filter expression
        new Object[]{key, name},               // Filter arguments
        null);                                 // Default search controls
```

The target context in this example is that named by `"ou=NewHires"`. The names in `SearchResults` in answer are relative to `"ou=NewHires"`. For example, if `getName()` returns `"cn=J. Duke"`, then its name relative to `ctx` will be `"cn=J. Duke, ou=NewHires"`.

If you performed the search by using `SearchControls.SUBTREE_SCOPE` or `Search-Controls.OBJECT_SCOPE` and the target context itself satisfied the search filter, then the name returned will be `""` (the empty name) because that is the name relative to the target context.

This isn't the whole story. If the search involves referrals (see the **Referrals** lesson (page 259)) or dereferencing aliases (see the **Miscellaneous** lesson (page 241)), then the corresponding `SearchResults` will have names that are not relative to the target context. Instead, they will be URLs that refer directly to the entry. To determine whether the name returned by getName() is relative or absolute, use isRelative(). If this method returns true, then the name is relative to the target context; if it returns false, then the name is a URL.

If the name is a URL and you need to use that URL, then you can pass it to the initial context, which understands URLs (see the **Miscellaneous** lesson (page 246)).

If you need to get the entry's full DN, then you can either do some bookkeeping to keep track of the ancestors of the SearchResult or use Context.getNameInNamespace().

Object

If the search was conducted requesting that the entry's object be returned (Search-Controls.setReturningObjFlag() was invoked with true), then the SearchResult will contain an object that represents the entry. To retrieve this object, you invoke getObject(). If a java.io.Serializable, Referenceable, or Reference object was previously bound to that LDAP name, then the attributes from the entry are used to reconstruct that object (see the example in the **Reading Objects from the Directory** lesson (page 183)). Otherwise, the attributes from the entry are used to create a DirContext instance that represents the LDAP entry. In either case, the LDAP provider invokes DirectoryManager.getObjectInstance() on the object and returns the results.

Class Name

If the search was conducted requesting that the entry's object be returned, then the class name is derived from the returned object. If the search requested attributes that included the retrieval of the "javaClassName" attribute of the LDAP entry, then the class name is the value of that attribute. Otherwise, the class name is "javax.naming.directory.DirContext". The class name is obtained from getClassName().

Attributes

When you perform a search, you can select the return attributes either by supplying a parameter to one of the search() methods or by setting the search controls using Search-Controls.setReturningAttributes(). If no attributes have been specified explicitly, then all of the LDAP entry's attributes are returned. To specify that no attributes be returned, you must pass an empty array (new String[0]).

To retrieve the LDAP entry's attributes, you invoke getAttributes() on the SearchResult.

Response Controls

See the **Controls and Extensions** lesson (page 298) for details on how to retrieve a search result's response controls.

Batch Size

When you invoke list(), listBindings(), or any of the search() methods, the LDAP service provider interacts with the LDAP server to retrieve the results and returns them in the form of a NamingEnumeration. The LDAP service provider can collect all of the results before returning the NamingEnumeration, or it can return each result as the caller invokes Naming-Enumeration.next() or NamingEnumeration.nextElement(). You can control how the LDAP service provider behaves in this respect by using the Context.BATCHSIZE ("java.naming.batchsize") environment property. This property contains the string representation of a decimal integer. The LDAP service provider uses its value to determine how many results to read from the server before unblocking—this number of results is the *batch size*—and allowing the client program to get the results by using next() or nextElement(). When the client program exhausts the batch, the LDAP service provider fetches another batch so that the client program can continue with the enumeration. If the batch size is zero, then the service provider will block until all results have been read. If this property was not set, then the default batch size is 1.

When you invoke search(), for example by using a batch size of *n*, the LDAP provider will block until it reads *n* results from the server before returning. So, setting the batch size to a smaller number allows the program to unblock sooner. However, some overhead attaches to processing each batch. If you are expecting a large number of results, then you might want to use a larger batch size to lower the number of context switches between the provider and your code. On the other hand, having a large batch also means that you need more memory to hold the results. These are the trade-offs that you'll need to consider when choosing a batch size.

Here's an example that sets the batch size to 10.

```
// Set the batch size to 10
env.put("java.naming.batchsize", "10");

// Create the initial context
DirContext ctx = new InitialDirContext(env);

// Perform the list
NamingEnumeration answer = ctx.list("ou=People");
```

Relationship to SearchControls.setCountLimit()

Note that the Context.BATCHSIZE environment property does not in any way affect how many results are returned or the order in which they are returned. It is completely unrelated to SearchControls.setCountLimit().

Batches at the Protocol Level

Context.BATCHSIZE controls the batch size only at the programmatic level. At the protocol level, an LDAP "search" operation causes the LDAP server to send all of the results to the client immediately. The LDAP provider stores all of the results that it receives—this might cause memory overflow problems.

LDAP servers that support either the Virtual List View or Paged Results control can be made to send results in batches at the protocol level. See the **Controls and Extensions** lesson (page 293) for details on how to use request controls with LDAP "search" operations.

Referrals

A *referral* is an entity that is used to redirect a client's request to another server. A referral contains the names and locations of other objects. It is sent by the server to indicate that the information that the client has requested can be found at another location (or locations), possibly at another server or several servers.

This lesson shows you how to handle referrals by using the JNDI. It starts off with an overview of referrals and a description of the mechanisms available in the JNDI for handling referrals. It then describes how to ignore them and how to handle them automatically and manually. Finally, it shows you how to create a referral entry and to update an existing referral entry.

Referrals in the LDAP

This section provides an overview of LDAP referrals.

Comparing Referrals with Aliases

In many ways, a referral is a generalization of an *alias*, which is discussed in the **Miscellaneous** lesson (page 241). An alias contains the DN of another object, whereas a referral contains one or more URLs of objects. The URLs are usually, but not necessarily, LDAP URLs. The LDAP URL contains the server's host/port and an object's DN. The host/port information can point to a directory server that differs from the one that returned the referral.

Whereas an alias is dereferenced and processed by the server, a referral is returned to the client, which is responsible for processing it.

Uses

Like an alias, a referral is useful for allowing an object to be identified by different names. Referrals can be used, for example, to accommodate the namespace changes and mergers that are inevitable as organizations evolve. In addition, they allow directory administrators to set up "search paths" for collecting results from multiple servers. They also can be used to deploy cache or read-only server replicas that return referrals for all update requests. Use of a read-only replica is among the many different load balancing strategies that can be implemented by using referrals.

Version 2 versus Version 3

The LDAP v2 provides limited support for referrals. An LDAP v2 server can be configured with a *default* referral so that if the information requested at the server does not exist, then the server will return a "partial result" error response that contains the referral URL. When the client receives this error, it will check whether the referral URL is present and use it instead of interpreting the response as a "partial result" error. The client uses the referral URL by contacting the server named in it to continue the requested operation.

The LDAP v3 explicitly supports referrals and allows servers to return them directly to the client. The server can return to the client a "referral" error response for any request that requires a response. This error response contains one or more URLs that are to be used to continue the operation. All of the URLs in the response are equivalent in that using any one should yield the correct result. The client should select one to continue the operation.

In addition, during an LDAP v3 "search" operation, a server can return a number of *continuation references*, which are of the same data type as a referral. The client is required to follow all continuation references. Like a referral, each continuation reference itself may contain a number of URLs that are assumed to be equivalent, and the client should use one of those URLs.

Unless a distinction is required, this lesson uses the term *referral* to mean the referral that is returned in either an error response or a continuation reference.

Referrals in the JNDI

A JNDI application uses the Context.REFERRAL ("java.naming.referral") environment property to indicate to the service providers how to handle referrals. Table 19 shows the values defined for this property. If this property was not set, then the default is to ignore referrals.

Unlike aliases, which are always ignored for LDAP operations that update the directory, the Context.REFERRAL property is in effect for all operations. See the **Creating and Updating Referrals** section (page 267) for a discussion of how to update referrals.

This property affects both "referral" error responses and continuation references.

TABLE 19: **Values for the "java.naming.referral" Property.**

Property Setting	Description
ignore	Ignore referrals.
follow	Automatically follow any referrals.
throw	Throw a ReferralException for each referral.

Interaction with the Manage Referral Control

The *Manage Referral* control (draft-ietf-ldapext-namedref-00.txt) tells the LDAP server to return referral entries as ordinary entries (instead of returning "referral" error responses or continuation references). If you are using the LDAP v3 and have set Context.REFERRAL to "ignore", then the LDAP service provider will automatically send this control along with the request. If you are using the LDAP v2, then the control will not be sent because it is not applicable in that protocol. When you set Context.REFERRAL to any other value, the control will not be sent regardless of the protocol version. When updating referral entries, you should always use "ignore".

When the LDAP service provider receives a referral despite your having set Context.REFERRAL to "ignore", it will throw a PartialResultException to indicate that more results might be forthcoming if the referral is followed. In this case, the server does not support the Manage Referral control and is supporting referral updates in some other way.

When Referrals Are Processed

Continuation references can be mixed in with search results returned by an LDAP "search" operation. For example, when searching a directory, the server might return several search results, in addition to a few continuation references that show where to obtain further results. These results and references might be interleaved at the protocol level. When the Context.REFERRAL property is set to "follow", the LDAP service provider processes all of the normal entries first, before following the continuation references. When this property is set to "throw", all normal entries are returned in the enumeration first, before the ReferralException is thrown.

By contrast, a "referral" error response is processed immediately when Context.REFERRAL is set to "follow" or "throw".

Server Configuration for Examples

The examples in this trail communicate with a new server whose directory contains referrals to the original server set up for this tutorial. The original server is assumed to be running on port 389 of the local machine, and the new server is assumed to be running on port 489 of the local machine. See Figure 3.

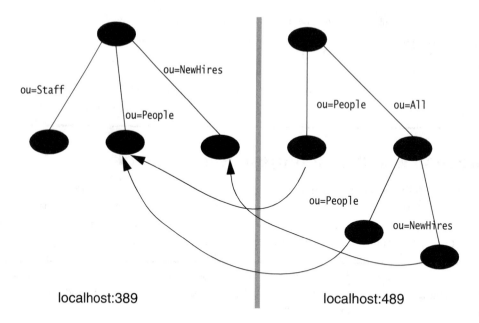

FIGURE 3:   Server Configuration for Referral Examples.

The following three referrals are set up from the new server (port 489) to the original server (port 389).

- The entry "ou=People, o=JNDITutorial" in the new server is a referral to the entry by the same name in the original server.
- The entry "ou=People, ou=All, o=JNDITutorial" in the new server is a referral to the "ou=People, o=JNDITutorial" entry in the original server.
- The entry "ou=NewHires, ou=All, o=JNDITutorial" is a referral to the "ou=NewHires, o=JNDITutorial" entry in the original server.

The initial context used in the examples in this lesson is initialized by using the following environment properties.

```
// Set up the environment for creating the initial context
Hashtable env = new Hashtable();
env.put(Context.INITIAL_CONTEXT_FACTORY,
    "com.sun.jndi.ldap.LdapCtxFactory");
env.put(Context.PROVIDER_URL, "ldap://localhost:489/o=JNDITutorial");
```

Unlike in the remaining examples in this tutorial, the port number is 489 instead of 389.

Before you go on: The examples in this lesson require you to set up a second server by using the configuration file refserver.ldif, available both on the accompanying CD and from the JNDI Web Site. The server must support LDAP v3 and draft-ietf-ldapext-namedref-00.txt. If the server does not support referrals in this way, then these examples won't work as shown. The configuration file contains referrals that point to the original server that you've set up and augmented for this lesson (using `tutorial.ldif` and `ldaptrail.ldif`). It assumes that the original server is on port 389 on the local machine. If you have set up the server on another machine or port, then you need to edit the "ref" entries in the `refserver.ldif` file and replace `"localhost:389"` with the appropriate setting. The second server is to be set up on port 489 on the local machine. If you set up the second server on another machine or port, then you need to adjust the setting of the `Context.PROVIDER_URL` environment property for the initial context accordingly.

Setting up a directory server is typically performed by the directory or system administrator. See the **Preparations** lesson (page 43) for more information.

Ignoring Referrals

If you set the `Context.REFERRAL` environment property to `"ignore"`, then any referral entries in the directory will be ignored and returned as plain entries. The LDAP provider will automatically send a Manage Referral control with the request for LDAP v3, telling the LDAP server to return the referral entries as plain LDAP entries. If the LDAP v2 is being used, then no control is sent.

Here's an example.

```
// Set the referral property; this is optional because
// "ignore" is the default
env.put(Context.REFERRAL, "ignore");

// Create the initial context
DirContext ctx = new InitialDirContext(env);

// Set the controls for performing a subtree search
SearchControls ctls = new SearchControls();
ctls.setSearchScope(SearchControls.SUBTREE_SCOPE);
// Perform the search
NamingEnumeration answer = ctx.search("", "(objectclass=*)", ctls);
```

Here is the output from running this example.

```
>>>
>>>ou=People
>>>ou=All
>>>ou=People, ou=All
>>>ou=NewHires, ou=All
```

Notice that the entries "ou=People", "ou=People, ou=All", and "ou=NewHires, ou=All" are returned as plain entries rather than as referrals.

Servers That Don't Support the Manage Referral Control

A server that does not support the Manage Referral control will ignore the control and send back referrals as it encounters them. In this case, when the LDAP provider receives the referral, it will throw a `PartialResultException` to indicate that there might be more results if the referral is followed.

Automatically Following Referrals

If you set the `Context.REFERRAL` environment property to `"follow"`, then referrals will be followed automatically. Here's an example.

```
// Set the referral property to "follow" referrals automatically
env.put(Context.REFERRAL, "follow");

// Create the initial context
DirContext ctx = new InitialDirContext(env);

// Set the controls for performing a subtree search
SearchControls ctls = new SearchControls();
ctls.setSearchScope(SearchControls.SUBTREE_SCOPE);

// Perform the search
NamingEnumeration answer = ctx.search("", "(objectclass=*)", ctls);
```

Running this example produces the following results.

```
>>>
>>>ou=All
>>>ldap://localhost:389/ou=People, o=JNDITutorial
>>>ldap://localhost:389/cn=Ted Geisel, ou=People, o=JNDITutorial
>>>ldap://localhost:389/cn=Jon Ruiz, ou=People, o=JNDITutorial
...
>>>ldap://localhost:389/ou=People, o=JNDITutorial
>>>ldap://localhost:389/cn=Ted Geisel, ou=People, o=JNDITutorial
>>>ldap://localhost:389/cn=Jon Ruiz, ou=People, o=JNDITutorial
...
>>>ldap://localhost:389/ou=NewHires,o=JNDITutorial
>>>ldap://localhost:389/cn=S. User,ou=NewHires,o=JNDITutorial
>>>ldap://localhost:389/cn=C. User,ou=NewHires,o=JNDITutorial
```

The example follows three referrals: `"ou=People"`, `"ou=People, ou=All"`, and `"ou=NewHires, ou=All"`.

Notice that the names of the referred entries are URLs instead of names that are relative to the context being searched. If you examine the `SearchResult` object for each of these referred entries and invoke `isRelative()` on them, then the method will return `false`. This indicates that the name is not relative and that it should be resolved relative to the initial context.

Manually Following Referrals

If you set the Context.REFERRAL environment property to "throw", then each referral encountered results in a ReferralException. A ReferralException contains *referral information*—information that describes the referral (such as a list of URLs)—and a *referral context*—the context to which the referral refers.

Here are the steps that a program usually follows when manually handling referrals.

1. Catch the exception.
2. Examine the referral information by using ReferralException.getReferralInfo(). For example, ask the user whether the referral should be followed.
3. If the referral is to be followed, then get the referral context by using Referral-Exception.getReferralContext() and reinvoke the original context method by using the same arguments supplied to the original invocation.
4. If the referral is not to be followed, then invoke ReferralException.skipReferral(). If this method returns true (which means that there are more referrals to be followed), then invoke ReferralException.getReferralContext() to continue. When you invoke a context method on the result, it will again throw a ReferralException for the next referral to be processed. Return to Step 1 to process it. If the method returns false, then there are no more referrals and this procedure can be terminated.

Here's an example.

```
// Set the referral property to throw ReferralException
env.put(Context.REFERRAL, "throw");

// Create the initial context
DirContext ctx = new InitialDirContext(env);

// Set the controls for performing a subtree search
SearchControls ctls = new SearchControls();
ctls.setSearchScope(SearchControls.SUBTREE_SCOPE);
// Do this in a loop because you don't know how
// many referrals there will be
for (boolean moreReferrals = true; moreReferrals;) {
    try {
        // Perform the search
        NamingEnumeration answer = ctx.search(">>>", "(objectclass=*)",
            ctls);

        // Print the answer
        while (answer.hasMore()) {
            System.out.println("" +
                ((SearchResult)answer.next()).getName());
        }
        // The search completes with no more referrals
        moreReferrals = false;

    } catch (ReferralException e) {
```

```
            if (! followReferral(e.getReferralInfo())) {
                moreReferrals = e.skipReferral();
            }

            // Point to the new context
            if (moreReferrals) {
                ctx = (DirContext) e.getReferralContext();
            }
        }
    }
```

For methods that return an enumeration, such as Context.list() and Dir-Context.search(), you must place the try/catch for the ReferralException around both the initial invocation and the while loop that iterates through the results. When the Referral-Exception is thrown, the existing enumeration becomes invalid and you must reinvoke the original context method to get a new enumeration. Notice also that the outer loop encloses both the method invocation on the context and the iteration of the results.

Authenticating to a Referral Context

By default, when you invoke ReferralException.getReferralContext(), the method uses the original context's environment properties, including its security-related properties, to create a connection to the referred server. Sometimes, upon examining the referral information, you might want to follow the referral by using different authentication information. You can do this by using ReferralException.getReferralContext(env) as follows.

```
    ...
    } catch (ReferralException e) {
    ...
        env.put(Context.SECURITY_PRINCIPAL, "newuser");
        env.put(Context.SECURITY_CREDENTIALS, "newpasswd");
        ctx = e.getReferralContext(env);
    }
```

If the authentication fails, that is, getReferralContext(env) throws an exception, then you can reauthenticate by first calling ReferralException.retryReferral() and then repeating the getReferralContext(env) call with updated environment properties. If you do not want to retry, then invoke ReferralException.skipReferral() before calling getReferral-Context(env).

Here is an example.

```
    ...
    } catch (ReferralException e) {
        if (!ask("Follow referral " + e.getReferralInfo())) {
            moreReferrals = e.skipReferral();
        } else {
            // Get credentials for the referral being followed
            getCreds(env);
        }

        // Do this in a loop in case getReferralContext()
```

```
       // fails with bad authentication info
     while (moreReferrals) {
         try {
             ctx = (DirContext)e.getReferralContext(env);
             break; // Success: got context
         } catch (AuthenticationException ne) {
             if (ask("Authentication failed. Retry")) {
                 getCreds(env);
                 e.retryReferral();
             } else {
                 // Give up and go on to the next referral
                 moreReferrals = e.skipReferral();
             }
         } catch (NamingException ne) {
             System.out.println("Referral failed: " + ne);
             // Give up and go on to the next referral
             moreReferrals = e.skipReferral();
         }
     }
   }
 }
```

In this example, the e.getReferralContext(env) call is placed inside of a loop so that if the call fails, it can be retried by using different credentials. The example defines a local method, getCreds(), for getting the principal name and credentials from Standard Input to update the environment properties, env, that are being used to get the referral context. When e.get-ReferralContext(env) fails, the user of the application can either choose to retry by using different credentials or skip the bad referral.

Passing Request Controls to a Referral Context

See the **Controls and Extensions** lesson (page 297) for details on how to set and change request controls of a referral context.

Creating and Updating Referrals

Note: The following discussion assumes that the LDAP server supports referrals as described in draft-ietf-ldapext-namedref-00.txt. If the server does not support referrals in this way, then the examples in this section won't work.

Representation in the Directory

A referral is represented in the LDAP directory as an object of class "referral". It contains a "ref" attribute, which is a multivalued attribute that contains one or more URLs. Each URL represents equivalent alternatives for following the referral. See draft-ietf-ldapext-namedref-00.txt for the schema definition of the "referral" object class and the "ref" attribute.

Disabling Following Referrals

You must ensure that the LDAP server will return referral entries as plain LDAP entries. You can do this by setting the Context.REFERRAL environment property to "ignore" or by unsetting it. ("ignore" is the default if the property is not set.) This is required if you are updating or deleting referrals and is optional if you are simply creating them. However, it is good practice to do this so that all programs that manage referrals are consistent.

Creating a Referral

You create a referral entry like you do any other type of entry: by using DirContext.bind() or DirContext.createSubcontext() and supplying the appropriate attributes. The referral entry must have as one of its object classes "referral", and it must have a "ref" attribute that has at least one URL string.

Here's an example that creates a referral called "cn=NewReferral" that points to the "cn=J. Duke, ou=NewHires, o=JNDITutorial" entry on another server.

```
// The object classes
Attribute objclass = new BasicAttribute("objectclass");
objclass.add("top");
objclass.add("referral");
objclass.add("extensibleObject"); // So that you can use cn as name
// The referral itself
Attribute ref = new BasicAttribute("ref",
    "ldap://localhost:389/cn=J. Duke, ou=NewHires, o=JNDITutorial");

// The name
Attribute cn = new BasicAttribute("cn", "NewReferral");

// Create the attributes to be associated with the new context
Attributes attrs = new BasicAttributes(true); // Case-ignore
attrs.put(objclass);
attrs.put(ref);
attrs.put(cn);

// Create the context
Context result = ctx.createSubcontext("cn=NewReferral", attrs);
```

You can use the CheckReferral.java sample program to examine the referral entry's attributes. If you run it without command line arguments, then it displays the referral entry itself. If you run it with a command line argument, then it displays the referred entry's attributes.

```
# java CheckReferral

ref: ldap://localhost:389/cn=J. Duke, ou=NewHires, o=JNDITutorial
objectclass: top, referral, extensibleObject
```

```
cn: NewReferral
```

```
# java CheckReferral follow
```

```
sn: Duke
objectclass: top, person, organizationalPerson, inetOrgPerson
mail: newbie@JNDITutorial.com
cn: J. Duke
```

Updating a Referral

You update a referral entry like any other type of entry: by using DirContext.modify-Attributes(). Here's an example that changes the referral's URL to "ldap://local-host:389/cn=C. User, ou=NewHires, o=JNDITutorial".

```
// Set up the new referral attribute
Attributes attrs = new BasicAttributes("ref",
    "ldap://localhost:389/cn=C. User, ou=NewHires, o=JNDITutorial",
    true); // Case-ignore
```

```
// Update the "ref" attribute
ctx.modifyAttributes(
    "cn=NewReferral", DirContext.REPLACE_ATTRIBUTE, attrs);
```
After running this program, if you reexamine the entry by using CheckReferral, then you will see the following.

```
# java CheckReferral
```

```
ref: ldap://localhost:389/cn=C. User, ou=NewHires, o=JNDITutorial
objectclass: top, referral, extensibleObject
cn: NewReferral
```

```
# java CheckReferral follow
```

```
sn: User
objectclass: top, person, organizationalPerson, inetOrgPerson
mail: cuser@JNDITutorial.com
userpassword: [B@1dacd887
cn: C. User
```

Deleting a Referral

You delete a referral entry like any other type of entry: by using Context.unbind() or Context.destroySubcontext(). Here's an example that removes the referral entry "cn=NewReferral".

```
// Remove the entry
ctx.destroySubcontext("cn=NewReferral");
```

Schema

This lesson gives an overview of LDAP schema and describes how it maps to the JNDI. It provides details about the schema content of object class definitions, attribute type definitions, syntax definitions, and matching rule definitions. It also contains two examples that illustrate practical uses of the schema.

Overview

A directory schema specifies, among other rules, the types of objects that a directory may have and the mandatory and optional attributes of each object type. The LDAP v3 defines a schema (RFC 2252 and RFC 2256) based on the X.500 standard for common objects found in a network, such as countries, localities, organizations, users/persons, groups, and devices. In the LDAP v3, the schema is available from the directory. That is, it is represented as entries in the directory and its information as attributes of those entries.

The LDAP v3 specifies that each directory entry may contain an operational attribute that identifies its *subschema subentry*. A subschema subentry contains the schema definitions for the object classes and attribute type definitions used by entries in a particular part of the directory tree. If a particular entry does not have a subschema subentry, then the subschema subentry of the root DSE, which is named by the empty DN, is used.

Version 2

Although schemas are not explicitly defined for the LDAP v2, a version 2 server can also publish schema information and make it accessible to the client. However, most such servers do not allow the schema information to be dynamically updated.

Schema in the JNDI

The JNDI contains methods that access schema information about object classes, attribute types, and attribute syntaxes. These methods are listed in Table 20 and illustrated in Figure 4.

TABLE 20: Schema-Related Methods in the JNDI.

Method	Description
`DirContext.getSchema()`	Returns the schema tree for the named object.
`DirContext.getSchema-ClassDefinition()`	Returns the object class definition for the named object.
`Attribute.getAttribute-Definition()`	Returns the attribute definition for this attribute.
`Attribute.getAttribute-SyntaxDefinition()`	Returns the syntax definition for this attribute.

`DirContext.getSchema()` is described in this section. The other methods are described in more detail elsewhere in this lesson.

The JNDI provides general descriptions of how these methods should behave but does not specify many details, such as the structure and contents of the schema tree, the attributes of the `DirContext` objects returned by the schema methods, or the effect of modifications to the schema tree and data on the directory itself. These details are currently determined by the underlying service provider and directory service because schema data is specific to each service. However, it makes sense for such details to be specified for a particular *style* of directory. For example, all LDAP-style directories should return schema information in a particular way. The *Guidelines for LDAP Service Providers* (http://java.sun.com/products/jndi/jndi-ldap-gl.html) describes the recommended schema tree and attributes for LDAP-style directories.

Relationship to the LDAP Schema

The methods in Table 20 are invoked on the object for which you want the schema information. When you are using the LDAP service provider, the objects returned by these methods are derived from schema information in the LDAP directory. The provider first tries to obtain the information from the subschema subentry of the object's corresponding LDAP entry. If this entry is not available, then it consults the root DSE's subschema subentry. If neither of these two sources is available, then an `OperationNotSupportedException` is thrown.

The sections **Object Class Definitions** (page 274), **Attribute Type Definitions** (page 278), **Attribute Syntax Definitions** (page 281), and **Attribute Matching Rule Defini-**

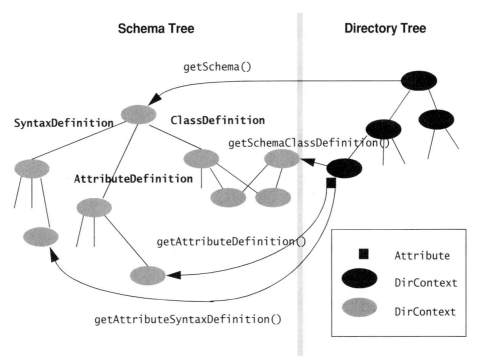

FIGURE 4: Relationship between Schema Tree and Directory Tree.

tions (page 283) give specifics about how the attributes in the subschema subentry are mapped to the objects returned by the JNDI methods.

The Schema Tree

The JNDI specifies that `DirContext.getSchema()` returns the root of the schema tree. The tree contains the bindings listed in Table 21.

TABLE 21:   Bindings in the JNDI Schema Tree.

Name	Binding
AttributeDefinition	The root of the attribute type definition namespace
ClassDefinition	The root of the object class definition namespace
SyntaxDefinition	The root of the attribute syntax definition namespace

Any or all of these bindings may be absent if the underlying directory does not publish such schema data or if the service provider does not support their retrieval. The Netscape Directory Server v4.1, for example, does not publish syntax definitions.

Service providers may also make available additional bindings in the schema tree, for example bindings for matching rules and extensions. Sun's LDAP service provider, for example, supports looking up matching rule definitions from the "MatchingRule" binding in the schema tree.

Here's an example that retrieves the schema tree root for the LDAP entry "ou=People" and lists its contents.

```
// Get the schema tree root
DirContext schema = ctx.getSchema("ou=People");

// List the contents of root
NamingEnumeration bds = schema.list("");
while (bds.hasMore()) {
    System.out.println(((NameClassPair)(bds.next())).getName());
}
```

Here's the output produced by this example.

```
AttributeDefinition
ClassDefinition
```

Object Class Definitions

All LDAP entries in the directory are *typed*. That is, each entry belongs to *object classes* that identify the type of data represented by the entry. The object class specifies the mandatory and optional attributes that can be associated with an entry of that class.

The object classes for all objects in the directory form a *class hierarchy*. The classes "top" and "alias" are at the root of the hierarchy. For example, the "organizationalPerson" object class is a subclass of the "Person" object class, which in turn is a subclass of "top". When creating a new LDAP entry, you must always specify all of the object classes to which the new entry belongs. Because many directories do not support object class subclassing, you also should always include all of the superclasses of the entry. For example, for an "organizationalPerson" object, you should list in its object classes the "organizationalPerson", "Person", and "top" classes.

Three types of object classes are possible:

- **Structural**. Indicates the attributes that the entry may have and where each entry may occur in the DIT.
- **Auxiliary**. Indicates the attributes that the entry may have.
- **Abstract**. Indicates a "partial" specification in the object class hierarchy; only structural and auxiliary subclasses may appear as entries in the directory.

In the schema tree, the name "ClassDefinition" is bound to a flat context containing DirContext objects that represent object class definitions in the schema. For example, if a directory supports a "person" object class, then the "ClassDefinition" context will have a binding with the name "person" that is bound to a DirContext object. Each object in the "ClassDefinition" context has the mandatory and optional attributes shown in Table 22. Only "NUMERICOID" is mandatory.

TABLE 22: Object Class Schema Attributes.

Attribute Identifier	Attribute Value Description
NUMERICOID (mandatory)	Unique object identifier (OID)
NAME	Object class's name
DESC	Object class's description
OBSOLETE	"true" if obsolete; "false" or absent otherwise
SUP	Names of superior object classes from which this object class is derived
ABSTRACT	"true" if the object class is abstract; "false" or absent otherwise
STRUCTURAL	"true" if the object class is structural; "false" or absent otherwise
AUXILIARY	"true" if the object class is auxiliary; "false" or absent otherwise
MUST	List of type names of attributes that must be present
MAY	List of type names of attributes that may be present
NOT	List of type names of attributes that must not be present

These attributes correspond to the definition of "ObjectClassDescription" in RFC 2252. All of the attribute values are represented by the java.lang.String class. Some directories do not publish all of the schema data. For example, the Netscape Directory Server v4.1 does not publish whether an object class is abstract, structural, or auxiliary. In such cases, the schema objects do not completely describe the object classes definitions.

Retrieving the Schema Object of an Object Class

To retrieve the schema object of an object class, you look for it in the schema tree. For example, you can obtain the schema object that represents the "person" object class by using the following code.

```
// Get the schema tree root
DirContext schema = ctx.getSchema("");

// Get the schema object for "person"
DirContext personSchema = (DirContext)schema.lookup(
    "ClassDefinition/person");
```

If you get the attributes of the `personSchema` schema object, then you will see the following.

```
NUMERICOID: 2.5.6.6
NAME: person
MAY: description, seealso, telephonenumber, userpassword
MUST: objectclass, sn, cn
DESC: Standard ObjectClass
SUP: top
```

In addition to using `lookup()`, you can use methods such as `list()` or `search()` to retrieve schema objects from the schema tree.

Getting an Entry's Object Classes

Given a `DirContext` object that represents an LDAP entry, you can get that entry's object classes by invoking `DirContext.getSchemaClassDefinition()` on it.

Following is an example that enumerates the object class definitions for the entry `"cn=Ted Geisel, ou=People"`. `getSchemaClassDefinition()` returns a context that contains the entry's object class definitions. Using this context, you can look up an individual definition, search for a definition, enumerate all definitions, or perform other `DirContext` operations.

```
// Create the initial context
DirContext ctx = new InitialDirContext(env);

// Get the context containing class definitions for
// the cn=Ted Geisel entry
DirContext tedClasses = ctx.getSchemaClassDefinition(
    "cn=Ted Geisel, ou=People");

// Enumerate the class definitions
NamingEnumeration enum = tedClasses.search("", null);
while (enum.hasMore()) {
    System.out.println(enum.next());
}
```

Adding a New Object Class

Before you go on: To update the schema, you must authenticate as the *directory administrator*. This is the name that you supplied to the directory administration program when you first configured the directory. For example, if you configured `"cn=Directory Manager"` as the administrator, then you need to do something like the following when creating the initial context.

```
env.put(Context.SECURITY_PRINCIPAL, "cn=Directory Manager");
env.put(Context.SECURITY_CREDENTIALS, "secret99");
```

Netscape v4.0 Bugs: The Netscape Directory Server v4.0 and earlier releases do not support schema entries that comply with RFC 2252. Specifically, contrary to RFC 2252, the Netscape server requires that OIDs (such as those for SUP and SYNTAX) be delimited by single quotation marks and MUST/ MAY lists be enclosed by parentheses. By default, the LDAP service provider produces schema entries that comply with RFC 2252 but are not acceptable to the Netscape server. To produce schema entries that are acceptable to the Netscape v4.0 server, you must add the following to the environment properties before creating the initial context:

```
env.put("com.sun.jndi.ldap.netscape.schemaBugs", "true");
```

Netscape v4.1 Bugs: The Netscape Directory Server v4.1 has fixed some of the schema-handling problems found in the version 4.0 server, so you should *not* use the "com.sun.jndi.ldap.netscape.schemaBugs" property with version 4.1. However, the version 4.1 server still requires that MUST/MAY lists be enclosed by parentheses. Sun's LDAP provider uses a quoted item instead of a parenthetical list for single-item MUST/MAY specifications. You can work around this problem by creating a single-valued "MUST"/"MAY" attribute and then adding a superfluous value, such as "objectclass", when you are modifying or creating an object class definition that has a single-item MUST/MAY list.

Adding a new object class to the schema is like adding a new entry to the directory. This is because the schema tree and schema objects are DirContext objects.

Following is an example that adds a new object class ("fooObjectClass") to the schema. It first declares the attributes that describe the new object class and then adds the object class definition to the schema by using DirContext.createSubcontext().

```
// Specify attributes for the schema object
Attributes attrs = new BasicAttributes(true); // Ignore case
attrs.put("NUMERICOID", "1.3.6.1.4.1.42.2.27.4.2.3.1.1.1");
attrs.put("NAME", "fooObjectClass");
attrs.put("DESC", "for JNDITutorial example only");
attrs.put("SUP", "top");
attrs.put("STRUCTURAL", "true");
Attribute must = new BasicAttribute("MUST", "cn");
must.add("objectclass");
attrs.put(must);

// Get the schema tree root
DirContext schema = ctx.getSchema("");

// Add the new schema object for "fooObjectClass"
DirContext newClass = schema.createSubcontext(
    "ClassDefinition/fooObjectClass", attrs);
```

Modifying an Object Class

You cannot modify an existing object class. You must first delete the existing object class definition and then add the updated version.

Deleting an Object Class

Before you go on: See the **Adding a New Object Class** section (page 276) for notes regarding updating the schema.

Deleting an existing object class from the schema is like deleting an entry from the directory. Here's an example that removes the object class "fooObjectClass" from the schema by using DirContext.destroySubcontext().

```
// Get the schema tree root
DirContext schema = ctx.getSchema("");

// Remove the schema object for "fooObjectClass"
schema.destroySubcontext("ClassDefinition/fooObjectClass");
```

Some servers might not let you delete an object class that's being used by entries in the directory. You might be able to get around this restriction by turning off schema checking.

Attribute Type Definitions

An attribute type definition specifies the attribute's syntax and how attributes of that type are compared and sorted. The attribute types in the directory form a class hierarchy. For example, the "commonName" attribute type is a subclass of the "name" attribute type. However, not many LDAP servers support attribute subclassing.

In the schema tree, the name "AttributeDefinition" is bound to a flat context that contains DirContext objects that represent attribute type definitions in the schema. For example, if a directory supports a "commonName" attribute, then the "AttributeDefinition" context will have a binding with the name "commonName" that is bound to a DirContext object.

Each object in the "AttributeDefinition" context has the mandatory and optional attributes listed in Table 23.

TABLE 23: **Attribute Type Schema Attributes.**

Attribute Identifier	Attribute Value Description
NUMERICOID (mandatory)	Unique object identifier (OID)
NAME	Attribute's name
DESC	Attribute's description
OBSOLETE	"true" if obsolete; "false" or absent otherwise
SUP	Name of superior attribute type from which this attribute's type is derived

TABLE 23: **Attribute Type Schema Attributes.**

Attribute Identifier	Attribute Value Description
EQUALITY	Name or OID of the matching rule if equality matching is allowed; absent otherwise
ORDERING	Name or OID of the matching rule if ordering matching is allowed; absent otherwise
SUBSTRING	Name or OID of the matching rule if substring matching is allowed; absent otherwise
SYNTAX	Numeric OID of the syntax of values of this type
SINGLE-VALUE	"true" if the attribute is not multivalued; "false" or absent otherwise
COLLECTIVE	"true" if the attribute is collective; "false" or absent otherwise
NO-USER-MODIFICATION	"true" if the attribute is not user-modifiable; "false" or absent otherwise
USAGE	Description of attribute usage

These attributes correspond to the definition of "AttributeTypeDescription" in RFC 2252. All of the attribute values are represented by the java.lang.String class. Some directories do not publish all of the schema data. For example, the Netscape Directory Server v4.1 does not publish the equality, ordering, and substring rules for its attribute definitions even though the server does support them for certain attributes. In these cases, the schema objects do not completely describe the attribute definitions.

Retrieving the Schema Object of an Attribute Type Definition

To retrieve the schema object of an attribute type definition, you look for it in the schema tree. For example, you can obtain the schema object representing the "cn" attribute by using the following code.

```
// Get the schema tree root
DirContext schema = ctx.getSchema("");

// Get the schema object for "cn"
DirContext cnSchema = (DirContext)schema.lookup(
    "AttributeDefinition/cn");
```

If you get the attributes of the cnSchema schema object, then you will see the following.

```
NUMERICOID: 2.5.4.3
NAME: cn
SYNTAX: 1.3.6.1.4.1.1466.115.121.1.15
DESC: Standard Attribute
```

You can use not only lookup() to retrieve schema objects from the schema tree, but also such methods as list() and search().

Getting an Attribute's Type Definition

Given an Attribute object that represents an LDAP attribute, you can get its schema object by invoking getAttributeDefinition() on it. Thus another way of getting the schema object for "cn" is to get a "cn" attribute and then invoke getAttributeDefinition(). Here's an example.

```
// Get an attribute of that type
Attributes attrs = ctx.getAttributes("cn=Ted Geisel, ou=People",
    new String[]{"cn"});
Attribute cnAttr = attrs.get("cn");

// Get its attribute type definition
DirContext cnSchema = cnAttr.getAttributeDefinition();
```

Adding a New Attribute Type Definition

Before you go on: See the **Object Class Definitions** section (page 276) for notes regarding updating the schema.

Adding a new attribute type definition to the schema is like adding a new entry to the directory. This is because the schema tree and schema objects are DirContext objects.

Here's an example that adds a new attribute type definition ("fooAttr") to the schema. It first declares the attributes that describe the new attribute type definition and then adds the definition to the schema by using DirContext.createSubcontext().

```
// Specify attributes for the schema object
Attributes attrs = new BasicAttributes(true); // Ignore case
attrs.put("NUMERICOID", "1.3.6.1.4.1.42.2.27.4.2.3.1.1.2");
attrs.put("NAME", "fooAttr");
attrs.put("DESC", "for JNDITutorial example only");
attrs.put("SYNTAX", "1.3.6.1.4.1.1466.115.121.1.15");

// Get the schema tree root
DirContext schema = ctx.getSchema("");

// Add the new schema object for "fooAttr"
DirContext newAttr = schema.createSubcontext(
    "AttributeDefinition/fooAttr", attrs);
```

Modifying an Attribute Type Definition

You cannot modify an existing attribute definition. You must first delete the existing attribute definition and then add the updated version.

Deleting an Attribute Type Definition

Before you go on: See the **Object Class Definitions** section (page 276) for notes regarding updating the schema.

Deleting an existing attribute type definition from the schema is like deleting an entry from the directory. Here's an example that removes the attribute type definition "fooAttr" from the schema by using DirContext.destroySubcontext().

```
// Get the schema tree root
DirContext schema = ctx.getSchema("");

// Remove the schema object for "fooAttr"
schema.destroySubcontext("AttributeDefinition/fooAttr");
```

Some servers might not let you delete an attribute type definition that's being used by entries in the directory. You might be able to get around this restriction by turning off schema checking.

Attribute Syntax Definitions

An attribute's syntax specifies the representation of the attribute's values. Examples of attribute syntaxes are Directory String, which specifies a case-insensitive character string encoded using the ISO 10646 character set, and Octet String, which specifies a sequence of octets.

In the schema tree, the name "SyntaxDefinition" is bound to a flat context containing DirContext objects that represent syntax definitions in the schema. For example, if a directory supports the 1.3.6.1.4.1.1466.115.121.1.15 (Directory String) syntax, then the "SyntaxDefinition" context will have a binding with the name "1.3.6.1.4.1.1466.115.121.1.15" that is bound to a DirContext object.

Each object in the "SyntaxDefinition" context has the mandatory and optional attributes listed in Table 24.

These attributes correspond to the definition of "SyntaxDescription" in RFC 2252. All of the attribute values are represented by the java.lang.String class.

TABLE 24: **Attribute Syntax Schema Attributes.**

Attribute Identifier	Attribute Value Description
NUMERICOID (mandatory)	Unique object identifier (OID)
DESC	Description of the syntax

Retrieving the Schema of an Attribute Syntax Definition

To retrieve the schema object of an attribute syntax, you look for it in the schema tree. For example, you can obtain the schema object that represents the Directory String syntax by using the following code. The OID for Directory String is 1.3.6.1.4.1.1466.115.121.1.15.

```
// Get the schema tree root
DirContext schema = ctx.getSchema("");

// Get the schema object for Directory String's syntax
DirContext dsSchema = (DirContext)schema.lookup(
    "SyntaxDefinition/1.3.6.1.4.1.1466.115.121.1.15");
```

If you get the attributes of the dsSchema schema object, then you will see the following.

```
NUMERICOID: 1.3.6.1.4.1.1466.115.121.1.15
DESC: Directory String
```

Note: This example won't work with the Netscape Directory Server v4.1 because that server does not publish syntax definitions in the schema.

You can use not only lookup() to retrieve schema objects from the schema tree, but also such methods as list() and search().

Getting an Attribute's Syntax Definition

Given an Attribute object representing an LDAP attribute, you can get its schema object by invoking getAttributeSyntaxDefinition() on it. For example, to retrieve the schema object for the Directory String syntax, you first fetch an attribute that uses that syntax (such as the "cn" attribute) and then invoke getAttributeSyntaxDefinition() on it. Here's an example.

```
// Get an attribute that uses that syntax
Attributes attrs = ctx.getAttributes("cn=Ted Geisel, ou=People",
    new String[]{"cn"});
Attribute cnAttr = attrs.get("cn");

// Get its attribute syntax definition
DirContext dsSyntax = cnAttr.getAttributeSyntaxDefinition();
```

Note: This example won't work with the Netscape Directory Server v4.1 because that server does not publish syntax definitions in the schema.

Creating, Modifying, or Updating an Attribute Syntax Definition

Dynamically creating, deleting, or modifying attribute syntaxes does not make sense. Even if the LDAP server allows you to add a syntax to (or delete a syntax from) its schema, the necessary implementation changes must be done on the LDAP server to support the new syntax. Most servers support a fixed set of syntaxes. Changing that set programmatically is usually not a supported feature.

Attribute Matching Rule Definitions

A *matching rule* specifies how attribute values are to be matched for equality, ordering, and substring comparison. Examples of matching rules are the case-exact ordering rule for English language-based strings and the case-ignore equality match for Directory String.

In the schema tree, the name `"MatchingRule"` is bound to a flat context that contains `DirContext` objects that represent matching rule definitions in the schema. For example, if a directory supports the "caseExactMatch" equality rule, then the `"MatchingRule"` context might have a binding with the name `"caseExactMatch"` that is bound to a `DirContext` object. Each object in the `"MatchingRule"` context has the mandatory and optional attributes shown in Table 25.

TABLE 25: Matching Rule Schema Attributes.

Attribute Identifier	Attribute Value Description
NUMERICOID (mandatory)	Unique object identifier (OID)
NAME	Matching rule's name
DESC	Matching rule's description
SYNTAX	Numeric OID of the syntax to which this matching rule applies
OBSOLETE	`"true"` if obsolete; `"false"` or absent otherwise

> **Note:** Many servers do not publish their matching rules. Even among those that do, some might not publish all of the rules.

These attributes correspond to the definition of "MatchingRuleDescription" in RFC 2252. All of the attribute values are represented by the `java.lang.String` class.

Retrieving the Schema of a Matching Rule Definition

To retrieve the schema object of a matching rule, you look for it in the schema tree. For example, you can obtain the schema object representing the "caseExactOrderingMatch-en" rule by using the following code.

```
// Get the schema tree root
DirContext schema = ctx.getSchema("");

// Get the schema object for the matching rule
DirContext mrSchema = (DirContext)schema.lookup(
    "MatchingRule/caseExactOrderingMatch-en");
```

If you get the attributes of the `mrSchema` schema object, then you will see the following.

```
SYNTAX: 1.3.6.1.4.1.1466.115.121.1.15
NAME: caseExactOrderingMatch-en
NUMERICOID: 2.16.840.1.113730.3.3.2.11.3
DESC: en
```

> **Note:** This example works only with directory servers that publish their matching rules, such as the Netscape Directory Server v4.1.

You can use not only `lookup()` to retrieve schema objects from the schema tree, but also such methods as `list()` or `search()`.

Creating, Modifying, or Updating a Matching Rule Definition

Dynamically creating, deleting, or modifying matching rules does not make sense. Most servers support a fixed set of matching rules. Changing that set programmatically is usually not a supported feature.

Two Practical Examples

How could you use this schema facility? This section shows two examples that use the schema. The first is a program that creates a new entry in the directory. It uses the schema to find out what attributes are required for the new entry. The second example is more ambitious. It creates an entry that may use new object classes, which in turn may use new attribute type definitions.

Using the Existing Schema

The following example is called UseSchema. It accepts as a command line argument the name of the entry to create. For example, to create a new entry called "cn=TestPerson" in the "ou=People" subtree, you enter at the prompt

```
# java UseSchema "cn=TestPerson, ou=People"
```

The program starts by asking you to enter the list of object classes for the new entry. After entering a list of object class names, you terminate the list by pressing Return. Working with this list of object class names, the program uses the schema to determine the list of mandatory and optional attributes required to create the new entry. This determination process is implemented by getAttributeLists().

```
static Vector[] getAttributeLists(DirContext schema,
    Vector objectClasses) throws NamingException {
    Vector mandatory = new Vector();
    Vector optional = new Vector();

    for (int i = 0; i < objectClasses.size(); i++) {
        String oc = (String)objectClasses.elementAt(i);
        Attributes ocAttrs =
            schema.getAttributes("ClassDefinition/" + oc);
        Attribute must = ocAttrs.get("MUST");
        Attribute may = ocAttrs.get("MAY");

        if (must != null) {
            addAttrNameToList(mandatory, must.getAll());
        }
        if (may != null) {
            addAttrNameToList(optional, may.getAll());
        }
    }
    return new Vector[] {mandatory, optional};
}
```

Note that for completeness, you should modify this example to recursively fetch the parents of the object classes and include them in your list of object classes to process. This is because some servers might follow subclassing rules and list only attributes of the most derived object class. Some servers list all of the attributes of the object class, including those inherited from superclasses.

The program looks up each object class name in the "ClassDefinition" portion of the schema tree and extracts from it the "MUST"/"MAY" attributes. These attributes contain lists of names of attributes that an entry of that object class must have and may have.

After constructing the list of mandatory and optional attribute names, the program uses getAttributeValues() to ask you to enter values for each attribute. (Press Return if you do not want to enter a value for an attribute.) The program uses each attribute's schema definition to get the attribute's syntax and then uses that syntax as part of the user prompt.

```
Attributes attrSchema = schema.getAttributes(
    "AttributeDefinition/" + name);
Attribute syntax = attrSchema.get("SYNTAX");
```

In practice, this is not very helpful because the syntax is an OID and few users will recognize what it represents. However, you can use the attribute schema definition in more useful ways, such as displaying its description and looking up the syntax to get its description.

After getting the attributes for the new entry, the program invokes DirContext.create-Subcontext() to create the new entry.

Augmenting the Existing Schema

Before you go on: See the **Object Class Definitions** section (page 276) for notes regarding updating the schema.

In the UseSchema example, you can enter only object classes defined in the schema. If you enter an object class that does not exist in the schema, then the program will throw a NameNot-FoundException.

The next example, AugmentSchema, allows you to enter object classes that have not been defined yet. You run the program by supplying the name of the entry to create as a command line argument as follows:

```
# java AugmentSchema "cn=TestPerson, ou=People"
```

As with the UseSchema program, you next enter a list of object classes for the new entry. With the AugmentSchema program, you may enter object classes that have not yet been defined. After getting this list, the program uses checkDefinition() to check whether the object classes have been defined. This method accepts as arguments the root of the schema tree, the list of object class names to check, the type of schema object (e.g., "ClassDefinition" or "AttributeDefinition"), and the list of attributes required for defining a schema object of that type. Here is the code for checkDefinition().

```
static void checkDefinition(DirContext schema, Vector names,
    String schemaType, String[]schemaAttrIDs)
    throws NamingException, IOException {
```

```
DirContext root = (DirContext)schema.lookup(schemaType);
for (int i = 0; i < names.size(); i++) {
    String name = (String)names.elementAt(i);
    try {
        // Check if the definition already exists in the schema
        root.lookup(name);
    } catch (NameNotFoundException e) {
        // Get the definition from the user
        Attributes schemaAttrs = getDefinition(schemaType, name,
            schemaAttrIDs);

        // Add the definition to the schema
        root.createSubcontext(name, schemaAttrs);
    }
}
}
```

For each object class that does not have a schema definition, the program creates a schema definition by asking you for the attributes needed to define it in the schema, such as its OID, name, and its list of mandatory and optional attributes. The program then creates an object class definition by invoking createSubcontext() on the schema tree.

Note: When using the Netscape Directory Server v4.1, you need to ensure that an object class's "MUST"/"MAY" attributes have more than one attribute value. See the **Object Class Definitions** section (page 277) for details.

After doing this for all object classes in the list, the program gets the object classes' lists of mandatory and optional attributes from the schema. It then checks these lists to make sure that they have attribute definitions in the schema, again by using checkDefinition(). For each attribute that does not have a definition in the schema, the program creates a schema definition by asking you for the attributes needed to define it in the schema, such as its OID, name, and syntax. The program then creates an attribute definition by invoking createSubcontext() on the schema tree.

The program gathers data for the attributes for the new entry and uses create-Subcontext() to create the new entry.

Controls and Extensions

The LDAP v3 was designed with extensibility in mind. It is extensible in two ways: by using controls and by using extensions.

Controls

The LDAP v3 allows the behavior of any operation to be modified through the use of controls. Any number of controls may be sent along with an LDAP request, and any number of controls may be returned with its results. For example, you can send a Sort control along with a "search" operation that tells the server to sort the results of the search according to the "name" attribute. Controls can be standard or proprietary.

The **Controls** sections of this lesson describe controls in detail and gives examples of how to use some of the more popular controls.

Extensions

In addition to the repertoire of predefined operations, such as "search" and "modify," the LDAP v3 defines an "extended" operation. The "extended" operation takes a request as the argument and returns a response. The request contains an identifier that identifies the request and the arguments of the request, and the response contains the results of performing the request. The pair of "extended" operation request/response is called an *extension*. For example, an extension is possible for Start TLS, which is a request for the client to the server to activate the TLS protocol. These extensions can be standard (defined by the LDAP community) or proprietary (defined by a particular directory vendor). The **Extensions** section (page 301) of this lesson describes extensions in more detail.

The javax.naming.ldap Package

Controls and extensions are supported by classes and interfaces in the `javax.naming.ldap` package. The core interface in this package is `LdapContext`, which defines methods on a context for performing "extended" operations and handling controls. The rest of the package contains classes and interfaces for representing controls and extensions.

Software Requirements: When using the examples in this lesson, you need the `ldapbp.jar` archive file in addition to the software requirements listed in the **Preparations** lesson (page 41). This file can be downloaded as part of the LDAP service provider from the JNDI Web site. It also is included on the CD that accompanies this book.

Server Requirements: The examples in this lesson depend on server support for certain features. Specifically, they use the Sort control and the Virtual List View control. The Netscape Directory Server v4.1 supports both of these, although it supports the Virtual List View control only for authenticated clients.

Controls

In the LDAP v3, a control can be either a *request control* or a *response control*. A request control is sent from the client to the server along with an LDAP operation. A response control is sent from the server to the client along with an LDAP response.

Either is represented by the interface `Control`. An application typically does not deal directly with this interface. Instead, it deals with classes that implement the interface. The application gets control classes either as part of a repertoire of controls standardized through the IETF or from directory vendors (vendor-specific controls). The request control classes should have constructors that accept arguments in a type-safe and user-friendly manner, and the response control classes should have access methods for getting the data of the response in a type-safe and user-friendly manner. Internally, the request/response control classes deal with encoding and decoding BER values. The next few pages include some examples of control implementation classes.

Criticality

When a client sends a request control to a server, it specifies the control's *criticality*. The criticality determines whether the server can ignore the request control. When a server receives a critical request control, it must either process the request with the control or reject the entire request. When it receives a noncritical request control, it must process the request either with the control or by ignoring the control. It can't reject the request simply because it does not support the control.

Whether a client specifies a request control as critical depends mainly on the nature of the control and how it is intended to be used. A designer who defines a control typically dictates or recommends whether the control be sent as critical or noncritical. When a server does not support a critical control, it is supposed to send back an "unsupported critical extension" error, which maps to the JNDI exception `OperationNotSupportedException`. However, some servers, such as the Microsoft Active Directory, might be nonconformant and send back a protocol error (`CommunicationException`) instead.

You use `Control.isCritical()` to determine whether a control is critical.

Identification

A designer defining a control must assign it a unique object identifier (OID). For example, the Sort control has an identifier of 1.2.840.113556.1.4.473.

You use `Control.getID()` to get a control's identifier.

Encoding

A control's definition specifies how it is to be encoded and transmitted between client and server. This encoding is done by using ASN.1 BER. Typically, an application does not need to deal with a control's encoding. This is because the implementation classes for a control deal with any encoding/decoding, as well as provide the application with type-friendly interfaces for constructing and accessing a control's fields. Service providers use `Control.getEncoded-Value()` to retrieve a control's encoded value for transmission to the server.

Request Controls

A request control is sent by a client to modify or augment an LDAP operation. You can use a control either to send more information to the server than is allowed by the operation's request or to modify the behavior of the operation altogether.

Request controls come in two types:

- Those that affect how a connection is created
- Those that affect context methods

The former is used when a connection needs to be established or re-established with an LDAP server. The latter is used when all other LDAP operations are sent to the LDAP server.

These two types of request controls must be differentiated because the JNDI is a high-level API that does not deal directly with connections. It is the job of the service provider to do any necessary connection management. Consequently, a single connection may be shared by multiple `Context` instances, and a service provider may use its own algorithms so as to conserve connection and network usage. Thus, when a method is invoked on the `Context` instance, the service provider might need to do some connection management in addition to performing the corresponding LDAP operations. For connection management, it uses the *connection request controls*, and for the normal LDAP operations, it uses the *context request controls*.

Unless explicitly qualified, the term *request controls* is meant here to mean context request controls.

Controls Supported by LDAP Servers

Support for specific controls is LDAP server-dependent. Eventually, when controls are standardized, LDAP servers might support a set of popular controls. However, some controls still might be proprietary and vendor-specific.

Here is a simple program for finding out the list of controls that an LDAP server supports.

```
// Create the initial context
DirContext ctx = new InitialDirContext();

// Read the supportedcontrol from the root DSE
Attributes attrs = ctx.getAttributes(
    "ldap://localhost:389", new String[]{"supportedcontrol"});
```

Here is the output produced by running this program against an LDAP server.

```
{supportedcontrol=supportedcontrol:
  2.16.840.1.113730.3.4.2,
  2.16.840.1.113730.3.4.3,
  2.16.840.1.113730.3.4.4,
  2.16.840.1.113730.3.4.5,
  1.2.840.113556.1.4.473,
  2.16.840.1.113730.3.4.9,
  2.16.840.1.113730.3.4.12
}
```

Implementations

The Control interface is generic for all request and response controls. Typically, you will deal with implementation classes that implement this interface rather than directly use the methods in this interface. Such implementation classes typically have type-friendly constructors and accessor methods. For example, Sun provides classes that implement some popular controls, such as Paged Results. This allows you to retrieve the results of an LDAP "search" operation in *pages*. To create a Paged Results control, you use its constructor, PagedResultsControl, as follows.

```
// Specify a page size of 20
Control prctl = new PagedResultsControl(20);
```

The next few pages offer other examples of how to construct and use controls.

Context Request Controls

You can associate request controls to be sent along with LDAP requests emitted by `Context` methods by using `LdapContext.setRequestControls()`. For example, you can set the context's request controls to include a control that tells the server to sort the results of `Context.list()` and `DirContext.search()`, assuming that the LDAP server supports server-side sorting, as shown in this example.

```
// Create the initial context with no connection request controls
LdapContext ctx = new InitialLdapContext(env, null);

// Create the critical Sort control that sorts based on "cn"
Control[] ctxCtls = new Control[]{
    new SortControl(new String[]{"cn"}, Control.CRITICAL)
};
// Set the context's request controls to be ctxCtls
ctx.setRequestControls(ctxCtls);

// Perform the list, which will sort by "cn"
NamingEnumeration answer = ctx.list("");
```

Once set, the controls remain in effect for the `Context` instance until they are replaced by the argument to another call to `setRequestControls()`. Next, after doing the list, you can perform a search by using the same `Context` instance; the results will still be sorted by the `"cn"` attribute.

```
// Perform the search, which will still sort by "cn"
// because context request controls are still in effect
answer = ctx.search("ou=People", "(cn=*)", null);
```

To tell a `Context` instance not to use any request controls, supply `null` as the argument to `setRequestControls()`.

```
// Set the context's request controls to be nothing
ctx.setRequestControls(null);
```

Finding Out the Context Request Controls That Are in Effect

To find out the request controls that are in effect for a context, you use `LdapContext.getRequestControls()`. Here is an example that sets the request controls to be a Sort control and then checks the controls by using `getRequestControls()`.

```
// Set the context's request controls to be ctxCtls
ctx.setRequestControls(ctxCtls);

// Check the controls that are in effect for context
Control[] reqCtls = ctx.getRequestControls();
if (reqCtls != null) {
    for (int i = 0; i < reqCtls.length; i++) {
        System.out.println(reqCtls[i]);
    }
}
```

Here is the output produced by this example.

```
com.sun.jndi.ldap.ctl.SortControl@1fa4d711
com.sun.jndi.ldap.ManageReferralControl@1fa4d59d
```

This output shows both the control that was added (the Sort control) as well as a Manage Referral control that the LDAP provider sends when referrals are being ignored (that is, the Context.REFERRAL environment property is unset or was set to "ignore"). To stop the LDAP provider from sending this control, you must set the Context.REFERRAL property to "throw" or "follow". See the **Referrals** lesson (page 261) for details.

Scope

A context's request controls remain in effect for all operations on the Context instance. However, unlike environment properties, a context's request controls are *not* inherited by contexts derived from this context. For example, if you perform a Context.lookup() and get back a context, then that context has no request controls. You must always explicitly set a context's request controls by using setRequestControls(), except when LdapContext.new-Instance() is used, as explained next.

Multithreaded Programming

Having a context's request controls in effect for all methods invoked on the context poses a bit of a challenge to multiple threads sharing a context handle. As always (independent of controls), such threads must synchronize their access to the context. In addition, they must ensure that the context has the right request controls set.

For example, to ensure that a method is executed with the right request controls, you might have code that looks as follows.

```
synchronized(ctx) {
    // Set the context's request controls to be myCtls
    ctx.setRequestControls(myCtls);

    // Perform the list by using the control
    NamingEnumeration answer = ctx.list("");

    // Do something useful with the answer

    // Get any response controls
    respCtls = ctx.getResponseControls();
}
```

This is cumbersome if you want a thread to have request controls that persist across multiple operations. Instead of doing this, you can use LdapContext.newInstance(). This method allows you to create a clone of the existing Context instance, with the request controls initialized to those supplied in the argument.

```
// Create a clone with the request controls set to newCtls
LdapContext cloneCtx = ctx.newInstance(newCtls);
```

When you subsequently update the clone's request controls, the updates won't affect the original context, and vice versa. Where appropriate and possible, the clone will share resources with the original context, such as the underlying connection to the LDAP server.

Here is an example that uses `newInstance()` to create a clone of a context and initializes the clone with a Sort control. It then performs a search in each context. The results from the clone are sorted, whereas those from the original are not.

```
// Create the initial context with no connection request controls
LdapContext ctx = new InitialLdapContext(env, null);

// Create the critical Sort that sorts based on "cn"
Control[] ctxCtls = new Control[]{
    new SortControl(new String[]{"cn"}, Control.CRITICAL)
};

// Create a clone with request controls set to ctxCtls
LdapContext cloneCtx = ctx.newInstance(ctxCtls);

// Perform the search by using the original context
NamingEnumeration answer = ctx.search("", "(cn=*)", null);

// Enumerate the answers (not sorted)
System.out.println("-----> Unsorted");
while (answer.hasMore()) {
    System.out.println(((SearchResult)answer.next()).getName());
}

// Perform the search by using a clone context; sort by "cn"
answer = cloneCtx.search("", "(cn=*)", null);

System.out.println("-----> Sorted");
// Enumerate the answers (sorted)
while (answer.hasMore()) {
    System.out.println(((SearchResult)answer.next()).getName());
}
```

Here is the output produced by the example.

```
# java NewInstance

-----> Unsorted
cn=Button
cn=Choice
cn=CheckboxGroup
cn=TextField
cn=CorbaHello
cn=RemoteHello
cn=RefHello
cn=Custom
cn=John Smith
-----> Sorted
cn=Button
cn=CheckboxGroup
```

```
cn=Choice
cn=CorbaHello
cn=Custom
cn=John Smith
cn=RefHello
cn=RemoteHello
cn=TextField
```

Connection Request Controls

Connection request controls are used whenever a connection needs to be established or re-established to an LDAP server. They do not affect other nonconnection-related LDAP operations, such as "search" or "modify." Conversely, context request controls do not affect connection-related LDAP operations. For example, setting a context's request controls to be a critical Sort control won't affect an LDAP "bind" operation.

You initialize a context's connection request controls by using the `InitialLdapContext` constructor. Here is an example.

```
// Create the control to use when establishing connection
Control[] connCtls = new Control[]{new SampleRequestControl()};

// Create the initial context
LdapContext ctx = new InitialLdapContext(env, connCtls);
```

This example creates a new `InitialLdapContext` instance with connection controls initialized to `SampleRequestControl`. Once set, the connection controls (`SampleRequestControl`) are inherited by all contexts derived from this context. Notice that this differs from context request controls, which are not inherited.

Changing the Connection Request Controls

You can change the connection request controls of a context by using `LdapContext.()`. This method establishes a new connection to the LDAP server by using the request controls supplied as the argument. If the argument is `null`, then no request controls are sent. Subsequent to the connection's being established, any implicit reconnections, for example those resulting from updated credentials, will also use the same controls.

`reconnect()` affects only the connection that is being used by the `Context` instance on which `reconnect()` is invoked. Any new `Context` instances that are derived from the context inherit the new connection controls, but contexts that previously shared the connection remain unchanged. That is, a context's connection request controls must be explicitly changed and is not affected by changes to another context's connection request controls.

In the following example, an `InitialLdapContext` is created with a `SampleRequest-Control`. The context's connection request controls are then set to `null` via a call to `reconnect()`, with `null` as the argument.

```
// Create the control to use when establishing the connection
Control[] connCtls = new Control[]{new SampleRequestControl()};

// Create the initial context
LdapContext ctx = new InitialLdapContext(env, connCtls);

// Do something useful with ctx

// Reconnect by using no controls
ctx.reconnect(null);
```

Finding Out the Connection Request Controls That Are in Effect

To find out the connection request controls that are in effect for a context, you use Ldap-Context.getConnectControls(). Here is an example that initializes the connection request controls to be SampleRequestControl and then checks the controls by using getConnectControls().

```
// Create the control to use when establishing the connection
Control[] connCtls = new Control[]{new SampleRequestControl()};

// Create the initial context
LdapContext ctx = new InitialLdapContext(env, connCtls);

// Check the controls in effect for connection establishment
Control[] reqCtls = ctx.getConnectControls();
```

Here is the output produced by this example.

```
SampleRequestControl@1fa4d891
com.sun.jndi.ldap.ManageReferralControl@1fa4d59d
```

This output shows both the control that was added (SampleRequestControl) as well as a Manage Referral control that the LDAP provider sends when referrals are being ignored (that is, the Context.REFERRAL environment property is unset or was set to "ignore"). To stop the LDAP provider from sending this control, you must set the Context.REFERRAL property to "throw" or "follow". See the **Referrals** lesson (page 261) for details.

Initializing a Referral Context's Connection Request Controls

Referrals are discussed in detail in the **Referrals** lesson (page 259). When you follow referrals automatically, the referral context inherits both the connection and the context request controls from the original context. When you handle referrals manually, you have the option of setting both controls for each referral context.

Here is an example. The referral context's connection request controls are set by being passed to LdapReferralException.getReferralContext(Hashtable, Control[]). After the referral context has been created, the context request controls are set via a call to `Ldap-Context.setRequestControls()`.

```
...
} catch (LdapReferralException e) {
    Control[] connCtls = new Control[]{new SampleRequestControl()};
    Control[] ctxCtls = new Control[]{
        new SortControl(new String[]{"cn"}, Control.CRITICAL)};

    // Get the referral context by using connection controls
    // when establishing the connection by using the referral
    ctx = (LdapContext) e.getReferralContext(env, connCtls);

    // Set the context request controls for the referral context
    ctx.setRequestControls(ctxCtls);
}
```

Response Controls

A response control allows a server to send more information to the client than is allowed by the operation's response. A one-to-one mapping between request controls and response controls is not needed. That is, a server can send response controls along with any response; they need not be in response to any client-initiated request control.

Because an LDAP server might send response controls with any response, you might be able to collect response controls after any `Context` method invocation. However, realistically, you would check for response controls only if you were expecting them.

`LdapContext.getResponseControls()` is used to retrieve a context's response controls. Each time that a method that communicates with the server is invoked on a context, the LDAP service provider clears any previously collected response controls and then collects all response controls resulting from the current method invocation.

For example, the following code fragment examines the response controls after a `Context.lookup()` call.

```
// Perform the lookup
Object answer = ctx.lookup("ou=People");

// Retrieve the response controls
Control[] respCtls = ctx.getResponseControls();
```

If you invoke two context methods and then use `getResponseControls()`, you will get only the response controls generated by the most recent context method.

Enumerations

Methods such as `Context.list()` and `DirContext.search()` return a `NamingEnumeration`. Each member of a `NamingEnumeration` might have response controls. One that does will implement the `HasControls` interface.

Here is an example that shows you how to retrieve the response controls from each member of a NamingEnumeration that is generated by a search.

```
// Perform the search
NamingEnumeration answer = ctx.search("ou=People", "(cn=*)", null);

// Examine the response controls (if any)
printControls("After search", ctx.getResponseControls());

// Enumerate the answers
while (answer.hasMore()) {
    SearchResult si = (SearchResult)answer.next();
    System.out.println(si);

    // Examine the response controls (if any)
    if (si instanceof HasControls) {
        printControls(si.getName(),
            ((HasControls)si).getControls());
    }
}

// Examine the response controls (if any)
printControls("After enumeration", ctx.getResponseControls());
```

This example performs a search, examines the response controls after the search, and then enumerates the search results. Next, it checks whether any member of the enumeration implements the HasControls interface and, for any that do, displays the response controls associated with the member. After the enumeration completes, it checks for context response controls by using ctx.getResponseControls(). This example defines a utility method, printControls(), that prints out a Control array.

Exceptions

If a context method throws an exception and the LDAP server had sent response controls with the error response that generated the exception, then you can retrieve the response controls by using ctx.getResponseControls(). Here is an example.

```
try {
    // Perform the lookup
    Object answer = ctx.lookup("ou=People");

    // Retrieve the response controls
    Control[] respCtls = ctx.getResponseControls();

    // Display respCtls
} catch (NamingException e) {
    // Retrieve the response controls
    Control[] respCtls = ctx.getResponseControls();

    // Handle the exception
}
```

Implementations

The `Control` interface is generic for all request and response controls. Typically, you will deal with implementation classes that implement this interface rather than directly use the methods in this interface. Such implementation classes typically have type-friendly and accessor methods. After getting the response controls by using `getResponseControls()`, you can cast the control to its most derived class and use the class-specific accessor methods.

For example, Sun provides classes that implement some popular controls, such as the server-side Sort control. The server-side Sort response control is represented by the `Sort-ResponseControl` class. You can use the following code to access information about the server-side Sort response control.

```
if (controls[i] instanceof SortResponseControl) {
    SortResponseControl src = (SortResponseControl)controls[i];

    if (src.isSorted()) {
        // Result was sorted ...
    }
}
...
```

To do this casting and use specific control classes, you must have some expectation of receiving such a control from the server and must have made the control classes available to your program. If either of these is lacking, then you can use only the methods in the `Control` interface to determine the identity of the control and to decode its contents.

Response Control Factories

The JNDI allows an application to use control implementation classes that are produced by any vendor. To help service providers achieve this goal, the JNDI provides the method

```
ControlFactory.getControlInstance(Control, Context, Hashtable)
```

for service providers to use to transform (that is, to *narrow*) generic controls received from an LDAP server into control classes that are made available to the application.

To narrow a control, you use a *control factory*, which is represented by the abstract class `ControlFactory`. A control received from an LDAP server begins life as a `Control` instance. The LDAP service provider uses `getControlInstance()` to narrow the `Control` instance into a more type-specific instance. This method searches the list of `ControlFactory` class implementations specified in the `LdapContext.CONTROL_FACTORIES` (`"java.naming.factory.control"`) environment property for a class that can narrow the control.

For example, if an application uses an LDAP server that returns a special response control, then the application can define a response control factory to parse the control and to provide type-friendly accessor methods. Here is an example of a response control factory.

```
public class SampleResponseControlFactory extends ControlFactory {
    public SampleResponseControlFactory() {
    }
```

```
public Control getControlInstance(Control ctl)
throws NamingException {
    String id = ctl.getID();

    // See if it's one of yours
    if (id.equals(SampleResponseControl.OID)) {
        return new SampleResponseControl(id, ctl.isCritical(),
            ctl.getEncodedValue());
    }

    // It's not one of yours, so return null and
    // let someone else try
    return null;
}
}
```

The factory class must have a public constructor that accepts no arguments. It also must provide an implementation for the abstract method `ControlFactory.getControl-Instance(Control)`. This method should check whether the input control is one that it can narrow. If it is, then the method should process the control and return an object of a more type-specific class. If it is not, then it should return `null` so that other factories may be tried.

"Extended" Operations

As mentioned earlier in this lesson, the LDAP v3 defines the "extended" operation, which takes a request as the argument and returns a response. The request contains an identifier that identifies the request and the arguments of the request. The response contains the results of performing the request. The pair of "extended" operation request/response is called an *extension*. For example, there can be an extension for Start TLS, which is a request for the client to the server to activate the TLS protocol. These extensions can be standard (defined by the LDAP community) or proprietary (defined by a particular directory vendor).

The `javax.naming.ldap` package defines the interface `ExtendedRequest` to represent the argument to an "extended" operation and the interface `ExtendedResponse` to represent the result of the operation. An extended response is usually paired with an extended request but not necessarily vice versa. That is, you can have an extended request that has no corresponding extended response. An unpaired extended response is called an unsolicited notification, described in detail in the **Event Notification** lesson (page 120).

An application typically does not deal directly with these interfaces. Instead, it deals with classes that *implement* these interfaces. The application gets these classes either as part of a repertoire of "extended" operations standardized through the IETF or from directory vendors for vendor-specific "extended" operations. The request classes should have constructors that accept arguments in a type-safe and user-friendly manner, whereas the response classes should have access methods for getting the data of the response in a type-safe and user-friendly manner. Internally, the request/response classes deal with encoding and decoding BER values.

Extensions Supported by LDAP Servers

Support for specific extensions is LDAP server-dependent. Eventually, when extensions are standardized, a set of popular extensions supported by most LDAP servers might be available. However, proprietary and vendor-specific extensions might still be around.

Here is a simple program for finding out the list of extensions that an LDAP server supports.

```
// Create the initial context
DirContext ctx = new InitialDirContext();

// Read supportedextension from the root DSE
Attributes attrs = ctx.getAttributes(
    "ldap://localhost:389", new String[]{"supportedextension"});
```

Here is the output produced by running this program against an LDAP server.

```
{supportedextension=supportedextension:
  1.3.6.1.4.1.1466.20037
}
```

Implementations

You typically will deal with implementation classes that implement ExtendedRequest and ExtendedResponse rather than directly use their methods. Such implementation classes typically have type-friendly constructors and accessor methods.

For example, suppose that an LDAP server supports a Get Time "extended" operation. It would supply classes such as GetTimeRequest and GetTimeResponse so that applications can use this feature. An application would use these classes as follows.

```
// Invoke the "extended" operation
GetTimeResponse resp =
    (GetTimeResponse) lctx.extendedOperation(new GetTimeRequest());

// Get the "extended" operation's (decoded) response
long time = resp.getTime();
```

The GetTimeRequest and GetTimeResponse classes might be defined as follows.

```
public class GetTimeRequest implements ExtendedRequest {
    // User-friendly constructor
    public GetTimeRequest() {
    };

    // Methods used by service providers
    public String getID() {
        return GETTIME_REQ_OID;
    }
    public byte[] getEncodedValue() {
        return null;  // No value is needed for the Get Time request
    }
    public ExtendedResponse createExtendedResponse(
        String id, byte[] berValue, int offset, int length)
```

```
            throws NamingException {
            return new GetTimeResponse(id, berValue, offset, length);
        }
    }

public class GetTimeResponse implements ExtendedResponse {
    long time;
    // Called by GetTimeRequest.createExtendedResponse()
    GetTimeResponse(String id, byte[] berValue, int offset,
        int length) throws NamingException {
        // Check the validity of the id
        long time =  ... // Decode berValue to get the time
    }

    // These are type-safe and user-friendly methods
    public java.util.Date getDate() {
        return new java.util.Date(time);
    }
    public long getTime() {
        return time;
    }
    // These are low-level methods
    public byte[] getEncodedValue() {
        return // berValue saved;
    }
    public String getID() {
        return GETTIME_RESP_OID;
    }
}
```

Frequently Asked Questions

This lesson answers the frequently asked questions users often have when using the JNDI to access LDAP services. These questions are classified in the following categories:

- Contexts
- Attributes
- Searches
- Names

You should consult the **Common Problems (and Their Solutions)** lesson (page 31) for descriptions of additional frequently encountered problems and their solutions.

Contexts

What is the relationship between a context and the connection to the LDAP server?

When you create an `InitialContext`, `InitialDirContext`, or `InitialLdapContext` by using the LDAP service provider, a connection is set up immediately with the target LDAP server. Any contexts and `NamingEnumerations` that are derived from this initial context share the same connection as the initial context.

For example, if you invoke `Context.lookup()` or `Context.listBindings()` from the initial context and get back other contexts, then all of those contexts will share the same connection. If you create a new initial context, then it will have its own connection.

When you change environment properties that are related to a connection, such as the principal name or credentials of the user, the context on which you make these changes will get its own connection (if the connection is shared). Contexts that are derived from this context in the future will share this new connection, but those that previously shared the context's connection are not affected (that is, they continue to use the old connection).

Similarly, if you use `LdapContext.reconnect()`, then the `Context` instance on which you invoke this method will get its own connection if the connection is shared.

How do I close the connection to the LDAP server?

To close the connection to the server, invoke `Context.close()` on *all* contexts originating from the initial context that created the connection. Make sure that all `NamingEnumeration` have been completed. For those context and enumeration objects that are no longer in scope, the Java runtime system will eventually garbage collect them, thus cleaning up the state that a `close()` would have done. To force the garbage collection, you can use the following code.

```
Runtime.getRuntime().gc();
Runtime.getRuntime().runFinalization();
```

Is the context safe for multithreaded access, or do I need to lock/synchronize access to a context?

The answer depends on the implementation. This is because the `Context` and `DirContext` interfaces do not specify synchronization requirements. Sun's LDAP implementation is optimized for single-threaded access. If you have multiple threads accessing the same `Context` instance, then each thread needs to lock the `Context` instance when using it. This also applies to any `NamingEnumeration` that is derived from the same `Context` instance. However, multiple threads can access *different* `Context` instances (even those derived from the same initial context) concurrently without locks.

Why does the LDAP provider ignore my security environment properties if I do not set the Context.SECURITY_CREDENTIALS ("java.naming.security.credentials") property or set it to the empty string?

If you supply an empty string, an empty `byte/char` array, or `null` to the `Context.SECURITY_CREDENTIALS` environment property, then an anonymous bind will occur even if the `Context.SECURITY_AUTHENTICATION` property was set to `"simple"`. This is because for simple authentication, the LDAP requires the password to be nonempty. If a password is not supplied, then the protocol automatically converts the authentication to `"none"`.

Why do I keep getting a CommunicationException when I try to create an initial context?

You might be talking to a server that supports only the LDAP v2. See the **Miscellaneous** lesson (page 237) for an example of how to set the version number.

I'm seeing some strange behavior. How do I find out what's really going on?

Try using the `"com.sun.jndi.ldap.trace.ber"` environment property. If the value of this property is an instance of `java.io.OutputStream`, then trace information about BER buffers sent and received by the LDAP provider is written to that stream. If the property's value is `null`, then no trace output is written.

For example, the following code will send the trace output to `System.err`:

```
env.put("com.sun.jndi.ldap.trace.ber", System.err);
```

How do I use a different authentication mechanism such as Kerberos?

First, you need to have Java classes that support Kerberos and/or GSSAPI. Then, you need to follow the instructions in the **Security** lesson (page 232) for making a SASL mechanism implementation available to the LDAP provider.

Attributes

When I ask for one attribute, I get back another. Why?

The attribute name that you are using might be a synonym for another attribute. In this case, the LDAP server might return the canonical attribute name instead of the one that you supplied. When you look in the `Attributes` returned by the server, you need to use the canonical name instead of the synonym.

For example, `"fax"` might be a synonym for the canonical attribute name `"facsimile-telephonenumber"`. If you ask for `"fax"`, then the server will return the attribute named `"facsimiletelephonenumber"`. See the **Directory Operations** lesson (page 60) for details on synonyms and other issues regarding attribute names.

How do I get back an attribute's value in a form other than a String or a byte array?

Currently you can't. The LDAP provider returns only attribute values that are either `java.lang.String` or `byte[]`. See the **Miscellaneous** lesson (page 238).

How do I know the type of an attribute's value?

An attribute's value can be either `java.lang.String` or `byte[]`. See the **Miscellaneous** lesson (page 238) for information on which attributes' values are returned as `byte[]`. To do this programmatically, you can use the `instanceof` operator to examine the attribute value that you get back from the LDAP provider.

Searches

Why does putting an "*" as an attribute value not work as expected in my search?

When you use the following form of search(), the attribute values are treated as literals; that is, the attribute in the directory entry is expected to contain exactly that value:

- search(Name name, Attributes matchingAttrs)

    To use wildcards, you should use the string filter forms of search(), as follows.

- search(Name name, String filter, SearchControls ctls)
- search(Name name, String filterExpr, Object[] filterArgs,
        SearchControls ctls)

For the last form, the wildcard characters must appear in the filterExpr argument, and not in filterArgs. The values in filterArgs are also treated as literals.

Why don't wildcards in search filters always work?

A wildcard that appears before or after the attribute value (such as in "attr=*I*") indicates that the server is to search for matching attribute values by using the attribute's substring matching rule. If the attribute's definition does not have a substring matching rule, then the server cannot find the attribute. You'll have to search by using an equality or "present" filter instead.

Why do I get back only *n* number of entries when I know there are more in the directory?

Some servers are configured to limit the number of entries that can be returned. Others also limit the number of entries that can be examined during a search. Check your server configuration.

How do I pass controls with my search?

See the **Controls and Extensions** lesson (page 293) for details.

How do I find out how many search results I got back?

You must keep count as you enumerate through the results. The LDAP does not provide this information.

Names

Why do I get an empty string as a name in my SearchResult?

getName() always returns a name *relative* to the *target context* of the search. So, if the target context satisfies the search filter, then the name returned will be "" (the empty name) because that is the name relative to the target context. See the **Searches** lesson (page 254) for details.

Why do I get a URL string as a name in my SearchResult?

The LDAP entry was retrieved by following either an alias or a referral, so its name is a URL. See the **Searches** lesson (page 254) for details.

Is the Name argument to the Context and DirContext methods a Compound-Name or a CompositeName?

The string forms accept the string representation of a composite name. That is, using a string name is equivalent to calling new CompositeName(stringName) and passing the results to the Context/DirContext method. The Name argument can be any object that implements the Name interface. If it is an instance of CompositeName, then the name is treated as a composite name; otherwise, it is treated as a compound name.

Can I pass the name I got back from NameParser to Context methods?

This is related to the previous question. Yes, you can. NameParser.parse() returns a compound name that implements the Name interface. This name can be passed to the Context methods, which will interpret it as a compound name.

What's the relationship between the name I use for the Context.SECURITY_PRINCIPAL property and the directory?

You can think of the principal name as coming from a different namespace than the directory. See draft-ietf-ldapext-authmeth-04.txt and the **Security** lesson (page 222) for details on LDAP authentication mechanisms. Sun's LDAP service provider accepts a string principal name, which it passes directly to the LDAP server. Some LDAP servers accept DNs, whereas others support the schemes proposed by draft-ietf-ldapext-authmeth-04.txt.

Why are there strange quotation marks and escapes in the names that I read from the directory?

Sun's LDAP name parser is conservative with respect to quoting rules, but it nevertheless produces "correct" names. Also, remember that the names of entries returned by NamingEnumerations are *composite names* that can be passed back to the Context and DirContext methods. So, if the name contains a character that conflicts with the composite name syntax (such as the forward slash character "/"), then the LDAP provider will provide an encoding to ensure that the slash character will be treated as part of the LDAP name rather than as a composite name separator.

How do I get an LDAP entry's full DN?

You can use `Context.getNameInNamespace()`.

Building a Service Provider

The lessons in the **Building a Service Provider** trail discuss how to write a service provider. Before embarking on this trail, you should have a good grasp of the fundamental and advanced JNDI topics described in **The Basics** (page 37), **Beyond the Basics** (page 75), and **Java**[TM] **Objects and the Directory** (page 151) trails. If you are building a service provider for a directory service, you also should first read the **Tips for LDAP Users** trail (page 201).

- **The Big Picture** lesson (page 315) describes the components of a service provider. It distinguishes between essential and optional components.
- **The Ground Rules** lesson (page 321) discusses general rules to follow when writing code for a service provider. It covers such topics as parameter passing, environment properties, and threads.
- **The Essential Components** lesson (page 331) describes how to write all of the essential components of a service provider and how to make it extensible. This includes building a context implementation, an initial context factory, and a name parser.
- The **Adding Directory Support** lesson (page 345) shows you how to add directory support to a service provider once you have the basic components. This lesson is useful to only those readers who are building a service provider for a directory service.
- The **Adding URL Support** lesson (page 357) shows you how to add URL support to a service provider once you have the basic components. URL support is an optional feature.
- The **Adding Federation Support** lesson (page 371) shows you how to add support for federation to a service provider once you have the basic components. Federation is an optional feature.
- The **Miscellaneous** lesson (page 387) shows you how to package a service provider and how to implement various advanced features such as referrals and event notification.

The Big Picture

Before you embark on writing a service provider, it is useful to get the big picture of the various components that comprise a service provider. The JNDI defines an architecture for building full function, very powerful service providers. However, not all service providers need to implement all of the features available. Seeing the big picture will enable you to know which components are mandatory, which are optional, and which may be supplied by other vendors or by application users. Understanding the big picture also makes the task of writing a service provider less daunting and less mysterious. This lesson describes this big picture.

If you have studied all of the other trails in this tutorial, then you likely have a pretty good understanding of the big picture. This lesson presents that picture from the perspective of the service provider developer. If you already understand this, then you might want to skip this lesson and go straight to the **The Ground Rules** lesson (page 321).

Essential Components

A basic service provider has the following necessary components.

- **Context implementation**. A class that implements the `Context` interface or one of its subinterfaces. This implementation is the guts of the provider. It is responsible for handling almost all of the requests submitted by the user application.
- **Initial context factory**. A class that implements the `InitialContextFactory` interface. This factory creates the root context that will satisfy method invocations on the `InitialContext` or its subclasses. The root context that is created by the initial context factory is typically an instance of the context implementation.
- **Name parser**. A class that implements the `NameParser` interface. The context implementation uses this parser to parse names that belong to its namespace.

Figure 5 illustrates how these three components interact. The arrows indicate instantiation paths.

Application/Applet/Servlet/ . . .

JNDI API

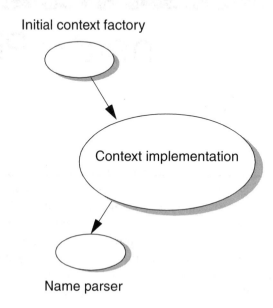

FIGURE 5:   Basic Components of a Service Provider.

Adding Extensibility

To make a context implementation extensible, you should use methods provided by the JNDI SPI framework. These methods are described in detail in the **The Essential Components** lesson (page 331). They use the object, state, and response control factories accessible to the application. These factories might be packaged with the service provider or be supplied by the application. Figure 6 depicts how a basic service provider interacts with these factories.

Optional Components

After building a basic service provider, you might want to add a couple of useful features, one to support URL string names and the other to access the context through other means than the initial context.

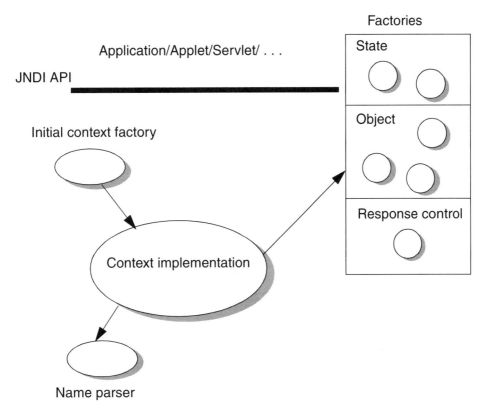

Factories

FIGURE 6: A Service Provider That Has Factories.

Supporting URL String Names

A useful feature to support is to allow applications to supply URL strings as name arguments to methods invoked on the `InitialContext` (and its subclasses). This feature is described in the **URLs** lesson (page 123). To support this feature, your service provider must have a *URL context factory*. This is a class that implements the `ObjectFactory` interface. Its job is to return a *URL context implementation* that accepts URL strings of a particular scheme. For example, an LDAP URL context implementation accepts URL strings of the `ldap` URL scheme. The URL context implementation typically works closely with the main context implementation (the one that accepts non-URL strings).

The **Adding URL Support** lesson (page 357) describes how to add support for URLs.

Putting a Handle on Things

Although you might not want to support full federation, a handle (that is, a reference) that can be bound in other naming systems can be useful for a context implementation. This allows the

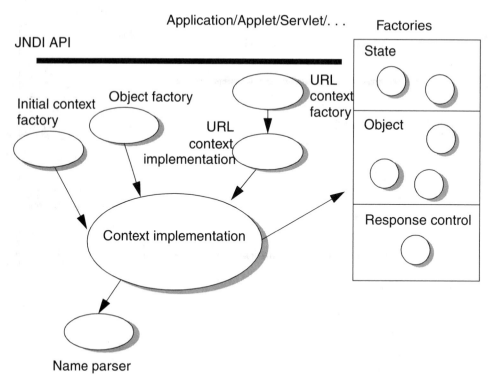

FIGURE 7: A Full-Featured Service Provider.

context to be federated at least as a terminal (i.e., leaf) naming system, as well as allows access to the context implementation through means other than the `InitialContext`. To support this feature, you need to decide on the format and content of the context's reference and define a corresponding object factory that accepts that reference. This object factory implements the `ObjectFactory` interface.

The **Adding Federation Support** lesson (page 371) describes how to add support for this feature.

Putting It All Together

Figure 7 shows the interactions between the components of a basic service provider and those necessary for URL support and object factory support.

Advanced Features

A context implementation must support methods defined in the `Context` interface and sub-interfaces in accordance with the JNDI specifications. Within that framework, however, a lot of leeway exists regarding the features that the context implementation supports. None of the features discussed in this section involve adding any new components. Rather, they involve embellishing a context implementation, typically by making existing methods support the feature or by adding new methods.

Federation Support

Federation concepts are described in the **Federation** lesson (page 131). Support for federation consists of the following:

- Determining the portion of the input name to process
- Contacting the *next naming system* (nns) to continue the operation

The JNDI SPI framework contains methods to assist in the latter.

A context implementation's support of federation is helpful but not required. The implementation can be used simply for accessing a particular naming/directory service—a valid and supported use of the JNDI.

The **Adding Federation Support** lesson (page 371) describes how to add support for federation.

Link Reference Support

A *link reference* is a symbolic link that can span multiple naming systems. It is represented by the `LinkRef` class. `Context.lookup()` and the resolution portion of all context methods are supposed to dereference link references automatically. `Context.lookupLink()` is used to read a link reference. Link references are described in the **Miscellaneous** lesson (page 142).

A context implementation that does not support binding of link references obviously does not have to deal with them. One that does support this feature should process the references according to the specification. It also should have mechanisms in place to catch link loops and/or to limit the number of links that can be followed.

The **Miscellaneous** lesson (page 390) describes how to add support for link references.

Referral Support

A *referral* is an entity used to redirect a client's request to another server. Containing the names and locations of other objects, it is sent by the server to indicate that the information that the client requested can be found at another location (or locations), possibly at another server or several servers.

Referrals are used by the LDAP (RFC 2251) and therefore apply only to LDAP-style directories. They are described in detail in the **Referrals** lesson (page 259).

The JNDI specifies the environment property `Context.REFERRAL` (`"java.naming.referral"`) that an application can use to control how referrals are processed by the context implementation. A context implementation that supports referrals must conform to this specification. It also should have mechanisms in place to catch referral loops and/or to limit the number of referrals that can be followed.

The **Miscellaneous** lesson (page 389) describes how to add support for referrals.

Schema Support

The `DirContext` and `Attribute` interfaces contain methods that enable programs to retrieve the schema of the directory entry/attribute. Schema in the LDAP are described in detail in the **Schema** lesson (page 271). These methods make sense only for a directory context implementation that publishes its schema. The schema might be read-only or read-write, depending on both the context implementation and the underlying directory service. To the degree possible, support for schemas should follow the guidelines given in the *Guidelines for LDAP Service Providers*, `http://java.sun.com/products/jndi/jndi-ldap-gl.html`.

The **Adding Directory Support** lesson (page 351) describes how to add support for schema.

Event Notification Support

Event notification support is defined in the `javax.naming.event` package. It is described in detail in the **Event Notification** lesson (page 111).

Support for event notification makes sense primarily for an underlying naming and directory service that supports event notification. Some context implementations might support this feature for those underlying services that do not support event notification, by using techniques such as polling to simulate the effects of notifications.

The **Miscellaneous** lesson (page 392) describes how to add support for events.

The Ground Rules

This lesson discusses some common issues that help you to write a service provider that conforms with the JNDI specifications. These issues concern parameter passing, environment properties, names, threads, and security.

If you have reviewed all of the other trails in this tutorial, then you likely have a fairly good understanding of these common issues. This lesson explains these issues from the perspective of the service provider developer and is useful as a refresher.

Parameters and Return Values

When writing a service provider, you must keep in mind certain rules on how to treat incoming parameters and outgoing return values. Not only do these rules affect the correctness of the service provider and ultimately the correctness of the program that uses it, but they also have security implications. These rules apply to method invocations on the Context interface and its subinterfaces and are discussed in the next subsections.

Parameters Are Owned by the Caller

When a service provider accepts a parameter from a caller as part of a context method invocation, it must not modify the parameter's contents. Suppose that a service provider receives a java.util.Hashtable as an environment parameter. Then it must not add, delete, or change any item in the Hashtable. If the provider must use a modified version of the Hashtable (for example, by deleting any security-related properties), then it must do so only after cloning the Hashtable.

In another example, when the provider gets a Name parameter, it must not add, delete, or change any component in the name.

Parameters Are Valid Only During Invocation

A service provider must not maintain any pointers to (mutable) parameters beyond the method invocation. If a service provider must retain information passed in the parameters, then it should clone or copy the information to locally accessible variables.

For example, if a caller invokes `LdapContext.setRequestControls()` with a non-null `Control[]`, then the service provider should copy the array before returning from the call. After the call, any changes that the caller makes to its array should not affect the service provider, and vice versa.

Return Values Are Owned by the Caller

When a service provider returns a (mutable) object to the caller, it should give up ownership of the object. The caller then is free to make changes to the returned object, and such changes should have no effect on the service provider.

For example, if two callers invoke `LdapContext.getRequestControls()`, then the `Control[]` that each receives is its own copy. Each caller can manipulate that result without affecting the other caller. Similarly, if two callers invoke `Context.getEnvironment()`, then the `java.util.Hashtable` that each receives can be manipulated independently without the other caller's being affected.

To support this behavior, the service provider typically needs to clone a mutable result (that can be returned to multiple callers) before returning it.

Environment Properties

Environment properties and how they are used by the application are described in detail in the **Environment Properties** lesson (page 95). This section describes how a service provider should handle environment properties.

Initialization

When a program uses the constructors from the `InitialContext` class or its subclasses, it supplies an optional environment parameter. The JNDI class libraries merge the contents of this parameter with other sources of environment properties (see the **Environment Properties** lesson (page 95)) and give the result to the service provider. More precisely, the JNDI gives the result to `InitialContextFactory.getInitialContext()`, which in turns creates the context implementation and supplies the resulting environment properties as a parameter. The context implementation does not have to worry about where the properties came from or with consulting the various sources. The JNDI class libraries will fetch and merge the properties before giving them to the underlying context implementation.

Ownership

Typically, the context implementation needs to remember the contents of the environment beyond the initialization of the context implementation. At a minimum, the context implementation needs the environment for processing `Context.getEnvironment()`. Like all other parameters received by a context implementation, the environment properties are owned by the caller and not by the context implementation. Therefore the context implementation needs to make a copy of the environment.

A common pattern in the context implementation's constructor is one that clones the environment, illustrated as follows.

```
if (inEnv != null) {
    myEnv = (Hashtable)inEnv.clone();
} else {
    myEnv = new Hashtable();
}
```

Inheritance

A `Context` instance is said to be *derived* from another `Context` instance if the latter was involved in the creation of the former. For example, if you obtain `Context` instance *B* by performing a `Context.lookup()` on `Context` instance *A*, then instance *B* is derived from instance *A*. Similarly, if you list a context and obtain a bunch of other `Context` instances, then those other instances are derived from the listed context.

A `Context` instance inherits its environment from the context from which it was derived, even across naming system boundaries. Following are the three places where a context implementation should pass on its environment.

- When a context implementation creates a `Context` instance, it should pass the parent `Context` instance's environment to the newly created `Context` instance. This can be done by cloning the environment or by using a copy-on-write policy so that each context's environment maintains its independence.
- When a context implementation invokes any of the following methods, it should pass the context's environment.

  - `NamingManager.getObjectInstance(Object, Name, Context, Hashtable)`
  - `DirectoryManager.getObjectInstance(Object, Name, Context, Hashtable, Attributes)`
  - `NamingManager.getStateToBind(Object, Name, Context, Hashtable)`
  - `DirectoryManager.getStateToBind(Object, Name, Context, Hashtable, Attributes)`
  - `ControlFactory.getControlInstance(Control, Context, Hashtable)`

  The factory, or the `Context` instance derived from the factory, resulting from these calls is responsible for cloning the environment as needed.
- When a context implementation that supports federation reaches its naming system

boundary, it constructs a `CannotProceedException` that pinpoints how far it has gotten and then invokes `NamingManager.getContinuationContext()` or `Directory-Manager.getContinuationDirContext()`. The context implementation should invoke `CannotProceedException.setEnvironment()` with the context's environment. Doing this passes the context's environment to the continuation context in the nns (next naming system). The context in the nns is responsible for cloning the environment as needed.

Note that inheritance occurs at the point at which the derived `Context` instance is created. Inheritance does *not* mean sharing. Each `Context` instance must maintain its own environment in such a way that any changes to its environment do not affect the environment of other `Context` instances.

Applicability

Possibly not all of the environment properties passed to a context will apply to that context implementation. The implementation is responsible for selecting and using those properties that apply to it and for maintaining and ignoring the ones that don't. The context is responsible for passing all properties, including those that it does not use, to `Context` instances derived from it. This allows the application to set up in one place the environment properties for all of the context implementations with which it will be interacting, instead of just those for the initial context.

Provider Resource Files

The JNDI SPI methods listed previously (`getObjectInstance()`, `getStateToBind()`, and `getControlInstance()`) not only use the properties found in the environment parameter, but also the context implementation's *provider resource file*. The JNDI locates the provider resource file by using the `Context` parameter. The name of the provider resource file is

```
[prefix/]jndiprovider.properties
```

where *prefix* is the package name of the `Context` parameter and each period character (".") is converted to a forward slash character ("/"). For example, suppose that the `Context` parameter is an instance of the class `com.sun.jndi.ldap.LdapCtx`. Its provider resource file will be named `com/sun/jndi/ldap/jndiprovider.properties`.

The JNDI SPI methods consult the provider resource file when determining the values of the following properties:

```
java.naming.factory.object
```

```
java.naming.factory.state
```

```
java.naming.factory.control
```

```
java.naming.factory.url.pkgs
```

These values are appended to the values found in the environment parameter.

Properties other than these may be set in the provider resource file at the service provider's discretion. These additional properties are ignored by the JNDI but might be used by the service provider. If your provider uses additional properties from the provider resource file, then you should document them clearly.

Provider-Specific Properties

The **Environment Properties** lesson (page 95) discusses the different categories of environment properties. Provider-specific environment properties are used only by a specific service provider. Before you define a provider-specific environment property, you should ensure that it must be provider-specific and cannot instead be service- or feature-specific. See the **Environment Properties** lesson for information on how to categorize environment properties.

When defining a provider-specific property, you should prefix it with the package name of your service provider. For example, if your context implementation has the class name `com.sun.jndi.ldap.LdapCtx`, then its provider-specific properties should have the prefix `"com.sun.jndi.ldap."`

Names

Names are discussed extensively in the **What's in a Name?** lesson (page 79). This section discusses in general how a service provider developer should treat the string and structured name parameters to methods in the `Context` interface and subinterfaces.

String Names

A string name is a composite name. Even if the context implementation that you are writing won't be supporting federation, following this rule is still a good idea so that users of your provider won't have to treat your provider differently in this respect.

Following this rule, you would write the overloads in the `Context` interface and subinterfaces that accept a `java.lang.String` name as simple wrappers around the overloads that accept a `Name`. As an example, here is a context implementation's definition of `Context.lookup()`.

```
Object lookup(String name) throws NamingException {
    return lookup(new CompositeName(name));
}
```

Composite Names

A structured name is represented by an object that implements the `Name` interface. It can represent either a composite name or a compound name. In either case, the name parameter belongs to the caller and you should not modify it (see the **Parameters and Return Values** section (page 321) for details).

A composite name is represented by an instance of CompositeName. If your context implementation does not support federation, then it can treat composite names in one of two ways. The simplest is for the context implementation to throw an InvalidNameException when it receives a CompositeName. However, this approach is Draconian in that it precludes the application from ever passing in a CompositeName, even if the CompositeName contains only the components that belong to the context implementation's namespace. A more compromising approach is for the context implementation to accept only CompositeNames that contain components that belong to its namespace. In this approach, the implementation extracts the components that belong to its namespace, and, for components that do not belong, it throws an InvalidNameException.

If your context implementation supports federation, then it should extract the components from the CompositeName that belong to its namespace. For components that do not belong, it should resolve its own components and then pass the remaining components to the nns. (More details about this are given in the **Adding Federation Support** lesson (page 371).) If the implementation receives only components for its namespace, then it should process the requested operation.

Here is some pseudocode that illustrates the nonfederated case.

```
Object lookup(Name name) throws NamingException {
    if (name instanceof CompositeName) {
        {mine, theirs} = splitName(name);
        if (theirs.size() == 0) {
            // Find this in internal tables
            return impl.get(mine);
        } else {
            // Don't support federation
            throw new InvalidNameException(name.toString() +
                " has more components than I can handle");
        }
    } else {
        // Process the compound name
        ...
    }
}
```

Compound Names

A compound name can be represented by any implementation of the Name interface except CompositeName or one of its subclasses. The easiest, though not the most efficient, way of making a context implementation accept a compound name is to turn it into a composite name.

Here is an example of mapping a compound name to a single-component composite name.

```
Object lookup(Name name) throws NamingException {
    if (name instanceof CompositeName) {
        // Process the composite name
        ...
```

```
    } else {
        // Process the compound name; turn it into single-component
        // CompositeName
        return lookup(new CompositeName().add(name.toString()));
    }
}
```

This is the most general solution. A context implementation typically can do this much more efficiently by using either the preparsed form (Name instance) directly or the stringified compound name. For example, an implementation might use the stringified compound name as a key to an internal hash table.

Threads and Synchronization

Threads and synchronization are discussed in the **Miscellaneous** lesson (page 146). This section discusses in general the issues that a service provider developer should be aware of regarding multithreaded access and the use of threads in service providers.

Context Implementations

The JNDI defines the Context interface and subinterfaces to which a service provider must implement. Thread-safety with respect to concurrent access is an implementation issue. However, the JNDI does make some common sense recommendations on what the API user and service provider should expect.

- Access to a single Context instance must be synchronized.
- Access to separate Context instances need not be synchronized, even when the separate instances are seemingly related.

The first rule means that the service provider need not worry about protecting access to resources used by a single Context instance against concurrent multithreaded access. Callers are responsible for synchronizing their accesses among themselves. This rule allows context implementations to be optimized for their most common thread usage mode.

The second rule reminds service provider writers that when Context instances from the same context implementation share resources, those resources must be protected against concurrent access. For example, multiple Context instances commonly share the same underlying network connection. The network connection in this example would need to be protected against concurrent access. This rule is motivated by the fact that the callers cannot be expected to be aware of any underlying relationship between different Context instances and surely cannot be expected to synchronize access to different Context instances. Therefore the service provider must ensure that different Context instances behave as individual, independent entities and hide any implementation relationships.

Factory Implementations

An object that implements any of the following interfaces and abstract classes (and their sub-interfaces) should be *reentrant*. That is, multiple threads should be able to invoke methods on a single instance of a factory concurrently.

- `InitialContextFactory`
- `ObjectFactory`
- `StateFactory`
- `ControlFactory`

Most factories are stateless, so this reentrancy requirement really is not much of an imposition on the implementation.

Use of Threads

Threads are a useful tool for building system software such as a context implementation, especially when the implementation needs to deal with the network. In fact, threads are indispensable if a context implementation is to support event notification as described in the `javax.naming.event` package (see the **Event Notification** lesson (page 111)).

You may use threads when building components of a service provider. However, be aware that the Java[TM] 2 Platform, Enterprise Edition, restricts components such as Enterprise Java-Beans[TM] from creating threads. This restriction means that if your service provider needs to create threads, then it should do so inside of a `doPrivileged` block. This allows the component's container to grant permission to the service provider for thread creation without granting the permission to the component.

Here is an example of a utility method for performing the thread creation inside of a `doPrivileged` block.

```
private Thread createThread(final Runnable r) {
    return (Thread) AccessController.doPrivileged(
        new PrivilegedAction() {
            public Object run() {
                return new Thread(r);
            }
        }
    );
}
```

Security Considerations

Security considerations from the API user's perspective are discussed in the **Miscellaneous** lesson (page 328). As a service provider developer, you should be aware of the following additional considerations.

Privileged Code

The Java 2 Platform, Standard Edition, defines a security model for system administrators and users to use to dynamically configure the security policy for running applications. You should be familiar with that security model before writing any service provider code. This discussion covers some issues pertinent to service provider code but is not a substitute for your reading and thoroughly understanding the *Java Security Guide* (`http://java.sun.com/products/jdk/1.2/docs/guide/security/`).

The security model allows you to mark sections of your code as *privileged* by wrapping each section inside of a `doPrivileged` block. The system administrator or user can then grant permissions to your code separate from those that it grants to other components of the application. Because service provider code is often considered "system" code and is granted all permissions by system administrators and users, you must be careful which permissions that the service provider requests. Or more precisely, you must be careful which sections of code that you put inside of `doPrivileged` blocks. Otherwise, you might be introducing security holes that can be exploited by malicious applications.

In general, a `doPrivileged` block should not be publicly accessible. Rather, it should be accessible in the smallest scope possible, with the package-private scope being the widest recommended scope. The code inside of a `doPrivileged` block should perform the narrowest functionality required.

For example, you should never have a `doPrivileged` block for reading arbitrary system properties, accessing local files, or creating network connections. On the other hand, it might be reasonable to have a `doPrivileged` block for reading a specific system property, reading a specific configuration file, or creating a network connection to the local machine on a specific port number.

In general, keep the number of `doPrivileged` blocks to a minimum. Always ask yourself if it is reasonable for the administrator or user to know that an application requires such a permission (and therefore is afforded the opportunity to deny the request) or is the action harmless enough that the provider should request the permission for the action on behalf of the application.

See the *Java Security Guide* for a general discussion of the Java security model and `doPrivileged` blocks.

Environment Properties

The **Miscellaneous** lesson (page 328) talks about security considerations associated with environment properties. The **Environment Properties** section (page 322) of this lesson describes how a provider should handle environment properties. The main security-related issue to note from these discussions is that, as a service provider writer, you should never return a context's copy of its environment properties. Rather, you should always return a clone or copy. This will forestall any possible tampering or accidental corruption of one of a `Context` instance's most important state—its environment properties.

If your context implementation is serializable, then you should avoid serializing any passwords or other security-sensitive environment properties.

Network Security

Most naming and directory services are accessed over the network. Although the data requested is protected by the server's authentication and access control mechanisms, some protocols do not protect (encrypt) the data that is sent as replies. This is not a problem particular to a client using the JNDI but rather a problem for any client accessing that service. Your service provider's documentation should describe the security implications associated with accessing its corresponding service over a network.

The Essential Components

This lesson shows you how to build all of the necessary components for a basic service provider. The components are shown in Figure 8. An overview of these components and their relationships to each other are described in **The Big Picture** lesson (page 331).

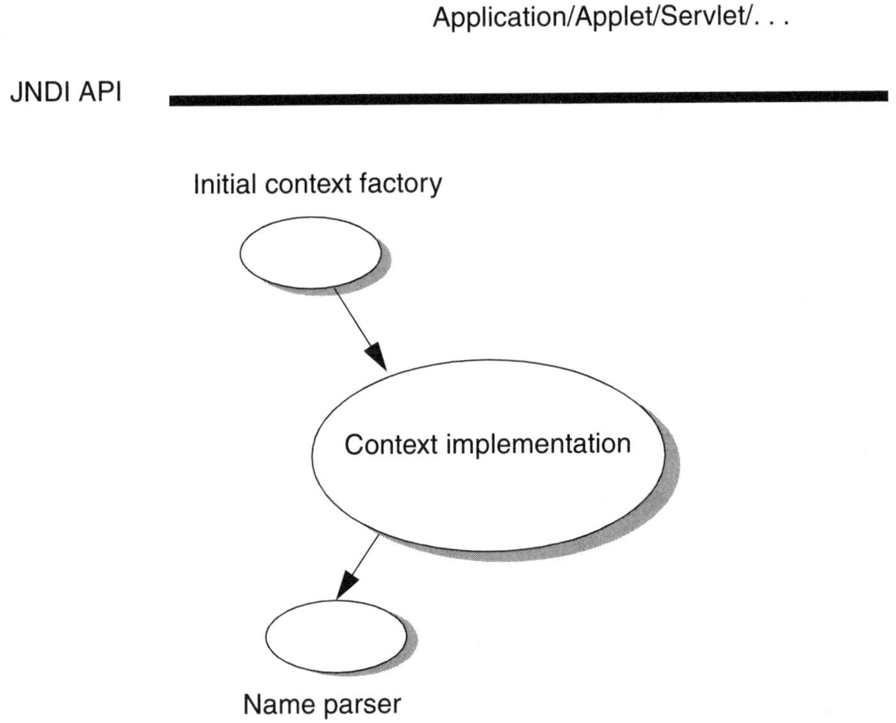

Application/Applet/Servlet/. . .

JNDI API

Initial context factory

Context implementation

Name parser

FIGURE 8: **Basic Components of a Service Provider.**

This lesson begins by demonstrating how to build the most fundamental component, the context implementation. It then shows you how to make that implementation extensible, by using utilities provided by the JNDI SPI framework. Finally, it describes how to build an initial context factory, which completes a basic service provider.

You should be familiar with **The Ground Rules** lesson (page 321) before proceeding with this lesson.

Note: The examples presented in this lesson are not meant to be prescriptive. Rather, they illustrate how some features can be implemented, but they do not always show the most efficient way of doing so. The most efficient and/or effective way to implement these features depends on the underlying service and the feature set of the context implementation.

Implementing a Context Implementation

A context implementation is a class that implements the `Context` interface. It is the guts of a service provider, which is responsible for handling almost all of the requests submitted by the user program.

The user program accesses a context implementation in two ways:

- Indirectly via method invocation on the `InitialContext` class
- Directly via method invocation on `Context` instances, obtained by calls such as `Context.lookup()`

A context implementation must provide a definition for each method in the `Context` interface. These methods can be categorized as follows:

- Lookup
- List (Enumeration)
- Update
- Names (name parser and other methods that deal with names)

Details on how to implement these methods and miscellaneous tips are discussed in the next sections.

Names

Almost all methods in the `Context` interface must process names. For consistency, you should use the same pattern in each method to process names. One way to achieve this conveniently is to define and use a utility method to process the input name. Two examples are given here, one for a context implementation of a flat namespace and one for a context implementation of a hierarchical namespace. Whether a context implementation supports a flat namespace or a hierarchical namespace is typically determined by the underlying naming/directory service or the requirements of the service provider.

As recommended in **The Ground Rules** lesson (page 325), for both examples, each method in the Context interface that accepts a java.lang.String name is defined simply to call its counterpart that accepts a Name. The rest of this discussion focuses on dealing with structured names.

A Flat Namespace Example

The first example implements a flat namespace and does not support federation. The methods that accept a Name use the following utility method to determine the components of the name that should be processed.

```
protected String getMyComponents(Name name)
throws NamingException {
    if (name instanceof CompositeName) {
        if (name.size() > 1) {
            throw new InvalidNameException(name.toString() +
                " has more components than namespace can handle");
        }
        return name.get(0);
    } else {
        // A compound name
        return name.toString();
    }
}
```

Because the context does not support federation, it accepts only single-component composite names or compound names. If it receives a multicomponent composite name, then it throws an InvalidNameException.

A Hierarchical Namespace Example

The second example implements a hierarchical namespace and does not support federation. The methods that accept a Name use the following utility method to determine the components of the name that should be processed.

```
protected Name getMyComponents(Name name) throws NamingException {
    if (name instanceof CompositeName) {
        if (name.size() > 1) {
            throw new InvalidNameException(name.toString() +
                " has more components than namespace can handle");
        }

        // Turn the component that belongs to you
        // into a compound name
        return myParser.parse(name.get(0));
    } else {
        // Already parsed
        return name;
    }
}
```

Unlike in the flat namespace example, this method returns a Name that represents a structured compound name instead of a java.lang.String. When the method gets a Composite-Name, it parses the first component into a compound name and returns it.

Lookup Methods

The flat namespace example uses in-memory storage; it does not support persistence. Whether a context implementation supports persistence typically is determined by the underlying naming/directory service or the requirements of the service provider.

Here is the implementation of lookup().

```
public Object lookup(Name name) throws NamingException {
    if (name.isEmpty()) {
        // Ask to look up this context itself; create and return
        // a new instance that has its own independent environment
        return (createCtx(myEnv));
    }

    // Extract the components that belong to this namespace
    String nm = getMyComponents(name);

    // Find the object in the internal hash table
    Object answer = bindings.get(nm);
    if (answer == null) {
        throw new NameNotFoundException(name + " not found");
    }
    return answer;
}
```

According to the JNDI specification, a lookup() of the empty name should return a copy of the context itself. After extracting the component that belongs to this context's namespace, the implementation proceeds to find the named binding from its internal data structure—a hash table. If it is not found, then it throws a NameNotFoundException. In an actual implementation, you would access the underlying naming/directory service instead of accessing a hash table.

This example does not support link references, so this method does not look for LinkRefs or treat them specially.

LookupLink

This example's definition of lookupLink() is the same as its definition of lookup(). This example does not support link references. See the **Miscellaneous** lesson (page 390) for a description of how to support link references.

List Methods

list() and listBindings() generate a NamingEnumeration. A NamingEnumeration is like a java.util.Enumeration, except that it contains methods that allow a NamingException to be thrown and it contains a close() method for freeing the resources associated with the enumeration. In the flat namespace example, list() and listBindings() simply perform a lookup() on the target context (that is, the context to be listed) and then do the listing by using the empty name as the argument. If the target does not name a Context, then it throws a Not-ContextException.

```java
public NamingEnumeration list(Name name) throws NamingException {
    if (name.isEmpty()) {
        // Generate enumeration of context's contents
        return new ListOfNames(bindings.keys());
    }
    // Perhaps "name" names a context
    Object target = lookup(name);
    if (target instanceof Context) {
        try {
            return ((Context)target).list("");
        } finally {
            ((Context)target).close();
        }
    }
    throw new NotContextException(name + " cannot be listed");
}
```

Implementation Note: Notice that the list() and listBindings() implementations take care to close the context that they looked up. This is good practice in case the context needs to be cleaned up. This also means that the enumeration returned by both methods should remain viable even after the Context instance from which it was obtained has been closed. When the Context instance's outstanding enumerations have been closed or completed, the final cleanup of the closed Context instance can occur.

The listing is generated by using the two internal classes ListOfNames and ListOfBindings. Here is the definition of ListOfNames.

```java
// Class for enumerating name/class pairs
class ListOfNames implements NamingEnumeration {
    protected Enumeration names;

    ListOfNames (Enumeration names) {
        this.names = names;
    }

    public boolean hasMoreElements() {
        try {
            return hasMore();
        } catch (NamingException e) {
            return false;
        }
    }

    public boolean hasMore() throws NamingException {
        return names.hasMoreElements();
    }
```

```
            public Object next() throws NamingException {
                String name = (String)names.nextElement();
                String className = bindings.get(name).getClass().getName();
                    return new NameClassPair(name, className);
            }
            public Object nextElement() {
                try {
                    return next();
                } catch (NamingException e) {
                    throw new NoSuchElementException(e.toString());
                }
            }
            public void close() {
            }
        }
```

The real work is done in the hasMore() and next() definitions. For the hash table example, ListOfNames is simply a wrapper around an Enumeration. In an actual implementation, the listing would be generated by accessing the underlying naming/directory service.

hasMoreElements() is a wrapper around hasMore(), whereas nextElement() is a wrapper around next(). hasMoreElements() and nextElement() satisfy the java.util.Enumeration interface and are used by clients that do not care about being notified of exceptions that occur during the enumeration. These are generic definitions that can be used by any implementation.

The ListOfBindings inner class is a subclass of ListOfNames. It overrides the definition of next() to return an instance of Binding instead of an instance of NameClassPair.

```
        public Object next() throws NamingException {
            String name = (String)names.nextElement();
            return new Binding(name, bindings.get(name));
        }
```

This is obviously a very simplified implementation. If the object in Binding is a Context, then it should be one that can be closed (which probably means that you want to clone it before returning it).

Update Methods

A context is updated by using the following operations:

- bind(Name name, Object obj)
- rebind(Name name, Object obj)
- unbind(Name name)
- rename(Name oldname, Name newname)
- createSubcontext(Name name)
- destroySubcontext(Name name)

Whether these methods are supported and how they are supported depend on the underlying naming/directory service. An actual context implementation would update the underlying naming/directory service. A context implementation for a read-only service, for example, would not support any of these methods. One for a flat namespace, such as the flat namespace example, would not support createSubcontext() and destroySubcontext().

Implementation Tip: bind() and rebind() can accept null as the object parameter if the context implementation supports only adding a name to the namespace without an associated object.

In the flat namespace example, bind(), rebind(), and unbind() are implemented much like lookup(), except that these methods update the internal data structure instead of read from it. Here is the definition of rebind().

```
public void rebind(Name name, Object obj) throws NamingException {
    if (name.isEmpty()) {
        throw new InvalidNameException("Cannot bind empty name");
    }

    // Extract the components that belong to this namespace
    String nm = getMyComponents(name);

    // Add the object to the internal hash table
    bindings.put(nm, obj);
}
```

Rename

rename() allows you to rename across *different* contexts. An actual context implementation could have problems supporting this fully because the underlying naming/directory service might not support this feature. Some services might support only renaming within the *same* context. In that case, the error might be indicated by the service itself and would result in a service-specific exception. Or, the context implementation might detect the problem and throw an OperationNotSupportedException.

Here is the definition of rename() from the simple flat namespace example.

```
public void rename(Name oldname, Name newname) throws NamingException {
    if (oldname.isEmpty() || newname.isEmpty()) {
        throw new InvalidNameException("Cannot rename empty name");
    }
    // Extract the components that belong to this namespace
    String oldnm = getMyComponents(oldname);
    String newnm = getMyComponents(newname);

    // Check whether the new name exists
    if (bindings.get(newnm) != null) {
        throw new NameAlreadyBoundException(newname.toString() +
            " is already bound");
    }

    // Check whether the old name is bound
    Object oldBinding = bindings.remove(oldnm);
```

```
        if (oldBinding == null) {
            throw new NameNotFoundException(oldname.toString() +
                " not bound");
        }

        bindings.put(newnm, oldBinding);
    }
```

Name Parser

Whether a context implementation supports a flat or hierarchical namespace depends on the underlying naming/directory service. For example, a context implementation for an LDAP directory service must support a hierarchical namespace, whereas a context implementation for the RMI registry must support a flat namespace because the underlying services dictate that.

A context implementation for a flat or hierarchical namespace needs a *name parser*, a class that implements the NameParser interface. The JNDI provides a utility class, Compound-Name, for developers to use when implementing NameParser. However, you are not required to use CompoundName. You can implement NameParser in any way as long as its parse() method returns an object that implements the Name interface. You should avoid using the Composite-Name class for this purpose because it would be interpreted as a composite name.

The hierarchical namespace example implements a syntax of right-to-left, dot-character (".") separated names. Here is its implementation of the NameParser interface.

```
class HierParser implements NameParser {
    private static final Properties syntax = new Properties();
    static {
        syntax.put("jndi.syntax.direction", "right_to_left");
        syntax.put("jndi.syntax.separator", ".");
        syntax.put("jndi.syntax.ignorecase", "false");
        syntax.put("jndi.syntax.escape", "\\");
        syntax.put("jndi.syntax.beginquote", "'");
    }

    public Name parse(String name) throws NamingException {
        return new CompoundName(name, syntax);
    }
}
```

The CompoundName class specifies properties that are used to define a naming syntax. For example, you can specify a syntax's atomic component separator, its escape and quotation characters, and whether the components are parsed right to left or left to right or are flat. Namespace syntax is determined by the underlying naming/directory service. You can use CompoundName only if the syntax of the underlying naming/directory service fits into CompoundName's syntax model.

The API user uses Context.getNameParser() to get a Context instance's name parser. The example implementation first performs a lookup() to verify that the input name is valid. It then returns the constant field myParser.

```
public NameParser getNameParser(Name name) throws NamingException {
    // Do lookup to verify that the name exists
    Object obj = lookup(name);
    if (obj instanceof Context) {
        ((Context)obj).close();
    }
    return myParser;
}
```

Each context implementation has only one instance of `HierParser`:

```
protected final static NameParser myParser = new HierParser();
```

This is done to satisfy the JNDI specification, which requires that a context implementation return a `NameParser` whose `equals()` method returns `true` for all `Context` instances from the same namespace. This requirement is useful for supporting federation. Even though this example does not support federation, the requirement is easy to fulfill.

More Names

The `Context` interface contains two name-related methods: `getNameInNamespace()` and `composeName()`. They allow the API user to manipulate names with respect to a context.

Fully Qualified Names

The API user uses `Context.getNameInNamespace()` to get a `Context` instance's fully qualified name within its namespace. The definition of this method depends on the underlying naming/directory service. In an actual implementation, this method might access the underlying naming/directory service or use bookkeeping information stored in the `Context` instance to generate an answer.

The hierarchical example maintains a back pointer to determine the fully qualified name of a context. Here is its `getNameInNamespace()` definition.

```
public String getNameInNamespace() throws NamingException {
    HierCtx ancestor = parent;

    // No ancestor; at root of namespace
    if (ancestor == null) {
        return "";
    }

    Name name = myParser.parse("");
    name.add(myAtomicName);

    // Get the parents' names
    while (ancestor != null && ancestor.myAtomicName != null) {
        name.add(0, ancestor.myAtomicName);
        ancestor = ancestor.parent;
    }

    return name.toString();
}
```

Compose Name

The API user uses `Context.composeName()` to compose names that span possibly multiple namespaces. The **What's in a Name?** lesson (page 92) describes this in more detail.

Because the hierarchical namespace example does not support federation, its `composeName()` name deals only with compound names. Here is its definition.

```
public Name composeName(Name name, Name prefix)
    throws NamingException {
    Name result;

    // Both are compound names; compose using compound name rules
    if (!(name instanceof CompositeName) &&
        !(prefix instanceof CompositeName)) {
        result = (Name)(prefix.clone());
        result.addAll(name);
        return new CompositeName().add(result.toString());
    }

    // Simplistic implementation; do not support federation
    throw new OperationNotSupportedException(
        "Do not support composing composite names");
}
```

Miscellaneous

This section describes additional miscellaneous issues that a context implementation must handle.

Resource Management

The Java programming language provides automatic garbage collection. This means that when an object is no longer being referenced, the Java runtime will automatically dispose of it. `close()` gives the API user a way to dispose of a `Context` instance and its associated resources before automatic garbage collection kicks in. This is important for network-based context implementations because network connections are a limited resource for both clients and servers. The flat namespace example does not provide any substantial implementation for `close()`. An actual implementation, especially one that must manage network connections, would define `close()` to clean up references and connections.

Environment Properties

The Ground Rules lesson (page 322) describes how a context implementation should treat its environment properties. Even though the flat namespace and hierarchical namespace examples don't use any environment properties, they must provide implementations for the environment-related methods.

As suggested by the **The Ground Rules** lesson, `getEnvironment()` should provide a read-only copy or a clone of its environment properties to its caller.

addToEnvironment() and removeFromEnvironment() are used by a program to update a context's environment. The flat namespace example simply updates its internal environment hash table. An actual implementation would examine the property name and act appropriately to update the Context instance's behavior accordingly.

Unsupported Operations

A context implementation must provide a valid implementation for lookup(). For all other methods, if a context implementation does not support a particular method, then the method definition should throw an OperationNotSupportedException.

For example, a context implementation for a read-only underlying naming service cannot support any method that involves updates. Here is an example of such a context implementation's definition of Context.bind().

```
public void bind(Name obj, Object obj) throws NamingException {
    throw new OperationNotSupportedException(
        "Read-only service does not support updates");
}
```

Building in Extensibility

If you followed the steps described in this lesson so far, then you should have a complete, functional context implementation. However, such a context implementation would be *closed* in the sense that the types of objects that can be read and stored by using the context implementation would be limited to what the context implementation was coded to accept. The JNDI provides utilities for making context implementations *extensible*. These utilities allow objects that are passed by the program to be transformed before they reach the context implementation, and allow objects that are read from the directory to be transformed before they reach the program.

Reading Objects

The **Object Factories** lesson (page 188) describes how a service provider should use Naming-Manager.getObjectInstance() or DirectoryManager.getObjectInstance() before returning an object to the user program from one of the following methods:

- Context.lookup(Name name)
- Context.lookupLink(Name name)
- Binding.getObject()
- SearchResult.getObject()

Following is how the hierarchical namespace example calls getObjectInstance() in its lookup() method. It uses the method in the NamingManager class because HierCtx implements only the Context interface. If a context implementation implements the DirContext interface, then it should use the one in the `DirectoryManager` class. See the **Adding Directory Support** lesson (page 354) for details.

```
// Code that determined that "inter" is the object bound to the
// atomic name "atom"
    ...

// Call getObjectInstance for using any object factories
try {
    return NamingManager.getObjectInstance(inter,
        new CompositeName().add(atom), this, myEnv);
} catch (Exception e) {
    NamingException ne = new NamingException(
        "getObjectInstance failed");
    ne.setRootCause(e);
    throw ne;
}
```

You should pass to `getObjectInstance()` the name of the object as a composite name and the context in which the name should be resolved. This need not be the deepest context (that is, the name need not be atomic). You should also pass in the context's environment properties in case the object factories need them.

Similarly, when returning the enumeration generated by `Context.listBindings()`, you should call `getObjectInstance()` for the object in each `Binding` in the enumeration. Here is the definition of the enumeration's `next()` method.

```
public Object next() throws NamingException {
    String name = (String)names.nextElement();
    Object obj = bindings.get(name);

    try {
        obj = NamingManager.getObjectInstance(obj,
            new CompositeName().add(name), HierCtx.this,
            HierCtx.this.myEnv);
    } catch (Exception e) {
        NamingException ne = new NamingException(
            "getObjectInstance failed");
        ne.setRootCause(e);
        throw ne;
    }

    return new Binding(name, obj);
}
```

This example shows a static approach, in which `getObjectInstance()` is called as you create each `Binding` instance. Another approach is to define your own `Binding` subclass and override `Binding.getObject()` to call `getObjectInstance()`. (The result of `getObject-Instance()` could be cached to avoid repeated invocations.)

Storing Objects

The **State Factories** lesson (page 173) describes how a service provider should use `Naming-Manager.getStateToBind()` or `DirectoryManager.getStateToBind()` before storing an object given by the user program to one of the following methods:

- `Context.bind(Name name, Object obj)`
- `DirContext.bind(Name name, Object obj, Attributes attrs)`
- `Context.rebind(Name name, Object obj)`
- `DirContext.rebind(Name name, Object obj, Attributes attrs)`

Here is how the hierarchical namespace example calls `getStateToBind()` in its `bind()` and `rebind()` methods. It uses the method in the `NamingManager` class because `HierCtx` implements only the `Context` interface. If a context implementation implements the `DirContext` interface, then it should use the one in the `DirectoryManager` class. See the **Adding Directory Support** lesson (page 354) for details.

```
// Code that determines that this is the context in which
// to bind the atomic name "atom" to the object "obj"
    ...
// Call getStateToBind for using any state factories
obj = NamingManager.getStateToBind(obj,
    new CompositeName().add(atom), this, myEnv);

// Add the object to the internal data structure
bindings.put(atom, obj);
```

You should pass to `getStateToBind()` the name of the object as a composite name and the context in which the name will be resolved. This need not be the deepest context (that is, the name need not be atomic). You should also pass in the context's environment properties in case the state factories need them.

Note that this implementation is simplistic because the example can store any type of object. A more realistic implementation would check the result of `getStateToBind()` to ensure that the object is of a type that it can store. See the **State Factories** lesson (page 171) for details.

Implementing an Initial Context Factory

The **Preparations** lesson (page 49) describes how to set up an *initial context* to access naming/directory services via the JNDI. For example, to use Sun's LDAP provider, use code that looks as follows.

```
Hashtable env = new Hashtable();
env.put(Context.INITIAL_CONTEXT_FACTORY,
    "com.sun.jndi.ldap.LdapCtxFactory");
env.put(Context.PROVIDER_URL, "ldap://localhost:389/o=jnditutorial");
```

```
Context ctx = new InitialContext(env);
// ... do something useful with ctx
```

The `InitialContext` class is simply a wrapper class that accesses the real context implementation—the `Context` instance created by the *initial context factory* class named by the `Context.INITIAL_CONTEXT_FACTORY` ("java.naming.factory.initial") environment property. This factory class must implement the `InitialContextFactory` interface. In the previous example, the initial context factory class is `com.sun.jndi.ldap.LdapCtxFactory`.

For a context implementation to be accessible from the initial context, a service provider must provide a class that implements the `InitialContextFactory` interface. Here is an example of an initial context factory for the hierarchical namespace example.

```
public class InitCtxFactory implements InitialContextFactory {
    public Context getInitialContext(Hashtable env) {
        return new HierCtx(env);
    }
}
```

This example is very simple: It calls the `HierCtx` constructor and returns an empty context. In an actual implementation, the initial context factory must create a `Context` instance for reaching all other parts of the namespace of the underlying naming/directory service. Also, an actual implementation would typically use the `Context.PROVIDER_URL` ("java.naming.provider.url") environment property to initialize the initial context. For example, in Sun's LDAP provider, the `Context.PROVIDER_URL` property indicates the directory server's machine address and port, as well as the DN (distinguished name) of the root naming context to use. In the previous example, the machine address and port are `localhost` and `389` and the DN is `"o=jnditutorial"`.

Adding Directory Support

Whether a context implementation supports directory operations depends to a large extent on the underlying service. If the underlying service is an LDAP directory service, for example, then a mismatch will result if the corresponding context implementation does not support directory operations. By contrast, if the underlying service is the RMI registry, supporting directory operations would make no sense because entries in the RMI registry do not have attributes.

To support directory operations, a context implementation must support methods defined in the `DirContext` interface in addition to those in the `Context` interface. This can be done either by defining a class that implements `DirContext` or by defining a subclass that implements `DirContext` and extends from a class that implements `Context`. In the example in this lesson, the latter is used, but there is really no difference between the two.

As with `Context` methods, a directory context implementation does not have to support all methods in the `DirContext` interface. For those that it does not support, it should throw an `OperationNotSupportedException`.

The directory operations can be categorized into five groups:

- Attribute retrieval
- Attribute updates
- Hybrid naming/directory operations
- Searches
- Schemas

Within this framework, however, is a lot of leeway in the features that the context implementation supports. None of the features discussed in this section involve adding any new components. Rather, they involve embellishing a context implementation, typically by making existing methods support the feature or by adding new methods.

This lesson also shows how to make a directory context implementation extensible in terms of the types of objects that it accepts for binding and those that it returns to the user program.

The Attribute Model

In some directory services, attributes are associated with the name of an object, whereas in other directory services, attributes are associated with the object itself. The JNDI does not specify a particular attribute model; both models are equally acceptable. The attribute model of the underlying service might affect the implementation of the context implementation.

Attribute Retrieval

The `DirContext` interface contains the following methods (plus their `java.lang.String` overloads) for retrieving the attributes of an object in a directory:

- `getAttributes(Name name)`
- `getAttributes(Name name, String[] attrIDs)`

Retrieving object attributes is the most basic of directory operations in the `DirContext` interface. Most directory context implementations support these methods.

Note that `getAttributes(name)` is just a shorthand form of writing

```
getAttributes(name, null);
```

Therefore its implementation should only call the longhand form, as follows.

```
public Attributes getAttributes(Name name) throws NamingException {
    return getAttributes(name, null);  // Same as attrIds == null
}
```

The implementation of `getAttributes()` depends on the attribute model of the underlying directory service. An actual implementation might need to do no more than pass the name and request to the underlying directory service for processing.

The hierarchical directory example uses a similar pattern as that for the `Context` operations in the hierarchical namespace example. Basically, it first determines whether the request is for this context or for a context or object named relative to this context. If it is for this context, then a copy of the context's attributes is returned. If it is for an immediate child object, then a copy of the object's attributes is returned. Otherwise, the next atomic name is resolved to a `DirContext` and the request is passed on to that context.

```
public Attributes getAttributes(Name name, String[] attrIds)
    throws NamingException {
    if (name.isEmpty()) {
        // Ask for attributes of this context
        return deepClone(myAttrs);
    }
    // Extract the components that belong to this namespace
    Name nm = getMyComponents(name);
    String atom = nm.get(0);
    Object inter = bindings.get(atom);

    if (nm.size() == 1) {
```

```
        // Atomic name; find the object in the
        // internal data structure
        if (inter == null) {
            throw new NameNotFoundException(name + " not found");
        }

        if (inter instanceof DirContext) {
            return ((DirContext)inter).getAttributes("", attrIds);
        } else {
            // Fetch the object's attributes from this context
            Attributes attrs = (Attributes) bindingAttrs.get(atom);
            if (attrs == null) {
                return new BasicAttributes();
            } else {
                return deepClone(attrs);
            }
        }
    } else {
        // Intermediate name; consume the name in this context
        // and then continue
        if (!(inter instanceof DirContext)) {
            throw new NotContextException(atom +
                " does not name a dircontext");
        }
        return ((DirContext)inter).getAttributes(
            nm.getSuffix(1), attrIds);
    }
}
```

Attribute Updates

The DirContext interface contains the following methods (plus their java.lang.String overloads) for retrieving the attributes of an object in a directory:

- modifyAttributes(Name name, int modOp, Attributes attrs)
- modifyAttributes(Name name, ModificationItem[] mods)

The form that accepts a modification operation (modOp) and an Attributes is typically used by an API user to specify the same operation to be applied to a bunch of attributes, such as adding several attributes. The API user can also use the form that accepts an array of ModificationItem for the same purpose, but the other form is more convenient. The form that accepts an array of ModificationItem is typically used by the API user to specify a series of different modifications to the same object.

A context implementation commonly implements the Attributes form by using the ModificationItem form. Here's how the example does this.

```
public void modifyAttributes(Name name, int mod_op,
    Attributes attrs) throws NamingException {
    if (attrs == null || attrs.size() == 0) {
        throw new IllegalArgumentException(
            "Cannot modify without an attribute");
```

```
        }
        // Turn it into a modification Enumeration and pass it on
        NamingEnumeration attrEnum = attrs.getAll();
        ModificationItem[] mods = new ModificationItem[attrs.size()];
        for (int i = 0; i < mods.length && attrEnum.hasMoreElements();
            i++) {
        mods[i] = new ModificationItem(mod_op,
            (Attribute)attrEnum.next());
        }

        modifyAttributes(name, mods);
    }
```

The implementation of both methods should guarantee that the series of modifications encapsulated by a single `modifyAttributes()` invocation is atomic. Whether atomicity is guaranteed is highly dependent on the underlying directory service, as is, in fact, the entire implementation of these methods. Other characteristics of the implementation include whether attribute names or identifiers are case-sensitive and whether the updates are sanctioned by any schema-checking features of the underlying directory service. Typically a context implementation does not need to take any special action to support or disallow these features. These are usually server-side features that are enforced when the modification requests reach the underlying service.

Hybrid Naming and Directory Operations

The `DirContext` interface contains the following methods (plus their `java.lang.String` overloads) that involve both updating the namespace and adding attributes:

- `createSubcontext(Name name, Attributes attrs)`
- `bind(Name name, Object obj, Attributes attrs)`
- `rebind(Name name, Object obj, Attributes attrs)`

How an API user uses these methods is discussed in the **Directory Operations** lesson (page 70).

`bind()` and `rebind()` can be used to bind a name as follows:

- To an object in the namespace
- To a set of attributes
- To both an object and a set of attributes

Depending on the underlying directory service, a context implementation might support one or all of these. If an implementation supports all three, then it should be ready to accept `null` as the object or `Attributes` parameter. Both parameters may be `null` in the same call if the context implementation supports adding only a name to the namespace, without also adding an associated object or attributes.

If the underlying directory supports storing only attributes, then the context implementation can decide whether it wants to support binding non-`null` objects and, if so, how to map

Java objects to attributes. See the **Representation in the Directory** lesson (page 195) for a discussion of object representations. See also later in this lesson a description of how to make the context implementation extensible in the types of objects that it will accept.

The implementation of these methods in particular depends on the attribute model of the underlying directory service. This is because one method invocation might involve both updating the namespace and adding attributes. If at all possible, the namespace update and attribute addition should occur atomically. Again, whether this is achievable depends on the facilities provided by the underlying directory service. An actual implementation might need to do no more than pass the name and request on to the underlying directory service for processing.

Implementation Tip: The semantics of `rebind()` require that the existing object's attributes be left untouched if the input `Attributes` parameter is `null`.

Implications on Pure Naming Operations

The context implementation not only must provide definitions for `createSubcontext()`, `bind()`, and `rebind()`. It also must ensure that the implementations of the pure naming methods take attributes into account. Following are the pure naming methods.

- `createSubcontext(Name name)`
- `destroySubcontext(Name name)`
- `bind(Name name, Object obj)`
- `rebind(Name name, Object obj)`
- `unbind(Name name)`

For example, you might implement these pure naming methods in terms of their counterparts that take an `Attributes` parameter. Here is a sample implementation of `bind(Name name, Object obj)`, written in terms of `bind(Name name, Object obj, Attributes attrs)`.

```
public void bind(Name name, Object obj) throws NamingException {
    bind(name, obj, null);
}
```

`unbind(Name name)` and `destroySubcontext(Name name)` need to get rid of the named object's attributes in addition to removing the object from the namespace.

Searches

The `DirContext` interface contains the following methods (plus their `java.lang.String` overloads) for searching a directory:

- `search(Name name, Attributes matches)`
- `search(Name name, Attributes matches, String[] retIDs)`

- search(Name name, String filter, SearchControls cons)
- search(Name name, String filterExpr, Object[] filterArgs,
    SearchControls cons)

As a developer of a context implementation, you need to be concerned only about two of them. This is because two of them usually can be written in terms of the other two.

The form that accepts a name and a set of matching attributes can be implemented by using the form that accepts the additional retIDs parameter, as follows.

```
public NamingEnumeration search(Name name,
    Attributes matchingAttrs) throws NamingException {
        return search(name, matchingAttrs, null);
}
```

A null value for the retIDs parameter means to return all attributes.

The form that accepts a filter expression and Object[] can be implemented by converting the filterExpr and filterArgs parameters into a string filter, as follows.

```
public NamingEnumeration search(Name name,
    String filterExpr, Object[] filterArgs, SearchControls cons)
    throws NamingException {
    // Fill in the expression
    String filter = format(filterExpr, filterArgs);

    return search(name, filter, cons);
}
```

format() is a utility method that takes a filter expression and arguments and returns a filter string that conforms to RFC 2254. See the hierarchical directory example (Tutorials/jndi/provider/dir/src/tut/HierDirCtx.java on the accompanying CD) for a sample implementation of this method.

You are then left with two methods to implement:

- The basic search that accepts a set of matching attributes and a list of attribute IDs to return
- The advanced search that accepts a string filter and a SearchControls parameter

Your implementation can support both, none, or only one of these methods. Typically, an implementation that supports the advanced search also supports the basic search. The basic search can be implemented in terms of the advanced search by converting the matching attributes into a string filter.

Theoretically, any context implementation can support both search methods, regardless of the capabilities of the underlying directory service. A context implementation for a directory service that does not support any searches can implement these methods by reading the directory data and then performing the searches in the context implementation itself. Similarly, a context implementation for a directory service that has only limited search capabilities can implement more-complicated searches by using the directory's limited capabilities. A context implementation for an LDAP directory service does not need to do much work, since the LDAP has full search capabilities. For directories with limited search capabilities, you need to evaluate whether it is cost-effective to provide full search capabilities despite possibly poor performance and heavy network load.

If your implementation does not support one of these methods, then the unsupported method should throw an `OperationNotSupportedException`.

The Basic Search

The basic search involves searching the named context for entries that contain the matching attributes. The method returns a `NamingEnumeration`; each item in the enumeration is a `SearchResult`. Each `SearchResult` consists of the entry's name relative to the named context and the entry's attributes selected by using the `retIDs` parameter. Because the search involves only the named context, the name is usually atomic, unless an alias or referral has been followed.

If the API user invokes `NamingEnumeration.close()`, then the context implementation should release resources associated with the search.

The Advanced Search

The complexity of implementing the advanced search has two dimensions. One dimension is the ability to process search filters that are arbitrarily complex. The other is the ability to satisfy the constraints specified in the `SearchControls` parameter. For example, an API user can specify a subtree search via this parameter. The advanced search maps easily onto directories that implement the LDAP or X.500 protocols. Context implementations for other protocols might need substantial work in order to support this method.

Like the basic search, the advanced search returns a `NamingEnumeration` of `SearchResults`. A `SearchResult` can contain, in addition to the name and requested attributes of the entry, the object bound to the name, provided that the API user requested it via the `SearchControls` parameter. See later in this lesson for a description of how to make the context implementation extensible in the types of objects that it can return in a `SearchResult`.

Schema

The `javax.naming.directory` package contains the following methods (plus their `java.lang.String` overloads) for dealing with directory schemas:

- `DirContext.getSchema(Name name)`
- `DirContext.getSchemaClassDefinition(Name name)`
- `Attribute.getAttributeDefinition()`
- `Attribute.getAttributeSyntaxDefinition()`

How an API user uses these methods is discussed in the **Schema** lesson (page 271).

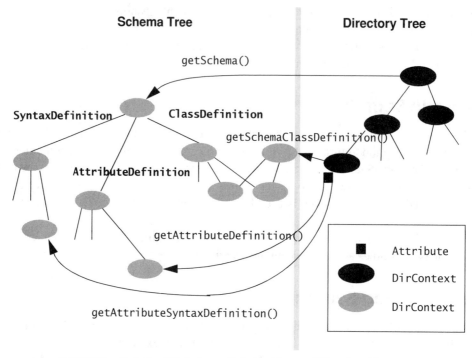

FIGURE 9:   Relationship between Schema Tree and Directory Tree.

getSchema(), getAttributeDefinition(), and getAttributeSyntaxDefinition() return a pointer to the schema tree, whereas getSchemaClassDefinition() returns a context whose children are from the schema tree. Figure 9 depicts the relationship between the directory tree and the schema tree.

If a context implementation does not support returning schema information, then these methods should throw an OperationNotSupportedException. Although a context implementation typically supports all or none of these four methods, it also may support only some of them. Further, some directory servers do not export all of the data required to completely populate the schema tree. Therefore a context implementation might not be able to return relevant data for all of these methods.

Implementation Strategies

A context implementation that supports schema methods should follow the recommendations in the *Guidelines for LDAP Service Providers* (http://java.sun.com/products/jndi/ jndi-ldap-gl.html) when choosing the names of attributes to use to describe schema data.

A common strategy is to build an in-memory schema tree that mirrors the one depicted in Figure 9. More than one schema tree per context implementation might exist because getSchema() accepts a Name argument. Whether there is one or more schema trees depends on the underlying directory service and/or server configuration. An LDAP server, for example, can be configured to have different schema trees for different parts of its directory tree. An API user who invokes getSchema() on different parts of the tree would expect to get back the corresponding (possibly different) schema trees.

Each node in the tree is a DirContext and represents a schema definition. The node has associated attributes that describe the schema definition. These attributes are described in the **Schema** lesson (page 271). The contents of each node (name and attributes) are determined by the underlying directory service and schema information on the server. For example, one context implementation might have a built-in (fixed) schema, whereas another might fetch the schema data dynamically from the directory service.

For getSchemaClassDefinition(), you need to create a new DirContext instance and bind as children the nodes that represent the named object's class definitions. For example, if the named object is of classes "top" and "person", the DirContext instance will have two child DirContext nodes, one representing the definition for "top" and the other for "person". The "top" and "person" DirContexts are nodes in the "ClassDefinition" branch of the schema tree (the one pointed to by getSchema()).

Attribute Definitions

To implement the schema methods in the Attribute interface, you need to provide a class that implements this interface or a subclass of BasicAttribute that overrides the two schema methods. Your context implementation, when asked to return any Attribute, will then return instances of this class. If you use an in-memory schema tree as suggested earlier in this lesson, then getAttributeDefinition() will return a node from the "AttributeDefinition" branch of the schema tree, whereas getAttributeSyntaxDefinition() will return a node from the "SyntaxDefinition" branch.

Advanced Features

The DirContext nodes returned by the schema methods are full-fledged DirContext objects. This means that they are free to implement, or not, all of the methods available in the DirContext interface.

A context implementation should support updates to the schema objects only to the extent that corresponding updates are reflected in the schema data of the underlying directory service. For example, you should never allow a DirContext to be removed from the schema tree unless the corresponding schema definition is removed from the underlying directory service.

To the degree possible, a context implementation should support basic searches (that is, single context level, attribute matches) on the schema tree. Support for the advanced search is nice, but its return on investment is not as great because the schema tree is not very deep.

Optimizations

The schema tree is typically very expensive to generate. Generating it involves first reading schema data from the directory service and parsing the data and then constructing an in-memory tree. To improve performance, a context implementation can cache the schema tree so that it can be shared by multiple contexts. Of course, such sharing should be allowed only if doing so does not compromise correctness and security.

Building in Extensibility

The Essential Components lesson (page 341) showed how to use JNDI utilities to make a context implementation extensible. When you are building a directory context implementation, you should replace those utilities with the ones described here.

Reading Objects

A directory context implementation should use `DirectoryManager.getObjectInstance()` before returning an object to the user program from one of the following methods:

- `Context.lookup()`
- `Context.lookupLink()`
- `Binding.getObject()`
- `SearchResult.getObject()`

Here is how the hierarchical directory example calls `getObjectInstance()` in its `lookup()`.

```
// Code that determines whether "inter" is the object bound to the
// atomic name "atom"
    ...
// Get the object's attributes
Attributes attrs;
if (inter instanceof DirContext) {
    attrs = ((DirContext)inter).getAttributes("");
} else {
    // Fetch the object's attributes from this context
    attrs = (Attributes) bindingAttrs.get(atom);
}
// Call getObjectInstance for using any object factories
try {
    return DirectoryManager.getObjectInstance(inter,
        new CompositeName().add(atom), this, myEnv, attrs);
} catch (Exception e) {
    NamingException ne = new NamingException(
        "getObjectInstance failed");
    ne.setRootCause(e);
    throw ne;
}
```

Similarly, when returning the enumeration generated by `Context.listBindings()` or overloads of `DirContext.search()`, you should call `getObjectInstance()` for the object in each `SearchResult` in the enumeration.

Here is the definition of the list enumeration's `next()` method.

```
public Object next() throws NamingException {
    String name = (String)names.nextElement();
    Object obj = bindings.get(name);

    try {
        // Get the attributes
        Attributes attrs;
        if (obj instanceof DirContext) {
            attrs = ((DirContext)obj).getAttributes("");
        } else {
            // Fetch the object's attributes from this context
            attrs = (Attributes) bindingAttrs.get(name);
        }

        obj = DirectoryManager.getObjectInstance(
            obj, new CompositeName().add(name), HierDirCtx.this,
            HierDirCtx.this.myEnv, attrs);
    } catch (Exception e) {
        NamingException ne = new NamingException(
            "getObjectInstance failed");
        ne.setRootCause(e);
        throw ne;
    }
    return new Binding(name, obj);
}
```

Storing Objects

A directory context implementation should use `DirectoryManager.getStateToBind()` before storing an object given by the user program to one of the following methods:

- `Context.bind()`
- `DirContext.bind()`
- `Context.rebind()`
- `DirContext.rebind()`

Here is how the hierarchical directory example calls `getStateToBind()` in its `bind()` and `rebind()` methods.

```
// Code that determines that this is the context in which
// to bind the atomic name "atom" to the object "obj"
    ...

// Call getStateToBind for using any state factories
DirStateFactory.Result res = DirectoryManager.getStateToBind(
    obj, new CompositeName().add(atom), this, myEnv, attrs);
// Add the object to the internal data structure
bindings.put(atom, res.getObject());
```

```
        // Add the attributes
        if (res.getAttributes() != null) {
            bindingAttrs.put(atom, deepClone(res.getAttributes()));
        }
```

DirectoryManager.getStateToBind() returns an instance of DirStateFactory.Result, which is a tuple consisting of the object to bind and the attributes to associate with the object. Upon receiving the result, the context implementation updates its internal bindings table and attributes table.

31

Adding URL Support

The **URLs** lesson (page 123) describes how the API user can pass a URL string to the initial context and have that URL be processed by a URL context implementation. This lesson shows you how to build a URL context implementation and make it available to the API user. This involves three steps:

1. Build an object factory that dispatches the request to the URL context implementation.
2. Build a context implementation to process the URL.
3. Set up the environment to make the object factory available to the user program.

   The JNDI uses the implementation as follows:

- To process URL strings passed as the name argument to methods in the `InitialContext` class and its subclasses
- To process URL strings in a `Reference` passed to `NamingManager.getObjectInstance()` and `DirectoryManager.getObjectInstance()`

This lesson describes these two ways in detail.

Prerequisite: Before embarking on this lesson, you should already know how to build a context implementation, the details of which are described in the **The Essential Components** lesson (page 331). If you are adding URL support to a directory context implementation, then you should also read the **Adding Directory Support** lesson (page 345).

URL Context Factory

A *URL context factory* is a special object factory that creates contexts for resolving URL strings. Like all object factories, it is a class that implements the `ObjectFactory` interface. A URL context factory must not only satisfy all of the requirements specified for object factories as stated in the **Object Factories** lesson (page 185). It also must adhere to the following rules.

- A `null` object argument to `getObjectInstance()` means that the factory should create a context for resolving arbitrary URL strings of the scheme associated with the factory. For example, such an invocation on a factory for the `ldap` scheme would return a context that accepts arbitrary LDAP URL strings, such as `"ldap://ldap.wiz.com/o=wiz,c=us"` and `"ldap://ldap.umich.edu/o=umich,c=us"`.
- If the object argument to `getObjectInstance()` is a URL string (`java.lang.String`) of a scheme acceptable to that factory, then the factory should return an object (which might not necessarily be a context) identified by the URL string. For example, if `getObjectInstance()` is given the string `"ldap://ldap.wiz.com/o=wiz,c=us"`, then it would return the object named by the DN `"o=wiz, c=us"` at the LDAP server `ldap.wiz.com`.
- If the object argument to `getObjectInstance()` is an array of URL strings (`java.lang.String[]`), then the factory should return the object named by any one of the URL strings. All of the URL strings in the array are assumed to be equivalent in terms of the object to which they refer. Verification of whether the strings are, or need to be, equivalent is up to the factory. The order of the URL strings in the array is insignificant.

If the factory receives any other type of object argument to `getObjectInstance()`, then its behavior is implementation-dependent.

The first rule applies to supporting the resolution of URL strings from the `Initial-Context`—this is described later in this lesson. The second and third rules apply to supporting the resolution of URL strings embedded in a `Reference`—this is also described later in this lesson. As indicated by the second and third rules, a URL *context* factory is not only a producer of *context* objects. It can produce any type of object named by a URL string.

Class Name's Naming Convention

The URL context factory's class name must use the following naming convention so that it can be located by the JNDI framework:

package_prefix.*scheme_id*.*scheme_id*URLContextFactory

where

- *package_prefix* is a valid prefix for a package in the Java programming language and
- *scheme_id* is the naming/directory service's URL scheme id (for example, `ldap` is the scheme id for services that support the LDAP).

For example, the class name `tut.foo.fooURLContextFactory` is for the `foo` URL scheme; it has the package prefix `"tut"`. In another example, the class name `com.sun.jndi.url.ldap.ldapURLContextFactory` is for the `ldap` URL scheme; it has the package prefix `"com.sun.jndi.url"`. Notice that *package_prefix* must not be empty.

Sample Implementation

This section offers an example of how to implement a URL context factory. This example is for illustrative purposes and is not meant to be prescriptive.

The example is for the `foo` URL scheme, which has the syntax

`foo:`*name in the* `HierCtx` *namespace*

`HierCtx` is an in-memory hierarchical namespace implementation. To make it work with the URL example, you need to create a static namespace that can be accessed by using a static method on the `HierCtx` class. Using a `foo` URL string, you can name the objects in this static namespace.

Like all object factories, a URL context factory must be public and have a public constructor that accepts no arguments.

```
public class fooURLContextFactory implements ObjectFactory {
    public fooURLContextFactory() {
    }
    ...
}
```

This factory's implementation of `getObjectInstance()` fairly well follows the three rules listed previously. The implementations of these rules use the following utility to create a context from the context implementation `fooURLContext`.

```
protected Context getURLContext(Hashtable env) {
    return new fooURLContext(env);
}
```

An actual implementation may or may not choose this strategy of using one context implementation to satisfy all three requirements. It is perfectly acceptable to have a factory that uses different context implementations.

In the following examples, `urlInfo` is the object argument to `getObjectInstance()`.

For the first rule, you simply return the root `fooURLContext`.

```
if (urlInfo == null) {
    return createURLContext(env);
}
```

For the second rule, you use the root `fooURLContext` to look up and return the object named by the URL string.

```
if (urlInfo instanceof String) {
    Context urlCtx = createURLContext(env);
    try {
```

```
            return urlCtx.lookup((String)urlInfo);
    } finally {
        urlCtx.close();
    }
}
```

Notice that before the method returns, it closes the root `fooURLContext`. In this particular example, this step is not really necessary because `fooURLContext` doesn't maintain any connections or resources. However, doing this is good practice so as to ensure that implementations that do maintain connections or resources are cleaned up properly.

For the third rule, you iterate over the array of URL strings until you find one that succeeds. You save one of the exceptions encountered along the way in case all of the URL strings fail and you need to indicate why.

```
if (urlInfo instanceof String[]) {

    // Try each URL until lookup() succeeds for one of them
    // If all URLs fail, throw one of the exceptions arbitrarily
    String[] urls = (String[])urlInfo;
    if (urls.length == 0) {
        throw (new ConfigurationException(
            "fooURLContextFactory: empty URL array"));
    }
    Context urlCtx = createURLContext(env);
    try {
        NamingException ne = null;
        for (int i = 0; i < urls.length; i++) {
            try {
                return urlCtx.lookup(urls[i]);
            } catch (NamingException e) {
                ne = e;
            }
        }
        throw ne;
    } finally {
        urlCtx.close();
    }
}
```

URL Context Implementation

A *URL context implementation* is a context that can handle arbitrary URL strings of the URL scheme supported by the context. It is a class that implements the `Context` interface or one of its subinterfaces. It differs from the (plain) context implementation described in the **The Essential Components** lesson (page 331) in the way that its methods accept and process the name argument.

Structured versus String Names

The Ground Rules lesson (page 325) suggests that you implement the context methods that accept strings in terms of their Name counterparts because string names should be treated like (JNDI) composite names. This rule does not apply to URL context implementations, because a URL string is not a JNDI composite name. A URL string should be processed according to the syntax defined by its URL scheme. In fact, the dependency is the other way around. That is, the overloads that accept Name should be implemented in terms of their string counterparts.

If you do not want to support federation, then you can throw an InvalidNameException when presented with a multicomponent Name.

```
public void bind(Name name, Object obj) throws NamingException {
    if (name.size() == 1) {
        bind(name.get(0), obj);
    } else {
        throw new InvalidNameException(
            "Cannot have composite names with URLs");
    }
}
```

If you do support federation, then when presented with a CompositeName whose first component is a valid URL string, you should treat the first component as a URL and the rest as components for federation (that is, resolving the URL will tell you which naming system to use to resolve the remaining part). If presented with a Name that is not a CompositeName, you should treat this as an error case and throw an InvalidNameException. This is because a URL embedded within a compound name is nonsensical.

This example doesn't check whether the input is a CompositeName. Here is the definition of bind() from the example.

```
public void bind(Name name, Object obj) throws NamingException {
    if (name.size() == 1) {
        bind(name.get(0), obj);
    } else {
        Context ctx = getContinuationContext(name);
        try {
            ctx.bind(name.getSuffix(1), obj);
        } finally {
            ctx.close();
        }
    }
}
```

All overloads that accept Name use a similar pattern. If the name contains a single component, then extract the first component and pass it to the overload that accepts a string name. This resembles the caller's using the overload that accepts a string name in the first place. Otherwise, use the utility method getContinuationContext() to resolve the first component (i.e., the URL string) and continue the operation in that context. Here is the definition of getContinuationContext().

```
protected Context getContinuationContext(Name n) throws
    NamingException {
    Object obj = lookup(n.get(0));
    CannotProceedException cpe = new CannotProceedException();
    cpe.setResolvedObj(obj);
    cpe.setEnvironment(myEnv);
    return NamingManager.getContinuationContext(cpe);
}
```

This utility method resolves the first component of the name and uses the result as the "resolved object" in a call to NamingManager.getContinuationContext() to get the target context in which to continue the operation on the remainder of the name.

The Root URL Context

Now that you have taken care of the overloads that accept Name, you can turn your attention to the overloads that accept java.lang.String. The implementations of these methods depend highly on their "non-URL" counterpart context implementation. For example, a URL context implementation for the LDAP URL is highly dependent on the context implementation for the LDAP service. A lookup of an LDAP URL in an LDAP URL context typically results in a lookup in an LDAP context (from the LDAP context implementation) using an LDAP DN. In this scenario, the URL context implementation is really just a front-end to the actual service's context implementation. Because of this close relationship, this example might not apply as well to some actual implementations.

The example uses the notion of a *root context* that is derived from the input URL string. It defines a utility method, getRootURLContext(), that accepts a URL string. This method returns a tuple that consists of a context that is derived from information in the URL and the remaining name from the URL to be resolved relative to the root context. For example, in the LDAP example, suppose that the input URL string is "ldap://favserver:289/o=jndituto-rial". The root context might be the context at the root of the LDAP server at machine favserver and port 289. In this case, the "ldap://favserver:289/" portion of the URL string will be consumed in producing the root context and the remaining name will be "o=jnditutorial".

In the foo URL example, the root context points to the root of the HierCtx static namespace and "foo:/" is consumed in producing the root context. The remaining name is represented as a single component CompositeName.

```
protected ResolveResult getRootURLContext(String url,
    Hashtable env) throws NamingException {
        if (!url.startsWith("foo:/")) {
            throw new IllegalArgumentException(url +
                " is not a foo URL");
        }
        String objName = url.length() > 5 ? url.substring(5) : null;

        // Represent the object name as empty or a single-component
        // composite name.
```

```
        CompositeName remaining = new CompositeName();

        if (objName != null) {
            remaining.add(objName);
        }

        // Get the handle to the static namespace to use for testing
        // In an actual implementation, this might be the root
        // namespace on a particular server
        Context ctx = tut.HierCtx.getStaticNamespace(env);

        return (new ResolveResult(ctx, remaining));
    }
```

The overloads that accept string names use this utility method to process the URL string and then complete the operation. Here is the definition of bind() from the example.

```
    public void bind(String name, Object obj) throws NamingException {
        ResolveResult res = getRootURLContext(name, myEnv);
        Context ctx = (Context)res.getResolvedObj();
        try {
            ctx.bind(res.getRemainingName(), obj);
        } finally {
            ctx.close();
        }
    }
```

Notice that before the method returns, it closes the root context. In this example, this step is not really necessary because fooURLContext doesn't maintain any connections or resources. However, doing this is good practice so as to ensure that implementations that do maintain connections or resources are cleaned up properly. This also means that stateful methods such as list() must ensure that the enumeration results that they return remain usable even after the context has been closed.

Special Considerations for rename()

rename() differs from the other context methods in that it accepts two names instead of one. With one name, you can use getRootURLContext() to get a workable context to complete the operation. With two names, you cannot call getRootURLContext() twice, once for each name, because each call might return a different context. rename() may have only one context in which to do the renaming.

To solve this for the example here, you first extract from both names a common prefix (by using the internal utility getURLPrefix()). Then you use getRootURLContext() to get the root context and remaining name of the original name. To get the remaining name of the new name, you use another internal utility, getURLSuffix(). Note that it is very important that all three methods—getRootURLContext(), getURLPrefix(), and getURLSuffix()—are in complete agreement regarding how a URL string is parsed and which parts are designated the prefix and suffix.

In particular, getRootURLContext() should consume the portion that is returned by getURLPrefix() to create its root context and return as remaining name the portion that getURLSuffix() will return. You also should take into account the restrictions on a context implementation's ability to perform renames across different servers or namespaces.

Here is the example of rename().

```
public void rename(String oldName, String newName)
    throws NamingException {
    String oldPrefix = getURLPrefix(oldName);
    String newPrefix = getURLPrefix(newName);
    if (!urlEquals(oldPrefix, newPrefix)) {
        throw new OperationNotSupportedException(
            "Renaming using different URL prefixes not supported : "
            + oldName + " " + newName);
    }

    ResolveResult res = getRootURLContext(oldName, myEnv);
    Context ctx = (Context)res.getResolvedObj();
    try {
        ctx.rename(res.getRemainingName(),
            getURLSuffix(newPrefix, newName));
    } finally {
        ctx.close();
    }
}
```

Here are the implementations of getURLPrefix() and getURLSuffix().

```
protected String getURLPrefix(String url) throws NamingException {
    int start = url.indexOf(":");

    if (start < 0) {
        throw new OperationNotSupportedException("Invalid URL: " +
            url);
    }
    ++start; // Skip ":"

    if (url.startsWith("//", start)) {
        start += 2;  // Skip the double forward slash

        // Find the last forward slash
        int posn = url.indexOf("/", start);
        if (posn >= 0) {
            start = posn;
        } else {
            start = url.length();  // Rest of the URL
        }
    }

    // Else 0 or 1 initial slashes; the start is unchanged
    return url.substring(0, start);
}
protected Name getURLSuffix(String prefix, String url)
    throws NamingException {
    String suffix = url.substring(prefix.length());
    if (suffix.length() == 0) {
```

```
        return new CompositeName();
    }
    if (suffix.charAt(0) == '/') {
        suffix = suffix.substring(1); // Skip the leading
                                      // forward slash
    }

    // Note: This is a simplified implementation;
    // a real implementation should transform any URL-encoded
    // characters into their Unicode char representations
    return new CompositeName().add(suffix);
}
```

Supporting Subinterfaces

An API user can pass a URL string to methods in the InitialDirContext class in the same way as for methods in the InitialContext class. To support this capability, the corresponding URL context implementation must support methods in the DirContext interface in addition to those in the Context interface, using the techniques described earlier in the **URL Context Implementation** section (page 360).

If your URL context implementation also supports federation, then it should define an internal utility method for getting the continuation context for performing directory operations. Here is an example.

```
protected DirContext getContinuationDirContext(Name n)
    throws NamingException {
    Object obj = lookup(n.get(0));
    CannotProceedException cpe = new CannotProceedException();
    cpe.setResolvedObj(obj);
    cpe.setEnvironment(myEnv);
    return DirectoryManager.getContinuationDirContext(cpe);
}
```

This method uses DirectoryManager.getContinuationDirContext() to get the continuation context. Overloads that accept Name use this utility in their implementations. Here is an example of how getAttributes() uses getContinuationDirContext().

```
public Attributes getAttributes(Name name, String[] attrIDs)
    throws NamingException  {
    if (name.size() == 1) {
        return getAttributes(name.get(0), attrIDs);
    } else {
        DirContext ctx = getContinuationDirContext(name);
        try {
            return ctx.getAttributes(name.getSuffix(1), attrIDs);
        } finally {
            ctx.close();
        }
    }
}
```

The implementation of the overloads that accept string names uses a similar pattern to that used by methods of the `Context` interface. Instead of expecting a `Context` as the resolved object from the internal utility `getRootURLContext()`, the `DirContext` methods should expect a `DirContext`. Here is an example of the `getAttributes()` implementation.

```
public Attributes getAttributes(String name, String[] attrIds)
    throws NamingException {
        ResolveResult res = getRootURLContext(name, myEnv);
        DirContext ctx = (DirContext)res.getResolvedObj();
        try {
            return ctx.getAttributes(res.getRemainingName(),
                attrIds);
        } finally {
            ctx.close();
        }
}
```

Supporting Nonstandard Subinterfaces

Adding URL support for methods in the `DirContext` interface makes sense because that interface contains methods that process names. Adding URL support doesn't make sense for subinterfaces whose methods have nothing to do with names. For example, you need not provide URL support for methods in the `LdapContext` interface because none of its methods deal with names.

Another reason that URL support might not be appropriate for some subinterfaces is that the model might not be appropriate. For example, the `EventContext` and `EventDirContext` interfaces contain methods that process names. However, these interfaces define a model in which listener registration is closely tied to the `Context` instance. This does not fit well with URLs, which are effectively *absolute names* that have no allegiance to a particular `Context` instance. (These two interfaces and the event model they support are described in the **Event Notification** lesson (page 111).)

Other, possibly proprietary, subinterfaces of `Context` might exist for which it makes sense to provide URL support. For such cases, you should follow the guidelines given earlier in this lesson and in this section when building your URL context implementation. Namely, the overloads that accept `Name` should use `getContinuationContext()` (if the context implementation supports federation), whereas the overloads that accept string names should use a utility similar to `getRootURLContext()`.

Here is an example. `BarContext` extends the `Context` interface by adding two new methods: barMethod(), which accepts a name argument, and bazMethod(), which does not. (A sample context implementation, `BarContextImpl`, which is based on the earlier `HierCtx` example, is supplied with this tutorial.) Its URL context implementation, `barURLContext`, implements the subinterface and extends from the earlier example `fooURLContext`. Here is `barURLContext`'s definition of its name-related method.

```
public Object barMethod(Name name) throws NamingException {
    if (name.size() == 1) {
```

```
            return barMethod(name.get(0));
    } else {
        Context ctx = getContinuationContext(name);
        if (!(ctx instanceof tut.BarContext)) {
            throw new NotContextException(
                "Cannot continue operation on nonBarContext");
        }
        try {
            return ((tut.BarContext)ctx).barMethod(
                name.getSuffix(1));
        } finally {
            ctx.close();
        }
    }
}

public Object barMethod(String name) throws NamingException {
    ResolveResult res = getRootURLContext(name, myEnv);
    tut.BarContext ctx = (tut.BarContext)res.getResolvedObj();
    try {
        return ctx.barMethod(res.getRemainingName());
    } finally {
        ctx.close();
    }
}
```

Methods that are not name-related, such as bazMethod(), typically won't be called from the URL context because of how URL contexts are accessed (see the discussion later in this lesson). However, you still need to provide implementations for them so as to satisfy Java programming language requirements. You then need to provide a URL context factory for this URL context implementation, as described earlier in this lesson.

You also should follow the instructions for extending the initial context described later in this lesson (page 368) for supporting URLs for subinterfaces. This last step is not necessary for the DirContext subinterface. This is because an initial context class, InitialDirContext, already exists that directs DirContext calls that involve the URL string names to the appropriate URL context implementation.

Making the Implementation Available

The JNDI looks for URL context factories by examining the Context.URL_PKG_PREFIXES ("java.naming.factory.url.pkgs") environment property. This property contains a colon-separated list of package prefixes of the class names for the URL context factories. The prefix "com.sun.jndi.url" is always appended to the possibly empty list of package prefixes.

In the foo URL example, the factory's fully qualified class name is tut.foo.fooURL-ContextFactory. Therefore, to include this factory in the list of URL context factories that the JNDI knows about, you set the Context.URL_PKG_PREFIXES property as follows:

```
java.naming.factory.url.pkgs=tut
```

The JNDI looks for a URL context factory based on its URL scheme id. Suppose that the JNDI is looking for a factory for the ldap URL scheme. It would look for the following classes:

```
tut.ldap.ldapURLContextFactory

com.sun.jndi.url.ldap.ldapURLContextFactory
```

Similarly, with the same property setting, the JNDI would look for the following classes for the foo URL scheme:

```
tut.foo.fooURLContextFactory

com.sun.jndi.url.foo.fooURLContextFactory
```

From this ordered list of class names, the JNDI will instantiate each class in turn and invoke getObjectInstance() on it until one class returns a non-null answer. The non-null answer becomes the URL context implementation that will be used for that URL scheme.

As a service provider developer, you typically package the components of your service provider (the context implementation for the naming/directory, URL context factory, and URL context implementation) into an archive (JAR) file. To make the URL context factory automatically available to any program that uses this JAR file, you should include in it a jndi.properties file that contains a setting for the Context.URL_PKG_PREFIXES property, as shown in the earlier example. See the **Environment Properties** lesson (page 100) for more information on how the JNDI reads and merges environment properties from different sources.

Relationship to the Initial Context

When the API user supplies a URL string to one of the methods in the InitialContext or InitialDirContext class, the JNDI extracts the URL scheme from the string and uses NamingManager.getURLContext() to find a URL context implementation that can process the URL string. This method uses the algorithm described earlier in this lesson.

If the JNDI successfully locates a URL context implementation, then it invokes the original context method by using the original arguments. This means that the complete URL string is passed on to the URL context implementation, where it is processed as described in the **URL Context Implementation** section (page 360) of this lesson.

If the JNDI cannot locate a URL context implementation to use to process the URL string, then it assumes that the input name is not a URL string. It then passes the name to the underlying initial context implementation (that named by the Context.INITIAL_CONTEXT_FACTORY ("java.naming.factory.initial") environment property).

Supporting Subinterfaces

To provide URL support from the initial context to a Context subinterface, you need to define a new class that extends from InitialContext or one of its subclasses. See the discussion earlier in this lesson (page 366) regarding factors to consider when deciding whether to add URL support for a subinterface.

For example, suppose that `BarContext` extends `Context` by adding two new methods: `barMethod()`, which accepts a name argument, and `bazMethod()`, which does not. This service has a URL scheme id of `bar`. (See its URL context implementation presented earlier in this lesson.) To define an initial context for this interface, you first specify its inheritance.

```
public class InitialBarContext
    extends InitialContext implements BarContext
```

This class extends from the `InitialContext` and implements the new interface, `BarContext`.

Then you define some constructors that are suitable for the class. Typically, you should plan on at least two constructors, one that accepts no arguments and one that accepts the environment parameter.

```
public InitialBarContext() throws NamingException {
    super();
}
public InitialBarContext(Hashtable env) throws NamingException {
    super(env);
}
```

Next, you provide utility methods for both methods that process names and those that don't. For methods that process names, define a utility method that returns either a URL context or the default underlying initial context by inspecting the name argument. Most of the work for this is done by the protected method `InitialContext.getURLOrDefaultInitCtx()`. The utility method needs only to check the type of the resulting context to make sure that it is compatible with that of the subinterface. You need two such methods, one for the string name and one for `Name`. Here is the string version.

```
protected BarContext getURLOrDefaultInitBarCtx(String name)
    throws NamingException {
    Context ctx = getURLOrDefaultInitCtx(name);
    if (!(ctx instanceof BarContext)) {
        throw new NoInitialContextException("Not a BarContext");
    }
    return (BarContext)ctx;
}
```

For methods that do not process names, define a utility method that returns the default underlying initial context. Most of the work for this is done by the protected method `Initial-Context.getDefaultInitCtx()`. The utility method needs only to check the type of the resulting context to make sure that it is compatible with that of the subinterface.

```
protected BarContext getDefaultInitBarCtx()
    throws NamingException {
    Context ctx = getDefaultInitCtx();
    if (!(ctx instanceof BarContext)) {
        throw new NoInitialContextException("Not a BarContext");
    }
    return (BarContext)ctx;
}
```

Once you have these methods, it is straightforward to provide implementations for all of the new methods. New name-related methods use getURLOrDefaultInitBarCtx(), whereas new non-name-related methods use getDefaultInitBarCtx(). Here are some examples.

```
public Object barMethod(String name) throws NamingException {
    return getURLOrDefaultInitBarCtx(name).barMethod(name);
}

public String bazMethod() throws NamingException {
    return getDefaultInitBarCtx().bazMethod();
}
```

To use this new initial context implementation, your program must import the new class. Here is an example that invokes one of the new methods by using a bar URL.

```
tut.BarContext ctx = new tut.InitialBarContext();

// Invoke the BarContext-specific method with the URL
Object answer = ctx.barMethod("bar:/a");
```

Running this example produces the output

```
The answer is a
```

Relationship to References

As suggested in the **Object Factories** lesson (page 188), a context implementation is supposed to invoke NamingManager.getObjectInstance() or DirectoryManager.getObject-Instance() before returning an object to the API user. If the object being returned is a Reference that has no factory (that is, its getFactoryClassName() method returns null), then these methods will check the Reference for an address of type "URL". When these methods find such an address, they will search for a URL context implementation to process the URL string in the address by using the algorithm described earlier in this lesson (page 367).

This feature provides a convenient way of using URLs as references. A program can create a reference with minimal information (a URL string) and bind it into a naming or directory service. When another program looks up the reference, the URL is automatically dereferenced into the object to which it refers. This mechanism is precisely the sort of thing needed to support federation: You can bind the URL of one naming service into the namespace of another naming service. This technique works especially well with well-known URL schemes (such as that for the LDAP) for which the URL context implementation is widely available. This is because you don't need to distribute its implementation.

Adding Federation Support

The **Federation** lesson (page 131) describes federation from an API user's perspective. That lesson discussed that federation basically involves three steps:

1. Figure out which part of a composite name to process.
2. Decide how to process the part that belongs to the current naming system.
3. Forward the operation to be completed in the nns (next naming system).

This lesson further details each step and gives examples of how to implement them. It also shows you how to make a context implementation act as an intermediate context for interfaces that it otherwise does not support. Finally, it shows you how to define an object factory for a context implementation so that it can be bound in other naming systems.

Naming System Boundaries

The **Federation** lesson (page 131) describes how a service provider determines which components of the composite name to process and which to pass on. **The Essential Components** lesson (page 332) contains two examples of how a context implementation selects components from the input composite name to process. Both of these examples concern context implementations that support strong separation and therefore simply select the first component of the composite name.

To support weak separation, you need to rewrite the utility method getMyComponents() and all of the context methods to eliminate the single component assumption. Following is a more general method that, given a composite or compound name, returns a two-element array. In that array, the first component contains the components to be processed by the current naming system and the second component contains the components to be processed by subsequent naming systems. This example handles strong separation.

```
protected Name[] parseComponents(Name name) throws NamingException {
    Name head, tail;
```

```
            if (name instanceof CompositeName) {
                int separator;
                // If there is no name to parse or
                // if you're already at the boundary
                if (name.isEmpty() || name.get(0).equals("")) {
                    separator = 0;
                } else {
                    separator = 1;
                }

                head = name.getPrefix(separator);
                tail = name.getSuffix(separator);
            } else {
                // Treat this like a compound name
                head = new CompositeName().add(name.toString());
                tail = null;
            }

            return new Name[]{head, tail};
    }
```

Following is the same method rewritten to support weak separation. For this particular context implementation, only leading components that contain the equals character ("=") are selected for the current naming system.

```
    protected Name[] parseComponents(Name name) throws NamingException {
        Name head, tail;
        if (name instanceof CompositeName) {
            int separator;
            // If there's no name to parse or
            // if you're already at the boundary
            if (name.isEmpty() || name.get(0).equals("")) {
                separator = 0;
            } else {
                // Find the leading components that have "="
                int total = name.size();
                int i;
                for (i = 0; i < total; i++) {
                    if (name.get(i).indexOf('=') < 0) {
                        break;
                    }
                }
                separator = i;
            }

            head = name.getPrefix(separator);
            tail = name.getSuffix(separator);
        } else {
            // Treat this like a compound name
            head = new CompositeName().add(name.toString());
            tail = null;
        }
        return new Name[]{head, tail};
    }
```

If the context implementation supports dynamic weak separation (that is, it determines the naming system boundary dynamically), then `parseComponents()` will return all components as belonging to the current naming system. Here is an example.

```
protected Name[] parseComponents(Name name) throws NamingException {
    Name head, tail;
    if (name instanceof CompositeName) {
        int separator;
        // If there is no name to parse or
        // if you're already at the boundary
        if (name.isEmpty() || name.get(0).equals("")) {
            separator = 0;
        } else {
            // All components are eligible
            separator = name.size();
        }

        head = name.getPrefix(separator);
        tail = name.getSuffix(separator);
    } else {
        // Treat this like a compound name
        head = new CompositeName().add(name.toString());
        tail = null;
    }

    return new Name[]{head, tail};
}
```

Once you have defined this method, your context methods can use it to extract the components. Here is an example.

```
Name[] nm = parseComponents(name);
Name mine = nm[0];
Name rest = nm[1];
```

The Current Naming System

After extracting the name components that belong to your current naming system, you must decide how to process those components. You have three choices.

- **Terminal**. Name resolution has reached the target naming system. Apply the operation to the name.
- **Terminal next naming system** (terminal nns). Name resolution has reached the target naming system. Apply the operation to the *nns pointer* (next naming system pointer) of the name.
- **Intermediate**. The current naming system is an intermediate naming system. Do the necessary name resolution to determine the nns to which to pass the operation.

Here is a sample implementation of `bind()` that implements these three choices.

```
public void bind(Name name, Object bindObj) throws NamingException {
```

```
        try {
            Name[] nm = parseComponents(name);
            Name mine = nm[0];
            Name rest = nm[1];

            if (rest == null || rest.isEmpty()) {
                // Terminal; just use head
                bind_internal(mine, bindObj);
            } else if (rest.get(0).equals("") && rest.size() == 1) {
                // Terminal nns
                bind_nns(mine, bindObj);
            } else if (mine.isEmpty() || isAllEmpty(rest)) {
                // Intermediate; resolve current components as intermediate
                Object obj = lookup_nns(mine);

                // Skip the leading forward slash
                throw fillInCPE(obj, mine, rest.getSuffix(1));
            } else {
                // Intermediate; resolve current components as intermediate
                Object obj = resolveIntermediate_nns(mine, rest);

                throw fillInCPE(obj, mine, rest);
            }
        } catch (CannotProceedException e) {
            Context cctx = NamingManager.getContinuationContext(e);
            cctx.bind(e.getRemainingName(), bindObj);
        }
    }
```

This example and the three alternatives are explained in more detail later in this lesson. Note that all other name-related methods in the Context interface should be implemented similarly.

Terminal

Once name resolution has reached the target naming system, you basically no longer need to worry about federation. In the example here, this case is handled by defining an *xxx_internal* method for each method in the Context interface. This technique is useful for clearly delineating the portion of the code that is local or internal to this context implementation.

Here is the example for bind().

```
private void bind_internal(Name name, Object obj) throws NamingException {
    if (name.isEmpty()) {
        throw new InvalidNameException("Cannot bind empty name");
    }

    // Extract the components that belong to this namespace
    String atom = getInternalName(name);
    if (bindings.get(atom) != null) {
        throw new NameAlreadyBoundException(
            "Use rebind to override");
    }
```

```
    // Call getStateToBind for using any state factories
    obj = NamingManager.getStateToBind(obj, name, this, myEnv);

    // Add the object to the internal data structure
    bindings.put(atom, obj);
}
```

If the context implementation supports dynamic weak separation (that is, it determines the naming system boundary dynamically), then the *xxx*_internal() methods will resolve the name to determine which parts belong to the current naming system. If the current naming system is determined not to be the terminal naming system, then the methods will throw a CannotProceedException, with the remaining components as the remaining name.

Terminal Next Naming System

When name resolution has reached the target naming system with a remaining name that has a trailing forward slash character ("/"), the operation is to be applied to the nns pointer of the remaining name. Recall from the **Federation** lesson (page 134) that a context implementation may implement the nns pointer as *explicit* (also called a *junction*) or *implicit*. In the example, this case is handled by defining an *xxx*_nns method for each method in the Context interface. As with the case of the *xxx*_internal naming technique, this technique is useful for delineating the part of the code that handles the nns pointer.

The implementation of the *xxx*_nns methods depends on how the context implementation handles nns pointers. For example, a context implementation might support implicit nns by having a table that records the nns for each name bound in a context. In that case, its bind_nns() method might look as follows.

```
private void bind_nns(Name name, Object obj) throws NamingException {
    if (name.isEmpty()) {
        // Set your nns
        myNNS = NamingManager.getStateToBind(obj,
            ((Name)(name.clone())).add(""), this, myEnv);
        return;
    }

    // Extract the components that belong to this namespace
    String atom = getInternalName(name);
    if (nnsBindings.get(atom) != null) {
        throw new NameAlreadyBoundException(
            "Use rebind to override");
    }

    // Call getStateToBind for using any state factories
    obj = NamingManager.getStateToBind(obj,
        ((Name)(name.clone())).add(""), this, myEnv);

    // Add the object to the internal nns data structure
    nnsBindings.put(atom, obj);
}
```

If the context implementation supports junctions, then it should look up the junction and apply the operation on the nns of the junction. This is illustrated by the example. Since this is a common pattern used by other context methods, an internal utility, processJunction_nns(), is defined for this purpose, as follows.

```
protected void processJunction_nns(Name name) throws NamingException {
    if (name.isEmpty()) {
        // Construct a new Reference that contains this context
        RefAddr addr = new RefAddr("nns") {
            public Object getContent() {
                return FedCtx.this;
            }
        };
        Reference ref = new Reference("java.lang.Object", addr);
        throw fillInCPE(ref, NNS_NAME, null);
    } else {
        // Look up the name to continue the operation in the nns
        Object target;
        try {
            target = lookup_internal(name);
        } catch (NamingException e) {
            e.appendRemainingComponent(""); // Add the nns back in
            throw e;
        }

        throw fillInCPE(target, name, NNS_NAME);
    }
}
```

If the name is empty, then the user is requesting the nns of the current context. In that case, an nns reference (see the **Federation** lesson (page 134)) is constructed by using the current context as the resolved object and the trailing forward slash character ("/") as the "alt" name. The "alt" name is the name of the resolved object resolved relative to the "alt" name context (which in this case is the current context). This information is used to create and throw a CannotProceedException. If the name is not empty, then you need to look up the named object from this current context and create a CannotProceedException that contains the trailing forward slash as the remaining name. The CannotProceedException is handled by the main bind() method, as discussed in the next section. bind_nns(), like other methods for handling the nns, simply uses the internal utility processJunction_nns().

```
private void bind_nns(Name name, Object obj) throws NamingException {
    processJunction_nns(name);
}
```

fillInCPE() is an internal utility that creates a CannotProceedException by using this context as the "alt" name context and this context's environment. Here is its definition.

```
protected CannotProceedException fillInCPE(Object resolvedObj,
    Name altName, Name remainingName) {
    CannotProceedException cpe = new CannotProceedException();
    // Generic stuff
    cpe.setEnvironment(myEnv);
    cpe.setAltNameCtx(this);
```

```
    // Specific stuff
    cpe.setResolvedObj(resolvedObj);
    cpe.setAltName(altName);
    cpe.setRemainingName(remainingName);
    return cpe;
}
```

Intermediate

If the parseComponents() utility method returns results that indicate that resolution is currently at an intermediate context, then you must resolve the name components intended for the current naming system to obtain the reference to the nns. How the resolution occurs depends on whether the implicit nns has been requested. The implicit nns has been requested if the name contains a leading forward slash character ("/") or if the name components that belong to the nns (rest) are all empty (this is indicated by one or more trailing forward slashes). In this case, the context implementation should use the internal utility lookup_nns() to obtain the nns and then continue the operation on the rest of the name components.

If the implicit nns has not been requested, then the name components that belong to this current naming system (mine) might name a junction or an implicit nns. To process this case, a utility is defined that can be used by all context methods called by resolve-Intermediate_nns().

```
protected Object resolveIntermediate_nns(Name name, Name rest,
    Name newName) throws NamingException {
    CannotProceedException cpe;
    try {
        final Object obj = lookup_internal(name);

        if (obj != null && getClass().isInstance(obj)) {
            // If "obj" is in the same type as this object, it must
            // not be a junction; continue the lookup with "/"

            cpe = fillInCPE(obj, name,
            ((Name)(NNS_NAME.clone())).addAll(rest));
            cpe.setRemainingNewName(newName);
        } else if (obj != null && !(obj instanceof Context)) {
            // obj is not even a context, so try to find its nns
            // dynamically by constructing a Reference that
            // contains obj
            RefAddr addr = new RefAddr("nns") {
                public Object getContent() {
                    return obj;
                }
            };
            Reference ref = new Reference("java.lang.Object", addr);

            // Resolved name has a trailing slash to indicate the nns
            CompositeName resName = (CompositeName)name.clone();
            resName.add(""); // Add the trailing forward slash

            cpe = fillInCPE(ref, resName, rest);
            cpe.setRemainingNewName(newName);
```

```
        } else {
            // Consume "/" and continue
            return obj;
        }
    } catch (NamingException e) {
        e.appendRemainingComponent(""); // Add the nns back in
        throw e;
    }
    throw cpe;
}
```

As defined in the example, this method supports junctions and dynamic implicit nns (see the **Federation** lesson (page 134)). If your context implementation supports static implicit nns, then it would probably look as follows instead.

```
private void resolveIntermediate_nns(Name name, Name rest,
    Name newName) throws NamingException {
    Object nns;
    if (name.isEmpty()) {
        nns = myNNS;    // Return this context's nns
    } else {
        // Extract the components that belong to this namespace
        String atom = getInternalName(name);

        // Get the nns from the internal table
        nns = nnsBindings.get(atom);
        if (nns == null) {
            throw new NameNotFoundException(atom + "/");
        }
    }
    // Call getObjectInstance for using any object factories
    try {
        return NamingManager.getObjectInstance(nns,
            ((Name)(name.clone())).add(""), this, myEnv);
    } catch (Exception e) {
        NamingException ne = new NamingException();
        ne.setRootCause(e);
        throw ne;
    }
}
```

The Next Naming System

Once you have done the processing for the current naming system, as described in the previous section, very little work is left to be done to complete the operation.

Here is a sample implementation of bind() from the previous section.

```
public void bind(Name name, Object bindObj) throws NamingException {
    try {
        Name[] nm = parseComponents(name);
        Name mine = nm[0];
        Name rest = nm[1];
```

```
        if (rest == null || rest.isEmpty()) {
            // Terminal; just use head
            bind_internal(mine, bindObj);
        } else if (rest.get(0).equals("") && rest.size() == 1) {
            // Terminal nns
            bind_nns(mine, bindObj);
        } else if (mine.isEmpty() || isAllEmpty(rest)) {
            // Intermediate; resolve current components as intermediate
            Object obj = lookup_nns(mine);

            // Skip the leading forward slash
            throw fillInCPE(obj, mine, rest.getSuffix(1));
        } else {
            // Intermediate; resolve current components as intermediate
            Object obj = resolveIntermediate_nns(mine, rest);

            throw fillInCPE(obj, mine, rest);
        }
    } catch (CannotProceedException e) {
        Context cctx = NamingManager.getContinuationContext(e);
        cctx.bind(e.getRemainingName(), bindObj);
    }
}
```

Evaluating the code within the try clause can result in any of three outcomes.

- The operation completes successfully.
- The operation results in an error and throws a NamingException.
- The operation needs to be continued in the nns and throws a CannotProceedException.

You handle the last outcome by attempting to find a continuation context, using get-ContinuationContext() or getContinuationDirContext(), based on information in the CannotProceedException. You then proceed to invoke the same method on the continuation context by using the remaining name.

The approach described here is based heavily on throwing and catching a Cannot-ProceedException. However, it is not the only approach. You could achieve the same results by using an iterative approach.

Resolving through Subinterfaces

The procedures described so far work fine when all of the context implementations involved in completing a method through a federation implement the same interfaces. What happens if some intermediate context implementations do not support all of the subinterfaces of Context? You do not want to require that an intermediate naming system support all subinterfaces in order for federation to work. This issue is more important for nonstandard subinterfaces because expecting wide support for those is unreasonable.

Suppose that you invoke a method in the DirContext interface on a federation consisting of five naming systems, only the first and last of which support DirContext. See Figure 10.

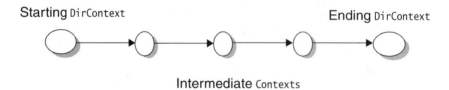

Starting DirContext

Ending DirContext

Intermediate Contexts

FIGURE 10:   Resolving through Subinterfaces.

For the method to be invoked successfully on the target context, the intermediate naming systems must be involved in the resolution phase of the operation and be able to indicate which operation to ultimately invoke. At first glance, achieving the resolution step by using lookup() might seem possible. This is problematic because you want the target *context* and not the named object. For example, if you are creating a subcontext, then you want the penultimate context named by the input name and not the named object.

The JNDI supports resolution through intermediate contexts by requiring that intermediate context implementations support the Resolver interface. This interface contains two overloaded forms of resolveToClass(): one form accepts a string name and a Class and the other accepts a Name and a Class. The JNDI uses resolveToClass() to partially resolve the input name, stopping at the first context that is an instance of the specified interface/class. A context implementation needs to implement the Resolver interface and provide implementations for this method.

Here is a sample implementation.

```
public ResolveResult resolveToClass(Name name, Class ctxType)
    throws NamingException {

    // If you're it, you can quit right now
    if (ctxType.isInstance(this)) {
        return new ResolveResult(this, name);
    }

    try {
        Name[] nm = parseComponents(name);
        Name mine = nm[0];
        Name rest = nm[1];
        Object nxt = null;

        if (rest == null || rest.isEmpty()) {
            // Terminal; just use head
            nxt = lookup_internal(mine);
        } else if (rest.get(0).equals("") && rest.size() == 1) {
            // Terminal nns
            nxt = lookup_nns(mine);
        } else if (mine.isEmpty() || isAllEmpty(rest)) {
            // Intermediate; resolve current components as intermediate
            Object obj = lookup_nns(mine);
```

```
            // Skip the leading forward slash
            throw fillInCPE(obj, mine, rest.getSuffix(1));
        } else {
            // Intermediate; resolve current components as intermediate
            Object obj = resolveIntermediate_nns(mine, rest);

            throw fillInCPE(obj, mine, rest);
        }

        if (ctxType.isInstance(nxt)) {
            return new ResolveResult(nxt, "");
        } else {
            // Have resolved the entire composite name but
            // cannot find the requested context type
            throw new NotContextException(
                "Not instanceof " + ctxType);
        }
    } catch (CannotProceedException e) {
        Context cctx = NamingManager.getContinuationContext(e);
        if (cctx instanceof Resolver) {
            return cctx.resolveToClass(e.getRemainingName(),
                ctxType);
        } else {
            // Have hit a nonResolver; give up
            e.fillInStackTrace();
            throw e;
        }
    }
}
}
```

In this method, you first check whether the current context implements the requested type. If so, you need to go no further. Otherwise, you proceed as with other context operations described in an earlier section (page 373) of this lesson. That is, you determine whether the current context is the terminal, terminal nns, or intermediate context. For the two terminal cases, if the answer is an instance of the requested type, then you return the answer and an empty remaining name in a `ResolveResult`. If you get a `CannotProceedException`, then use it to find a continuation context. This context must implement the `Resolver` interface. Otherwise, you can't use it to find the target context.

Continuation Contexts for Subinterfaces

The following JNDI methods use `resolveToClass()` to find the continuation context of the appropriate type:

- `NamingManager.getContinuationContext()`
- `DirectoryManager.getContinuationDirContext()`

If your context implementation supports another subinterface, then it should define a similar method for that subinterface. For example, suppose that you need to support the `BarContext` subinterface. Then you would define a method called `getContinuationBarContext()`. Here is an example.

```
public BarContext getContinuationBarContext(
    CannotProceedException cpe) {
    return new ContinuationBarCtx(cpe);
}
```

You then define an implementation for the continuation context, `ContinuationBarCtx`. This class must implement both `Resolver` and the subinterface `BarContext`. The following utility methods are defined for getting the target context for `Context` and `BarContext` methods.

```
// Gets the default target context, and caches it
protected Context getTargetContext() throws NamingException {
    if (cctx == null) {
        cctx = NamingManager.getContinuationContext(cpe);
    }
    return cctx;
}

protected ResolveResult getTargetContext(Name name)
    throws NamingException {

    Context ctx = getTargetContext();

    if (ctx instanceof BarContext)
        return new ResolveResult(ctx, name);

    // Have found the resolver; ask it to find BarContext
    if (ctx instanceof Resolver) {
        Resolver res = (Resolver)ctx;
        return res.resolveToClass(name, BarContext.class);
    }

    // Resolve all of the way by using lookup()
    // This may allow the operation
    // to succeed if it doesn't require the penultimate context
    Object ultimate = ctx.lookup(name);
    if (ultimate instanceof BarContext) {
        return (new ResultResult(ultimate, new CompositeName()));
    }

    throw (NamingException)cpe.fillInStackTrace();
}
```

The `BarContext` methods can then be implemented as follows in the continuation context.

```
public void BarMethod(Name name) throws NamingException {
    ResolveResult res = getTargetContext(name);
    return ((BarContext)res.getResolvedObj()).barMethod(
        res.getRemainingName());
}
```

The method uses the resolved `BarContext` and the remaining name to continue the operation.

All of the `Context` methods are implemented by using a `getTargetContext()` method that accepts no argument. These implementations exist to satisfy the `Context` interface. Typically, the context implementation would use `NamingManager.getContinuationContext()`

directly instead the subinterface's continuation context for methods in the `Context` interface, as shown in the previous section (page 378) of this lesson.

Here is a sample implementation of `lookup()` in the continuation context.

```
public Object lookup(Name name) throws NamingException {
    Context ctx = getTargetContext();
    return ctx.lookup(name);
}
```

A context implementation that implements the subinterface would use `getContinuationBar-Context()` in the same way that it uses `NamingManager.getContinuationContext()`. Here is an example.

```
public Object barMethod(Name name) throws NamingException {
    try {
        ...
    } catch (CannotProceedException e) {
        BarContext cctx =
            ContinuationBarCtx.getContinuationBarContext(e);
        return cctx.barMethod(e.getRemainingName());
    }
}
```

Creating a Federation

You create a federation in either of two ways:

- By explicit administration
- By dynamic composition

In the former way, you explicitly bind the reference of one naming system into a context in another naming system. For example, you might record reference information about the local departmental LDAP naming system into a DNS system such that applications can subsequently resolve a composite name that contains the DNS name and the LDAP name. In the latter way, you have the federation be created dynamically as the resolution of a composite name proceeds. For example, a file system contains different types of files. Some of those files might be ZIP formatted. You can create a federation by using a composite name that contains the filename and its entry within the ZIP file. In this way, the federation is created dynamically with no external assistance and can be as varied as the types of files and their corresponding service providers.

An explicit binding consists of a name and a reference. Depending on the naming system in which the reference is bound, the actual reference might take different forms. For example, a departmental LDAP naming system might be *bound* into the DNS via a DNS SRV record that contains the LDAP servers' IP addresses and DNs. Or, the JNDI reference of an application naming system might be bound in an LDAP naming system. Also, a naming system might be represented differently in different superior naming systems. For example, the same naming system might be bound by using different data in the DNS and in the LDAP. Regardless of its storage format, a reference is eventually represented programmatically by a `Reference`. The **Java Objects and the Directory** lesson (page 151) describes how a `Reference` can be transformed to and from its actual representation.

From a service provider developer's perspective, it is a good idea to define a reference for the context implementation. This encourages users of the provider to use a consistent reference when referring to contexts in the implementation and when binding contexts from the implementation into foreign naming systems.

References

A context's reference should contain the data required to create a `Context` instance. If the context represents state on a naming or directory server, then its reference should at a minimum contain information on how to contact the server and how to identify its state within the server. Sometimes this task is complicated by the fact that access to the server might be controlled and require authentication. You are advised not to place security-sensitive information such as passwords in a reference. Rather, the reference should be generic and the context's authentication information ignored.

If the service provider already has a URL context implementation and a factory for the context implementation, then you can leverage that when designing the context's reference. For example, you can simply make the reference contain the URL(s) of the context. This not only makes access to the context more consistent, but also significantly simplifies the implementation of the corresponding object factory.

Object Factories

Once you have defined the format of the reference for your context implementation, you can write an object factory for it. Thus applications will be able to access your context implementation via references instead of names.

Following is an example of an object factory written to use the URL context factory of the same context implementation. For example, suppose that your context implementation supports the foo URL scheme and has the URL context factory `tut.foo.fooURLContextFactory`. The corresponding object factory `FooCtxFactory` might look as follows.

```
public class FooCtxFactory implements ObjectFactory {
    public FooCtxFactory() {
    }
    public Object getObjectInstance(Object ref, Name name,
        Context nameCtx, Hashtable env) throws Exception {

        if ((ref instanceof Reference) &&
            myClassName.equals(
                ((Reference)ref).getFactoryClassName())) {

            // Create a URL context factory
            ObjectFactory factory = new tut.foo.fooURLContextFactory();
```

```
        // Extract the URL(s) from the Reference
        String[] urls = getURLs((Reference)ref);

        // Ask the URL context factory to process the URL(s)
        return factory.getObjectInstance(urls, name, nameCtx, env);
    }

    // This is not meant for this factory
    return null;
    }
}
```

getURLs() is a utility that extracts the URL strings from the reference's addresses.

Referenceable

A symmetric relationship is not needed for binding the context. Simply because you can look up a context from a foreign naming system does not necessarily mean that you can programmatically bind (the reference of) the same context into that foreign naming system. The binding could have been added administratively through tools specific for that foreign naming server.

Nevertheless, you can plan for programmatic binding support by making your context implementation *referenceable*. To do this, make the implementation implement the Referenceable interface. Also, provide an implementation for getReference(). This method should return a reference that can be fed back into the provider's object factory.

Miscellaneous

This lesson shows you how to bundle all of the components of your service provider. It also gives you some tips on how to implement the following advanced features:

- Referrals
- Link references
- Event notification
- LDAP v3 controls and extensions

Adding support for each of these features requires quite a bit of work. This lesson touches on only some aspects of their implementations. This is because the actual implementations will be closely tied to the underlying service and how you have structured the other components of your service provider.

Packaging

The Big Picture lesson (page 315) discussed that a service provider typically contains several components. A service provider is delivered most commonly by packaging all of its components into a JAR file. This JAR should contain the class files of the different components and the JNDI resource files. The resource files allow programs to use the service provider with minimal configuration.

Here are the contents of the JAR for a typical sample service provider.

```
tut/SampleContextImpl.class
tut/SampleContextImpl$Parser.class
tut/SampleContextImpl$ListEnum.class
tut/SampleContextImpl$BindingEnum.class
tut/SampleContextImpl$SearchEnum.class
tut/SampleInitialContextFactory.class
tut/OneObjectFactory.class
tut/TwoObjectFactory.class
tut/ThreeObjectFactory.class
```

```
tut/OneStateFactory.class
tut/TwoStateFactory.class

tut/SampleResponseControlFactory.class
tut/OneResponseControl.class
tut/TwoResponseControl.class
tut/ThreeResponseControl.class

tut/SampleObjectFactory.class

tut/sam/samURLContextFactory.class
tut/sam/samURLContext.class

tut/jndiprovider.properties
jndi.properties
```

This sample provider is in the package tut. It contains a context implementation (tut.SampleContextImpl and its inner classes) and an initial context factory (tut.Sample-InitialContextFactory). It uses several object, state, and response control factories, some of which are included in the provider's resource file, tut/jndiprovider.properties. This file's contents are as follows:

```
java.naming.factory.object=tut.ThreeObjectFactory

java.naming.factory.state=tut.OneStateFactory:tut.TwoStateFactory

java.naming.factory.control=tut.SampleResponseControlFactory
```

Including this file makes the listed factories visible only to this context implementation, as described in the **Environment Properties** lesson (page 108). The two object factories, tut.OneObjectFactory and tut.TwoObjectFactory, are not included in the jndi-provider.properties file because they are always referenced by their class names. (In other words, any reference that uses one of these factories will have its class name in getFactory-ClassName().)

The provider also contains an object factory for the context implementation itself, called tut.SampleObjectFactory. This class is responsible for creating an instance of tut.Sample-ContextImpl, when given a reference for it.

The provider supports the sam URL scheme and provides the corresponding URL context factory and implementation classes tut.sam.samURLContextFactory and tut.sam.sam-URLContext. The JAR contains a jndi.properties file that names the package prefix of the sam URL context factory. This allows the URL context factory to be considered automatically when the JNDI is looking for URL context factories. The contents of the jndi.properties file are as follows:

```
java.naming.factory.initial=tut.SampleInitialContextFactory

java.naming.factory.url.pkgs=tut
```

This file also includes a setting for the initial context factory. This will cause any program that uses this JAR to use, by default, tut.SampleInitialContextFactory as the initial context factory.

Adding Referral Support

Prerequisite: You should be familiar with referrals before reading this section. Referrals are covered in the **Referrals** lesson (page 259).

A service provider typically supports referrals only when the underlying naming/directory service provides such a feature. Only the LDAP and LDAP-like services support referrals.

How referrals are supported is an integral part of the service provider implementation. It permeates every aspect of how responses from the underlying LDAP service are processed. This section touches on only a few topics related to implementing referrals.

Referral Exception

A referral is represented by the abstract class `ReferralException` or its subclass `LdapReferralException`. The latter should be used by service providers that support LDAP controls.

Providing a concrete implementation for this class is key to providing referral support. The implementation's main task is to return a *referral context* for `getReferralContext()`. This method has a couple of overloads, including one declared in `LdapReferralException`. It is responsible for generating a `Context` instance that represents the location identified by the referral. A referral is defined as a URL in the LDAP. One way to create the referral context is to use the JNDI's support for URLs, for example by creating a `Reference` using the URL and then using `NamingManager.getObjectInstance()` to get the context.

Once the user program has a referral context, it is supposed to invoke on the context the original method that caused the `ReferralException` to be thrown by using the original arguments. Some of the original arguments might be affected by the referral's contents, including the name, search scope, search filter, and returning attributes. (See `draft-ietf-ldapext-namedref-00.txt` for details.) Your implementation of the referral context is responsible for modifying and/or replacing the supplied arguments with the ones from the referral. Here is an example of how `bind()` might be implemented in the referral context.

```
public void bind(Name name, Object obj) throws NamingException {
    // This referral has been skipped; throw a ReferralException
    if (skipThisReferral) {
        throw new ReferralExceptionImpl(untriedReferrals);
    }

    // Override the name from the referral URL, if appropriate
    Name nm = (urlName == null ? name : urlName);

    // Invoke the method on the real referral context
    refCtx.bind(nm, obj);
}
```

Skipping Referrals

A single LDAP referral entry might contain several alternate but equivalent referral URLs. A `ReferralException` actually represents a single referral URL. As a result, the user program can choose from the alternates by using `skipReferral()`. The implementation of a `Referral-Exception` must take this into account and generate possibly multiple `ReferralExceptions` from a single LDAP referral entry. After the user program calls `skipReferral()`, it must then call `getReferralContext()` to get to a valid context. That context's sole purpose is to provide a context whose methods simply throw a `ReferralException` for the *next* referral URL in the list of alternates.

Note that if the user program successfully follows one alternate, then all other untried alternates should be discarded.

Referral Modes

A JNDI program determines how it wants to handle referrals by using the `Context.REFERRAL` (`"java.naming.referral"`) environment property. In this way, the user program can specify whether it wants referrals to be followed automatically, followed manually, or ignored. As a service provider developer, you must handle all three cases.

When referrals are followed automatically, you should include a mechanism to limit the number of referrals followed so as to prevent referrals from being followed indefinitely due to misconfigured servers. This can be done by, for example, maintaining a count in the referral exception and referral context and then updating them as each referral exception is processed.

When referrals are followed manually, you must do some bookkeeping to track which is the "current" referral, as explained in the previous section.

LDAP referrals currently are specified by an Internet-draft, `draft-ietf-ldapext-named-ref-00.txt`. Not all servers support this Internet-draft. Your LDAP service provider must decide how to support referrals. If it uses this Internet-draft, then it might not be fully interoperable with servers that do not. This might cause the servers always to return referrals in LDAP responses regardless of what your provider does. One way to handle this mismatch is for your provider to throw a `PartialResultException` to indicate that there might be more results than those returned.

Adding Link Reference Support

Prerequisite: You should be familiar with link references before reading this section. Link references are discussed in the **Miscellaneous** lesson (page 142).

A service provider typically supports link references if it supports lookups that can return link references. However, because most naming/directory services have their own notions of (native) symbolic links (such as aliases and/or referrals), link references might be supported only by service providers that also support federation.

As with support for referrals, support for link references is an integral part of the service provider implementation. It affects all operations that involve name resolution. Furthermore, link references can be implemented in different ways. Following are some tips that you can follow, but the implementation that works for your service provider will depend on the features of the underlying naming/directory service. Especially important in this respect is how you've structured your code to handle federation.

Dereferencing a Link

A link reference is represented by the class LinkRef. Here is an example of a method for dereferencing a LinkRef.

```
public static Object derefLink(LinkRef ref, Context currCtx,
    Hashtable env) throws NamingException {

    String link = ref.getLinkName();

    if (link.startsWith("./")) {
        // A relative link; assume that currCtx is the immediate
        // context in which the link is bound
        return currCtx.lookup(link.substring(2));
    } else {
        // An absolute link; resolve it to the initial context
        Context ctx = new InitialContext(env);
        try {
            return ctx.lookup(link);
        } finally {
            ctx.close();  // Close when you're done
        }
    }
}
```

When to Dereference

lookupLink() should not dereference links. All other normal resolution of names for all methods in the Context interface and its subinterfaces always follows links.

Detecting Cycles

Resolution of the link name itself might cause the resolution to pass through other links. The result might be a cycle of links whose resolution can't terminate normally.

Several approaches are possible to detect and avoid cycles. One is to maintain a fixed-sized stack. In this case, each followed link is pushed onto the stack with the corresponding remaining name. When the stack is full, your provider should throw a `LinkLoopException`. Resolution of a link proceeds by resolving each link on the stack. When resolution of the link on the top of the stack completes, it is popped off and resolution on the next link on the stack begins. When the stack is empty, the resolution of the original link is complete.

Adding Event Notification Support

Prerequisite: You should be familiar with the event model used by the JNDI before reading this section. The event model is covered in the **Event Notification** lesson (page 111).

A service provider typically supports event notification only when the underlying naming/directory service provides such a feature. However, a service provider may support event notification even if the underlying service does not. It simply needs to do more work and perhaps offer the feature by polling the underlying service for changes.

Architectural Overview

Event notification can be implemented in several different ways. Following is one sample architecture. However, the one that works for your service provider will depend on the features of the underlying naming/directory service.

To add event notification support, you need the following three components.

- **Bookkeeper**. Maintains the list of listeners and is responsible for implementing the registration/deregistration methods in the `EventContext` and `EventDirContext` interfaces.
- **Notifier**. Notifies the listener(s) of an event. The occurrence of an event is typically triggered by an asynchronous change in the underlying service. The notifier detects the change (for example, via a message from the underlying service or by polling the state of the underlying service) and puts a corresponding event in the event queue.
- **Event queue**. Maintains a queue of events that have occurred and fires the events to the registered listeners.

To implement event notification, your context implementation must implement either the `EventContext` or `EventDirContext` interface. The bookkeeper might be a part of the context implementation or a utility used by the context implementation. When a program registers a listener, the bookkeeper records the listener and the target in which it is interested. It then uses—creates or uses one from a thread pool—a notifier to track the target. Typically, the notifier is a thread that listens for changes to the target. When the notifier detects a change that will trigger an event, it creates an event that contains the appropriate information and puts it in the event queue. The notifier then returns to listening for future changes. The event queue is monitored by an event queue manager thread, whose job is to remove an event from the queue and dispatch it to the appropriate listeners.

Implementation Tips

Here are some tips to keep in mind when developing your context implementation.

- Handling listener registration.
  Listener registration is associated with a Context *instance* and not the representation of the context in the underlying service. For example, suppose that you are using the LDAP service. You cannot expect to register a listener with one Context instance and remove it from another Context instance, even if both represent the same LDAP entry. Therefore your implementation should maintain separate listener lists for separate Context instances.
- When to deregister.
  Some events cause automatic deregistration. If a listener receives an exception or if the Context instance with which it has registered is closed, then the listener is automatically deregistered and will receive no further events. Your notifier implementation should pay attention to the exception events that it generates and tell the bookkeeper to deregister listeners that receive such events (but only *after* the exception events have been delivered).
- Using threads.
  Regardless of whether you choose to follow the sample architecture described previously in this section, support for event notification requires the use of threads. Furthermore, these threads manipulate shared data such as Context instances, event queues, and listener lists. Be sure to have a good understanding of the threads model in the Java programming language.

Adding Support for Controls and Extensions

Prerequisite: You should be familiar with LDAP v3 controls and extensions before reading this section. These topics are covered in the **Controls and Extensions** lesson (page 289).

A service provider typically supports LDAP v3 controls and extensions only when the underlying naming/directory service supports such features. Only the LDAP and LDAP-like services support these features.

To support controls and extensions, the context implementation must implement the Ldap-Context interface. In addition, how controls and extensions are supported is closely tied to how your implementation processes LDAP requests and responses. This section gives some general hints on how to implement these features.

Controls

In the LDAP v3, you can send a request control along with any LDAP request and receive a response control along with any LDAP response. Although request and response controls are commonly paired, a one-to-one correspondence between the two is not required. For example, you can receive a response control with an LDAP response without having sent any request control with the corresponding request.

The context implementation must be able to *encode* arbitrary request controls (supplied by the API user) with any LDAP request and be able to *decode* arbitrary response controls that accompany LDAP responses. The *encoding* of request controls is actually done by the individual implementations of the `Control` interface via `Control.getEncodedValue()`. The *decoding* of response controls is done by the response control implementations, which the context implementation selects via `ControlFactory.getControlInstance()`.

Two types of request controls are available.

- **Connection request control**. Affects how a connection is created
- **Context request control**. Affects context methods

Connection request controls are initialized by the API user's argument to the `Initial-LdapContext` constructor or `LdapReferralException.getReferralContext()` and modified via `LdapContext.reconnect()`. The context implementation must maintain a context's connection request controls in the environment property `"java.naming.ldap.control.connect"` and pass this property on to `Context` instances that it creates. In this way, the derived `Context` instances will inherit the connection controls.

The context implementation should maintain context request controls on a per `Context` instance basis and not pass them on to derived contexts. Context request controls are initialized by the API user's argument to `LdapContext.newInstance()` and modified via `Ldap-Context.setRequestControls()`.

"Extended" Operations

An API user invokes an "extended" operation by creating an `ExtendedRequest` and then invoking `extendedOperation()`. The context implementation is then responsible for encoding the extended request and submitting it as an LDAP "extended" operation to the LDAP server. The encoding is actually done by the individual implementations of the `ExtendedRequest` interface via `ExtendedRequest.getEncodedValue()`. When the server returns the corresponding extended response, the context implementation passes the response to `Extended-Request.createExtendedResponse()` to generate a response for the initial caller of `extendedOperation()`.

From this description, the onus of handling "extended" operations appears to be on the developers of the `ExtendedRequests`. However, this is true only for "extended" operations that have no effect on the context implementation. It is common for "extended" operations to affect the state of the context implementation. For example, the Start TLS operation enables Transport Layer Security (TLS) on an existing LDAP connection. Adding support for such an oper-ation requires changes to any existing context implementation and likely depends on internal interfaces of the context implementation. So usually, defining a general framework for han-dling arbitrary "extended" operations is difficult. Typically, the context implementation would maintain a list of "extended" operations that it would support natively. It would then inspect the object identifier of the extended responses for those operations and modify its behavior accordingly. There really is no good way to handle "extended" operations that it does not know about because it can't tell whether it should ignore or flag the operation.

## PART II

Class Libraries Reference

javax.naming

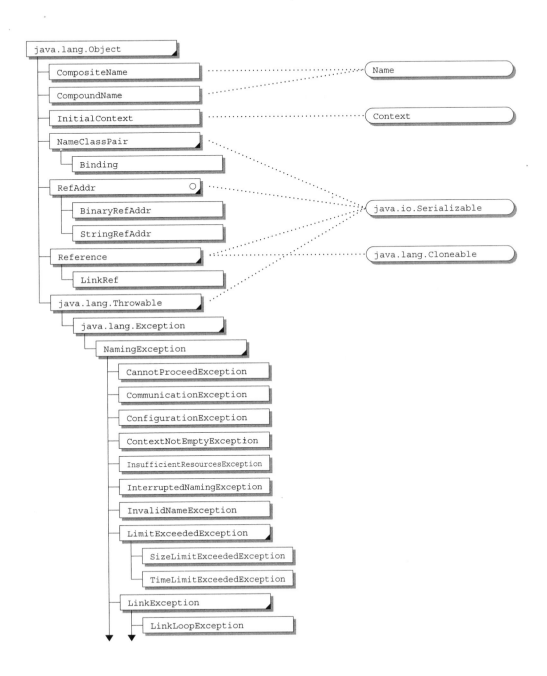

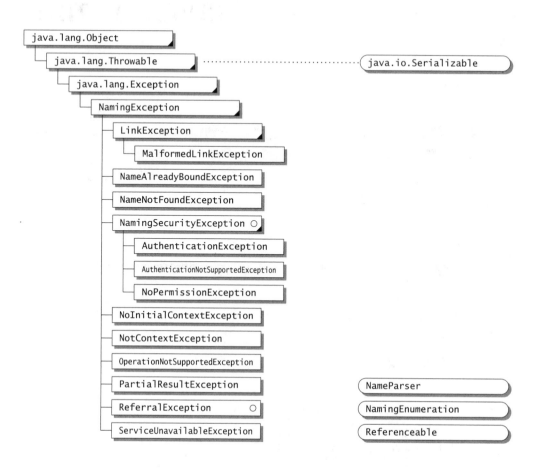

Description

The javax.naming package defines the naming operations and related classes of the JNDI.

Context

This package defines the notion of a *context*, represented by the Context interface. A context consists of a set of name-to-object *bindings*. Context is the core interface for looking up, binding, unbinding, and renaming objects and for creating and destroying subcontexts.

lookup() is the most commonly used operation. You supply to lookup() the name of the object that you want to look up, and it returns the object bound to that name. For example, the following code fragment looks up a printer and sends a document to the printer object to be printed.

```
Printer printer = (Printer)ctx.lookup("treekiller");
printer.print(report);
```

Names

Every naming method in the Context interface has two overloads: one that accepts a Name argument and one that accepts a string name. Name is an interface that represents a generic name—an ordered sequence of zero or more components. For these methods, Name can be used to represent a *composite name* (CompositeName) so that you can name an object by using a name that spans multiple namespaces.

The overloads that accept Name are useful for applications that need to manipulate names: composing names, comparing components, and so on. The overloads that accept string names are likely to be more useful for simple applications, such as those that simply read in a name and look up the corresponding object.

Bindings

The Binding class represents a name-to-object binding. It is a tuple that contains the name of the bound object, the name of the object's class, and the object itself.

The Binding class is actually a subclass of NameClassPair, which consists of the object's name and the object's class name. The NameClassPair is useful when you want only information about the object's class and do not want to pay the extra cost of getting the object.

References

Objects are stored in naming and directory services in different ways. If an object store supports storing Java objects, then it might support storing an object in its serialized form. However, some naming and directory services do not support storing Java objects. Furthermore, for some objects in the directory, Java programs are but one group of applications that access them. In this case, a serialized Java object might not be the most appropriate representation.

The JNDI defines a *reference*, represented by the Reference class, which contains information on how to construct a copy of the object. It attempts to turn references looked up from the directory into the Java objects that they represent so that JNDI clients have the illusion that what is stored in the directory are Java objects.

The Initial Context

In the JNDI, all naming and directory operations are performed relative to a context. There are no absolute roots. Therefore the JNDI defines an *initial context*, InitialContext, that provides a starting point for naming and directory operations. Once you have an initial context, you can use it to look up other contexts and objects.

Exceptions

The JNDI defines a class hierarchy for exceptions that can be thrown in the course of performing naming and directory operations. The root of this class hierarchy is NamingException.

A program interested in dealing with a particular exception can catch the corresponding subclass of the exception. Otherwise, it should catch NamingException.

Class and Interface Summary

Contexts

Context	A naming context that consists of a set of name-to-object bindings.
InitialContext	The starting context for performing naming operations.
NamingEnumeration	A list that is returned by methods in the javax.naming and javax.naming.directory packages.

Names

CompositeName	A composite name (a sequence of component names spanning multiple namespaces).
CompoundName	A compound name (a name from a hierarchical namespace).
Name	A generic name (an ordered sequence of components).
NameParser	A parser of names from a hierarchical namespace.

References

BinaryRefAddr	The binary form of the address of a communications endpoint.
LinkRef	A Reference whose content is a name, called the *link name*, that is bound to an atomic name in a context.
RefAddr	The address of a communications endpoint.
Reference	A reference to an object that is found outside of the naming/directory system.
Referenceable	An object that can provide a Reference to itself.
StringRefAddr	The string form of the address of a communications endpoint.

Bindings

Binding	A name-to-object binding found in a context.
NameClassPair	The object name and class name pair of a binding found in a context.

Exceptions

AuthenticationException	Thrown when an authentication error occurs while accessing the naming or directory service.
AuthenticationNotSupported-Exception	Thrown when the particular flavor of authentication requested is not supported.
CannotProceedException	Thrown to indicate that the operation has reached a point in the name where the operation cannot proceed further.
CommunicationException	Thrown when the client is unable to communicate with the directory or naming service.
ConfigurationException	Thrown when a configuration problem occurs.
ContextNotEmptyException	Thrown when an attempt was made to destroy a context that is not empty.
InsufficientResourcesException	Thrown when resources are not available to complete the requested operation.
InterruptedNamingException	Thrown when the naming operation being invoked was interrupted.
InvalidNameException	Thrown when the name being specified does not conform to the naming syntax of a naming system.
LimitExceededException	Thrown when a method terminated abnormally due to a user- or system-specified limit.
LinkException	Thrown to describe problems encountered while resolving links.
LinkLoopException	Thrown when a loop is detected when either an attempt was made to resolve a link or an implementation-specific limit on link counts was reached.
MalformedLinkException	Thrown when a malformed link is encountered while resolving or constructing a link.
NameAlreadyBoundException	Thrown by methods to indicate that a binding cannot be added because the name is already bound to another object.
NameNotFoundException	Thrown when a component of the name cannot be resolved because it is not bound.
NamingException	The superclass of all exceptions thrown by operations in the Context and DirContext interfaces.
NamingSecurityException	The superclass of security-related exceptions thrown by operations in the Context and DirContext interfaces.
	Continued

`NoInitialContextException`	Thrown when no initial context implementation can be created.
`NoPermissionException`	Thrown when an attempt was made to perform an operation for which the client had no permission.
`NotContextException`	Thrown when a naming operation proceeds to a point where a context is required to continue the operation but the resolved object is not a context.
`OperationNotSupportedException`	Thrown when a context implementation does not support the operation being invoked.
`PartialResultException`	Thrown to indicate that the result being returned or returned so far is partial and that the operation cannot be completed.
`ReferralException`	An abstract class used to represent a referral exception, which is generated in response to a *referral* such as that returned by LDAP v3 servers.
`ServiceUnavailableException`	Thrown when an attempt was made to communicate with a directory or naming service and that service was not available.
`SizeLimitExceededException`	Thrown when a method produced a result that exceeded a size-related limit.
`TimeLimitExceededException`	Thrown when a method does not terminate within the specified time limit.

javax.naming.directory

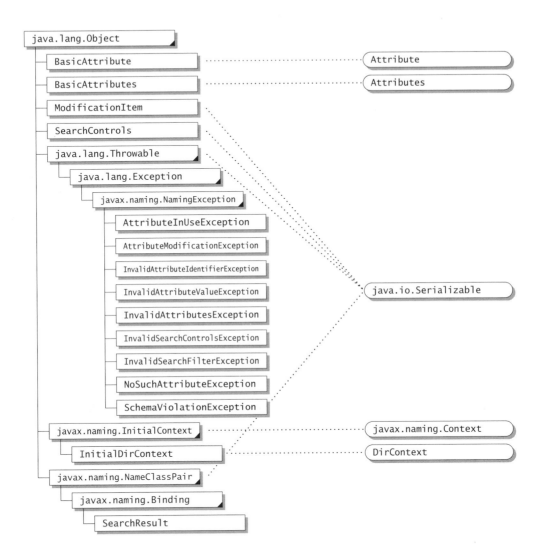

Description

The javax.naming.directory package defines the directory operations of the JNDI. It allows applications to retrieve and update attributes associated with objects stored in a directory and to search for objects by using specified attributes.

The Directory Context

The DirContext interface represents a *directory context*. It defines methods for examining and updating attributes associated with a *directory object*, sometimes called a *directory entry*.

405

You use getAttributes() to retrieve the attributes associated with a directory object (for which you supply the name). Attributes are modified using modifyAttributes(). You can add, replace, or remove attributes and/or attribute values by using this operation.

DirContext also behaves as a naming context by extending the Context interface in the javax.naming package. This means that any directory object can also provide a naming context. For example, the directory object for a person might contain the attributes of that person, as well as provide a context for naming objects relative to that person, such as printers and home directory.

Searches

DirContext contains methods for performing content-based searching of the directory. In the simplest and most common usage, the application specifies a set of attributes—possibly with specific values—to match and then submits this attribute set to search(). Other overloaded forms of search() support more sophisticated *search filters*.

Class and Interface Summary

Contexts

DirContext	A context that contains methods for examining and updating attributes associated with objects and for searching the directory.
InitialDirContext	The starting context for performing directory operations.
ModificationItem	A modification item.
SearchControls	A collection of parameters used for specifying factors that control a search, such as the scope of the search and what gets returned as a result of the search.
SearchResult	An item in the NamingEnumeration returned as a result of the search.

Attributes

Attribute	An attribute associated with a named object.
Attributes	A collection of attributes.
BasicAttribute	A basic implementation of the Attribute interface.
BasicAttributes	A basic implementation of the Attributes interface.

Exceptions

`AttributeInUseException`	Thrown when an operation attempts to add an attribute that already exists.
`AttributeModificationException`	Thrown when an attribute change was attempted (e.g., to add, remove, or modify the attribute, its identifier, or its values) that conflicts with the attribute's (schema) definition or the attribute's state.
`InvalidAttributeIdentifier-Exception`	Thrown when an attempt was made to add or create an attribute that has an invalid attribute identifier.
`InvalidAttributesException`	Thrown when an attempt was made to add or modify an attribute set that has been specified incompletely or incorrectly.
`InvalidAttributeValueException`	Thrown when an attempt was made to add to an attribute a value that conflicts with the attribute's schema definition.
`InvalidSearchControlsException`	Thrown when the specification of the `SearchControls` for a search operation is invalid.
`InvalidSearchFilterException`	Thrown when the specification of a search filter is invalid.
`NoSuchAttributeException`	Thrown when an attempt was made to access an attribute that does not exist.
`SchemaViolationException`	Thrown when a method in some way violates the schema.

javax.naming.event

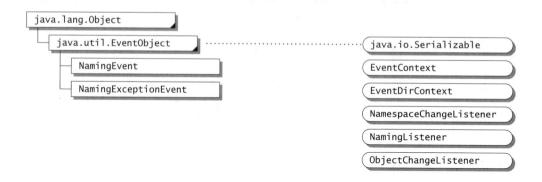

```
java.lang.Object
    java.util.EventObject ............................ java.io.Serializable
        NamingEvent                                     EventContext
        NamingExceptionEvent                            EventDirContext
                                                        NamespaceChangeListener
                                                        NamingListener
                                                        ObjectChangeListener
```

Description

The javax.naming.event package defines the event notification operations of the JNDI.

Naming Events

This package defines a NamingEvent class to represent an event that is generated by a naming/directory service. It also defines subinterfaces of Context and DirContext, called Event-Context and EventDirContext, through which applications can register their interest in events fired by the context.

NamingEvent represents an event that occurs in a naming or directory service. Two categories of naming events are possible:

- Those that affect the namespace (add/remove/rename an object)
- Those that affect the objects' contents

Each category is handled by a corresponding listener: NamespaceChangeListener or ObjectChangeListener.

Threading Issues

When an event is dispatched to a listener, the listener method (such as objectChanged()) may be executed in a thread other than the one in which the call to addNamingListener() was executed. The service provider determines which thread to use. When an event is dispatched to multiple listeners, the service provider may choose (and is generally encouraged) to execute the listener methods concurrently in separate threads.

When a listener instance invokes NamingEvent.getEventContext(), it must consider that other threads might be working with that context concurrently. When a listener is registered via addNamingListener(), the registering thread must consider that the service provider likely will later invoke the listeners in newly created threads. As Context instances are not guaranteed to be thread-safe in general, all context operations must be synchronized as needed.

Exception Handling

When a listener registers for events with a context, the context might need to do some internal processing in order to collect information required to generate the events. For example, it might need to ask the server to register interest in changes on the server that will eventually be translated into events. If an exception occurs that prevents information about the events from being collected, then the listener will never be notified of the events. When such an exception occurs, a NamingExceptionEvent is fired to notify the listener. The listener's naming-ExceptionThrown() method is invoked, and the listener is automatically deregistered.

Class and Interface Summary

Contexts

EventContext	A context that contains methods for registering/deregistering listeners that are to be notified of events fired when objects named in a context change.
EventDirContext	A context that contains methods for registering listeners that are to be notified of events fired when objects named in a directory context change.

Listeners

NamespaceChangeListener	Specifies the methods that a listener interested in namespace changes must implement.
NamingListener	The root of listener interfaces that handle NamingEvents.
ObjectChangeListener	Specifies the method that a listener of a NamingEvent with event type of OBJECT_CHANGED must implement.

Events

NamingEvent	Fired by a naming/directory service.
NamingExceptionEvent	Fired when the procedures/processes used to collect information for notifying listeners of NamingEvents throw a NamingException.

javax.naming.ldap

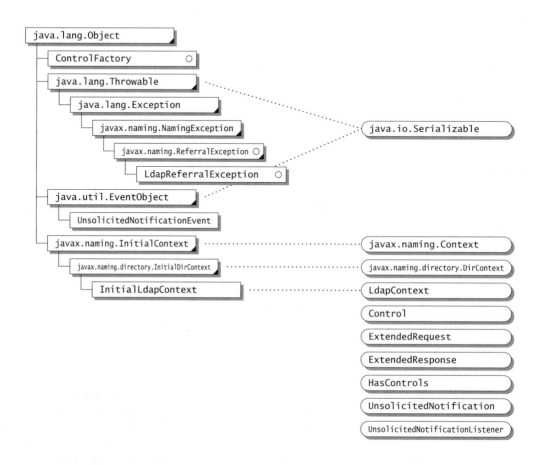

Description

The `javax.naming.ldap` package extends the directory operations of the JNDI. It is used by applications and service providers that deal with LDAP v3 "extended" operations and controls, as defined by RFC 2251. The core interface in this package is `LdapContext`, which defines methods on a context for performing "extended" operations and handling controls.

"Extended" Operations

This package defines the interface `ExtendedRequest` to represent the argument to an "extended" operation and the interface `ExtendedResponse` to represent the result of the "extended" operation. An extended response is always paired with an extended request but the reverse is not necessarily true. That is, you can have an extended request that has no corresponding extended response.

An application typically does not deal directly with these interfaces. Instead, it deals with classes that *implement* these interfaces. It gets these classes either as part of a repertoire of "extended" operations standardized through the IETF or from directory vendors, for vendor-specific "extended" operations. The request classes should have constructors that accept arguments in a type-safe and user-friendly manner, and the response classes should have access methods for getting the data of the response in a type-safe and user-friendly manner. Internally, the request/response classes deal with encoding and decoding BER values.

Controls

This package defines the interface `Control` to represent an LDAP v3 control. The interface can be a control that is sent to an LDAP server (*request control*) or a control returned by an LDAP server (*response control*). Unlike extended requests and extended responses, the pairing of request controls and response controls is not required. You can send a request control and expect no response control back, or vice versa.

An application typically does not deal directly with this interface. Instead, it deals with classes that *implement* this interface. It gets control classes either as part of a repertoire of controls standardized through the IETF or from directory vendors, for vendor-specific controls. The request control classes should have constructors that accept arguments in a type-safe and user-friendly manner, and the response control classes should have access to methods for getting the data of the response in a type-safe and user-friendly manner. Internally, the request/response control classes deal with encoding and decoding BER values. A service provider that receives response controls uses the `ControlFactory` class to produce specific classes that implement the `Control` interface.

An LDAP server can return response controls with an LDAP operation and with enumeration results, such as those returned by a "search" operation. The `LdapContext` provides `getResponseControls()` for getting the response controls sent with an LDAP operation. The `HasControls` interface is used to retrieve response controls associated with enumeration results.

Class and Interface Summary

Contexts

`InitialLdapContext`	The starting context for performing LDAP v3-style "extended" operations and controls.
`LdapContext`	A context in which you can perform operations with LDAP v3-style controls and perform LDAP v3-style "extended" operations.

Controls

Control	An LDAP v3 control as defined in RFC 2251.
ControlFactory	A factory for creating LDAP v3 controls.
HasControls	An interface for returning controls along with objects returned in NamingEnumerations.

"Extended" Operations

ExtendedRequest	An LDAP v3 "extended" operation request as defined in RFC 2251.
ExtendedResponse	An LDAP v3 "extended" operation response as defined in RFC 2251.

Unsolicited Notifications

UnsolicitedNotification	An unsolicited notification as defined in RFC 2251.
UnsolicitedNotification-Event	An event fired in response to an unsolicited notification sent by the LDAP server.
UnsolicitedNotification-Listener	A listener for handling UnsolicitedNotificationEvent.

Exception

LdapReferralException	An abstract class used to represent a referral exception from which you can create a referral context by using controls.

javax.naming.spi

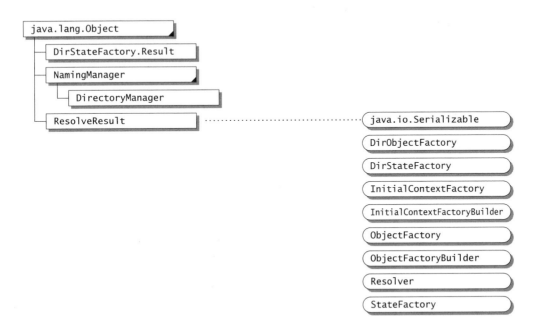

Description

The `javax.naming.spi` package defines the service provider interface (SPI) of the JNDI. The JNDI SPI provides the means for creating JNDI service providers, through which JNDI applications access different naming and directory services.

Plug-In Architecture

This package allows different implementations to be plugged in dynamically, including those for the *initial context* and those for contexts that can be reached from the initial context.

Java Object Support

This package provides support for implementors of `javax.naming.Context.lookup()` and related methods to return Java objects that are natural and intuitive for the Java programmer. For example, when you look up a printer name from the directory, you naturally expect to get back a printer object on which to operate.

This package also provides support for implementors of `javax.naming.Context.bind()` and related methods to store Java objects in forms acceptable by the underlying naming/directory service.

Multiple Naming Systems (Federation)

JNDI operations allow applications to supply names that span multiple naming systems. In the process of completing an operation, one service provider might need to interact with another service provider, for example to pass on the operation to be continued in the nns (next naming system). This package provides support for different providers to cooperate to complete JNDI operations.

Class and Interface Summary

Static Manager Classes

DirectoryManager	Contains methods for supporting DirContext implementations.
NamingManager	Contains methods for creating context objects and objects referred to by location information in the naming or directory service.

Object Factories

DirObjectFactory	A factory for creating an object when given an object and attributes about the object.
ObjectFactory	A factory for creating an object.
ObjectFactoryBuilder	A builder that creates object factories.

State Factories

DirStateFactory	A factory for obtaining the state of an object and corresponding attributes for binding.
DirStateFactory.Result	An object/attributes pair for returning the result of DirStateFactory.getStateToBind().
StateFactory	A factory for obtaining the state of an object for binding.

Initial Context Factories

`InitialContextFactory`	A factory that creates an initial context.
`InitialContextFactory-` `Builder`	A builder that creates initial context factories.

Federation

`Resolver`	An *intermediate context* for name resolution.
`ResolveResult`	The result of the resolution of a name.

Attribute

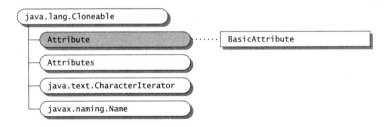

```
java.lang.Cloneable
    Attribute  ............  BasicAttribute
    Attributes
    java.text.CharacterIterator
    javax.naming.Name
```

Syntax

```
public interface Attribute extends Cloneable, java.io.Serializable
```

Description

The `Attribute` interface represents an attribute associated with a named object.

In a directory, named objects can have attributes associated with them. The `Attribute` interface represents an attribute associated with a named object. An attribute contains zero or more, possibly `null`, values. The attribute values can be ordered or unordered (see `isOrdered()`). If the values are unordered, then no duplicates are allowed. If the values are ordered, then duplicates are allowed.

The content and representation of an attribute and its values are defined by the attribute's *schema*. The schema contains information about the attribute's syntax and other properties about the attribute. See `getAttributeDefinition()` and `getAttributeSyntaxDefinition()` for details regarding how to get schema information about an attribute if the underlying directory service supports schemas.

Equality of two attributes is determined by the implementation class. A simple implementation can use `Object.equals()` to determine equality of attribute values, whereas a more sophisticated implementation might use schema information. Similarly, one implementation might provide a static storage structure that simply returns the values passed to its constructor, whereas another might define `get()` and `getAll()` to get the values dynamically from the directory.

Updates to `Attribute` (such as adding or removing a value) do not affect the attribute's representation in the directory. Updates to the directory can be done only via operations in the `DirContext` interface.

MEMBER SUMMARY
Copy Method
`clone()`   Makes a copy of this attribute.
Continued

A

MEMBER SUMMARY	
Update Methods	
add()	Adds an attribute value to this attribute.
clear()	Removes all values from this attribute.
remove()	Removes an attribute value from this attribute.
set()	Sets an attribute value in the ordered list of attribute values.
Query and Access Methods	
contains()	Determines whether a value is in this attribute.
get()	Retrieves one of this attribute's values.
getAll()	Retrieves an enumeration of this attribute's values.
getID()	Retrieves the identifier of this attribute.
isOrdered()	Determines whether this attribute's values are ordered.
size()	Retrieves the number of values in this attribute.
Schema Methods	
getAttributeDefinition()	Retrieves the attribute's schema definition.
getAttributeSyntaxDefinition()	Retrieves the syntax definition associated with this attribute.

See Also

BasicAttribute.

Example

See the **Directory Operations** lesson (page 61).

add()

PURPOSE   Adds an attribute value to this attribute.

SYNTAX   boolean add(Object attrVal)
               void add(int ix, Object attrVal)

DESCRIPTION   This method adds a new value to this attribute. If the attribute values are unordered and attrVal is already in the attribute, then the first form of the method does nothing. If the attribute values are ordered, then this form adds attrVal to the end of the list of attribute values.

The second form of this method adds an attribute value attrVal to the ordered list of attribute values at index ix. Values located at indices at or greater than ix are shifted down toward the end of the list (and their indices incremented by

A

1). If the attribute values are unordered and already have `attrVal`, then an `IllegalStateException` is thrown.

The implementation determines whether a value is already in the attribute. It may use `Object.equals()` or schema information to determine whether two attribute values are equal.

PARAMETERS

`attrVal`   The possibly `null` attribute value to add. If `null`, then `null` is the value added.

`ix`   The index in the ordered list of attribute values at which to add the new value. $0 \leq ix \leq size()$.

RETURNS   The first form of the method returns `true` if a value was added; `false` otherwise.

EXCEPTIONS

`IllegalStateException`
             If the attribute values are unordered and `attrVal` is one of those values.

`IndexOutOfBoundsException`
             If `ix` is outside of the specified range.

SEE ALSO   `contains()`.

EXAMPLE   See the **Directory Operations** lesson (page 70).

clear()

PURPOSE   Removes all values from this attribute.

SYNTAX   `void clear()`

clone()

PURPOSE   Makes a copy of this attribute.

SYNTAX   `Object clone()`

DESCRIPTION This method makes a copy of this attribute. The copy contains the same attribute values as the original attribute; the attribute values are not themselves cloned. Changes to the copy will not affect the original, and vice versa.

RETURNS   A non-`null` copy of this attribute.

OVERRIDES   `java.lang.Object.clone()`.

contains()

PURPOSE   Determines whether a value is in this attribute.

A

SYNTAX   `boolean contains(Object attrVal)`

DESCRIPTION   This method determines whether a value is in this attribute. The implementation determines the equality of two attribute values, by using `Object.equals()` or schema information.

PARAMETERS
attrVal   The possibly `null` value to check. If `attrVal` is `null`, then check whether this attribute has an attribute value whose value is `null`.

RETURNS   `true` if `attrVal` is one of this attribute's values; `false` otherwise.

SEE ALSO   `BasicAttribute.equals()`, `java.lang.Object.equals()`.

EXAMPLE   See the **Object Factories** lesson (page 192).

get()

PURPOSE   Retrieves one of this attribute's values.

SYNTAX   `Object get() throws NamingException`
                `Object get(int ix) throws NamingException`

DESCRIPTION   This method retrieves one of this attribute's values. If no index was specified and the attribute has more than one value and is unordered, then any one of the values is returned. If no index was specified and the attribute has more than one value and is ordered, then the first value is returned.

                If an index, `ix`, has been specified, then this method returns the value at the `ix` index of the list of attribute values. If the attribute values are unordered, then it returns the value that happens to be at that index.

PARAMETERS
ix   The index of the value in the ordered list of attribute values. $0 \leq ix < size()$.

RETURNS   The possibly `null` attribute value at index `ix`, or any object if `ix` has not been specified, or `null` if the attribute value is `null`.

EXCEPTIONS
IndexOutOfBoundsException
                If `ix` is outside of the specified range.
java.util.NoSuchElementException
                If this attribute has no values.
NamingException
                If a naming exception is encountered while retrieving the value.

EXAMPLE   See the **Object Factories** lesson (page 192).

getAll()

PURPOSE   Retrieves an enumeration of this attribute's values.

SYNTAX   `NamingEnumeration getAll() throws NamingException`

A

DESCRIPTION   This method retrieves an enumeration of this attribute's values. The behavior of this enumeration is unspecified if this attribute's values are added, changed, or removed while the enumeration is in progress. If the attribute values are ordered, then the enumeration's items will be ordered.

RETURNS   A non-`null` enumeration of this attribute's values. Each element of the enumeration is a possibly `null` object. The object's class is the class of the attribute value. The element is `null` if the attribute's value is `null`. If the attribute has zero values, then an empty enumeration is returned.

EXCEPTIONS

`NamingException`
> If a naming exception is encountered while retrieving the values.

SEE ALSO   `isOrdered()`.

EXAMPLE   See the **Directory Operations** lesson (page 61).

getAttributeDefinition()

PURPOSE   Retrieves this attribute's schema definition.

SYNTAX   `DirContext getAttributeDefinition() throws NamingException`

DESCRIPTION   This method retrieves this attribute's schema definition. This definition contains such information as whether the attribute is multivalued or single-valued and the matching rules to use when comparing the attribute's values.

The information that you can retrieve from an attribute definition is directory-dependent. If an implementation does not support schemas, then it should throw an `OperationNotSupportedException`. Otherwise, it should define this method to return the appropriate information.

RETURNS   This attribute's schema definition. `null` if the implementation supports schemas but this particular attribute does not have any schema information.

EXCEPTIONS

`NamingException`
> If a naming exception occurs while getting the schema.

`OperationNotSupportedException`
> If getting the schema is not supported.

EXAMPLE   See the **Schema** lesson (page 280).

getAttributeSyntaxDefinition()

PURPOSE   Retrieves the syntax definition associated with this attribute.

SYNTAX   `DirContext getAttributeSyntaxDefinition() throws NamingException`

DESCRIPTION   This method retrieves the syntax definition associated with this attribute. This definition specifies the format of the attribute's value(s). Note that this differs from the attribute value's representation as a Java object. Syntax definition refers to the directory's notion of *syntax*.

                     For example, a value might be a Java `String` object, but its directory syntax might be "Printable String" or "Telephone Number". Or a value might be a byte array and its directory syntax "JPEG" or "Certificate". For example, if this attribute's syntax is "JPEG", then this method would return the syntax definition for "JPEG".

                     The information that you can retrieve from a syntax definition is directory-dependent.

                     If an implementation does not support schemas, then it should throw an `OperationNotSupportedException`. Otherwise, it should define this method to return the appropriate information.

RETURNS   The attribute's syntax definition. `null` if the implementation supports schemas but this particular attribute does not have any schema information.

EXCEPTIONS

`NamingException`
                     If a naming exception occurs while getting the schema.

`OperationNotSupportedException`
                     If getting the schema is not supported.

EXAMPLE   See the **Schema** lesson (page 282).

getID()

PURPOSE   Retrieves the identifier of this attribute.

SYNTAX   `String getID()`

RETURNS   The identifier of this attribute. Cannot be `null`.

EXAMPLE   See the **Directory Operations** lesson (page 61).

isOrdered()

PURPOSE   Determines whether this attribute's values are ordered.

SYNTAX   `boolean isOrdered()`

DESCRIPTION   This method determines whether this attribute's values are ordered. If an attribute's values are ordered, then duplicate values are allowed. If its values are unordered, then they are presented in any order and there are no duplicate values.

RETURNS   `true` if this attribute's values are ordered; `false` otherwise.

SEE ALSO   `add()`, `get()`, `remove()`, `set()`.

remove()

PURPOSE   Removes an attribute value from this attribute.

SYNTAX   `Object remove(int ix)`
                 `boolean remove(Object attrVal)`

DESCRIPTION   This method removes an attribute value from this attribute. The first form removes an value from the ordered list of attribute values at the `ix` index of the list. If the attribute values are unordered, then it removes the value that happens to be at that index. Values located at indices greater than `ix` are shifted up toward the front of the list (and their indices decremented by 1).

                 The second form removes `attrVal` from this attribute. If `attrVal` is not in the attribute, then it does nothing. If the attribute values are ordered, then the first occurrence of `attrVal` is removed and attribute values at indices greater than the removed value are shifted up toward the head of the list (and their indices decremented by 1).

                 The implementation determines the equality of attribute values, by using `Object.equals()` or schema information.

PARAMETERS
  attrVal   The possibly `null` value to remove from this attribute. If `null`, then remove the attribute value that is `null`.

  ix   The index of the value to remove. $0 \leq ix < size()$.

RETURNS   The first form returns the possibly `null` attribute value at index `ix` that was removed; `null` if the attribute value is `null`. The second form returns `true` if the value was removed; `false` otherwise.

EXCEPTIONS
  IndexOutOfBoundsException
                 If `ix` is outside of the specified range.

set()

PURPOSE	Sets an attribute value in the ordered list of attribute values.
SYNTAX	`Object set(int ix, Object attrVal)`
DESCRIPTION	This method sets an attribute value in the ordered list of attribute values. It sets the value at the `ix` index of the list of attribute values to be `attrVal` and removes the old value. If the attribute values are unordered, then it sets the value that happens to be at that index to `attrVal`, unless `attrVal` is already one of the values. In that case, an `IllegalStateException` is thrown.

PARAMETERS

`attrVal`	The possibly `null` attribute value to use. If `null`, then `null` replaces the old value.
`ix`	The index of the value in the ordered list of attribute values. $0 \leq ix < size()$.
RETURNS	The possibly `null` attribute value at index ix that was replaced. `null` if the attribute value was `null`.

EXCEPTIONS

`IllegalStateException`
> If `attrVal` already exists and the attribute values are unordered.

`IndexOutOfBoundsException`
> If `ix` is outside of the specified range.

size()

PURPOSE	Retrieves the number of values in this attribute.
SYNTAX	`int size()`
RETURNS	The nonnegative number of values in this attribute.

AttributeInUseException

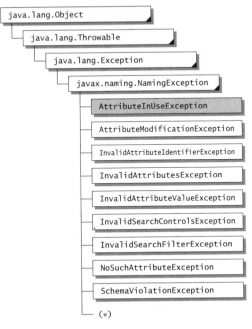

(*) 18 classes from other packages not shown.

Syntax

public class AttributeInUseException extends NamingException

Description

An AttributeInUseException is thrown when an operation attempts to add an attribute that already exists.

Synchronization and serialization issues that apply to NamingException apply directly here.

MEMBER SUMMARY
Constructor
AttributeInUseException()   Constructs an instance of AttributeInUseException.

AttributeInUseException()

PURPOSE	Constructs an instance of `AttributeInUseException`.
SYNTAX	`public AttributeInUseException()` `public AttributeInUseException(String msg)`
DESCRIPTION	These constructors construct an instance of `AttributeInUseException` by using an optional `msg` supplied. If `msg` is not supplied, then `msg` defaults to `null`. All other fields default to `null`.
PARAMETERS	
`msg`	Additional detail about this exception. May be `null`.
SEE ALSO	`java.lang.Throwable.getMessage()`.

A

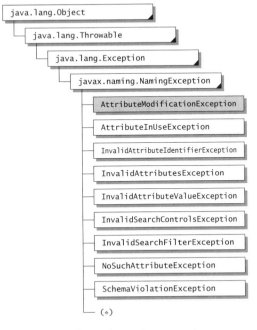

A

```
java.lang.Object
    java.lang.Throwable
        java.lang.Exception
            javax.naming.NamingException
                AttributeModificationException
                AttributeInUseException
                InvalidAttributeIdentifierException
                InvalidAttributesException
                InvalidAttributeValueException
                InvalidSearchControlsException
                InvalidSearchFilterException
                NoSuchAttributeException
                SchemaViolationException
                (*)
```

(*) 18 classes from other packages not shown.

Syntax
`public class AttributeModificationException extends NamingException`

Description

An `AttributeModificationException` is thrown when an attempt is made to add, remove, or modify an attribute, its identifier, or its values that conflicts with the attribute's schema definition or the attribute's state. It is thrown in response to `DirContext.modifyAttributes()`. It contains a list of modifications that have not been performed, in the order that they were supplied to `modifyAttributes()`. If the list is `null`, none of the modifications were performed successfully.

An `AttributeModificationException` instance is not synchronized against concurrent multithreaded access. Multiple threads trying to access and modify a single `Attribute-ModificationException` instance should lock the object.

See Also
`DirContext.modifyAttributes()`.

A

MEMBER SUMMARY	
Constructor	
`AttributeModificationException()`	Constructs an instance of `AttributeModificationException`.
Unexecuted Modification Methods	
`getUnexecutedModifications()`	Retrieves the unexecuted modification list.
`setUnexecutedModifications()`	Sets the unexecuted modification list.
Object Method	
`toString()`	Generates the string representation of this exception.

AttributeModificationException()

PURPOSE   Constructs an instance of `AttributeModificationException`.

SYNTAX   `public AttributeModificationException()`
`public AttributeModificationException(String msg)`

DESCRIPTION   These constructors construct an instance of `AttributeModification-Exception` by using an optional `msg` supplied. If `msg` is not supplied, `msg` defaults to `null`. All other fields default to `null`.

PARAMETERS

  `msg`   Additional detail about this exception. May be `null`. If `null`, this exception has no detail message.

SEE ALSO   `java.lang.Throwable.getMessage()`.

getUnexecutedModifications()

PURPOSE   Retrieves the unexecuted modification list.

SYNTAX   `public ModificationItem[] getUnexecutedModifications()`

DESCRIPTION   This method retrieves the unexecuted modification list. Items in the list appear in the same order in which they were originally supplied in `DirContext.modifyAttributes()`. The first item in the list is the first one that was not executed. A `null` list means that none of the operations originally submitted to `modifyAttributes()` were executed.

RETURNS   The possibly `null` unexecuted modification list.

SEE ALSO   `setUnexecutedModifications()`.

A

setUnexecutedModifications()

PURPOSE   Sets the unexecuted modification list.

SYNTAX   `public void setUnexecutedModifications(ModificationItem[] e)`

DESCRIPTION   This method sets the unexecuted modification list to be e. Items in the list must appear in the same order in which they were originally supplied in `Dir-Context.modifyAttributes()`. The first item in the list is the first one that was not executed. A `null` list means that none of the operations originally submitted to `modifyAttributes()` were executed.

PARAMETERS

e   The possibly `null` list of unexecuted modifications.

SEE ALSO   `getUnexecutedModifications()`.

toString()

PURPOSE   Generates the string representation of this exception.

SYNTAX   `public String toString()`

DESCRIPTION   This method generates the string representation of this exception. The string consists of information about where the error occurred and the first unexecuted modification. It is for debugging and is not meant to be interpreted programmatically.

RETURNS   The non-`null` string representation of this exception.

OVERRIDES   `javax.naming.NamingExcepton.toString()`.

Attributes

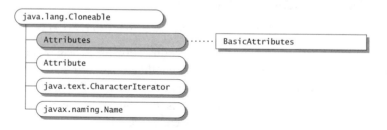

```
java.lang.Cloneable
    Attributes ......... BasicAttributes
    Attribute
    java.text.CharacterIterator
    javax.naming.Name
```

Syntax

```
public interface Attributes extends Cloneable, java.io.Serializable
```

Description

The `Attributes` interface represents a collection of attributes.

In a directory, named objects can have attributes associated with them. The `Attributes` interface represents a collection of attributes. For example, you can request from the directory the attributes associated with an object. Those attributes are returned in an object that implements the `Attributes` interface.

Attributes in an object that implements the `Attributes` interface are unordered. The object can have zero or more attributes, each with a unique attribute identifier. `Attributes` is either case-sensitive or case-insensitive (case-ignore). This property is determined at the time that the `Attributes` object is created (see the `BasicAttributes` constructor for an example). In a case-insensitive `Attributes`, the case of its attribute identifiers is ignored when searching for or adding attributes. In a case-sensitive `Attributes`, the case is significant.

Updates to `Attributes` (such as adding or removing an attribute) do not affect the corresponding representation in the directory. Updates to the directory can be done only by using operations in the `DirContext` interface.

MEMBER SUMMARY	
Query and Access Methods	
`get()`	Retrieves the attribute with the given attribute identifier from this attribute set.
`getAll()`	Retrieves an enumeration of the attributes in this attribute set.
`getIDs()`	Retrieves an enumeration of the identifiers of the attributes in this attribute set.
`isCaseIgnored()`	Determines whether the attribute set ignores the case of attribute identifiers when retrieving or adding attributes.
`size()`	Retrieves the number of attributes in this attribute set.

MEMBER SUMMARY	
Update Methods	
put()	Adds a new attribute to this attribute set.
remove()	Removes an attribute from this attribute set.
Copy Method	
clone()	Makes a copy of this attribute set.

See Also

Attribute, BasicAttributes.

Example

See the **Directory Operations** lesson (page 64).

clone()

PURPOSE	Makes a copy of this attribute set.
SYNTAX	`Object clone()`
DESCRIPTION	This method makes a copy of this attribute set. The new set contains the same attributes as the original set; the attributes are not themselves cloned. Changes to the copy will not affect the original, and vice versa.
RETURNS	A non-null copy of this attribute set.
OVERRIDES	`java.lang.Object.clone()`.
EXAMPLE	See the **State Factories** lesson (page 176).

get()

PURPOSE	Retrieves the attribute with the given attribute identifier from this attribute set.
SYNTAX	`Attribute get(String attrID)`
PARAMETERS	
attrID	The non-null identifier of the attribute to retrieve. If this attribute set ignores the character case of its attribute identifiers, then the case of attrID is ignored.
RETURNS	The attribute identified by attrID; null if not found.
SEE ALSO	`put()`, `remove()`.
EXAMPLE	See the **State Factories** lesson (page 176).

A

getAll()

PURPOSE   Retrieves an enumeration of the attributes in this attribute set.

SYNTAX   `NamingEnumeration getAll()`

DESCRIPTION This method retrieves an enumeration of the attributes in this attribute set. The effects of updates to this attribute set on this enumeration are undefined.

RETURNS   A non-null enumeration of the attributes in this attribute set. Each element of the enumeration is of class `Attribute`. If this attribute set has zero attributes, then an empty enumeration is returned.

EXAMPLE   See the **Directory Operations** lesson (page 61).

getIDs()

PURPOSE   Retrieves an enumeration of the identifiers of the attributes in this attribute set.

SYNTAX   `NamingEnumeration getIDs()`

DESCRIPTION This method retrieves an enumeration of the identifiers of the attributes in this attribute set. The effects of updates to this attribute set on this enumeration are undefined.

RETURNS   A non-null enumeration of the attributes' identifiers in this attribute set. Each element of the enumeration is of class `java.lang.String`. If this attribute set has zero attributes, then an empty enumeration is returned.

isCaseIgnored()

PURPOSE   Determines whether this attribute set ignores the case of attribute identifiers when attributes are being retrieved or add.

SYNTAX   `boolean isCaseIgnored()`

RETURNS   `true` if case is ignored; `false` otherwise.

put()

PURPOSE   Adds a new attribute to this attribute set.

SYNTAX   `Attribute put(String attrID, Object val)`
             `Attribute put(Attribute attr)`

DESCRIPTION   This method adds a new attribute to this attribute set. The new attribute can be specified either as an `Attribute` instance (attr) or as an attribute identifier (attrID) and its value (val).

PARAMETERS
attr   The non-null attribute to add. If the attribute set ignores the character case of its attribute identifiers, then the case of attr's identifier is ignored.

attrID   The non-null identifier of the attribute to add. If this attribute set ignores the character case of its attribute identifiers, then the case of attrID is ignored.

val   The possibly null value of the attribute to add. If null, then null is the value added.

RETURNS   The `Attribute` with an attrID or attr's identifier that was previously in this attribute set; null if no such attribute exists.

SEE ALSO   `remove()`.

EXAMPLE   See the **Directory Operations** lesson (page 64).

remove()

PURPOSE   Removes an attribute from this attribute set.

SYNTAX   `Attribute remove(String attrID)`

DESCRIPTION   This method removes the attribute with the attribute identifier attrID from this attribute set. If the attribute does not exist, this method does nothing.

PARAMETERS
attrID   The non-null identifier of the attribute to remove. If this attribute set ignores the character case of its attribute identifiers, then the case of attrID is ignored.

RETURNS   The `Attribute` with the same identifier as attrID that was previously in this attribute set; null if no such attribute exists.

size()

PURPOSE   Retrieves the number of attributes in this attribute set.

SYNTAX   `int size()`

RETURNS   The nonnegative number of attributes in this attribute set.

javax.naming
AuthenticationException

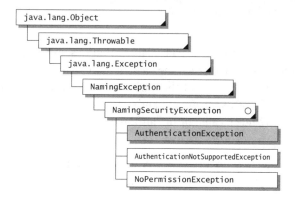

```
java.lang.Object
    java.lang.Throwable
        java.lang.Exception
            NamingException
                NamingSecurityException        ○
                    AuthenticationException
                    AuthenticationNotSupportedException
                    NoPermissionException
```

Syntax
```
public class AuthenticationException extends NamingSecurityException
```

Description

An AuthenticationException is thrown when an authentication error occurs while the naming or directory service is being accessed. An authentication error can happen, for example, when the credentials supplied by the user program are invalid or otherwise fail to authenticate the user to the naming/directory service.

If the program wants to handle this exception in particular, then it should catch the AuthenticationException explicitly before attempting to catch the NamingException. After catching the AuthenticationException, the program could reattempt the authentication by updating the resolved context's environment properties with the appropriate credentials.

Synchronization and serialization issues that apply to NamingException apply directly here.

MEMBER SUMMARY
Constructor
AuthenticationException()　　　Constructs an instance of AuthenticationException.

Example
See the **Referrals** lesson (page 266).

AuthenticationException()

PURPOSE   Constructs an instance of `AuthenticationException`.

SYNTAX   `public AuthenticationException()`
                   `public AuthenticationException(String msg)`

DESCRIPTION   These constructors construct an instance of `AuthenticationException` by using the optional `msg` supplied. All other fields default to `null`.

PARAMETERS

`msg`   Additional detail about this exception. May be `null`. If `null`, then this exception has no detail message.

SEE ALSO   `java.lang.Throwable.getMessage()`.

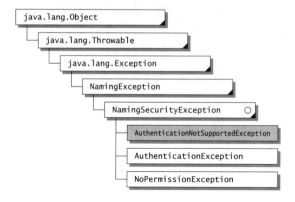

Syntax

```
public class AuthenticationNotSupportedException extends
    NamingSecurityException
```

Description

An AuthenticationNotSupportedException is thrown when the particular flavor of authentication requested is not supported. For example, if the program is attempting to use strong authentication but the directory/naming service supports only simple authentication, then this exception will be thrown.

The identification of a particular flavor of authentication is provider- and server-specific. It may be specified by using specific authentication schemes, such those identified as using SASL, or a generic authentication specifier (such as "simple" and "strong").

A program that wants to handle this exception in particular should catch the AuthenticationNotSupportedException explicitly before attempting to catch the NamingException. After catching the AuthenticationNotSupportedException, the program could reattempt the authentication using a different authentication flavor by updating the resolved context's environment properties accordingly.

Synchronization and serialization issues that apply to NamingException apply directly here.

MEMBER SUMMARY
Constructor
AuthenticationNotSupportedException()   Constructs an instance of AuthenticationNotSupportedException.

Example

See the **Security** lesson (page 224).

AuthenticationNotSupportedException()

PURPOSE   Constructs an instance of AuthenticationNotSupportedException.

SYNTAX   public AuthenticationNotSupportedException()
               public AuthenticationNotSupportedException(String msg)

DESCRIPTION   These constructors construct an instance of AuthenticationNotSupported-
               Exception by using an optional msg supplied. If msg is not supplied, msg
               defaults to null. All other fields default to null.

PARAMETERS
   msg   Additional detail about this exception. May be null.

SEE ALSO   java.lang.Throwable.getMessage().

BasicAttribute

```
java.lang.Object
      BasicAttribute ......( Attribute )
```

B

Syntax

```
public class BasicAttribute implements Attribute
```

Description

The `BasicAttribute` class provides a basic implementation of the `Attribute` interface.

This implementation does not support the schema methods `getAttributeDefinition()` and `getAttributeSyntaxDefinition()`. The methods simply throw an `OperationNot-SupportedException`. Subclasses of `BasicAttribute` should override these methods, if they support them.

The `BasicAttribute` class by default uses `Object.equals()` to determine equality of attribute values when testing for equality or when searching for values, *except* when the value is an array. For an array, it uses `Object.equals()` to check each element of the array. Subclasses of `BasicAttribute` can use schema information when doing similar equality checks by overriding methods in which such use of schema is meaningful.

The `BasicAttribute` class by default returns the values that are passed to its constructor and/or manipulated by using the `add()`/`set()`/`remove()` methods. Subclasses of `Basic-Attribute` can override `get()` and `getAll()` to get the values dynamically from the directory (or implement the `Attribute` interface directly instead of subclassing `BasicAttribute`).

Updates to `BasicAttribute` (such as adding or removing a value) do not affect the corresponding representation of the attribute in the directory. Updates to the directory can be done only by using operations in the `DirContext` interface.

A `BasicAttribute` instance is not synchronized against concurrent multithreaded access. Multiple threads trying to access and modify a `BasicAttribute` should lock the object.

MEMBER SUMMARY	
Constructor	
BasicAttribute()	Constructs an instance of BasicAttribute.
Update Methods	
add()	Adds a new value to this attribute.
clear()	Removes all values from this attribute.
remove()	Removes a specified value from this attribute.
set()	Sets an attribute value in the ordered list of attribute values.

MEMBER SUMMARY	
Copy Method	
clone()	Makes a copy of this attribute.
Query and Access Methods	
contains()	Determines whether a value is in this attribute.
get()	Retrieves one of this attribute's values.
getAll()	Retrieves an enumeration of this attribute's values.
getID()	Retrieves the identifier of this attribute.
isOrdered()	Determines whether this attribute's values are ordered.
size()	Retrieves the number of values in this attribute.
Schema Methods	
getAttributeDefinition()	Retrieves this attribute's schema definition.
getAttributeSyntaxDefinition()	Retrieves this attribute's syntax definition.
Object Methods	
equals()	Determines whether an object is equal to this attribute.
hashCode()	Calculates the hash code of this attribute.
toString()	Generates the string representation of this attribute.
Protected Fields	
attrID	Holds the attribute's identifier.
ordered	A flag that records whether this attribute's values are ordered.
values	Holds this attribute's values.

Example

See the **Directory Operations** lesson (page 71).

add()

PURPOSE   Adds a new value to this attribute.

SYNTAX
```
public boolean add(Object attrVal)
public void add(int ix, Object attrVal)
```

DESCRIPTION   This method adds a new value to this attribute. See `Attribute.add()` for a complete description.

By default, the first form of this method uses `Object.equals()` to compare `attrVal` with this attribute's values, except when `attrVal` is an array. For an array, `Object.equals()` is used to check each element of the array.

A subclass may use schema information to determine equality.

B

PARAMETERS

attrVal The possibly null attribute value to add. If null, then null is the value added.

ix The index in the ordered list of attribute values at which to add the new value.
$0 \leq ix \leq size()$.

RETURNS The first form of the method returns true if a value was added; false otherwise.

EXCEPTIONS

IllegalStateException
If the attribute values are unordered and attrVal is one of those values.

IndexOutOfBoundsException
If ix is outside of the specified range.

SEE ALSO Attribute.add(), contains().

EXAMPLE See the **Directory Operations** lesson (page 71).

attrID

PURPOSE Holds the attribute's identifier.

SYNTAX `protected String attrID`

DESCRIPTION This field holds the attribute's identifier. It is initialized by the public constructor and cannot be null unless methods in BasicAttribute that use attrID have been overridden.

BasicAttribute()

PURPOSE Constructs an instance of BasicAttribute.

SYNTAX
```
public BasicAttribute(String id)
public BasicAttribute(String id, Object value)
public BasicAttribute(String id, boolean ordered)
public BasicAttribute(String id, Object value, boolean ordered)
```

DESCRIPTION These constructors construct an instance of BasicAttribute. If value is not supplied, then the new instance has no attribute value. If ordered is not supplied, then the attribute is unordered.

PARAMETERS

id The attribute's identifier. Cannot be null.

ordered true means that the attribute's values will be ordered; false otherwise.

value This attribute's value. If null, then a null value is added to the attribute.

EXAMPLE See the **Directory Operations** lesson (page 71).

clear()

PURPOSE	Removes all values from this attribute.
SYNTAX	`public void clear()`
SEE ALSO	`Attribute.clear()`.

B

clone()

PURPOSE	Makes a copy of this attribute.
SYNTAX	`public Object clone()`
DESCRIPTION	See `Attribute.clone()` for a complete description.
RETURNS	A non-null copy of this attribute.
OVERRIDES	`java.lang.Object.clone()`.
SEE ALSO	`Attribute.clone()`.

contains()

PURPOSE	Determines whether a value is in this attribute.
SYNTAX	`public boolean contains(Object attrVal)`
DESCRIPTION	This method determines whether a value is in this attribute. See `Attribute.contains()` for a complete description.
	By default, it uses `Object.equals()` to compare `attrVal` with this attribute's values, except when `attrVal` is an array. For an array, it uses `Object.equals()` to check each element of the array.
	A subclass may use schema information to determine equality.
PARAMETERS	
`attrVal`	The possibly `null` value to check. If `null`, then checks whether this attribute has an attribute value whose value is `null`.
RETURNS	`true` if `attrVal` is one of this attribute's values; `false` otherwise.
SEE ALSO	`Attribute.contains()`, `java.lang.Object.equals()`, `BasicAttribute.equals()`.
EXAMPLE	See the **Object Factories** lesson (page 192).

equals()

PURPOSE	Determines whether an object is equal to this attribute.

441

SYNTAX	`public boolean equals(Object obj)`
DESCRIPTION	This method determines whether an object, `obj`, is equal to this attribute. Two attributes are equal if their attribute identifiers, syntaxes, and values are equal. If the attribute values are unordered, then the order in which the values were added is irrelevant. If the attribute values are ordered, then the order of the values must match. If `obj` is `null` or not an `Attribute`, then `false` is returned.
	By default, this method uses `Object.equals()` to compare the attribute identifier and its values, except when a value is an array. For an array, it uses `Object.equals()` to check each element of the array.
	A subclass may override this to use schema syntax information and matching rules, which define what it means for two attributes to be equal. How and whether a subclass uses the schema information is determined by the subclass. If a subclass overrides `equals()`, it should also override `hashCode()` such that two attributes that are equal have the same hash code.
PARAMETERS	
obj	The possibly `null` object to check.
RETURNS	`true` if `obj` is equal to this attribute; `false` otherwise.
OVERRIDES	`java.lang.Object.equals()`.
SEE ALSO	`contains()`, `hashCode()`.

get()

PURPOSE	Retrieves one of this attribute's values.
SYNTAX	`public Object get() throws NamingException` `public Object get(int ix) throws NamingException`
DESCRIPTION	This method retrieves one of this attribute's values. See `Attribute.get()` for a complete description.
	By default, the first form returns one of the values that is passed to the constructor and/or manipulated by using the `add()`/`set()`/`remove()` methods.
	A subclass may override this method to retrieve the value dynamically from the directory.
PARAMETERS	
ix	The index of the value in the ordered list of attribute values. $0 \leq ix < size()$.
RETURNS	The possibly `null` attribute value at index `ix`, or any object if `ix` has not been specified, or `null` if the attribute value is `null`.

EXCEPTIONS

`IndexOutOfBoundsException`
> If `ix` is outside of the specified range.

`java.util.NoSuchElementException`
> If this attribute has no values.

`NamingException`
> If a naming exception is encountered while retrieving the value.

SEE ALSO   `Attribute.get()`.

EXAMPLE   See the **Examples** lesson (page 29).

getAll()

PURPOSE   Retrieves an enumeration of this attribute's values.

SYNTAX   `public NamingEnumeration getAll() throws NamingException`

DESCRIPTION   This method retrieves an enumeration of this attribute's values. See `Attribute.getAll()` for a complete description.

By default, it returns the values that are passed to the constructor and/or manipulated by using the `add()`/`set()`/`remove()` methods.

A subclass may override this method to retrieve the values dynamically from the directory.

RETURNS   A non-`null` enumeration of the attribute's values. Each element of the enumeration is a possibly `null` object. The object's class is the class of the attribute value. The element is `null` if the attribute's value is `null`. If the attribute has zero values, then an empty enumeration is returned.

EXCEPTIONS

`NamingException`
> If a naming exception is encountered while retrieving the values.

SEE ALSO   `Attribute.getAll()`, `isOrdered()`.

getAttributeDefinition()

PURPOSE   Retrieves this attribute's schema definition.

SYNTAX   `public DirContext getAttributeDefinition() throws NamingException`

DESCRIPTION   This method retrieves this attribute's schema definition. See `Attribute.getAttributeDefinition()` for a complete description.

By default, it throws an `OperationNotSupportedException`.

A subclass should override this method if it supports schema.

RETURNS   Does not return a value unless it is overridden by a subclass.

EXCEPTIONS

`NamingException`

If a naming exception occurs while getting the schema.

`OperationNotSupportedException`

If getting the schema is not supported.

SEE ALSO   `Attribute.getAttributeDefinition().`

EXAMPLE   See the **Schema** lesson (page 280).

getAttributeSyntaxDefinition()

PURPOSE   Retrieves the syntax definition associated with this attribute.

SYNTAX   `public DirContext getAttributeSyntaxDefinition() throws`
`                    NamingException`

DESCRIPTION   This method retrieves the syntax definition associated with this attribute. See
`Attribute.getAttributeSyntaxDefinition()` for a complete description.

By default, it throws an `OperationNotSupportedException`.

A subclass should override this method if it supports schema.

RETURNS   Does not return a value unless it is overridden by a subclass.

EXCEPTIONS

`NamingException`

If a naming exception occurs while getting the schema.

`OperationNotSupportedException`

If getting the schema is not supported.

SEE ALSO   `Attribute.getAttributeSyntaxDefinition().`

EXAMPLE   See the **Schema** lesson (page 282).

getID()

PURPOSE   Retrieves the identifier of this attribute.

SYNTAX   `public String getID()`

RETURNS   The identifier of this attribute. Cannot be `null`.

EXAMPLE   See the **Directory Operations** lesson (page 61).

B

hashCode()

PURPOSE	Calculates the hash code of this attribute.
SYNTAX	`public int hashCode()`
DESCRIPTION	This method calculates the hash code of this attribute.

The hash code is computed by adding the hash code of this attribute's identifier and that of all of its values, except for values that are arrays. For an array, the hash codes of all of the elements of the array are summed.

If a subclass overrides `hashCode()`, it should override `equals()` as well so that two attributes that are equal have the same hash code.

RETURNS	An `int` that represents the hash code of this attribute.
OVERRIDES	`java.lang.Object.hashCode()`.
SEE ALSO	`equals()`.

isOrdered()

PURPOSE	Determines whether this attribute's values are ordered.
SYNTAX	`public boolean isOrdered()`
DESCRIPTION	See `Attribute.isOrdered()` for a complete description.
RETURNS	`true` if this attribute's values are ordered; `false` otherwise.
SEE ALSO	`add()`, `Attribute.isOrdered()`, `get()`, `remove()`, `set()`.

ordered

PURPOSE	A flag for recording whether this attribute's values are ordered.
SYNTAX	`protected boolean ordered`
DESCRIPTION	This field holds a `boolean` that indicates whether this attribute's values are ordered.

remove()

PURPOSE	Removes a specified value from this attribute.
SYNTAX	`public Object remove(int ix)` `public boolean remove(Object attrval)`
DESCRIPTION	This method removes a specified value from this attribute. See `Attribute.remove()` for a complete description.

445

By default, it uses `Object.equals()` to compare `attrVal` with this attribute's values, except when `attrVal` is an array. For an array, it uses `Object.equals()` to check each element of the array. A subclass may use schema information to determine equality.

PARAMETERS

`attrval`   The possibly `null` value to remove from this attribute. If `null`, then removes the attribute value that is `null`.

`ix`   The index of the value to remove. $0 \leq ix < size()$.

RETURNS   The first form returns the possibly `null` attribute value at index `ix` that was removed; `null` if the attribute value is `null`. The second form returns `true` if the value was removed; `false` otherwise.

EXCEPTIONS

`IndexOutOfBoundsException`

              If `ix` is outside of the specified range.

SEE ALSO   `Attribute.remove()`.

set()

PURPOSE   Sets an attribute value in the ordered list of attribute values.

SYNTAX   `public Object set(int ix, Object attrVal)`

DESCRIPTION   See `Attribute.set()` for a complete description.

PARAMETERS

`attrVal`   The possibly `null` attribute value to use. If `null`, then `null` replaces the old value.

`ix`   The index of the value in the ordered list of attribute values. $0 \leq ix < size()$.

RETURNS   The possibly `null` attribute value at index `ix` that was replaced; `null` if the attribute value was `null`.

EXCEPTIONS

`IllegalStateException`

              If `attrVal` already exists and the attribute values are unordered.

`IndexOutOfBoundsException`

              If `ix` is outside of the specified range.

SEE ALSO   `Attribute.set()`.

size()

PURPOSE   Retrieves the number of values in this attribute.

SYNTAX   `public int size()`

RETURNS   The nonnegative number of values in this attribute.

toString()

PURPOSE   Generates the string representation of this attribute.

SYNTAX   `public String toString()`

DESCRIPTION   This method generates the string representation of this attribute. The string consists of the attribute's identifier and its values. It is for debugging and is not meant to be interpreted programmatically.

RETURNS   The non-`null` string representation of this attribute.

OVERRIDES   `java.lang.Object.toString()`.

values

PURPOSE   Holds the attribute's values.

SYNTAX   `protected transient Vector values`

DESCRIPTION   This field holds the attribute's values. It is initialized by public constructors and cannot be `null` unless methods in `BasicAttribute` that use values have been overridden.

BasicAttributes

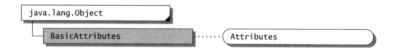

Syntax

```
public class BasicAttributes implements Attributes
```

Description

The BasicAttributes class provides a basic implementation of the Attributes interface.

An instance of BasicAttributes is either case-sensitive or case-insensitive (case-ignore). This property is determined when the BasicAttributes constructor is called. In a case-insensitive BasicAttributes, the case of its attribute identifiers is ignored when searching for an attribute or adding attributes. In a case-sensitive BasicAttributes, the case is significant.

When the BasicAttributes class needs to create an Attribute, it uses BasicAttribute. There is no other dependency on BasicAttribute.

Updates to BasicAttributes (such as adding or removing an attribute) do not affect the attribute's corresponding representation in the directory. Updates to the directory can be done only by using operations in the DirContext interface.

A BasicAttributes instance is not synchronized against concurrent multithreaded access. Multiple threads trying to access and modify a single BasicAttributes instance should lock the object.

MEMBER SUMMARY	
Constructor	
BasicAttributes()	Constructs an instance of BasicAttributes.
Update Methods	
put()	Adds a new attribute to this attribute set.
remove()	Removes an attribute from this attribute set.
Query and Access Methods	
get()	Retrieves the attribute that has the given attribute identifier from this attribute set.
getAll()	Retrieves an enumeration of the attributes in this attribute set.
getIDs()	Retrieves an enumeration of the identifiers of the attributes in this attribute set.
isCaseIgnored()	Determines whether this attribute set ignores the case of attribute identifiers when attributes are retrieved or added.
size()	Retrieves the number of attributes in the attribute set.

MEMBER SUMMARY	
Copy Method	
clone()	Makes a copy of this attribute set.
Object Methods	
equals()	Determines whether this BasicAttributes is equal to another object.
hashCode()	Calculates the hash code of this BasicAttributes.
toString()	Generates the string representation of this attribute set.

See Also
Attributes.

Example
See the **Directory Operations** lesson (page 64).

BasicAttributes()

PURPOSE   Constructs an instance of BasicAttributes.

SYNTAX
```
public BasicAttributes()
public BasicAttributes(boolean ignoreCase)
public BasicAttributes(String attrID, Object val)
public BasicAttributes(String attrID, Object val, boolean
    ignoreCase)
```

DESCRIPTION   These constructors construct an instance of BasicAttributes. If ignoreCase is not specified, then it defaults to false. If ignoreCase is true, then the character case of attribute identifiers is ignored; otherwise, the case is significant. The character case of attribute identifiers is significant when subsequently retrieving or adding attributes.

If attrID and val are not specified, then the new instance has no attributes. If attrID and val are specified, then the attribute specified by attrID and val is added to the newly created attribute.

PARAMETERS

attrID   The non-null identifier of the attribute to add.

ignoreCase   true means that this attribute set will ignore the case of its attribute identifiers when attributes are retrieved or added; false means case is respected.

val   The value of the attribute to add. If null, then a null value is added to the attribute.

EXAMPLE   See the **Referrals** lesson (page 268).

B

clone()

PURPOSE	Makes a copy of this attribute set.
SYNTAX	`public Object clone()`
RETURNS	A non-null copy of this attribute set.
OVERRIDES	`java.lang.Object.clone()`.
SEE ALSO	`Attributes.clone()`.
EXAMPLE	See the **State Factories** lesson (page 176).

equals()

PURPOSE	Determines whether this `BasicAttributes` is equal to another object.
SYNTAX	`public boolean equals(Object obj)`
DESCRIPTION	This method determines whether this `BasicAttributes` is equal to an object, `obj`. `obj` is equal if it is an instance of `Attributes` and if it and this `Basic-Attributes` treat the case of attribute identifiers in the same way and contain the same attributes. This method checks each `Attribute` in this `Basic-Attributes` for equality by using `Object.equals()`, which might have been overridden by implementations of `Attribute`.
	If a subclass overrides `equals()`, then it should override `hashCode()` as well so that two `Attributes` instances that are equal have the same hash code.
PARAMETERS	
obj	The possibly `null` object against which to compare.
RETURNS	`true` if `obj` is equal to this `BasicAttributes`.
OVERRIDES	`java.lang.Object.equals()`.
SEE ALSO	`hashCode()`.

get()

PURPOSE	Retrieves the attribute that has the given attribute identifier from this attribute set.
SYNTAX	`public Attribute get(String attrID)`
PARAMETERS	
attrID	The non-null identifier of the attribute to retrieve. If this attribute set ignores the character case of its attribute identifiers, then the case of `attrID` is ignored.
RETURNS	The attribute identified by `attrID`; `null` if not found.

SEE ALSO   `Attributes.get()`, `put()`, `remove()`.

EXAMPLE   See the **State Factories** lesson (page 176).

getAll()

PURPOSE   Retrieves an enumeration of the attributes in this attribute set.

SYNTAX   `public NamingEnumeration getAll()`

RETURNS   A non-null enumeration of the attributes in this attribute set. Each element of the enumeration is of class `Attribute`. If the attribute set has zero attributes, then an empty enumeration is returned.

SEE ALSO   `Attributes.getAll()`.

EXAMPLE   See the **Directory Operations** lesson (page 61).

getIDs()

PURPOSE   Retrieves an enumeration of the identifiers of the attributes in this attribute set.

SYNTAX   `public NamingEnumeration getIDs()`

RETURNS   A non-null enumeration of the identifiers of the attributes in this attribute set. Each element of the enumeration is of class `java.lang.String`. If this attribute set has zero attributes, then an empty enumeration is returned.

SEE ALSO   `Attributes.getIDs()`.

hashCode()

PURPOSE   Calculates the hash code of this `BasicAttributes`.

SYNTAX   `public int hashCode()`

DESCRIPTION   This method calculates the hash code of this `BasicAttributes`.

The hash code is computed by summing the hash codes of the attributes of this object. If this `BasicAttributes` ignores the case of its attribute identifiers, then 1 is added to the hash code.

If a subclass overrides `hashCode()`, then it should override `equals()` as well so that two `Attributes` instances that are equal have the same hash code.

RETURNS   An `int` that represents the hash code of this `BasicAttributes` instance.

OVERRIDES   `java.lang.Object.hashCode()`.

SEE ALSO   `equals()`.

isCaseIgnored()

PURPOSE	Determines whether this attribute set ignores the case of attribute identifiers when retrieving or adding attributes.
SYNTAX	`public boolean isCaseIgnored()`
RETURNS	`true` if case is ignored; `false` otherwise.

put()

PURPOSE	Adds a new attribute to this attribute set.
SYNTAX	`public Attribute put(String attrID, Object val)` `public Attribute put(Attribute attr)`
PARAMETERS	
`attr`	The non-`null` attribute to add. If this attribute set ignores the character case of its attribute identifiers, then the case of `attr`'s identifier is ignored.
`attrID`	The non-`null` identifier of the attribute to add. If this attribute set ignores the character case of its attribute identifiers, then the case of `attrID` is ignored.
`val`	The possibly `null` value of the attribute to add. If `null`, then `null` is the value added.
RETURNS	The `Attribute` with `attrID` or `attr`'s identifier that was previously in this attribute set.
DESCRIPTION	`null` if no such attribute exists.
SEE ALSO	`Attributes.put()`, `remove()`.
EXAMPLE	See the **Referrals** lesson (page 268).

remove()

PURPOSE	Removes an attribute from this attribute set.
SYNTAX	`public Attribute remove(String attrID)`
PARAMETERS	
`attrID`	The non-`null` identifier of the attribute to remove. If this attribute set ignores the character case of its attribute identifiers, then the case of `attrID` is ignored.
RETURNS	The `Attribute` with the same identifier as `attrID` that was previous in the attribute set; `null` if no such attribute exists.
SEE ALSO	`Attributes.remove()`.

size()

PURPOSE	Retrieves the number of attributes in this attribute set.
SYNTAX	`public int size()`
RETURNS	The nonnegative number of attributes in this attribute set.

toString()

PURPOSE	Generates the string representation of this attribute set.
SYNTAX	`public String toString()`
DESCRIPTION	This method generates the string representation of this attribute set. The string consists of each attribute identifier and the contents of each attribute. It is for debugging and is not meant to be interpreted programmatically.
RETURNS	A non-`null` string that lists the contents of this attribute set.
OVERRIDES	`java.lang.Object.toString()`.

BinaryRefAddr

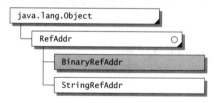

Syntax

```
public class BinaryRefAddr extends RefAddr
```

Description

The `BinaryRefAddr` class represents the binary form of the address of a communications end-point.

A `BinaryRefAddr` consists of a type that describes the communication mechanism and an opaque buffer that contains the address description specific to that mechanism. The format and interpretation of the address type and the contents of the opaque buffer are based on the agreement of three parties: the client that uses the address, the object/server that can be reached by using the address, and the administrator or program that creates the address.

Examples of a binary reference address is an BER X.500 presentation address and a serialized form of a service's object handle. A binary reference address is immutable in the sense that its fields, once created, cannot be replaced. However, accessing the `byte` array used to hold the opaque buffer is possible. Programs are strongly advised not to change this `byte` array. Changes to this array need to be explicitly synchronized.

MEMBER SUMMARY	
Constructor	
BinaryRefAddr()	Constructs an instance of `BinaryRefAddr`.
RefAddr Method	
getContent()	Retrieves the contents of this address as an `Object`.
Object Methods	
equals()	Determines whether obj is equal to this address.
hashCode()	Computes the hash code of this address by using its address type and contents.
toString()	Generates the string representation of this address.

B

BinaryRefAddr()

PURPOSE   Constructs an instance of `BinaryRefAddr`.

SYNTAX
```
public BinaryRefAddr(String addrType, byte[] src)
public BinaryRefAddr(String addrType, byte[] src, int offset, int
    count)
```

DESCRIPTION   These constructors construct an instance of `BinaryRefAddr` by using its address type and a `byte` array for contents. `offset` and `count` specify the region of `src` to use.

PARAMETERS

  addrType   A non-null string that describes the type of the address.

  count   The number of bytes to extract from `src`.

  offset   The 0-based starting index in `src` at which to get the bytes.

  src   The non-null contents of the address as a `byte` array.

equals()

PURPOSE   Determines whether `obj` is equal to this address.

SYNTAX   `public boolean equals(Object obj)`

DESCRIPTION   This method determines whether `obj` is equal to this address. `obj` is equal if it contains the same address type and the contents of both are byte-wise equivalent.

PARAMETERS

  obj   The possibly `null` object to check.

RETURNS   `true` if the object is equal; `false` otherwise.

OVERRIDES   `RefAddr.equals()`.

SEE ALSO   `hashCode()`.

getContent()

PURPOSE   Retrieves the contents of this address as an `Object`.

SYNTAX   `public Object getContent()`

DESCRIPTION   This method retrieves the contents of this address as an `Object`. The result is a `byte` array. Changes to this array will affect this `BinaryRefAddr`'s contents. Programs are advised not to change this array's contents and to lock the buffer if they need to change it.

455

| RETURNS | The non-null buffer that contains this address's contents. |
| OVERRIDES | RefAddr.getContent(). |

hashCode()

PURPOSE	Computes the hash code of this address by using its address type and contents.
SYNTAX	`public int hashCode()`
DESCRIPTION	This method computes the hash code of this address by using its address type and contents. Two BinaryRefAddrs have the same hash code if they have the same address type and the same contents. It is possible for two Binary-RefAddrs that have different address types and/or contents to have the same hash code.
RETURNS	The hash code of this address as an `int`.
OVERRIDES	RefAddr.hashCode().
SEE ALSO	equals().

toString()

PURPOSE	Generates the string representation of this address.
SYNTAX	`public String toString()`
DESCRIPTION	This method generates the string representation of this address. The string consists of the address's type and contents with labels. The first 32 bytes of the contents are displayed (in hexadecimal). If there are more than 32 bytes, then "..." is used to indicate more. This string is for debugging and is not meant to be interpreted programmatically.
RETURNS	The non-null string representation of this address.
OVERRIDES	RefAddr.toString().

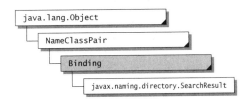

Syntax
`public class Binding extends NameClassPair`

Description

The `Binding` class represents a name-to-object binding found in a context.

A context consists of name-to-object bindings. The `Binding` class represents such a binding and consists of a name and an object. `Context.listBindings()` returns an enumeration of `Binding`.

A service provider that generate contents of a binding dynamically should subclass this class.

A `Binding` instance is not synchronized against concurrent access by multiple threads. Threads that need to access a `Binding` concurrently should synchronize among themselves and provide the necessary locking.

MEMBER SUMMARY	
Constructor	
`Binding()`	Constructs an instance of `Binding`.
Binding Methods	
`getClassName()`	Retrieves the class name of the object bound to the name of this binding.
`getObject()`	Retrieves the object bound to the name of this binding.
`setObject()`	Sets the object associated with this binding.
Object Method	
`toString()`	Generates the string representation of this binding.

Example

See the **Naming Operations** lesson (page 55).

Binding()

PURPOSE   Constructs an instance of a `Binding`.

SYNTAX

```
public Binding(String name, Object obj)
public Binding(String name, Object obj, boolean isRelative)
public Binding(String name, String className, Object obj)
public Binding(String name, String className, Object obj, boolean
    isRelative)
```

DESCRIPTION   These constructors construct an instance of a `Binding` when given its name, object, and, optionally, its class name and whether the name is relative. If `isRelative` is omitted, then it defaults to `true`. If `className` is omitted, then it defaults to the class of `obj`. If `isRelative` is true, then `name` is named relative to the target context of the operation that returned the binding. If `isRelative` is `false`, then `name` is named relative to the initial context.

PARAMETERS

`className`   The possibly `null` class name of the object. If `null`, then the class name of `obj` is used.

`isRelative`   If `true`, then `name` is relative to the context in which it was bound.

`name`   The non-`null` name of the object.

`obj`   The possibly `null` object bound to name.

SEE ALSO   `NameClassPair.isRelative()`, `NameClassPair.setClassName()`, `NameClassPair.setRelative()`.

EXAMPLE   See **The Essential Components** lesson (page 336).

getClassName()

PURPOSE   Retrieves the class name of the object bound to the name of this binding.

SYNTAX   `public String getClassName()`

DESCRIPTION   This method retrieves the class name of the object bound to the name of this binding. If the class name has been set explicitly, then return it. Otherwise, if this binding contains a non-`null` object, then use that object's class name. Otherwise, `null` is returned.

RETURNS   A possibly `null` string that contains the class name of bound object.

OVERRIDES   `NameClassPair.getClassName()`.

getObject()

PURPOSE   Retrieves the object bound to the name of this binding.

SYNTAX	`public Object getObject()`
RETURNS	The bound object; `null` if this binding does not contain an object.
SEE ALSO	`setObject()`.
EXAMPLE	See the **Reading Objects from the Directory** lesson (page 182).

B

setObject()

PURPOSE	Sets the object associated with this binding.
SYNTAX	`public void setObject(Object obj)`
PARAMETERS	
obj	The possibly `null` object to use.
SEE ALSO	`getObject()`.

toString()

PURPOSE	Generates the string representation of this binding.
SYNTAX	`public String toString()`
DESCRIPTION	This method generates the string representation of this binding. The string consists of the string representation of the name/class pair and the string representation of this binding's object, separated by ":". It is for debugging and is not meant to be interpreted programmatically.
RETURNS	The non-`null` string representation of this binding.
OVERRIDES	`NameClassPair.toString()`.

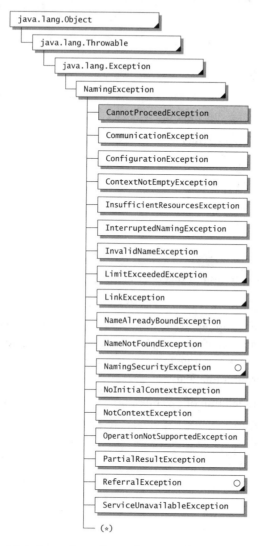

```
java.lang.Object
    java.lang.Throwable
        java.lang.Exception
            NamingException
                CannotProceedException
                CommunicationException
                ConfigurationException
                ContextNotEmptyException
                InsufficientResourcesException
                InterruptedNamingException
                InvalidNameException
                LimitExceededException
                LinkException
                NameAlreadyBoundException
                NameNotFoundException
                NamingSecurityException        ○
                NoInitialContextException
                NotContextException
                OperationNotSupportedException
                PartialResultException
                ReferralException              ○
                ServiceUnavailableException
                (*)
```

(*) 9 classes from other packages not shown.

Syntax

```
public class CannotProceedException extends NamingException
```

Description

A CannotProceedException is thrown to indicate that the operation reached a point in the name where the operation could not proceed any further.

When performing an operation on a composite name, a naming service provider may reach a part of the name that does not belong to its namespace. At that point, it can construct a CannotProceedException and then invoke methods provided by javax.naming.spi.NamingManager (such as getContinuationContext()) to locate another provider to continue the operation. If this is not possible, then this exception is raised to the caller of the context operation.

A program that wants to handle this exception in particular should catch the CannotProceedException explicitly before attempting to catch the NamingException.

A CannotProceedException instance is not synchronized against concurrent multi-threaded access. Multiple threads trying to access and modify a CannotProceedException should lock the object.

C

MEMBER SUMMARY	
Constructor	
CannotProceedException()	Constructs an instance of CannotProceedException.
Access Methods	
getAltName()	Retrieves the altName field of this exception.
getAltNameCtx()	Retrieves the altNameCtx field of this exception.
getEnvironment()	Retrieves the environment that was in effect when this exception was created.
getRemainingNewName()	Retrieves the remaining new name field of this exception.
setAltName()	Sets the altName field of this exception.
setAltNameCtx()	Sets the altNameCtx field of this exception.
setEnvironment()	Sets the environment that will be returned when getEnvironment() is called.
setRemainingNewName()	Sets the remaining new name field of this exception.
Fields	
altName	Contains the name of the resolved object, relative to the context altNameCtx.
altNameCtx	Contains the context relative to which altName is specified.
environment	Contains the environment relevant for the Context or DirContext method that cannot proceed.
remainingNewName	Contains the remaining unresolved part of the second name argument to Context.rename().

See Also

`javax.naming.spi.DirectoryManager.getContinationDirContext()`,
`javax.naming.spi.NamingManager.getContinuationContext()`.

Example

See the **Adding Federation Support** lesson (page 377).

altName

PURPOSE	Contains the name of the resolved object, relative to the context `altNameCtx`.
SYNTAX	`protected Name altName`
DESCRIPTION	This field contains the name of the resolved object, relative to the context `altNameCtx`. It is a composite name. If `null`, then no name is specified. For details on how to use this, see `javax.naming.spi.ObjectFactory.getObjectInstance()`.
	This field is initialized to `null`. It should not be manipulated directly. Rather, it should be accessed and updated by using `getAltName()` and `setAltName()`.
SEE ALSO	`altNameCtx`, `getAltName()`, `javax.naming.spi.ObjectFactory.getObjectInstance()`, `setAltName()`.

altNameCtx

PURPOSE	Contains the context relative to which `altName` is specified.
SYNTAX	`protected Context altNameCtx`
DESCRIPTION	This field contains the context relative to which `altName` is specified. If `null`, then the default initial context is implied. See `javax.naming.spi.ObjectFactory.getObjectInstance()` for details on how to use this.
	This field is initialized to `null`. It should not be manipulated directly. Rather, it should be accessed and updated by using `getAltNameCtx()` and `setAltNameCtx()`.
SEE ALSO	`altName`, `getAltNameCtx()`, `javax.naming.spi.ObjectFactory.getObjectInstance()`, `setAltNameCtx()`.

CannotProceedException()

PURPOSE	Constructs an instance of `CannotProceedException`.

SYNTAX	`public CannotProceedException()` `public CannotProceedException(String msg)`
DESCRIPTION	These constructors construct an instance of `CannotProceedException` by using an optional `msg` supplied. If `msg` is not supplied, then `msg` defaults to `null`. All unspecified fields default to `null`.
PARAMETERS	
`msg`	Additional detail about this exception. May be `null`.
SEE ALSO	`java.lang.Throwable.getMessage()`.
EXAMPLE	See the **Adding Federation Support** lesson (page 376).

environment

PURPOSE	Contains the environment relevant for the `Context` or `DirContext` method that cannot proceed.
SYNTAX	`protected Hashtable environment`
DESCRIPTION	This field contains the environment relevant for the `Context` or `DirContext` method that cannot proceed. This field is initialized to `null`. It should not be manipulated directly. Rather, it should be accessed and updated by using `getEnvironment()` and `setEnvironment()`.
SEE ALSO	`getEnvironment()`, `setEnvironment()`.

getAltName()

PURPOSE	Retrieves the `altName` field of this exception.
SYNTAX	`public Name getAltName()`
DESCRIPTION	This method retrieves the `altName` field of this exception. This field is the name of the resolved object, relative to the context `altNameCtx`. It will be used during a subsequent call to `javax.naming.spi.ObjectFactory.getObjectInstance()`.
RETURNS	The name of the resolved object, relative to `altNameCtx`. It is a composite name. If `null`, then no name was specified.
SEE ALSO	`getAltNameCtx()`, `javax.naming.spi.ObjectFactory.getObjectInstance()`, `setAltName()`.

getAltNameCtx()

PURPOSE	Retrieves the `altNameCtx` field of this exception.
SYNTAX	`public Context getAltNameCtx()`
DESCRIPTION	This method retrieves the `altNameCtx` field of this exception. This is the context relative to which `altName` is named. It will be used during a subsequent call to `javax.naming.spi.ObjectFactory.getObjectInstance()`.
RETURNS	The context relative to which `altName` is named. If `null`, then the default initial context is implied.
SEE ALSO	`getAltName()`, `javax.naming.spi.ObjectFactory.getObjectInstance()`, `setAltNameCtx()`.

getEnvironment()

PURPOSE	Retrieves the environment that was in effect when this exception was created.
SYNTAX	`public Hashtable getEnvironment()`
DESCRIPTION	This method retrieves the environment that was in effect when this exception was created.
RETURNS	Possibly `null` environment property set. If `null`, then no environment was recorded for this exception.
SEE ALSO	`setEnvironment()`.

getRemainingNewName()

PURPOSE	Retrieves the remaining new name field of this exception.
SYNTAX	`public Name getRemainingNewName()`
DESCRIPTION	This method retrieves the remaining new name field of this exception. This field is used when this exception is thrown during a `rename()` operation.
RETURNS	The possibly `null` part of the new name that was not resolved. It is a composite name. If `null`, the remaining new name field was not set.
SEE ALSO	`setRemainingNewName()`.

remainingNewName

PURPOSE	Contains the remaining unresolved part of the second name argument to `Context.rename()`.

SYNTAX	`protected Name remainingNewName`
DESCRIPTION	This method contains the remaining unresolved part of the second name argument to `Context.rename()`. This information is necessary for continuing the `Context.rename()` operation.
	This field is initialized to `null`. It should not be manipulated directly. Rather, it should be accessed and updated by using `getRemainingNewName()` and `setRemainingNewName()`.
SEE ALSO	`getRemainingNewName()`, `setRemainingNewName()`.

C

setAltName()

PURPOSE	Sets the `altName` field of this exception.
SYNTAX	`public void setAltName(Name altName)`
PARAMETERS	
altName	The name of the resolved object, relative to `altNameCtx`. It is a composite name. If `null`, then no name was supplied.
SEE ALSO	`getAltName()`, `setAltNameCtx()`.
EXAMPLE	See the **Adding Federation Support** lesson (page 377).

setAltNameCtx()

PURPOSE	Sets the `altNameCtx` field of this exception.
SYNTAX	`public void setAltNameCtx(Context altNameCtx)`
PARAMETERS	
altNameCtx	The context relative to which `altName` is named. If `null`, then the default initial context is implied.
SEE ALSO	`getAltNameCtx()`, `setAltName()`.
EXAMPLE	See the **Adding Federation Support** lesson (page 376).

setEnvironment()

PURPOSE	Sets the environment that will be returned when `getEnvironment()` is called.
SYNTAX	`public void setEnvironment(Hashtable env)`
PARAMETERS	
env	A possibly `null` environment property set.

SEE ALSO   `getEnvironment()`.

EXAMPLE   See the **Adding Federation Support** lesson (page 376).

setRemainingNewName()

PURPOSE   Sets the remaining new name field of this exception.

SYNTAX   `public void setRemainingNewName(Name newName)`

DESCRIPTION   This method sets the remaining new name field of this exception. This is the value returned by `getRemainingNewName()`.

newName is a composite name. If the intent is to set this field by using a compound name or string, then you must stringify the compound name and use the string to create a composite name that has a single component. You can then invoke this method by using the resulting composite name.

A copy of newName is made and stored. Subsequent changes to newName do not affect the copy in this `NamingException`, and vice versa.

PARAMETERS

newName   The possibly `null` name to which to set the remaining new name field.

SEE ALSO   `getRemainingNewName()`.

EXAMPLE   See the **Adding Federation Support** lesson (page 377).

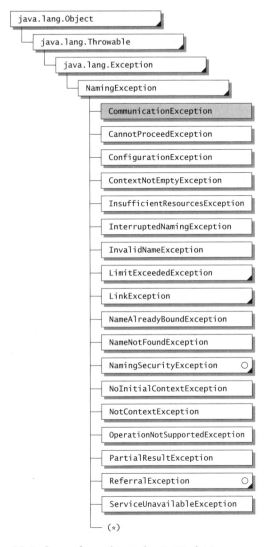

```
java.lang.Object
    java.lang.Throwable
        java.lang.Exception
            NamingException
                CommunicationException
                CannotProceedException
                ConfigurationException
                ContextNotEmptyException
                InsufficientResourcesException
                InterruptedNamingException
                InvalidNameException
                LimitExceededException
                LinkException
                NameAlreadyBoundException
                NameNotFoundException
                NamingSecurityException        ○
                NoInitialContextException
                NotContextException
                OperationNotSupportedException
                PartialResultException
                ReferralException              ○
                ServiceUnavailableException
                (*)
```

(*) 9 classes from other packages not shown.

Syntax

```
public class CommunicationException extends NamingException
```

CommunicationException()

Description

A CommuncationException is thrown when the client is unable to communicate with the directory or naming service.

The inability to communicate with the service might result from many factors, such as network partitioning, hardware or interface problems, or failures on either the client or server side. This exception is used to capture such communication problems.

Synchronization and serialization issues that apply to NamingException apply directly here.

C

MEMBER SUMMARY

Constructor
CommunicationException()   Constructs an instance of CommunicationException.

CommunicationException()

PURPOSE   Constructs an instance of CommunicationException.

SYNTAX   public CommunicationException()
                public CommunicationException(String msg)

DESCRIPTION   These constructors construct an instance of CommunicationException by using an optional msg supplied. If msg is not supplied, then msg defaults to null.

PARAMETERS
  msg   Additional detail about this exception. May be null.

SEE ALSO   java.lang.Throwable.getMessage().

Syntax

```
public class CompositeName implements Name
```

Description

The CompositeName class represents a *composite name*—a sequence of component names that span multiple namespaces.

Each component is a string name from the namespace of a naming system. If the component comes from a hierarchical namespace, then that component can be further parsed into its atomic parts by using the CompoundName class.

The components of a composite name are numbered. The indexes of a composite name with N components range from 0 up to, but not including, N. This range may be written as $[0, N)$. The most significant component is at index 0. An empty composite name has no components.

The JNDI Composite Name Syntax

The JNDI defines a standard string representation for composite names. This string is the concatenation of the components of a composite name from left to right, with components separated by the component separator (a forward slash character ("/")). The JNDI syntax defines the following meta characters:

- Escape (backward slash ("\"))
- Quotation characters (single (" ' ") and double (" " "))
- Component separator (forward slash character ("/"))

Any occurrence of a leading quotation mark, an escape preceding any meta character, an escape at the end of a component, or a component separator character in an unquoted component must be preceded by an escape character when that component is being included in a composite name string. Alternatively, to avoid adding escape characters as described, you can quote the entire component by using matching single or matching double quotation marks. A single quotation mark occurring within a double-quoted component is not considered a meta character (and need not be escaped), and vice versa.

A leading component separator (the composite name string begins with a separator) denotes a leading empty component (a component consisting of an empty string). A trailing component separator (the composite name string ends with a separator) denotes a trailing empty component. Adjacent component separators denote an empty component.

When two composite names are compared, the case of the characters is significant.

Composite Name Examples

Table 26 shows examples of some composite names. Each row shows the string form of a composite name and its corresponding structural form (`CompositeName`).

TABLE 26:   How String Names Map to Structured Composite Names.

String Name	CompositeName
`""`	`{}` (the empty name == new `CompositeName("")` == new `CompositeName()`)
`"x"`	`{"x"}`
`"x/y"`	`{"x", "y"}`
`"x/"`	`{"x", ""}`
`"/x"`	`{"", "x"}`
`"/"`	`{""}`
`"//"`	`{"", ""}`
`"/x/"`	`{"", "x", ""}`
`"x//y"`	`{"x", "", "y"}`

Composition Examples

Table 27 gives some composition examples. The String Name column shows composing string composite names, and the Composite Name column shows composing the corresponding `CompositeNames`. Notice that composing the string forms of two composite names simply involves concatenating together their string forms, along with appropriate placement(s) of the composite name component separator.

TABLE 27:   Composition of String Names and Structured Composite Names.

String Name	CompositeName
`"x/y"` + `"/"` = `x/y/`	`{"x", "y"}` + `{""}` = `{"x", "y", ""}`
`""` + `"x"` = `"x"`	`{}` + `{"x"}` = `{"x"}`
`"/"` + `"x"` = `"/x"`	`{""}` + `{"x"}` = `{"", "x"}`
`"x"` + `""` + `""` = `"x"`	`{"x"}` + `{}` + `{}` = `{"x"}`

Multithreaded Access

A `CompositeName` instance is not synchronized against concurrent multithreaded access. Multiple threads trying to access and modify a `CompositeName` should lock the object.

MEMBER SUMMARY	
Constructor and Creation Methods	
CompositeName()	Constructs an instance of CompositeName.
getPrefix()	Creates a composite name whose components consist of a prefix of the components in this composite name.
getSuffix()	Creates a composite name whose components consist of a suffix of the components in this composite name.
Access and Query Methods	
get()	Retrieves a component of this composite name.
getAll()	Retrieves the components of this composite name as an enumeration of strings.
isEmpty()	Determines whether this composite name is empty.
size()	Retrieves the number of components in this composite name.
Update Methods	
add()	Adds a single component to this composite name.
addAll()	Adds the components of a composite name, in order, to this composite name.
remove()	Deletes a component from this composite name.
Comparison Methods	
compareTo()	Compares this composite name with the specified Object for order.
endsWith()	Determines whether a composite name is a suffix of this composite name.
startsWith()	Determines whether a composite name is a prefix of this composite name.
Object Methods	
clone()	Generates a copy of this composite name.
equals()	Determines whether two composite names are equal.
hashCode()	Computes the hash code of this composite name.
toString()	Generates the string representation of this composite name.

C

Example

See the **What's in a Name?** lesson (page 82).

add()

PURPOSE   Adds a single component to this composite name.

SYNTAX

```
public Name add(String comp) throws InvalidNameException
public Name add(int posn, String comp) throws
    InvalidNameException
```

471

DESCRIPTION This method adds a single component to this composite name. The first form adds a single component to the end of this composite name.

The second form adds a single component at position posn within this composite name. Components of this composite name at or after posn are shifted up by 1 (away from index 0) to accommodate the new component.

PARAMETERS

comp   The non-null component to add.

posn   The index at which to add the new component. Must be in the range [0, size()].

RETURNS   The updated CompositeName (not a new one). Cannot be null.

EXCEPTIONS

ArrayIndexOutOfBoundsException
                If posn is outside of the specified range.

InvalidNameException
                If adding comp would violate the name's syntax.

EXAMPLE   See the **What's in a Name?** lesson (page 84).

addAll()

PURPOSE   Adds the components of a composite name, in order, to this composite name.

SYNTAX   public Name addAll(Name comp) throws InvalidNameException
            public Name addAll(int posn, Name comp) throws
                InvalidNameException

DESCRIPTION This method adds the components of a composite name, in order, to this composite name. The first form adds the components, in order, at the end of this composite name.

The second form adds the components at position posn within this composite name. Components of this composite name at or after posn are shifted up (away from index 0) to accommodate the new components.

PARAMETERS

comp   The non-null components to add.

posn   The index in this name at which to add the new components. Must be in the range [0, size()]

RETURNS   The updated CompositeName (not a new one). Cannot be null.

EXCEPTIONS

ArrayIndexOutOfBoundsException
                If posn is outside of the specified range.

InvalidNameException

If comp is not a composite name.

EXAMPLE   See the **What's in a Name?** lesson (page 84).

clone()

PURPOSE   Generates a copy of this composite name.

SYNTAX   `public Object clone()`

DESCRIPTION   This method generates a copy of this composite name. Changes to the components of this composite name won't affect the new copy, and vice versa.

RETURNS   A non-null copy of this composite name.

OVERRIDES   `java.lang.Object.clone()`.

EXAMPLE   See **The Essential Components** lesson (page 340).

compareTo()

PURPOSE   Compares this composite name with the specified object for order.

SYNTAX   `public int compareTo(Object obj)`

DESCRIPTION   This method compares this CompositeName with the object, obj, for order. It returns a negative integer, zero, or a positive integer depending on whether this CompositeName is, respectively, less than, equal to, or greater than obj.

If obj is null or not an instance of CompositeName, then a ClassCastException is thrown.

See equals() for what it means for two composite names to be equal. If two composite names are equal, then 0 is returned.

The ordering of composite names follows the lexicographical rules for string comparison, with the extension that these rules apply to all of the components in the composite name. The effect is as if all of the components were lined up in their specified order and the lexicographical rules applied over the two lineups generated by the two composite names that are being compared. If this composite name is lexicographically lesser than obj, then a negative number is returned. If it is lexicographically greater than obj, then a positive number is returned.

PARAMETERS
obj   The non-null object against which to compare.

RETURNS   A negative integer, zero, or a positive integer, depending on whether this `CompositeName` is, respectively, less than, equal to, or greater than `obj`.

EXCEPTIONS

`ClassCastException`
           If `obj` is not a `CompositeName`.

EXAMPLE   See the **What's in a Name?** lesson (page 84).

CompositeName()

PURPOSE   Constructs an instance of `CompositeName`.

SYNTAX
```
public CompositeName()
public CompositeName(String n) throws InvalidNameException
protected CompositeName(Enumeration comps)
```

DESCRIPTION   These constructors construct an instance of `CompositeName`. The first constructor constructs a new, empty composite name that returns `true` when `isEmpty()` is invoked on it.

The second constructor constructs the instance by parsing the string n by using the composite name syntax (left-to-right, forward slash ("/")-separated). The composite name syntax is described in detail in the class description.

The protected constructor constructs the instance by using the components specified by `comps`. It is intended to be used by subclasses of `CompositeName` when they override methods such as `clone()`, `getPrefix()`, and `getSuffix()`.

PARAMETERS

`comps`   A non-`null` enumeration that contains the components for the new composite name. Each element is of class `java.lang.String`. The enumeration will be consumed to extract its elements.

`n`   The non-`null` string to parse.

EXCEPTIONS

`InvalidNameException`
           If n has invalid composite name syntax.

EXAMPLE   See the **What's in a Name?** lesson (page 84).

endsWith()

PURPOSE   Determines whether a composite name is a suffix of this composite name.

SYNTAX   `public boolean endsWith(Name n)`

DESCRIPTION	This method determines whether a composite name is a suffix of this composite name. A composite name n is a suffix if it is equal to getSuffix(size()-n.size())—in other words, this composite name ends with n. If n is null or not a composite name, then false is returned.
PARAMETERS	
n	The possibly null name to check.
RETURNS	true if n is a CompositeName and is a suffix of this composite name; false otherwise.
EXAMPLE	See the **What's in a Name?** lesson (page 85).

equals()

PURPOSE	Determines whether two composite names are equal.
SYNTAX	`public boolean equals(Object obj)`
DESCRIPTION	This method determines whether two composite names are equal. If obj is null or not a composite name, then false is returned. Two composite names are equal if each component in one is equal to the corresponding component in the other. This implies that both have the same number of components and that each component's equals() test against the corresponding component in the other name returns true.
PARAMETERS	
obj	The possibly null object against which to compare.
RETURNS	true if obj is equal to this composite name; false otherwise.
OVERRIDES	`java.lang.Object.equals()`.
SEE ALSO	`hashCode()`.
EXAMPLE	See the **What's in a Name?** lesson (page 85).

get()

PURPOSE	Retrieves a component of this composite name.
SYNTAX	`public String get(int posn)`
PARAMETERS	
posn	The 0-based index of the component to retrieve. Must be in the range [0, size()).
RETURNS	The non-null component at index posn.

EXCEPTIONS

`ArrayIndexOutOfBoundsException`
    If `posn` is outside of the specified range.

EXAMPLE See the **What's in a Name?** lesson (page 83).

getAll()

PURPOSE Retrieves the components of this composite name as an enumeration of strings.

SYNTAX `public Enumeration getAll()`

DESCRIPTION This method retrieves the components of this composite name as an enumeration of strings. The effects of updates to this composite name on this enumeration are undefined.

RETURNS A non-`null` enumeration of the components of this composite name. Each element of the enumeration is of class `java.lang.String`.

EXAMPLE See the **What's in a Name?** lesson (page 83).

getPrefix()

PURPOSE Creates a composite name whose components consist of a prefix of the components in this composite name.

SYNTAX `public Name getPrefix(int posn)`

DESCRIPTION This method creates a composite name whose components consist of a prefix of the components in this composite name. Subsequent changes to this composite name do not affect the name that is returned.

PARAMETERS

posn The 0-based index of the component at which to stop. Must be in the range `[0, size()]`.

RETURNS A composite name consisting of the components at indexes in the range `[0, posn)`.

EXCEPTIONS

`ArrayIndexOutOfBoundsException`
    If `posn` is outside of the specified range.

EXAMPLE See the **What's in a Name?** lesson (page 83).

getSuffix()

PURPOSE	Creates a composite name whose components consist of a suffix of the components in this composite name.
SYNTAX	`public Name getSuffix(int posn)`
DESCRIPTION	This method creates a composite name whose components consist of a suffix of the components in this composite name. Subsequent changes to this composite name do not affect the name that is returned.
PARAMETERS	
posn	The 0-based index of the component at which to start. Must be in the range `[0, size()]`.
RETURNS	A composite name consisting of the components at indexes in the range `[posn, size())`. If posn is equal to `size()`, then an empty composite name is returned.
EXCEPTIONS	
`ArrayIndexOutOfBoundsException`	
	If posn is outside of the specified range.
EXAMPLE	See the **What's in a Name?** lesson (page 83).

hashCode()

PURPOSE	Computes the hash code of this composite name.
SYNTAX	`public int hashCode()`
DESCRIPTION	This method computes the hash code of this composite name. The hash code is the sum of the hash codes of the individual components of this composite name.
RETURNS	An `int` representing the hash code of this name.
OVERRIDES	`java.lang.Object.hashCode()`.
SEE ALSO	`equals()`.

isEmpty()

PURPOSE	Determines whether this composite name is empty.
SYNTAX	`public boolean isEmpty()`
DESCRIPTION	This method determines whether this composite name is empty. A composite name is empty if it has zero components.

C

RETURNS   true if this composite name is empty; false otherwise.

EXAMPLE   See the **What's in a Name?** lesson (page 85).

remove()

PURPOSE   Deletes a component from this composite name.

SYNTAX   `public Object remove(int posn) throws InvalidNameException`

DESCRIPTION   This method deletes a component from this composite name. The component of this composite name at position posn is removed, and components at indices greater than posn are shifted down (toward index 0) by 1.

PARAMETERS
posn   The index of the component to delete. Must be in the range [0, size()).

RETURNS   The component removed (a java.lang.String).

EXCEPTIONS
ArrayIndexOutOfBoundsException
                If posn is outside of the specified range (includes the case in which the composite name is empty).
InvalidNameException
                If deleting the component would violate the name's syntax.

EXAMPLE   See the **What's in a Name?** lesson (page 84).

size()

PURPOSE   Retrieves the number of components in this composite name.

SYNTAX   `public int size()`

RETURNS   The nonnegative number of components in this composite name.

EXAMPLE   See the **What's in a Name?** lesson (page 85).

startsWith()

PURPOSE   Determines whether a composite name is a prefix of this composite name.

SYNTAX   `public boolean startsWith(Name n)`

DESCRIPTION   This method determines whether a composite name is a prefix of this composite name. The composite name n is a prefix if it is equal to getPrefix(n.size())—in other words, this composite name starts with n. If n is null or not a composite name, then false is returned.

PARAMETERS

n   The possibly `null` name to check.

RETURNS   `true` if n is a `CompositeName` and is a prefix of this composite name; `false` otherwise.

EXAMPLE   See the **What's in a Name?** lesson (page 85).

toString()

PURPOSE   Generates the string representation of this composite name.

SYNTAX   `public String toString()`

DESCRIPTION   This method generates the string representation of this composite name. To create the string, enumerate in order each component of the composite name, separating each component by a forward slash character ("/"). Quoting and escape characters are applied where necessary according to the JNDI syntax, which is described in the class description. An empty component is represented by an empty string.

The string thus generated can be passed to the `CompositeName` constructor to create a new equivalent composite name.

RETURNS   A non-`null` string representation of this composite name.

OVERRIDES   `java.lang.Object.toString()`.

EXAMPLE   See the **What's in a Name?** lesson (page 85).

CompoundName

```
java.lang.Object
    CompoundName  ......  Name
```

Syntax

```
public class CompoundName implements Name
```

Description

The CompoundName class represents a *compound name*—a name from a hierarchical name space. Each component in a compound name is an atomic name.

The components of a compound name are numbered. The indexes of a compound name with N components range from 0 up to, but not including, N. This range may be written as $[0, N)$. The most significant component is at index 0. An empty compound name has no components.

Compound Name Syntax

The syntax of a compound name is specified by using a set of properties, as shown in Table 28.

TABLE 28: Compound Name Syntax Properties.

Property Name	Description
jndi.syntax.direction	Direction for parsing ("right_to_left", "left_to_right", "flat"). If the direction is unspecified, then it defaults to "flat", which means that the namespace is flat with no hierarchical structure.
jndi.syntax.separator	Separator between atomic name components. Required unless the direction is "flat".
jndi.syntax.ignorecase	If present, then "true" means to ignore the case when comparing name components. If not "true", or if the property is not present, then case is considered when comparing name components.
jndi.syntax.escape	If present, then specifies the escape string for overriding separators, escapes, and quotation marks.
jndi.syntax.beginquote	If present, then specifies the string that delimits the start of a quoted string.

TABLE 28: **Compound Name Syntax Properties.**

Property Name	Description
jndi.syntax.endquote	If present, then specifies the string that delimits the end of a quoted string. If not present, then use the "jndi.syntax.beginquote" property as the end quotation mark.
jndi.syntax.beginquote2	Alternative set of begin/end quotation marks.
jndi.syntax.endquote2	Alternative set of begin/end quotation marks.
jndi.syntax.trimblanks	If present, then "true" means to trim any leading and trailing whitespaces in a name component for comparison purposes. If not "true", or if the property is not present, then blanks are significant.
jndi.syntax.separator.ava	If present, then specifies the string that separates attribute/value-assertions when specifying multiple attribute/value pairs (e.g., ",", in "age=65,gender=male").
jndi.syntax.separator.typeval	If present, then specifies the string that separates the attribute from the value (e.g., "=" in "age=65").

These properties are interpreted according to the following rules.

1. In a string without quotation marks or escapes, any instance of the separator delimits two atomic names. Each atomic name is called a *component*.
2. A separator, quotation mark, or escape is escaped if it is preceded immediately (on the left) by the escape.
3. If there are two sets of quotation marks, then a specific begin quotation mark must be matched by its corresponding end quotation mark.
4. A nonescaped begin quotation mark that precedes a component must be matched by a nonescaped end quotation mark at the end of the component. A component thus quoted is called a *quoted component*. It is parsed by removing the being and end quotation marks and by treating the intervening characters as ordinary characters, unless one of the rules involving quoted components listed next applies.

   - Quotation marks embedded in nonquoted components are treated as ordinary strings and need not be matched.
   - A separator that is escaped or appears between nonescaped quotation marks is treated as an ordinary string and not as a separator.
   - An escape string within a quoted component acts as an escape only when followed by the corresponding end quotation mark string. This can be used to embed an escaped quotation mark within a quoted component.

5. An escaped escape string is not treated as an escape string.

6. An escape string that does not precede a meta string (quotation marks or separator) and is not at the end of a component is treated as an ordinary string.

7. A leading separator (the compound name string begins with a separator) denotes a leading empty atomic component (consisting of an empty string). A trailing separator (the compound name string ends with a separator) denotes a trailing empty atomic component. Adjacent separators denote an empty atomic component.

The string form of the compound name follows the syntax described here. When the components of the compound name are turned into their string representation, then the reserved syntax rules described previously apply (e.g., embedded separators are escaped or quoted). In this way, parsing the same string will yield the same components of the original compound name.

Multithreaded Access

A CompoundName instance is not synchronized against concurrent multithreaded access. Multiple threads trying to access and modify a CompoundName should lock the object.

MEMBER SUMMARY	
Constructor and Creation Methods	
CompoundName()	Constructs an instance of CompoundName.
getPrefix()	Creates a compound name whose components consist of a prefix of the components in this compound name.
getSuffix()	Creates a compound name whose components consist of a suffix of the components in this compound name.
Access and Query Methods	
get()	Retrieves a component of this compound name.
getAll()	Retrieves the components of this compound name as an enumeration of strings.
isEmpty()	Determines whether this compound name is empty.
size()	Retrieves the number of components in this compound name.
Update Methods	
add()	Adds a single component to this compound name.
addAll()	Adds the components of a compound name, in order, to this compound name.
remove()	Deletes a component from this compound name.
Comparison Methods	
compareTo()	Compares this CompoundName with the specified Object for order.
endsWith()	Determines whether a compound name is a suffix of this compound name.
startsWith()	Determines whether a compound name is a prefix of this compound name.

MEMBER SUMMARY	
Object Methods	
clone()	Creates a copy of this compound name.
equals()	Determines whether obj is syntactically equal to this compound name.
hashCode()	Computes the hash code of this compound name.
toString()	Generates the string representation of this compound name, using the syntax rules of the compound name.
Protected Fields	
mySyntax	Holds the syntax properties for this compound name.
impl	Holds the implementation of this compound name.

See Also

CompositeName.

Example

See the **What's in a Name?** lesson (page 87).

add()

PURPOSE   Adds a single component to this compound name.

SYNTAX
```
public Name add(String comp) throws InvalidNameException
public Name add(int posn, String comp) throws
    InvalidNameException
```

DESCRIPTION   This method adds a single component to this compound name. If posn is not specified, then the component is added to the end of this name. If posn is specified, then components at or after posn are shifted up by 1 (away from index 0) to accommodate the new component.

PARAMETERS

comp   The non-null component to add.

posn   The index at which to add the new component. Must be in the range [0, size()].

RETURNS   The updated CompoundName (not a new one). Cannot be null.

EXCEPTIONS

ArrayIndexOutOfBoundsException
     If posn is outside of the specified range.

InvalidNameException
     If adding comp would violate the compound name's syntax.

EXAMPLE   See the **What's in a Name?** lesson (page 87).

addAll()

PURPOSE	Adds the components of a compound name, in order, to this compound name.
SYNTAX	`public Name addAll(Name n) throws InvalidNameException` `public Name addAll(int posn, Name n) throws InvalidNameException`
DESCRIPTION	This method adds the components of a compound name, in order, to this compound name. If `posn` is not specified, then the components are added to the end of this compound name. If `posn` is specified, then components at or after `posn` are shifted up (away from index 0) to accommodate the new components.

Implementation Note: Currently the syntax properties of n are not used or checked. They might be in the future.

PARAMETERS	
n	The non-null components to add.
posn	The index in this name at which to add the new components. Must be in the range [0, `size()`].
RETURNS	The updated `CompoundName` (not a new one). Cannot be `null`.
EXCEPTIONS	

`InvalidNameException`

If n is not a compound name, or if the addition of the components violates the syntax of this compound name (e.g., exceeds the number of components).

clone()

PURPOSE	Creates a copy of this compound name.
SYNTAX	`public Object clone()`
DESCRIPTION	This method creates a copy of this compound name. Changes to the components of this compound name won't affect the new copy, and vice versa. The clone and this compound name share the same syntax.
RETURNS	A non-null copy of this compound name.
OVERRIDES	`java.lang.Object.clone()`.

compareTo()

PURPOSE	Compares this `CompoundName` with the specified `Object` for order.
SYNTAX	`public int compareTo(Object obj)`

DESCRIPTION   This method compares this CompoundName with the object, obj, for order. It returns a negative integer, zero, or a positive integer depending on whether this name is, respectively, less than, equal to, or greater than obj.

If obj is null or not an instance of CompoundName, then a ClassCast-Exception is thrown.

See equals() for what it means for two compound names to be equal. If two compound names are equal, then 0 is returned.

The ordering of compound names depends on the syntax of the compound name. By default, it follows the lexicographical rules for string comparison, with the extension that these rules apply to all of the components in the compound name and that comparison of individual components is affected by the "jndi.syntax.ignorecase" and "jndi.syntax.trimblanks" properties, identical to how they affect equals(). If this compound name is lexicographically lesser than obj, then a negative number is returned. If this compound name is lexicographically greater than obj, then a positive number is returned.

Implementation Note: Currently the syntax properties of the two compound names are not compared when checking order. They might be in the future.

PARAMETERS
obj   The non-null object against which to compare.

RETURNS   A negative integer, zero, or a positive integer depending on whether this name is, respectively, less than, equal to, or greater than obj.

EXCEPTIONS
ClassCastException
               If obj is not a CompoundName.

SEE ALSO   equals().

CompoundName()

PURPOSE   Constructs an instance of CompoundName.

SYNTAX   public CompoundName(String n, Properties syntax) throws
                   InvalidNameException
               protected CompoundName(Enumeration comps, Properties syntax)

DESCRIPTION   These constructors construct an instance of CompoundName.

The public constructor constructs a CompoundName instance by parsing the string n by using the syntax specified by the syntax properties supplied.

The protected constructor constructs a CompoundName instance by using the components specified in comps and syntax. It is intended to be used by subclasses of CompoundName when they override methods such as clone(), get-Prefix(), and getSuffix().

PARAMETERS

comps   A non-null enumeration of the components to add. Each element of the enumeration is of class String. The enumeration will be consumed to extract its elements.

n   The non-null string to parse.

syntax   A non-null properties that specify the syntax of this compound name. See the class description for information on the contents of properties.

EXCEPTIONS

InvalidNameException

If n violates the syntax specified by syntax.

EXAMPLE   See **The Essential Components** lesson (page 338).

endsWith()

PURPOSE   Determines whether a compound name is a suffix of this compound name.

SYNTAX   public boolean endsWith(Name n)

DESCRIPTION   This method determines whether a compound name, n, is a suffix of this compound name. n is a suffix if it is equal to getSuffix(size()-n.size())—in other words, this compound name ends with n. If n is null or not a compound name, then false is returned.

                Implementation Note: Currently the syntax properties of n are not used when doing the comparison. They might be in the future.

PARAMETERS

n   The possibly null compound name to check.

RETURNS   true if n is a CompoundName and is a suffix of this compound name; false otherwise.

SEE ALSO   startsWith().

equals()

PURPOSE   Determines whether an object is syntactically equal to this compound name.

SYNTAX   public boolean equals(Object obj)

DESCRIPTION   This method determines whether the object, obj, is syntactically equal to this compound name. If obj is null or not a CompoundName, then false is returned.

Two compound names are equal if each component in one is "equal" to the corresponding component in the other.

Equality is also defined in terms of the syntax of this compound name. The default implementation of `CompoundName` uses the syntax properties `"jndi.syntax.ignorecase"` and `"jndi.syntax.trimblanks"` when comparing two components for equality. If case is ignored, then two strings with the same sequence of characters but with different cases are considered equal. If blanks are being trimmed, then leading and trailing blanks are ignored for the purpose of the comparison.

Both compound names must have the same number of components.

Implementation Note: Currently the syntax properties of the two compound names are not compared for equality. They might be in the future.

PARAMETERS
obj   The possibly `null` object against which to compare.

RETURNS   `true` if `obj` is equal to this compound name; `false` otherwise.

OVERRIDES   `java.lang.Object.equals()`.

SEE ALSO   `compareTo()`, `hashCode()`.

get()

PURPOSE   Retrieves a component of this compound name.

SYNTAX   `public String get(int posn)`

PARAMETERS
posn   The `0`-based index of the component to retrieve. Must be in the range `[0, size())`.

RETURNS   The component at index `posn`.

EXCEPTIONS
`ArrayIndexOutOfBoundsException`
            If `posn` is outside of the specified range.

getAll()

PURPOSE   Retrieves the components of this compound name as an enumeration of strings.

SYNTAX   `public Enumeration getAll()`

487

DESCRIPTION   This method retrieves the components of this compound name as an enumeration of strings. The effects of updates to this compound name on this enumeration are undefined.

RETURNS   A non-null enumeration of the components of this compound name. Each element of the enumeration is of class java.lang.String.

getPrefix()

PURPOSE   Creates a compound name whose components consist of a prefix of the components in this compound name.

SYNTAX   public Name getPrefix(int posn)

DESCRIPTION   This method creates a compound name whose components consist of a prefix of the components in this compound name. The result and this compound name share the same syntax. Subsequent changes to this compound name do not affect the name that is returned, and vice versa.

PARAMETERS

posn   The 0-based index of the component at which to stop. Must be in the range [0, size()].

RETURNS   A compound name that consists of the components at indexes in the range [0, posn).

EXCEPTIONS

ArrayIndexOutOfBoundsException
     If posn is outside of the specified range.

getSuffix()

PURPOSE   Creates a compound name whose components consist of a suffix of the components in this compound name.

SYNTAX   public Name getSuffix(int posn)

DESCRIPTION   This method creates a compound name whose components consist of a suffix of the components in this compound name. The result and this compound name share the same syntax. Subsequent changes to this compound name do not affect the name that is returned.

PARAMETERS

posn   The 0-based index of the component at which to start. Must be in the range [0, size()].

RETURNS   A compound name that consists of the components at indexes in the range [posn, size()). If posn is equal to size(), then an empty compound name is returned.

EXCEPTIONS

ArrayIndexOutOfBoundsException
          If posn is outside of the specified range.

hashCode()

PURPOSE   Computes the hash code of this compound name.

SYNTAX   `public int hashCode()`

DESCRIPTION   This method computes the hash code of this compound name. The hash code is the sum of the hash codes of the canonicalized forms of individual components of this compound name. Each component is canonicalized according to the compound name's syntax before its hash code is computed. For a case-insensitive name, for example, the uppercase form of a name has the same hash code as its lowercase equivalent.

RETURNS   An `int` that represents the hash code of this name.

OVERRIDES   `java.lang.Object.hashCode()`.

SEE ALSO   `equals()`.

impl

PURPOSE   Holds the implementation of this compound name.

SYNTAX   `protected transient NameImpl impl`

DESCRIPTION   This field holds the implementation of this compound name. It is initialized by the constructors and cannot be `null`. It should be treated by subclasses as a read-only variable.

isEmpty()

PURPOSE   Determines whether this compound name is empty.

SYNTAX   `public boolean isEmpty()`

DESCRIPTION   This method determines whether this compound name is empty. A compound name is empty if it has zero components.

RETURNS   `true` if this compound name is empty; `false` otherwise.

C

mySyntax

PURPOSE	Syntax properties for this compound name.
SYNTAX	`protected transient Properties mySyntax`
DESCRIPTION	This field holds the syntax properties for this compound name. It is initialized by the constructors and cannot be `null`. It should be treated as a read-only variable by subclasses. Any necessary changes to `mySyntax` should be made within constructors and not after the compound name has been instantiated.

remove()

PURPOSE   Deletes a component from this compound name.

SYNTAX   `public Object remove(int posn) throws InvalidNameException`

DESCRIPTION This method deletes a component from this compound name. The component at position `posn` is removed, and components at indices greater than `posn` are shifted down (toward index 0) by 1.

PARAMETERS
posn   The index of the component to delete. Must be in the range [0, `size()`).

RETURNS   The component removed (a `java.lang.String`).

EXCEPTIONS
ArrayIndexOutOfBoundsException
            If `posn` is outside of the specified range (includes case when the compound name is empty).
InvalidNameException
            If deleting the component would violate the compound name's syntax.

EXAMPLE   See the **What's in a Name?** lesson (page 87).

size()

PURPOSE   Retrieves the number of components in this compound name.

SYNTAX   `public int size()`

DESCRIPTION This method retrieves the number of components in this compound name.

RETURNS   The nonnegative number of components in this compound name.

startsWith()

PURPOSE   Determines whether a compound name is a prefix of this compound name.

SYNTAX   `public boolean startsWith(Name n)`

DESCRIPTION   This method determines whether a compound name, n, is a prefix of this compound name. n is a prefix if it is equal to `getPrefix(n.size())`—in other words, this compound name starts with n. If n is `null` or not a compound name, then `false` is returned.

Implementation Note: Currently the syntax properties of n are not used when doing the comparison. They might be in the future.

PARAMETERS
    n   The possibly `null` compound name to check.

RETURNS   `true` if n is a `CompoundName` and is a prefix of this compound name; `false` otherwise.

toString()

PURPOSE   Generates the string representation of this compound name, using the syntax rules of the compound name.

SYNTAX   `public String toString()`

DESCRIPTION   This method generates the string representation of this compound name, using the syntax rules of the compound name. The syntax rules are described in the class description. An empty component is represented by an empty string.

The string thus generated can be passed to the `CompoundName` constructor that has the same syntax properties in order to create a new, equivalent compound name.

RETURNS   A non-`null` string representation of this compound name.

OVERRIDES   `java.lang.Object.toString()`.

EXAMPLE   See the **What's in a Name?** lesson (page 87).

491

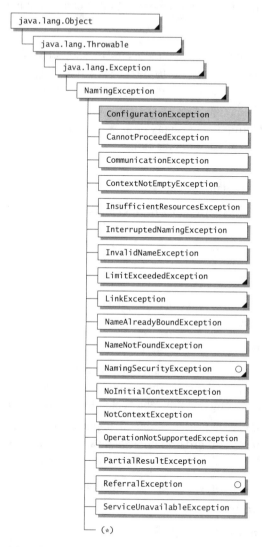

java.lang.Object

java.lang.Throwable

java.lang.Exception

NamingException

ConfigurationException

CannotProceedException

CommunicationException

ContextNotEmptyException

InsufficientResourcesException

InterruptedNamingException

InvalidNameException

LimitExceededException

LinkException

NameAlreadyBoundException

NameNotFoundException

NamingSecurityException ○

NoInitialContextException

NotContextException

OperationNotSupportedException

PartialResultException

ReferralException ○

ServiceUnavailableException

(*)

(*) 9 classes from other packages not shown.

Syntax
```
public class ConfigurationException extends NamingException
```

Description

A `ConfigurationException` is thrown when there is a configuration problem. This problem can arise when the installation of a provider was not done correctly, or if the server has configuration problems, or if configuration information required to access the provider or service is malformed or missing. For example, a request to use SSL as the security protocol when the service provider software was not configured with the SSL component would cause such an exception. Another example is if the provider requires that a URL be specified as one of the environment properties but the client failed to provide it.

C

    Synchronization and serialization issues that apply to `NamingException` apply directly here.

MEMBER SUMMARY

Constructor
`ConfigurationException()`   Constructs an instance of `ConfigurationException`.

ConfigurationException()

PURPOSE   Constructs an instance of `ConfigurationException`.

SYNTAX   `public ConfigurationException()`
           `public ConfigurationException(String msg)`

DESCRIPTION   These constructors construct an instance of `ConfigurationException` by using an optional `msg` that gives details about this exception. If `msg` is not supplied, then `msg` defaults to `null`. All other fields default to `null`.

PARAMETERS
msg   Additional detail about this exception. May be `null`.

SEE ALSO   `java.lang.Throwable.getMessage()`.

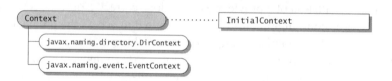

Syntax
```
public interface Context
```

Description

The Context interface represents a naming context, which consists of a set of name-to-object bindings. It contains methods for examining and updating these bindings.

Names

Each name passed as an argument to a context method is relative to that context. The empty name is used to name the context itself. A name parameter may never be null.

Most of its methods have overloaded versions, with one taking a Name parameter and one taking a String. These overloaded versions are equivalent in that if the Name and String parameters are simply different representations of the same name, then the overloaded versions of the same methods behave the same.

For systems that support federation, String name arguments to context methods are composite names. Name arguments that are instances of CompositeName are treated as composite names, whereas Name arguments that are not instances of CompositeName are treated as compound names (which might be instances of CompoundName or other implementations of compound names). This allows the results of NameParser.parse() to be used as arguments to context methods.

Furthermore, for systems that support federation, all names returned in a NamingEnumeration from list() and listBindings() are composite names represented as strings. See CompositeName for the string syntax of names.

For systems that do not support federation, the name arguments (in either Name or String forms) and the names returned in NamingEnumeration may be names in their own namespace rather than names in a composite namespace, at the discretion of the service provider.

Exceptions

All methods in this interface can throw a NamingException or any of its subclasses. See NamingException and its subclasses for details on each exception.

Concurrent Access

A Context instance is not guaranteed to be synchronized against concurrent access by multiple threads. Threads that need to access a single Context instance concurrently should synchronize among themselves and provide the necessary locking. Multiple threads that each manipulate a different Context instance need not synchronize. You can use lookup() to get a new Context instance that represents the same naming context. Do this by passing it an empty name.

For purposes of concurrency control, a context operation that returns a Naming-Enumeration is not considered to have completed either while the enumeration is still in use or while any referrals generated by that operation are still being followed.

Parameters

A Name parameter passed to any context method or one of its subinterfaces will not be modified by the service provider. The service provider may keep a reference to it for the duration of the operation, including any enumeration of the method's results and the processing of any referrals generated. The caller should not modify the object during this time. A Name returned by any such method is owned by the caller. The caller may subsequently modify it; the service provider may not.

Environment Properties

JNDI applications need a way to communicate various preferences and properties that define the environment in which naming and directory services are accessed. For example, a context might require the specification of security credentials in order to access the service. Another context might require that server configuration information be supplied. These are called, collectively, the *environment* of a context. The Context interface provides methods for retrieving and updating this environment.

The environment is inherited from the parent context as context methods proceed from one context to the next. Changes to the environment of one context do not directly affect the environments of other contexts.

The point when environment properties are used and/or verified for validity is implementation-dependent. For example, service providers use some of the security-related properties to log in to the directory. This login process might occur when the context is created or the first time that a method is invoked on the context. When, and whether, this occurs is implementation-dependent. When environment properties are added or removed from the context, verifying the validity of the changes also is implementation-dependent. For example, verification of some properties might occur when the change is made, or at the time that the next operation is performed on the context, or not at all.

Any object that has a reference to a context may examine that context's environment. Sensitive information such as clear-text passwords should not be stored there unless the implementation is known to protect it.

C

Resource Files

To simplify the task of setting up the environment required by a JNDI application, application components and service providers may be distributed along with *resource files*. A JNDI resource file is a file in the properties file format (see `java.util.Properties.load()`) and that contains a list of key/value pairs. The key is the name of the property (e.g., `"java.naming.factory.object"`), and the value is a string in the format defined for that property. Here is an example of a JNDI resource file.

```
java.naming.factory.object=\
    com.sun.jndi.ldap.AttrsToCorba:com.wiz.from.Person
java.naming.factory.state=\
    com.sun.jndi.ldap.CorbaToAttrs:com.wiz.from.Person
java.naming.factory.control=com.sun.jndi.ldap.ResponseControlFactory
```

The JNDI class library reads the resource files and makes the property values freely available. Thus JNDI resource files should be considered "world readable," and sensitive information such as clear-text passwords should not be stored in them.

There are two kinds of JNDI resource files: *provider* and *application*.

Provider Resource Files

Each service provider has an optional resource that lists properties specific to that provider. The name of this resource is

```
[prefix/]jndiprovider.properties
```

where *prefix* is the package name of the provider's context implementation(s), with each period character (".") converted to a forward slash character ("/"). For example, suppose that a service provider defines a context implementation with class name `com.sun.jndi.ldap.LdapCtx`. The provider resource for this provider is named `com/sun/jndi/ldap/jndiprovider.properties`. If the class is not in a package, then the resource's name is simply `jndiprovider.properties`.

Certain methods in the JNDI class library use the following standard JNDI properties that specify lists of JNDI factories:

```
java.naming.factory.object
java.naming.factory.state
java.naming.factory.control
java.naming.factory.url.pkgs
```

The JNDI library consults the provider resource file when determining the values of these properties. Properties other than these may be set in the provider resource file at the discretion of the service provider. The service provider's documentation should clearly state which properties are allowed; other properties in the file will be ignored.

Application Resource Files

An application, when deployed, will generally have several codebase directories and JARs in its classpath. Similarly, when an applet is deployed, it will have a codebase and archives that specify where to find the applet's classes. The JNDI locates (by using `ClassLoader.get-`

Resources()) all *application resource files* named jndi.properties in the classpath. In addition, if the file *java.home*/lib/jndi.properties exists and is readable, then the JNDI treats it as an additional application resource file. (*java.home* indicates the directory named by the "java.home" system property.) All properties in these files are placed in the environment of the initial context. This environment is then inherited by other contexts.

For each property found in more than one application resource file, the JNDI uses the first value found or, in a few cases (where it makes sense to do so), it concatenates all of the values (details are given later in this description). For example, if the "java.naming.factory.object" property is found in three jndi.properties resource files, then the list of object factories is a concatenation of the property values from all three files. When this scheme is used, each deployable component is responsible for listing the factories that it exports. The JNDI automatically collects and uses all of these export lists when searching for factory classes.

Application resource files are available beginning with the Java 2 Platform, except that the file in *java.home*/lib may be used on earlier Java platforms as well.

Search Algorithm for Properties

When the JNDI constructs an initial context, the context's environment is initialized with properties that are defined in the environment parameter that is passed to the constructor, the system properties, the applet parameters, and the application resource files. See Initial-Context for details. This initial environment is then inherited by other Context instances.

When the JNDI class library needs to determine the value of a property, it does so by merging the values from the following two sources, in order:

- The environment of the context being operated on
- The provider resource file (jndiprovider.properties) for the context being operated on

For each property found in both of these two sources, the JNDI determines the property's value as follows. If the property is one of the standard JNDI properties that specify a list of JNDI factories (listed previously), then the values are concatenated into a single colon-separated list. For other properties, only the first value found is used.

When a service provider needs to determine the value of a property, it generally will take that value directly from the environment. A service provider may define provider-specific properties to be placed in its own provider resource file. In this case, it should merge values as described in the previous paragraph. In this way, each service provider developer can specify a list of factories to use with that service provider. These can be modified by the application resources specified by the deployer of the application or applet, which in turn can be modified by the user.

Example

See the **Naming Operations** lesson (page 53) and the **Environment Properties** lesson (page 95).

MEMBER SUMMARY	
Context Methods	
bind()	Binds a name to an object.
close()	Closes this context.
composeName()	Composes the name of this context with a name relative to this context.
createSubcontext()	Creates and binds a context.
destroySubcontext()	Destroys the named context and removes it from the namespace.
getNameInNamespace()	Retrieves the full name of this context within its own namespace.
getNameParser()	Retrieves the parser associated with the named context.
list()	Enumerates the names bound in the named context, along with the class names of objects bound to them.
listBindings()	Enumerates the names bound in the named context, along with the objects bound to them.
lookup()	Retrieves the named object.
lookupLink()	Retrieves the named object, following links except for the terminal atomic component of the name.
rebind()	Binds a name to an object, overwriting any existing binding.
rename()	Binds a new name to the object bound to an old name, and unbinds the old name.
unbind()	Unbinds the named object.
Environment Methods	
addToEnvironment()	Adds a new environment property to the environment of this context.
getEnvironment()	Retrieves the environment in effect for this context.
removeFromEnvironment()	Removes an environment property from the environment of this context.
Environment Property Names	
APPLET	Holds the name of the environment property for specifying an applet for the initial context constructor to use when searching for other properties.
AUTHORITATIVE	Holds the name of the environment property for specifying the authoritativeness of the service requested.
BATCHSIZE	Holds the name of the environment property for specifying the batch size to use when returning data via the service's protocol.
DNS_URL	Holds the name of the environment property for specifying the DNS host and domain names to use for the JNDI URL context.
INITIAL_CONTEXT_FACTORY	Holds the name of the environment property for specifying the initial context factory to use.

C

MEMBER SUMMARY	
LANGUAGE	Holds the name of the environment property for specifying the preferred language to use with the service.
OBJECT_FACTORIES	Holds the name of the environment property for specifying the list of object factories to use.
PROVIDER_URL	Holds the name of the environment property for specifying configuration information for the service provider to use.
REFERRAL	Holds the name of the environment property for specifying how referrals encountered by the service provider are to be processed.
SECURITY_AUTHENTICATION	Holds the name of the environment property for specifying the security level to use.
SECURITY_CREDENTIALS	Holds the name of the environment property for specifying the credentials of the principal for authenticating the caller to the service.
SECURITY_PRINCIPAL	Holds the name of the environment property for specifying the identity of the principal for authenticating the caller to the service.
SECURITY_PROTOCOL	Holds the name of the environment property for specifying the security protocol to use.
STATE_FACTORIES	Holds the name of the environment property for specifying the list of state factories to use.
URL_PKG_PREFIXES	Holds the name of the environment property for specifying the list of package prefixes to use when loading in URL context factories.

addToEnvironment()

PURPOSE	Adds a new environment property to the environment of this context.
SYNTAX	`public Object addToEnvironment(String propName, Object propVal)` `throws NamingException`
DESCRIPTION	This method adds a new environment property to the environment of this context. If the property already exists, then its value is overwritten. See the class description for more details on environment properties.
PARAMETERS	
propName	The name of the environment property to add. May not be `null`.
propVal	The value of the property to add. May not be `null`.
RETURNS	The previous value of the property, or `null` if the property was not previously in the environment.

EXCEPTIONS
`NamingException`

      If a naming exception is encountered.

SEE ALSO   `getEnvironment()`, `removeFromEnvironment()`.

EXAMPLE   See the **Environment Properties** lesson (page 106).

APPLET

PURPOSE   Holds the name of the environment property for specifying an applet for the initial context constructor to use when searching for other properties.

SYNTAX   `public final static String APPLET`

DESCRIPTION   This constant holds the name of the environment property for specifying an applet for the initial context constructor to use when searching for other properties. The value of this property is the `java.applet.Applet` instance that is being executed. This property may be specified in the environment parameter passed to the initial context constructor. When this property is set, each property that the initial context constructor looks for in the system properties is first sought in the applet's parameter list. If this property is unspecified, then the initial context constructor will search for properties only in the environment parameter passed to it, the system properties, and application resource files.

     The value of this constant is `"java.naming.applet"`.

SEE ALSO   `addToEnvironment()`, `removeFromEnvironment()`, `InitialContext`.

EXAMPLE   See the **Environment Properties** lesson (page 102).

AUTHORITATIVE

PURPOSE   Holds the name of the environment property for specifying the authoritativeness of the service requested.

SYNTAX   `public final static String AUTHORITATIVE`

DESCRIPTION   This constant holds the name of the environment property for specifying the authoritativeness of the service requested. If the value of this property is the string `"true"`, then the access is to the most authoritative source (i.e., bypass any cache or replicas). If the value is anything else, then the source need not be (but may be) authoritative. If it is unspecified, then the value defaults to `"false"`.

     The value of this constant is `"java.naming.authoritative"`.

SEE ALSO   `addToEnvironment()`, `removeFromEnvironment()`.

BATCHSIZE

PURPOSE   Holds the name of the environment property for specifying the batch size to use when returning data via the service's protocol.

SYNTAX   `public final static String BATCHSIZE`

DESCRIPTION This constant holds the name of the environment property for specifying the batch size to use when returning data via the service's protocol. This is a hint to the provider to return the results of operations in batches of the specified size so that the provider can optimize its performance and its use of resources.

The value of the property is the string representation of an integer. If it is unspecified, then the batch size is determined by the service provider.

The value of this constant is `"java.naming.batchsize"`.

SEE ALSO   `addToEnvironment()`, `removeFromEnvironment()`.

EXAMPLE   See the **Searches** lesson (page 256).

bind()

PURPOSE   Binds a name to an object.

SYNTAX   `public void bind(Name name, Object obj) throws NamingException`
`public void bind(String name, Object obj) throws NamingException`

DESCRIPTION This method binds a name to an object, `obj`. All intermediate contexts and the target context (that named by all but the terminal atomic component of the name) must already exist.

PARAMETERS
name   The name to bind. May not be empty.
obj   The object to bind; possibly `null`.

EXCEPTIONS
`javax.naming.directory.InvalidAttributesException`
            If `obj` does not supply all mandatory attributes.
`NameAlreadyBoundException`
            If `name` is already bound.
`NamingException`
            If a naming exception is encountered.

SEE ALSO   `javax.naming.directory.DirContext.bind()`, `rebind()`.

EXAMPLE   See the **Naming Operations** lesson (page 56).

close()

PURPOSE   Closes this context.

SYNTAX   `public void close() throws NamingException`

DESCRIPTION   This method closes this context. It releases this context's resources immediately, instead of waiting for them to be released automatically by the garbage collector.

This method is idempotent. That is, invoking it on a context that has already been closed has no effect. Invoking any other method on a closed context is not allowed and results in undefined behavior.

EXCEPTIONS
`NamingException`
                If a naming exception is encountered.

EXAMPLE   See **The Essential Components** lesson (page 339).

composeName()

PURPOSE   Composes the name of this context with a name relative to this context.

SYNTAX   `public Name composeName(Name name, Name prefix) throws`
                `    NamingException`
                `public String composeName(String name, String prefix) throws`
                `    NamingException`

DESCRIPTION   This method composes the name of this context with a name relative to this context. Given a name (`name`) relative to this context and the name (`prefix`) of this context relative to one of its ancestors, this method returns the composition of the two names by using the syntax appropriate for the naming system(s) involved. That is, if `name` names an object relative to this context, then the result is the name of the same object but it is relative to the ancestor context. None of the names may be `null`.

For example, if this context is named `"wiz.com"` relative to the initial context, then

                `composeName("east", "wiz.com")`

might return `"east.wiz.com"`. If instead this context is named `"org/research"`, then

                `composeName("user/jane", "org/research")`

might return `"org/research/user/jane"` whereas

                `composeName("user/jane", "research")`

returns "research/user/jane".

PARAMETERS

name   A name relative to this context.

prefix   The name of this context relative to one of its ancestors.

RETURNS   The composition of prefix and name.

EXCEPTIONS

NamingException

If a naming exception is encountered.

EXAMPLE   See the **What's in a Name?** lesson (page 93).

createSubcontext()

PURPOSE   Creates and binds a new context.

SYNTAX   public Context createSubcontext(Name name) throws
                  NamingException
              public Context createSubcontext(String name) throws
                  NamingException

DESCRIPTION   This method creates a context with the given name and binds it in the target
              context (that named by all but the terminal atomic component of the name).
              All intermediate contexts and the target context must already exist.

PARAMETERS

name   The name of the context to create, May not be empty.

RETURNS   The newly created context.

EXCEPTIONS

javax.naming.directory.InvalidAttributesException

If the creation of the subcontext requires the specification of mandatory
attributes.

NameAlreadyBoundException

If name is already bound.

NamingException

If a naming exception is encountered.

SEE ALSO   javax.naming.directory.DirContext.createSubcontext().

EXAMPLE   See the **Naming Operations** lesson (page 58).

destroySubcontext()

PURPOSE   Destroys the named context and removes it from the namespace.

SYNTAX   `public void destroySubcontext(Name name) throws NamingException`
              `public void destroySubcontext(String name) throws`
                  `NamingException`

DESCRIPTION   This method destroys the named context and removes it from the namespace. Any attributes associated with the name are also removed. Intermediate contexts are not destroyed.

This method is idempotent. It succeeds even if the terminal atomic name is not bound in the target context, but it throws a `NameNotFoundException` if any of the intermediate contexts do not exist.

In a federated naming system, a context from one naming system may be bound to a name in another. One can subsequently look up and perform operations on the foreign context by using a composite name. However, an attempt to destroy the context by using this composite name will fail with a `NotContextException`. This is because the foreign context is not a *subcontext* of the context in which it is bound. Instead, use `unbind()` to remove the binding of the foreign context. Destroying the foreign context requires that `destroySubcontext()` be performed on a context from the foreign context's *native* naming system.

PARAMETERS

name   The name of the context to be destroyed. May not be empty

EXCEPTIONS

`ContextNotEmptyException`
         If the named context is not empty.

`NameNotFoundException`
         If an intermediate context does not exist.

`NamingException`
         If a naming exception is encountered.

`NotContextException`
         If the name is bound but either does not name a context or does not name a context of the appropriate type.

EXAMPLE   See the **Naming Operations** lesson (page 58).

DNS_URL

PURPOSE   Holds the name of the environment property for specifying the DNS host and domain names to use for the JNDI URL context.

SYNTAX   `public final static String DNS_URL`

DESCRIPTION   This constant holds the name of the environment property for specifying the DNS host and domain names to use for the JNDI URL context (for example, "dns://somehost/wiz.com"). This property may be specified in the environment, an applet parameter, a system property, or a resource file. If it is not specified in any of these sources and the program attempts to use a JNDI URL that contains a DNS name, then a `ConfigurationException` will be thrown.

The value of this constant is "java.naming.dns.url".

SEE ALSO   addToEnvironment(), removeFromEnvironment().

getEnvironment()

PURPOSE   Retrieves the environment in effect for this context.

SYNTAX   `public Hashtable getEnvironment() throws NamingException`

DESCRIPTION   See the class description for more details on environment properties.

               The caller should not make any changes to the object returned. The effects of changes on the context are undefined. The environment of this context may be changed by using `addToEnvironment()` and `removeFromEnvironment()`.

RETURNS   The environment of this context. Never `null`.

EXCEPTIONS
  `NamingException`
               If a naming exception is encountered.

SEE ALSO   addToEnvironment(), removeFromEnvironment().

EXAMPLE   See the **Environment Properties** lesson (page 105).

getNameInNamespace()

PURPOSE   Retrieves the full name of this context within its own namespace.

SYNTAX   `public String getNameInNamespace() throws NamingException`

DESCRIPTION   This method retrieves the full name of this context within its own namespace.

               Many naming services have a notion of a "full name" for objects in their respective namespaces. For example, an LDAP entry has a DN and a DNS node has a fully qualified name. This method allows the client application to retrieve this name.

               The string returned by this method is not a JNDI composite name and should not be passed directly to context methods. In naming systems for which the notion of full name does not make sense, an `OperationNotSupported-Exception` is thrown.

RETURNS   This context's name in its own namespace. Never `null`.

C

EXCEPTIONS
`NamingException`
    If a naming exception is encountered.
`OperationNotSupportedException`
    If the naming system does not have the notion of a full name.

EXAMPLE   See the **What's in a Name?** lesson (page 89).

getNameParser()

PURPOSE   Retrieves the parser associated with the named context.

SYNTAX
```
public NameParser getNameParser(Name name) throws
    NamingException
public NameParser getNameParser(String name) throws
    NamingException
```

DESCRIPTION This method retrieves the parser associated with the named context. In a federation of namespaces, different naming systems parse names differently. This method allows an application to get a parser for parsing names into their atomic components by using the naming convention of a particular naming system. Within any single naming system, `NameParser` objects returned by this method must be equal (determined by using the `equals()` test).

PARAMETERS
`name`   The name of the context from which to get the parser.

RETURNS   A name parser that can parse compound names into their atomic components.

EXCEPTIONS
`NamingException`
    If a naming exception is encountered.

SEE ALSO   `CompoundName`.

EXAMPLE   See the **What's in a Name?** lesson (page 87).

INITIAL_CONTEXT_FACTORY

PURPOSE   Holds the name of the environment property for specifying the initial context factory to use.

SYNTAX   `public final static String INITIAL_CONTEXT_FACTORY`

DESCRIPTION This constant holds the name of the environment property for specifying the initial context factory to use. The value of the property should be the fully qualified class name of the factory class that will create an initial context. This property may be specified in the environment parameter that is passed to the initial context constructor, an applet parameter, a system property, or an application resource file. If it is not specified in any of these sources, then a `NoInitialContextException` is thrown when an initial context is required to complete an operation.

The value of this constant is `"java.naming.factory.initial"`.

SEE ALSO `addToEnvironment()`, `APPLET`, `InitialContext`, `javax.naming.directory.InitialDirContext`, `javax.naming.spi.InitialContextFactory`, `javax.naming.spi.NamingManager.getInitialContext()`, `NoInitialContextException`, `removeFromEnvironment()`.

EXAMPLE See the **Preparations** lesson (page 50).

LANGUAGE

PURPOSE Holds the name of the environment property for specifying the preferred language to use with the service.

SYNTAX `public final static String LANGUAGE`

DESCRIPTION This constant holds the name of the environment property for specifying the preferred language to use with the service. The value of the property is a colon-separated list of language tags as defined in RFC 1766. If this property is unspecified, then the service provider determines the language preference.

The value of this constant is `"java.naming.language"`.

SEE ALSO `addToEnvironment()`, `removeFromEnvironment()`.

list()

PURPOSE Enumerates the names bound in the named context, along with the class names of objects bound to them.

SYNTAX `public NamingEnumeration list(Name name) throws NamingException`
`public NamingEnumeration list(String name) throws`
`    NamingException`

DESCRIPTION This method enumerates the names bound in the named context, along with the class names of objects bound to them. The contents of any subcontexts are not included.

If a binding is added to or removed from this context, then its effect on an enumeration previously returned is undefined.

PARAMETERS

name　　　　　　　The name of the context to list.

RETURNS　　　　　An enumeration of the names and class names of the bindings in this context. Each element of the enumeration is of type `NameClassPair`.

EXCEPTIONS

`NamingException`

　　　　　　　　　If a naming exception is encountered.

SEE ALSO　　　　　`listBindings()`, `NameClassPair`.

EXAMPLE　　　　　See the **Naming Operations** lesson (page 54).

listBindings()

PURPOSE　　　　　Enumerates the names bound in the named context, along with the objects bound to them.

SYNTAX　　　　　```
public NamingEnumeration listBindings(Name name) throws
    NamingException
public NamingEnumeration listBindings(String name) throws
    NamingException
```

DESCRIPTION　　　This method enumerates the names bound in the named context, along with the objects bound to them. The contents of any subcontexts are not included.

　　　　　　　　　If a binding is added to or removed from this context, then its effect on an enumeration previously returned is undefined.

PARAMETERS

name　　　　　　　The name of the context to list.

RETURNS　　　　　An enumeration of the bindings in this context. Each element of the enumeration is of type `Binding`.

EXCEPTIONS

`NamingException`

　　　　　　　　　If a naming exception is encountered.

SEE ALSO　　　　　`list()`, `Binding`.

EXAMPLE　　　　　See the **Naming Operations** lesson (page 55).


## lookup()

PURPOSE　　　　　Retrieves the named object.

SYNTAX　　　　　```
public Object lookup(Name name) throws NamingException
public Object lookup(String name) throws NamingException
```

DESCRIPTION   This method returns the object named by `name`.

If `name` is empty, then this method returns a new instance of this context. This new instance represents the same naming context as this context, but its environment may be modified independently and it may be accessed concurrently.

PARAMETERS
`name`   The name of the object to look up.

RETURNS   The object bound to `name`.

EXCEPTIONS
`NamingException`
    If a naming exception is encountered.

SEE ALSO   `lookupLink()`.

EXAMPLE   See the **Naming Operations** lesson (page 54).

lookupLink()

PURPOSE   Retrieves the named object by following links, except for the terminal atomic component of the name.

SYNTAX   `public Object lookupLink(Name name) throws NamingException`
`public Object lookupLink(String name) throws NamingException`

DESCRIPTION   This method retrieves the named object by following links, except for the terminal atomic component of the name. If the object bound to `name` is not a link, then it returns the object itself.

PARAMETERS
`name`   The name of the object to look up.

RETURNS   The object bound to `name`, not following the terminal link (if any).

EXCEPTIONS
`NamingException`
    If a naming exception is encountered.

SEE ALSO   `lookup()`.

EXAMPLE   See the **Miscellaneous** lesson (page 143).

OBJECT_FACTORIES

PURPOSE   Holds the name of the environment property for specifying the list of object factories to use.

SYNTAX   `public final static String OBJECT_FACTORIES`

C

DESCRIPTION   This constant holds the name of the environment property for specifying the list of object factories to use. The value of the property should be a colon-separated list of the fully qualified class names of factory classes that, when given information about an object, will create the object. This property may be specified in the environment, an applet parameter, a system property, or one or more resource files.

The value of this constant is `"java.naming.factory.object"`.

SEE ALSO   `addToEnvironment()`, `APPLET`, `javax.naming.spi.NamingManager.getObjectInstance()`, `javax.naming.spi.ObjectFactory`, `removeFromEnvironment()`.

EXAMPLE   See the **Storing Objects in the Directory** lesson (page 162).

PROVIDER_URL

PURPOSE   Holds the name of the environment property for specifying configuration information for the service provider to use.

SYNTAX   `public final static String PROVIDER_URL`

DESCRIPTION   This constant holds the name of the environment property for specifying configuration information for the service provider to use. The value of the property should contain a URL string (e.g., `"ldap://somehost:389"`). This property may be specified in the environment, an applet parameter, a system property, or a resource file. If it is not specified in any of these sources, then the service provider determines the default configuration.

The value of this constant is `"java.naming.provider.url"`.

SEE ALSO   `addToEnvironment()`, `APPLET`, `removeFromEnvironment()`.

EXAMPLE   See the **Preparations** lesson (page 50).

rebind()

PURPOSE   Binds a name to an object, overwriting any existing binding.

SYNTAX   `public void rebind(Name name, Object obj) throws NamingException`
`public void rebind(String name, Object obj) throws`
`    NamingException`

DESCRIPTION   This method binds a name to an object, overwriting any existing binding. All intermediate contexts and the target context (that named by all but the terminal atomic component of the name) must already exist.

If the object is a `DirContext`, then any existing attributes associated with the name are replaced with those of the object. Otherwise, any existing attributes associated with the name remain unchanged.

PARAMETERS

name   If a naming exception is encountered.

obj   The object to bind. Possibly `null`.

EXCEPTIONS

`javax.naming.directory.InvalidAttributesException`
                If `obj` did not supply all mandatory attributes.

`NamingException`
                If a naming exception is encountered.

SEE ALSO   `bind()`, `javax.naming.directory.DirContext.rebind()`.

EXAMPLE   See the **Naming Operations** lesson (page 56).

REFERRAL

PURPOSE   Holds the name of the environment property for specifying how referrals encountered by the service provider are to be processed.

SYNTAX   `public final static String REFERRAL`

                This constant holds the name of the environment property for specifying how referrals encountered by the service provider are to be processed. The value of the property is one of the strings listed in Table 29.

TABLE 29:   Values for the "java.naming.referral" Property.

Value	Description
follow	Follow referrals automatically.
ignore	Ignore referrals.
throw	Throw a `ReferralException` when a referral is encountered.

If this property is not specified, then the default is determined by the provider. The value of this constant is `"java.naming.referral"`.

SEE ALSO   `addToEnvironment()`, `ReferralException`, `removeFromEnvironment()`.

EXAMPLE   See the **Referrals** lesson (page 263).

removeFromEnvironment()

PURPOSE   Removes an environment property from the environment of this context.

SYNTAX
```
public Object removeFromEnvironment(String propName) throws
    NamingException
```

DESCRIPTION   This method removes an environment property from the environment of this context. See the class description for more details on environment properties.

PARAMETERS
propName   The name of the environment property to remove. May not be `null`.

RETURNS   The previous value of the property, or `null` if the property was not in the environment.

EXCEPTIONS
NamingException
                 If a naming exception is encountered.

SEE ALSO   `addToEnvironment()`, `getEnvironment()`.

EXAMPLE   See the **Environment Properties** lesson (page 106).

rename()

PURPOSE   Binds a new name to the object bound to an old name, and unbinds the old name.

SYNTAX
```
public void rename(Name oldName, Name newName) throws
    NamingException
public void rename(String oldName, String newName) throws
    NamingException
```

DESCRIPTION   This method binds a new name to the object bound to an old name, and unbinds the old name. Both names are relative to this context. Any attributes associated with the old name become associated with the new name. Intermediate contexts of the old name are not changed.

PARAMETERS
newName   The name of the new binding. May not be empty.
oldName   The name of the existing binding. May not be empty.

EXCEPTIONS
NameAlreadyBoundException
                 If `newName` is already bound.
NamingException
                 If a naming exception is encountered.

SEE ALSO   `bind()`, `rebind()`.

EXAMPLE   See the **Naming Operations** lesson (page 57).

SECURITY_AUTHENTICATION

PURPOSE   Holds the name of the environment property for specifying the security level to use.

SYNTAX   `public final static String SECURITY_AUTHENTICATION`

DESCRIPTION   This constant holds the name of the environment property for specifying the security level to use. Its value is one of the following strings: `"none"`, `"simple"`, or `"strong"`. If this property is unspecified, then the behavior is determined by the service provider.

The value of this constant is `"java.naming.security.authentication"`.

SEE ALSO   `addToEnvironment()`, `removeFromEnvironment()`.

EXAMPLE   See the **Security** lesson (page 228).

SECURITY_CREDENTIALS

PURPOSE   Holds the name of the environment property for specifying the credentials of the principal for authenticating the caller to the service.

SYNTAX   `public final static String SECURITY_CREDENTIALS`

DESCRIPTION   This constant holds the name of the environment property for specifying the credentials of the principal for authenticating the caller to the service. The value of the property depends on the authentication scheme. For example, it could be a hashed password, clear-text password, key, or certificate. If this property is unspecified, then the behavior is determined by the service provider.

The value of this constant is `"java.naming.security.credentials"`.

SEE ALSO   `addToEnvironment()`, `removeFromEnvironment()`.

EXAMPLE   See the **Security** lesson (page 223).

SECURITY_PRINCIPAL

PURPOSE   Holds the name of the environment property for specifying the identity of the principal for authenticating the caller to the service.

SYNTAX   `public final static String SECURITY_PRINCIPAL`

DESCRIPTION	This constant holds the name of the environment property for specifying the identity of the principal for authenticating the caller to the service. The format of the principal depends on the authentication scheme. If this property is unspecified, then the service provider determines the behavior.
	The value of this constant is `"java.naming.security.principal"`.
SEE ALSO	`addToEnvironment()`, `removeFromEnvironment()`.
EXAMPLE	See the **Security** lesson (page 223).

C

SECURITY_PROTOCOL

PURPOSE	Holds the name of the environment property for specifying the security protocol to use.
SYNTAX	`public final static String SECURITY_PROTOCOL`
DESCRIPTION	This constant holds the name of the environment property for specifying the security protocol to use. Its value is a string determined by the service provider (e.g., `"ssl"`). If this property is unspecified, then the service provider determines the behavior.
	The value of this constant is `"java.naming.security.protocol"`.
SEE ALSO	`addToEnvironment()`, `removeFromEnvironment()`.
EXAMPLE	See the **Security** lesson (page 233).

STATE_FACTORIES

PURPOSE	Holds the name of the environment property for specifying the list of state factories to use.
SYNTAX	`public final static String STATE_FACTORIES`
DESCRIPTION	This constant holds the name of the environment property for specifying the list of state factories to use. The value of the property should be a colon-separated list of the fully qualified class names of state factory classes that, when given an object, will return the object's state for storage in a naming/directory service. This property may be specified in the environment, an applet parameter, a system property, or one or more resource files.
	The value of this constant is `"java.naming.factory.state"`.
SEE ALSO	`addToEnvironment()`, `APPLET`, `javax.naming.spi.NamingManager.getStateToBind()`, `javax.naming.spi.StateFactory`, `removeFromEnvironment()`.
EXAMPLE	See the **Environment Properties** lesson (page 97).

unbind()

PURPOSE Unbinds the named object.

SYNTAX
```
public void unbind(Name name) throws NamingException
public void unbind(String name) throws NamingException
```

DESCRIPTION This method unbinds the named object. It removes the terminal atomic name in `name` from the target context, that named by all but the terminal atomic part of `name`.

This method is idempotent. It succeeds even if the terminal atomic name is not bound in the target context, but it throws a `NameNotFoundException` if any of the intermediate contexts do not exist.

Any attributes associated with the name are removed. Intermediate contexts are not changed.

PARAMETERS
`name` The name to unbind. May not be empty.

EXCEPTIONS
`NameNotFoundException`
        If an intermediate context does not exist.
`NamingException`
        If a naming exception is encountered.

EXAMPLE See the **Naming Operations** lesson (page 57).

URL_PKG_PREFIXES

PURPOSE Holds the name of the environment property for specifying the list of package prefixes to use when loading in URL context factories.

SYNTAX
```
public final static String URL_PKG_PREFIXES
```

DESCRIPTION This constant holds the name of the environment property for specifying the list of package prefixes to use when loading in URL context factories. The value of the property should be a colon-separated list of package prefixes for the class name of the factory class that will create a URL context factory.

This property may be specified in the environment, an applet parameter, a system property, or one or more resource files. The prefix `"com.sun.jndi.url"` is always appended to the possibly empty list of package prefixes.

The value of this constant is `"java.naming.factory.url.pkgs"`.

SEE ALSO `addToEnvironment()`, `APPLET`, `InitialContext`, `javax.naming.spi.NamingManager.getObjectInstance()`,

```
javax.naming.spi.NamingManager.getURLContext(),
javax.naming.spi.ObjectFactory, removeFromEnvironment().
```

EXAMPLE   See the **Adding URL Support** lesson (page 367).

C

C

(*) 9 classes from other packages not shown.

Syntax

```
public class ContextNotEmptyException extends NamingException
```

Description

A `ContextNotEmptyException` is thrown when attempting to destroy a context that is not empty.

If the program wants to handle this exception in particular, then it should catch a `Context-NotEmptyException` explicitly before attempting to catch a `NamingException`. For example, after catching a `ContextNotEmptyException`, the program might try to remove the contents of the context before reattempting the destroy.

Synchronization and serialization issues that apply to `NamingException` apply directly here.

MEMBER SUMMARY
Constructor
`ContextNotEmptyException()`   Constructs an instance of `ContextNotEmptyException`.

ContextNotEmptyException()

PURPOSE	Constructs an instance of `ContextNotEmptyException`.
SYNTAX	`public ContextNotEmptyException()` `public ContextNotEmptyException(String msg)`
DESCRIPTION	These constructors construct an instance of `ContextNotEmptyException` by using the optional `msg` supplied. If `msg` is not supplied, then `msg` defaults to `null`. All other fields default to `null`.
PARAMETERS	
`msg`	Additional detail about this exception. May be `null`.
SEE ALSO	`java.lang.Throwable.getMessage()`.

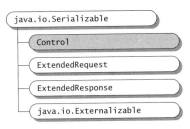

Syntax

`public interface Control extends java.io.Serializable`

Description

The `Control` interface represents an LDAP v3 control as defined in RFC 2251. The LDAP v3 protocol uses controls to send and receive additional data to affect the behavior of predefined operations.

Controls can be sent along with any LDAP operation to the server. These are called *request controls*. For example, a Sort control can be sent with an LDAP "search" operation to request that the results be returned in a particular order. Solicited and unsolicited controls can also be returned with responses from the server. Such controls are called *response controls*. For example, an LDAP server might define a special control to return change notifications.

This interface is used to represent both request and response controls.

MEMBER SUMMARY	
Access Methods	
`getEncodedValue()`	Retrieves the ASN.1 BER encoded value of the LDAP control.
`getID()`	Retrieves the object identifier assigned to the LDAP control.
`isCritical()`	Determines the criticality of the LDAP control.
Constants	
`CRITICAL`	Indicates a critical control.
`NONCRITICAL`	Indicates a noncritical control.

See Also

`ControlFactory`, `LdapContext`.

Example

See the **Controls and Extensions** lesson (page 293).

CRITICAL

PURPOSE	Indicates a critical control.
SYNTAX	`public static final boolean CRITICAL`
DESCRIPTION	This constant is used to indicate a critical control. The value of this constant is `true`.
EXAMPLE	See the **Controls and Extensions** lesson (page 293).

getEncodedValue()

PURPOSE	Retrieves the ASN.1 BER encoded value of the LDAP control.
SYNTAX	`public byte[] getEncodedValue()`
DESCRIPTION	This method retrieves the ASN.1 BER encoded value of the LDAP control. The result is the raw BER bytes, including the tag and length of the control's value. It does not include the control's OID or criticality. `null` is returned if the value is absent.
RETURNS	A possibly `null` byte array that represents the ASN.1 BER encoded value of the LDAP control.
EXAMPLE	See the **Controls and Extensions** lesson (page 301).

getID()

PURPOSE	Retrieves the object identifier assigned to the LDAP control.
SYNTAX	`public String getID()`
RETURNS	The non-`null` object identifier string.
EXAMPLE	See the **Controls and Extensions** lesson (page 301).

isCritical()

PURPOSE	Determines the criticality of the LDAP control.
SYNTAX	`public boolean isCritical()`

DESCRIPTION   This method determines the criticality of the LDAP control. A critical control must not be ignored by the server. If the server receives a critical control that it does not support, regardless of whether the control makes sense for the operation, then the operation will not be performed and an `OperationNot-SupportedException` will be thrown.

RETURNS   `true` if this control is critical; `false` otherwise.

EXAMPLE   See the **Controls and Extensions** lesson (page 301).

C

NONCRITICAL

PURPOSE   Indicates a noncritical control.

SYNTAX   `public static final boolean NONCRITICAL`

DESCRIPTION   This constant is used to indicate a non-critical control. The value of this constant is `false`.

ControlFactory

```
java.lang.Object
    ControlFactory                    O
```

Syntax

```
public abstract class ControlFactory
```

Description

The ControlFactory abstract class represents a factory for creating LDAP v3 controls as defined in RFC 2251. When a service provider receives a response control, it uses control factories to return the specific/appropriate control class implementation.

MEMBER SUMMARY	
Constructor	
ControlFactory()	Constructs an instance of ControlFactory.
Factory Method	
getControlInstance()	Creates a control.

See Also

Control, LdapContext.

Example

Suppose that an LDAP server sends back a Change ID control in response to a successful modification. It supplies a class ChangeIDControl so that the application can use this feature. The application will perform an update and then try to get the Change ID.

```
// Perform the update
Context ctx = ectx.createSubsubcontext("cn=newobj");

// Get the response controls
Control[] respCtls = ectx.getResponseControls();
if (respCtls != null) {
    // Find the one that you want
    for (int i = 0; i < respCtls; i++) {
        if(respCtls[i] instanceof ChangeIDControl) {
            ChangeIDControl cctl = (ChangeIDControl)respCtls[i];
            System.out.println(cctl.getChangeID());
        }
    }
}
```

The vendor might supply the following ChangeIDControl and VendorXControlFactory classes. The service provider will use VendorXControlFactory when it receives response controls from the LDAP server.

```java
public class ChangeIDControl implements Control {
    long id;

    // Constructor used by ControlFactory
    public ChangeIDControl(String OID, byte[] berVal)
        throws NamingException {
        // Check the validity of the OID
        id = // Extract the change ID from berVal
    };

    // Type-safe and user-friendly method
    public long getChangeID() {
        return id;
    }

    // Low-level methods
    public String getID() {
        return CHANGEID_OID;
    }
    public byte[] getEncodedValue() {
        return // Original berVal
    }
    ...
}
public class VendorXControlFactory extends ControlFactory {
    public VendorXControlFactory () {
    }

    public Control getControlInstance(Control orig)
        throws NamingException {
        if (isOneOfMyControls(orig.getID())) {
            ...
            // Determine which of yours it is, and call its constructor
            return (new ChangeIDControl(orig.getID(),
                orig.getEncodedValue()));
        }
        return null;  // Not one of yours
    }
}
```

ControlFactory()

PURPOSE   Constructs an instance of ControlFactory.

SYNTAX   protected ControlFactory()

DESCRIPTION   This constructor is used by subclasses to construct an instance of Control-Factory.

EXAMPLE   See the class example.

getControlInstance()

PURPOSE   Creates a control.

SYNTAX
```
public abstract Control getControlInstance(Control ctl) throws
    NamingException
public static Control getControlInstance(Control ctl, Context
    ctx, Hashtable env) throws NamingException
```

DESCRIPTION   The abstract (instance) form of this method creates a control by using this
ControlFactory. The service provider uses the factory to return controls that
it reads from the LDAP protocol as specialized control classes. Without this
mechanism, the provider would be returning controls that contained only data
in BER-encoded format.

Typically, ctl is a basic control that contains BER-encoded data. The factory
is used to create a specialized control implementation, usually by decoding the
BER encoded data, that provides methods to access that data in a type-safe and
friendly manner. For example, a factory might use the BER-encoded data in
the basic control and return an instance of VirtualListReplyControl.

If this factory cannot create a control by using the argument supplied, then it
should return null. A factory should throw an exception only if it is sure that it
is the only intended factory and that no other control factories should be tried.
This might happen, for example, if the BER data in the control does not match
what is expected of a control that has the given OID. Because this method
throws a NamingException, any other internally generated exception that
should be propagated must be wrapped inside of a NamingException.

The static form of this method creates a control by using known control factories. The following rules are used to create the control.

1. Use, in order, the control factories specified in the Ldap-
   Context.CONTROL_FACTORIES property of the environment and of the
   provider resource file associated with ctx. The value of this property is a
   colon-separated list of factory class names that are tried in order. The
   first one that succeeds in creating the control is the one used.
2. If none of the factories succeed in returning a control, then return ctl.
3. If an exception is encountered while creating the control, then the exception is passed up to the caller.

Note that a control factory must be public and must have a public constructor
that accepts no arguments.

PARAMETERS
ctl   The non-null control object that contains the OID and BER data.
ctx   The possibly null context in which the control is being created. If null, then
               no such information is available.

env   The possibly `null` environment of the context. This is used to find the value of the `LdapContext.CONTROL_FACTORIES` property.

RETURNS   The abstract form returns a possibly `null` `Control`. The static form returns a control object created by using `ctl` or `ctl` if a control object cannot be created by using the algorithm described previously.

EXCEPTIONS
`NamingException`
             If `ctl` contains invalid data that prevents it from being used to create a control. A factory should throw an exception only if it knows how to produce the control (identified by the OID) but is unable to because of, for example, invalid BER data.
             For the static form of this method, an exception thrown by one of the factories accessed is propagated up to the caller. If an error is encountered while loading and instantiating the factory and object classes, then the exception is wrapped inside of a `NamingException` and rethrown.

EXAMPLE   See the class example.

C

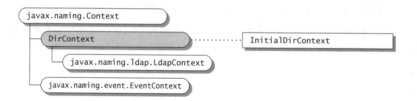

Syntax
```
public interface DirContext extends Context
```

Description
The DirContext interface contains methods for examining and updating attributes associated with objects and for searching the directory.

Names
Each name passed as an argument to a DirContext method is relative to that context. The empty name is used to name the context itself. The name parameter may never be null.

Most of the methods have two overloaded versions, one that takes a Name parameter and one that takes a String. These overloaded versions are equivalent in that if the Name and String parameters are just different representations of the same name, then the overloaded versions of the same methods behave in the same way.

See Context for a discussion on the interpretation of the name argument to the context methods. These same rules apply to the name argument to the DirContext methods.

Attribute Models
Two basic models set out what attributes should be associated with. In the first, attributes may be directly associated with a DirContext object. An attribute operation on the named object is roughly equivalent to a lookup on the name (which returns the DirContext object), followed by the attribute operation invoked on the DirContext object in which the caller supplies an empty name. The attributes can be viewed as being stored along with the object (note that this does not imply that the implementation must do so).

In the second model, attributes are associated with a name (typically an atomic name) in a DirContext. An attribute operation on the named object is roughly equivalent to a lookup on the name of the parent DirContext of the named object, followed by the attribute operation invoked on the parent in which the caller supplies the terminal atomic name. The attributes can be viewed as being stored in the parent DirContext (again, this does not imply that the implementation must do so). Objects that are not DirContexts can have attributes, provided that their parents are DirContexts.

D

The JNDI supports both of these models. The individual service providers decide where to "store" attributes. JNDI clients are safest when they do not make assumptions about whether an object's attributes are stored as part of the object or stored within the parent object and associated with the object's name.

Attribute Type Names

In `getAttributes()` and `search()`, you supply the attributes to return by giving a list of attribute names (strings). The attributes that you get back might not have the same names as the attribute names that you specified. This is because some directories support features that cause them to return other attributes. Such features include attribute subclassing, attribute name synonyms, and attribute language codes.

In attribute subclassing, attributes are defined in a class hierarchy. In some directories, for example, the `"name"` attribute might be the superclass of all name-related attributes, including `"commonName"` and `"surName"`. Asking for the `"name"` attribute might return both the `"commonName"` and `"surName"` attributes.

With attribute type synonyms, a directory can assign multiple names to the same attribute. For example, `"cn"` and `"commonName"` might both refer to the same attribute. Asking for `"cn"` might return the `"commonName"` attribute.

Some directories support the language codes for attributes. Asking the directory for the `"description"` attribute, for example, might result in all of the following attributes being returned:

```
description
description;lang-en
description;lang-de
description;lang-fr
```

Operational Attributes

Some directories have the notion of *operational attributes,* attributes associated with a directory object for administrative purposes. An example of operational attributes is the access control list for an object.

In `getAttributes()` and `search()`, you can specify that all attributes associated with the requested objects be returned. You do this by supplying `null` as the list of attributes to return. The attributes returned do *not* include operational attributes. To retrieve operational attributes, you must name them explicitly.

Named Context

Certain methods require that the name resolve to a context (for example, when searching a single-level context). The documentation of such methods uses the term *named context* to describe their `name` parameters. For these methods, if the named object is not a `DirContext`, then a `NotContextException` is thrown. Aside from these methods, no other requirement exists that the *named object* be a `DirContext`.

Parameters

An `Attributes`, `SearchControls`, or array object passed as a parameter to any method will not be modified by the service provider. The service provider may keep a reference to the object for the duration of the operation, including any enumeration of the method's results and the processing of any referrals generated. The caller should not modify the object during this time. An `Attributes` object returned by any method is owned by the caller. The caller may subsequently modify it, but the service provider will not.

Exceptions

All methods in this interface can throw a `NamingException` or any of its subclasses. See `NamingException` and its subclasses for details on each exception.

MEMBER SUMMARY	
Directory Methods	
`getAttributes()`	Retrieves the attributes associated with a named object.
`modifyAttributes()`	Modifies the attributes associated with a named object.
`search()`	Searches a context or subcontexts.
Hybrid Naming and Directory Service Methods	
`bind()`	Binds a name to an object, along with associated attributes.
`createSubcontext()`	Creates and binds a new context, along with associated attributes.
`rebind()`	Binds a name to an object, along with associated attributes, overwriting any existing binding.
Schema Methods	
`getSchema()`	Retrieves the schema associated with the named object.
`getSchemaClass-` `Definition()`	Retrieves a context that contains the schema objects of the named object's class definitions.
Constants for Modifying Attributes	
`ADD_ATTRIBUTE`	Specifies adding an attribute that has the specified values.
`REMOVE_ATTRIBUTE`	Specifies deleting the specified attribute values from the attribute.
`REPLACE_ATTRIBUTE`	Specifies replacing an attribute with specified values.

Example

See the **Directory Operations** lesson (page 59) and the **Searches** lesson (page 249).

ADD_ATTRIBUTE

PURPOSE   Specifies adding an attribute that has the specified values.

SYNTAX   `public final static int ADD_ATTRIBUTE`

DESCRIPTION   This constant specifies adding an attribute that has the specified values.

If the attribute does not exist, then the directory creates the attribute. The resulting attribute has a union of the specified value set and the prior value set. Adding an attribute that has no value will cause an `InvalidAttributeValue-Exception` to be thrown if the attribute must have at least one value. For a single-valued attribute that already has a value, an `AttributeInUseException` is thrown. If an attempt is made to add more than one value to a single-valued attribute, then an `InvalidAttributeValueException` is thrown.

The value of this constant is 1.

SEE ALSO   `ModificationItem`, `modifyAttributes()`, `REMOVE_ATTRIBUTE`, `REPLACE_ATTRIBUTE`.

EXAMPLE   See the **Directory Operations** lesson (page 63).

bind()

PURPOSE   Binds a name to an object, along with associated attributes.

SYNTAX
```
public void bind(Name name, Object obj, Attributes attrs) throws
    NamingException
public void bind(String name, Object obj, Attributes attrs)
    throws NamingException
```

DESCRIPTION   This method binds a name to an object, along with associated attributes. If `attrs` is `null`, then the resulting binding will have the attributes associated with `obj` if `obj` is a `DirContext`, and no attributes otherwise. If `attrs` is non-`null`, then the resulting binding will have `attrs` as its attributes; any attributes associated with `obj` will be ignored.

PARAMETERS

`attrs`   The attributes to associate with the binding.

`name`   The name to bind. May not be empty.

`obj`   The object to bind; possibly `null`.

EXCEPTIONS

`InvalidAttributesException`
     If some mandatory attributes of the binding are not supplied.

`NameAlreadyBoundException`
     If `name` is already bound.

    NamingException

         If a naming exception is encountered.

SEE ALSO   `Context.bind()`, `rebind()`.

EXAMPLE   See the **Directory Operations** lesson (page 71).

createSubcontext()

PURPOSE   Creates and binds a new context, along with associated attributes.

SYNTAX
```
public DirContext createSubcontext(Name name, Attributes attrs)
    throws NamingException
public DirContext createSubcontext(String name, Attributes
    attrs) throws NamingException
```

DESCRIPTION   This method creates and binds a new context, along with associated attributes. It creates a new subcontext with the given name, binds it in the target context (that named by all but the terminal atomic component of the name), and associates the supplied attributes with the newly created object. All intermediate and target contexts must already exist. If attrs is null, then this method is equivalent to `Context.createSubcontext()`.

PARAMETERS

  attrs   The attributes to associate with the newly created context.

  name   The name of the context to create. May not be empty.

RETURNS   The newly created context.

EXCEPTIONS

  InvalidAttributesException

         If attrs does not contain all of the mandatory attributes required for creation.

  NameAlreadyBoundException

         If name is already bound.

  NamingException

         If a naming exception is encountered.

SEE ALSO   `Context.createSubcontext()`.

EXAMPLE   See the **Directory Operations** lesson (page 70).

getAttributes()

PURPOSE   Retrieves the attributes associated with a named object.

SYNTAX
```
public Attributes getAttributes(Name name) throws
    NamingException
```

```
public Attributes getAttributes(String name) throws
    NamingException
public Attributes getAttributes(Name name, String[] attrIds)
    throws NamingException
public Attributes getAttributes(String name, String[] attrIds)
    throws NamingException
```

DESCRIPTION   This method retrieves the attributes associated with a named object. If `attrIds` was not specified, then the method returns all of the object's attributes. See the class description regarding attribute models, attribute type names, and operational attributes.

If the object does not have an attribute specified, then the directory will ignore the nonexistent attribute and return those requested attributes that the object does have.

A directory might return more attributes than was requested (see *Attribute Type Names* in the class description), but it may not return arbitrary, unrelated attributes. See also *Operational Attributes* in the class description.

PARAMETERS

  attrIds   The identifiers of the attributes to retrieve. `null` indicates that all attributes should be retrieved; an empty array indicates that none should be retrieved.

  name   The name of the object from which to retrieve attributes.

RETURNS   The requested attributes; never `null`. Returns an empty attribute set if `name` has no attributes or none of the requested attributes are found.

EXCEPTIONS

NamingException

       If a naming exception is encountered.

EXAMPLE   See the **Directory Operations** lesson (page 61).

getSchema()

PURPOSE   Retrieves the schema associated with the named object.

SYNTAX
```
public DirContext getSchema(Name name) throws NamingException
public DirContext getSchema(String name) throws NamingException
```

DESCRIPTION   This method retrieves the schema associated with the named object. The schema describes rules regarding the structure of the namespace and the attributes stored in it. It specifies the types of objects that may added to the directory and where they may be added, as well as the mandatory and optional attributes that an object can have. The range of support for schemas is directory-specific.

This method returns the root of the schema information tree that applies to the named object. Several named objects (or even an entire directory) might share the same schema.

Issues such as the structure and contents of the schema tree, permission to modify the contents of the schema tree, and the effect of such modifications on the directory are dependent on the underlying directory.

PARAMETERS

name The name of the object whose schema to retrieve.

RETURNS The schema associated with the context; never null.

EXCEPTIONS

NamingException
  If a naming exception is encountered.

OperationNotSupportedException
  If the schema is not supported.

EXAMPLE See the **Schema** lesson (page 275).

getSchemaClassDefinition()

PURPOSE Retrieves a context that contains the schema objects of the named object's class definitions.

SYNTAX
```
public DirContext getSchemaClassDefinition(Name name) throws
    NamingException
public DirContext getSchemaClassDefinition(String name) throws
    NamingException
```

DESCRIPTION This method retrieves a context that contains the schema objects of the named object's class definitions. One category of information found in directory schemas is *class definitions*. An "object class" definition specifies the object's *type* and the attributes (mandatory and optional) that the object must/may have. Note that the term *object class* is used in the directory sense rather than in the Java sense. For example, if the named object is a directory object of the "Person" class, then getSchemaClassDefinition() will return a DirContext that represents the (directory's) object class definition of "Person".

The information that can be retrieved from an object class definition is directory-dependent.

PARAMETERS

name The name of the object whose object class definition to retrieve.

RETURNS The DirContext that contains the named object's class definitions; never null.

EXCEPTIONS

NamingException
> If a naming exception is encountered.

OperationNotSupportedException
> If the schema is not supported.

EXAMPLE   See the **Schema** lesson (page 276).

modifyAttributes()

D

PURPOSE   Modifies the attributes associated with a named object.

SYNTAX
```
public void modifyAttributes(Name name, int mod_op, Attributes
    attrs) throws NamingException
public void modifyAttributes(String name, int mod_op, Attributes
    attrs) throws NamingException
public void modifyAttributes(Name name, ModificationItem[] mods)
    throws NamingException
public void modifyAttributes(String name, ModificationItem[]
    mods) throws NamingException
```

DESCRIPTION   This method modifies the attributes associated with a named object. The first two form modify the attributes associated with a named object, with the modification specified by mod_op and attrs. The order of the modifications is not specified.

The last two forms modify the attributes by using an ordered list of modifications, mods. The modifications are performed in the order specified. Each modification specifies a modification operation code and an attribute on which to operate.

For all forms of this method, the modifications are performed atomically where possible.

PARAMETERS

attrs   The attributes to be used for the modification. May not be null.

mod_op   The modification operation, one of ADD_ATTRIBUTE, REPLACE_ATTRIBUTE, or REMOVE_ATTRIBUTE.

mods   The ordered list of modifications. May not be null.

name   The name of the object whose attributes will be updated.

EXCEPTIONS

AttributeModificationException
> If the modification cannot be completed successfully.

NamingException
> If a naming exception is encountered.

SEE ALSO   `ADD_ATTRIBUTE, REPLACE_ATTRIBUTE, REMOVE_ATTRIBUTE.`

EXAMPLE   See the **Directory Operations** lesson (page 62).

rebind()

PURPOSE   Binds a name to an object, along with associated attributes, overwriting any existing binding.

SYNTAX   ```
public void rebind(Name name, Object obj, Attributes attrs)
    throws NamingException
public void rebind(String name, Object obj, Attributes attrs)
    throws NamingException
```

DESCRIPTION   This method binds a name to an object, along with associated attributes, over-writing any existing binding. If `attrs` is `null` and `obj` is a `DirContext`, then the attributes from `obj` are used. If `attrs` is `null` and `obj` is not a `DirContext`, then any existing attributes associated with the object already bound in the directory remain unchanged. If `attrs` is non-`null`, then any existing attributes associated with the object already bound in the directory are removed and `attrs` is associated with the named object. If `obj` is a `DirContext` and `attrs` is non-`null`, then the attributes of `obj` are ignored.

PARAMETERS
`attrs`        The attributes to associate with the binding.
`name`         The name to bind. May not be empty.
`obj`          The object to bind; possibly `null`.

EXCEPTIONS
`InvalidAttributesException`
               If some mandatory attributes of the binding are not supplied.
`NamingException`
               If a naming exception is encountered.

SEE ALSO      `bind(), Context.bind().`

EXAMPLE       See the **Directory Operations** lesson (page 72).


## REMOVE_ATTRIBUTE

PURPOSE       Specifies deleting the specified attribute values from the attribute.

SYNTAX        `public final static int REMOVE_ATTRIBUTE`

DESCRIPTION   This constant specifies deleting the specified attribute values from the attribute. The resulting attribute has the set difference of its prior value set and the specified value set. If no values are specified, then the directory deletes the
```

entire attribute. If the attribute does not exist or if some or all members of the specified value set do not exist, then this absence may be ignored and either the operation will succeed or a `NamingException` might be thrown to indicate the absence. Removing the last value also removes the attribute if the attribute is required to have at least one value.

The value of this constant is 3.

SEE ALSO   `ADD_ATTRIBUTE, ModificationItem, modifyAttributes(), REPLACE_ATTRIBUTE.`

EXAMPLE   See the **Directory Operations** lesson (page 63).

REPLACE_ATTRIBUTE

PURPOSE   Specifies replacing an attribute with specified values.

SYNTAX   `public final static int REPLACE_ATTRIBUTE`

DESCRIPTION   This constant specifies replacing an attribute with specified values. If the attribute already exists, then the directory replaces all existing values with new specified values. If the attribute does not exist, then the directory creates it. If no value is specified, then it deletes all of the values of the attribute. Removing the last value also removes the attribute if the attribute is required to have at least one value. If an attempt is made to add more than one value to a single-valued attribute, then an `InvalidAttributeValueException` will be thrown.

The value of this constant is 2.

SEE ALSO   `ADD_ATTRIBUTE, ModificationItem, modifyAttributes(), REMOVE_ATTRIBUTE.`

EXAMPLE   See the **Directory Operations** lesson (page 63).

search()

PURPOSE   Searches a context or subcontexts.

SYNTAX
```
public NamingEnumeration search(Name name, Attributes
    matchingAttributes) throws NamingException
public NamingEnumeration search(String name, Attributes
    matchingAttributes) throws NamingException
public NamingEnumeration search(Name name, Attributes
    matchingAttributes, String[] attributesToReturn) throws
    NamingException
public NamingEnumeration search(String name, Attributes
    matchingAttributes, String[] attributesToReturn) throws
    NamingException
```

```
public NamingEnumeration search(Name name, String filter,
    SearchControls cons) throws NamingException
public NamingEnumeration search(String name, String filter,
    SearchControls cons) throws NamingException
public NamingEnumeration search(Name name, String filterExpr,
    Object[] filterArgs, SearchControls cons) throws
    NamingException
public NamingEnumeration search(String name, String filterExpr,
    Object[] filterArgs, SearchControls cons) throws
    NamingException
```

DESCRIPTION   This method searches a context or subcontexts. Two types of searches are possible: *basic* and *filter-based*.

The first four forms of this method perform a basic search. They search in a
single context for objects that contain a specified set of attributes (`matching-
Attributes`) and retrieve selected attributes (`attributesToReturn`). If
`attributesToReturn` is not specified, then it defaults to `null`, meaning return
all attributes. (The search is performed by using the default `SearchControls`
settings.)

For an object to be selected, each attribute in `matchingAttributes` must
match some attribute of the object. If `matchingAttributes` is empty or `null`,
then all objects in the target context are returned.

An attribute A_1 in `matchingAttributes` is considered to match an attribute A_2
of an object if A_1 and A_2 have the same identifier and each value of A_1 is equal
to some value of A_2. This implies that the order of values is not significant and
that A_2 may contain "extra" values not found in A_1 without affecting the comparison. It also implies that if A_1 has no values, then testing for a match is
equivalent to testing for the presence of an attribute A_2 that has the same identifier.

The precise definition of *equality* used in comparing attribute values is determined by the underlying directory service. The service might use
`Object.equals()`, for example, or might use a schema to specify a different
equality operation. For matching based on operations other than equality (such
as substring comparison), use a filter-based search.

The last four forms of the method perform a filter-based search. They search in
the named context or object for entries that satisfy the given search filter.
These forms perform the search specified by the search controls, `cons`.

The format and interpretation of `filter` are in accordance with RFC 2254,
with the following interpretations for `attr` and `value` mentioned in the RFC.
- `attr` is the attribute's identifier.
- `value` is the string that represents the attribute's value. The translation of
  this string representation into the attribute's value is directory-specific.

For the assertion "someCount=127", for example, `attr` is "someCount" and `value` is "127". The provider determines, based on the attribute identifier ("someCount") (and possibly its schema), that the attribute's value is an integer. It then parses the string "127" appropriately.

Any non-ASCII characters in the filter string should be represented by the appropriate Java (Unicode) characters and not encoded as UTF-8 octets. Alternatively, the "backslash-hexcode" notation described in RFC 2254 may be used.

If the directory does not support a string representation of some or all of its attributes, then use the form of the search method that accepts filter arguments in the form of `java.lang.Objects`. The service provider for such a directory will then translate the filter arguments to its service-specific representation for filter evaluation.

Like `filter`, the interpretation of `filterExpr` is based on RFC 2254. It may also contain variables of the form {i}—where i is an integer—that refer to objects in the `filterArgs` array. The interpretation of `filterExpr` is otherwise identical to that of `filter`. A variable {i} that appears in a search filter indicates that the filter argument `filterArgs[i]` is to be used in that place. Such variables may be used wherever an `attr`, `value`, or `matchingrule` production appears in the filter grammar of RFC 2254, Section 4. When a string-valued filter argument is substituted for a variable, the filter is interpreted as if the string were given in place of the variable, with any characters having special significance within filters (such as "*") having been escaped according to the rules of RFC 2254.

RFC 2254 defines certain operators for the filter, including substring matches, equals, approximate match, greater than, and less than. These operators are mapped to operators with corresponding semantics in the underlying directory. For example, for the equals operator, suppose that the directory has a matching rule that defines the "equality" of the attributes in the filter. This rule would be used to check the equality of the attributes specified in the filter with the attributes of objects in the directory. Similarly, if the directory has a matching rule for ordering, then this rule would be used for making *greater than* and *less than* comparisons. Not all of the operators defined in RFC 2254 apply to all attributes. When an operator is not applicable, an `InvalidSearchFilter-Exception` is thrown.

For all forms of this method, the result is returned in an enumeration of `SearchResults`. Each `SearchResult` contains the name of the object and other information about the object (see `SearchResult`). The name is either relative to the target context of the search (which is named by the `name` parameter) or a URL string. If the target context is included in the enumeration (as is possible

D

when `cons` specifies a search scope of `SearchControls.OBJECT_SCOPE` or `SearchControls.SUBTREE_SCOPE`), then its name is the empty string. The `SearchResult` may also contain attributes of the matching object if `attributesToReturn` or `cons` specifies that attributes are to be returned. If the object does not have a requested attribute, then that nonexistent attribute will be ignored. Those requested attributes that the object does have will be returned. A directory might return more attributes than were requested (see *Attribute Type Names* in the class description) but may not return arbitrary, unrelated attributes. See also *Operational Attributes* in the class description.

When changes are made to this `DirContext`, the effect on enumerations returned by prior calls to this method is undefined.

PARAMETERS

`attributesToReturn`
  The attributes to return. `null` indicates that all attributes are to be returned; an empty array indicates that none are to be returned.

`cons` The search controls that control the search. If `null`, then the default search controls are used (equivalent to `new SearchControls()`).

`filter` The filter to use for the search.

`filterArgs` The array of arguments to substitute for the variables in `filterExpr`. The value of `filterArgs[i]` will replace each occurrence of `{i}` in `filterExpr`. `null` is equivalent to an empty array.

`filterExpr` The filter expression to use for the search. The expression may contain variables of the form `{i}`, where i is a nonnegative integer. May not be `null`.

`matchingAttributes`
  The attributes for which to search. If empty or `null`, then all objects in the target context are returned.

`name` The name of the context to search.

RETURNS A non-`null` enumeration of `SearchResult` objects. Each `SearchResult` contains the attributes identified by `attributesToReturn` or `cons` and the name of the corresponding object, named relative to the context named by `name`.

EXCEPTIONS

`ArrayIndexOutOfBoundsException`
  If `filterExpr` contains `{i}` expressions, where i is outside of the bounds of the array `filterArgs`.

`InvalidSearchControlsException`
  If the search controls contain invalid settings.

`InvalidSearchFilterException`
  If the search filter specified is not supported or understood by the underlying directory.

NamingException

        If a naming exception is encountered.

SEE ALSO   `java.text.MessageFormat`, `SearchControls`, `SearchResult`.

EXAMPLE   See the **Directory Operations** lesson (page 63).

D

DirectoryManager

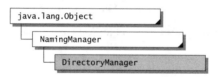

```
java.lang.Object
    NamingManager
        DirectoryManager
```

Syntax

`public class DirectoryManager extends NamingManager`

Description

The `DirectoryManager` class contains methods for supporting `DirContext` implementations. It is an extension of `NamingManager` and contains methods that service providers use to access object factories and state factories and to get continuation contexts for supporting federation.

`DirectoryManager` is safe for concurrent access by multiple threads.

Except as otherwise noted, a `Name`, `Attributes`, or environment parameter passed to any method is owned by the caller. The implementation will not modify the object or keep a reference to it, although it may keep a reference to a clone or copy.

MEMBER SUMMARY	
Factory Methods	
getObjectInstance()	Creates an instance of an object for the specified object, attributes, and environment.
getStateToBind()	Retrieves the state of an object for binding when given the original object and its attributes.
Federation Method	
getContinuationDirContext()	Creates a context in which to continue a `DirContext` operation.

See Also

`javax.naming.CannotProceedException`, `NamingManager`.

getContinuationDirContext()

PURPOSE   Creates a context in which to continue a `DirContext` operation.

SYNTAX   `public static DirContext getContinuationDirContext(`
                `CannotProceedException cpe) throws NamingException`

DESCRIPTION   This method creates a context in which to continue a `DirContext` operation. It operates like `NamingManager.getContinuationContext()`, except that the continuation context returned is a `DirContext`.

PARAMETERS
cpe   The non-`null` exception that triggered this continuation.

RETURNS   A non-`null` `DirContext` object for continuing the operation.

EXCEPTIONS
`NamingException`
               If a naming exception occurs.

SEE ALSO   `NamingManager.getContinuationContext()`.

EXAMPLE   See the **Adding Federation Support** lesson (page 381).

getObjectInstance()

PURPOSE   Creates an instance of an object for the specified object, attributes, and environment.

SYNTAX   ```
               public static Object getObjectInstance(Object refInfo, Name name,
                   Context nameCtx, Hashtable env, Attributes attrs) throws
                   Exception
               ```

DESCRIPTION    This method creates an instance of an object for the specified object, attributes, and environment. It operates the same as `NamingManager.getObject-Instance()`, except for the following differences.
               - It accepts an `Attributes` parameter that contains attributes associated with the object. The `DirObjectFactory` might use these attributes to save having to look them up from the directory.
               - It uses object factories that implement either `ObjectFactory` or `Dir-ObjectFactory`. If a factory implements `DirObjectFactory`, then this method calls `DirObjectFactory.getObjectInstance()`; otherwise, it calls `ObjectFactory.getObjectInstance()`.

               Service providers that implement the `DirContext` interface should use this method and not `NamingManager.getObjectInstance()`.

PARAMETERS
attrs          The possibly `null` attributes associated with `refInfo`. This might not be the complete set of attributes for `refInfo`; you might be able to read more attributes from the directory.
env            The possibly `null` environment to be used in the creation of the object factory and the object.

**541**
               ```

name	The name of this object relative to `nameCtx`. Specifying a name is optional; if it is omitted, then `name` should be `null`.
nameCtx	The context relative to which the `name` parameter is specified. If `null`, then `name` is relative to the default initial context.
refInfo	The possibly `null` object for which to create an object.

RETURNS   An object created by using `refInfo` and `attrs`; or `refInfo` if an object cannot be created by a factory.

EXCEPTIONS

Exception   If one of the factories accessed throws an exception, or if an error was encountered while loading and instantiating the factory and object classes. A factory should throw an exception only if it does not want other factories to be used in an attempt to create an object. See `DirObjectFactory.getObject-Instance()`.

NamingException

     If a naming exception was encountered while attempting to get a URL context, or if one of the factories accessed throws a `NamingException`.

SEE ALSO   `DirObjectFactory`, `DirObjectFactory.getObjectInstance()`, `NamingManager.getURLContext()`.

EXAMPLE   See the **Adding Directory Support** lesson (page 354).

getStateToBind()

PURPOSE   Retrieves the state of an object for binding when given the original object and its attributes.

SYNTAX   ```
public static DirStateFactory.Result getStateToBind(Object obj,
    Name name, Context nameCtx, Hashtable env, Attributes attrs)
    throws NamingException
```

DESCRIPTION  This method retrieves the state of an object for binding when given the original object and its attributes.

This method operates like `NamingManager.getStateToBind()`, except for the following differences.

- It accepts an `Attributes` parameter that contains attributes that were passed to the `DirContext.bind()` method.
- It returns a non-null `DirStateFactory.Result` instance that contains the object to be bound and the attributes to accompany the binding. Either the object or the attributes may be `null`.
- It uses state factories that implement either `StateFactory` or `DirState-Factory`. If a factory implements `DirStateFactory`, then this method calls `DirStateFactory.getStateToBind()`; otherwise, it calls `State-Factory.getStateToBind()`.
```

Service providers that implement the DirContext interface should use this method and not NamingManager.getStateToBind().

See NamingManager.getStateToBind() for a description of how the list of state factories to be tried is determined.

The return value of this method is owned by the caller; the implementation will not subsequently modify it. It will contain either a new Attributes object that is likewise owned by the caller or a reference to the original attrs parameter.

PARAMETERS

attrs   The possibly null Attributes that is to be bound with the object.

env   The possibly null environment to be used in creating the state factory and the object's state.

name   The name of this object relative to nameCtx, or null if no name is specified.

nameCtx   The context relative to which the name parameter is specified, or null if name is relative to the default initial context.

obj   The non-null object for which to get state to bind.

RETURNS   A non-null DirStateFactory.Result that contains the object and attributes to be bound. If no state factory returns a non-null answer, then the result will contain the object (obj) itself with the original attributes.

EXCEPTIONS

NamingException

            If a naming exception is encountered while using the factories. A factory should throw an exception only if it does not want other factories to be used in an attempt to create an object. See DirStateFactory.getStateToBind().

SEE ALSO   DirStateFactory, DirStateFactory.getStateToBind(), NamingManager.getStateToBind().

EXAMPLE   See the **Adding Directory Support** lesson (page 355).

DirObjectFactory

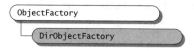

ObjectFactory
DirObjectFactory

Syntax

```
public interface DirObjectFactory extends ObjectFactory
```

Description

The DirObjectFactory interface represents a factory for creating an object. To create the object, it uses an object and attributes about the object.

The JNDI framework allows for object implementations to be loaded in dynamically via *object factories*. See ObjectFactory for details.

A DirObjectFactory extends ObjectFactory by allowing an Attributes instance to be supplied to getObjectInstance(). DirObjectFactory implementations are intended to be used by DirContext service providers. The service provider, in addition reading an object from the directory, might already have attributes that are useful for the object factory to check to see whether the factory is supposed to process the object. For example, an LDAP-style service provider might have read the "objectclass" attribute of the object. A CORBA object factory might be interested only in LDAP entries with "objectclass=corbaObject". By using the attributes supplied by the LDAP service provider, the CORBA object factory can quickly eliminate objects that it does not need to worry about, and non-CORBA object factories can quickly eliminate CORBA-related LDAP entries.

MEMBER SUMMARY	
Factory Method	
getObjectInstance()	Creates an object by using the location or reference information and the attributes specified.

See Also

DirectoryManager.getObjectInstance(), NamingManager.getObjectInstance(), ObjectFactory.

Example

See the **Object Factories** lesson (page 192).

getObjectInstance()

PURPOSE

Creates an object by using the location or reference information and the attributes specified.

SYNTAX

```
public Object getObjectInstance(Object obj, Name name, Context
    nameCtx, Hashtable env, Attributes attrs) throws Exception
```

DESCRIPTION

This method creates an object by using the location or reference information and the attributes specified. Special requirements of this object are supplied via env. An example of an environment property is user identity information.

DirectoryManager.getObjectInstance() successively loads in object factories. If it encounters a DirObjectFactory, then it invokes DirObjectFactory.getObjectInstance(); otherwise, it invokes Object-Factory.getObjectInstance(). It does this until a factory produces a non-null answer.

Any exception thrown by an object factory is passed on to the caller of DirectoryManager.getObjectInstance(), and the search for other factories that may produce a non-null answer is halted. An object factory should throw an exception only if it is sure that it is the only intended factory and that no other object factories should be tried. If this factory cannot create an object by using the arguments supplied, then it should return null.

Because DirObjectFactory extends ObjectFactory, it effectively has two getObjectInstance() methods, one differing from the other by the attrs argument. Given a factory that implements DirObjectFactory, Directory-Manager.getObjectInstance() will use only the method that accepts the attrs argument, whereas NamingManager.getObjectInstance() will use only the one that does not accept that argument.

See ObjectFactory for a description of URL context factories and other properties of object factories that apply equally to DirObjectFactory.

The name, attrs, and env parameters are owned by the caller. The implementation will not modify these objects or keep references to them, although it may keep references to clones or copies of them.

PARAMETERS

attrs

The possibly null attributes containing some of obj's attributes. attrs might not necessarily have all of obj's attributes. If the object factory requires more attributes, then it needs to get them, either by using obj or by using name and nameCtx. The factory must not modify attrs.

env

The possibly null environment that is used to create the object.

name

The name of this object relative to nameCtx, or null if no name is specified.

nameCtx	The context relative to which the name parameter is specified, or `null` if `name` is relative to the default initial context.
obj	The possibly `null` object that contains location or reference information that can be used to create an object.
RETURNS	The object created; `null` if an object cannot be created.
EXCEPTIONS	
`Exception`	
	If this object factory encounters an exception while attempting to create an object and no other object factories are to be tried.
SEE ALSO	`DirectoryManager.getObjectInstance()`, `NamingManager.getURLContext()`.
EXAMPLE	See the **Object Factories** lesson (page 192).

D

Syntax

```
public interface DirStateFactory extends StateFactory
```

Description

The `DirStateFactory` interface represents a factory for obtaining an object's state and corresponding attributes for binding.

The JNDI framework allows for object implementations to be loaded in dynamically via object factories.

A `DirStateFactory` extends `StateFactory` by allowing an `Attributes` instance to be supplied to and returned by `getStateToBind()`. `DirStateFactory` implementations are intended to be used by `DirContext` service providers. A caller that binds an object by using `DirContext.bind()` might also specify a set of attributes to be bound along with the object. The object and attributes to be bound are passed to a factory's `getStateToBind()`. If the factory processes the object and attributes, then it returns a corresponding pair of object and attributes to be bound. If the factory does not process the object, then it must return `null`.

For example, a caller might bind a printer object with some printer-related attributes:

```
ctx.rebind("inky", printer, printerAttrs);
```

An LDAP service provider for `ctx` uses a `DirStateFactory` (indirectly via `Directory-Manager.getStateToBind()`) and gives it `printer` and `printerAttrs`. A factory for an LDAP directory might turn `printer` into a set of attributes and merge that set with `printer-Attrs`. The service provider then might use the resulting attributes to create an LDAP entry and update the directory.

Because `DirStateFactory` extends `StateFactory`, it has two `getStateToBind()` methods, one differing from the other by the `Attributes` argument. Given a factory that implements `DirStateFactory`, `DirectoryManager.getStateToBind()` will use only the form that accepts the `Attributes` argument, whereas `NamingManager.getStateToBind()` will use only the form that does not accept that argument.

Either form of a `DirStateFactory`'s `getStateToBind()` may be invoked multiple times, possibly with different parameters used. The implementation is thread-safe.

See Also

`DirectoryManager.getStateToBind()`, `DirStateFactory.Result`, `NamingManager.getStateToBind()`, `StateFactory`.

MEMBER SUMMARY	
Factory Method	
getStateToBind()	Retrieves the state of an object for binding, when given the object and attributes to be transformed.

Example

See the **State Factories** lesson (page 175).

getStateToBind()

PURPOSE
: Retrieves the state of an object for binding, when given the object and attributes to be transformed.

SYNTAX
: ```
public DirStateFactory.Result getStateToBind(Object obj, Name
    name, Context nameCtx, Hashtable env, Attributes inAttrs)
    throws NamingException;
```

DESCRIPTION
: This method retrieves the state of an object for binding, when given the object and attributes to be transformed. `DirectoryManager.getStateToBind()` successively loads in state factories. If a factory implements `DirStateFactory`, then `DirectoryManager` invokes this method; otherwise, it invokes `StateFactory.getStateToBind()`. It does this until a factory produces a non-null answer.

An exception thrown by a factory is passed on to the caller of `DirectoryManager.getStateToBind()`, and the search for other factories that might produce a non-null answer is halted. A factory should throw an exception only if it is sure that it is the only intended factory and that no other factories should be tried. If this factory cannot create an object by using the arguments supplied, then it should return `null`.

The `name` and `nameCtx` parameters may optionally be used to specify the name of the object being created. See the description of *Name and Context Parameters* in `ObjectFactory` for details. If a factory uses `nameCtx`, then it should synchronize its use against concurrent access, since context implementations are not guaranteed to be thread-safe.

The `name`, `inAttrs`, and `env` parameters are owned by the caller. The implementation will not modify these objects or keep references to them, although it may keep references to clones or copies of them. The return value of this method also is owned by the caller; the implementation will not subsequently modify it. It will contain either a new `Attributes` object that is likewise owned by the caller or a reference to the original `inAttrs` parameter.
```

PARAMETERS

env   The possibly `null` environment to be used in the creation of the object's state.

inAttrs   The possibly `null` attributes to be bound with the object. The factory must not modify `inAttrs`.

name   The name of this object relative to `nameCtx`, or `null` if no name is specified.

nameCtx   The context relative to which the `name` parameter is specified, or `null` if `name` is relative to the default initial context.

obj   A possibly `null` object whose state to retrieve.

RETURNS   A `DirStateFactory.Result` that contains the object's state for binding and the corresponding attributes to be bound; `null` if the object doesn't use this factory.

D

EXCEPTIONS

NamingException
           If this factory encounters an exception while attempting to get the object's state and no other factories are to be tried.

SEE ALSO   `DirectoryManager.getStateToBind()`.

EXAMPLE   See the **State Factories** lesson (page 175).

DirStateFactory.Result

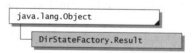

```
java.lang.Object
```
```
DirStateFactory.Result
```

Syntax

```
public static class DirStateFactory.Result
```

D

Description

DirStateFactory.Result is an object/attributes pair used to return the result of DirState-Factory.getStateToBind().

MEMBER SUMMARY	
Constructor	
DirStateFactory.Result()	Constructs an instance of Result.
Access Methods	
getAttributes()	Retrieves the attributes to be bound.
getObject()	Retrieves the object to be bound.

See Also

DirectoryManager.getStateToBind(), DirStateFactory.

Example

See the **State Factories** lesson (page 174).

DirStateFactory.Result()

PURPOSE	Constructs an instance of Result.
SYNTAX	public DirStateFactory.Result(Object obj, Attributes outAttrs)
PARAMETERS	
obj	The possibly null object to be bound.
outAttrs	The possibly null attributes to be bound.
EXAMPLE	See the **State Factories** lesson (page 177).

getAttributes()

PURPOSE   Retrieves the attributes to be bound.

SYNTAX   `public Attributes getAttributes()`

RETURNS   The possibly `null` attributes to be bound.

EXAMPLE   See the **State Factories** lesson (page 174).

getObject()

PURPOSE   Retrieves the object to be bound.

SYNTAX   `public Object getObject()`

RETURNS   The possibly `null` object to be bound.

EXAMPLE   See the **State Factories** lesson (page 174).

javax.naming.event
EventContext

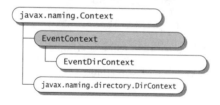

Syntax

```
public interface EventContext extends Context
```

Description

The `EventContext` interface contains methods for registering/deregistering listeners to be notified of events fired when objects named in a context change.

Target

The `name` parameter in the `addNamingListener()` methods is called the *target*. The target, along with the scope, identify the object(s) in which the listener is interested. Registering interest in a target that does not exist is possible, but the extent to which this can be supported by the service provider and underlying protocol/service might be limited.

If a service supports only registration for existing targets, then an attempt to register for a nonexistent target will result in a `NameNotFoundException`'s being thrown as early as possible, preferably at the time that `addNamingListener()` is called. If that is not possible, then the listener will receive the exception through the `NamingExceptionEvent`.

Also, for service providers that support only registration for existing targets, when the target that a listener has registered for is subsequently removed from the namespace, the listener will be notified via a `NamingExceptionEvent` (that contains a `NameNotFoundException`).

An application can use `targetMustExist()` to check whether an `EventContext` supports the registration of nonexistent targets.

Event Source

The `EventContext` instance on which you invoke the registration methods is the *event source* of the events that are (potentially) generated. The source is *not necessarily* the object named by the target. Only when the target is the empty name is the object named by the target the source. In other words, the target along with the scope parameter are used to identify the object(s) in which the listener is interested, but the event source is the `EventContext` instance with which the listener has registered.

For example, suppose that a listener makes the following registration.

```
NamespaceChangeListener listener = ...;
src.addNamingListener("x", SUBTREE_SCOPE, listener);
```

When an object named "x/y" is subsequently deleted, the corresponding NamingEvent (evt) must contain the following.

```
evt.getEventContext() == src
evt.getOldBinding().getName().equals("x/y")
```

Furthermore, listener registration/deregistration is with the EventContext *instance* and not with the corresponding object in the namespace. If the program intends at some point to remove a listener, then it needs to keep a reference to the EventContext instance on which it invoked addNamingListener() (just as it needs to keep a reference to the listener in order to remove it later). It cannot expect to do a lookup() and get another instance of a EventContext on which to perform the deregistration.

Lifetime of Registration
A registered listener becomes deregistered when any of the following occurs.

- It is removed by using removeNamingListener().
- It receives a NamingExceptionEvent.
- Context.close() is invoked on the EventContext instance with which it has registered.

Until then, an EventContext instance that has outstanding listeners will continue to exist and be maintained by the service provider.

Listener Implementations
The registration/deregistration methods accept a NamingListener instance. Subinterfaces of NamingListener exist for different event types of NamingEvents. For example, the ObjectChangeListener interface is for the NamingEvent.OBJECT_CHANGED event type.

To register interest in multiple event types, the listener implementation should implement multiple NamingListener subinterfaces and use a single invocation of addNamingListener(). Doing this not only reduces the number of method calls, and possibly the code size of the listeners, but also allows some service providers to optimize the registration.

Threading Issues
Like Context instances in general, EventContext instances are not guaranteed to be thread-safe. Care must be taken when multiple threads are accessing the same EventContext concurrently. See the javax.naming.event package description for more information on threading issues.

Example
See the **Event Notification** lesson (page 115).

MEMBER SUMMARY	
Registration/Deregistration Methods	
addNamingListener()	Adds a listener for receiving naming events.
removeNamingListener()	Removes a listener from receiving naming events.
Query Method	
targetMustExist()	Determines whether a listener can register interest in a target that does not exist.
Search Scope Constants	
OBJECT_SCOPE	Expresses interest in events that concern the object named by the target.
ONELEVEL_SCOPE	Expresses interest in events that concern objects in the context named by the target.
SUBTREE_SCOPE	Expresses interest in events that concern objects in the subtree of the object named by the target.

addNamingListener()

PURPOSE   Adds a listener for receiving naming events.

SYNTAX
```
public void addNamingListener(Name target, int scope,
    NamingListener l) throws NamingException;
public void addNamingListener(String target, int scope,
    NamingListener l) throws NamingException;
```

DESCRIPTION   This method adds a listener for receiving naming events fired when the object(s) identified by a target and scope change.

The event source of those events is this context. See the class description for a discussion on event source and target. See the descriptions of the constants OBJECT_SCOPE, ONELEVEL_SCOPE, and SUBTREE_SCOPE to see how scope affects the registration.

target needs to name a context only when scope is ONELEVEL_SCOPE. target may name a noncontext if scope is either OBJECT_SCOPE or SUBTREE_SCOPE. Using SUBTREE_SCOPE for a noncontext might be useful, for example if the caller does not know in advance whether target is a context and only wants to register interest in the (possibly degenerate subtree) rooted at target.

When the listener is notified of an event, it may be invoked in a thread other than the one in which addNamingListener() is executed. Care must be taken when multiple threads are accessing the same EventContext concurrently. See the javax.naming.event package description for more information on threading issues.

E

PARAMETERS

l   The non-null listener to register.

scope   One of OBJECT_SCOPE, ONELEVE_SCOPE, or SUBTREE_SCOPE.

target   A non-null name to be resolved relative to this context.

EXCEPTIONS

NamingException

                     If a problem is encountered while adding the listener.

SEE ALSO   removeNamingListener().

EXAMPLE   See the **Event Notification** lesson (page 115).

E

OBJECT_SCOPE

PURPOSE   Expresses interest in events that concern the object named by the target.

SYNTAX   public final static int OBJECT_SCOPE

DESCRIPTION   This constant is used to express interest in events that concern the object named by the target.

                 The value of this constant is 0.

EXAMPLE   See the **Event Notification** lesson (page 116).

ONELEVEL_SCOPE

PURPOSE   Expresses interest in events that concern objects in the context named by the target.

SYNTAX   public final static int ONELEVEL_SCOPE

DESCRIPTION   This constant is used to express interest in events that concern objects in the context named by the target, excluding the context named by the target.

                 The value of this constant is 1.

EXAMPLE   See the **Event Notification** lesson (page 115).

removeNamingListener()

PURPOSE   Removes a listener from receiving naming events.

SYNTAX   public void removeNamingListener(NamingListener l) throws
                     NamingException

DESCRIPTION   This method removes a listener from receiving naming events fired by this EventContext. The listener may have registered more than once with this

EventContext, perhaps with different target/scope arguments. After this method is invoked, the listener will no longer receive events with this Event-Context instance as the event source (except for those events already in the process of being dispatched). If the listener was not, or is no longer, registered with this EventContext instance, then this method does nothing.

PARAMETERS

l   The non-null listener.

EXCEPTIONS

NamingException

If a problem is encountered while removing the listener.

SEE ALSO   addNamingListener().

EXAMPLE   See the **Event Notification** lesson (page 117).

SUBTREE_SCOPE

PURPOSE   Expresses interest in events that concern objects in the subtree of the object named by the target.

SYNTAX   `public final static int SUBTREE_SCOPE`

DESCRIPTION   This constant is used to express interest in events that concern objects in the subtree of the object named by the target, including the object named by the target.

The value of this constant is 2.

EXAMPLE   See the **Event Notification** lesson (page 116).

targetMustExist()

PURPOSE   Determines whether a listener can register interest in a target that does not exist.

SYNTAX   `public boolean targetMustExist() throws NamingException`

RETURNS   true if the target must exist; false if the target need not exist.

EXCEPTIONS

NamingException

If the context's behavior in this regard cannot be determined.

EXAMPLE   See the **Event Notification** lesson (page 116).

EventDirContext

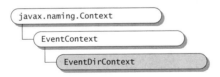

Syntax

```
public interface EventDirContext extends EventContext, DirContext
```

E

Description

The EventDirContext interface contains methods for registering listeners to be notified of events fired when objects named in a directory context change.

The methods in this interface support the identification of objects by RFC 2254 search filters. Using the search filter, you can register interest in objects that do not exist at the time of registration but that later come into existence and satisfy the filter. However, the extent to which this can be supported by the service provider and underlying protocol/service might be limited. If the caller submits a filter that cannot be supported in this way, then addNaming-Listener() throws an InvalidSearchFilterException.

See EventContext for a description of event source and target and for information about listener registration/deregistration that also applies to methods in this interface. See the javax.naming.event package description for information on threading issues.

A SearchControls or array object passed as a parameter to any method is owned by the caller. The service provider will not modify the object or keep a reference to it.

MEMBER SUMMARY	
Registration Method	
addNamingListener()	Adds a listener for receiving naming events.

Example

See the **Event Notification** lesson (page 117).

addNamingListener()

PURPOSE	Adds a listener for receiving naming events.
SYNTAX	public void addNamingListener(Name target, String filter, SearchControls ctls, NamingListener l) throws NamingException

```
public void addNamingListener(String target, String filter,
    SearchControls ctls, NamingListener l) throws NamingException
public void addNamingListener(Name target, String filterExpr,
    Object[] filterArgs, SearchControls ctls, NamingListener l)
    throws NamingException;
public void addNamingListener(String target, String filterExpr,
    Object[] filterArgs, SearchControls ctls, NamingListener l)
    throws NamingException
```

DESCRIPTION   This method adds a listener for receiving naming events fired when changes
are made to objects that are identified by the search filter, `filter`, or a search
filter expression, `filterExpr`, with arguments (`filterArgs`) at the object
named by `target`. See `javax.naming.directory.DirContext.search()` for
descriptions of the format of `filter`, `filterExpr`, and `filterArgs`.

The `scope`, `returningObj` flag, and `returningAttributes` flag from the
search controls, `ctls`, are used to control the selection of objects that the listener is interested in and determine the information that is returned in the even-
tual `NamingEvent` object. Note that the requested information to be returned
might not be present in the `NamingEvent` object if it is unavailable or could not
be obtained by the service provider or service.

PARAMETERS
ctls   The possibly `null` search controls to use. If `null`, then the default search controls are used.

filter   The non-`null` filter to use for the search.

filterArgs   The array of arguments to substitute for the variables in `filterExpr`. The
value of `filterArgs[i]` will replace each occurrence of $\{i\}$. `null` is equivalent to an empty array.

filterExpr   The filter expression to use for the search. The expression may contain variables of the form $\{i\}$, where i is a nonnegative integer. May not be `null`.

l   The non-`null` listener.

target   The name of the object or context to search.

EXCEPTIONS
NamingException
               If a problem is encountered while adding the listener.

SEE ALSO   `EventContext.removeNamingListener()`,
               `javax.naming.directory.DirContext.search()`,
               `javax.naming.directory.SearchControls`.

EXAMPLE   See the **Event Notification** lesson (page 117).

ExtendedRequest

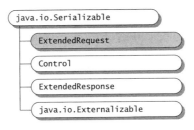

```
java.io.Serializable
    ExtendedRequest
    Control
    ExtendedResponse
    java.io.Externalizable
```

E

Syntax

`public interface ExtendedRequest extends java.io.Serializable`

Description

The `ExtendedRequest` interface represents an LDAP v3 "extended" operation request as defined in RFC 2251.

```
ExtendedRequest ::= [APPLICATION 23] SEQUENCE {
    requestName [0] LDAPOID,
    requestValue [1] OCTET STRING OPTIONAL
}
```

It consists of an object identifier string and an optional ASN.1 BER encoded value.

The service provider uses methods in this class to construct the bits to send to the LDAP server. Applications typically deal only with the classes that implement this interface, supplying them with any information required for a particular "extended" operation request. It would then pass such a class as an argument to `LdapContext.extendedOperation()` for performing the LDAP v3 "extended" operation.

MEMBER SUMMARY	
Access Methods	
`getEncodedValue()`	Retrieves the ASN.1 BER encoded value of the LDAP "extended" operation request.
`getID()`	Retrieves the object identifier of the request.
Response Creation Method	
`createExtendedResponse()`	Creates the response object that corresponds to this request.

See Also

`ExtendedResponse`, `LdapContext.extendedOperation()`.

Example

Suppose that the LDAP server supports a Get Time "extended" operation. It would supply the GetTimeRequest and GetTimeResponse classes.

```
public class GetTimeRequest implements ExtendedRequest {
    public GetTimeRequest() { ... };
    public ExtendedResponse createExtendedResponse(String id,
        byte[] berValue, int offset, int length) throws NamingException {
        return new GetTimeResponse(id, berValue, offset, length);
    }
    ...
}
public class GetTimeResponse implements ExtendedResponse {
    private long time;
    public GetTimeResponse(String id, byte[] berValue, int offset,
        int length) throws NamingException {
        time = ... // Decode berValue to get the time
    }
    public java.util.Date getDate() {
        return new java.util.Date(time)
    };
    public long getTime() {
        return time;
    };
    ...
}
```

A program would then use these classes as follows.

```
GetTimeResponse resp = (GetTimeResponse) ectx.extendedOperation(
    new GetTimeRequest());
long time = resp.getTime();
```

createExtendedResponse()

PURPOSE   Creates the response object that corresponds to this request.

SYNTAX   public ExtendedResponse createExtendedResponse(String id, byte[]
                berValue, int offset, int length) throws NamingException

DESCRIPTION   This method creates the response object that corresponds to this request. After the service provider sends the "extended" operation request to the LDAP server, it will receive a response from the server. If the operation fails, then the provider will throw a NamingException. If the operation succeeds, then the provider will invoke this method by using the data that it got back in the response. It is this method's job to return a class that implements the ExtendedResponse interface that is appropriate for the "extended" operation request.

                For example, a Start TLS extended request class would need to know how to process a Start TLS extended response. It does this by creating a class that implements ExtendedResponse.

PARAMETERS

berValue	The possibly null ASN.1 BER encoded value of the response control. This value is the raw BER bytes, including the tag and length of the response value. It does not include the response OID.
id	The possibly null object identifier of the response control.
length	The number of bytes in berValue to use.
offset	The starting position in berValue of the bytes to use.

RETURNS   A non-null object.

EXCEPTIONS

NamingException

     If cannot create an extended response due to an error.

SEE ALSO   ExtendedResponse.

EXAMPLE   See class example.

E

getEncodedValue()

PURPOSE   Retrieves the ASN.1 BER encoded value of the LDAP "extended" operation request.

SYNTAX   `public byte[] getEncodedValue()`

DESCRIPTION   This method retrieves the ASN.1 BER encoded value of the LDAP "extended" operation request. null is returned if the value is absent.

     The result is the raw BER bytes, including the tag and length of the request value. It does not include the request OID. This method is called by the service provider to get the bits to put into the "extended" operation to be sent to the LDAP server.

RETURNS   A possibly null byte array that represents the ASN.1 BER encoded contents of the LDAP ExtendedRequest.requestValue component.

EXCEPTIONS

IllegalStateException

     If the encoded value cannot be retrieved because the request contains insufficient or invalid data/state.

EXAMPLE   See the class example.

getID()

PURPOSE   Retrieves the object identifier of the request.

SYNTAX   `public String getID()`

getID()

RETURNS   The non-null object identifier string that represents the LDAP Extended-
              Request.requestName component.

EXAMPLE   See the class example.

E

ExtendedResponse

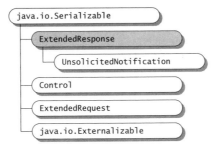

E

Syntax

```
public interface ExtendedResponse extends java.io.Serializable
```

Description

The `ExtendedReponse` interface represents an LDAP "extended" operation response as defined in RFC 2251.

```
ExtendedResponse ::= [APPLICATION 24] SEQUENCE {
    COMPONENTS OF LDAPResult,
    responseName [10] LDAPOID OPTIONAL,
    response [11] OCTET STRING OPTIONAL
}
```

It consists of an optional object identifier and an optional ASN.1 BER encoded value.

The application can use the methods in this class to get low-level information about the "extended" operation response. However, typically, it will use methods specific to the class that implements this interface. Such a class should have decoded the BER buffer in the response and should provide methods that allow the user to access that data in the response in a type-safe and friendly manner.

MEMBER SUMMARY	
Access Methods	
`getEncodedValue()`	Retrieves the ASN.1 BER encoded value of the LDAP "extended" operation response.
`getID()`	Retrieves the object identifier of the response.

See Also

`ExtendedRequest`, `LdapContext.extendedOperation()`.

Example

Suppose that the LDAP server supports a Get Time "extended" operation. It would supply `GetTimeRequest` and `GetTimeResponse` classes. The `GetTimeResponse` class might look like the following.

```
public class GetTimeResponse implements ExtendedResponse {
    public java.util.Date getDate() {...};
    public long getTime() {...};
    ....
}
```

A program would then use these classes as follows.

```
GetTimeResponse resp = (GetTimeResponse) ectx.extendedOperation(
    new GetTimeRequest());
java.util.Date now = resp.getDate();
```

getEncodedValue()

PURPOSE   Retrieves the ASN.1 BER encoded value of the LDAP "extended" operation response.

SYNTAX   `public byte[] getEncodedValue()`

DESCRIPTION   This method retrieves the ASN.1 BER encoded value of the LDAP "extended" operation response. `null` is returned if the value is absent from the response sent by the LDAP server. The result is the raw BER bytes, including the tag and length of the response value. It does not include the response OID.

RETURNS   A possibly `null` byte array that represents the ASN.1 BER encoded contents of the LDAP `ExtendedResponse.response` component.

EXAMPLE   See the class example.

getID()

PURPOSE   Retrieves the object identifier of the response.

SYNTAX   `public String getID()`

DESCRIPTION   This method retrieves the object identifier of the response. The LDAP protocol specifies that the response object identifier is optional. If the server does not send it, then the response will contain no ID (i.e., `null`).

RETURNS   A possibly `null` object identifier string that represents the LDAP `Extended-Response.responseName` component.

EXAMPLE   See the class example.

HasControls

Syntax
```
public interface HasControls
```

Description
The HasControls interface is used to return controls with objects returned in Naming-
Enumerations.

MEMBER SUMMARY

Access Method

getControls()   Retrieves an array of Control objects from the object that
                 implements this interface.

See Also
```
javax.naming.Context.list(), javax.naming.Context.listBindings(),
javax.naming.directory.DirContext.search(),
javax.naming.ldap.LdapContext.getResponseControls().
```

Example
Suppose that a server sends back controls with the results of a "search" operation. The service provider would return a NamingEnumeration of objects that are both SearchResult and implement HasControls.

```
NamingEnumeration enum = ectx.search((Name)name, filter, sctls);
while (enum.hasMore()) {
    Object entry = enum.next();
    // Get search result
    SearchResult res = (SearchResult)entry;
    // do something with it

    // Get entry controls
    if (entry instanceof HasControls) {
        Control[] entryCtls = ((HasControls)entry).getControls();
        // Do something with controls
    }
}
```

getControls()

PURPOSE   Retrieves an array of `Control` objects from the object that implements this interface.

SYNTAX   `public Control[] getControls() throws NamingException`

DESCRIPTION   This method retrieves an array of `Control` objects from the object that implements this interface. It is `null` if there are no controls.

RETURNS   A possibly `null` array of `Control` objects.

EXCEPTIONS

  `NamingException`

           If cannot return controls due to an error.

EXAMPLE   See the class example.

H

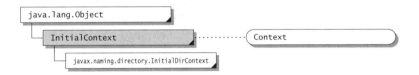

```
java.lang.Object
     InitialContext ............ Context
          javax.naming.directory.InitialDirContext
```

Syntax

```
public class InitialContext implements Context
```

Description

The `InitialContext` class is the starting context for performing naming operations.

All naming operations are relative to a context. The initial context implements the `Context` interface and provides the starting point for resolving names.

Environment Properties

When the initial context is constructed, its environment is initialized with properties that are defined in the environment parameter that is passed to the constructor and in any application resource files. In addition, a small number of standard JNDI properties may be specified as system properties or as applet parameters (through the use of `Context.APPLET`). These special properties are listed in the field detail sections of the `Context` and `LdapContext` interface documentation.

The JNDI determines each property's value by merging the values from the following two sources, in order:

1. The first occurrence of the property from the constructor's environment parameter and, for appropriate properties, the applet parameters and system properties
2. The application resource files (`jndi.properties`)

For each property found in both of these two sources, or in more than one application resource file, the property's value is determined as follows. If the property is one of the standard JNDI properties that specify a list of JNDI factories (see `Context`), then all of the values are concatenated into a single colon-separated list. For other properties, only the first value found is used.

Implementation Class

The initial context implementation is determined at runtime. The default policy uses the environment property `Context.INITIAL_CONTEXT_FACTORY` (`"java.naming.factory.initial"`), which contains the class name of the initial context factory. An exception to this policy is made when resolving URL strings, as described shortly.

A NoInitialContextException is thrown when an initial context cannot be instantiated. It can be thrown during any interaction with the InitialContext, not only when the InitialContext is constructed. For example, the implementation of the initial context might lazily retrieve the context only when actual methods are invoked on it. The application should not depend on when the existence of an initial context is determined.

When the environment property "java.naming.factory.initial" is non-null, the InitialContext constructor will attempt to create the initial context specified therein. At that time, the initial context factory involved might throw an exception if it encounters a problem. However, it is provider implementation-dependent as to when the factory verifies and indicates to the users of the initial context that there is an environment property- or connection-related problem. It can do so lazily—by delaying until an operation is performed on the context—or eagerly, at the time that the context is constructed.

URL Support

When a URL string (a String of the form *scheme_id:rest_of_name*) is passed as a name parameter to any method, a URL context factory for handling that scheme is located and used to resolve the URL. If no such factory is found, then the initial context specified by "java.naming.factory.initial" is used. Similarly, when a CompositeName object whose first component is a URL string is passed as a name parameter to any method, then a URL context factory is located and used to resolve the first name component. See NamingManager.getURLContext() for a description of how URL context factories are located.

This default policy of locating the initial context and URL context factories may be overridden by calling NamingManager.setInitialContextFactoryBuilder().

Concurrent Access

An InitialContext instance is not synchronized against concurrent access by multiple threads. Multiple threads each manipulating a different InitialContext instance need not synchronize. Threads that need to access a single InitialContext instance concurrently should synchronize among themselves and provide the necessary locking.

MEMBER SUMMARY

Constructor

InitialContext()	Constructs an instance of InitialContext.

Protected Methods and Fields Useful to Subclasses

defaultInitCtx	Holds the result of calling NamingManager.getInitialContext().
getDefaultInitCtx()	Retrieves the underlying initial context implementation.
getURLOrDefaultInitCtx()	Retrieves a URL context or the underlying initial context implementation for resolving a name.

MEMBER SUMMARY	
`gotDefault`	Indicates whether the underlying initial context implementation has been obtained.
`init()`	Initializes the initial context by using the supplied environment.
`myProps`	Holds the environment associated with this `InitialContext`.
Context Methods	
`bind()`	Binds a name to an object.
`close()`	Closes this context.
`composeName()`	Composes the name of this context with a name relative to this context.
`createSubcontext()`	Creates and binds a new context.
`destroySubcontext()`	Destroys the named context, and removes it from the namespace.
`getNameInNamespace()`	Retrieves the full name of this context within its own namespace.
`getNameParser()`	Retrieves the parser associated with the named context.
`list()`	Enumerates the names bound in the named context, along with the class names of objects bound to them.
`listBindings()`	Enumerates the names bound in the named context, along with the objects bound to them.
`lookup()`	Retrieves the named object.
`lookupLink()`	Retrieves the named object, following links except for the terminal atomic component of the name.
`rebind()`	Binds a name to an object, overwriting any existing binding.
`rename()`	Binds a new name to the object bound to an old name, and unbinds the old name.
`unbind()`	Unbinds the named object.
Environment Methods	
`addToEnvironment()`	Adds a new environment property to the environment of this context.
`getEnvironment()`	Retrieves the environment in effect for this context.
`removeFromEnvironment()`	Removes an environment property from the environment of this context.

Example

See the **Preparations** lesson (page 49) and the **URLs** lesson (page 123).

addToEnvironment()

PURPOSE   Adds a new environment property to the environment of this context.

| SYNTAX | `public Object addToEnvironment(String propName, Object propVal)`
`    throws NamingException` |

PARAMETERS

| propName | The name of the environment property to add. May not be `null`. |
| propVal | The value of the property to add. May not be `null`. |

| RETURNS | The previous value of the property, or `null` if the property was not previously in the environment. |

EXCEPTIONS

`NamingException`
> If a naming exception is encountered.

| SEE ALSO | `Context.addToEnvironment()`. |

bind()

| PURPOSE | Binds a name to an object. |

| SYNTAX | `public void bind(Name name, Object obj) throws NamingException`
`public void bind(String name, Object obj) throws NamingException` |

PARAMETERS

| name | The name to bind. May not be empty. |
| obj | The object to bind; possibly `null`. |

EXCEPTIONS

`javax.naming.directory.InvalidAttributesException`
> If the object did not supply all mandatory attributes.

`NameAlreadyBoundException`
> If name is already bound.

`NamingException`
> If a naming exception is encountered.

| SEE ALSO | `Context.bind()`. |

close()

| PURPOSE | Closes this context. |

| SYNTAX | `public void close() throws NamingException` |

EXCEPTIONS

`NamingException`
> If a naming exception is encountered.

| SEE ALSO | `Context.close()`. |

composeName()

PURPOSE	Composes the name of this context with a name relative to this context.

SYNTAX	`public Name composeName(Name name, Name prefix) throws`
	`    NamingException`
	`public String composeName(String name, String prefix) throws`
	`    NamingException`

DESCRIPTION	Since an initial context can never be named relative to itself, `prefix` must be an empty name.

PARAMETERS

`name`	A name relative to this context.
`prefix`	The name of this context relative. Must be an empty name.

RETURNS	The composition of `prefix` and `name`.

EXCEPTIONS

`NamingException`

        If a naming exception is encountered.

SEE ALSO	`Context.composeName()`.

createSubcontext()

PURPOSE	Creates and binds a new context.

SYNTAX	`public Context createSubcontext(Name name) throws`
	`    NamingException`
	`public Context createSubcontext(String name) throws`
	`    NamingException`

PARAMETERS

`name`	The name of the context to create. May not be empty.

RETURNS	The newly created context.

EXCEPTIONS

`javax.naming.directory.InvalidAttributesException`

        If the creation of the subcontext requires that mandatory attributes be specified.

`NameAlreadyBoundException`

        If `name` is already bound.

`NamingException`

        If a naming exception is encountered.

SEE ALSO	`Context.createSubcontext()`.

defaultInitCtx

PURPOSE	Holds the result of calling `NamingManager.getInitialContext()`.
SYNTAX	`protected Context defaultInitCtx`
DESCRIPTION	This field holds the result of calling `NamingManager.getInitialContext()`. It is set by `getDefaultInitCtx()` the first time that `getDefaultInitCtx()` is called. Subsequent invocations of `getDefaultInitCtx()` return the value of `defaultInitCtx`.
SEE ALSO	`getDefaultInitCtx()`.

destroySubcontext()

PURPOSE   Destroys the named context, and removes it from the namespace.

SYNTAX
```
public void destroySubcontext(Name name) throws NamingException
public void destroySubcontext(String name) throws
    NamingException
```

PARAMETERS

name   The name of the context to be destroyed. May not be empty.

EXCEPTIONS

`ContextNotEmptyException`
    If the named context is not empty.
`NameNotFoundException`
    If an intermediate context does not exist.
`NamingException`
    If a naming exception is encountered.
`NotContextException`
    If `name` is bound but does not name a context or does not name a context of the appropriate type.

SEE ALSO   `Context.destroySubcontext()`.

getDefaultInitCtx()

PURPOSE   Retrieves the underlying initial context implementation.

SYNTAX   `protected Context getDefaultInitCtx() throws NamingException`

DESCRIPTION   This method retrieves the underlying initial context implementation by calling `NamingManager.getInitialContext()` and caching it in `defaultInitCtx`. It sets `gotDefault` to indicate that this has been tried before.

RETURNS   The non-`null` cached underlying initial context implementation.

EXCEPTIONS

`NamingException`

>If a naming exception is encountered.

`NoInitialContextException`

>If cannot find an underlying initial context implementation.

SEE ALSO   `defaultInitCtx, gotDefault, getURLOrDefaultInitCtx()`.

EXAMPLE   See the **Adding URL Support** lesson (page 369).

getEnvironment()

PURPOSE   Retrieves the environment in effect for this context.

SYNTAX   `public Hashtable getEnvironment() throws NamingException`

RETURNS   The environment of this context. Never `null`.

EXCEPTIONS

`NamingException`

>If a naming exception is encountered.

SEE ALSO   `Context.getEnvironment()`.

getNameInNamespace()

PURPOSE   Retrieves the full name of this context within its own namespace.

SYNTAX   `public String getNameInNamespace() throws NamingException`

RETURNS   This context's name in its own namespace. Never `null`.

EXCEPTIONS

`NamingException`

>If a naming exception is encountered.

`OperationNotSupportedException`

>If the naming system does not have the notion of a full name.

SEE ALSO   `Context.getNameInNamespace()`.

getNameParser()

PURPOSE   Retrieves the parser associated with the named context.

SYNTAX   `public NameParser getNameParser(Name name) throws`
        `NamingException`
        `public NameParser getNameParser(String name) throws`
        `NamingException`

PARAMETERS

name   The name of the context from which to get the parser.

RETURNS   A name parser that can parse compound names into their atomic components.

EXCEPTIONS

NamingException

                If a naming exception is encountered

SEE ALSO   Context.getNameParser().

getURLOrDefaultInitCtx()

PURPOSE   Retrieves a URL context or the underlying initial context implementation for resolving a name.

SYNTAX   ```
protected Context getURLOrDefaultInitCtx(Name name) throws
    NamingException
protected Context getURLOrDefaultInitCtx(String name) throws
    NamingException
```

DESCRIPTION     This method retrieves a URL context or the underlying initial context implementation for resolving the name name. If name is a Name and if its first component is a URL string, then this method attempts to find a URL context for the URL string. If no context is found, or if the first component of name is not a URL string, then it returns getDefaultInitCtx().

                The second form retrieves a context for resolving the string name name. If name is a URL string, then this method attempts to find a URL context for it. If no context is found or if name is not a URL string, then getDefaultInitCtx() is returned.

                When creating a subclass of InitialContext, use this method as follows. Define a new method that uses this method to get an initial context of the desired subclass.

```
protected XXXContext getURLOrDefaultInitXXXCtx(Name name)
    throws NamingException {
    Context answer = getURLOrDefaultInitCtx(name);
    if (!(answer instanceof XXXContext)) {
        if (answer == null) {
            throw new NoInitialContextException();
        } else {
            throw new NotContextException("Not an XXXContext");
        }
    }
    return (XXXContext)answer;
}
```

                When providing implementations for the new methods in the subclass, use this newly defined method to get the initial context.
```

```
public Object XXXMethod1(Name name, ...) throws NamingException {
    return getURLOrDefaultInitXXXCtx(name).XXXMethod1(name, ...);
}
```

PARAMETERS

name   The non-null name for which to get the context.

RETURNS   A URL context for name or the cached initial context. The result cannot be null.

EXCEPTIONS

NamingException

If a naming exception is encountered.

NoInitialContextException

If cannot find an initial context.

SEE ALSO   javax.naming.spi.NamingManager.getURLContext().

EXAMPLE   See the **Adding URL Support** lesson (page 369).

gotDefault

PURPOSE   Indicates whether the underlying initial context implementation has been obtained.

SYNTAX   `protected boolean gotDefault`

DESCRIPTION   This field indicates whether the underlying initial context implementation has been obtained by calling NamingManager.getInitialContext(). If true, its result is in defaultInitCtx.

SEE ALSO   defaultInitCtx, getDefaultInitCtx().

init()

PURPOSE   Initializes the initial context by using the supplied environment.

SYNTAX   `protected void init(Hashtable env) throws NamingException`

DESCRIPTION   This method initializes the initial context implementation by using the supplied environment, env. Environment properties are discussed in the class description. This method will modify env and save a reference to it. The caller then may no longer modify it.

PARAMETERS

env   The environment used to create the initial context; null indicates an empty environment.

InitialContext()

EXCEPTIONS

`NamingException`

If a naming exception is encountered.

SEE ALSO   `InitialContext().`

InitialContext()

PURPOSE   Constructs an instance of `InitialContext`.

SYNTAX
```
public InitialContext() throws NamingException
public InitialContext(Hashtable env) throws NamingException
protected InitialContext(boolean lazy) throws NamingException
```

DESCRIPTION These constructors construct an instance of `InitialContext`. The first form constructs an initial context with no environment properties. It is equivalent to

```
new InitialContext(null)
```

The second form constructs an initial context by using the supplied environment, env. Environment properties are discussed in the class description. This constructor will not modify env or save a reference to it, but it may save a clone of it.

The third form constructs an initial context with the option of not initializing it. This might be used by a constructor in a subclass when the value of the environment parameter is not known when the `InitialContext` constructor is called. The subclass's constructor will call this constructor, compute the value of the environment, and then call `init()` before returning.

PARAMETERS

env   The environment used to create the initial context; `null` indicates an empty environment.

lazy   `true` means do not initialize the initial context; `false` is equivalent to calling `new InitialContext()`.

EXCEPTIONS

`NamingException`

If a naming exception is encountered.

SEE ALSO   `init().`

list()

PURPOSE   Enumerates the names bound in the named context, along with the class names of objects bound to them.

SYNTAX   `public NamingEnumeration list(Name name) throws NamingException`

```
public NamingEnumeration list(String name) throws
    NamingException
```

PARAMETERS

name   The name of the context to list.

RETURNS   An enumeration of the names and class names of the bindings in this context. Each element of the enumeration is of type `NameClassPair`.

EXCEPTIONS

`NamingException`

      If a naming exception is encountered.

SEE ALSO   `Context.list()`.

listBindings()

PURPOSE   Enumerates the names bound in the named context, along with the objects bound to them.

SYNTAX

```
public NamingEnumeration listBindings(Name name) throws
    NamingException
public NamingEnumeration listBindings(String name) throws
    NamingException
```

PARAMETERS

name   The name of the context to list.

RETURNS   An enumeration of the bindings in this context. Each element of the enumeration is of type `Binding`.

EXCEPTIONS

`NamingException`

      If a naming exception is encountered.

SEE ALSO   `Context.listBindings()`.

lookup()

PURPOSE   Retrieves the named object.

SYNTAX

```
public Object lookup(Name name) throws NamingException
public Object lookup(String name) throws NamingException
```

PARAMETERS

name   The name of the object to look up.

RETURNS   The object bound to `name`.

EXCEPTIONS

`NamingException`

If a naming exception is encountered.

SEE ALSO　　　`Context.lookup()`.

lookupLink()

PURPOSE　　　Retrieves the named object, following links except for the terminal atomic component of the name.

SYNTAX

```
public Object lookupLink(Name name) throws NamingException
public Object lookupLink(String name) throws NamingException
```

PARAMETERS

name　　　The name of the object to look up.

RETURNS　　　The object bound to `name`, not following the terminal link (if any).

EXCEPTIONS

`NamingException`

If a naming exception is encountered.

SEE ALSO　　　`Context.lookupLink()`.

myProps

PURPOSE　　　The environment associated with this `InitialContext`.

SYNTAX　　　`protected Hashtable myProps`

DESCRIPTION　　　The environment associated with this `InitialContext`. It is initialized to `null` and is updated either by the constructor that accepts an environment or by `init()`.

SEE ALSO　　　`addToEnvironment()`, `getEnvironment()`, `removeFromEnvironment()`.

removeFromEnvironment()

PURPOSE　　　Removes an environment property from the environment of this context.

SYNTAX

```
public Object removeFromEnvironment(String propName) throws
    NamingException
```

PARAMETERS

propName　　　The name of the environment property to remove. May not be `null`.

RETURNS　　　The previous value of the property, or `null` if the property was not in the environment.

EXCEPTIONS

`NamingException`

If a naming exception is encountered.

SEE ALSO   `Context.removeFromEnvironment()`.

rename()

PURPOSE   Binds a new name to the object bound to an old name, and unbinds the old name.

SYNTAX

```
public void rename(Name oldName, Name newName) throws
    NamingException
public void rename(String oldName, String newName) throws
    NamingException
```

PARAMETERS

`newName`   The name of the new binding. May not be empty.

`oldName`   The name of the existing binding. May not be empty.

EXCEPTIONS

`NameAlreadyBoundException`

If `newName` is already bound.

`NamingException`

If a naming exception is encountered.

SEE ALSO   `Context.rename()`.

unbind()

PURPOSE   Unbinds the named object.

SYNTAX

```
public void unbind(Name name) throws NamingException
public void unbind(String name) throws NamingException
```

PARAMETERS

`name`   The name to unbind. May not be empty.

EXCEPTIONS

`NameNotFoundException`

If an intermediate context does not exist.

`NamingException`

If a naming exception is encountered.

SEE ALSO   `Context.unbind()`.

InitialContextFactory

InitialContextFactory

Syntax

```
public interface InitialContextFactory
```

Description

The InitialContextFactory interface represents a factory that creates an initial context.

The JNDI framework allows for different initial context implementations to be specified at runtime. The initial context is created by using an *initial context factory*. An initial context factory must implement the InitialContextFactory interface, which provides a method for creating instances of initial contexts that implement the Context interface. In addition, the factory class must be public and must have a public constructor that accepts no arguments.

MEMBER SUMMARY	
Factory Method	
getInitialContext()	Creates an initial context for beginning name resolution.

See Also

```
InitialContextFactoryBuilder, javax.naming.InitialContext,
javax.naming.directory.InitialDirContext,
javax.naming.ldap.InitialLdapContext, NamingManager.getInitialContext().
```

Example

See **The Essentials Components** lesson (page 343).

getInitialContext()

PURPOSE   Creates an initial context for beginning name resolution.

SYNTAX   ```
            public Context getInitialContext(Hashtable env) throws
                NamingException
            ```

DESCRIPTION This method creates an initial Context (or one of its subclass) for beginning name resolution. Special requirements of this context are supplied by using env.
            ```

The env parameter is owned by the caller. The implementation will not modify the object or keep a reference to it, although it may keep a reference to a clone or copy of it.

PARAMETERS

env   The possibly `null` environment that specifies the information to be used in the creation of the initial context.

RETURNS   A non-`null` initial context object that implements the `Context` interface.

EXCEPTIONS

NamingException

If cannot create an initial context.

EXAMPLE   See **The Essentials Components** lesson (page 343).

InitialContextFactoryBuilder

Syntax
```
public interface InitialContextFactoryBuilder
```

Description

The `InitialContextFactoryBuilder` interface represents a builder that creates initial context factories.

The JNDI framework allows for different initial context implementations to be specified at runtime. An initial context is created by using an initial context factory. By calling `Naming-Manager.setInitialContextFactoryBuilder()`, a program can install its own builder that creates initial context factories, thereby overriding the default policies used by the framework. The `InitialContextFactoryBuilder` interface must be implemented by such a builder.

MEMBER SUMMARY
Factory Method
`createInitialContextFactory()` Creates an initial context factory by using the specified environment.

See Also

`InitialContextFactory`, `NamingManager.getInitialContext()`,
`NamingManager.hasInitialContextFactoryBuilder()`,
`NamingManager.setInitialContextFactoryBuilder()`.

createInitialContextFactory()

PURPOSE   Creates an initial context factory by using the specified environment.

SYNTAX
```
public InitialContextFactory
    createInitialContextFactory(Hashtable env) throws
    NamingException
```

DESCRIPTION   This method creates an initial context factory by using the specified environment. The env parameter is owned by the caller. The implementation will not modify the object or keep a reference to it, although it may keep a reference to a clone or copy of it.

PARAMETERS

env Environment used in creating an initial context implementation. May be `null`.

RETURNS A non-`null` initial context factory.

EXCEPTIONS

`NamingException`

If cannot create an initial context factory.

InitialDirContext

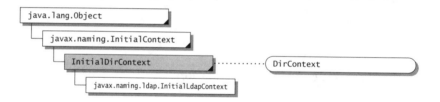

```
java.lang.Object
    javax.naming.InitialContext
        InitialDirContext ............ DirContext
            javax.naming.ldap.InitialLdapContext
```

Syntax

```
public class InitialDirContext extends InitialContext implements DirContext
```

Description

The `InitialDirContext` class is the starting context for performing directory operations. The documentation in the class description of `InitialContext` (including that for synchronization) applies here.

MEMBER SUMMARY

Constructor

`InitialDirContext()`	Constructs an instance of `InitialDirContext`.

Directory Methods

`getAttributes()`	Retrieves the attributes associated with a named object.
`modifyAttributes()`	Modifies the attributes associated with a named object.
`search()`	Searches a context or subcontexts.

Hybrid Naming and Directory Service Methods

`bind()`	Binds a name to an object, along with associated attributes.
`createSubcontext()`	Creates and binds a new context, along with associated attributes.
`rebind()`	Binds a name to an object, along with associated attributes, overwriting any existing binding.

Schema Methods

`getSchema()`	Retrieves the schema associated with the named object.
`getSchemaClass-Definition()`	Retrieves a context that contains the schema objects of the named object's class definitions.

See Also

`javax.naming.ldap.InitialLdapContext`.

Example

See the **Directory Operations** lesson (page 59) and the **Miscellaneous** lesson (page 246).

bind()

PURPOSE   Binds a name to an object, along with associated attributes.

SYNTAX
```
public void bind(Name name, Object obj, Attributes attrs) throws
    NamingException
public void bind(String name, Object obj, Attributes attrs)
    throws NamingException
```

PARAMETERS

`attrs`   The attributes to associate with the binding.

`name`   The name to bind. May not be empty.

`obj`   The object to bind; possibly `null`.

EXCEPTIONS

`InvalidAttributesException`
    If some mandatory attributes of the binding are not supplied.

`NameAlreadyBoundException`
    If `name` is already bound.

`NamingException`
    If a naming exception is encountered.

SEE ALSO   `DirContext.bind()`.

createSubcontext()

PURPOSE   Creates and binds a new context, along with associated attributes.

SYNTAX
```
public DirContext createSubcontext(Name name, Attributes attrs)
    throws NamingException
public DirContext createSubcontext(String name, Attributes
    attrs) throws NamingException
```

PARAMETERS

`attrs`   The attributes to associate with the newly created context.

`name`   The name of the context to create. May not be empty.

RETURNS   The newly created context.

EXCEPTIONS

`InvalidAttributesException`
    If `attrs` does not contain all of the mandatory attributes required for creating the new context.

NameAlreadyBoundException
>   If name is already bound.

NamingException
>   If a naming exception is encountered.

SEE ALSO   DirContext.createSubcontext().

getAttributes()

PURPOSE   Retrieves the attributes associated with a named object.

SYNTAX   public Attributes getAttributes(Name name) throws
>   NamingException
>   public Attributes getAttributes(String name) throws
>   NamingException
>   public Attributes getAttributes(Name name, String[] attrIds)
>   throws NamingException
>   public Attributes getAttributes(String name, String[] attrIds)
>   throws NamingException

PARAMETERS

attrIds   The identifiers of the attributes to retrieve. null indicates that all attributes should be retrieved; an empty array indicates that none should be retrieved.

name   The name of the object from which to retrieve attributes.

RETURNS   The requested attributes; never null. Returns an empty attribute set if name has no attributes or none of the requested attributes are found.

EXCEPTIONS

NamingException
>   If a naming exception is encountered.

SEE ALSO   DirContext.getAttributes().

getSchema()

PURPOSE   Retrieves the schema associated with the named object.

SYNTAX   public DirContext getSchema(Name name) throws NamingException
>   public DirContext getSchema(String name) throws NamingException

PARAMETERS

name   The name of the object whose schema to retrieve.

RETURNS   The schema associated with the context; never null.

EXCEPTIONS

NamingException
>   If a naming exception is encountered.

OperationNotSupportedException
> If the schema is not supported.

SEE ALSO   `DirContext.getSchema().`

getSchemaClassDefinition()

PURPOSE   Retrieves a context that contains the schema objects of the named object's class definitions.

SYNTAX   `public DirContext getSchemaClassDefinition(Name name) throws`
> `NamingException`
`public DirContext getSchemaClassDefinition(String name) throws`
> `NamingException`

PARAMETERS

`name`   The name of the object whose object class definition to retrieve.

RETURNS   The `DirContext` that contains the named object's class definitions; never `null`.

EXCEPTIONS

`NamingException`
> If a naming exception is encountered.
`OperationNotSupportedException`
> If the schema is not supported.

SEE ALSO   `DirContext.getSchemaClassDefinition().`

InitialDirContext()

PURPOSE   Constructs an instance of `InitialDirContext`.

SYNTAX   `public InitialDirContext() throws NamingException`
`public InitialDirContext(Hashtable env) throws NamingException`
`protected InitialDirContext(boolean lazy) throws NamingException`

DESCRIPTION   These constructors construct an instance of `InitialDirContext`. The first constructor constructs an `InitialDirContext` and is equivalent to

```
new InitialDirContext(null)
```

The second constructor constructs an `InitialDirContext` by using the supplied env. Environment properties are discussed in the `javax.naming.InitialContext` class description. This constructor will not modify env or save a reference to it, but it may save a clone of it.

The protected constructor constructs an `InitialDirContext` with the option of not initializing it. This might be used by a constructor in a subclass when the value of the env parameter is not known when the `InitialDirContext` constructor is called. The subclass's constructor will call this constructor, compute the value of the environment, and then call `InitialContext.init()` before returning.

PARAMETERS

env   The environment used to create the `InitialDirContext`. `null` indicates an empty environment.

lazy   `true` means do not initialize the initial `DirContext`; `false` is equivalent to calling `new InitialDirContext()`.

EXCEPTIONS

`NamingException`

If a naming exception is encountered.

SEE ALSO   `InitialContext.init()`.

modifyAttributes()

PURPOSE   Modifies the attributes associated with a named object.

SYNTAX   `public void modifyAttributes(Name name, int mod_op, Attributes attrs) throws NamingException`
            `public void modifyAttributes(String name, int mod_op, Attributes attrs) throws NamingException`
            `public void modifyAttributes(Name name, ModificationItem[] mods) throws NamingException`
            `public void modifyAttributes(String name, ModificationItem[] mods) throws NamingException`

PARAMETERS

attrs   The attributes to be used for the modification; may not be `null`.

mod_op   The modification operation, one of `ADD_ATTRIBUTE`, `REPLACE_ATTRIBUTE`, or `REMOVE_ATTRIBUTE`.

mods   The ordered list of modifications. May not be `null`.

name   The name of the object whose attributes will be updated.

EXCEPTIONS

`AttributeModificationException`

If the modification cannot be completed successfully.

`NamingException`

If a naming exception is encountered.

SEE ALSO   `DirContext.modifyAttributes()`.

rebind()

PURPOSE   Binds a name to an object, along with associated attributes, overwriting any existing binding.

SYNTAX
```
public void rebind(Name name, Object obj, Attributes attrs)
    throws NamingException
public void rebind(String name, Object obj, Attributes attrs)
    throws NamingException
```

PARAMETERS

`attrs`   The attributes to associate with the binding.

`name`   The name to bind. May not be empty.

`obj`   The object to bind; possibly `null`.

EXCEPTIONS

`InvalidAttributesException`

      If some mandatory attributes of the binding are not supplied.

`NamingException`

      If a naming exception is encountered.

SEE ALSO   `DirContext.rebind()`.

search()

PURPOSE   Searches a context or subcontexts.

SYNTAX
```
public NamingEnumeration search(Name name, Attributes
    matchingAttributes) throws NamingException
public NamingEnumeration search(String name, Attributes
    matchingAttributes) throws NamingException
public NamingEnumeration search(Name name, Attributes
    matchingAttributes, String[] attributesToReturn) throws
    NamingException
public NamingEnumeration search(String name, Attributes
    matchingAttributes, String[] attributesToReturn) throws
    NamingException
public NamingEnumeration search(Name name, String filter,
    SearchControls cons) throws NamingException
public NamingEnumeration search(String name, String filter,
    SearchControls cons) throws NamingException
public NamingEnumeration search(Name name, String filterExpr,
    Object[] filterArgs, SearchControls cons) throws
    NamingException
public NamingEnumeration search(String name, String filterExpr,
    Object[] filterArgs, SearchControls cons) throws
    NamingException
```

I

PARAMETERS

attributesToReturn

> The attributes to return. `null` indicates that all attributes are to be returned; an empty array indicates that none are to be returned.

cons
> The search controls that control the search. If `null`, then the default search controls are used (equivalent to a new `SearchControls()`).

filter
> The filter to use for the search.

filterArgs
> The array of arguments to substitute for the variables in `filterExpr`. The value of `filterArgs[i]` will replace each occurrence of `{i}` in `filterExpr`. If `null`, then equivalent to an empty array.

filterExpr
> The filter expression to use for the search. The expression may contain variables of the form `{i}`, where i is a nonnegative integer. May not be `null`.

matchingAttributes

> The attributes for which to search. If empty or `null`, then all objects in the target context are returned.

name
> The name of the context to search.

RETURNS
> A non-null enumeration of `SearchResult` objects. Each `SearchResult` contains the attributes identified by `attributesToReturn` or `cons` and the name of the corresponding object, named relative to the context named by `name`.

EXCEPTIONS

ArrayIndexOutOfBoundsException

> If `filterExpr` contains `{i}` expressions, where i is outside of the bounds of the array `filterArgs`.

InvalidSearchControlsException

> If the search controls contain invalid settings.

InvalidSearchFilterException

> If the search filter specified is not supported or not understood by the underlying directory.

NamingException

> If a naming exception is encountered.

SEE ALSO   `DirContext.search()`.

InitialLdapContext

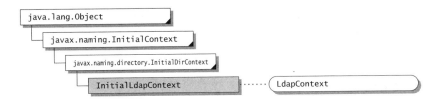

Syntax

`public class InitialLdapContext extends InitialDirContext implements LdapContext`

Description

The `InitialLdapContext` class is the starting context for performing LDAP v3-style "extended" operations and controls.

See `javax.naming.InitialContext` and `javax.naming.InitialDirContext` for details on synchronization and the policy on how to create an initial context.

Request Controls

When you create an initial context (`InitialLdapContext`), you can specify a list of request controls to be used as the request controls for any implicit LDAP "bind" operation performed by the context(s) derived from the context. These are called *connection request controls*. Use `getConnectControls()` to get a context's connection request controls.

The request controls supplied to the initial context constructor are *not* used as the context request controls for subsequent context operations such as searches and lookups. Context request controls are set and updated by using `setRequestControls()`.

In summary, two different sets of request controls can be associated with a context: connection and context. This differentiation is required for those applications needing to send critical controls that might not be applicable to both the context operation and any implicit LDAP "bind" operation. A typical user program would do the following.

```
InitialLdapContext lctx = new InitialLdapContext(env, critConnCtls);
lctx.setRequestControls(critModCtls);
lctx.modifyAttributes(name, mods);
Controls[] respCtls = lctx.getResponseControls();
```

This program first specifies the critical controls for creating the initial context (`critConnCtls`) and then sets the context's request controls (`critModCtls`) for the context operation. If for some reason `lctx` needs to reconnect to the server, then it will use `critConnCtls`. See the `LdapContext` interface for more discussion about request controls.

Service provider implementors should read the *Service Provider* section in the `Ldap-Context` class description for implementation details.

MEMBER SUMMARY
Constructor
`InitialLdapContext()`   Constructs an instance of `InitialLdapContext`.

Example

See the **Controls and Extensions** lesson (page 293).

InitialLdapContext()

PURPOSE   Constructs an instance of `InitialLdapContext`.

SYNTAX
```
public InitialLdapContext() throws NamingException
public InitialLdapContext(Hashtable env, Control[] connCtls)
    throws NamingException
```

DESCRIPTION   These constructors construct an instance of `InitialLdapContext`. The first constructor constructs an initial context by using no environment properties or connection request controls. It is equivalent to

```
new InitialLdapContext(null, null)
```

The second constructor constructs an initial context by using environment properties and connection request controls. See `javax.naming.Initial-Context` for a discussion of environment properties. This constructor will not modify its parameters or save references to them, but it may save a clone or copy of them.

`connCtls` is used as the underlying context implementation's connection request controls. See the class description for details.

PARAMETERS

  `connCtls`   Connection request controls for the initial context. If `null`, then no connection request controls are used.

  `env`   Environment used to create the initial context. `null` indicates an empty environment.

EXCEPTIONS

  `NamingException`

       If a naming exception is encountered.

SEE ALSO   `LdapContext.reconnect()`, `reconnect()`.

EXAMPLE   See the **Controls and Extensions** lesson (page 293).

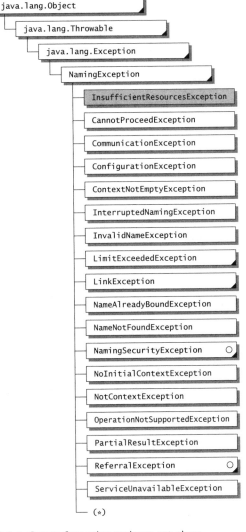

java.lang.Object

java.lang.Throwable

java.lang.Exception

NamingException

InsufficientResourcesException

CannotProceedException

CommunicationException

ConfigurationException

ContextNotEmptyException

InterruptedNamingException

InvalidNameException

LimitExceededException

LinkException

NameAlreadyBoundException

NameNotFoundException

NamingSecurityException　○

NoInitialContextException

NotContextException

OperationNotSupportedException

PartialResultException

ReferralException　○

ServiceUnavailableException

(*)

(*) 9 classes from other packages not shown.

Syntax
```
public class InsufficientResourcesException extends NamingException
```

InsufficientResourcesException()

Description

An `InsufficientResourcesException` is thrown when resources are not available to complete the requested operation. This might result from a lack of resources on the server or on the client. This exception can be used to represent the lack of any type of resource. The lack of resources might be due to physical limits and/or administrative quotas. Examples of limited resources are internal buffers, memory, and network bandwidth.

`InsufficientResourcesException` differs from `LimitExceededException` in that the latter is due to user/system specified limits. See `LimitExceededException` for details.

Synchronization and serialization issues that apply to `NamingException` apply directly here.

MEMBER SUMMARY
Constructor
`InsufficientResourcesException()`   Constructs an instance of `Insufficient-` `ResourcesException.`

InsufficientResourcesException()

PURPOSE   Constructs an instance of `InsufficientResourcesException`.

SYNTAX   `public InsufficientResourcesException()`
                 `public InsufficientResourcesException(String msg)`

DESCRIPTION   These constructors construct an instance of `InsufficientResources-` `Exception` by using an optional `msg` supplied. If `msg` is not supplied, then `msg` defaults to `null`. All other fields default to `null`.

PARAMETERS
  msg   Additional detail about this exception. May be `null`.

SEE ALSO   `java.lang.Throwable.getMessage()`.

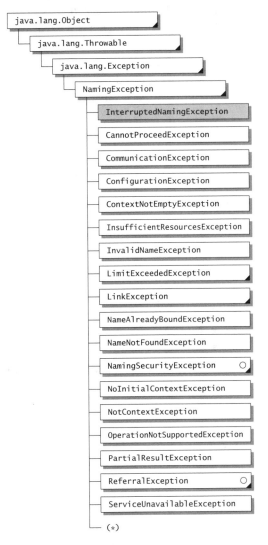

java.lang.Object

java.lang.Throwable

java.lang.Exception

NamingException

InterruptedNamingException

CannotProceedException

CommunicationException

ConfigurationException

ContextNotEmptyException

InsufficientResourcesException

InvalidNameException

LimitExceededException

LinkException

NameAlreadyBoundException

NameNotFoundException

NamingSecurityException ○

NoInitialContextException

NotContextException

OperationNotSupportedException

PartialResultException

ReferralException ○

ServiceUnavailableException

(*)

(*) 9 classes from other packages not shown.

Syntax
```
public class InterruptedNamingException extends NamingException
```

InterruptedNamingException()

Description

An InterruptedNamingException is thrown when the naming operation being invoked has been interrupted. For example, an application might interrupt a thread that is performing a search. If the search supports being interrupted, then it will throw an InterruptedNaming-Exception. Whether an operation is interruptible and when depends on its implementation (as provided by the service provider). Different implementations have different ways of protecting their resources and objects from being damaged due to unexpected interrupts.

Synchronization and serialization issues that apply to NamingException apply directly here.

MEMBER SUMMARY

Constructor

InterruptedNamingException()	Constructs an instance of InterruptedNaming-Exception.

InterruptedNamingException()

PURPOSE	Constructs an instance of InterruptedNamingException.
SYNTAX	public InterruptedNamingException() public InterruptedNamingException(String msg)
DESCRIPTION	These constructors construct an instance of InterruptedNamingException by using an optional msg supplied. If msg is not supplied, then msg defaults to null. All other fields default to null.
PARAMETERS	
msg	Additional detail about this exception. May be null.
SEE ALSO	java.lang.Throwable.getMessage().

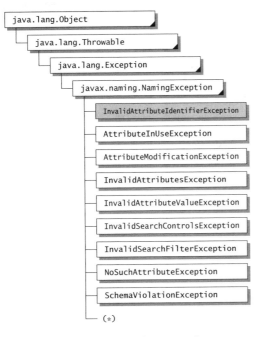

```
java.lang.Object
    java.lang.Throwable
        java.lang.Exception
            javax.naming.NamingException
                InvalidAttributeIdentifierException
                AttributeInUseException
                AttributeModificationException
                InvalidAttributesException
                InvalidAttributeValueException
                InvalidSearchControlsException
                InvalidSearchFilterException
                NoSuchAttributeException
                SchemaViolationException
                (*)
```

(*) 18 classes from other packages not shown.

Syntax

`public class InvalidAttributeIdentifierException extends NamingException`

Description

An `InvalidAttributeIdentifierException` is thrown when an attempt is made to add or create an attribute with an invalid attribute identifier. The validity of an attribute identifier is directory-specific.

Synchronization and serialization issues that apply to `NamingException` apply directly here.

MEMBER SUMMARY
Constructor
`InvalidAttributeIdentifierException()` Constructs an instance of `Invalid-AttributeIdentifierException`.

InvalidAttributeIdentifierException()

PURPOSE	Constructs an instance of `InvalidAttributeIdentifierException`.
SYNTAX	`public InvalidAttributeIdentifierException()` `public InvalidAttributeIdentifierException(String msg)`
DESCRIPTION	These constructors construct an instance of `InvalidAttributeIdentifier-Exception` by using an optional `msg` supplied. If `msg` is not supplied, then `msg` defaults to `null`. All other fields default to `null`.
PARAMETERS	
`msg`	Additional detail about this exception. May be `null`.
SEE ALSO	`java.lang.Throwable.getMessage()`.

I

InvalidAttributesException

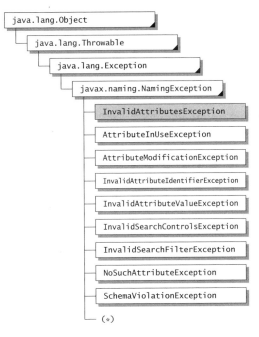

```
java.lang.Object
    └── java.lang.Throwable
            └── java.lang.Exception
                    └── javax.naming.NamingException
                            ├── InvalidAttributesException
                            ├── AttributeInUseException
                            ├── AttributeModificationException
                            ├── InvalidAttributeIdentifierException
                            ├── InvalidAttributeValueException
                            ├── InvalidSearchControlsException
                            ├── InvalidSearchFilterException
                            ├── NoSuchAttributeException
                            ├── SchemaViolationException
                            └── (*)
```

(*) 18 classes from other packages not shown.

Syntax

```
public class InvalidAttributesException extends NamingException
```

Description

An InvalidAttributesException is thrown when an attempt is made to add or modify an attribute set that has been specified incompletely or incorrectly. This could happen, for example, when attempting to add or modify a binding or to create a new subcontext without specifying all of the mandatory attributes required for creating the object. Another example is when specifying incompatible attributes within the same attribute set or attributes in conflict with that specified by the object's schema.

Synchronization and serialization issues that apply to NamingException apply directly here.

InvalidAttributesException()

MEMBER SUMMARY

Constructor

InvalidAttributesException()	Constructs an instance of InvalidAttributes-Exception.

InvalidAttributesException()

PURPOSE   Constructs an instance of InvalidAttributesException.

SYNTAX   public InvalidAttributesException()
               public InvalidAttributesException(String msg)

DESCRIPTION   These constructors construct an instance of InvalidAttributesException by
               using an optional msg supplied. If msg is not supplied, then msg defaults to
               null. All other fields default to null.

PARAMETERS
  msg   Additional detail about this exception. May be null.

SEE ALSO   java.lang.Throwable.getMessage().

InvalidAttributeValueException

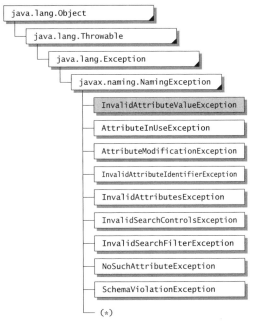

```
java.lang.Object
    java.lang.Throwable
        java.lang.Exception
            javax.naming.NamingException
                InvalidAttributeValueException
                AttributeInUseException
                AttributeModificationException
                InvalidAttributeIdentifierException
                InvalidAttributesException
                InvalidSearchControlsException
                InvalidSearchFilterException
                NoSuchAttributeException
                SchemaViolationException
                (*)
```

(*) 18 classes from other packages not shown.

Syntax

```
public class InvalidAttributeValueException extends NamingException
```

Description

An InvalidAttributeValueException is thrown when an attempt is made to add to an attribute a value that conflicts with the attribute's schema definition. This could happen, for example, when attempting to add an attribute that has no value when the attribute is required to have at least one value, or when attempting to add more than one value to a single-valued attribute, or when attempting to add a value that conflicts with the attribute's syntax.

Synchronization and serialization issues that apply to NamingException apply directly here.

InvalidAttributeValueException()

MEMBER SUMMARY	
Constructor	
InvalidAttributeValueException()	Constructs an instance of Invalid-AttributeValueException.

InvalidAttributeValueException()

PURPOSE   Constructs an instance of InvalidAttributeValueException.

SYNTAX   public InvalidAttributeValueException()
               public InvalidAttributeValueException(String msg)

DESCRIPTION   These constructors construct an instance of InvalidAttributeValue-Exception by using an optional msg supplied. If msg is not supplied, then msg defaults to null. All other fields default to null.

PARAMETERS

msg   Additional detail about this exception. May be null.

SEE ALSO   java.lang.Throwable.getMessage().

```
java.lang.Object
    java.lang.Throwable
        java.lang.Exception
            NamingException
                InvalidNameException
                CannotProceedException
                CommunicationException
                ConfigurationException
                ContextNotEmptyException
                InsufficientResourcesException
                InterruptedNamingException
                LimitExceededException
                LinkException
                NameAlreadyBoundException
                NameNotFoundException
                NamingSecurityException        ○
                NoInitialContextException
                NotContextException
                OperationNotSupportedException
                PartialResultException
                ReferralException              ○
                ServiceUnavailableException
                (*)
```

(*) 9 classes from other packages not shown.

Syntax

```
public class InvalidNameException extends NamingException
```

Description

An InvalidNameException is thrown to indicate that the name being specified does not conform to the naming syntax of a naming system. It is thrown by any method that does name parsing (such as those in Context, DirContext, CompositeName, and CompoundName).

Synchronization and serialization issues that apply to NamingException apply directly here.

MEMBER SUMMARY
Constructor
InvalidNameException()   Constructs an instance of InvalidNameException.

InvalidNameException()

PURPOSE	Constructs an instance of InvalidNameException.
SYNTAX	public InvalidNameException() public InvalidNameException(String msg)
DESCRIPTION	These constructors construct an instance of InvalidNameException by using an optional msg supplied. If msg is not supplied, then msg defaults to null. All other fields default to null.
PARAMETERS	
msg	Additional detail about this exception. May be null.
SEE ALSO	java.lang.Throwable.getMessage().

InvalidSearchControlsException

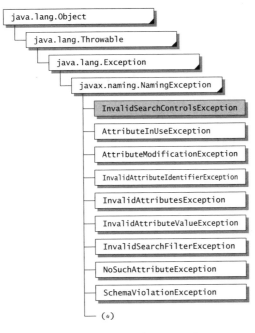

(*) 18 classes from other packages not shown.

Syntax

```
public class InvalidSearchControlsException extends NamingException
```

Description

An InvalidSearchControlsException is thrown when the specification of the Search-
Controls for a search operation is invalid. For example, if the scope is set to a value other than
OBJECT_SCOPE, ONELEVEL_SCOPE, or SUBTREE_SCOPE, then this exception is thrown.

Synchronization and serialization issues that apply to NamingException apply directly
here.

MEMBER SUMMARY
Constructor
InvalidSearchControlsException()   Constructs an instance of InvalidSearch- ControlsException.

See Also

`DirContext.search(). javax.naming.event.EventDirContext.addNamingListener(),`
`SearchControls.`

InvalidSearchControlsException()

PURPOSE   Constructs an instance of `InvalidSearchControlsException`.

SYNTAX   `public InvalidSearchControlsException()`
                `public InvalidSearchControlsException(String msg)`

DESCRIPTION   These constructors construct an instance of `InvalidSearchControls-`
                `Exception` with an optional explanation (`msg`) supplied. If `msg` is not supplied,
                then `msg` defaults to `null`. All other fields default to `null`.

PARAMETERS
  `msg`   Additional detail about this exception. May be `null`.

SEE ALSO   `java.lang.Throwable.getMessage()`.

InvalidSearchFilterException

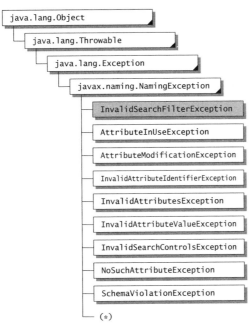

```
java.lang.Object
    java.lang.Throwable
        java.lang.Exception
            javax.naming.NamingException
                InvalidSearchFilterException
                AttributeInUseException
                AttributeModificationException
                InvalidAttributeIdentifierException
                InvalidAttributesException
                InvalidAttributeValueException
                InvalidSearchControlsException
                NoSuchAttributeException
                SchemaViolationException
                (*)
```

(*) 18 classes from other packages not shown.

Syntax

```
public class InvalidSearchFilterException extends NamingException
```

Description

An InvalidSearchFilterException is thrown when the specification of a search filter is invalid. The expression of the filter may be invalid, or a problem might exist regarding one of the parameters passed to the filter.

Synchronization and serialization issues that apply to NamingException apply directly here.

MEMBER SUMMARY
Constructor
InvalidSearchFilterException()   Constructs an instance of InvalidSearch-FilterException.

See Also

DirContext.search(), javax.naming.event.EventDirContext.addNamingListener().

InvalidSearchFilterException()

PURPOSE	Constructs an instance of InvalidSearchFilterException.
SYNTAX	public InvalidSearchFilterException() public InvalidSearchFilterException(String msg)
DESCRIPTION	These constructors construct an instance of InvalidSearchFilterException with an optional explanation (msg) supplied. If msg is not supplied, then msg defaults to null. All other fields default to null.
PARAMETERS	
msg	Additional detail about this exception. May be null.
SEE ALSO	java.lang.Throwable.getMessage().

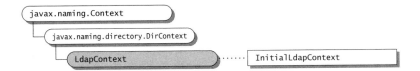

Syntax

```
public interface LdapContext extends DirContext
```

Description

The `LdapContext` interface represents a context in which you can perform operations with LDAP v3-style controls and perform LDAP v3-style "extended" operations. For applications that do not require such controls or "extended" operations, the more generic `javax.naming.directory.DirContext` should be used instead.

Usage Details about Controls

This interface provides support for LDAP v3 controls. At a high level, this support allows a user program to set request controls for LDAP operations that are executed in the course of the user program's invocation of `Context/DirContext` methods and to read response controls resulting from LDAP operations. At the implementation level, developers of both the user program and service providers need to understand certain details in order to correctly use request and response controls, as discussed next.

Request Controls

Request controls come in two types:

- Those that affect how a connection is created
- Those that affect context methods

The former are used whenever a connection needs to be established or reestablished with an LDAP server. The latter are used when all other LDAP operations are sent to the LDAP server. These two types of request controls need to be distinguished because the JNDI is a high-level API that does not deal directly with connections. It is the job of service providers to do any necessary connection management. Consequently, a single connection may be shared by multiple `Context` instances and a service provider is free to use its own algorithms to conserve connection and network usage. Thus, when a method is invoked on a `Context` instance, the service provider might need to do some connection management in addition to performing the corresponding LDAP operations. For connection management, it uses the *connection request controls* and for the normal LDAP operations, it uses the *context request controls*.

Unless explicitly qualified, the term *request control* refers to context request control.

Context Request Controls

A `Context` instance gets its request controls in either of two ways:

```
ldapContext.newInstance(reqCtls);

ldapContext.setRequestControls(reqCtls);
```

where `ldapContext` is an instance of `LdapContext`. Specifying `null` or an empty array for *reqCtls* means no request controls. `newInstance()` creates an instance (clone) of `ldapContext` by using *reqCtls*, whereas `setRequestControls()` updates `ldapContext`'s request controls to *reqCtls*.

Unlike environment properties, request controls of a `Context` instance are *not* inherited by `Context` instances that are derived from it. Derived `Context` instances have `null` as their context request controls. You must set the request controls of a derived `Context` instance explicitly by using `setRequestControls()`.

A `Context` instance's request controls are retrieved by using the method `getRequest-Controls()`.

Connection Request Controls

Connection request controls are set in either of three ways:

```
new InitialLdapContext(env, connCtls);

refException.getReferralContext(env, connCtls);

ldapContext.reconnect(connCtls);
```

where `refException` is an instance of `LdapReferralException` and `ldapContext` is an instance of `LdapContext`. Specifying `null` or an empty array for *connCtls* means no connection request controls.

Like environment properties, connection request controls of a context *are* inherited by contexts that are derived from it. Typically, you initialize the connection request controls by using the `InitialLdapContext` constructor or `LdapReferralContext.getReferral-Context()`. These connection request controls are inherited by contexts that share the same connection, that is, contexts derived from the initial or referral contexts.

Use `reconnect()` to change the connection request controls of a context. Invoking `ldap-Context.reconnect()` affects only the connection used by `ldapContext` and any new `Context` instances that are derived from `ldapContext`. Contexts that previously shared the connection with `ldapContext` remain unchanged. That is, a context's connection request controls must be explicitly changed and are not affected by changes to another context's connection request controls.

A `Context` instance's connection request controls are retrieved by using `getConnect-Controls()`.

Service Provider Requirements

A service provider supports connection and context request controls in the following ways. Context request controls must be associated on a per `Context` instance basis, whereas connection request controls must be associated on a per connection instance basis. The service provider must look for the connection request controls in the environment property `"java.naming.ldap.control.connect"` and pass this property on to `Context` instances that it creates.

Response Controls
The method `LdapContext.getResponseControls()` is used to retrieve the response controls generated by LDAP operations executed as the result of invoking a `Context`/`DirContext` operation. The result is all of the response controls generated by the underlying LDAP operations, including those generated by any implicit reconnection. To get only the reconnection response controls, use `reconnect()` followed by `getResponseControls()`.

Parameters
A `Control[]` array passed as a parameter to any method is owned by the caller. The service provider will not modify the array or keep a reference to it, although it may keep references to the individual `Control` objects in the array. A `Control[]` array returned by any method is immutable and may not subsequently be modified by either the caller or the service provider.

MEMBER SUMMARY	
Extension Method	
`extendedOperation()`	Performs an "extended" operation.
Control Methods	
`getConnectControls()`	Retrieves the connection request controls in effect for this context.
`getRequestControls()`	Retrieves the request controls in effect for this context.
`getResponseControls()`	Retrieves the response controls produced as a result of the last method invoked on this context.
`newInstance()`	Creates an instance of this context initialized by using request controls.
`reconnect()`	Reconnects to the LDAP server by using the supplied controls and this context's environment.
`setRequestControls()`	Sets the request controls for methods subsequently invoked on this context.
Environment Property Name	
`CONTROL_FACTORIES`	Holds the name of the environment property for specifying the list of control factories to use.

Example
See the **Controls and Extensions** lesson (page 289).

CONTROL_FACTORIES

PURPOSE   Holds the name of the environment property for specifying the list of control factories to use.

SYNTAX   `public static final String CONTROL_FACTORIES`

DESCRIPTION   This constant holds the name of the environment property for specifying the list of control factories to use. The value of the property should be a colon-separated list of the fully qualified class names of factory classes that will create a control when given another control. See `ControlFactory.getControlInstance()` for details. This property may be specified in the environment, an applet parameter, a system property, or one or more resource files.

The value of this constant is `"java.naming.factory.control"`.

SEE ALSO   `ControlFactory`, `javax.naming.Context.addToEnvironment()`, `javax.naming.Context.removeFromEnvironment()`.

EXAMPLE   See the **Miscellaneous** lesson (page 388).

extendedOperation()

PURPOSE   Performs an "extended" operation.

SYNTAX   `public ExtendedResponse extendedOperation(ExtendedRequest request) throws NamingException`

DESCRIPTION   This method performs an "extended" operation. It is used to support LDAP v3 "extended" operations.

PARAMETERS
request   The non-`null` request to be performed.

RETURNS   The possibly `null` response of the operation. `null` means that the operation did not generate any response.

EXCEPTIONS
NamingException
          If an error occurs while performing the "extended" operation.

EXAMPLE   See the `ExtendedRequest` class example.

getConnectControls()

PURPOSE   Retrieves the connection request controls in effect for this context.

SYNTAX   `public Control[] getConnectControls() throws NamingException`

DESCRIPTION   This method retrieves the connection request controls in effect for this context. The controls are owned by the JNDI implementation and are immutable. Neither the array nor the controls may be modified by the caller.

RETURNS   A possibly-`null` array of controls. `null` means that no connection request controls were set for this context.

EXCEPTIONS

`NamingException`
    If an error occurs while getting the request controls.

EXAMPLE   See the **Controls and Extensions** lesson (page 297).

getRequestControls()

PURPOSE   Retrieves the request controls in effect for this context.

SYNTAX   `public Control[] getRequestControls() throws NamingException`

DESCRIPTION   This method retrieves the request controls in effect for this context. The request controls are owned by the JNDI implementation and are immutable. Neither the array nor the controls may be modified by the caller.

RETURNS   A possibly `null` array of controls. `null` means that no request controls have been set for this context.

EXCEPTIONS

`NamingException`
    If an error occurs while getting the request controls.

SEE ALSO   `setRequestControls()`.

EXAMPLE   See the **Controls and Extensions** lesson (page 293).

getResponseControls()

PURPOSE   Retrieves the response controls produced as a result of the last method invoked on this context.

SYNTAX   `public Control[] getResponseControls() throws NamingException`

DESCRIPTION   This method retrieves the response controls produced as a result of the last method invoked on this context. The response controls are owned by the JNDI implementation and are immutable. Neither the array nor the controls may be modified by the caller. These response controls might have been generated by a successful or failed operation.

613

When a context method that may return response controls is invoked, response controls from the previous method invocation are cleared. `getResponse-Controls()` returns all of the response controls that are generated by LDAP operations and used by the context method in the order received from the LDAP server. Invoking `getResponseControls()` does not clear the response controls. You can call it many times (and get back the same controls) until the next context method that might return controls is invoked.

RETURNS   A possibly `null` array of controls. If `null`, then the previous method invoked on this context did not produce any controls.

EXCEPTIONS
`NamingException`

If an error occurs while getting the response controls.

EXAMPLE   See the **Controls and Extensions** lesson (page 298).

newInstance()

PURPOSE   Creates an instance of this context initialized by using request controls.

SYNTAX   `public LdapContext newInstance(Control[] requestControls) throws`
`            NamingException`

DESCRIPTION   This method creates an instance of this context initialized by using request controls. It is a convenience method for creating an instance of this context for the purposes of multithreaded access. For example, if multiple threads want to use different context request controls, then each thread may use this method to get its own copy of this context and set/get context request controls without having to synchronize with other threads.

The new context has the same environment properties and connection request controls as this context. See the class description for details. Implementations might also allow this context and the new context to share the same network connection or other resources if doing so does not impede the independence of either context.

PARAMETERS
`requestControls`

The possibly `null` request controls to use for the new context. If `null`, then the context is initialized with no request controls.

RETURNS   A non-`null` `LdapContext` instance.

EXCEPTIONS
`NamingException`

If an error occurs while creating the instance.

SEE ALSO   `InitialLdapContext`.

EXAMPLE   See the **Controls and Extensions** lesson (page 294).

reconnect()

PURPOSE   Reconnects to the LDAP server by using the supplied controls and this context's environment.

SYNTAX   `public void reconnect(Control[] connCtls) throws NamingException`

DESCRIPTION   This method reconnects this context to the LDAP server by using the supplied controls and this context's environment. It is a means to explicitly initiate an LDAP "bind" operation. For example, you can use this method to set request controls for the LDAP "bind" operation or to explicitly connect to the server to get response controls returned by the LDAP "bind" operation.

This method sets `connCtls` to be this context's new connection request controls. This context's context request controls are not affected. After this method has been invoked, any subsequent implicit reconnections will be done by using `connCtls`. `connCtls` are also used as connection request controls for new `Context` instances derived from this context. These connection request controls are not affected by `setRequestControls()`.

Service provider implementors should read the *Service Provider* section in the class description for implementation details.

PARAMETERS
`connCtls`   The possibly `null` controls to use. If `null`, then no controls are used.

EXCEPTIONS
`NamingException`
                If an error occurs while reconnecting.

SEE ALSO   `getConnectControls()`, `newInstance()`.

EXAMPLE   See the **Controls and Extensions** lesson (page 296).

setRequestControls()

PURPOSE   Sets the request controls for methods subsequently invoked on this context.

SYNTAX   `public void setRequestControls(Control[] requestControls) throws`
                `    NamingException`

DESCRIPTION   This method sets the request controls for methods subsequently invoked on this context.

This method removes any previous request controls and adds `request-Controls` for use by subsequent methods invoked on this context. It does not affect this context's connection request controls.

Note that `requestControls` will be in effect until the next invocation of `set-RequestControls()`. You need to explicitly invoke `setRequestControls()` with `null` or an empty array to clear the controls if you no longer want them to affect the context methods. To check which request controls are in effect for this context, use `getRequestControls()`.

PARAMETERS

`requestControls`

The possibly `null` controls to use. If `null`, then no controls are used.

EXCEPTIONS

`NamingException`

If an error occurs while setting the request controls.

SEE ALSO   `getRequestControls()`.

EXAMPLE   See the **Controls and Extensions** lesson (page 293).

L

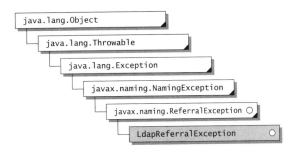

LdapReferralException

Syntax

```
public abstract class LdapReferralException extends ReferralException
```

Description

The `LdapReferralException` abstract class represents an LDAP referral exception. It extends the base `ReferralException` by providing a `getReferralContext()` that accepts request controls. Because `LdapReferralException` is an abstract class, concrete implementations of it determine its synchronization and serialization properties.

A `Control[]` array passed as a parameter to `getReferralContext()` is owned by the caller. The service provider will not modify the array or keep a reference to it, although it may keep references to the individual `Control` objects in the array.

MEMBER SUMMARY
Constructor
`LdapReferralException()`   Constructs an instance of `LdapReferralException`.
Referral Management Method
`getReferralContext()`   Retrieves the context at which to continue the context method by following the referral.

Example

See the **Controls and Extensions** lesson (page 297).

getReferralContext()

PURPOSE   Retrieves the context at which to continue the context method by following the referral.

SYNTAX

```
public abstract Context getReferralContext() throws
    NamingException
public abstract Context getReferralContext(Hashtable env) throws
    NamingException
public abstract Context getReferralContext(Hashtable env,
    Control[] reqCtls) throws NamingException
```

DESCRIPTION

This method retrieves the context at which to continue the context method by following the referral, by using env as its environment properties and reqCtls as its request controls. If env is not specified, then the referral context is created by using the environment properties of the context that threw the ReferralException. If reqCtls is not specified, then no request controls are used.

reqCtls is used when creating the connection to the referred server. These controls will be used as the connection request controls for the context and Context instances derived from the context. reqCtls will also be the context's request controls for subsequent context operations. See the LdapContext class description for details.

Regardless of whether a referral is encountered directly during a context operation or indirectly, for example, during a search enumeration, the referral exception should provide a context at which to continue the operation. To continue the operation, the client program should reinvoke the context method by using the same arguments as the original invocation. See ReferralException for details on how to use this method.

The first form of this method is equivalent to

```
getReferralContext(ctx.getEnvironment(), null);
```

where ctx is the context that threw the ReferralException.

The second form of this method is equivalent to

```
getReferralContext(env, null);
```

These two forms are overridden in this class for documentation purposes only.

The third form of this method should be used when the caller needs to supply request controls for creating the referral context. It might need to do this, for example, when it needs to supply special controls relating to authentication.

Service provider implementors should read the *Service Provider* section in the LdapContext class description for implementation details.

PARAMETERS

env

The possibly null environment properties to use for the new context. null means to use no environment properties.

reqCtls

The possibly null request controls to use for the new context. null or an empty array means to use no request controls.

RETURNS   The non-null context at which to continue the context method.

EXCEPTIONS

NamingException

 If a naming exception occurs. Call either retryReferral() or skip-Referral() to continue processing referrals.

EXAMPLE   See the **Controls and Extensions** lesson (page 297).

LdapReferralException()

PURPOSE   Constructs an instance of LdapReferralException.

SYNTAX   protected LdapReferralException()
                 protected LdapReferralException(String msg)

DESCRIPTION   These constructors construct an instance of LdapReferralException by using the optional msg supplied. If msg is not supplied, then it defaults to null. All other fields default to null.

PARAMETERS

msg   Additional detail about this exception. May be null.

SEE ALSO   java.lang.Throwable.getMessage().

L

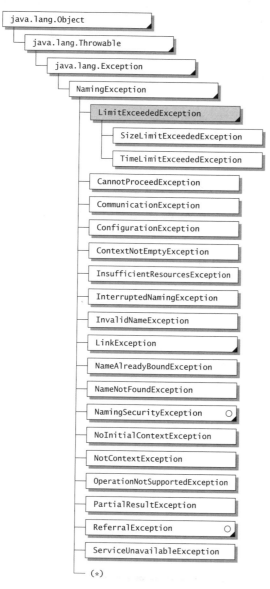

```
java.lang.Object
    java.lang.Throwable
        java.lang.Exception
            NamingException
                LimitExceededException
                    SizeLimitExceededException
                    TimeLimitExceededException
                CannotProceedException
                CommunicationException
                ConfigurationException
                ContextNotEmptyException
                InsufficientResourcesException
                InterruptedNamingException
                InvalidNameException
                LinkException
                NameAlreadyBoundException
                NameNotFoundException
                NamingSecurityException        ○
                NoInitialContextException
                NotContextException
                OperationNotSupportedException
                PartialResultException
                ReferralException              ○
                ServiceUnavailableException
                (*)
```

(*) 9 classes from other packages not shown.

Syntax

public class LimitExceededException extends NamingException

L

Description

A `LimitExceededException` is thrown when a method terminates abnormally due to a user- or system-specified limit. This differs from a `InsufficientResourceException` in that `Limit-ExceededException` is due to a user/system-specified limit. For example, running out of memory to complete the request would be an insufficient resource. The client's asking for 10 answers and getting back 11 is a size limit exception.

Examples of these limits include client and server configuration limits such as size, time, and number of hops.

Synchronization and serialization issues that apply to `NamingException` apply directly here.

MEMBER SUMMARY

Constructor
`LimitExceededException()`   Constructs an instance of `LimitExceededException`.

LimitExceededException()

PURPOSE   Constructs an instance of `LimitExceededException`.

SYNTAX   `public LimitExceededException()`
                 `public LimitExceededException(String msg)`

DESCRIPTION   These constructors construct an instance of `LimitExceededException` by using an optional `msg` supplied. If `msg` is not supplied, then `msg` defaults to `null`. All other fields default to `null`.

PARAMETERS

`msg`   Additional detail about this exception. May be `null`.

SEE ALSO   `java.lang.Throwable.getMessage()`.

L

621

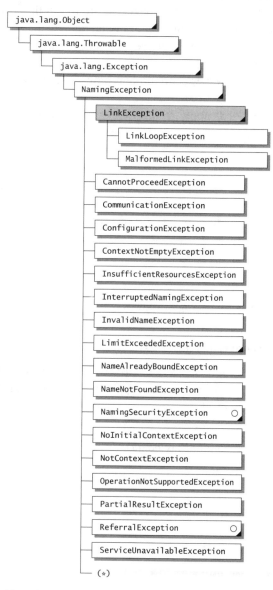

java.lang.Object

java.lang.Throwable

java.lang.Exception

NamingException

LinkException

LinkLoopException

MalformedLinkException

CannotProceedException

CommunicationException

ConfigurationException

ContextNotEmptyException

InsufficientResourcesException

InterruptedNamingException

InvalidNameException

LimitExceededException

NameAlreadyBoundException

NameNotFoundException

NamingSecurityException ○

NoInitialContextException

NotContextException

OperationNotSupportedException

PartialResultException

ReferralException ○

ServiceUnavailableException

(*)

(*) 9 classes from other packages not shown.

Syntax
```
public class LinkException extends NamingException
```

Description

A LinkException describes problems encountered while resolving links. Additional information is added to the base NamingException for pinpointing the problem with the link.

Analogous to how NamingException captures name resolution information, LinkException captures link-name resolution information, pinpointing the problem encountered while resolving a link. All of the fields may be null. Table 30 contains descriptions of these fields.

TABLE 30: Link-Name Resolution Information.

Field	Description
Link Resolved Name	Portion of the link name that has been resolved.
Link Resolved Object	Object to which the resolution of the link name proceeded.
Link Remaining Name	Portion of the link name that has not been resolved.
Link Explanation	Detail explaining why link resolution failed.

A LinkException instance is not synchronized against concurrent multithreaded access. Multiple threads trying to access and modify a single LinkException instance should lock the object.

L

MEMBER SUMMARY	
Constructor	
LinkException()	Constructs an instance of LinkException.
Link Field Accessor Methods	
getLinkExplanation()	Retrieves the explanation associated with the problem encountered while resolving a link.
getLinkRemainingName()	Retrieves the remaining unresolved portion of the link name.
getLinkResolvedName()	Retrieves the leading portion of the link name that was resolved successfully.
getLinkResolvedObj()	Retrieves the object to which resolution was successful.
setLinkExplanation()	Sets the explanation associated with the problem encountered when resolving a link.
setLinkRemainingName()	Sets the link remaining name field of this exception.
setLinkResolvedName()	Sets the link resolved name field of this exception.
setLinkResolvedObj()	Sets the link resolved object field of this exception.
Protected Fields	
linkExplanation	Contains the explanation of why the resolution of the link failed.
	Continued

623

MEMBER SUMMARY	
Protected Fields (*Continued*)	
linkRemainingName	Contains the remaining link name that has not been resolved.
linkResolvedName	Contains the part of the link that has been successfully resolved.
linkResolvedObj	Contains the object to which the resolution of the part of the link was successful.
String Method	
toString()	Generates the string representation of this exception.

getLinkExplanation()

PURPOSE   Retrieves the explanation associated with the problem encountered while resolving a link.

SYNTAX   `public String getLinkExplanation()`

RETURNS   The possibly null detail string explaining more about the problem with resolving a link. If null, then this exception has no link detail message.

SEE ALSO   `setLinkExplanation().`

getLinkRemainingName()

PURPOSE   Retrieves the remaining unresolved portion of the link name.

SYNTAX   `public Name getLinkRemainingName()`

RETURNS   The part of the link name that was not resolved. A composite name, it can be null, meaning that the link remaining name field was not set.

SEE ALSO   `setLinkRemainingName().`

getLinkResolvedName()

PURPOSE   Retrieves the leading portion of the link name that was resolved successfully.

SYNTAX   `public Name getLinkResolvedName()`

RETURNS   The part of the link name that was resolved successfully. A composite name, it can be null, meaning that the link resolved name field was not set.

SEE ALSO   `getLinkResolvedObj(), setLinkResolvedName().`

getLinkResolvedObj()

PURPOSE	Retrieves the object to which resolution was successful.
SYNTAX	`public Object getLinkResolvedObj()`
DESCRIPTION	This method retrieves the object to which resolution was successful. This is the object to which the resolved link name is bound.
RETURNS	The possibly `null` object that was resolved so far. If `null`, then the link resolved object field was not set.
SEE ALSO	`getLinkResolvedName()`, `setLinkResolvedObj()`.

LinkException()

PURPOSE	Constructs an instance of `LinkException`.
SYNTAX	`public LinkException()` `public LinkException(String msg)`
DESCRIPTION	These constructors construct an instance of `LinkException` with an optional `msg` supplied. If `msg` is not supplied, then `msg` defaults to `null`. All other non-link-related and link-related fields default to `null`.
PARAMETERS	
msg	Additional detail about this exception. May be `null`.
SEE ALSO	`java.lang.Throwable.getMessage()`.

L

linkExplanation

PURPOSE	Contains the explanation of why the resolution of the link failed.
SYNTAX	`protected String linkExplanation`
DESCRIPTION	This field contains the explanation of why the resolution of the link failed. It may be `null`. It is initialized by the constructors. You should access and manipulate this field through its get and set methods.
SEE ALSO	`getLinkExplanation()`, `setLinkExplanation()`.

linkRemainingName

PURPOSE	Contains the remaining link name that has not been resolved.
SYNTAX	`protected Name linkRemainingName`

625

DESCRIPTION   This field contains the remaining link name that has not been resolved. It is a composite name and may be `null`. It is initialized by the constructors. You should access and manipulate this field through its get and set methods.

SEE ALSO   `getLinkRemainingName()`, `setLinkRemainingName()`.

linkResolvedName

PURPOSE   Contains the part of the link that has been successfully resolved.

SYNTAX   `protected Name linkResolvedName`

DESCRIPTION   This field contains the part of the link that has been successfully resolved. It is a composite name and may be `null`. It is initialized by the constructors. You should access and manipulate this field through its get and set methods.

SEE ALSO   `getLinkResolvedName()`, `setLinkResolvedName()`.

linkResolvedObj

PURPOSE   Contains the object to which the resolution of the part of the link was successful.

SYNTAX   `protected Object linkResolvedObj`

DESCRIPTION   This field contains the object to which the resolution of the part of the link was successful. It may be `null`. This field is initialized by the constructors. You should access and manipulate this field through its get and set methods.

SEE ALSO   `getLinkResolvedObj()`, `setLinkResolvedObj()`.

setLinkExplanation()

PURPOSE   Sets the explanation associated with the problem encountered while resolving a link.

SYNTAX   `public void setLinkExplanation(String msg)`

PARAMETERS
  msg   Additional detail about this exception. May be `null`. If `null`, then no detail is recorded.

SEE ALSO   `getLinkExplanation()`.

setLinkRemainingName()

PURPOSE   Sets the link remaining name field of this exception.

SYNTAX   `public void setLinkRemainingName(Name name)`

DESCRIPTION   This method sets the link remaining name field of this exception. `name` is a composite name. If the intent is to set this field by using a compound name or string, then you must stringify the compound name and create a composite name with a single component by using the string. You can then invoke this method by using the resulting composite name.

A copy of `name` is made and stored. Subsequent changes to `name` do not affect the copy in this `LinkException`, and vice versa.

PARAMETERS
name   The name to which to set the remaining link name. May be `null`. If `null`, then it sets the link remaining name field to `null`.

SEE ALSO   `getLinkRemainingName()`.

setLinkResolvedName()

PURPOSE   Sets the link resolved name field of this exception.

SYNTAX   `public void setLinkResolvedName(Name name)`

DESCRIPTION   This method sets the link resolved name field of this exception.

name is a composite name. If the intent is to set this field by using a compound name or string, then you must stringify the compound name and create a composite name with a single component by using the string. You can then invoke this method by using the resulting composite name.

A copy of `name` is made and stored. Subsequent changes to `name` do not affect the copy in this `LinkException`, and vice versa.

PARAMETERS
name   The name to which to set resolved link name. May be `null`. If `null`, then it sets the link resolved name field to `null`.

SEE ALSO   `getLinkResolvedName()`.

setLinkResolvedObj()

PURPOSE   Sets the link resolved object field of this exception.

SYNTAX   `public void setLinkResolvedObj(Object obj)`

DESCRIPTION   This method sets the link resolved object field of this exception, thereby indicating the last successfully resolved object of the link name.

PARAMETERS

obj   The object to which to set the link resolved object. May be `null`. If `null`, then
              the link resolved object field is set to `null`.

SEE ALSO   `getLinkResolvedObj()`.

toString()

PURPOSE   Generates the string representation of this exception.

SYNTAX
```
public String toString()
public String toString(boolean detail)
```

DESCRIPTION   This method generates the string representation of this exception. This string
              consists of the `NamingException` information plus the additional information
              regarding resolving the link. If `detail` is `true`, then the string also contains
              information on the link resolved object. If `detail` is `false` or not supplied,
              then the string consists of the `NamingException` information plus the link's
              remaining name. This string is for debugging and is not meant to be interpreted
              programmatically.

PARAMETERS

detail   If `true`, then add information about the link resolved object.

RETURNS   The non-`null` string representation of this link exception.

OVERRIDES   `NamingException.toString()`.

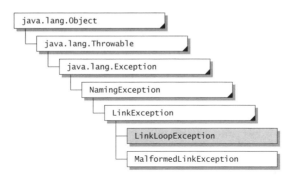

Syntax

`public class LinkLoopException extends LinkException`

Description

A `LinkLoopException` is thrown when a loop is detected either while attempting to resolve a link or when an implementation-specific limit on link counts has been reached.

Synchronization and serialization issues that apply to `LinkException` apply directly here.

MEMBER SUMMARY
Constructor
`LinkLoopException()`   Constructs an instance of `LinkLoopException`.

LinkLoopException()

PURPOSE	Constructs an instance of `LinkLoopException`.
SYNTAX	`public LinkLoopException()` `public LinkLoopException(String msg)`
DESCRIPTION	These constructors construct an instance of `LinkLoopException` with an optional `msg` supplied. If `msg` is not supplied, then `msg` defaults to `null`. All other fields default to `null`.
PARAMETERS	
`msg`	Additional detail about this exception. May be `null`.
SEE ALSO	`java.lang.Throwable.getMessage()`.

L

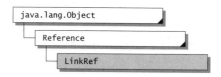

Syntax

```
public class LinkRef extends Reference
```

Description

The LinkRef class represents a Reference whose content is a name, called the *link name*, that is bound to an atomic name in a context. The name is either a URL or a name to be resolved relative to the initial context. If the first character of the name is a period character ("."), then the name is relative to the context in which the link is bound.

Normal resolution of names in context operations always follow links. The resolution of the link name itself might cause the resolution to pass through other links. This gives rise to the possibility of a cycle of links whose resolution cannot terminate normally. As a simple means to avoid such nonterminating resolutions, service providers may define limits on the number of links that may be involved in any single operation invoked by the caller.

A LinkRef contains a single StringRefAddr, whose type is "LinkAddress" and whose content is the link name. The class name field of the Reference is that of this (LinkRef) class.

LinkRef is bound to a name by using the normal Context.bind()/rebind() and Dir-Context.bind()/rebind(). Context.lookupLink() is used to retrieve the link itself if the terminal atomic name is bound to a link.

Many naming systems support a native notion of link that may be used within the naming system itself. The JNDI does not specify whether any relationship exists between such native links and JNDI links.

A LinkRef instance is not synchronized against concurrent access by multiple threads. Threads that need to access a LinkRef instance concurrently should synchronize among themselves and provide the necessary locking.

MEMBER SUMMARY	
Constructor	
LinkRef()	Constructs an instance of LinkRef for a name.
Link Method	
getLinkName()	Retrieves the name of this link.

See Also
Context.lookupLink().

getLinkName()

PURPOSE   Retrieves the name of this link.

SYNTAX   public String getLinkName() throws NamingException

RETURNS   The non-null name of this link.

EXCEPTIONS
 MalformedLinkException
          If a link name cannot be extracted.
 NamingException
          If a naming exception is encountered.

EXAMPLE   See the **Miscellaneous** lesson (page 391).

LinkRef()

PURPOSE   Constructs an instance of LinkRef for a name.

SYNTAX   public LinkRef(Name linkName)
                 public LinkRef(String linkName)

PARAMETERS
 linkName   The non-null composite name for which to create this link.

L

javax.naming
MalformedLinkException

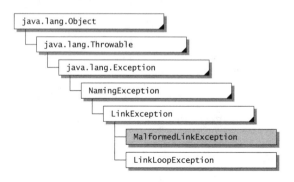

Syntax

```
public class MalformedLinkException extends LinkException
```

Description

A `MalformedLinkException` is thrown when a malformed link is encountered while resolving or constructing a link.

Synchronization and serialization issues that apply to `LinkException` apply directly here.

MEMBER SUMMARY
Constructor
`MalformedLinkException()`   Constructs an instance of `MalformedLinkException`.

MalformedLinkException()

PURPOSE	Constructs an instance of `MalformedLinkException`.
SYNTAX	`public MalformedLinkException()` `public MalformedLinkException(String msg)`
DESCRIPTION	These constructors create an instance of `MalformedLinkException` with an optional `msg` supplied. If `msg` is not supplied, then `msg` defaults to `null`. All other fields default to `null`.
PARAMETERS	
msg	Additional detail about this exception. May be `null`.
SEE ALSO	`java.lang.Throwable.getMessage()`.

Syntax

```
public class ModificationItem implements java.io.Serializable
```

Description

The ModificationItem class represents a modification item. It consists of modification code and an attribute on which to operate.

A ModificationItem instance is not synchronized against concurrent multithreaded access. Multiple threads trying to access and modify a single ModificationItem instance should lock the object.

MEMBER SUMMARY	
Constructor	
ModificationItem()	Constructs an instance of ModificationItem.
Access Methods	
getAttribute()	Retrieves the attribute associated with this Modification-Item.
getModificationOp()	Retrieves the modification code of this ModificationItem.
Object Method	
toString()	Generates the string representation of this ModificationItem.

See Also

DirContext.modifyAttributes().

Example

See the **Directory Operations** lesson (page 62).

getAttribute()

PURPOSE   Retrieves the attribute associated with this ModificationItem.

SYNTAX   public Attribute getAttribute()

M

RETURNS	The non-null attribute to use for the modification.

getModificationOp()

PURPOSE	Retrieves the modification code of this ModificationItem.
SYNTAX	`public int getModificationOp()`
RETURNS	The modification code. One of DirContext.ADD_ATTRIBUTE, DirContext.REPLACE_ATTRIBUTE, or DirContext.REMOVE_ATTRIBUTE.

ModificationItem()

PURPOSE	Constructs an instance of ModificationItem.
SYNTAX	`public ModificationItem(int mod_op, Attribute attr)`
PARAMETERS	
attr	The non-null attribute to use for modification.
mod_op	The modification to apply. Must be one of DirContext.ADD_ATTRIBUTE, DirContext.REPLACE_ATTRIBUTE, or DirContext.REMOVE_ATTRIBUTE.
EXCEPTIONS	
IllegalArgumentException	If attr is null, or if mod_op is not one of the modifications specified here.
EXAMPLE	See the **Directory Operations** lesson (page 62).

toString()

PURPOSE	Generates the string representation of this ModificationItem.
SYNTAX	`public String toString()`
DESCRIPTION	This method generates the string representation of this ModificationItem, which consists of the modification operation and its related attribute. The string is for debugging and is not meant to be interpreted programmatically.
RETURNS	The non-null string representation of this modification item.
OVERRIDES	`java.lang.Object.toString()`.

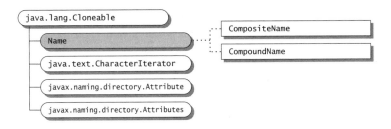

Syntax

```
public interface Name extends Cloneable, java.io.Serializable
```

Description

The Name interface represents a *generic name*—an ordered sequence of components. It can be a *composite name* (names that span multiple namespaces) or a *compound name* (names that are used within an individual hierarchical naming system).

Name may have different implementations, for example composite names, URLs, or namespace-specific compound names. The components of a name are numbered. The indexes of a name with N components range from 0 up to, but not including, N. This range may be written as [0, N). The most significant component is at index 0. An empty name has no components.

None of this interface's methods accept null as a valid value for a parameter that is a name or a name component. Likewise, methods that return a name or name component never return null.

A Name instance is not guaranteed to be synchronized against concurrent multithreaded access if that access is not read-only.

N

MEMBER SUMMARY	
Update Methods	
add()	Adds a single component to this name.
addAll()	Adds the components of a name, in order, to this name.
get()	Retrieves a component of this name.
getAll()	Retrieves the components of this name as an enumeration of strings.
isEmpty()	Determines whether this name is empty.
remove()	Removes a component from this name.
size()	Returns the number of components in this name.
	Continued

MEMBER SUMMARY	
Create Methods	
clone()	Generates a copy of this name.
getPrefix()	Creates a name whose components consist of a prefix of the components of this name.
getSuffix()	Creates a name whose components consist of a suffix of the components of this name.
Comparison Methods	
compareTo()	Compares this name with another name for order.
endsWith()	Determines whether this name ends with a specified suffix.
startsWith()	Determines whether this name starts with a specified prefix.

See Also

CompositeName, CompoundName.

Example

See CompositeName and CompoundName.

add()

N

PURPOSE   Adds a single component to this name.

SYNTAX   public Name add(String comp) throws InvalidNameException
             public Name add(int posn, String comp) throws
                InvalidNameException

DESCRIPTION This method adds a single component at position posn in this name. Components of this name at or after posn are shifted up by 1 (away from index 0) to accommodate the new component. If posn is not specified, then the component is added to the end of this name.

PARAMETERS
 comp   The component to add.
 posn   The index at which to add the new component. Must be in the range [0, size()].

RETURNS   The updated name (not a new one).

EXCEPTIONS
 InvalidNameException
         If adding comp would violate the syntax rules of this name.

addAll()

PURPOSE   Adds the components of a name, in order, to this name.

SYNTAX
```
public Name addAll(Name n) throws InvalidNameException
public Name addAll(int posn, Name n) throws InvalidNameException
```

DESCRIPTION   This method adds the components of a name, n, in order, at position posn in this name. Components of this name at or after posn are shifted up (away from 0) to accommodate the new components. If posn is not specified, then n is added at the end of this name.

PARAMETERS

n   The components to add.

posn   The index in this name at which to add the new components. Must be in the range [0, size()].

RETURNS   The updated name (not a new one).

EXCEPTIONS

ArrayIndexOutOfBoundsException

                If posn is outside of the specified range.

InvalidNameException

                If n is not a valid name, or if the addition of the components would violate the syntax rules of this name.

clone()

PURPOSE   Generates a new copy of this name.

SYNTAX   `public Object clone()`

DESCRIPTION   Subsequent changes to the components of this name will not affect the new copy, and vice versa.

RETURNS   A copy of this name.

OVERRIDES   `java.lang.Object.clone()`.

compareTo()

PURPOSE   Compares this name with another name for order.

SYNTAX   `public int compareTo(Object obj)`

DESCRIPTION   This method compares this name with another name for order. It returns a negative integer, zero, or a positive integer depending on whether this name, respectively, is less than, equal to, or greater than obj.

N

As with `Object.equals()`, the notion of ordering for names depends on the class that implements this interface. For example, the ordering may be based on lexicographical ordering of the name components. Specific attributes of the name, such as how it treats case, may affect the ordering. In general, two names of different classes may not be compared.

PARAMETERS

obj   The non-null object against which to compare.

RETURNS   A negative integer, zero, or a positive integer depending no whether this name, respectively, is less than, equal to, or greater than `obj`.

EXCEPTIONS

ClassCastException

If `obj` is not a `Name` of a type that may be compared with this name.

SEE ALSO   `java.lang.Comparable.compareTo()`.

endsWith()

PURPOSE   Determines whether this name ends with a specified suffix.

SYNTAX   `public boolean endsWith(Name n)`

DESCRIPTION   This method determines whether this name ends with the suffix `n`. A name `n` is a suffix if it is equal to `this.getSuffix(size()-n.size())`.

PARAMETERS

n   The name to check.

RETURNS   `true` if `n` is a suffix of this name; `false` otherwise.

SEE ALSO   `startsWith()`.

get()

PURPOSE   Retrieves a component of this name.

SYNTAX   `public String get(int posn)`

PARAMETERS

posn   The 0-based index of the component to retrieve. Must be in the range [0, `size()`).

RETURNS   The component at index `posn`.

EXCEPTIONS

ArrayIndexOutOfBoundsException

If `posn` is outside of the specified range.

getAll()

PURPOSE   Retrieves the components of this name as an enumeration of strings.

SYNTAX   `public Enumeration getAll()`

DESCRIPTION   This method retrieves the components of this name as an enumeration of strings. The effect on the enumeration of updates to this name is undefined. If the name has zero components, then an empty (non-`null`) enumeration is returned.

RETURNS   An enumeration of the components of this name, each a `String`.

getPrefix()

PURPOSE   Creates a name whose components consist of a prefix of the components of this name.

SYNTAX   `public Name getPrefix(int posn)`

DESCRIPTION   This method creates a name whose components consist of a prefix of the components of this name. Subsequent changes to this name will not affect the name that is returned, and vice versa.

PARAMETERS

posn   The 0-based index of the component at which to stop. Must be in the range [`0`, `size()`].

RETURNS   A name that consists of the components at indexes in the range [`0`, `posn`).

EXCEPTIONS

`ArrayIndexOutOfBoundsException`
               If posn is outside of the specified range.

SEE ALSO   `getSuffix()`.

getSuffix()

PURPOSE   Creates a name whose components consist of a suffix of the components of this name.

SYNTAX   `public Name getSuffix(int posn)`

DESCRIPTION   This method creates a name whose components consist of a suffix of the components of this name. Subsequent changes to this name do not affect the name that is returned, and vice versa.

PARAMETERS

posn   The 0-based index of the component at which to start. Must be in the range
                [0, size()].

RETURNS   A name that consists of the components at indexes in the range [posn, size()).
                If posn is equal to size(), then an empty name is returned.

EXCEPTIONS

ArrayIndexOutOfBoundsException
                If posn is outside of the specified range.

SEE ALSO   getPrefix().

isEmpty()

PURPOSE   Determines whether this name is empty.

SYNTAX   `public boolean isEmpty()`

DESCRIPTION   This method determines whether this name is empty. An empty name is a
                name that has zero components.

RETURNS   true if this name is empty; false otherwise.

SEE ALSO   size().

remove()

PURPOSE   Removes a component from this name.

SYNTAX   `public Object remove(int posn) throws InvalidNameException`

DESCRIPTION   This method removes a component at the specified position from this name.
                Components with indexes greater than this position are shifted down (toward
                index 0) by 1.

PARAMETERS

posn   The index of the component to remove. Must be in the range [0, size()).

RETURNS   The component removed (a String).

EXCEPTIONS

ArrayIndexOutOfBoundsException
                If posn is outside of the specified range.

InvalidNameException
                If deleting the component would violate the syntax rules of the name.

size()

PURPOSE	Returns the number of components in this name.
SYNTAX	`public int size()`
RETURNS	The number of components in this name.

startsWith()

PURPOSE	Determines whether this name starts with a specified prefix.
SYNTAX	`public boolean startsWith(Name n)`
DESCRIPTION	This method determines whether this name starts with the prefix n. A name n is a prefix if it is equal to `getPrefix(n.size())`.
PARAMETERS	
n	The name to check.
RETURNS	`true` if n is a prefix of this name; `false` otherwise.
SEE ALSO	`endsWith()`.

N

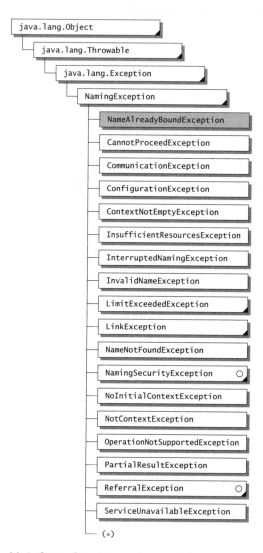

(*) 9 classes from other packages not shown.

Syntax

```
public class NameAlreadyBoundException extends NamingException
```

Description

A `NameAlreadyBoundException` is thrown by methods to indicate that a binding cannot be added because the name is already bound to another object.

Synchronization and serialization issues that apply to `NamingException` apply directly here.

MEMBER SUMMARY

Constructor

NameAlreadyBoundException()	Constructs an instance of NameAlreadyBound-Exception.

NameAlreadyBoundException()

PURPOSE	Constructs an instance of `NameAlreadyBoundException`.
SYNTAX	`public NameAlreadyBoundException()` `public NameAlreadyBoundException(String msg)`
DESCRIPTION	These constructors construct an instance of `NameAlreadyBoundException` by using an optional `msg` supplied. If no `msg` is supplied, then `msg` defaults to `null`. All other fields default to `null`.
PARAMETERS	
`msg`	Additional detail about this exception. May be `null`.
SEE ALSO	`java.lang.Throwable.getMessage()`.

N

NameClassPair

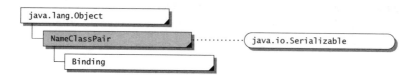

Syntax

`public class NameClassPair implements java.io.Serializable`

Description

The NameClassPair class represents the object name/class name pair of a binding found in a context.

A context consists of name-to-object bindings. This class represents the name and the class of the bound object. It consists of a name and a string that represents the package-qualified class name.

Use subclassing for naming systems that generate contents of a name/class pair dynamically.

A NameClassPair instance is not synchronized against concurrent access by multiple threads. Threads that need to access a NameClassPair concurrently should synchronize among themselves and provide the necessary locking.

MEMBER SUMMARY	
Constructor	
NameClassPair()	Constructs an instance of NameClassPair.
Accessor Methods	
getClassName()	Retrieves the class name of the object bound to the name of this binding.
getName()	Retrieves the name of this binding.
isRelative()	Determines whether the name of this binding is relative to the target context.
setClassName()	Sets the class name of this binding.
setName()	Sets the name of this binding.
setRelative()	Sets whether the name of this binding is relative to the target context.
String Method	
toString()	Generates the string representation of this name/class pair.

See Also
Context.list().

Example
See the **Naming Operations** lesson (page 54).

getClassName()

PURPOSE	Retrieves the class name of the object bound to the name of this binding.
SYNTAX	public String getClassName()
DESCRIPTION	This method retrieves the class name of the object bound to the name of this binding. If a reference or some other indirect information is bound, then this method retrieves the class name of the eventual object that will be returned by Binding.getObject().
RETURNS	The possibly null class name of the object bound; null if the object is null.
SEE ALSO	Binding.getClassName(), Binding.getObject(), setClassName().
EXAMPLE	See the **Reading Objects from the Directory** lesson (page 181).

getName()

N

PURPOSE	Retrieves the name of this binding.
SYNTAX	public String getName()
DESCRIPTION	This method retrieves the name of this binding. If isRelative() is true, then this name is relative to the target context (which is named by the first parameter of Context.list()). If isRelative() is false, then this name is a URL string.
RETURNS	The non-null name of this binding.
SEE ALSO	isRelative(), setName().
EXAMPLE	See the **URLs** lesson (page 128).

isRelative()

PURPOSE	Determines whether the name of this binding is relative to the target context.
SYNTAX	public boolean isRelative()

DESCRIPTION	This method determines whether the name of this binding is relative to the target context (which is named by the first parameter of the Context.list() method).
RETURNS	true if the name of this binding is relative to the target context; false if the name of this binding is a URL string.
SEE ALSO	getName(), setRelative().
EXAMPLE	See the **URLs** lesson (page 128).

NameClassPair()

PURPOSE	Constructs an instance of NameClassPair.
SYNTAX	public NameClassPair(String name, String className) public NameClassPair(String name, String className, boolean isRelative)
DESCRIPTION	These constructors construct an instance of NameClassPair, when given its name, class name, and whether it is relative to the listing context. If isRelative is not supplied, then isRelative default to true.
PARAMETERS	
className	The non-null name of the class of the object.
isRelative	true if name is relative to the target context; false if name is relative to the initial context (i.e., a URL string).
name	The non-null name of the object.
EXAMPLE	See **The Essential Components** lesson (page 336).

setClassName()

PURPOSE	Sets the class name of this binding.
SYNTAX	public void setClassName(String name)
PARAMETERS	
name	The possibly null string to use as the class name. If null, then Binding.getClassName() will return the actual class name of the object in the binding. The class name will be null if the object bound is null.
SEE ALSO	Binding.getClassName(), getClassName().

setName()

PURPOSE	Sets the name of this binding.

SYNTAX	`public void setName(String name)`
PARAMETERS	
name	The non-null string to use as the name.
SEE ALSO	`getName()`, `setRelative()`.

setRelative()

PURPOSE	Sets whether the name of this binding is relative to the target context.
SYNTAX	`public void setRelative(boolean r)`
DESCRIPTION	This method sets whether the name of this binding is relative to the target context (which is named by the first parameter of `Context.list()`).
PARAMETERS	
r	If `true`, then the name of this binding is relative to the target context; if `false`, then the name of this binding is a URL string.
SEE ALSO	`isRelative()`, `setName()`.

toString()

PURPOSE	Generates the string representation of this name/class pair.
SYNTAX	`public String toString()`
DESCRIPTION	This method generates the string representation of this name/class pair. The string consists of the name and class name separated by a colon character (":"). This string is for debugging and is not meant to be interpreted programmatically.
RETURNS	The string representation of this name/class pair.
OVERRIDES	`java.lang.Object.toString()`.
EXAMPLE	See the **Naming Operations** lesson (page 54).

N

NameNotFoundException

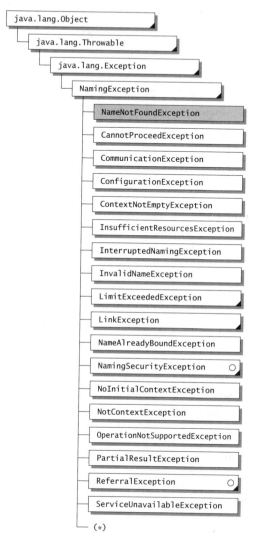

```
java.lang.Object
    java.lang.Throwable
        java.lang.Exception
            NamingException
                NameNotFoundException
                CannotProceedException
                CommunicationException
                ConfigurationException
                ContextNotEmptyException
                InsufficientResourcesException
                InterruptedNamingException
                InvalidNameException
                LimitExceededException
                LinkException
                NameAlreadyBoundException
                NamingSecurityException        ○
                NoInitialContextException
                NotContextException
                OperationNotSupportedException
                PartialResultException
                ReferralException              ○
                ServiceUnavailableException
                (*)
```

(*) 9 classes from other packages not shown.

Syntax

```
public class NameNotFoundException extends NamingException
```

Description

A `NameNotFoundException` is thrown when a component of the name cannot be resolved because it is not bound.

Synchronization and serialization issues that apply to `NamingException` apply directly here.

MEMBER SUMMARY
Constructor
`NameNotFoundException()`   Constructs an instance of `NameNotFoundException`.

NameNotFoundException()

PURPOSE	Constructs an instance of `NameNotFoundException`.
SYNTAX	`public NameNotFoundException()` `public NameNotFoundException(String msg)`
DESCRIPTION	These constructors construct an instance of `NameNotFoundException` by using the optional `msg` supplied. If `msg` is not supplied, then `msg` defaults to `null`. All other fields default to `null`.
PARAMETERS	
`msg`	Additional detail about this exception. May be `null`.
SEE ALSO	`java.lang.Throwable.getMessage()`.

N

NameParser

NameParser

Syntax

```
public interface NameParser
```

Description

The NameParser interface is used to parse names from a hierarchical namespace. It contains knowledge of the syntactic information (such as left-to-right orientation and name separator) needed to parse names. equals(), when used to compare two NameParsers, returns true if and only if the two NameParsers serve the same namespace.

MEMBER SUMMARY	
Parse Method	
parse()	Parses a name into its components.

See Also

CompoundName, Context.getNameParser().

parse()

PURPOSE	Parses a name into its components.
SYNTAX	Name parse(String name) throws NamingException
DESCRIPTION	This method parses a name into its components.
PARAMETERS	
name	The non-null string name to parse.
RETURNS	A non-null parsed form of the name derived by using the naming convention of this parser.
EXCEPTIONS	
InvalidNameException	If name does not conform to the syntax defined for the namespace.
NamingException	If a naming exception is encountered.
EXAMPLE	See the **What's in a Name?** lesson (page 87).

N

NamespaceChangeListener

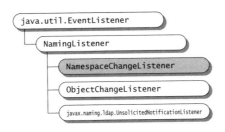

```
java.util.EventListener
    NamingListener
        NamespaceChangeListener
        ObjectChangeListener
        javax.naming.ldap.UnsolicitedNotificationListener
```

Syntax

```
public interface NamespaceChangeListener extends NamingListener
```

Description

The NamespaceChangeListener interface specifies the methods that a listener interested in namespace changes must implement. Specifically, the listener is interested in NamingEvents with event types of OBJECT_ADDED, OBJECT_RENAMED, or OBJECT_REMOVED.

Such a listener must do the following.

1. Implement this interface and its methods.
2. Implement NamingListener.namingExceptionThrown() so that it will be notified of exceptions thrown while attempting to collect information about the events.
3. Register with the source by using its addNamingListener() method.

A listener that wants to be notified of OBJECT_CHANGED event types should also implement the ObjectChangeListener interface.

MEMBER SUMMARY

Callback Methods

objectAdded()	Called when an object has been added.
objectRemoved()	Called when an object has been removed.
objectRenamed()	Called when an object has been renamed.

Example

See the **Event Notification** lesson (page 112).

objectAdded()

PURPOSE   Called when an object has been added.

SYNTAX	`void objectAdded(NamingEvent evt)`
DESCRIPTION	This method is called when an object has been added. The binding of the newly added object can be obtained by using `evt.getNewBinding()`.
PARAMETERS	
`evt`	The non-null event.
SEE ALSO	`NamingEvent.OBJECT_ADDED`.
EXAMPLE	See the **Event Notification** lesson (page 112).

objectRemoved()

PURPOSE	Called when an object has been removed.
SYNTAX	`void objectRemoved(NamingEvent evt)`
DESCRIPTION	This method is called when an object has been removed. The binding of the newly removed object can be obtained by using `evt.getOldBinding()`.
PARAMETERS	
`evt`	The non-null event.
SEE ALSO	`NamingEvent.OBJECT_REMOVED`.
EXAMPLE	See the **Event Notification** lesson (page 112).

N

objectRenamed()

PURPOSE	Called when an object has been renamed.
SYNTAX	`void objectRenamed(NamingEvent evt)`
DESCRIPTION	This method is called when an object has been renamed. The binding of the renamed object can be obtained by using `evt.getNewBinding()`. Its old binding (before the rename) can be obtained by using `evt.getOldBinding()`. One of these may be `null` if the old/new binding is outside of the scope in which the listener has registered interest.
PARAMETERS	
`evt`	The non-null event.
SEE ALSO	`NamingEvent.OBJECT_RENAMED`.
EXAMPLE	See the **Event Notification** lesson (page 112).

NamingEnumeration

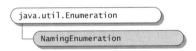

Syntax

```
public interface NamingEnumeration extends Enumeration
```

Description

The NamingEnumeration interface is used to enumerate lists that are returned by methods in the javax.naming and javax.naming.directory packages. It extends java.util.Enumeration to allow exceptions to be thrown during the enumeration.

When a method such as Context.list(), Context.listBindings(), or Dir-Context.search() returns a NamingEnumeration, any exceptions encountered are reserved until all results have been returned. At the end of the enumeration, the exception(s) are thrown (by hasMore()).

For example, suppose that list() is returning only a partial answer. list() first will return a NamingEnumeration. After NamingEnumeration's next() has returned the last of the results, then invoking hasMore() will cause a PartialResultException to be thrown.

In another example, suppose that a search method is invoked with a specified size limit of *n* and the answer consists of more than *n* results. First, search() will return a NamingEnumeration. Then, after the *n*th result has been returned by invocations of next() on the Naming-Enumeration, hasMore() will be invoked, thereby causing a SizeLimitExceedException to be thrown.

Note that if the program uses hasMoreElements() and nextElement() instead to iterate through the NamingEnumeration, then because these methods cannot throw exceptions, no exception will be thrown. Instead, in the previous example, after the *n*th result has been returned by nextElement(), invoking hasMoreElements() will return false.

Note also that a NoSuchElementException is thrown if the program invokes next() or nextElement() when no elements are left in the enumeration. The program can always avoid this exception by using hasMore() and hasMoreElements() to check whether the end of the enumeration has been reached.

If an exception is thrown during an enumeration, then the enumeration will become invalid. Subsequent invocation of any method on that enumeration will yield undefined results.

MEMBER SUMMARY	
Enumeration Methods	
close()	Closes this enumeration.
hasMore()	Determines whether this enumeration contains any more elements.
next()	Retrieves the next element in this enumeration.

See Also

Context.list(), Context.listBindings(),
javax.naming.directory.Attribute.getAll(),
javax.naming.directory.Attributes.getAll(), javax.naming.directory.search().

Example

See the **Naming Operations** lesson (page 54).

close()

PURPOSE   Closes this enumeration.

SYNTAX   `public void close() throws NamingException`

DESCRIPTION   This method closes this enumeration. After this method has been invoked on this enumeration, the enumeration becomes invalid and subsequent invocation of any of its methods will yield undefined results. This method is intended for aborting an enumeration so as to free up resources. If an enumeration proceeds to the end—that is, until `hasMoreElements()` or `hasMore()` returns `false`—then resources will be freed up automatically and `close()` will not need to be called explicitly.

                This method indicates to the service provider that it is free to release resources associated with the enumeration and can notify servers to cancel any outstanding requests. `close()` is a hint to implementations for managing their resources. Implementations are encouraged to use appropriate algorithms to manage their resources when the client omits the `close()` calls.

EXCEPTIONS
 NamingException
                If a naming exception is encountered while closing the enumeration.

hasMore()

PURPOSE   Determines whether the enumeration has any more elements.

SYNTAX   `public boolean hasMore() throws NamingException`

DESCRIPTION   This method determines whether the enumeration has any more elements. It allows the application to catch and handle naming exceptions encountered while determining whether there are more elements.

RETURNS   `true` if there is more in the enumeration; `false` otherwise.

EXCEPTIONS

`NamingException`

If a naming exception is encountered while attempting to determine whether the enumeration contains another element. See `NamingException` and its subclasses for the possible naming exceptions.

SEE ALSO   `java.util.Enumeration.hasMoreElements()`.

EXAMPLE   See the **Naming Operations** lesson (page 54).

next()

PURPOSE   Retrieves the next element in the enumeration.

SYNTAX   `public Object next() throws NamingException`

DESCRIPTION   This method retrieves the next element in the enumeration. It allows the application to catch and handle naming exceptions encountered while retrieving the next element.

N

Note that `next()` can also throw the runtime exception `NoSuchElementException` to indicate that the caller is attempting to enumerate beyond the end of the enumeration. This differs from a `NamingException`, which indicates that a problem occurred in obtaining the next element, for example due to a referral or server unavailability.

RETURNS   The possibly `null` element in the enumeration. `null` is valid only for enumerations that can return `null` (e.g., `Attribute.getAll()` returns an enumeration of attribute values, and an attribute value may be `null`).

EXCEPTIONS

`java.util.NoSuchElementException`

If attempting to get the next element when none is available.

`NamingException`

If a naming exception is encountered while attempting to retrieve the next element. See `NamingException` and its subclasses for the possible naming exceptions.

SEE ALSO   `java.util.Enumeration.nextElement()`.

EXAMPLE   See the **Naming Operations** lesson (page 54).

NamingEvent

```
java.lang.Object
    java.util.EventObject
        NamingEvent
        NamingExceptionEvent
        javax.naming.ldap.UnsolicitedNotificationEvent
```

Syntax

```
public class NamingEvent extends java.util.EventObject
```

Description

The NamingEvent class represents an event fired by a naming/directory service. Its state consists of the following:

- The event source: the EventContext that fired this event
- The event type
- The new binding: information about the object after the change
- The old binding: information about the object before the change
- Change information: information about the change that triggered this event; usually service provider-specific or server-specific

The event source is always the same EventContext *instance* with which the listener has registered. Furthermore, the names of the bindings in the NamingEvent are always relative to that instance. For example, suppose that a listener makes the following registration.

```
NamespaceChangeListener listener = ...;
src.addNamingListener("x", SUBTREE_SCOPE, listener);
```

When an object named "x/y" is subsequently deleted, the corresponding NamingEvent (evt) must contain the following.

```
evt.getEventContext() == src
evt.getOldBinding().getName().equals("x/y")
```

Care must be taken when multiple threads are accessing the same EventContext concurrently. See the javax.naming.event package description for more information on threading issues.

Example

See the **Event Notification** lesson (page 118).

MEMBER SUMMARY	
Constructor	
NamingEvent()	Constructs an instance of NamingEvent.
Access Methods	
getChangeInfo()	Retrieves the change information for this event.
getEventContext()	Retrieves the event source that fired this event.
getNewBinding()	Retrieves the binding of the object after the change.
getOldBinding()	Retrieves the binding of the object before the change.
getType()	Returns the type of this event.
Event Dispatch Method	
dispatch()	Invokes the appropriate listener method on this event.
NamingEvent Types	
OBJECT_ADDED	Indicates that a new object has been added.
OBJECT_CHANGED	Indicates that an existing object has been changed.
OBJECT_REMOVED	Indicates that an object has been removed.
OBJECT_RENAMED	Indicates that an object has been renamed.
Protected Fields	
changeInfo	Contains information about the change that generated this event.
newBinding	Contains information about the object after the change.
oldBinding	Contains information about the object before the change.
type	Contains the type of this event.

N

changeInfo

PURPOSE	Contains information about the change that generated this event.
SYNTAX	protected Object changeInfo
DESCRIPTION	This field contains information about the change that generated this event.
SEE ALSO	getChangeInfo().

dispatch()

PURPOSE	Invokes the appropriate listener method on this event.
SYNTAX	public void dispatch(NamingListener listener)
DESCRIPTION	This method invokes the appropriate listener method on this event. The default implementation of this method handles the following event types: OBJECT_ADDED, OBJECT_REMOVED, OBJECT_RENAMED, and OBJECT_CHANGED.

The listener method is executed in the same thread as this method. See the `javax.naming.event` package description for more information on threading issues.

PARAMETERS

`listener`   The non-null listener.

getChangeInfo()

PURPOSE   Retrieves the change information for this event.

SYNTAX   `public Object getChangeInfo()`

DESCRIPTION   This method retrieves the change information for this event. The value of the change information is service-specific. For example, it could be an identifier that identifies a change in a change log on the server.

RETURNS   The possibly `null` change information of this event.

getEventContext()

PURPOSE   Retrieves the event source that fired this event.

SYNTAX   `public EventContext getEventContext()`

DESCRIPTION   This method retrieves the event source that fired this event. It returns the same object as `EventObject.getSource()`.

              If the result of this method is used to access the event source, for example to look up the object or get its attributes, then it needs to be locked. This is because `Context` implementations are not guaranteed to be thread-safe (and `EventContext` is a subinterface of `Context`). See the `javax.naming.event` package description for more information on threading issues.

RETURNS   The non-null context that fired this event.

EXAMPLE   See the **Event Notification** lesson (page 119).

getNewBinding()

PURPOSE   Retrieves the binding of the object after the change.

SYNTAX   `public Binding getNewBinding()`

DESCRIPTION   This method retrieves the binding of the object after the change.

              The binding must be non-null if the object existed after the change relative to the source context (`getEventContext()`). That is, it must be non-null for

OBJECT_ADDED and OBJECT_CHANGED. For OBJECT_RENAMED, it is null if the object after the rename is outside of the scope for which the listener registered interest; it is non-null if the object is inside of the scope after the rename.

The name in the binding is resolved relative to the event source getEvent-Context(). The object returned by Binding.getObject() may be null if such information is unavailable.

RETURNS   The possibly null binding of the object after the change.

EXAMPLE   See the **Event Notification** lesson (page 119).

getOldBinding()

PURPOSE   Retrieves the binding of the object before the change.

SYNTAX   `public Binding getOldBinding()`

DESCRIPTION   This method retrieves the binding of the object before the change.

The binding must be non-null if the object existed before the change relative to the source context (getEventContext()). That is, it must be non-null for OBJECT_REMOVED and OBJECT_CHANGED. For OBJECT_RENAMED, it is null if the object before the rename is outside of the scope for which the listener has registered interest. It is non-null if the object is inside of the scope before the rename.

The name in the binding is resolved relative to the event source getEvent-Context(). The object returned by Binding.getObject() may be null if such information is unavailable.

RETURNS   The possibly null binding of the object before the change.

EXAMPLE   See the **Event Notification** lesson (page 113).

getType()

PURPOSE   Returns the type of this event.

SYNTAX   `public int getType()`

RETURNS   The type of this event.

SEE ALSO   OBJECT_ADDED, OBJECT_CHANGED, OBJECT_REMOVED, OBJECT_RENAMED.

NamingEvent()

PURPOSE   Constructs an instance of NamingEvent.

SYNTAX	`public NamingEvent(EventContext source, int type, Binding newBd,` `    Binding oldBd, Object changeInfo)`
DESCRIPTION	This constructor constructs an instance of `NamingEvent`.
	The names in `newBd` and `oldBd` are resolved relative to the event source `source`.
	For an `OBJECT_ADDED` event type, `newBd` must not be `null`. For an `OBJECT_REMOVED` event type, `oldBd` must not be `null`. For an `OBJECT_CHANGED` event type, `newBd` and `oldBd` must not be `null`. For an `OBJECT_RENAMED` event type, one of `newBd` or `oldBd` may be `null` if the new or old binding is outside of the scope for which the listener has registered.

PARAMETERS

`changeInfo`	A possibly `null` object that contains information about the change.
`newBd`	A possibly `null` binding before the change. See the method description.
`oldBd`	A possibly `null` binding after the change. See the method description.
`source`	The non-`null` context that fired this event.
`type`	The type of the event.
SEE ALSO	`OBJECT_ADDED, OBJECT_CHANGED, OBJECT_REMOVED, OBJECT_RENAMED`.

newBinding

PURPOSE	Contains information about the object after the change.
SYNTAX	`protected Binding newBinding`
DESCRIPTION	This field contains information about the object after the change.
SEE ALSO	`getNewBinding()`.

OBJECT_ADDED

PURPOSE	Indicates that a new object has been added.
SYNTAX	`public static final int OBJECT_ADDED`
DESCRIPTION	This constant represents the naming event type for indicating that a new object has been added. The value of this constant is 0.

OBJECT_CHANGED

PURPOSE	Indicates that an object has been changed.
SYNTAX	`public static final int OBJECT_CHANGED`

DESCRIPTION   This constant represents the naming event type for indicating that an object has been changed. The changes might include the object's attributes and even the object itself. Note that some services might fire multiple events for a single modification. For example, the modification might be implemented by first removing the old binding and then adding a new binding that contains the same name but a different object.

The value of this constant is 3.

OBJECT_REMOVED

PURPOSE   Indicates that an object has been removed.

SYNTAX   `public static final int OBJECT_REMOVED`

DESCRIPTION   This constant represents the naming event type for indicating that an object has been removed. The value of this constant is 1.

OBJECT_RENAMED

PURPOSE   Indicates that an object has been renamed.

SYNTAX   `public static final int OBJECT_RENAMED`

DESCRIPTION   This constant represents the naming event type for indicating that an object has been renamed. Some services might fire multiple events for a single logical "rename" operation. For example, the "rename" operation might be implemented by adding a binding with the new name and removing the old binding.

The old/new binding in `NamingEvent` may be `null` if the old or new name is outside of the scope for which the listener has registered.

When an interior node in the namespace tree has been renamed, the topmost node that is part of the listener's scope should be used to generate a rename event. The extent to which this can be supported is provider-specific. For example, a service might generate rename notifications for all descendants of the changed interior node and the corresponding provider might not be able to prevent those notifications from being propagated to the listeners.

The value of this constant is 2.

oldBinding

PURPOSE   Contains information about the object before the change.

SYNTAX   `protected Binding oldBinding`

N

DESCRIPTION	This field contains information about the object before the change.
SEE ALSO	getOldBinding().

type

PURPOSE	Contains the type of this event.
SYNTAX	`protected int type`
DESCRIPTION	This field contains the type of this event.
SEE ALSO	getType(), OBJECT_ADDED, OBJECT_CHANGED, OBJECT_REMOVED, OBJECT_RENAMED.

N

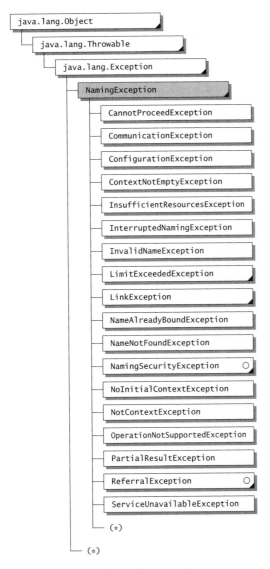

```
java.lang.Object
    └── java.lang.Throwable
            └── java.lang.Exception
                    └── NamingException
                            ├── CannotProceedException
                            ├── CommunicationException
                            ├── ConfigurationException
                            ├── ContextNotEmptyException
                            ├── InsufficientResourcesException
                            ├── InterruptedNamingException
                            ├── InvalidNameException
                            ├── LimitExceededException
                            ├── LinkException
                            ├── NameAlreadyBoundException
                            ├── NameNotFoundException
                            ├── NamingSecurityException        ○
                            ├── NoInitialContextException
                            ├── NotContextException
                            ├── OperationNotSupportedException
                            ├── PartialResultException
                            ├── ReferralException               ○
                            ├── ServiceUnavailableException
                            └── (*)
                    └── (*)
```

(*) classes from other packages not shown.

Syntax

```
public class NamingException extends Exception
```

663

Description

The NamingException is the superclass of all exceptions thrown by operations in the Context and DirContext interfaces. The nature of the failure is described by the name of the subclass. This exception captures the information pinpointing where the operation failed, such as the point to which resolution last proceeded. Table 31 shows the fields of a NamingException.

TABLE 31: NamingException Fields.

Field	Description
Resolved Name	Portion of the name that has been resolved.
Resolved Object	Object to which the resolution of the name proceeded.
Remaining Name	Portion of the name that has not been resolved.
Explanation	Detail explaining why name resolution failed.
Root Exception	The exception that caused this NamingException to be thrown.

null is an acceptable value for any of these fields. When null, it means that no such information has been recorded for that field.

A NamingException instance is not synchronized against concurrent multithreaded access. Multiple threads trying to access and modify a single NamingException instance should lock the object.

N

MEMBER SUMMARY	
Constructor	
NamingException()	Constructs an instance of NamingException.
Accessor Methods	
appendRemainingComponent()	Adds a component as the last component in the remaining name.
appendRemainingName()	Adds components as the last components in the remaining name.
getExplanation()	Retrieves the explanation associated with this exception.
getRemainingName()	Retrieves the remaining unresolved portion of the name.
getResolvedName()	Retrieves the leading portion of the name that was resolved successfully.
getResolvedObj()	Retrieves the object to which resolution was successful.
getRootCause()	Retrieves the root cause of this exception, if any.
setRemainingName()	Sets the remaining name field of this exception.
setResolvedName()	Sets the resolved name field of this exception.
setResolvedObj()	Sets the resolved object field of this exception.
setRootCause()	Records the root cause of this exception.

MEMBER SUMMARY	
Protected Fields	
remainingName	Contains the remaining name to be resolved.
resolvedName	Contains the part of the name that has been successfully resolved.
resolvedObj	Contains the object to which the resolution of the part of the name was successful.
rootException	Contains the original exception that caused this exception to be thrown.
Output Methods	
printStackTrace()	Prints this exception's stack trace.
toString()	Generates the string representation of this exception.

Example

See the **Preparations** lesson (page 47).

appendRemainingComponent()

PURPOSE   Adds a component as the last component in the remaining name.

SYNTAX   `public void appendRemainingComponent(String name)`

PARAMETERS

name   The component to add. If name is `null`, then this method does nothing.

SEE ALSO   `appendRemainingName()`, `getRemainingName()`, `setRemainingName()`.

appendRemainingName()

PURPOSE   Adds components as the last components in the remaining name.

SYNTAX   `public void appendRemainingName(Name name)`

DESCRIPTION This method add components from name as the last components in the remaining name. name is a composite name. If the intent is to append a compound name, then you should stringify the compound name and invoke the overloaded form that accepts a `java.lang.String` parameter.

Subsequent changes to name do not affect the remaining name fields in this `NamingException`, and vice versa.

PARAMETERS

name   The possibly `null` name that contains ordered components to add. If name is `null`, then this method does nothing.

665

SEE ALSO 　　　appendRemainingComponent(), getRemainingName(),
　　　　　　　　setRemainingName().

getExplanation()

PURPOSE 　　　Retrieves the explanation associated with this exception.

SYNTAX 　　　public String getExplanation()

RETURNS 　　　Additional detail about this exception. May be null. null means that there is
　　　　　　　　no detail message for this exception.

SEE ALSO 　　　java.lang.Throwable.getMessage().

getRemainingName()

PURPOSE 　　　Retrieves the remaining unresolved portion of the name.

SYNTAX 　　　public Name getRemainingName()

RETURNS 　　　The part of the name that has not been resolved. A composite name, it may be
　　　　　　　　null, meaning that the remaining name field has not been set.

SEE ALSO 　　　appendRemainingComponent(), appendRemainingName(),
　　　　　　　　setRemainingName().

getResolvedName()

PURPOSE 　　　Retrieves the leading portion of the name that was resolved successfully.

SYNTAX 　　　public Name getResolvedName()

RETURNS 　　　The part of the name that was resolved successfully. A composite name, it may
　　　　　　　　be null, meaning that the resolved name field has not been set.

SEE ALSO 　　　getResolvedObj(), setResolvedName().

getResolvedObj()

PURPOSE 　　　Retrieves the object to which resolution was successful.

SYNTAX 　　　public Object getResolvedObj()

DESCRIPTION 　This method retrieves the object to which resolution was successful. This is the
　　　　　　　　object to which the resolved name is bound.

RETURNS 　　　The possibly null object that was resolved so far. null means that the
　　　　　　　　resolved object field has not been set.

SEE ALSO 　　　getResolvedName(), setResolvedObj().

getRootCause()

PURPOSE	Retrieves the root cause of this exception, if any.
SYNTAX	`public Throwable getRootCause()`
DESCRIPTION	This method retrieves the root cause of this exception, if any. The service provider uses the root cause of a naming exception to indicate a non-naming-related exception to the caller and uses the `NamingException` structure to indicate how far the naming operation proceeded.
RETURNS	The possibly `null` exception that caused this naming exception. `null` means that no root cause was set for this naming exception.
SEE ALSO	`rootException`, `setRootCause()`.

NamingException()

PURPOSE	Constructs an instance of `NamingException`.
SYNTAX	`public NamingException()` `public NamingException(String msg)`
DESCRIPTION	This method constructs an instance of `NamingException` by using an optional `msg` supplied. If `msg` is not supplied, then `msg` defaults to `null`. All unspecified fields default to `null`.
PARAMETERS	
msg	Additional detail about this exception. May be `null`.
SEE ALSO	`java.lang.Throwable.getMessage()`.

N

printStackTrace()

PURPOSE	Prints this exception's stack trace.

SYNTAX	`public void printStackTrace()`
	`public void printStackTrace(java.io.PrintStream ps)`
	`public void printStackTrace(java.io.PrintWriter pw)`

DESCRIPTION	This method prints this exception's stack trace. If this exception has a root exception, then the stack trace of the root exception is printed instead.
	The first form of the method prints the stack trace to `System.err`. The second form prints the stack trace to the print stream `ps`. The third form prints the stack trace to a print writer `pw`.

PARAMETERS

ps	The non-null print stream to which to print.
pw	The non-null print writer to which to print.

remainingName

PURPOSE   Contains the remaining name to be resolved.

SYNTAX   `protected Name remainingName`

DESCRIPTION   This field contains the remaining name to be resolved. The name is a composite name and may be `null`. This field is initialized by the constructors. You should access and manipulate it through its get, set, and append methods.

SEE ALSO   `appendRemainingComponent()`, `appendRemainingName()`, `getRemainingName()`, `setRemainingName()`.

resolvedName

PURPOSE   Contains the part of the name that has been successfully resolved.

SYNTAX   `protected Name resolvedName`

DESCRIPTION   This field contains the part of the name that has been successfully resolved. The name is a composite name and may be `null`. It is initialized by the constructors. You should access and manipulate it through its get and set methods.

SEE ALSO   `getResolvedName()`, `setResolvedName()`.

resolvedObj

PURPOSE   Contains the object to which the resolution of the part of the name was successful.

SYNTAX   `protected Object resolvedObj`

DESCRIPTION   This field contains the object to which resolution of the part of the name was successful. It may be `null`. It is initialized by the constructors. You should access and manipulate this field through its get and set methods.

SEE ALSO   `getResolvedObj()`, `setResolvedObj()`.

rootException

PURPOSE   Contains the original exception that caused this exception to be thrown.

SYNTAX   `protected Throwable rootException`

N

DESCRIPTION   This field contains the original exception that caused this exception to be thrown. It is set if additional information is available that could be obtained from the original exception or if the original exception could not be mapped to a subclass of `NamingException`. This field may be `null`. It is initialized by the constructors. You should access and manipulate it through its get and set methods.

SEE ALSO   `getRootCause()`, `setRootCause()`.

setRemainingName()

PURPOSE   Sets the remaining name field of this exception.

SYNTAX   `public void setRemainingName(Name name)`

DESCRIPTION   This method sets the remaining name field of this exception.

    `name` is a composite name. If the intent is to set this field by using a compound name or string, then you must "stringify" the compound name and create a composite name with a single component by using the string. You can then invoke this method by using the resulting composite name.

    A copy of `name` is made and stored. Subsequent changes to `name` do not affect the copy in this exception, and vice versa.

PARAMETERS
name   The possibly `null` name to which to set the remaining name. If `null`, then it sets the remaining name field to `null`.

SEE ALSO   `appendRemainingComponent()`, `appendRemainingName()`, `getRemainingName()`.

setResolvedName()

PURPOSE   Sets the resolved name field of this exception.

SYNTAX   `public void setResolvedName(Name name)`

DESCRIPTION   This method sets the resolved name field of this exception. `name` is a composite name. If the intent is to set this field by using a compound name or string, then you must stringify the compound name and create a composite name with a single component by using the string. You can then invoke this method by using the resulting composite name.

    A copy of `name` is made and stored. Subsequent changes to `name` do not affect the copy in this exception, and vice versa.

N

PARAMETERS

name   The possibly `null` name to which to set the resolved name. If `null`, then it sets the resolved name field to `null`.

SEE ALSO   `getResolvedName()`.

setResolvedObj()

PURPOSE   Sets the resolved object field of this exception.

SYNTAX   `public void setResolvedObj(Object obj)`

PARAMETERS

obj   The possibly `null` object to which to set the resolved object. If `null`, then the resolved object field is set to `null`.

SEE ALSO   `getResolvedObj()`.

setRootCause()

PURPOSE   Records the root cause of this exception.

SYNTAX   `public void setRootCause(Throwable e)`

DESCRIPTION This method records the root cause of this exception. If e is `this`, then this method does nothing.

PARAMETERS

e   The possibly `null` exception that caused the naming operation to fail. `null` means that this naming exception has no root cause.

SEE ALSO   `getRootCause()`, `rootException`.

toString()

PURPOSE   Generates the string representation of this exception.

SYNTAX   `public String toString()`
             `public String toString(boolean detail)`

DESCRIPTION This method generates the string representation of this exception. The string consists of this exception's class name, its detailed message, and, if it has a root cause, the string representation of the root cause exception, followed by the remaining name (if it is not `null`). If detail is `true`, then the string also includes the string representation of the resolved object (if it is not `null`).

             This string is for debugging and is not meant to be interpreted programmatically.

PARAMETERS

detail   If true, then include details about the resolved object in addition to the other information.

RETURNS   The non-null string that contains the string representation of this exception.

OVERRIDES   java.lang.Object.toString().

N

NamingExceptionEvent

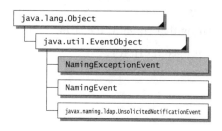

Syntax

```
public class NamingExceptionEvent extends java.util.EventObject
```

Description

The NamingExceptionEvent class represents an event that is fired when the procedures/processes used to collect information for notifying listeners of NamingEvents throw a NamingException. This can happen, for example, if the server that the listener is using aborts subsequent to the addNamingListener() call.

MEMBER SUMMARY	
Constructor	
NamingExceptionEvent()	Constructs an instance of NamingExceptionEvent.
Access Methods	
getEventContext()	Retrieves the EventContext that fired this event.
getException()	Retrieves the exception that was thrown.
Event Dispatch Method	
dispatch()	Invokes namingExceptionThrown() on a listener by using this event.

Example

See the **Event Notification** lesson (page 113).

dispatch()

PURPOSE	Invokes namingExceptionThrown() on a listener by using this event.
SYNTAX	`public void dispatch(NamingListener listener)`

PARAMETERS
listener   The non-null naming listener on which to invoke the method.

getEventContext()

PURPOSE   Retrieves the EventContext that fired this event.

SYNTAX   `public EventContext getEventContext()`

DESCRIPTION   This method retrieves the EventContext that fired this event. It returns the same object as EventObject.getSource().

RETURNS   The non-null EventContext that fired this event.

SEE ALSO   `java.util.EventObject.getSource()`.

getException()

PURPOSE   Retrieves the exception that was thrown.

SYNTAX   `public NamingException getException()`

RETURNS   The exception that was thrown.

EXAMPLE   See the **Event Notification** lesson (page 113).

N

NamingExceptionEvent()

PURPOSE   Constructs an instance of NamingExceptionEvent.

SYNTAX   `public NamingExceptionEvent(EventContext source, NamingException exc)`

DESCRIPTION   This constructor constructs an instance of NamingExceptionEvent by using the context in which the NamingException was thrown and the exception that was thrown.

PARAMETERS
exc   The non-null NamingException that was thrown.
source   The non-null context in which the exception was thrown.

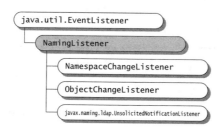

Syntax

```
public interface NamingListener extends java.util.EventListener
```

Description

The NamingListener interface is the root of listener interfaces that handle NamingEvents. It does not make sense for a listener to implement only this interface. Rather, a listener typically implements a subinterface of NamingListener, such as ObjectChangeListener or NamespaceChangeListener.

This interface contains a single method, namingExceptionThrown(), that must be implemented so that the listener can be notified of exceptions that are thrown (by the service provider) while it is gathering information about the events in which it is interested. When this method is invoked, the listener will be automatically deregistered from the EventContext with which it is registered.

For example, suppose that a listener implements ObjectChangeListener and registers with a EventContext. Then, if the connection to the server is subsequently broken, the listener will receive a NamingExceptionEvent and may take some corrective action, such as notifying the user of the application.

MEMBER SUMMARY
Callback Method
namingExceptionThrown()   Called when a naming exception is thrown.

Example

See NamespaceChangeListener and ObjectChangeListener.

N

namingExceptionThrown()

PURPOSE   Called when a naming exception is thrown.

SYNTAX   `void namingExceptionThrown(NamingExceptionEvent evt)`

DESCRIPTION   This method is called when a naming exception is thrown while attempting to fire a `NamingEvent`.

PARAMETERS
 evt   The non-`null` event.

EXAMPLE   See the **Event Notification** lesson (page 113).

N

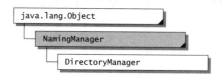

Syntax

`public class NamingManager`

Description

The `NamingManager` class contains methods for creating context objects and objects referred to by location information in the naming or directory service. It cannot be instantiated. It has only static methods.

The mention of URL in the documentation for this class refers to a URL string as defined by RFC 1738 and its related RFCs. The URL is any string that conforms to the syntax described therein and might not always have corresponding support in the `java.net.URL` class or in Web browsers.

`NamingManager` is safe for concurrent access by multiple threads.

Except as otherwise noted, a `Name` or environment parameter passed to any method is owned by the caller. The implementation will not modify the object or keep a reference to it, although it might keep a reference to a clone or copy of it.

MEMBER SUMMARY	
Initial Context Methods	
`getInitialContext()`	Creates an initial context by using the specified environment properties.
`getURLContext()`	Creates a context for the given URL scheme id.
`hasInitialContextFactoryBuilder()`	Determines whether an initial context factory builder has been set.
`setInitialContextFactoryBuilder()`	Sets the `InitialContextFactory` builder.
Object and State Factory Methods	
`getObjectInstance()`	Creates an instance of an object for the specified object and environment.
`getStateToBind()`	Retrieves the state of an object for binding.
`setObjectFactoryBuilder()`	Sets the `ObjectFactory` builder.
Federation Method	
`getContinuationContext()`	Creates a context in which to continue a context operation.

MEMBER SUMMARY	
Environment Property Name	
CPE	The name of the environment property into which getContinuationContext() stores the value of its CannotProceedException parameter.

See Also

DirectoryManager.

CPE

PURPOSE   The name of the environment property into which getContinuation-Context() stores the value of its CannotProceedException parameter.

SYNTAX   `public static final String CPE`

DESCRIPTION   This constant holds the name of the environment property into which get-ContinuationContext() stores the value of its CannotProceedException parameter. This property is inherited by the continuation context and may be used by that context's service provider to inspect the fields of the exception.

The value of this constant is "java.naming.spi.CannotProceedException".

SEE ALSO   DirectoryManager.getContinuationDirContext(), getContinuationContext().

getContinuationContext()

PURPOSE   Creates a context in which to continue a context operation.

SYNTAX   `public static Context`
         `getContinuationContext(CannotProceedException cpe) throws`
         `NamingException`

DESCRIPTION   This method creates a context in which to continue a context operation.

In performing an operation on a name that spans multiple namespaces, a context from one naming system might need to pass the operation on to the nns (next naming system). The context implementation does this by first constructing a CannotProceedException that contains information pinpointing how far it has proceeded. It then obtains a continuation context from the JNDI by calling getContinuationContext(). The context implementation should then

N

resume the context operation by invoking the same operation on the continuation context, using the remainder of the name to be resolved.

Before using the `cpe` parameter, this method updates the environment associated with that object by setting the value of the property to `cpe`. This property will be inherited by the continuation context and may be used by that context's service provider to inspect the fields of this exception.

PARAMETERS

cpe   The non-`null` exception that triggered this continuation.

RETURNS   A non-`null` `Context` object for continuing the operation.

EXCEPTIONS

NamingException

          If a naming exception occurred.

SEE ALSO   CPE, `DirectoryManager.getContinuationDirContext()`.

EXAMPLE   See the **Adding Federation Support** lesson (page 374).

getInitialContext()

PURPOSE   Creates an initial context by using the specified environment properties.

SYNTAX   `public static Context getInitialContext(Hashtable env) throws NamingException`

DESCRIPTION   This method creates an initial context by using the specified environment properties.

          If an `InitialContextFactoryBuilder` has been installed, then it is used to create the factory for creating the initial context. Otherwise, the class specified in the `Context.INITIAL_CONTEXT_FACTORY` environment property is used. Note that an initial context factory (an object that implements the `InitialContextFactory` interface) must be public and must have a public constructor that accepts no arguments.

PARAMETERS

env   The possibly `null` environment properties used when creating the context.

RETURNS   A non-`null` initial context.

EXCEPTIONS

NamingException

          If some other naming exception is encountered.

NoInitialContextException

          If the `Context.INITIAL_CONTEXT_FACTORY` property is not found or names a nonexistent class or a class that cannot be instantiated, or if the initial context could not be created for some other reason.

SEE ALSO   `javax.naming.InitialContext,`
`javax.naming.directory.InitialDirContext,`
`javax.naming.ldap.InitialLdapContext.`

getObjectInstance()

PURPOSE   Creates an instance of an object for the specified object and environment.

SYNTAX   `public static Object getObjectInstance(Object refInfo, Name name,`
`    Context nameCtx, Hashtable env) throws Exception`

DESCRIPTION   This method creates an instance of an object for the specified object and environment.

Any object factory builder that has been installed is used to create a factory for creating the object. Otherwise, the following rules apply to creating the object.

1. If `refInfo` is a `Reference` or `Referenceable` that contains a factory class name, then use the named factory to create the object. Return `refInfo` if the factory cannot be created. Under the JDK^{TM} 1.1, if the factory class must be loaded from a location specified in the reference, then a `SecurityManager` must have been installed; otherwise, the factory creation will fail. Pass up to the caller any exception encountered while creating the factory.

2. If `refInfo` is a `Reference` or `Referenceable` with no factory class name and the address or addresses are `StringRefAddrs` with address type `"URL"`, then try the URL context factory that corresponds to each URL's scheme id to create the object (see `getURLContext()`). If that fails, then continue to the next rule.

3. Use, in this order, the object factories specified in the environment's `Context.OBJECT_FACTORIES` property and in the provider resource file associated with `nameCtx`. The value of this property is a colon-separated list of factory class names that are tried in order. The first one that succeeds in creating an object is the one used. If no factory can be loaded, then return `refInfo`. Pass up to the caller any exception encountered while creating the object.

Service providers that implement the `DirContext` interface should use `DirectoryManager.getObjectInstance()` and not this method. Service providers that implement only the `Context` interface should use this method.

Note that an object factory (an object that implements the `ObjectFactory` interface) must be public and must have a public constructor that accepts no arguments.

The `name` and `nameCtx` parameters may optionally be used to specify the name of the object being created. `name` is the name of the object, relative to the context `nameCtx`. This information could be useful to the object factory or to the

N

object implementation. If several possible contexts are available from which the object could be named—as will often be the case—then it is up to the caller to select one. A good rule of thumb is to select the *deepest* context available. If nameCtx is null, then name is relative to the default initial context. If no name is specified, then the name parameter should be null.

PARAMETERS

env
: The possibly null environment to be used in creating the object factory and the object.

name
: The name of this object relative to nameCtx. Specifying a name is optional. If it is omitted, then name should be null.

nameCtx
: The context relative to which the name parameter is specified. If null, then name is relative to the default initial context.

refInfo
: The possibly null object for which to create an object.

RETURNS
: An object created by using refInfo; or, refInfo is returned if an object cannot be created by using the algorithm described previously.

EXCEPTIONS

Exception
: If one of the factories accessed throws an exception, or if an error is encountered while loading and instantiating the factory and object classes. A factory should throw an exception only if it does not want other factories to be used in an attempt to create an object. See ObjectFactory.getObjectInstance().

NamingException
: If a naming exception is encountered while attempting to get a URL context, or if one of the factories accessed throws a NamingException.

SEE ALSO
: getURLContext(), ObjectFactory, ObjectFactory.getObjectInstance().

EXAMPLE
: See **The Essential Components** lesson (page 341).

getStateToBind()

PURPOSE
: Retrieves the state of an object for binding.

SYNTAX
: public static Object getStateToBind(Object obj, Name name, Context nameCtx, Hashtable env) throws NamingException

DESCRIPTION
: This method retrieves the state of an object for binding.

Service providers that implement the DirContext interface should use DirectoryManager.getStateToBind() and not this method. Those that implement only the Context interface should use this method.

This method uses, in order, the specified state factories in the Context.STATE_FACTORIES property from the environment properties and those from the provider resource file associated with `nameCtx`. The value of this property is a colon-separated list of factory class names that are tried in order. The first one that succeeds in returning the object's state is the one used. If no object's state can be retrieved in this way, then return the object itself. Pass up to the caller any exception encountered while retrieving the state.

Note that a state factory (an object that implements the `StateFactory` interface) must be public and must have a public constructor that accepts no arguments.

The `name` and `nameCtx` parameters may optionally be used to specify the name of the object being created. See the description of *Name and Context Parameters* in `ObjectFactory.getObjectInstance()` for details. This method may return a `Referenceable` object. The service provider obtaining this object may choose to store it directly or to extract its reference (by using `Reference-able.getReference()`) and store that instead.

PARAMETERS

  env   The possibly `null` environment to be used in creating the state factory and the object's state.

  name   The name of this object relative to `nameCtx`, or `null` if no name is specified.

  nameCtx   The context relative to which the `name` parameter is specified, or `null` if `name` is relative to the default initial context.

  obj   The non-`null` object for which to get state to bind.

RETURNS   The non-`null` object representing `obj`'s state for binding. It could be the object (`obj`) itself.

EXCEPTIONS

`NamingException`

               If one of the factories accessed throws an exception, or if an error is encountered while loading and instantiating the factory and object classes. A factory should throw an exception only if it does not want other factories to be used in an attempt to create an object. See `StateFactory.getStateToBind()`.

SEE ALSO   `DirectoryManager.getStateToBind()`, `StateFactory`, `StateFactory.getStateToBind()`.

EXAMPLE   See **The Essential Components** lesson (page 343).

getURLContext()

PURPOSE   Creates a context for the given URL scheme id.

SYNTAX   `public static Context getURLContext(String scheme, Hashtable env)`
                    `throws NamingException`

DESCRIPTION This method creates a context for the given URL scheme id.

The resulting context is used to resolve URLs of the scheme id `scheme`. The resulting context is not tied to a specific URL. It is able to handle arbitrary URLs with the specified scheme.

The class name of the factory that creates the resulting context has the naming convention

scheme-id`URLContextFactory`

(e.g., `ftpURLContextFactory` for the `ftp` scheme id) in the package specified as follows.

The `Context.URL_PKG_PREFIXES` environment property (which may contain values taken from applet parameters, system properties, or application resource files) contains a colon-separated list of package prefixes. Each package prefix in the property is tried in the order specified to load the factory class. The default package prefix is `"com.sun.jndi.url"` (if none of the specified packages work, this default is tried). The complete package name is constructed by using the package prefix, concatenated with the scheme id.

For example, if the scheme is `ldap` and the `Context.URL_PKG_PREFIXES` property contains `"com.widget:com.wiz.jndi"`, then the naming manager will attempt to load the following classes until one is successfully instantiated:

```
com.widget.ldap.ldapURLContextFactory
com.wiz.jndi.ldap.ldapURLContextFactory
com.sun.jndi.url.ldap.ldapURLContextFactory
```

If none of the package prefixes work, then `null` is returned.

If a factory is instantiated, then it is invoked with the following parameters to produce the resulting context:

```
factory.getObjectInstance(null, env);
```

For example, invoking `getObjectInstance()` as shown here on a LDAP URL context factory would return a context that can resolve LDAP URLs such as

```
ldap://ldap.wiz.com/o=wiz,c=us
ldap://ldap.umich.edu/o=umich,c=us
```

Note that an object factory (an object that implements the `ObjectFactory` interface) must be public and must have a public constructor that accepts no arguments.

PARAMETERS

env The possibly `null` environment properties to be used in creating the object factory and the context.

scheme The non-`null` scheme id of the URLs supported by the context.

RETURNS   A context for resolving URLs with the scheme id `scheme`; `null` if the factory for creating the context is not found.

EXCEPTIONS

`NamingException`
> If a naming exception occurs while creating the context.

SEE ALSO   `getObjectInstance, ObjectFactory.getObjectInstance().`

hasInitialContextFactoryBuilder()

PURPOSE   Determines whether an initial context factory builder has been set.

SYNTAX   `public static boolean hasInitialContextFactoryBuilder()`

RETURNS   `true` if an initial context factory builder has been set; `false` otherwise.

SEE ALSO   `setInitialContextFactoryBuilder().`

setInitialContextFactoryBuilder()

PURPOSE   Sets the `InitialContextFactory` builder.

SYNTAX   `public static synchronized void`
                   `setInitialContextFactoryBuilder(InitialContextFactoryBuilder`
                   `builder) throws NamingException`

DESCRIPTION   This method sets the `InitialContextFactory` builder to be `builder`. The builder can be installed only if the executing thread is allowed by the security manager to do so. Once installed, the builder cannot be replaced.

PARAMETERS

`builder`   The initial context factory builder to install. If `null`, then no builder is set.

EXCEPTIONS

`IllegalStateException`
> If a builder is already installed.

`NamingException`
> `builder` cannot be installed for a nonsecurity reason.

`SecurityException`
> `builder` cannot be installed for a security reason.

SEE ALSO   `hasInitialContextFactoryBuilder(),`
               `java.lang.SecurityManager.checkSetFactory().`

N

setObjectFactoryBuilder()

PURPOSE   Sets the object factory builder.

SYNTAX

```
public static synchronized void
    setObjectFactoryBuilder(ObjectFactoryBuilder builder) throws
    NamingException
```

DESCRIPTION   This method sets the object factory builder to be `builder`. The `Object-FactoryBuilder` determines the policy used when trying to load object factories. See `getObjectInstance()` and the `ObjectFactory` class for descriptions of the default policy. `setObjectFactoryBuilder()` overrides this default policy by installing an `ObjectFactoryBuilder`. Subsequent object factories will be loaded and created by using the installed builder.

                        The builder can be installed only if the executing thread is allowed (by the security manager's `checkSetFactory()`) to do so. Once installed, the builder cannot be replaced.

PARAMETERS

`builder`   The factory builder to install. If `null`, then no builder is installed.

EXCEPTIONS

`IllegalStateException`
                If a factory is already installed.

`NamingException`
                `builder` cannot be installed for a nonsecurity reason.

`SecurityException`
                `builder` cannot be installed for a security reason.

SEE ALSO   `java.lang.SecurityManager.checkSetFactory()`, `getObjectInstance()`, `ObjectFactory`, `ObjectFactoryBuilder`.

N

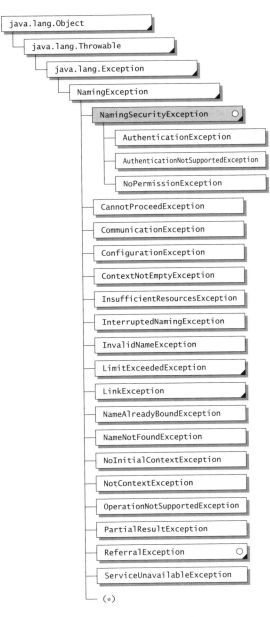

```
java.lang.Object
    └── java.lang.Throwable
            └── java.lang.Exception
                    └── NamingException
                            ├── NamingSecurityException      ○
                            │       ├── AuthenticationException
                            │       ├── AuthenticationNotSupportedException
                            │       └── NoPermissionException
                            ├── CannotProceedException
                            ├── CommunicationException
                            ├── ConfigurationException
                            ├── ContextNotEmptyException
                            ├── InsufficientResourcesException
                            ├── InterruptedNamingException
                            ├── InvalidNameException
                            ├── LimitExceededException
                            ├── LinkException
                            ├── NameAlreadyBoundException
                            ├── NameNotFoundException
                            ├── NoInitialContextException
                            ├── NotContextException
                            ├── OperationNotSupportedException
                            ├── PartialResultException
                            ├── ReferralException            ○
                            ├── ServiceUnavailableException
                            └── (*)
```

(*) 9 classes from other packages not shown.

N

685

Syntax

```
public abstract class NamingSecurityException extends NamingException
```

Description

NamingSecurityException is the superclass of security-related exceptions thrown by operations in the Context and DirContext interfaces. The nature of the failure is described by the name of the subclass.

If the program wants to handle this exception in particular, it should catch the Naming-SecurityException explicitly before attempting to catch the NamingException. A program might want to do this, for example, if it wants to treat security-related exceptions differently from other sorts of naming exception.

Synchronization and serialization issues that apply to NamingException apply directly here.

MEMBER SUMMARY
Constructor
NamingSecurityException()   Constructs an instance of NamingSecurityException.

NamingSecurityException()

PURPOSE   Constructs an instance of NamingSecurityException.

SYNTAX   ```
public NamingSecurityException()
public NamingSecurityException(String msg)
```

DESCRIPTION     These constructors construct an instance of NamingSecurityException by using the optional msg supplied. If msg is not supplied, then msg defaults to null. All other fields default to null.

PARAMETERS

msg             Additional detail about this exception. May be null.

SEE ALSO        java.lang.Throwable.getMessage().
```

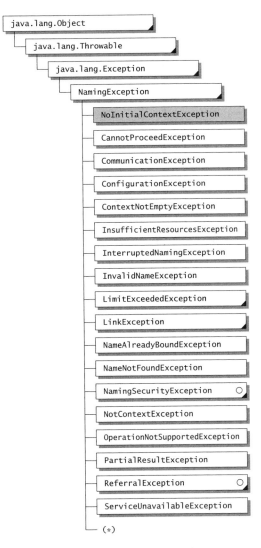

```
java.lang.Object
    java.lang.Throwable
        java.lang.Exception
            NamingException
                NoInitialContextException
                CannotProceedException
                CommunicationException
                ConfigurationException
                ContextNotEmptyException
                InsufficientResourcesException
                InterruptedNamingException
                InvalidNameException
                LimitExceededException
                LinkException
                NameAlreadyBoundException
                NameNotFoundException
                NamingSecurityException        ○
                NotContextException
                OperationNotSupportedException
                PartialResultException
                ReferralException              ○
                ServiceUnavailableException
                (*)
```

(*) 9 classes from other packages not shown.

Syntax
```
public class NoInitialContextException extends NamingException
```

N

Description

A NoInitialContextException is thrown when no initial context implementation can be created. The policy of how an initial context implementation is selected is described in the documentation of the InitialContext class.

This exception can be thrown during any interaction with the InitialContext and not only when the InitialContext is constructed. For example, the implementation of the initial context might lazily retrieve the context only when actual methods are invoked on it. The application should not have any dependency on when the existence of an initial context is determined.

Synchronization and serialization issues that apply to NamingException apply directly here.

MEMBER SUMMARY	
Constructor	
NoInitialContextException()	Constructs an instance of NoInitialContext-Exception.

See Also

InitialContext, javax.naming.directory.InitialDirContext,
javax.naming.ldap.InitialLdapContext.

NoInitialContextException()

PURPOSE	Constructs an instance of NoInitialContextException.
SYNTAX	public NoInitialContextException() public NoInitialContextException(String msg)
DESCRIPTION	These constructors construct an instance of NoInitialContextException with an optional msg supplied. If msg is not supplied, then msg defaults to null. All other fields default to null.
PARAMETERS	
msg	Additional detail about this exception. May be null.
SEE ALSO	java.lang.Throwable.getMessage().

NoPermissionException

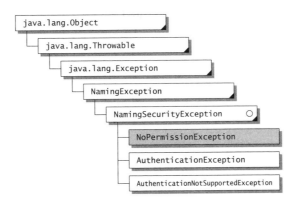

Syntax

```
public class NoPermissionException extends NamingSecurityException
```

Description

A `NoPermissionException` is thrown when attempting to perform an operation for which the client has no permission. The access control/permission model is dictated by the directory/naming server.

Synchronization and serialization issues that apply to `NamingException` apply directly here.

N

MEMBER SUMMARY

Constructor
`NoPermissionException()`   Constructs an instance of `NoPermissionException`.

NoPermissionException()

PURPOSE   Constructs an instance of `NoPermissionException`.

SYNTAX   ```
public NoPermissionException()
public NoPermissionException(String msg)
```

DESCRIPTION     These constructors construct an instance of `NoPermissionException` by using an optional `msg` supplied. If `msg` is not supplied, then `msg` defaults to `null`. All other fields default to `null`.
```

NoPermissionException()

PARAMETERS

msg   Additional detail about this exception. May be `null`.

SEE ALSO   `java.lang.Throwable.getMessage()`.

NoSuchAttributeException

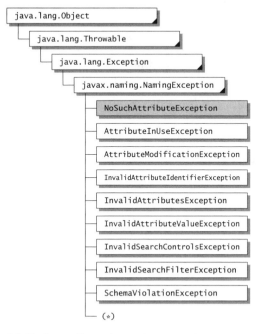

java.lang.Object

java.lang.Throwable

java.lang.Exception

javax.naming.NamingException

NoSuchAttributeException

AttributeInUseException

AttributeModificationException

InvalidAttributeIdentifierException

InvalidAttributesException

InvalidAttributeValueException

InvalidSearchControlsException

InvalidSearchFilterException

SchemaViolationException

(*)

(*) 18 classes from other packages not shown.

Syntax
`public class NoSuchAttributeException extends NamingException`

Description
A `NoSuchAttributeException` is thrown when attempting to access an attribute that does not exist.

Synchronization and serialization issues that apply to `NamingException` apply directly here.

MEMBER SUMMARY
Constructor
`NoSuchAttributeException()`　　Constructs an instance of `NoSuchAttributeException`.

NoSuchAttributeException()

PURPOSE   Constructs an instance of NoSuchAttributeException.

SYNTAX   public NoSuchAttributeException()
          public NoSuchAttributeException(String msg)

DESCRIPTION   These constructors construct an instance of NoSuchAttributeException by using an optional msg supplied. If msg is not supplied, then msg defaults to null. All other fields default to null.

PARAMETERS

msg   Additional detail about this exception. May be null.

SEE ALSO   java.lang.Throwable.getMessage().

N

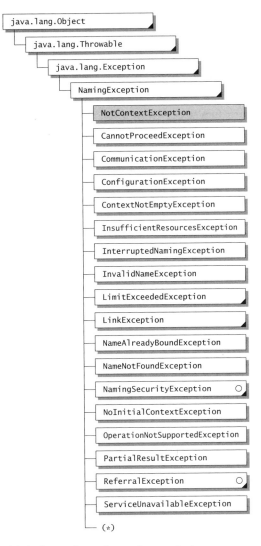

java.lang.Object

java.lang.Throwable

java.lang.Exception

NamingException

NotContextException

CannotProceedException

CommunicationException

ConfigurationException

ContextNotEmptyException

InsufficientResourcesException

InterruptedNamingException

InvalidNameException

LimitExceededException

LinkException

NameAlreadyBoundException

NameNotFoundException

NamingSecurityException   ○

NoInitialContextException

OperationNotSupportedException

PartialResultException

ReferralException   ○

ServiceUnavailableException

(*)

(*) 9 classes from other packages not shown.

Syntax
```
public class NotContextException extends NamingException
```

Description

A NotContextException is thrown when a naming operation proceeds to a point where a context is required in order to continue the operation but the resolved object is not a context. For example, Context.destroy() requires that the named object be a context. If it is not, then a NotContextException is thrown. As another example, this exception is thrown when a non-context is encountered during the resolution phase of the context methods.

It also is thrown when a particular subtype of a context is required, such as a DirContext, and the resolved object is a context but not of the required subtype.

Synchronization and serialization issues that apply to NamingException apply directly here.

MEMBER SUMMARY
Constructor
NotContextException()   Constructs an instance of NotContextException.

Example

See the **Adding Federation Support** lesson (page 381).

NotContextException()

PURPOSE	Constructs an instance of NotContextException.
SYNTAX	public NotContextException() public NotContextException(String msg)
DESCRIPTION	These constructors construct an instance of NotContextException by using an optional msg supplied. If msg is not supplied, then msg defaults to null. All other fields default to null.
PARAMETERS msg	Additional detail about this exception. May be null.
SEE ALSO	java.lang.Throwable.getMessage().
EXAMPLE	See the **Adding Federation Support** lesson (page 381).

N

ObjectChangeListener

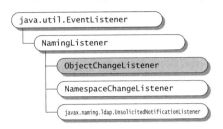

Syntax

```
public interface ObjectChangeListener extends NamingListener
```

Description

The `ObjectChangeListener` interface specifies the method that a listener of a `NamingEvent` with event type of `OBJECT_CHANGED` must implement.

An `OBJECT_CHANGED` event type is fired when (the content of) an object has changed. This might mean that its attributes have been modified, added, or removed and/or that the object itself has been replaced. You can determine how the object has changed by examining the `NamingEvent`'s old and new bindings.

A listener interested in `OBJECT_CHANGED` event types must do the following.

1. Implement this interface and its method (`objectChanged()`).
2. Implement `NamingListener.namingExceptionThrown()` so that it will be notified of exceptions thrown while attempting to collect information about the events.
3. Register with the source by using the source's `addNamingListener()` method.

A listener that wants to be notified of namespace change events should also implement the `NamespaceChangeListener` interface.

MEMBER SUMMARY	
Callback Method	
objectChanged()	Called when an object has been changed.

Example

An application might register its interest in changes to context objects as follows.

```
EventContext src =
    (EventContext)(new InitialContext()).lookup("o=wiz,c=us");
src.addNamingListener("ou=users", EventContext.ONELEVEL_SCOPE,
    new ChangeHandler());
```

ChangeHandler is defined as follows.

```
class ChangeHandler implements ObjectChangeListener {
    public void objectChanged(NamingEvent evt) {
        System.out.println(evt.getNewBinding());
    }
    public void namingExceptionThrown(NamingExceptionEvent evt) {
        System.out.println(evt.getException());
    }
}
```

objectChanged()

PURPOSE   Called when an object has been changed.

SYNTAX   `void objectChanged(NamingEvent evt)`

DESCRIPTION   This method is called when an object has been changed.

The binding of the changed object can be obtained by using `evt.getNew-Binding()`. Its old binding (before the change) can be obtained by using `evt.getOldBinding()`.

PARAMETERS

evt   The non-null naming event.

SEE ALSO   `NamingEvent.OBJECT_CHANGED`.

EXAMPLE   See the class example.

O

Syntax
`public interface ObjectFactory`

Description
The `ObjectFactory` interface represents a factory for creating an object.

The JNDI framework allows for object implementations to be loaded in dynamically via *object factories*. For example, suppose that a printer bound in the namespace is being looked up. If the print service binds printer names to `References`, then the printer `Reference` could be used to create a printer object so that the caller of `lookup()` can directly operate on the printer object after the lookup.

An `ObjectFactory` is responsible for creating objects of a specific type. In this example, you might have a `PrinterObjectFactory` for creating `Printer` objects.

An object factory must implement the `ObjectFactory` interface. In addition, the factory class must be public and must have a public constructor that accepts no parameters.

An object factory's `getObjectInstance()` method may be invoked multiple times, possibly by the use of different parameters. The implementation is thread-safe.

The mention of URL in the documentation for this class refers to a URL string as defined by RFC 1738 and its related RFCs. It is any string that conforms to the syntax described therein and may not always have corresponding support in the `java.net.URL` class or in Web browsers.

O

MEMBER SUMMARY	
Factory Method	
`getObjectInstance()`	Creates an object by using the location or reference information specified.

See Also
`DirObjectFactory, DirectoryManager.getObjectInstance(),`
`NamingManager.getObjectInstance()`.

Example
See the **Object Factories** lesson (page 190).

getObjectInstance()

PURPOSE   Creates an object by using the location or reference information specified.

SYNTAX   ```
              public Object getObjectInstance(Object obj, Name name, Context
                  nameCtx, Hashtable env) throws Exception
              ```

DESCRIPTION   This method creates an object by using the location or reference information specified.

Special requirements of this object are supplied via `env`. An example of such an environment property is user identity information.

`NamingManager.getObjectInstance()` successively loads in object factories and invokes this method on them until one produces a non-`null` answer. When an object factory throws an exception, the exception is passed on to the caller of `NamingManager.getObjectInstance()` (and no search is made for other factories that might produce a non-`null` answer). An object factory should throw an exception only if it is sure that it is the only intended factory and that no other object factories should be tried. If this factory cannot create an object by using the arguments supplied, then it should return `null`.

A *URL context factory* is a special `ObjectFactory` that creates contexts for resolving URLs or objects whose locations are specified by URLs. A URL context factory's `getObjectInstance()` method will obey the following rules.

1. If `obj` is `null`, then create a context for resolving URLs of the scheme associated with this factory. The resulting context is not tied to a specific URL; it is able to handle arbitrary URLs with this factory's scheme id. For example, invoking `getObjectInstance()` with `obj` set to `null` on an LDAP URL context factory will return a context that can resolve LDAP URLs such as `"ldap://ldap.wiz.com/o=wiz,c=us"` and `"ldap://ldap.umich.edu/o=umich,c=us"`.

2. If `obj` is a URL string, then create an object (typically a context) identified by the URL. For example, suppose that this is an LDAP URL context factory. If `obj` is `"ldap://ldap.wiz.com/o=wiz,c=us"`, then `getObjectInstance()` will return the context named by the DN `"o=wiz, c=us"` at the LDAP server `ldap.wiz.com`. This context can then be used to resolve LDAP names (such as `"cn=George"`) relative to that context.

3. If `obj` is an array of URL strings, then the URLs are assumed to be equivalent in terms of the context to which they refer. Verification of whether the URLs are, or need to be, equivalent is up to the context factory. The order of the URLs in the array is not significant. The object returned by `getObjectInstance()` is like that of the single URL case (rule 2): It is the object named by the URLs.

4. If `obj` is of any other type, then the behavior of `getObjectInstance()` is determined by the context factory implementation.
              ```

The `name` and `env` parameters are owned by the caller. The implementation will not modify these objects or keep references to them, although it may keep references to clones or copies of them.

Name and Context Parameters

The `name` and `nameCtx` parameters may optionally be used to specify the name of the object being created. `name` is the name of the object, relative to the context `nameCtx`. If several contexts are possible from which the object could be named—as is often the case—then it is up to the caller to select one. A good rule of thumb is to select the *deepest* context available. If `nameCtx` is `null`, then `name` is relative to the default initial context. If no name is specified, then the `name` parameter should be `null`. If a factory uses `nameCtx`, then it should synchronize its use against concurrent access, since context implementations are not guaranteed to be thread-safe.

PARAMETERS

env	The possibly `null` environment that is used in creating the object.
name	The name of this object relative to `nameCtx`, or `null` if no name is specified.
nameCtx	The context relative to which the `name` parameter is specified, or `null` if `name` is relative to the default initial context.
obj	The possibly `null` object that contains location or reference information that can be used in creating an object.

RETURNS   The object created; `null` if an object cannot be created.

EXCEPTIONS

`Exception`

If this object factory encounters an exception while attempting to create an object and no other object factories are to be tried.

SEE ALSO   `DirectoryManager.getObjectInstance()`,
`NamingManager.getObjectInstance()`,
`NamingManager.getURLContext()`.

EXAMPLE   See the **Object Factories** lesson (page 190).

O

ObjectFactoryBuilder

Syntax

```
public interface ObjectFactoryBuilder
```

Description

The `ObjectFactoryBuilder` interface represents a builder that creates object factories.

The JNDI framework allows for object implementations to be loaded in dynamically via *object factories*. For example, suppose that a printer bound in the namespace is looked up. If the print service binds printer names to `References`, then the printer `Reference` could be used to create a printer object so that the caller of `lookup()` can directly operate on the printer object after the lookup.

An `ObjectFactory` is responsible for creating objects of a specific type. The JNDI uses a default policy for using and loading object factories. You can override this default policy by calling `NamingManager.setObjectFactoryBuilder()` with an `ObjectFactoryBuilder`, which contains the program-defined way of creating/loading object factories. Any `Object-FactoryBuilder` implementation must implement this interface for creating object factories.

MEMBER SUMMARY
Factory Method
`createObjectFactory()`   Creates an instance of `ObjectFactory` object factory by using the environment supplied.

See Also

`DirectoryManager.getObjectInstance()`, `NamingManager.getObjectInstance()`, `NamingManager.setObjectFactoryBuilder()`, `ObjectFactory`.

createObjectFactory()

PURPOSE	Creates an instance of `ObjectFactory` by using the environment supplied.
SYNTAX	`public ObjectFactory createObjectFactory(Object obj, Hashtable env) throws NamingException`
DESCRIPTION	This method creates an instance of `ObjectFactory` by using the environment supplied.

The environment parameter is owned by the caller. The implementation will not modify the object or keep a reference to it, although it may keep a reference to a clone or copy of it.

PARAMETERS

env   Environment to use when creating the factory. May be null.

obj   The possibly null object for which to create a factory.

RETURNS   A non-null instance of ObjectFactory.

EXCEPTIONS

NamingException

If an object factory cannot be created.

O

OperationNotSupportedException

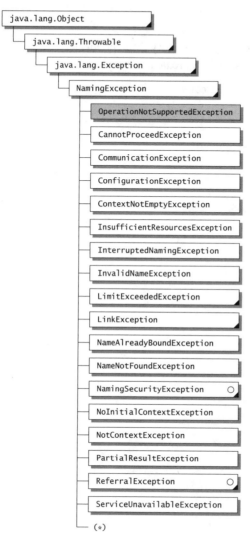

```
java.lang.Object
    java.lang.Throwable
        java.lang.Exception
            NamingException
                OperationNotSupportedException
                CannotProceedException
                CommunicationException
                ConfigurationException
                ContextNotEmptyException
                InsufficientResourcesException
                InterruptedNamingException
                InvalidNameException
                LimitExceededException
                LinkException
                NameAlreadyBoundException
                NameNotFoundException
                NamingSecurityException      ○
                NoInitialContextException
                NotContextException
                PartialResultException
                ReferralException            ○
                ServiceUnavailableException
                (*)
```

(*) 9 classes from other packages not shown.

Syntax

```
public class OperationNotSupportedException extends NamingException
```

Description

An OperationNotSupportedException is thrown when a context implementation does not support the operation being invoked. For example, a server that does not support Context.bind() will throw a OperationNotSupportedException when bind() is invoked on it.

Synchronization and serialization issues that apply to NamingException apply directly here.

MEMBER SUMMARY
Constructor
OperationNotSupportedException()   Constructs an instance of OperationNotSupportedException.

Example

See **The Essential Components** lesson (page 341).

OperationNotSupportedException()

PURPOSE   Constructs an instance of OperationNotSupportedException.

SYNTAX   public OperationNotSupportedException()
public OperationNotSupportedException(String msg)

DESCRIPTION   These constructors construct an instance of OperationNotSupported-Exception by using an optional msg supplied. If msg is not supplied, then msg defaults to null. All other fields default to null.

PARAMETERS
msg   Additional detail about this exception. May be null.

SEE ALSO   java.lang.Throwable.getMessage().

O

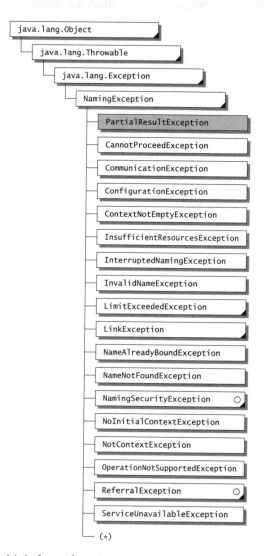

```
java.lang.Object
    java.lang.Throwable
        java.lang.Exception
            NamingException
                PartialResultException
                CannotProceedException
                CommunicationException
                ConfigurationException
                ContextNotEmptyException
                InsufficientResourcesException
                InterruptedNamingException
                InvalidNameException
                LimitExceededException
                LinkException
                NameAlreadyBoundException
                NameNotFoundException
                NamingSecurityException      ○
                NoInitialContextException
                NotContextException
                OperationNotSupportedException
                ReferralException            ○
                ServiceUnavailableException
                (*)
```

(*) 9 classes from other packages not shown.

Syntax

```
public class PartialResultException extends NamingException
```

Description

A `PartialResultException` is thrown to indicate that the result being returned or returned so far is partial and that the operation cannot be completed. For example, when a context is being listed, this exception indicates that the returned results represent only some of the bindings in the context.

Synchronization and serialization issues that apply to `NamingException` apply directly here.

MEMBER SUMMARY
Constructor
`PartialResultException()`   Constructs an instance of `PartialResultException`.

PartialResultException()

PURPOSE   Constructs an instance of `PartialResultException`.

SYNTAX   `public PartialResultException()`
                 `public PartialResultException(String msg)`

DESCRIPTION   These constructors construct an instance of `PartialResultException` by using the optional `msg` specified. If `msg` is not supplied, then `msg` defaults to `null`. All other fields default to `null`.

PARAMETERS

   msg   Additional detail about this exception. May be `null`.

SEE ALSO   `java.lang.Throwable.getMessage()`.

P

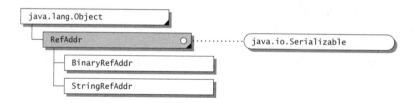

Syntax

```
public abstract class RefAddr implements java.io.Serializable
```

Description

The RefAddr class represents the address of a communication endpoint. It consists of a type that describes the communication mechanism and an address content that is determined by an RefAddr subclass.

For example, an address type could be "BSD Printer Address", which specifies that it is an address to be used with the BSD printing protocol. Its content could be the machine name that identifies the location of the printer server that understands this protocol.

A RefAddr is contained within a Reference.

Because RefAddr is an abstract class, concrete implementations of it determine its synchronization properties.

MEMBER SUMMARY	
Constructor	
RefAddr()	Constructs an instance of RefAddr by using its address type.
Address Methods and Field	
addrType	Contains the type of this address.
getContent()	Retrieves the contents of this address.
getType()	Retrieves the address type of this address.
Object Methods	
equals()	Determines whether an object is equal to this RefAddr.
hashCode()	Computes the hash code of this address by using its address type and contents.
toString()	Generates the string representation of this address.

See Also

BinaryRefAddr, StringRefAddr.

R

Example

See the **Object Factories** lesson (page 190).

addrType

PURPOSE	Contains the type of this address.
SYNTAX	`protected String addrType`
DESCRIPTION	This field contains the type of this address.

equals()

PURPOSE	Determines whether an object is equal to this `RefAddr`.
SYNTAX	`public boolean equals(Object obj)`
DESCRIPTION	This method determines whether an object, `obj`, is equal to this `RefAddr`. `obj` is equal to this `RefAddr` if all of the following conditions are `true`:

- Non-`null`
- Instance of `RefAddr`
- `obj` has the same address type as this `RefAddr` (by using `String.compareTo()`)
- Both the contents of `obj` and this `RefAddr` are `null` or they are equal (determined by using the `equals()` test)

PARAMETERS	
`obj`	A possibly `null` object to check.
RETURNS	`true` if `obj` is equal to this `RefAddr`; `false` otherwise.
OVERRIDES	`java.lang.Object.equals()`.
SEE ALSO	`getContent()`, `getType()`, `hashCode()`.

getContent()

PURPOSE	Retrieves the contents of this address.
SYNTAX	`public abstract Object getContent()`
RETURNS	The possibly `null` address contents.
EXAMPLE	See the **Object Factories** lesson (page 190).

getType()

PURPOSE	Retrieves the address type of this address.
SYNTAX	`public String getType()`
RETURNS	The non-null address type of this address.

hashCode()

PURPOSE	Computes the hash code of this address by using its address type and contents.
SYNTAX	`public int hashCode()`
DESCRIPTION	This method computes the hash code of this address by using its address type and contents. The hash code is the sum of the hash codes of the address type and the address contents.
RETURNS	The hash code of this address as an `int`.
OVERRIDES	`java.lang.Object.hashCode()`.
SEE ALSO	`equals()`.

RefAddr()

PURPOSE	Constructs an instance of `RefAddr` by using its address type.
SYNTAX	`protected RefAddr(String addrType)`
PARAMETERS	
addrType	A non-null string that describes the type of the address.

R

toString()

PURPOSE	Generates the string representation of this address.
SYNTAX	`public String toString()`
DESCRIPTION	This method generates the string representation of this address. The string consists of the address's type and contents with labels. The string is for display only and is not meant to be parsed.
RETURNS	The non-null string representation of this address.
OVERRIDES	`java.lang.Object.toString()`.

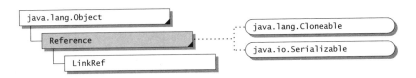

Syntax
```
public class Reference implements Cloneable, java.io.Serializable
```

Description
The Reference class represents a reference to an object that is found outside of the naming/directory system. It provides a way to record address information about objects that are not directly bound to the naming/directory system.

A Reference consists of an ordered list of addresses and class information about the object being referenced. Each address in the list identifies a *communication endpoint* for the same conceptual object. The endpoint is information that indicates how to contact the object. It could be, for example, a network address, a location in memory on the local machine, or another process on the same machine. The order of the addresses in the list might be significant to object factories that interpret the reference.

Multiple addresses might arise for various reasons, such as replication or the object offers interfaces over more than one communication mechanism. The addresses are indexed starting with zero.

A Reference also contains information to assist in creating an instance of the object to which this Reference refers. It contains the class name of that object, as well as the class name and location of the factory to be used to create the object. The class factory location is a space-separated list of URLs that represent the classpath used to load the factory. When the factory class (or any class or resource on which it depends) needs to be loaded, each URL is used (in order) in an attempt to load the class.

A Reference instance is not synchronized against concurrent access by multiple threads. Threads that need to access a single Reference concurrently should synchronize among themselves and provide the necessary locking.

See Also
RefAddr.

Example
See the **Object Factories** lesson (page 190).

R

MEMBER SUMMARY	
Constructor	
Reference()	Constructs an instance of Reference.
Access Methods	
get()	Retrieves an address from this reference.
getAll()	Retrieves an enumeration of the addresses in this reference.
getClassName()	Retrieves the class name of the object to which this reference refers.
getFactoryClassLocation()	Retrieves the location of the factory of the object to which this reference refers.
getFactoryClassName()	Retrieves the class name of the factory of the object to which this reference refers.
size()	Retrieves the number of addresses in this reference.
Update Methods	
add()	Adds an address to the list of addresses.
clear()	Deletes all addresses from this reference.
remove()	Deletes the address at index posn from the list of addresses.
Object Methods	
clone()	Makes a copy of this reference by using its class name list of addresses, class factory name, and class factory location.
equals()	Determines whether obj is a reference with the same addresses (in the same order) as this reference.
hashCode()	Computes the hash code of this reference.
toString()	Generates the string representation of this reference.

R

add()

PURPOSE   Adds an address to the list of addresses.

SYNTAX
```
public void add(RefAddr addr)
public void add(int posn, RefAddr addr)
```

DESCRIPTION   This method adds an address to the list of addresses.

The first form adds an address to the end of the list. The second form adds an address to the list of addresses at index posn. All addresses at index posn or greater are shifted up the list by 1 (away from index 0).

PARAMETERS
addr   The non-null address to add.
posn   The 0-based index of the list at which to insert addr.

EXCEPTIONS
ArrayIndexOutOfBoundsException
> If posn is not in the specified range.

clear()

PURPOSE	Deletes all addresses from this reference.
SYNTAX	`public void clear()`

clone()

PURPOSE	Makes a copy of this reference by using its class name list of addresses, class factory name, and class factory location.
SYNTAX	`public Object clone()`
DESCRIPTION	This method makes a copy of this reference by using its class name list of addresses, class factory name, and class factory location. Changes to the newly created copy do not affect this Reference, and vice versa.
OVERRIDES	`java.lang.Object.clone()`.

equals()

PURPOSE	Determines whether an object is a reference with the same addresses (in the same order) as this reference.
SYNTAX	`public boolean equals(Object obj)`
DESCRIPTION	This method determines whether an object, obj, is a reference with the same addresses (in the same order) as this reference. The addresses are checked by using RefAddr.equals(). In addition to having the same address, the reference also needs to have the same class name as this reference. The class factory and class factory location are not checked. If obj is null or not an instance of Reference, then false is returned.
PARAMETERS	
obj	The possibly null object to check.
RETURNS	true if obj is equal to this reference; false otherwise.
OVERRIDES	`java.lang.Object.equals()`.
SEE ALSO	`hashCode()`.

R

get()

PURPOSE	Retrieves an address from this reference.
SYNTAX	`public RefAddr get(String addrType)` `public RefAddr get(int posn)`
DESCRIPTION	This method retrieves an address from this reference. The first form retrieves the first address that has the address type `addrType`. `String.compareTo()` is used to test the equality of the address types. The second form retrieves the address at index `posn`.
PARAMETERS	
addrType	The non-null address type for which to find the address.
posn	The index of the address to retrieve. Must be in the range [0, `size()`).
RETURNS	The address in this reference with address type `addrType` (`null` if no such address exists) for the first form, or the address at the 0-based index `posn` for the second form.
EXCEPTIONS	
`ArrayIndexOutOfBoundsException`	If `posn` is not in the specified range.
EXAMPLE	See the **Object Factories** lesson (page 190).

getAll()

PURPOSE	Retrieves an enumeration of the addresses in this reference.
SYNTAX	`public Enumeration getAll()`
DESCRIPTION	This method retrieves an enumeration of the addresses in this reference. When addresses are added, changed, or removed from this reference, its effects on this enumeration are undefined.
RETURNS	A non-null enumeration of the addresses (`RefAddr`) in this reference. If this reference has zero addresses, then an enumeration with zero elements is returned.

getClassName()

PURPOSE	Retrieves the class name of the object to which this reference refers.
SYNTAX	`public String getClassName()`
RETURNS	The non-null fully qualified class name of the object (e.g., `"java.lang.String"`).
EXAMPLE	See the **Object Factories** lesson (page 190).

R

getFactoryClassLocation()

PURPOSE	Retrieves the location of the factory of the object to which this reference refers.
SYNTAX	`public String getFactoryClassLocation()`
DESCRIPTION	This method retrieves the location of the factory of the object to which this reference refers. If it is a codebase, then it is an ordered list of URLs, separated by spaces, listing locations from where the factory class definition should be loaded.
RETURNS	The possibly `null` string that contains the location for loading in the factory's class.
SEE ALSO	`getFactoryClassName()`.

getFactoryClassName()

PURPOSE	Retrieves the class name of the factory of the object to which this reference refers.
SYNTAX	`public String getFactoryClassName()`
RETURNS	The possibly `null` fully qualified class name of the factory.
SEE ALSO	`getFactoryClassLocation()`.

hashCode()

PURPOSE	Computes the hash code of this reference.
SYNTAX	`public int hashCode()`
DESCRIPTION	The hash code is the sum of the hash codes of the reference's addresses.
RETURNS	A hash code of this reference as an `int`.
OVERRIDES	`java.lang.Object.hashCode()`.
SEE ALSO	`equals()`.

R

Reference()

PURPOSE	Constructs an instance of `Reference`.
SYNTAX	`public Reference(String className)` `public Reference(String className, RefAddr addr)`

> ```
> public Reference(String className, String factory, String
>     factoryLoc)
> public Reference(String className, RefAddr addr, String factory,
>     String factoryLoc)
> ```

DESCRIPTION These constructors create an instance of `Reference` that has the class name `className`. If the class factory and class factory location are not supplied, then they default to `null`. If `addr` is not supplied, then the newly created reference contains zero addresses.

PARAMETERS

addr   The non-null address of the object.

className   The non-null class name of the object to which this reference refers.

factory   The possibly `null` class name of the object's factory.

factoryLoc The possibly `null` location from which to load the factory (e.g., a URL string).

SEE ALSO   `javax.naming.spi.NamingManager.getObjectInstance()`,
            `javax.naming.spi.ObjectFactory`.

EXAMPLE   See the **Storing Objects in the Directory** lesson (page 159).

remove()

PURPOSE   Deletes the address at index `posn` from the list of addresses.

SYNTAX   `public Object remove(int posn)`

DESCRIPTION This method deletes the address at index `posn` from the list of addresses. All addresses at an index greater than `posn` are shifted down the list by 1 (toward index 0).

PARAMETERS

posn   The 0-based index of the address to delete.

RETURNS   The address removed.

EXCEPTIONS

`ArrayIndexOutOfBoundsException`
            If `posn` is not in the specified range.

size()

PURPOSE   Retrieves the number of addresses in this reference.

SYNTAX   `public int size()`

RETURNS   The nonnegative number of addresses in this reference.

toString()

PURPOSE   Generates the string representation of this reference.

SYNTAX   `public String toString()`

DESCRIPTION This method generates the string representation of this reference. The string consists of the class name to which this reference refers and the string representation of each of its addresses. This string is for display only and is not meant to be parsed.

RETURNS   The non-null string representation of this reference.

OVERRIDES   `java.lang.Object.toString()`.

R

Referenceable

Referenceable

Syntax
```
public interface Referenceable
```

Description
The Referenceable interface is implemented by an object that can provide a Reference to itself.

A Reference represents a way to record address information about objects that themselves are not directly bound to the naming system. An object can implement the Referenceable interface as a way for programs that use that object to determine its Reference. For example, when an object is being bound and implements the Referenceable interface, then getReference() can be invoked on the object to get its Reference to use for binding.

MEMBER SUMMARY	
Referenceable Method	
getReference()	Retrieves the Reference of this object.

Example
See the **Storing Objects in the Directory** lesson (page 159).

getReference()

PURPOSE	Retrieves the Reference of this object.
SYNTAX	Reference getReference() throws NamingException
RETURNS	The non-null Reference of this object.
EXCEPTIONS	
NamingException	
	If a naming exception is encountered while retrieving the reference.
EXAMPLE	See the **Storing Objects in the Directory** lesson (page 159).

```
java.lang.Object
    java.lang.Throwable
        java.lang.Exception
            NamingException
                ReferralException                              ○
                    javax.naming.ldap.LdapReferralException  ○
                CannotProceedException
                CommunicationException
                ConfigurationException
                ContextNotEmptyException
                InsufficientResourcesException
                InterruptedNamingException
                InvalidNameException
                LimitExceededException
                LinkException
                NameAlreadyBoundException
                NameNotFoundException
                NamingSecurityException                        ○
                NoInitialContextException
                NotContextException
                OperationNotSupportedException
                PartialResultException
                ServiceUnavailableException
                (*)
```

(*) 9 classes from other packages not shown.

Syntax

```
public abstract class ReferralException extends NamingException
```

Description

The ReferralException abstract class is used to represent a referral exception, which is generated in response to a *referral* such as that returned by LDAP v3 servers.

A service provider offers a subclass of ReferralException by providing implementations for getReferralInfo() and getReferralContext() (and appropriate constructors and/or corresponding set methods).

The following code sample shows one way to use ReferralException.

```
while (true) {
    try {
        bindings = ctx.listBindings(name);
        while (bindings.hasMore()) {
            b = bindings.next();
            ...
        }
        break;
    } catch (ReferralException e) {
        ctx = e.getReferralContext();
    }
}
```

Because ReferralException is an abstract class, concrete implementations determine its synchronization and serialization properties.

An environment parameter passed to getReferralContext() is owned by the caller. The service provider will not modify the object or keep a reference to it, but it may keep a reference to a clone of it.

MEMBER SUMMARY	
Constructor	
ReferralException()	Constructs an instance of ReferralException.
Referral Information Method	
getReferralInfo()	Retrieves information (such as URLs) related to this referral.
Referral Management Methods	
getReferralContext()	Retrieves the context at which to continue the context method by following the referral.
retryReferral()	Retries the referral currently being processed.
skipReferral()	Discards the referral about to be processed.

See Also

javax.naming.ldap.LdapReferralException.

Example

See the **Referrals** lesson (page 265).

getReferralContext()

PURPOSE   Retrieves the context at which to continue the context method by following the referral.

SYNTAX
```
public abstract Context getReferralContext() throws
    NamingException
public abstract Context getReferralContext(Hashtable env) throws
    NamingException
```

DESCRIPTION   This method retrieves the context at which to continue the context method by following the referral, by using env as its environment properties. If env is not supplied, then the referral context is created by using the environment properties of the context that threw the `ReferralException`. Specifically, the first form of this method is equivalent to

```
getReferralContext(ctx.getEnvironment());
```

where `ctx` is the context that threw the `ReferralException`.

env should be used when the caller needs to use different environment properties for the referral context. It might do this, for example, when it needs to supply different authentication information to the referred server in order to create the referral context.

Regardless of whether a referral is encountered directly during a context operation or indirectly, for example during a search enumeration, the referral exception should provide a context at which to continue the operation. To continue the operation, the client program should reinvoke the context method by using the same arguments as for the original invocation.

PARAMETERS

env   The possibly `null` environment properties to use for the new context. `null` means to use no environment properties.

RETURNS   The non-`null` context at which to continue the context method.

EXCEPTIONS

NamingException

     If a naming exception is encountered. Call either `retryReferral()` or `skipReferral()` to continue processing referrals.

EXAMPLE   See the **Referrals** lesson (page 265).

getReferralInfo()

PURPOSE   Retrieves information (such as URLs) related to this referral.

SYNTAX
```
public abstract Object getReferralInfo()
```

DESCRIPTION   This method retrieves information (such as URLs) related to this referral. The program may examine or display this information to the user to determine whether to continue with the referral or whether additional information needs to be supplied in order to continue with the referral.

RETURNS   Non-null referral information related to this referral.

EXAMPLE   See the **Referrals** lesson (page 265).

ReferralException()

PURPOSE   Constructs an instance of `ReferralException`.

SYNTAX
```
protected ReferralException()
protected ReferralException(String msg)
```

DESCRIPTION   These constructors construct an instance of `ReferralException` with an optional `msg` supplied. If `msg` is not supplied, then `msg` defaults to `null`. All other fields default to `null`.

These constructors are used by subclasses of `ReferralException`.

PARAMETERS

msg   Additional detail about this exception. May be `null`.

SEE ALSO   `java.lang.Throwable.getMessage()`.

retryReferral()

PURPOSE   Retries the referral currently being processed.

SYNTAX   `public abstract void retryReferral()`

DESCRIPTION   This method retries the referral currently being processed. A call to this method should be followed by a call to `getReferralContext()` to allow the current referral to be retried.

EXAMPLE   The following code fragment shows a typical usage.

```
} catch (ReferralException e) {
    while (true) {
        try {
            ctx = e.getReferralContext(env);
            break;
        } catch (NamingException ne) {
            if (! shallIRetry()) {
                return;
            }
            // Modify environment properties (env), if necessary
            e.retryReferral();
        }
    }
}
```

R

skipReferral()

PURPOSE   Discards the referral about to be processed.

SYNTAX   `public abstract boolean skipReferral()`

DESCRIPTION This method discards the referral about to be processed. A call to this method should be followed by a call to `getReferralContext()` to allow the processing of other referrals to continue.

RETURNS   `true` if more referral processing is pending; `false` otherwise.

EXAMPLE   The following code fragment shows a typical usage.

```
} catch (ReferralException e) {
    if (!shallIFollow(e.getReferralInfo())) {
        if (!e.skipReferral()) {
            return;
        }
    }
    ctx = e.getReferralContext();
}
```

R

Resolver

Resolver

Syntax

```
public interface Resolver
```

Description

The Resolver interface represents an intermediate context for name resolution.

The Resolver interface contains methods that are implemented by contexts that do not support subtypes of Context but that can act as intermediate contexts for resolution purposes.

A Name parameter passed to any method is owned by the caller. The service provider will not modify the object or keep a reference to it. A ResolveResult object returned by any method is owned by the caller. The caller may subsequently modify it; the service provider may not.

MEMBER SUMMARY
Resolver Method
resolveToClass()   Partially resolves a name.

See Also

```
DirectoryManager.getContinuationDirContext(),
NamingManager.getContinuationContext().
```

R

Example

See the **Adding Federation Support** lesson (page 379).

resolveToClass()

PURPOSE	Partially resolves a name.

SYNTAX	`public ResolveResult resolveToClass(Name name, Class`
	`    contextType) throws NamingException`
	`public ResolveResult resolveToClass(String name, Class`
	`    contextType) throws NamingException`

DESCRIPTION	This method partially resolves a name, stopping at the first context that is an instance of a given subtype of Context.

PARAMETERS

contextType The type of object to resolve; should be a subtype of Context.

name The name to resolve.

RETURNS The object that was found, along with the unresolved suffix of name. May not be null.

EXCEPTIONS

NamingException

If a naming exception is encountered.

NotContextException

If no context of the appropriate type is found.

EXAMPLE See the **Adding Federation Support** lesson (page 379).

R

javax.naming.spi
ResolveResult

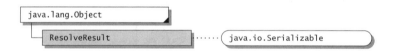

```
java.lang.Object
     ResolveResult  ........  java.io.Serializable
```

Syntax

```
public class ResolveResult implements java.io.Serializable
```

Description

The `ResolveResult` class represents the result of the resolution of a name. It contains the object to which the name was resolved and the portion of the name that was not resolved.

A `ResolveResult` instance is not synchronized against concurrent multithreaded access. Multiple threads trying to access and modify a single `ResolveResult` instance should lock the object.

MEMBER SUMMARY

Constructor
`ResolveResult()`	Constructs an instance of `ResolveResult`.

Access and Update Methods
`appendRemainingComponent()`	Adds a single component to the end of the remaining name.
`appendRemainingName()`	Adds components to the end of the remaining name.
`getRemainingName()`	Retrieves the remaining unresolved portion of the name.
`getResolvedObj()`	Retrieves the object to which resolution was successful.
`setRemainingName()`	Sets the remaining name field of this result.
`setResolvedObj()`	Sets the resolved object field of this result.

Protected Fields
`remainingName`	Contains the remaining name to be resolved.
`resolvedObj`	Contains the object that was resolved to successfully.

See Also

`Resolver`.

Example

See the **Adding Federation Support** lesson (page 381).

R

appendRemainingComponent()

PURPOSE   Adds a single component to the end of the remaining name.

SYNTAX   `public void appendRemainingComponent(String name)`

PARAMETERS
name   The component to add. May be `null`. If `null`, doesn't do anything.

SEE ALSO   `appendRemainingName()`, `getRemainingName()`.

appendRemainingName()

PURPOSE   Adds components to the end of the remaining name.

SYNTAX   `public void appendRemainingName(Name name)`

PARAMETERS
name   The components to add. May be `null`. If `null`, doesn't do anything.

SEE ALSO   `appendRemainingComponent()`, `getRemainingName()`,
               `setRemainingName()`.

getRemainingName()

PURPOSE   Retrieves the remaining unresolved portion of the name.

SYNTAX   `public Name getRemainingName()`

RETURNS   The remaining unresolved portion of the name. May not be `null`, but may be
               empty.

SEE ALSO   `appendRemainingComponent()`, `appendRemainingName()`,
               `setRemainingName()`.

EXAMPLE   See the **Adding Federation Support** lesson (page 382).

getResolvedObj()

PURPOSE   Retrieves the object to which resolution was successful.

SYNTAX   `public Object getResolvedObj()`

RETURNS   The object to which resolution was successful. May not be `null`.

SEE ALSO   `setResolvedObj()`.

EXAMPLE   See the **Adding Federation Support** lesson (page 382).

R

remainingName

PURPOSE	Contains the remaining name to be resolved.
SYNTAX	`protected Name remainingName`
DESCRIPTION	This field contains the remaining name to be resolved. It may be `null` only when constructed by using a subclass. Constructors should always initialize this field.
SEE ALSO	`appendRemainingComponent()`, `appendRemainingName()`, `getRemainingName()`, `setRemainingName()`.

resolvedObj

PURPOSE	Contains the object that was resolved to successfully.
SYNTAX	`protected Object resolvedObj`
DESCRIPTION	This field contains the object that was resolved to successfully. It may be `null` only when constructed by using a subclass. Constructors should always initialize this field.
SEE ALSO	`getResolvedObj()`, `setResolvedObj()`.

ResolveResult()

PURPOSE	Constructs an instance of `ResolveResult`.

SYNTAX	`public ResolveResult(Object robj, String rcomp)`
	`public ResolveResult(Object robj, Name rname)`
	`protected ResolveResult()`

DESCRIPTION	These constructors construct an instance of `ResolveResult` with the resolved object and remaining name that is supplied. The protected constructor initializes both of these to `null`.
PARAMETERS	
rcomp	The single remaining name component to be resolved. May not be `null`, but may be empty.
rname	The non-`null` remaining name to be resolved.
robj	The non-`null` object resolved to.

setRemainingName()

PURPOSE	Sets the remaining name field of this result.
SYNTAX	`public void setRemainingName(Name name)`

R

DESCRIPTION   This method sets the remaining name field of this result to name. A copy of name is made so that modifying the copy within this ResolveResult does not affect name, and vice versa.

PARAMETERS
name   The name to which to set the remaining name. May not be null.

SEE ALSO   appendRemainingComponent(), appendRemainingName(), getRemainingName().

setResolvedObj()

PURPOSE   Sets the resolved object field of this result.

SYNTAX   public void setResolvedObj(Object obj)

PARAMETERS
obj   The object to use to set the resolved object field. May not be null.

SEE ALSO   getResolvedObj().

R

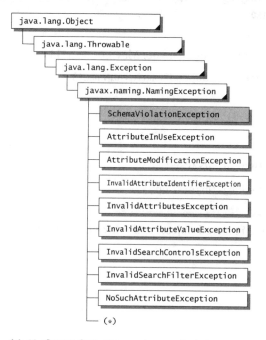

```
java.lang.Object
    java.lang.Throwable
        java.lang.Exception
            javax.naming.NamingException
                SchemaViolationException
                AttributeInUseException
                AttributeModificationException
                InvalidAttributeIdentifierException
                InvalidAttributesException
                InvalidAttributeValueException
                InvalidSearchControlsException
                InvalidSearchFilterException
                NoSuchAttributeException
                (*)
```

(*) 18 classes from other packages not shown.

Syntax

```
public class SchemaViolationException extends NamingException
```

Description

A SchemaViolationException is thrown when a method violates the schema.

An example of schema violation is modifying an object's attributes such that the modification violates the object's schema definition. Another example is renaming or moving an object to a part of the namespace such that the rename or move violates the namespace's schema definition.

Synchronization and serialization issues that apply to NamingException apply directly here.

MEMBER SUMMARY
Constructor
SchemaViolationException()   Constructs an instance of SchemaViolationException.

SchemaViolationException()

PURPOSE   Constructs an instance of `SchemaViolationException`.

SYNTAX   `public SchemaViolationException()`
               `public SchemaViolationException(String msg)`

DESCRIPTION   These constructors construct an instance of `SchemaViolationException` by using an optional `msg` supplied. If `msg` is not supplied, then `msg` defaults to `null`. All other fields default to `null`.

PARAMETERS
`msg`   Additional detail about this exception. May be `null`.

SEE ALSO   `java.lang.Throwable.getMessage()`.

S

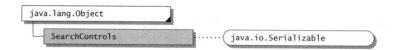

Syntax

```
public class SearchControls implements java.io.Serializable
```

Description

The SearchControls class encapsulates factors that determine the scope of a search and what is returned as the search results.

A SearchControls instance is not synchronized against concurrent multithreaded access. Multiple threads trying to access and modify a single SearchControls instance should lock the object.

MEMBER SUMMARY	
Constructor	
SearchControls()	Constructs an instance of SearchControls.
Access Methods	
getCountLimit()	Retrieves the maximum number of entries that will be returned as a result of the search.
getDerefLinkFlag()	Determines whether links will be dereferenced during the search.
getReturningAttributes()	Retrieves the attributes that will be returned as part of the search.
getReturningObjFlag()	Determines whether objects will be returned as part of the result.
getSearchScope()	Retrieves the search scope of this SearchControls.
getTimeLimit()	Retrieves the time limit of this SearchControls in milliseconds.
Update Methods	
setCountLimit()	Sets the maximum number of entries to be returned as a result of the search.
setDerefLinkFlag()	Enables/disables link dereferencing during the search.
setReturningAttributes()	Specifies the attributes that will be returned as part of the search.
setReturningObjFlag()	Enables/disables returning objects returned as part of the result.
setSearchScope()	Sets the search scope.

S

MEMBER SUMMARY	
setTimeLimit()	Sets the time limit of this SearchControls in milliseconds.
Search Scope Constants	
OBJECT_SCOPE	Specifies a "search" operation on the named object.
ONELEVEL_SCOPE	Specifies a "search" operation on one level of the named context.
SUBTREE_SCOPE	Specifies a "search" operation on the entire subtree rooted at the named object.

See Also

DirContext.search(), javax.naming.event.EventDirContext.addNamingListener().

Example

See the **Directory Operations** lesson (page 67).

getCountLimit()

PURPOSE   Retrieves the maximum number of entries that will be returned as a result of the search.

SYNTAX   public long getCountLimit()

RETURNS   The maximum number of entries that will be returned. 0 indicates that all entries will be returned.

SEE ALSO   setCountLimit().

getDerefLinkFlag()

PURPOSE   Determines whether links will be dereferenced during the search.

SYNTAX   public boolean getDerefLinkFlag()

RETURNS   true if links will be dereferenced; false otherwise.

SEE ALSO   setDerefLinkFlag().

getReturningAttributes()

PURPOSE   Retrieves the attributes that will be returned as part of the search.

SYNTAX   public String[] getReturningAttributes()

S

DESCRIPTION	This method retrieves the attributes that will be returned as part of the search. `null` indicates that all attributes will be returned; an empty array indicates that no attributes are to be returned.
RETURNS	An array of attribute ids that identify the attributes that will be returned. May be `null`.
SEE ALSO	`setReturningAttributes()`.

getReturningObjFlag()

PURPOSE	Determines whether objects will be returned as part of the result.
SYNTAX	`public boolean getReturningObjFlag()`
RETURNS	true if objects will be returned; `false` otherwise.
SEE ALSO	`setReturningObjFlag()`.

getSearchScope()

PURPOSE	Retrieves the search scope of this `SearchControls`.
SYNTAX	`public int getSearchScope()`
RETURNS	The search scope of this `SearchControls`. It is one of `OBJECT_SCOPE`, `ONELEVEL_SCOPE`, or `SUBTREE_SCOPE`.
SEE ALSO	`setSearchScope()`.

getTimeLimit()

PURPOSE	Retrieves the time limit of this `SearchControls` in milliseconds.
SYNTAX	`public int getTimeLimit()`
RETURNS	The time limit of this `SearchControls` in milliseconds. `0` means to wait indefinitely.
SEE ALSO	`setTimeLimit()`.

OBJECT_SCOPE

PURPOSE	Specifies a "search" operation on the named object.
SYNTAX	`public final static int OBJECT_SCOPE`
DESCRIPTION	This constant specifies a "search" operation on the named object. The `Naming-Enumeration` that results from `DirContext.search()` by using `OBJECT_SCOPE`

S

will contain one or zero elements. The enumeration contains one element if the named object satisfies the search filter specified in `DirContext.search()`. The element will have as its name the empty string. This is because the names of the elements in the `NamingEnumeration` are relative to the target context; in this case, the target context is the named object.

The enumeration contains zero elements if the named object does not satisfy the search filter specified in `DirContext.search()`.

The value of this constant is `0`.

EXAMPLE See the **Directory Operations** lesson (page 68).

ONELEVEL_SCOPE

PURPOSE Specifies a "search" operation on one level of the named context.

SYNTAX `public final static int ONELEVEL_SCOPE`

DESCRIPTION This constant specifies a "search" operation on one level of the named context. The `NamingEnumeration` that results from `DirContext.search()` by using `ONELEVEL_SCOPE` contains elements with objects in the named context that satisfy the search filter specified in `DirContext.search()`. The names of elements in the `NamingEnumeration` are atomic names relative to the named context.

The value of this constant is `1`.

SearchControls()

PURPOSE Constructs an instance of `SearchControls`.

SYNTAX `public SearchControls()`
`public SearchControls(int scope, long countlim, int timelim,`
  `String[] attrs, boolean retobj, boolean deref)`

DESCRIPTION These constructors construct an instance of `SearchControls`.

The constructor that accepts no arguments uses the following defaults:

- Search one level
- No maximum return limit for search results
- No time limit for search
- Return all attributes associated with objects that satisfy the search filter
- Do not return the named object (return only the name and the class)
- Do not dereference links during the search

PARAMETERS

`attrs`	The identifiers of the attributes to return along with the entry. If `null`, then return all attributes. If empty, then return no attributes.
`countlim`	The maximum number of entries to return. If `0`, then return all entries that satisfy the filter.
`deref`	If `true`, then dereference links during the search.
`retobj`	If `true`, then return the object bound to the name of the entry; if `false`, do not return the object.
`scope`	The search scope. One of `OBJECT_SCOPE`, `ONELEVEL_SCOPE`, or `SUBTREE_SCOPE`.
`timelim`	The number of milliseconds to wait before returning. If `0`, then wait indefinitely.

EXAMPLE   See the **Directory Operations** lesson (page 68).

setCountLimit()

PURPOSE   Sets the maximum number of entries to be returned as a result of the search.

SYNTAX   `public void setCountLimit(long limit)`

PARAMETERS

`limit`   The maximum number of entries that will be returned. `0` indicates no limit and all entries will be returned.

SEE ALSO   `getCountLimit()`.

EXAMPLE   See the **Directory Operations** lesson (page 69).

setDerefLinkFlag()

PURPOSE   Enables/disables link dereferencing during the search.

SYNTAX   `public void setDerefLinkFlag(boolean on)`

PARAMETERS

`on`   If `true`, then links will be dereferenced; if `false`, then links are not followed.

SEE ALSO   `getDerefLinkFlag()`.

setReturningAttributes()

PURPOSE   Specifies the attributes that will be returned as part of the search.

SYNTAX   `public void setReturningAttributes(String[] attrs)`

DESCRIPTION   This method specifies the attributes that will be returned as part of the search. `null` indicates that all attributes will be returned. An empty array indicates that no attributes will be returned.

PARAMETERS
`attrs`   An array of attribute ids that identify the attributes that will be returned. May be `null`.

SEE ALSO   `getReturningAttributes()`.

EXAMPLE   See the **Directory Operations** lesson (page 67).

setReturningObjFlag()

PURPOSE   Enables/disables returning objects returned as part of the result.

SYNTAX   `public void setReturningObjFlag(boolean on)`

DESCRIPTION   This method enables/disables returning objects returned as part of the result. If disabled, then only the name and class of the object is returned. If enabled, then the object will be returned.

PARAMETERS
`on`   If `true`, then objects will be returned; if `false`, then objects will not be returned.

SEE ALSO   `getReturningObjFlag()`.

EXAMPLE   See the **Reading Objects from the Directory** lesson (page 183).

setSearchScope()

PURPOSE   Sets the search scope.

SYNTAX   `public void setSearchScope(int scope)`

PARAMETERS
`scope`   The search scope of this `SearchControls`. One of `OBJECT_SCOPE`, `ONELEVEL_SCOPE`, or `SUBTREE_SCOPE`.

SEE ALSO   `getSearchScope()`.

EXAMPLE   See the **Directory Operations** lesson (page 68).

setTimeLimit()

PURPOSE   Sets the time limit of this `SearchControls` in milliseconds.

SYNTAX   `public void setTimeLimit(int ms)`

S

PARAMETERS

ms   The time limit of this `SearchControls` in milliseconds. 0 means to wait indefinitely.

SEE ALSO   `getTimeLimit()`.

EXAMPLE   See the **Directory Operations** lesson (page 70).

SUBTREE_SCOPE

PURPOSE   Specifies a "search" operation on the entire subtree rooted at the named object.

SYNTAX   `public final static int SUBTREE_SCOPE`

DESCRIPTION   This constant specifies a "search" operation on the entire subtree rooted at the named object. If the named object is not a `DirContext`, then search only the object. If the named object is a `DirContext`, then search the subtree rooted at the named object, including the named object itself.

The search will not cross naming system boundaries.

The `NamingEnumeration` that results from `DirContext.search()` by using `SUBTREE_SCOPE` contains elements of objects from the subtree (including the named context) that satisfy the search filter specified in `DirContext.search()`. The names of elements in the `NamingEnumeration` are either relative to the named context or a URL string. If the named context satisfies the search filter, then it is included in the enumeration, with the empty string as its name.

The value of this constant is 2.

EXAMPLE   See the **Directory Operations** lesson (page 68).

S

SearchResult

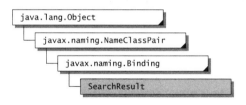

```
java.lang.Object
    javax.naming.NameClassPair
        javax.naming.Binding
            SearchResult
```

Syntax
```
public class SearchResult extends Binding
```

Description
The `SearchResult` class represents an item in the `NamingEnumeration` that is returned as a result of `DirContext.search()`.

A `SearchResult` instance is not synchronized against concurrent multithreaded access. Multiple threads trying to access and modify a single `SearchResult` instance should lock the object.

MEMBER SUMMARY	
Constructor	
SearchResult()	Constructs an instance of `SearchResult`.
Access and Update Methods	
getAttributes()	Retrieves the attributes in this `SearchResult`.
setAttributes()	Sets the attributes of this `SearchResult`.
Object Method	
toString()	Generates the string representation of this `SearchResult`.

S

See Also
`DirContext.search()`, `javax.naming.event.NamingEvent.getNewBinding()`, `javax.naming.event.NamingEvent.getOldBinding()`, `javax.naming.NamingEnumeration`.

Example
See the **Directory Operations** lesson (page 64).

getAttributes()

PURPOSE   Retrieves the attributes in this `SearchResult`.

SYNTAX   `public Attributes getAttributes()`

RETURNS   The non-null attributes in this `SearchResult`. Can be empty.

SEE ALSO   `setAttributes()`.

EXAMPLE   See the **Directory Operations** lesson (page 64).

setAttributes()

PURPOSE   Sets the attributes of this `SearchResult`.

SYNTAX   `public void setAttributes(Attributes attrs)`

PARAMETERS

  `attrs`   The non-null attributes to use. May be empty.

SEE ALSO   `getAttributes()`.

SearchResult()

PURPOSE   Constructs an instance of `SearchResult`.

SYNTAX   `public SearchResult(String name, String className, Object obj,`
           `Attributes attrs)`
         `public SearchResult(String name, String className, Object obj,`
           `Attributes attrs, boolean isRelative)`

DESCRIPTION These constructors construct an instance of `SearchResult` by using the result's name and its class name, bound object, and attributes. If `isRelative` is specified, then it specifies whether `name` is relative to the target context. If `isRelative` is not specified, then it defaults to `true`.

PARAMETERS

  `attr`   The attributes that were requested to be returned with this search item. May not be `null`.

  `className` The possibly `null` class name of the object. If `null`, then the class name of `obj` is used.

  `isRelative` If `true`, then `name` is relative to the context in which it was bound.

  `name`   The non-null name of the object.

  `obj`   The possibly `null` object bound to `name`.

SEE ALSO   `javax.naming.NameClassPair.getClassName()`,
             `javax.naming.Binding.getObject()`.

S

toString()

PURPOSE   Generates the string representation of this `SearchResult`.

SYNTAX   `public String toString()`

DESCRIPTION   This method generates the string representation of this `SearchResult`. The string consists of the string representations of `Binding` and of this `SearchResult`'s attributes, separated by the colon character (":"). The content of this string is for debugging and is not meant to be interpreted programmatically.

RETURNS   The string representation of this binding. May not be `null`.

OVERRIDES   `javax.naming.Binding.toString()`.

S

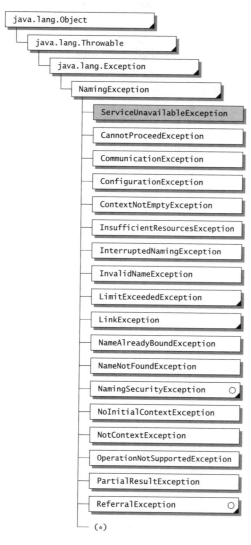

```
java.lang.Object
  java.lang.Throwable
    java.lang.Exception
      NamingException
        ServiceUnavailableException
        CannotProceedException
        CommunicationException
        ConfigurationException
        ContextNotEmptyException
        InsufficientResourcesException
        InterruptedNamingException
        InvalidNameException
        LimitExceededException
        LinkException
        NameAlreadyBoundException
        NameNotFoundException
        NamingSecurityException        ○
        NoInitialContextException
        NotContextException
        OperationNotSupportedException
        PartialResultException
        ReferralException              ○
        (*)
```

(*) 9 classes from other packages not shown.

Syntax

```
public class ServiceUnavailableException extends NamingException
```

Description

A `ServiceUnavailableException` is thrown when attempting to communicate with a directory or naming service and that service is not available.

The service might be unavailable for different reasons. For example, the server might be too busy to service the request or it might not be registered to service any requests.

Synchronization and serialization issues that apply to `NamingException` apply directly here.

MEMBER SUMMARY
Constructor
`ServiceUnavailableException()` Constructs an instance of `ServiceUnavailable-Exception`.

ServiceUnavailableException()

PURPOSE Constructs an instance of `ServiceUnavailableException`.

SYNTAX `public ServiceUnavailableException()`
`public ServiceUnavailableException(String msg)`

DESCRIPTION These constructors construct an instance of `ServiceUnavailableException` by using an optional `msg` supplied. If `msg` is not supplied, then `msg` defaults to `null`. All other fields default to `null`.

PARAMETERS
msg Additional detail about this exception. May be `null`.

SEE ALSO `java.lang.Throwable.getMessage()`.

S

SizeLimitExceededException

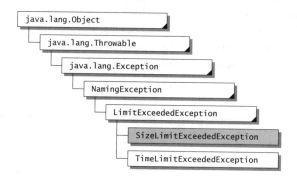

Syntax

```
public class SizeLimitExceededException extends LimitExceededException
```

Description

A `SizeLimitExceededException` is thrown when a method produces a result that exceeds a size-related limit. This can happen, for example, if the result contains more objects than the user requested or when the size of the result exceeds some implementation-specific limit.

Synchronization and serialization issues that apply to `NamingException` apply directly here.

MEMBER SUMMARY
Constructor
`SizeLimitExceededException()`   Constructs an instance of `SizeLimitExceeded-Exception`.

See Also

`javax.naming.directory.SearchControls.getCountLimit()`,
`javax.naming.directory.SearchControls.setCountLimit()`.

Example

See the **Directory Operations** lesson (page 69).

SizeLimitExceededException()

PURPOSE   Constructs an instance of `SizeLimitExceededException`.

SYNTAX   `public SizeLimitExceededException()`
                  `public SizeLimitExceededException(String msg)`

DESCRIPTION These constructors construct an instance of `SizeLimitExceededException` by using an optional `msg` supplied. If no `msg` is supplied, then `msg` defaults to `null`. All other fields default to `null`.

PARAMETERS
  `msg`   Additional detail about this exception. May be `null`.

SEE ALSO   `java.lang.Throwable.getMessage()`.

S

Syntax

```
public interface StateFactory
```

Description

The StateFactory interface represents a factory for obtaining the state of an object for binding.

The JNDI framework allows for object implementations to be loaded in dynamically via *object factories*. For example, suppose that a printer bound in the namespace is looked up. If the print service binds printer names to References, then the printer Reference could be used to create a printer object so that the caller of lookup() can directly operate on the printer object after the lookup.

An ObjectFactory is responsible for creating objects of a specific type. In the previous example, you might have a PrinterObjectFactory for creating Printer objects.

For the reverse process, when an object is bound into the namespace, the JNDI provides *state factories*. Continuing with the printer example, suppose that the printer object is updated and rebound:

```
ctx.rebind("inky", printer);
```

The service provider for ctx uses a state factory to obtain the state of printer for binding into its namespace. A state factory for the Printer type object might return a more compact object for storage in the naming system.

A state factory must implement the StateFactory interface. In addition, the factory class must be public and must have a public constructor that accepts no parameters.

A state factory's getStateToBind() method may be invoked multiple times, possibly by using different parameters. The implementation is thread-safe.

StateFactory is intended for use with service providers that implement only the Context interface. DirStateFactory is intended for use with service providers that implement the Dir-Context interface.

MEMBER SUMMARY	
Factory Method	
getStateToBind()	Retrieves the state of an object for binding.

See Also

DirStateFactory, DirectoryManager.getStateToBind(),
NamingManager.getStateToBind().

Example

See the **State Factories** lesson (page 175).

getStateToBind()

PURPOSE   Retrieves the state of an object for binding.

SYNTAX
```
public Object getStateToBind(Object obj, Name name, Context
    nameCtx, Hashtable env) throws NamingException
```

DESCRIPTION   This method retrieves the state of an object for binding.

NamingManager.getStateToBind() successively loads in state factories and invokes this method on them until one produces a non-null answer. DirectoryManager.getStateToBind() successively loads in state factories. If a factory implements DirStateFactory, then DirectoryManager invokes DirStateFactory.getStateToBind(); otherwise, it invokes State-Factory.getStateToBind().

An exception thrown by a factory is passed on to the caller of Naming-Manager.getStateToBind() and DirectoryManager.getStateToBind() and the search for other factories that might produce a non-null answer is halted. A factory should throw an exception only if it is sure that it is the only intended factory and that no other factories should be tried. If this factory cannot create an object by using the arguments supplied, then it should return null.

The name and nameCtx parameters may optionally be used to specify the name of the object being created. See the description of *Name and Context Parameters* in ObjectFactory.getObjectInstance() for details. If a factory uses nameCtx, then it should synchronize its use against concurrent access, since context implementations are not guaranteed to be thread-safe.

The name and env parameters are owned by the caller. The implementation will not modify these objects or keep references to them, although it may keep references to clones or copies of them.

PARAMETERS

env   The possibly null environment to be used in the creation of the object's state.

name   The name of this object relative to nameCtx, or null if no name is specified.

nameCtx   The context relative to which the name parameter is specified, or null if name is relative to the default initial context.

`obj`	A non-null object whose state is to be retrieved.
RETURNS	The object's state for binding; `null` if the factory is not returning any changes.
EXCEPTIONS	

`NamingException`

     If this factory encounters an exception while attempting to get the object's state and no other factories are to be tried.

SEE ALSO	`DirStateFactory`, `DirectoryManager.getStateToBind()`, `NamingManager.getStateToBind()`.
EXAMPLE	See the **State Factories** lesson (page 175).

S

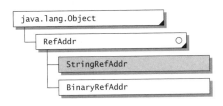

Syntax
```
public class StringRefAddr extends RefAddr
```

Description
The `StringRefAddr` class represents the string form of the address of a communication end-point. It consists of a type that describes the communication mechanism and a string whose contents are specific to that communication mechanism. The format and interpretation of the address type and the contents of the address are based on the agreement of three parties: the client that uses the address, the object/server that can be reached by using the address, and the administrator or program that creates the address.

Examples of a string reference address are a host name and a URL.

A string reference address is immutable; that it, once created, it cannot be changed. Multi-threaded access to a single `StringRefAddr` need not be synchronized.

MEMBER SUMMARY	
Constructor	
StringRefAddr()	Constructs an instance of StringRefAddr by using its address type and contents.
Address Method	
getContent()	Retrieves the contents of this address as a string.

Example
See the **Storing Objects in the Directory** lesson (page 159).

getContent()

PURPOSE	Retrieves the contents of this address as a string.
SYNTAX	`public Object getContent()`

S

StringRefAddr()

DESCRIPTION   This method retrieves the contents of this address as a string.

RETURNS   The possibly `null` address contents.

OVERRIDES   `RefAddr.getContent()`.

EXAMPLE   See the **Object Factories** lesson (page 190).

StringRefAddr()

PURPOSE   Constructs an instance of `StringRefAddr` by using its address type and contents.

SYNTAX   `public StringRefAddr(String addrType, String addr)`

PARAMETERS
  addr   The possibly `null` contents of the address in the form of a string.
  addrType   A non-`null` string that describes the type of the address.

EXAMPLE   See the **Storing Objects in the Directory** lesson (page 159).

S

TimeLimitExceededException

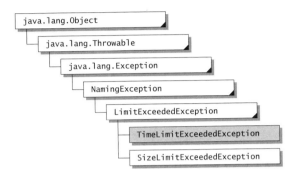

```
java.lang.Object
    java.lang.Throwable
        java.lang.Exception
            NamingException
                LimitExceededException
                    TimeLimitExceededException
                    SizeLimitExceededException
```

Syntax

`public class TimeLimitExceededException extends LimitExceededException`

Description

A `TimeLimitExceededException` is thrown when a method does not terminate within the specified time limit. This can happen, for example, if the user specifies that the method should take no longer than 10 seconds and the method fails to complete within that time limit.

Synchronization and serialization issues that apply to `NamingException` apply directly here.

MEMBER SUMMARY
Constructor
`TimeLimitExceededException()` Constructs an instance of `TimeLimitExceeded-` `Exception`.

See Also

```
javax.naming.directory.SearchControls.getTimeLimit(),
javax.naming.directory.SearchControls.setTimeLimit().
```

Example

See the **Directory Operations** lesson (page 70).

TimeLimitExceededException()

PURPOSE   Constructs an instance of `TimeLimitExceededException`.

SYNTAX   `public TimeLimitExceededException()`
       `public TimeLimitExceededException(String msg)`

DESCRIPTION These constructors construct an instance of `TimeLimitExceededException` by using the optional `msg` supplied. If `msg` is not supplied, then `msg` defaults to `null`. All other fields default to `null`.

PARAMETERS

`msg`   Additional detail about this exception. May be `null`.

SEE ALSO   `java.lang.Throwable.getMessage()`.

T

UnsolicitedNotification

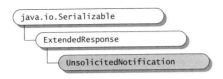

Syntax

`public interface UnsolicitedNotification extends ExtendedResponse, HasControls`

Description

The `UnsolicitedNotification` interface represents an unsolicited notification as defined in RFC 2251.

An unsolicited notification is sent by the LDAP server to the LDAP client without any provocation from the client. Its format is that of an extended response (`ExtendedResponse`).

MEMBER SUMMARY	
Access Methods	
`getException()`	Retrieves the exception constructed by using information sent by the server.
`getReferrals()`	Retrieves the referral(s) sent by the server.

See Also

`javax.naming.event.EventContext`, `javax.naming.event.EventDirContext`, `UnsolicitedNotificationException`, `UnsolicitedNotificationListener`.

getException()

PURPOSE	Retrieves the exception constructed by using information sent by the server.
SYNTAX	`public NamingException getException()`
RETURNS	A possibly `null` exception constructed by using information sent by the server. If `null`, the server indicated a "success" status.

getReferrals()

PURPOSE	Retrieves the referral(s) sent by the server.

U

SYNTAX   `public String[] getReferrals()`

RETURNS   A possibly `null` array of referrals, each represented by a URL string. If `null`, then no referral was sent by the server.

U

UnsolicitedNotificationEvent

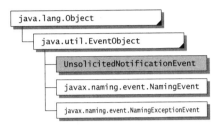

Syntax

```
public class UnsolicitedNotificationEvent extends java.util.EventObject
```

Description

The UnsolicitedNotificationEvent class represents an event fired in response to an unsolicited notification sent by the LDAP server. *Unsolicited notification* is defined in RFC 2251.

MEMBER SUMMARY	
Constructor	
UnsolicitedNotificationEvent()	Constructs an instance of Unsolicited-NotificationEvent.
Access Method	
getNotification()	Returns the unsolicited notification.
Dispatch Method	
dispatch()	Invokes notificationReceived() on a listener by using this event.

See Also

UnsolicitedNotification, UnsolicitedNotificationListener.

U

Example

See the **Event Notification** lesson (page 120).

dispatch()

PURPOSE	Invokes notificationReceived() on a listener by using this event.
SYNTAX	public void dispatch(UnsolicitedNotificationListener listener)

PARAMETERS

`listener`   The non-null listener on which to invoke `notificationReceived()`.

getNotification()

PURPOSE   Returns the unsolicited notification.

SYNTAX   `public UnsolicitedNotification getNotification()`

RETURNS   The non-null unsolicited notification that caused this event to be fired.

EXAMPLE   See the **Event Notification** lesson (page 120).

UnsolicitedNotificationEvent()

PURPOSE   Constructs an instance of `UnsolicitedNotificationEvent`.

SYNTAX   `public UnsolicitedNotificationEvent(Object src,`
                        `UnsolicitedNotification notice)`

PARAMETERS

`notice`   The non-null unsolicited notification.

`src`   The non-null source that fired the event.

U

UnsolicitedNotificationListener

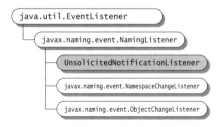

Syntax

```
public interface UnsolicitedNotificationListener extends NamingListener
```

Description

The `UnsolicitedNotificationListener` interface is used to handle `UnsolicitedNotifica-tionEvents`.

Unsolicited notification is defined in RFC 2251. It allows the server to send unsolicited notifications to the client.

A listener for `UnsolicitedNotificationEvents` must do the following.

1. Implement this interface and its method.
2. Implement `NamingListener.namingExceptionThrown()` so that it will be notified of exceptions thrown while attempting to collect unsolicited notification events.
3. Register with the context by using one of the `addNamingListener()` methods from `EventContext` or `EventDirContext`. Only the `NamingListener` argument of these methods applies; the remainder are ignored for an `UnsolicitedNotificationListener`. (These arguments might apply to the listener if it implements other listener interfaces.)

MEMBER SUMMARY
Callback Method
`notificationReceived()`   Called when an unsolicited notification has been received.

See Also

```
javax.naming.event.NamingListener, UnsolicitedNotification,
UnsolicitedNotificationEvent.
```

Example

See the **Event Notification** lesson (page 120).

U

755

notificationReceived()

PURPOSE   Called when an unsolicited notification has been received.

SYNTAX   `void notificationReceived(UnsolicitedNotificationEvent evt)`

DESCRIPTION   This method is called when an unsolicited notification has been received.

PARAMETERS

`evt`   The non-null `UnsolicitedNotificationEvent`.

EXAMPLE   See the **Event Notification** lesson (page 120).

U

LDAP Schemas

Schema for Java Objects

The schema for Java™ objects is described in RFC 2173 (`http://www.ietf.org/rfc/rfc2713.txt`).

Attribute Types

```
( 1.3.6.1.4.1.42.2.27.4.1.6
    NAME 'javaClassName'
    DESC 'Fully qualified name of distinguished Java class or interface'
    EQUALITY caseExactMatch
    SYNTAX 1.3.6.1.4.1.1466.115.121.1.15
    SINGLE-VALUE
)

( 1.3.6.1.4.1.42.2.27.4.1.7
    NAME 'javaCodebase'
    DESC 'URL(s) specifying the location of class definition'
    EQUALITY caseExactIA5Match
    SYNTAX 1.3.6.1.4.1.1466.115.121.1.26
)

( 1.3.6.1.4.1.42.2.27.4.1.8
    NAME 'javaSerializedData'
    DESC 'Serialized form of a Java object'
    SYNTAX 1.3.6.1.4.1.1466.115.121.1.40
    SINGLE-VALUE
)

( 1.3.6.1.4.1.42.2.27.4.1.10
    NAME 'javaFactory'
    DESC 'Fully qualified Java class name of a JNDI object factory'
    EQUALITY caseExactMatch
    SYNTAX 1.3.6.1.4.1.1466.115.121.1.15
    SINGLE-VALUE
)

( 1.3.6.1.4.1.42.2.27.4.1.11
    NAME 'javaReferenceAddress'
    DESC 'Addresses associated with a JNDI Reference'
```

```
        EQUALITY caseExactMatch
        SYNTAX 1.3.6.1.4.1.1466.115.121.1.15
    )

    ( 1.3.6.1.4.1.42.2.27.4.1.12
      NAME 'javaDoc'
      DESC 'The Java documentation for the class'
      EQUALITY caseExactIA5Match
      SYNTAX 1.3.6.1.4.1.1466.115.121.1.26
    )

    ( 1.3.6.1.4.1.42.2.27.4.1.13
      NAME 'javaClassNames'
      DESC 'Fully qualified Java class or interface name'
      EQUALITY caseExactMatch
      SYNTAX 1.3.6.1.4.1.1466.115.121.1.15
    )
```

Attribute Type From RFC 2256

```
    ( 2.5.4.13
      NAME 'description'
      EQUALITY caseIgnoreMatch
      SUBSTR caseIgnoreSubstringsMatch
      SYNTAX 1.3.6.1.4.1.1466.115.121.1.15{1024}
    )
```

Object Classes

```
    ( 1.3.6.1.4.1.42.2.27.4.2.1
      NAME 'javaContainer'
      DESC 'Container for a Java object'
      SUP top
      STRUCTURAL
      MUST ( cn )
    )

    ( 1.3.6.1.4.1.42.2.27.4.2.4
      NAME 'javaObject'
      DESC 'Java object representation'
      SUP top
      ABSTRACT
      MUST ( javaClassName )
      MAY ( javaClassNames $ javaCodebase $ javaDoc $ description )
    )

    ( 1.3.6.1.4.1.42.2.27.4.2.5
      NAME 'javaSerializedObject'
      DESC 'Java serialized object'
      SUP javaObject
      AUXILIARY
      MUST ( javaSerializedData )
    )

    ( 1.3.6.1.4.1.42.2.27.4.2.7
      NAME 'javaNamingReference'
      DESC 'JNDI reference'
      SUP javaObject
```

```
    AUXILIARY
    MAY ( javaReferenceAddress $ javaFactory )
)

( 1.3.6.1.4.1.42.2.27.4.2.8
    NAME 'javaMarshalledObject'
    DESC 'Java marshalled object'
    SUP javaObject
    AUXILIARY
    MUST ( javaSerializedData )
)
```

Matching Rule From ISO X.520

```
( 2.5.13.5
    NAME 'caseExactMatch'
    SYNTAX 1.3.6.1.4.1.1466.115.121.1.15
)
```

Schema for CORBA Objects

The schema for CORBA objects is described in RFC 2174 (http://www.ietf.org/rfc/rfc2714.txt).

Attribute Types

```
( 1.3.6.1.4.1.42.2.27.4.1.14
    NAME 'corbaIor'
    DESC 'Stringified interoperable object reference of a CORBA object'
    EQUALITY caseIgnoreIA5Match
    SYNTAX 1.3.6.1.4.1.1466.115.121.1.26
    SINGLE-VALUE
)

( 1.3.6.1.4.1.42.2.27.4.1.15
    NAME 'corbaRepositoryId'
    DESC 'Repository ids of interfaces implemented by a CORBA object'
    EQUALITY caseExactMatch
    SYNTAX 1.3.6.1.4.1.1466.115.121.1.15
)
```

Attribute Type From RFC 2256

```
( 2.5.4.13
    NAME 'description'
    EQUALITY caseIgnoreMatch
    SUBSTR caseIgnoreSubstringsMatch
    SYNTAX 1.3.6.1.4.1.1466.115.121.1.15{1024}
)
```

Object Classes

```
( 1.3.6.1.4.1.42.2.27.4.2.9
  NAME 'corbaObject'
  DESC 'CORBA object representation'
  SUP top
  ABSTRACT
  MAY ( corbaRepositoryId description )
)

( 1.3.6.1.4.1.42.2.27.4.2.10
  NAME 'corbaContainer'
  DESC 'Container for a CORBA object'
  SUP top
  STRUCTURAL
  MUST ( cn )
)

( 1.3.6.1.4.1.42.2.27.4.2.11
  NAME 'corbaObjectReference'
  DESC 'CORBA interoperable object reference'
  SUP corbaObject
  AUXILIARY
  MUST ( corbaIor )
)
```

Matching Rule From ISO X.520

```
( 2.5.13.5
  NAME 'caseExactMatch'
  SYNTAX 1.3.6.1.4.1.1466.115.121.1.15
)
```

Index

D

F

J

L

M

N

O

Q

query
components in a URL, (Tips for LDAP Users - Miscellaneous); 247

R

RDN (relative distinguished name)
X.500, (Tips for LDAP Users - Comparison of the LDAP and JNDI Models); 208

reading
attributes, (The Basics - Directory Operations); 61
objects
(Building a Service Provider - Adding Directory Support); 355
(Building a Service Provider - The Essential Components); 341

Reading Objects from the Directory lesson
Java Objects and the Directory trail; 179

rebind() method
`Context`; 510
`DirContext`; 534
`InitialDirContext`; 589

reconnect() method
`LdapContext`; 615

reconnecting
to LDAP server, `LdapContext.reconnect()`; 615

reentrancy
as service provider requirements, (Building a Service Provider - The Ground Rules); 328

RefAddr class; 706
`addrType`; 707
`equals()`; 707
`getContent()`; 707
`getType()`; 708
`hashCode()`; 708
`toString()`; 708

Reference class; 709
`add()`; 710
`clear()`; 711
`clone()`; 711
`equals()`; 711
`get()`; 712
`getAll()`; 712
`getClassName()`; 712
`getFactoryClassLocation()`; 713
`getFactoryClassName()`; 713
(Getting Started - JNDI Overview); 19

`hashCode()`; 713
`remove()`; 714
`size()`; 714
`toString()`; 715

Referenceable interface; 716
`getReference()`; 716

referenceable objects, (Java Objects and the Directory - Storing Objects in the Directory); 158
binding, (Java Objects and the Directory - Storing Objects in the Directory); 160
directory representation of, (Java Objects and the Directory - Representation in the Directory); 196
object factories and, (Java Objects and the Directory - Storing Objects in the Directory); 159

references
binary reference address, `BinaryRefAddr`; 454
binding, (Java Objects and the Directory - Storing Objects in the Directory); 160
binding remote objects by using, (Java Objects and the Directory - Storing Objects in the Directory); 165
characteristics and uses, (Java Objects and the Directory - Storing Objects in the Directory); 159
cloning, `Reference.clone()`; 711
communication endpoint, `Reference`; 709
CORBA object, binding, (Java Objects and the Directory - Storing Objects in the Directory); 168
example, (Java Objects and the Directory - Object Factories); 190
federation, URLs as, (Beyond the Basics - URLs); 128
(Getting Started - Naming and Directory Concepts); 8
glossary definition, (Getting Started - Naming and Directory Concepts); 14
hash code, calculating, Reference.hashCode(); 713
link
(Beyond the Basics - Miscellaneous); 142
relative, (Beyond the Basics - Miscellaneous); 143
supporting, (Building a Service Provider - Miscellaneous); 390
supporting, (Building a Service Provider - The Big Picture); 319
to objects outside of the naming/directory system, `Reference`; 709
Reference, (Getting Started - JNDI Overview); 19
removing, `Reference.remove()`; 714

U